Fundamentals of Managerial Economics: Second Edition

Fundamentals of Managerial Economics

Second Edition

James L. Pappas
University of Wisconsin–Madison

Mark Hirschey
University of Colorado at Denver

The Dryden Press

Chicago   New York   Philadelphia   San Francisco   Montreal   Toronto
London   Sydney   Tokyo   Mexico City   Rio de Janeiro   Madrid

Acquisitions Editor: Elizabeth Widdicombe
Project Editor: Rebecca Ryan
Managing Editor: Jane Perkins
Design Director: Alan Wendt
Design Supervisor: Jeanne Calabrese
Production Manager: Mary Jarvis
Permissions Editor: Doris Milligan

Text and Cover Designer: Harry Voigt
Copy Editor: Susan Thornton
Indexer: Bernice Eisen
Compositor: G&S Typesetters, Inc.
Text Type: 10/12 Palatino

Library of Congress Cataloging in Publication Data
Pappas, James L.
    Fundamentals of managerial economics.
    First ed. by James L. Pappas and Eugene F. Brigham.
    Includes bibliographies and index.
    1. Managerial economics.   I. Hirschey, Mark.
II. Title.
HD30.22.P36   1985   338.5'024658   84-13699
ISBN 0-03-071033-2

Printed in the United States of America
567-038-987654321

Address orders:
383 Madison Avenue
New York, NY 10017

Address editorial correspondence:
One Salt Creek Lane
Hinsdale, IL 60521

CBS College Publishing
The Dryden Press
Holt, Rinehart and Winston
Saunders College Publishing

About the cover

The cover is a graphic representation of Figure 5.1 which
illustrates a production surface.

To Bonnie, Kristen, and Kari—JLP
To Christine and Nicholas—MH

The Dryden Press Series in Economics

Asch and Seneca
Government and the Marketplace

Breit and Elzinga
The Antitrust Casebook

Breit and Ransom
The Academic Scribblers,
Revised Edition

Campbell and Campbell
An Introduction to Money and
Banking, *Fifth Edition*

Dolan
Basic Economics, *Third Edition*

Dolan
Basic Macroeconomics, *Third Edition*

Dolan
Basic Microeconomics, *Third Edition*

Heertje, Rushing, and Skidmore
Economics

Hyman
Public Finance

Johnson and Roberts
Money and Banking: A Market-
Oriented Approach, *Second Edition*

Kidwell and Peterson
Financial Institutions, Markets, and
Money, *Second Edition*

Leftwich and Eckert
The Price System and Resource
Allocation, *Ninth Edition*

Lindsay
Applied Price Theory

Morley
Inflation and Unemployment,
Second Edition

Morley
Macroeconomics

Nicholson
Intermediate Microeconomics and
Its Application, *Third Edition*

Nicholson
Microeconomic Theory: Basic Principles and Extensions, *Third Edition*

Pappas and Hirschey
Fundamentals of Managerial
Economics, *Second Edition*

Pappas, Brigham, and Hirschey
Managerial Economics,
Fourth Edition

Poindexter
Macroeconomics, *Second Edition*

Puth
American Economic History

Richardson
Urban Economics

Welch and Welch
Economics: Theory and Practice

Preface

Fundamentals of Managerial Economics provides a thorough treatment of those aspects of economic theory and analysis that are most important in managerial decision making. The presentation focuses on tools and techniques of economic analysis most useful in the decision-making process.

While both micro- and macroeconomic relationships influence managerial decisions, *Fundamentals of Managerial Economics* concentrates primarily on microeconomic topics. The demand for a firm's goods and services plays a major role in determining the profitability of operations. Demand theory and analysis are, therefore, core subjects in the study of managerial economics. Similarly, the success of a firm depends on the efficiency with which resources are acquired and utilized. Production and cost analysis, which examines the economics of resource allocation and employment, provides insight into this important area.

Fundamentals of Managerial Economics thoroughly develops and integrates the areas of demand and supply analysis. This approach gives the student a strong foundation for problem analysis. Of course, managerial decisions must be considered within the broader context of the firm's environment as defined by industry, government, and the public. Thus, the study of market structure and of the role of government in the market economy is an important, albeit controversial, aspect of managerial economics. Our coverage of these areas is meant to be both stimulating and comprehensive. Finally, investment decisions and competitive strategy are treated as areas in which the tools of managerial economics can be utilized in the process of long-term planning.

Fundamentals of Managerial Economics attempts to depict the firm as a cohesive, unified organization. A basic valuation model is constructed and used as the underlying economic model of the firm. Each topic in the text is then related to an element of the model. In this way, efficient management is shown to involve an interplay of accounting, marketing, production, personnel, and finance functions. This is particularly valuable for demonstrating that the solution of business problems requires an interdisciplinary approach. According to our students, considering the relationship of various topics as they apply to a business firm—or a business administration curriculum—as a whole, rather than as a series of discrete, unrelated topics, is one of the most valuable characteristics of the study of managerial economics.

Each chapter in *Fundamentals of Managerial Economics* contains solved problems, questions, and unsolved problems. These are designed to assist the student in acquiring a working facility with the tools and techniques of economic analysis. We have found classroom discussion of solved problems a valuable learning device and a most effective means of illustrating basic economic principles developed in the text. Furthermore, students utilize solved problems as a guide to understanding and answering the unsolved questions and problems.

Relation to *Managerial Economics*

Fundamentals of Managerial Economics differs from our other textbook, *Managerial Economics,* in several ways. First, a number of the more complex topics examined in *Managerial Economics* have been omitted. These include the lagrangian method for solving constrained optimization problems, duality concepts in linear programming, and transfer pricing concepts. Second, *Managerial Economics* assumes a working knowledge of calculus. Because *Fundamentals of Managerial Economics* takes a problem-solving approach to the study of managerial economics with a focus on the economics of the decision process, not the mathematics, the text requires no math facility beyond simple algebra. For the more mathematically inclined reader, we have provided calculus-based footnotes on important marginal concepts. Third, *Fundamentals of Managerial Economics* expands our coverage of the theory and practice of managerial decision making through an extended coverage of forecasting, pricing practices, and competitive strategy. We believe this expanded coverage will increase students' appreciation of the power of economic analysis and their understanding of how the tools and techniques of managerial economics can be applied in practical problem solving.

Instructor's Manual

The *Instructor's Manual* for *Fundamentals of Managerial Economics* provides suggested discussion topics for each of the end-of-chapter questions and complete solutions for the end-of-chapter problems. Also included is a set of check figures for the problems. We copy the check figures and distribute them to our students. The combination of solved problems in the text and check figures for the unsolved problems helps reduce student anxiety and provides the benefit of immediate feedback on a student's ability to use the tools of economic analysis.

Changes in the Second Edition

Just as the world in which managerial decisions are made is always in flux, so a textbook must undergo continual modification and updating to maintain its value as an educational resource. In addition to smoothing out those sections of the prior edition that proved most difficult to students, the second edition of *Fundamentals of Managerial Economics* contains several substantial changes. Some materials have been eliminated; others are shifted to provide an improved flow. Several chapters incorporate new topics or expand the treatment of those already existing. Also, we have added many new illustrations. Specific changes include the following:

• Every effort has been made to provide a variety of new, interesting and insightful questions and problems for each chapter. The end-of-chapter problems have been extensively revised and thoroughly class tested. The problem sets now are broader both in terms of the variety of decision situations covered and the range of difficulty encountered. They have been revised to reinforce the relationship between economic analysis and managerial decision making. At the end of each chapter we have also added solved problems to aid the student in tackling the problem sets.

• An appendix on the *mathematics of marginal analysis* has been added to Chapter 2 for readers who want to examine this topic in greater depth.

• The topic of *risk analysis* has been postponed until after the basic demand, production, cost, and pricing concepts are covered. This provides a more focused approach to introducing managerial economics. (Chapter 11)

- The material on *demand estimation* has been integrated into the Demand Analysis chapter to improve the flow of the chapter and the transition to the subject of demand estimation. (Chapter 4)

- In Chapter 5, covering *production*, the development of optimal input combinations has been modified to emphasize the relationships among factor productivity, value of output, and resource employment. Also, output elasticities have been introduced as a means of analyzing the returns to scale in a production system.

- Chapter 7, on *linear programming*, has been placed following the chapter on cost analysis. This change improves the transition from production to cost topics and allows for discussion of a wider range of linear programming applications.

- Material on *market concentration* has been incorporated into Chapter 8 on market structure. This leads to a more explicit treatment of identifying and analyzing the markets in which a firm sells its products.

- Chapter 10, on *regulation and antitrust*, now follows the market structure and pricing chapters. It has been revised extensively and includes an expanded treatment of both equity and efficiency issues in the regulation of the economy. Furthermore, it examines questions of property rights and the role of government in the assistance and direction of the private economy.

- Chapter 13 is a new treatment of *competitive strategy*. It introduces the methods by which the tools and techniques of managerial economics are used to formulate and implement effective competitive strategy.

Acknowledgments

We are grateful to the many individuals who aided in the preparation of *Fundamentals of Managerial Economics*. We received valuable suggestions and comments from both instructors and students who used the first edition. In addition, numerous reviewers provided assistance in clarifying our presentation. Among those who have been especially helpful in the development of this edition of *Fundamentals of Managerial Economics* are: Barry Brownstein, University of Baltimore; Frank Millerd, Wilfrid Laurier University; Steven M. Rock, Illinois Institute of Technology; M. Scahill, Saint John Fisher College; Daniel C. Smith, The University of Toledo; Richard A. Stanford, Furman University; Stanley P. Stephenson, The Pennsylvania State University; and Dr. Irvin B. Tucker, III, University of North Carolina-Charlotte.

Our students and colleagues also provided us with a stimulating environment and intellectual support. We would like to thank Christine Hauschel for her help in proofreading pages. Finally, we are indebted to The Dryden Press staff—particularly Liz Widdicombe, Bill Schoof, Debby Ruck, Jeanne Calabrese, Mary Jarvis and Becky Ryan—for their special efforts in this endeavor. Susan Thornton provided invaluable assistance as the copy editor of the manuscript.

Although every effort has been made to minimize textual errors, we recognize that some undoubtedly will have slipped through. We are anxious to eliminate them and invite readers to correspond with us concerning corrections, suggestions for further improvements in clarity, or other comments.

Economic efficiency is an essential ingredient in the successful management of both private- and public-sector organizations. Its importance to the well-being of the entire economic system cannot be overstated. The field of managerial economics continues to undergo significant changes in response to the challenges imposed by the complexities of managerial decision making in a rapidly evolving environment. It is exciting to participate in these developments.

We sincerely hope that *Fundamentals of Managerial Economics* will contribute to a better understanding of the application of economic theory and methodology to managerial practice and thus help lead to a more efficient economic system.

January 1985

James L. Pappas
Madison, Wisconsin

Mark Hirschey
Denver, Colorado

About the
Authors

James L. Pappas, Ph.D. (UCLA) is Professor of Finance and Managerial Economics in the Graduate School of Business, University of Wisconsin-Madison. Professor Pappas is active in executive education and serves as Academic Dean of the Graduate School of Banking at the University of Wisconsin. He is a member of several professional organizations and has served as an officer of the Financial Management Association. Articles by Professor Pappas have appeared in *Decision Sciences, Engineering Economist, Financial Analyst Journal, Journal of Business, Journal of Finance, Journal of Industrial Economics, Journal of Marketing Research, Southern Economic Journal* and other journals. He has served on the Editorial Board of *Financial Management*. He is also co-author of *Managerial Economics*, Fourth Edition. Professor Pappas teaches graduate and undergraduate courses in managerial economics and finance.

Mark Hirschey, Ph.D (University of Wisconsin-Madison) is Associate Professor of Business Economics in the Graduate School of Business Administration, University of Colorado at Denver. He previously served on the faculty of the Graduate School of Business at the University of Wisconsin-Madison. He is a member of several professional organizations and president of the Association of Managerial Economists. Articles by Professor Hirschey have appeared in the *Journal of Accounting Research, Journal of Business, Journal of Business and Economic Statistics, Journal of Industrial Economics, Managerial and Decision Economics, Review of Economics and Statistics,* and *Southern Economic Journal* among others. He is editor of *Managerial and Decision Economics* and serves as advisory editor for the *Review of Industrial Organization*. He is also co-author of *Managerial Economics*, Fourth Edition. Professor Hirschey currently teaches undergraduate and graduate courses in managerial economics.

Contents

Chapter 1

Introduction:
The Nature and
Scope of Managerial
Economics

Although one finds the term **managerial economics** defined in a variety of ways, the differences are typically more semantic than real. Some define managerial economics as applied microeconomics. Others define the field in terms of management science and operations research concepts. There are also those who see managerial economics as primarily providing an integrative framework for analyzing business decision problems. In actuality, all of those views are useful, for each provides an important insight into managerial economics.

Managerial economics is the application of economic theory and methodology to business and administrative decision making. More specifically, managerial economics relates to the use of tools and techniques of economic analysis to analyze and solve managerial problems. In a sense, managerial economics provides the link between traditional economics and the decision sciences in managerial decision making, as is illustrated in Figure 1.1. While we focus throughout the text primarily on business applications, it is important to recognize that the concepts of managerial economics apply equally to other types of organizations. The principles of managerial economics pertain to the efficient allocation of scarce resources. As such, these principles are

Figure 1.1
The Role of Managerial Economics in Managerial Decision Making

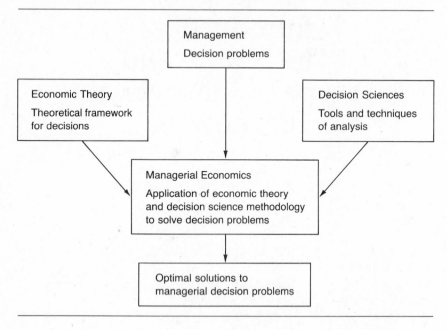

equally relevant to the management of nonbusiness, nonprofit organizations such as government agencies, cooperatives, schools, hospitals, museums, and similar institutions. This point will be amplified by the examples and problems drawn from the government and nonprofit sectors in the chapters that follow.

The Scope of Managerial Economics

We can more clearly understand the generality of the concepts of managerial economics by examining the relationship of managerial economics to (1) economics, (2) decision sciences, and (3) related fields that have impact on managerial decision making.

Relationship of Managerial Economics to Traditional Economics

Understanding the relationship between managerial economics and more traditional fields in economics is facilitated by considering the structure of traditional economic studies as shown in Table 1.1. The

Table 1.1
Classification of Traditional Economic Studies

Theory:	*Microeconomics* focuses on individual consumers, firms, and industries. *Macroeconomics* focuses on aggregations of economic units, especially national economies.
Traditional fields:	Agricultural economics Comparative economic systems Econometrics Economic development Economic history Industrial organization International trade Labor economics Money and banking Public economics Urban and regional economics
Emphasis:	*Normative economics* focuses on prescriptive statements; that is, it establishes rules to help attain specified goals. *Positive economics* focuses on description; that is, it describes the manner in which economic forces operate without attempting to state how they should operate.

traditional fields of economic study presented in the table overlap to some extent. Not only are micro and macro theory interrelated, but there are also micro and macro aspects of each area listed. Moreover, the areas themselves overlap; for example, econometric techniques provide a common set of tools of analysis that apply to each other area. Similarly, economic systems as studied in positive, or descriptive, economics must be understood before meaningful normative rules can be formulated. Nevertheless, the focus of each field of study is sufficiently well defined to warrant the breakdown suggested.

Since each area of economics has some bearing on managerial decision making, managerial economics draws from them all. In practice, some are more relevant to the business firm than others, and hence to managerial economics. To illustrate, both microeconomics and macroeconomics are important in managerial economics, but the microeconomic theory of the firm is especially significant. It may be said that the theory of the firm is the single most important element in managerial economics. However, because the individual firm is influenced by the general economy, which is the domain of macroeconomics, managerial economics draws from this area as well.

The emphasis of managerial economics is certainly on normative theory. We want to establish decision rules that will help managers attain the goals of their firm, agency, or organization; this is the essence of the word *normative*. If managers are to establish valid decision rules, however, they must thoroughly understand the environment in which they operate. For this reason positive or descriptive economics is important.

Relationship of Managerial Economics to the Decision Sciences

Economics provides the theoretical framework for analyzing managerial decision problems. Similarly, the decision sciences provide the means to actually construct decision models, analyze the impact of alternative courses of action, and evaluate the results obtained from the models. Managerial economics draws heavily upon *optimization techniques* that help management choose from among available alternatives to achieve the firm's established goals. *Statistical tools* are used to estimate relationships between important variables in decision problems. Because most managerial decision problems involve activities and events that occur in the future, *forecasting techniques* play an important role in managerial decision making and, therefore, in the study of managerial economics.

As in economics, the dichotomy used here to classify the decision sciences is not absolute. Optimization procedures are inherent in statistical relationships, and both optimization techniques and statistical relationships play important parts in developing forecasting methodologies.

In addition to the overlaps within the classifications of economics and decision science, there is substantial overlap between them. For example, many of the basic corollaries of economics—including the well-known microeconomic axiom that states that profit maximization requires operation at the activity level where marginal revenue equals marginal cost—are derived from basic optimization principles. Because of these interrelationships, managerial economics differs from traditional economics and the decision sciences primarily in its focus rather than in substance.

Relationship of Managerial Economics to Business Administration

Having delineated the role of economics and the decision sciences in managerial economics, it should prove useful to place managerial economics in perspective as a part of the study of business administration. In general, business administration is organized into four major categories, as is illustrated in Table 1.2. The functional areas are well situated

Table 1.2
Classifications of Business Administration Studies

Functional areas:	Accounting
	Finance
	Marketing
	Personnel
	Production
Tool areas:	Accounting
	Management information systems
	Managerial economics
	Organizational behavior
	Quantitative methods: operations research, statistics
Special areas:	Banking
	Insurance
	International business
	Real estate
	Regulation
Integrating courses:	Business policy
	Managerial economics

because both businesses and business schools are generally structured to include these departments. The special areas are also fairly well defined, and their place in the business administration curriculum is relatively clear-cut. The tool areas and integrating courses are not so easily categorized. Accounting, for example, is a function within the firm, but it is also a tool used throughout the firm. Accordingly, accounting is listed both as a functional area and as a tool.

The real question is this: Where does managerial economics fit into the picture? Again, the answer is not clear-cut. Although some firms have economics departments, these departments are usually small, and economics per se is not a major function within the firm. One possibility is to include managerial economics as a special area, but in our judgment it would be somewhat out of character there.

As we see it, managerial economics fits into the classification of business administration studies in two places. First, it serves as a *tool course*, wherein certain economic theories, methods, and techniques of analysis are covered in preparation for their use in the functional areas. Second, managerial economics serves as an *integrating course*, combining the various functional areas and showing not only how they interact with one another as the firm attempts to achieve its goals, but also how the firm interacts with the environment in which it operates.

The Theory of the Firm

A useful way to begin studying managerial economics is to develop a theory of firm behavior with which to analyze managerial decision making. A business enterprise is a combination of people, physical assets, and information (technical, sales, coordinative, and so on). The people directly involved include stockholders, management, labor, suppliers, and customers. In addition to these direct participants, all of society is indirectly involved in the firm's operations, because businesses use resources that are otherwise available for other purposes, pay taxes if operations are profitable, provide employment, and generally produce most of the material output of society.

Firms exist because they are useful in the process of allocating and employing resources for the production and distribution of goods and services. They are basically economic entities. As such, their activities can best be analyzed in the context of an economic model of the firm.

The basic model of the business enterprise is derived from what economists call the *theory of the firm*. In its earliest version, the goal of the firm was assumed to be profit maximization: The owner-manager of the firm was assumed to strive single-mindedly to maximize the firm's short-run profits. Later, when the emphasis on profits was shifted or broadened to encompass uncertainty and the time dimension, the primary goal became expected wealth maximization rather than short-run profit maximization. This goal of wealth or value maximization is recognized today as the *primary* objective of a business.

Definition of Value

Since the basis of the economic model is maximization of the value of the firm, it is appropriate to clarify the meaning of value. Actually, many concepts of value are found in economics and business literature—book value, market value, liquidating value, going-concern value, and so on. For our purposes **value of the firm** can be defined as the present value of the firm's expected future net cash flows. Cash flows may, for now, be equated to profits; therefore the value of the firm today, its *present value*, is the value of its expected future profits, discounted back to the present at an appropriate interest rate.[1]

---

[1] We assume that the reader is familiar with the concepts of present value and compound interest. For those who are not, we have included a detailed treatment of the subject in Appendix A at the end of the textbook. This material is useful for a complete understanding of Chapter 11, "Decision Making under Uncertainty," and it is essential to an understanding of Chapter 12, "Long-Term Investment Decisions: Capital Budgeting."

For current purposes one merely needs to recognize that $1 in hand today is worth more than $1 to be received a year from now; because the $1 today can be invested and,

The essence of the model with which we are concerned throughout the book may be expressed as follows:

Value of the Firm = Present Value of Expected Future Profits

$$= \frac{\pi_1}{(1 + i)^1} + \frac{\pi_2}{(1 + i)^2} + \ldots + \frac{\pi_n}{(1 + i)^n}$$

$$= \sum_{t=1}^{n} \frac{\pi_t}{(1 + i)^t} . \tag{1.1}$$

Here π_1, π_2, and so forth represent the expected profits in each year, t and i is the appropriate interest, or discount, rate. The final form for Equation 1.1 is simply a shorthand expression in which sigma (Σ) stands for "sum up" or "add together." Thus, the term

$$\sum_{t=1}^{n}$$

simply says add together as t goes from 1 to n the values of the term to the right. For this expression the process is as follows: Let $t = 1$ and find the value of the term $\pi_1/(1 + i)^1$, the present value of year one profit; then let $t = 2$ and calculate $\pi_2/(1 + i)^2$, the present value of year two profit; continue until $t = n$, the last year included in the analysis; then sum these present value terms of yearly profits to find the value of the firm.

Since profits are equal to total revenues (TR) minus total costs (TC), Equation 1.1 may be rewritten as follows:

$$\text{Value} = \sum_{t=1}^{n} \frac{TR_t - TC_t}{(1 + i)^t} . \tag{1.2}$$

The marketing department of a firm has a major responsibility for sales; the production department, a major responsibility for costs; and the finance department, a major responsibility for acquiring capital to support the firm's activities and, hence, for the discount factor in the denominator. There are many important overlaps among these functional areas: The marketing department, for example, can help reduce the costs associated with a given level of output by affecting customer order size and timing, and the production department can stimulate sales by improving quality and making new products available to sales

---

with interest, can grow to an amount larger than $1 by the end of the year. If we had $1 and invested it at 10 percent interest, it would grow to $1.10 in one year. Thus, $1 is defined as the present value of $1.10 due in one year when the appropriate interest rate is 10 percent.

personnel. Further, other departments within the firm—for example, accounting, personnel, transportation, and engineering—provide information or services vital to both sales expansion and cost control. These activities all affect the risks of the firm and thereby the discount rate used to determine present values. We see, therefore, that decisions throughout the firm can be appraised in terms of their effects on the determinants of value as expressed in Equations 1.1 and 1.2.

A fundamental assumption, then, in managerial economics is that the firm seeks to maximize its value as expressed in Equations 1.1 and 1.2. This statement is highly simplified; the remainder of this book will amplify and qualify it and will show how economic theory can be used to help management achieve the value maximization goal.

Constraints and the Theory of the Firm

In order to make value maximizing decisions, managers must consider both short- and long-run implications, as well as the ways various external restrictions or constraints affect their ability to achieve organizational objectives. Managerial decision making typically involves optimizing the value of some objective function subject to constraints imposed by technology, resource scarcity, contractual obligations, and government restrictions.

While a tremendous variety of constraints can arise in managerial decision problems, most fall within three broad categories, namely resource constraints, output quantity or quality constraints, and legal constraints. Given the important role that constraints play in managerial decision making, we will briefly examine some examples of constrained decision problems.

Firms and other organizations, such as hospitals, schools, and government agencies, frequently are faced with limited availability of essential inputs. Examples of such resource constraints include limitations on the availability of skilled labor, key raw materials, energy, machinery, warehouse space, and other such factors. Managers often face similar capital constraints due to limitations on the amount of capital resources available for a particular project or activity.

Managerial decisions can also be constrained by contractual output requirements. A specific minimum level of output often must be produced to meet delivery requirements. In other instances, output must meet certain minimum quality requirements. Some common examples of output quality constraints are nutritional requirements for feed mixtures, audience exposure requirements for marketing promotions, reliability requirements for electronic products, and requirements for minimum customer service levels.

Legal restrictions that affect both production and marketing activities can also play an important role in managerial decisions. Laws that define minimum wages, health and safety standards, pollution emission standards, fuel efficiency requirements, and fair pricing and marketing practices all limit managerial flexibility.

The important role played by constraints in managerial decision making makes the topic of *constrained optimization* a basic element of managerial economics. In later chapters we will consider important economic implications of constraints self-imposed by firms as well as those imposed on firms by society. This analysis is important because both value maximization and productive and allocative efficiency in society depend upon the efficient use of scarce (limited) economic resources.

Limitations of the Theory of the Firm

Many critics have questioned why the assumed profit or wealth maximization criterion is used as a foundation for the study of firm behavior. Are not the managers of firms interested, at least to some extent, in power, prestige, leisure, employee welfare, community well-being, and society in general? Further, do managers really try to *maximize*, or do they *satisfice*? That is, do they seek satisfactory results rather than *optimal* results, as the economic theory asserts? Would the manager of a firm really seek the *sharpest* needle in a haystack (maximize), or would he or she stop upon finding one sharp enough for sewing (satisfice)?

It is extremely difficult to determine whether management is trying to maximize firm value or whether it is merely attempting to satisfy owners while pursuing other goals. For example, how can one tell whether a community activity undertaken by a firm leads to long-run value maximization? Are high salaries and substantial perquisites really necessary to attract and retain managers who can keep the firm ahead of the competition? When a risky venture is turned down, how can one say whether this reflects conservatism or risk avoidance on the part of management, or whether it in fact reflects an appropriate decision from the standpoint of value maximization, given the risks of the venture compared with its potential return?

It is impossible to give definitive answers to questions like those above, and this problem led to the development of numerous alternative theories of firm behavior. Some of the more prominent alternatives are models in which size or growth maximization is the assumed primary objective of management, models that assume managers are most concerned with their own personal utility or welfare maximization, and models that treat the firm as a collection of individuals with widely divergent goals, rather than a single identifiable unit.

Each of these theories, or models, of managerial behavior has added to our knowledge and understanding of the firm. Still, none can sup-

plant the basic microeconomic model of the firm as a basis for analyzing managerial decisions. It is worthwhile to examine why in some
detail.

The economic theory of the firm, as it has evolved to date, states
that a manager seeks to maximize the value of the firm, subject to constraints imposed by resource limitations, technology, and society. The
theory does not explicitly recognize other goals, including the possibility that managers might take actions that would benefit someone
other than stockholders—perhaps the managers themselves or society
in general—but would *reduce* stockholder wealth. Thus, the model
seems to ignore the possibilities of satisficing, managerial self-dealing,
and voluntary social responsibility on the part of business.

Given that firms assert the existence of multiple goals, engage in
active "social responsibility" programs, and exhibit what appears to be
satisficing behavior, is the economic model of the firm really adequate
as a basis for our study of managerial decision making? We think it is.
First, we believe that the typically vigorous competition both in product markets, where firms sell their output, and in the capital market,
where they acquire the funds necessary to engage in productive enterprise, forces managements to heed value maximization in their decisions. Stockholders are, of course, interested in value maximization
since it affects their rates of return on common stock investments. Managers who pursue their own interests instead of those of the stockholder
run the risk of being replaced. While stockholder revolts are relatively
rare among large established firms, buyout pressure from unfriendly
firms ("raiders") has been significant during recent years. Unfriendly
takeovers are especially unfriendly to inefficient managements who are
replaced. Further, recent studies of managerial compensation indicate a
strong correlation between firm profits and managers' salaries. Thus,
managers appear to have a strong economic incentive to consider value
maximization in their decisions.

Second, even if value maximization oversimplifies some multi-goal
objective of firms, the concepts and understanding developed from
a study of the economic theory of the firm help improve managerial
decisions. Further, the foundation provided by such study forms the
basis both for extending the model and for evaluating alternative models that are proposed for use in managerial decision making.

Third, the costs as well as the benefits of any action must be considered before a reasoned decision can be made. This rule applies to a
decision to satisfice rather than to maximize. Thus, before a firm can
decide on a satisfactory level of achievement, a manager must examine
the costs of such an action. The analysis involved in the maximizing
model provides information on such costs.

Fourth, the value maximization model provides insight into a firm's
voluntary social responsibility activities, though at first glance the

model seems to preclude this possibility. The criticism that the microeconomic theory of the firm emphasizes profits and value maximization while ignoring the issue of social responsibility is important enough to warrant a slightly extended discussion and we shall return to it later in the chapter. It will prove useful, however, to examine first the concept of profits, which is central to the theory of the firm.

Profits

In order to understand both the theory of firm behavior and the role of the firm in a free enterprise economy one must understand the nature of profits. Indeed, profits are such a key element in the free enterprise system that it would fail to operate without profits and the profit motive. Given its importance, it is appropriate to analyze the nature of profits in some detail.

Business versus Economic Profit

Controversy about *profit* extends even to the definition of the term. The general public and the business community typically define profit by using an accounting concept. Here **profit** is the residual of income minus the explicit (accounting) costs of doing business. It is the amount available to the equity capital or ownership position after payment for all other resources used by the firm. For clarification this definition of profit is often referred to as **business profit**.

The economist also defines profit as the excess of revenues over the costs of doing business. To the economist, however, the inputs provided by the firm's owner(s), e.g., entrepreneurial effort and capital, are other resources that must be paid for if they are to be employed in that use as opposed to some other. Thus, the economist includes a normal rate of return on equity capital and an opportunity cost for the effort of the owner-entrepreneur as costs of doing business, just as the interest paid on debt and wages paid to labor are considered costs in calculating business profits. The normal rate of return on equity is the minimum return necesssary to obtain it for a particular use. Similarly, the opportunity cost of owner effort is determined by the value that could be received in an alternative activity. Profit to an economist, then, is the excess of business profit over the implicit costs of the equity or owner provided inputs used by the firm. This profit concept is frequently referred to as **economic profit**, to distinguish it from the business profit concept.

The concepts of business profit and economic profit help to sharpen one's focus on the issue of why profits exist and what their role is in a free enterprise economy. The concept of economic profit recognizes a

required payment for the use of owner provided inputs. There is a normal rate of return, or profit, for example, that is necessary to induce
individuals to invest some of their funds in a particular activity rather
than to spend them for current consumption or invest them elsewhere.
This normal profit is simply a price for capital. It is no different than
the price for other resources, such as labor, materials, and energy. A
similar price exists for the entrepreneurial effort of a firm's owner-
manager or for other resources owners bring to the firm. These opportunity costs for owner provided inputs provide a primary explanation
for the existence of business profits.

The existence of economic profits is a more complex issue. What
explains the difference between the economist's concept of normal
profits as a price of equity capital and other owner provided inputs,
and the actual business profits earned by firms? In long-run equilibrium, economic profits would be zero if all firms operated in perfectly competitive markets. In other words, all firms would report
business profit rates reflecting only a normal rate of return on equity
investment and payment for other owner supplied inputs. We know,
however, that reported profit rates tend to vary widely among firms.
Profit rates have ranged from very low in the railroad and textile industries, for example, to very high in the pharmaceutical, office equipment, and other high-technology industries. While we can explain
some of this variation as risk premiums (higher profits) necessary to
compensate investors if one business is inherently riskier than another,
significant economic profits (or losses) are undoubtedly earned by different firms at any point in time. Examining several theories that have
been proposed to explain the existence of these economic profits will
provide further insight into their critical role in a market economy and
in managerial decision making.

Frictional Theory of Economic Profits

One explanation of economic profits (or losses) offered by economists
is that markets are seldom in long-run equilibrium, but often in disequilibrium because of unanticipated changes in product demand or
cost conditions. In other words, shocks occur in the economy, producing disequilibrium conditions that lead to either positive or negative
economic profits for some firms. For example, the emergence of a new
product such as the automobile might lead to a marked increase in
the demand for steel, and this could cause profits of steel firms to rise
above the normal level for a period of time. Alternatively, a rise in the
use of plastics or aluminum in automobiles might drive the steel firms'
profits down. In the long run, barring impassable barriers to entry and
exit, resources would flow into or out of the steel industry, driving

rates of return back to normal levels, but during interim periods profits might be above or below normal because of frictional factors that prevent instantaneous adjustment to new market conditions.

Monopoly Theory of Economic Profits

A second rationale, the monopoly theory, is an extension of the frictional theory. It asserts that some firms, because of such factors as economies of scale, capital requirements, or patent protection, can build monopoly positions that allow them to keep their profits above normal for long periods. Monopoly, a most interesting topic, is discussed at length in Chapters 8 and 10, where we consider why it exists, its effects, and how society attempts to mitigate the potential costs it can impose.

Innovation Theory of Economic Profits

A third theory of profit, the innovation theory, is also related to frictions. Under the innovation theory, above-normal profits arise as a result of successful innovation. For example, the theory suggests that Xerox Corporation, which historically earned a high rate of return because it successfully developed and marketed a superior copying device, continued to receive these supernormal returns until other firms entered the field to compete with Xerox and drive its high profits down to a normal level.

Compensatory Theory of Economic Profits

The compensatory theory of economic profits holds that above-normal rates of return may simply constitute a reward to firms that are extraordinarily successful in meeting customer needs, maintaining efficient operations, and so forth. For example, if firms that operate at the industry's average level of efficiency receive normal rates of return, it is reasonable that firms that operate at above-average levels of efficiency will earn above-normal rates of return. Similarly, inefficient firms can be expected to earn relatively unsatisfactory (below-normal) rates of return.

The Role of Profits

Each of the above theories is descriptive of economic profits obtained for different reasons, and perhaps several are applicable in some cases. To illustrate, a very efficient farmer may earn an above-normal rate of return in accordance with the compensatory theory, but during a wartime farming boom already above-average profits may be augmented by frictional profits. Similarly, Xerox's profit position might be explained in part by all four theories: the company certainly benefited from successful innovation; it is exceptionally well managed and has earned compensatory profits; it earned high frictional profits while 3M, IBM, Savin, and other firms were tooling up in response to the rapid growth in demand for office copiers; and it has earned monopoly profits, because it is protected to some extent by its patents.

Economic profits are an important keystone to a market-based economy. First, above-normal profits serve as a valuable signal that firm or industry output should be increased. Indeed, expansion by established firms or entry by new competitors often occurs quickly during periods of high profit. Just as above-normal profits provide a signal for expansion and entry, below-normal profits provide a signal for contraction and exit. Without economic profits we would lose one of the most important indicators affecting the allocation of scarce economic resources. Also, above-normal profits can constitute an important reward for innovation and efficiency, just as below-normal profits can constitute a penalty for stagnation and inefficiency. Thus, profits play a critical role both in providing an incentive for innovation and productive efficiency, and in allocating scarce resources.

An understanding of how profits affect business behavior provides important insight about the relationship between the firm and society. We turn now to an examination of the role of the firm in society and to a look at the social responsibility of business.

Role of Business in Society

As suggested earlier, an important element in the study of managerial economics is the interrelationship between the firm and society. Managerial economics can clarify the vital role firms play in society and can point out ways of improving their benefits to society.

The evidence that business in the United States has contributed significantly to the social welfare is both clear and convincing. Not only has the economy sustained a significant and unprecedented rate of growth over many decades, but the benefits of that growth have been widely distributed. Suppliers of capital, labor, and other resources have all received substantial returns for their contributions. Consumers have benefited from both the quantity and quality of goods and services available for consumption. Taxes on the business profits of firms, as well as on the payments made to suppliers of labor, materials, capital, and other inputs, have provided the revenues for government to increase its service to society. All of these contributions to social welfare stem directly from the efficiency of businesses that serve the economy.

Does this mean that firms do not or should not exercise social responsibility in a broader, perhaps more philanthropic, sense? Not necessarily. Firms exist by public consent to serve the needs of society. Only through the satisfactory execution of this mandate will business survive. As the needs and expectations of society (and hence the social requirements placed on the economic system) change, business must adapt and respond to its changing environment.

If social welfare could be measured, business firms might be expected to operate in a manner that would maximize some index of social well-being. The maximization of social welfare leads to important yet unanswerable questions. For example, how should goods be produced? What combination of goods and services (including negative by-products such as pollution) should be produced? And how should goods and services be distributed? These are some of the most vital questions faced in a free enterprise system, and as such, they are important issues in managerial economics.

In a market economy, the economic system produces and allocates goods and services according to the forces of supply and demand. Firms determine what consumers desire, bid for the resources necessary to produce these products, then make and distribute them. The suppliers of capital, labor, and raw materials must all be compensated out of the proceeds from the sale of the output, and competition (bargaining) takes place among these groups. Further, the firm competes with other firms for the consumer's dollar.

Although this process of market-determined production and allocation of goods and services is for the most part highly efficient, there are potential difficulties in a totally unconstrained market economy that can prevent maximization of social welfare. Society has developed a variety of methods to alleviate these problems through the political system.

One possible difficulty with an unconstrained market economy is that certain groups could gain excessive economic power, permitting them to obtain too large a share of the value created by firms. To illustrate, the economics of producing and distributing electric power are such that only one firm can efficiently serve a given community. Further, there are no good substitutes for electric lighting. As a result, the electric companies are in a position to exploit consumers; they could charge high prices and earn excessive profits. Society's solution to this potential exploitation is direct regulation. Prices charged by electric companies and certain other monopolistic enterprises are controlled and held down to a level that is thought to be just sufficient to provide stockholders with a fair rate of return on their investment. The regulatory process is simple in concept; in practice it is costly, difficult to operate, and in many ways arbitrary. It is a poor substitute for competition, but it is a substitute that is sometimes necessary.

A second problem in a market economy occurs when, because of economies of scale or other conditions, a limited number of firms serve a given market. If the firms compete with one another, no difficulty occurs; however, if they conspire with one another in setting prices, they may be able to restrict output, obtain excessive profits, and thereby reduce social welfare. Antitrust laws are designed to prevent such collusion, as well as to prevent the merging of competing firms when the effect of merger would be to lessen competition substantially. Like direct regulation, antitrust laws contain arbitrary elements and are costly to administer, but they, too, are necessary if economic justice, as defined by the body politic, is to be served.

A third problem is that under certain conditions, workers can be exploited. As a result, laws were developed to equalize the bargaining power of employers and workers. These labor laws require firms to submit to collective bargaining and to refrain from certain unfair practices. The question of whether labor's bargaining position is too strong in some instances has also been raised. For example, can powerful national unions such as the Teamsters use the threat of a strike to obtain "excessive" increases in wages, which may in turn be passed on to consumers in the form of higher prices and, thus, cause inflation? Those who believe this is the case have suggested that the antitrust laws should be applied to labor unions, especially to those bargaining with numerous small employers.

A fourth problem faced by the economic system is that firms may impose external costs on society through their production activities. For example, they may dump wastes into the air or the water or deface the earth, as in strip mining. If a steel mill creates polluted air, which causes people to paint their houses in three years instead of five or to clean their clothes more frequently or to suffer lung ailments or other health impairments, the mill imposes a cost on society in general. Failure to shift these costs back onto the firm—and, ultimately, to the consumers of its output—means that the firm and its customers unfairly benefit because the firm does not pay the full costs of its activities. This results in an economically inefficient allocation of resources between industries and firms. Currently, much attention is being directed to the problem of internalizing social costs. Some of the practices used to internalize social costs include setting health and safety standards for products and production systems, establishing emissions limits on manufacturing processes and on products that pollute, and imposing fines on or closing firms that do not meet established standards.

All the measures discussed above—utility regulation, antitrust laws, labor laws, and pollution control restrictions—are examples of actions taken by society to modify the behavior of business firms and to make this behavior more consistent with broad social goals. As we shall see, these constraints have a most important bearing on the operations of a business firm and, hence, on managerial decision making.

What does all this mean with respect to the microeconomic theory of the firm? Is the model too narrow in scope and thus inadequate for examining issues of social responsibility and for developing models of business decisions that adequately incorporate the role of business in society? On the contrary, the model not only provides an appropriate framework for analyzing the **social responsibility of business**, but it also helps us determine the cost to society of changing the requirements imposed on business.

Business firms are primarily economic entities and as such can be expected to analyze social responsibility in the context of the economic model of the firm. This is an important consideration in examining the set of inducements that can channel the efforts of business in new directions that society desires. Similar considerations should also be taken into account before political pressures or regulations are imposed on firms to constrain their operations. For example, from the consumer's standpoint it is preferable to pay lower rates for gas, electric, and telephone services; but if public pressures on these regulated firms drive rates down too low, then profits will fall below the level necessary to provide an adequate return to investors; capital will not flow into the industries, and service will deteriorate. When such issues are considered, the economic model of the firm provides useful insights. The model emphasizes the close interrelationship between the firm and society. This in turn indicates the importance to business in participating actively to develop and formulate its role in helping to achieve society's goals.

Structure of this Text

Objectives

Reflecting the concept of managerial economics developed above, this text is designed to accomplish the following objectives:

1. To present those aspects of economics and the decision sciences that are most important and relevant in managerial decision making.

2. To provide a rationale or framework to help one understand the nature of the firm as an integrated whole, as opposed to a loosely connected set of functional departments.

3. To demonstrate the interrelation between the firm and society and to illustrate the key role of business as an agent of social and economic welfare.

Outline of Topics

In Chapter 1 we present the basic economic model of the firm and
introduce value maximization, the central focus of the firm. Chapter 2
introduces a number of important economic concepts and fundamental principles of economic analysis. These relationships and tools form
the basis of managerial decision making. In Chapter 3, the application
of the theory of demand to business decisions is examined. Chapter 4
explores tools and techniques available for forecasting important decision variables for managerial decision making.

Chapter 5 looks at production, the manufacture and distribution of
goods and services. Chapter 6 develops cost relationships and methods
of analysis, explores how to estimate cost functions, and examines
their use in management decisions. In Chapter 7 linear programming,
an important tool for decision making when constraints limit managers, is presented.

Chapter 8 relates the roles of demand, production, and costs in determining market structures and explains the manner in which their
relationship affects the nature of competition in an industry. In Chapter 9 material from earlier chapters is used to show how firms can develop successful pricing policies. Chapter 10 illustrates the interaction
between government and the private market. Here the role of government in regulating and controlling business for the public interest is
examined and a basis is provided for evaluating both benefits and costs
of such government activity.

In Chapter 11 the basic model of the firm is expanded to include decision making under conditions of risk. Chapter 12 explores long run investment decisions, or capital budgeting, showing how firms combine
demand analysis, production and cost analysis, and risk analysis to
make the key investment decisions that shape their futures. Finally,
Chapter 13 introduces competitive strategy, and looks at the methods
and applications of strategic analysis and planning.

Summary

In the first section of this chapter we defined *managerial economics* as
the application of economic theory and methodology to the practice of
managerial decision making. We also discussed the contributions from
traditional economic study and the decision sciences.

As a first step in our analysis of managerial decision making, this
chapter examined the *economic theory of the firm* as the basic model of
how a firm operates. This model is based on the premise that managers seek to maximize the value of their firms, subject to a variety of
constraints. Although we briefly discussed alternative models, includ-

ing satisficing and multiple-goal models, we stressed the economic model, which has proved most useful for analyzing the behavior of the firm.

An important element in the model is the firm's profit stream: The value of the firm is the present value of expected future profits. Because profits are so critical to understanding both the theory of the firm and the role of the firm in a free enterprise economy, the nature of profits, including both the theories used to explain their existence and problems encountered in defining and measuring them, received attention. We also examined the role of business in society and concluded that the interaction of the firm with society is an important aspect of managerial decision making. Understanding how business activities support the goals of society is a key component of managerial economics.

The reader should always have in mind the overall nature of managerial economics, because only in this way can one see how each individual topic fits into the general scheme of things and how each section builds toward a general model of business behavior. To help provide a road map for managerial economics, we presented a topical outline in the final section of the chapter.

Questions

1.1 Why is it appropriate to view firms as primarily economic entities?

1.2 Explain how the valuation model given in Equation 1.2 could be used to describe the integrated nature of managerial decision making across the functional areas of business.

1.3 In terms of the valuation model discussed in this chapter, explain the effects of each of the following:

a) The firm is required to install new equipment to reduce air pollution.

b) The firm's marketing department, through heavy expenditures on advertising, increases sales substantially.

c) The production department purchases new equipment that lowers manufacturing costs.

d) The firm raises prices. Quantity demanded in the short run is unaffected, but in the longer run unit sales can be expected to decline.

e) The Federal Reserve System takes actions that lower interest rates dramatically.

f) The firm is confronting inflation in the general economy by exactly passing increased costs through to sales so that business profits (sales minus costs) remain constant. At the same time inflation is causing generally higher interest rates, and hence the discount rate increases.

1.4 It is sometimes argued that managers of large publicly owned firms make decisions so as to maximize their own welfare as opposed to that of stockholders. Does the existence of such behavior create problems in using the microeconomic theory of the firm as a basis for examining managerial decision making?

1.5 Do you feel that it is reasonable to expect firms to take actions that are in the public interest but are detrimental to stockholders? Is regulation always necessary and appropriate to induce firms to act in the public interest?

1.6 How is the popular notion of business profit different from the economic concept as described in this chapter? What role does the idea of normal profits play in this difference?

1.7 Which do you think provides the more appropriate basis for evaluating the operations of a business: the accounting profit concept or the economic profit concept? Why?

1.8 What factors should one consider in examining the adequacy (or excesses) of profits for a firm or industry?

Solved Problem 1.1

Steve Westin has invested $40,000 in a new health spa. Business has been good and the health spa shows an accounting profit of $26,000 for the last year. This profit is after taxes but does not include payment of any salary to Westin, who has the potential to earn $20,000 at another job. During the year inflation was approximately 10 percent and money-market interest rates available to investors were 10 to 12 percent. Considering the risk involved in operating a health spa, Westin believes that a 14 percent after-tax rate of return is appropriate for this type of investment.

    a) Given this information, calculate the *economic* profit earned by Westin.

    b) What accounting profits would the firm have to earn in order for economic profits to be zero?

    c) Assume the $26,000 accounting profit represents the cash flow stream earned in the business and that Westin expects this income to be earned in each of the next four years, at which time he believes the business could be sold for $50,000. What is the current value of the health spa? (Ignore tax implications.)

Solution

    a) The economic profit of Westin's business can be calculated by adjusting accounting profits for the opportunity cost of both equity capital and Westin's effort. In this instance, economic profits are calculated as follows:

Business profit		$26,000
Equity capital opportunity cost (0.14 x $40,000)	$ 5,600	
Westin's managerial opportunity cost	20,000	
Total opportunity cost of owner supplied inputs		−$25,600
Economic profit		$400

b) Business profits would have to equal $25,600 in order for economic profits to equal zero.

c) The current value of the firm is the present value of the expected future cash flows (CF) attributable to capital. These cash flows equal gross cash flow ($26,000) minus the management's salary ($20,000), or $6,000 per year for four years, plus the $50,000 that the firm can be sold for in four years.

$$\text{Value} = \sum_{t=1}^{n} \frac{CF_t}{(1 + i)^t}$$

$$= \frac{\$6,000}{(1 + 0.14)^1} + \frac{\$6,000}{(1 + 0.14)^2} + \frac{\$6,000}{(1 + 0.14)^3} + \frac{\$6,000}{(1 + 0.14)^4}$$

$$+ \frac{\$50,000}{(1 + 0.14)^4}$$

$$= \$5,263.16 + \$4,616.81 + \$4,049.83 + \$3,552.48 + \$29,604.01$$

$$= \$47,086.29$$

Problem

1.1 Kari Duncan has invested $15,000 in a copy center franchise. The $15,000 included $10,000 of her own funds and $5,000 from a business loan she obtained at her bank. The investment resulted in her owning a self-service photocopying store in a regional shopping mall. During Duncan's first year of business, the store generated $69,000 in revenues. Expenses were:

Salaries	$38,000
Supplies	15,000
Rent	7,800
Utilities	900
Franchise Expense	700
Interest on Bank Loan	700
Taxes	2,500
	$65,600

The salary expense included $18,000 to Duncan, a salary that is comparable to what she could earn in another position. During the year the prime rate of interest fluctuated around 11.5 percent, and Duncan estimated she could earn 10 percent on her funds in a money market fund if they weren't invested in the business. She would require 15 percent as an expected return to induce her to invest in the common stock of a small retailing business with risk similar to that of the copy center franchise.

a) Determine the "business profits" of Duncan's copy center.

b) Determine the "economic profits" of Duncan's copy center.

c) Name *two* theories of economic profits that could account for the results you found in part b above, and under which you would expect to see economic profits driven to zero under equilibrium conditions.

d) Recalculate the economic profits under an assumption that Kari Duncan could earn a salary of $15,000 managing a comparable business which she did not own.

e) Assume that the business profits calculated in part a represent the cash flow stream earned in the business and that Duncan expects this income to be earned in each of the next three years, at which time she believes the business could be sold for $15,000. What is the current value of the copy center?

References

Asakura, Kanji. "Management in Japanese Society." *Managerial and Decision Economics* 3 (March 1982): 16–23.

Beasley, W. Howard. "Can Managerial Economics Aid the Chief Executive Officer?" *Managerial and Decision Economics* 2 (September 1981): 129–132.

Boland, Lawrence. "On the Futility of Criticizing the Neoclassical Maximization Hypothesis." *American Economic Review* 71 (September 1981): 1031–1036.

Bower, Joseph L. "Managing for Efficiency, Managing for Equity." *Harvard Business Review* 61 (July–August 1983): 82–90.

Carroll, Archie B., and Frank Hoy. "Integrating Corporate Social Responsibility into Strategic Management." *Journal of Business Strategy* 4 (Winter 1984): 48–57.

Ciscel, David H., and Thomas M. Carroll. "The Determinants of Executive Salaries: An Econometric Survey." *Review of Economics and Statistics* 62 (February 1980): 7–13.

Cochran, Philip L., and Robert A. Wood. "Corporate Social Responsibility and Financial Performance." *Academy of Management Journal* 27 (March 1984): 42–56.

Cohen, Michael D., and Robert Alexrod. "Coping with Complexity: The Adaptive Value of Changing Utility." *American Economic Review* 74 (March 1984): 30–42.

Demsetz, Harold. "The Structure of Ownership and the Theory of the Firm." *Journal of Law and Economics* 26 (June 1983): 375–389.

Fama, Eugene F., and Michael C. Jensen. "Separation of Ownership and Control." *Journal of Law and Economics* 26 (June 1983): 301–325.

Friedman, Milton. "The Methodology of Positive Economics." In *Essays in Positive Economics*. Chicago: University of Chicago Press, 1953.

Hirschey, Mark, and James L. Pappas. "Regulatory and Life Cycle Influences on Managerial Incentives." *Southern Economic Journal* 48 (October 1981): 327–334.

Howard, John A. "Marketing Theory of the Firm." *Journal of Marketing* 47 (Fall 1983): 90–100.

Jensen, Michael C., and William H. Meckling. "Theory of the Firm: Managerial Behavior, Agency Costs and Ownership Structure." *Journal of Financial Economics* 3 (October 1976): 305–360.

Jensen, Michael C., and Richard S. Ruback. "The Market for Corporate Control: The Scientific Evidence." *Journal of Financial Economics* 11 (April 1983): 5–50.

Machlup, Fritz. "Theories of the Firm: Marginalist, Behavioral, Managerial." *American Economic Review* 57 (March 1967): 1–33.

Rappaport, Alfred. "How to Design Value-Contributing Executive Incentives." *Journal of Business Strategy* 4 (Fall 1983): 49–59.

Seitz, Neil. "Shareholder Goals, Firm Goals and Firm Financing Decisions." *Financial Management* 11 (Autumn 1982): 20–26.

Simon, Herbert A. "Rational Decision Making in Business Organizations." *American Economic Review* 69 (September 1979): 493–513.

Wong, Robert E. "Profit Maximization and Alternative Theories: A Dynamic Reconciliation." *American Economic Review* 65 (September 1975): 689–694.

Chapter 2

Basic Economic Relationships

Key Terms
Incremental concept
Marginal concept
Optimization
Value maximization

Managerial decision making is the process of determining the best possible solution to a given problem. If only one solution, or action, is possible, no decision problem exists. If a number of alternative courses of action are available, however, the alternative that produces a result most consistent with the decision maker's goal is the optimal action. The process of finding this best action, or decision, is the concern of managerial economics.

One major problem associated with the decision-making process is defining alternatives in terms of the goals or objectives of the decision maker. Not only must decision makers be able to recognize the available options in a given situation, they must also be able to specify those options in terms of the appropriate decision variables and relevant costs and benefits. This delineation of available alternatives, often the most difficult facet of the decision-making process, is enhanced through application of the principles of managerial economics.

Analyzing and evaluating the alternatives available in a decision situation is the second requirement for decision making. Here, the concepts and methodologies of economic analysis are applied to the set of feasible alternatives to aid in selecting the optimal course of action, given the decision maker's objective.

In this chapter we introduce a number of basic economic concepts and fundamental principles of economic analysis. These fundamental relationships are essential to all aspects of managerial economics. In addition to providing an introduction to the tools and techniques of optimization, the material provides insight into the theory of the firm presented in the preceding chapter and the complexities of goal-oriented managerial activities.

Maximizing the Value of the Firm

In managerial economics the primary objective of management is assumed to be maximization of the firm's value. This objective of **value maximization**, which was introduced in Chapter 1, is expressed in Equation 2.1:

$$\text{Value} = \sum_{t=1}^{n} \frac{\text{Profit}_t}{(1+i)^t} = \sum_{t=1}^{n} \frac{\text{Total Revenue}_t - \text{Total Cost}_t}{(1+i)^t} \tag{2.1}$$

Maximizing Equation 2.1 is a complex task, involving the determinants of revenues, costs, and discount rates in each future year of some unspecified time horizon. Revenues, costs, and discount rates are interrelated, complicating the problem even more. A closer inspection of the relationships involved in Equation 2.1 should help clarify both the concept and the complexities.

A firm's total revenues are directly determined by the quantity of its products sold and the prices received. This is nothing more than a recognition that total revenue (TR) is the product of price (P) times quantity (Q), i.e., $TR = P \times Q$. For managerial decision making the important considerations relate to factors that affect prices and quantities, and to the interrelationships between them. These factors include the choice of products the firm designs, manufactures, and sells; the advertising strategies it employs; the pricing policy it establishes; the general state of the economy it encounters; and the nature of the competition it faces in the marketplace. In short, the revenue relationship encompasses both demand and supply considerations.

The cost relationships involved in producing a firm's products are similarly complex. An analysis of costs requires examination of alternative production systems, technological options, input possibilities, and so on. The prices of factors of production play an important role in cost determination, and thus factor supply considerations are important.

Finally, there is the relationship between the discount rate and the company's product mix, physical assets, and financial structure. These factors affect the cost and availability of financial resources for the firm and ultimately determine the discount rate used by investors to establish a value for the firm.

To evaluate the choices available to management and to determine the optimal course of action, marketing, production, and financial decisions—as well as decisions related to personnel, product distribution, and so on—must be combined into a single integrated system, one that shows how any action affects all parts of the firm. The economic model of the firm provides a basis for this integration, while the principles of economic analysis enable one to analyze the important interrelationships.

The complexity involved in this integrated decision-analysis approach typically limits the use of the procedure to major planning decisions. For many day-to-day operating decisions, much less complicated partial optimization techniques are employed. Partial optimization abstracts somewhat from the complexity of the integrated decision process by concentrating on more limited objectives within the firm's various operating departments. For example, the marketing department is usually required to determine the price and advertising policy that will achieve some sales goal, given the firm's product line and constraints on marketing expenditures. The production department is expected to minimize the cost of producing a specified quantity of output of a stated quality level. Here again, the fundamentals of economic analysis provide the basis for optimal managerial decisions.

The decision process, regardless of whether related to fully integrated or to partial optimization problems, takes place in two steps. First, the economic relationships must be expressed in a form suitable for analysis; generally, this means expressing the problem in analytical terms. Second, various techniques are applied to determine the optimal solution to the problem at hand. In the material that follows, we first introduce a number of concepts useful for expressing decision problems in an economic framework. Then, several economic relationships frequently used in the second part of the decision-making process are examined.

Methods of Expressing Economic Relationships

Equations, tables in which relationships are enumerated, and graphs in in which these relations are plotted are all frequently used to express economic relations. A table or a graph may be sufficient for the purpose at hand. When the problem is complex, however, equations are useful so that the powerful tools of mathematical analysis and computer simulation may be used.

Functional Relationships: Equations

Perhaps the easiest way to examine various means of expressing economic relationships and, at the same time, to gain insight into the economics of optimization is to consider several functional relationships
that play key roles in the basic valuation model. Consider first the relationship between output, Q, and total revenue, TR. Using functional
notation, we can express the relationship in general terms with the
following equation:

$$TR = f(Q). \qquad (2.2)$$

Equation 2.2 is read "Total revenue is a function of output." The value
of the dependent variable—total revenue—is determined by the independent variable—output. In an equation such as this one, the variable to the left of the equals sign is called the *dependent variable*, as its
value *depends* on the size of the variable or variables to the right of
the equals sign. The variables on the right-hand side of the equals sign
are called *independent variables*, because their values are assumed to be
determined outside, or *independently*, of the model expressed in the
equation.

Equation 2.2 does not indicate the specific relationship between output and total revenue; it merely states that some relationship exists. A
more specific expression of the functional relationship is provided by
the equation:

$$TR = P \cdot Q, \qquad (2.3)$$

where P represents the price at which each unit Q is sold. Here, the
manner in which the value of the dependent variable is related to the
independent variable is more precisely specified. Total revenue is equal
to price times the quantity of output sold. If, for example, price is constant at $1.50 regardless of the quantity sold, then the relationship be-
tween quantity sold and total revenue is precisely stated by the function:

$$TR = \$1.50 \cdot Q. \qquad (2.4)$$

Functional Relationships: Tables and Graphs

In addition to equations, tables and graphs are often used to express
economic relationships. The data in Table 2.1, for example, express exactly the same functional relationship specified by Equation 2.4, and
this same function is graphically illustrated in Figure 2.1. All three
methods of expressing relationships play an important role in presenting and analyzing data for managerial decision making.

Table 2.1
Relationship between Total Revenue and Output:
Total Revenue = $1.50 × Output

Total Revenue	Output
$1.50	1
3.00	2
4.50	3
6.00	4
7.50	5
9.00	6

Figure 2.1
Graph of the Relationship between Total Revenue and Output

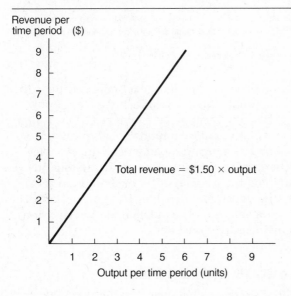

Revenue per time period ($)

Total revenue = $1.50 × output

Output per time period (units)

Total, Average, and Marginal Relationships

Total, average, and marginal relationships are very useful in optimization analysis. The definitions of totals and averages are too well known to warrant restating, but it is perhaps appropriate to define the term *marginal*. A marginal relationship is defined as *the change in the dependent variable of a function associated with a unitary change in one of the inde-*

Table 2.2
Total, Marginal, and Average Relationships
for a Hypothetical Profit Function

Units of Output Q (1)	Total Profits π[a] (2)	Marginal Profits $\Delta\pi$[b] (3)	Average Profits $\bar{\pi}$[c] (4)
0	$ 0	$ 0	—
1	19	19	$19
2	52	33	26
3	93	41	31
4	136	43	34
5	175	39	35
6	210	35	35
7	217	7	31
8	208	−9	26

[a]The Greek letter π (pi) is frequently used in economic and business literature to denote profits.
[b]The symbol Δ (delta) denotes difference or change. Thus, marginal profit is expressed as: $\Delta\pi = \pi_Q - \pi_{Q-1}$.
[c]Average profit ($\bar{\pi}$) equals total profit (π) divided by total output (Q): $\bar{\pi} = \pi/Q$.

pendent variables.[1] In the total revenue function, marginal revenue is the change in total revenue associated with a one-unit change in output.

Because the essence of the optimizing process involves analysis of changes, the **marginal concept** is of critical importance. Typically, we analyze an objective function by changing the independent variables to see what effect these changes have on the dependent variable. In other words, we are examining the *marginal* effect of changes in the independent variables on the dependent variable. The purpose of this analysis is to locate that set of values for the independent, or decision, variables that optimizes the objective function.

Relationship between Totals and Marginals
Table 2.2 shows the relationship between totals, marginals, and averages for a hypothetical profit function. Columns 1 and 2 show the output and profit relationship; column 3 shows marginal profits for one-unit changes in output; column 4 gives the average per unit profit at each level of output.

[1]Appendix 2.A at the end of this chapter provides a more complete development of the marginal concept. Although the material in this text does not require knowledge of the concepts in the Appendix, we believe the reader will find that it provides a more comprehensive understanding of the marginal relationships and their role in managerial decision making.

Marginal profit refers to the change in profit associated with each one unit change in output. The marginal profit of the first unit of output is $19. This is the change from the $0 profits related to an output of 0 units to the $19 profit earned when one unit is produced. Likewise, the $33 marginal profit associated with the second unit of output is the increase in total profits ($52–$19) that results when output is increased from one to two units.

The importance of the relationship between marginal and total values in decision analysis lies in the fact that when the marginal is positive, the total is increasing, and when the marginal is negative, the total is decreasing. The data in Table 2.2 can also be used to illustrate this point. The marginal profit associated with each of the first seven units of output is positive, and the total profits increase with output over this range. Since the marginal profit of the eighth unit is negative, however, profits are reduced if output is raised to that level. Thus, maximization of the profit function—or any function for that matter—occurs at the point where the marginal relationship shifts from positive to negative. This important relationship is examined again later in this chapter.

Relationship between Averages and Marginals

The relationship between average and marginal values is also important in some decision analyses. Since the marginal represents the change in the total, it follows that when the marginal is greater than the average, the average must be increasing. For example, if a firm operates five retail stores with average sales of $350,000 per store and it opens a sixth store (the marginal store) that generates sales of $400,000, the average sales per store increase. Likewise if sales at the new (marginal) store are less than $350,000, average sales per store will decrease.

The data in Table 2.2 can be used to illustrate the relationship between marginal and average values. In going from four units of output to five, marginal profit, $39, is greater than the $34 average profit at four units; hence, average profit increases—to $35. The marginal profit associated with the sixth unit, however, is $35, the same as the average for the first five units, so average profit remains unchanged between five and six units. Finally, the marginal profit of the seventh unit is below the average profits at six units, causing average profit to fall.

Graphing the Total, Marginal, and Average Relationships

Knowledge of the geometrical relationships between totals, marginals, and averages can provide information useful in managerial decision making. Figure 2.2a presents a graph of the profit to output relation-

Figure 2.2

Geometric Representation of Total, Marginal, and Average Relationships:
(a) Total Profits (b) Marginal and Average Profits

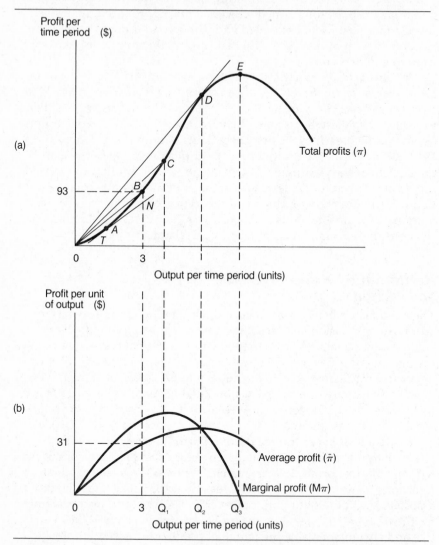

ship given in Table 2.2. Each point on the curve represents an output–total profit combination, as do columns 1 and 2 of Table 2.2. The marginal and average profit figures from Table 2.2 have been plotted in Figure 2.2b.

Just as there is an arithmetic relationship between the totals, marginals, and averages in the table, so too is there a corresponding geometric relationship. To see this relationship, consider first the average profit per unit of output at any point along the total profits curve. The average profit figure is equal to total profit divided by the corresponding number of units of output. Geometrically, this relationship is represented by the slope of a line from the origin to the point of interest on the total profits curve. For example, consider the slope of the line from the origin to point B in Figure 2.2a. Slope is a measure of the steepness of a line, and it is defined as the increase (or decrease) in height per unit of movement out along the horizontal axis. The slope of a straight line passing through the origin is determined by dividing the Y coordinate at any point on the line by the corresponding X coordinate. That is, using Δ (read delta) to denote change, slope $= \Delta Y / \Delta X = (Y_2 - Y_1)/(X_2 - X_1)$. Since X_1 and Y_1 are zero for any line going through the origin, slope $= Y_2/X_2$ or, more generally, slope $= Y/X$. Thus, the slope of the line $0B$ can be calculated by dividing \$93 (the Y coordinate at point B) by 3 (the X coordinate at point B). Notice, however, that in this process we are dividing total profits by the corresponding units of output. This is the definition of average profit at that point. *Thus, at any point along a total curve, the corresponding average figure is given by the slope of a straight line from the origin to that point.* These average figures can also be graphed directly as in Figure 2.2b. There, each point on the average profit curve is the corresponding total profit divided by the output quantity.

The marginal relationship has a similar geometric association with the total curve. In Table 2.2 each marginal figure was shown to be the change in total profit associated with the last unit increase in output. This rise (or fall) in the total profit associated with a one-unit increase in output is the *slope* of the total profit curve at that point.

Slopes of nonlinear curves are typically found geometrically by drawing a line tangent to the curve at the point of interest and determining the slope of the tangent. (A tangent is a line that touches but does not intersect the curve.) In Figure 2.2a, for example, the marginal profit at point A is equal to the slope of the total profit curve at that point, which is equal to the slope of the tangent labeled *TAN*. Therefore, *at any point along a total curve, the corresponding marginal figure is given by the slope of a line drawn tangent to the total curve at that point.* These slope, or marginal, figures can also be graphed directly as shown by the marginal profit curve in Figure 2.2b.

Several important relationships between the total, marginal, and average figures may now be examined. First, note that the slope of the total profit curve is increasing from the origin to point C. That is, lines drawn tangent to the total profit curve become steeper as the point of tangency approaches point C, so marginal profit is increasing up to this point. This is also illustrated in Figure 2.2b, where the marginal profit curve increases up to output Q_1, corresponding to point C on the total profit curve. At point C, called an *inflection point*, the slope of the total profit curve is maximized; thus, marginal (but not average or total) profits are maximized at that output. Between points C and E total profit continues to increase because marginal profit is still positive even though it is declining. At point E the total profit curve has a slope of zero and thus is neither rising nor falling. Marginal profit at this point is zero, and total profit is maximized. Beyond E (output Q_3 in Figure 2.2b) the total profit curve has a negative slope, and marginal profit is negative.

In addition to the total-average and total-marginal relationships, the relation between marginals and averages is also demonstrated in Figure 2.2b. At low output levels, where the marginal profit curve lies above the average, the average is rising. Although marginal profit reaches a maximum at output Q_1 and declines thereafter, the average curve continues to rise so long as the marginal lies above it. At output Q_2, marginal and average profits are equal, and here the average profit curve reaches its maximum value. Beyond Q_2, the marginal curve lies below the average, and the average is falling.

Use of Marginals for Economic Analysis

We can use the geometric relationships between totals and marginals to examine the role of marginal analysis in economic decision making further. The process of decision making frequently requires one to find the maximum value of a function. For a function to be at a maximum, its marginal value (slope) must be zero. Evaluating the slope, or marginal value, of a function, therefore, enables one to determine the point at which it is maximized. To illustrate, consider the following profit function:

$$\pi = -\$10,000 + \$400Q - \$2Q^2.$$

Here π = total profit, and Q is output in units. As shown in Figure 2.3, if output is zero, the firm incurs a \$10,000 loss (fixed costs are \$10,000); but as output rises, profit increases. A breakeven point is reached at 28 units of output; that is, revenues equal costs and profit is zero at that activity level. Profit is maximized at 100 units and declines thereafter. The marginal profit function graphed in Figure 2.3 begins at a level of \$400 and declines continuously. For output quantities from 0 to 100 units marginal profit is positive, and total profit increases with each additional unit of output; at $Q = 100$ marginal profit is zero, and total profit is at its maximum. Beyond $Q = 100$ marginal profit is negative, and total profit is decreasing.

A second example of the importance of the marginal concept in economic decision analysis is provided by the important and well-known

Figure 2.3
Profit as a Function of Output

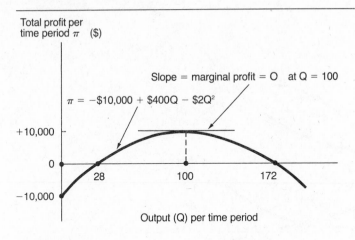

Total profit per
time period π ($)

Slope = marginal profit = 0   at Q = 100

$\pi = -\$10{,}000 + \$400Q - \$2Q^2$

+10,000

0

−10,000

28   100   172

Output (Q) per time period

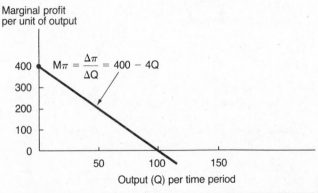

Marginal profit
per unit of output

400   $M\pi = \dfrac{\Delta\pi}{\Delta Q} = 400 - 4Q$

300

200

100

0

50   100   150

Output (Q) per time period

microeconomic corollary that marginal revenue equals marginal cost
when profits are maximized. Figure 2.4 illustrates the relationship.
Here, hypothetical revenue and cost functions are shown. Total profit
is equal to total revenue minus total cost and is, therefore, equal to the
vertical distance between the two curves at any output level. This distance is maximized at output Q_B, where marginal revenue, MR, and
marginal cost, MC, are equal, i.e., $MR = MC$ at the profit maximizing
output level.

The reason that Q_B is the profit maximizing output can be intuitively
explained by considering the shapes of the two curves to the right of
point A. At A total revenue equals total cost, and we have a breakeven
point; that is, an output quantity where profits are zero. At output
quantities just beyond Q_A, marginal revenue is greater than marginal
cost, meaning that total revenue is rising faster than total cost, so the

Figure 2.4
Total Revenue, Total Cost, and Profit Maximization

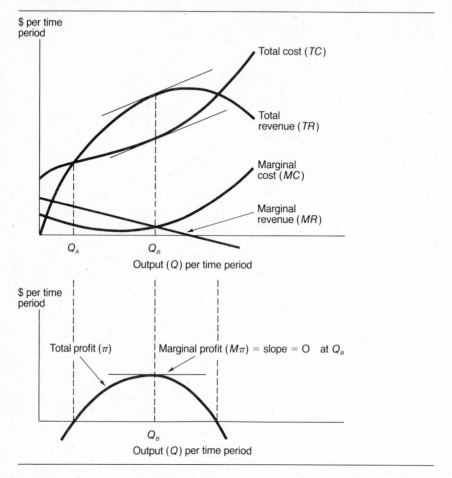

curves are spreading farther apart and profits are increasing. This diverging of the curves continues as long as total revenue is rising faster than total cost, in other words, as long as $MR > MC$. Once the slope of the total revenue curve is exactly equal to the slope of the total cost curve—in other words, where marginal revenue equals marginal cost—the two curves will be parallel and no longer diverging. This occurs at output Q_B. Beyond Q_B the slope of the cost curve is greater than that of the revenue curve (marginal cost is greater than marginal revenue), so the distance between them is decreasing and total profits decline.

This relationship between marginal revenue, marginal cost, and profit maximization can also be demonstrated by considering the general profit expression, $\pi = TR - TC$. Because total profit is total revenue minus total cost, marginal profit ($M\pi$) will be marginal revenue (MR) minus marginal cost (MC). That is,

$$M\pi = MR - MC.$$

Now, because maximization of a function requires that the marginal of the function be equal to zero, profit maximization will occur where

$$M\pi = MR - MC = 0,$$

or where

$$MR = MC.$$

Thus, in determining the optimal activity level for a firm the marginal relationship tells us that so long as the increase in revenues associated with expanding output exceeds the increase in costs, continued expansion is profitable. The optimal output is found where marginal revenue is equal to marginal cost, marginal profit is zero, and total profit is maximized.

The Incremental Concept in Economic Analysis

The marginal concept introduced above is a key component in the economic decision-making process. It is important to recognize, however, that marginal relationships are limited for managerial decision making by the fact that they measure only impact associated with *unitary changes*. In many managerial decision situations, one is interested in the effect of changes or differences that result from alternatives that are of a much broader nature. For example, one might be interested in analyzing the effects on revenues, costs, and profits of doubling a firm's production level. Or, one might be interested in analyzing the profit impact of introducing a new product, or in assessing the cost impact of changing the production system used to produce the current products of the firm. In all managerial decision making, *differences* or *changes* are the key elements in the selection of an optimal course of action. The marginal concept, while correct for analyzing unitary changes, is too narrow to provide a general methodology for evaluating alternative courses of action.

The **incremental concept** is the economist's generalization of the marginal concept. Incremental analysis involves examining the impact of alternative courses of action on revenues, costs, and profit. The focus is on changes or differences between the available alternatives. The incremental change is defined as the total change resulting from the decision. For example, the incremental revenue associated with adding a new item to a firm's product line would be measured as the difference between the firm's total revenue with the product and without the product.

The fundamental relationships of incremental analysis are essentially the same as with marginal analysis. Total profit increases so long as incremental profit is positive; with a negative incremental profit, total profit declines. Similarly, incremental profit is positive (and total profit increases) if the incremental revenue associated with a decision exceeds the incremental cost. The incremental concept is so intuitively obvious that it is easy to overlook both its significance in managerial decision making and the complexity that may be involved in correctly applying it.

For this reason, the incremental concept is often violated in practice. For example, a firm may refuse to sell excess computer time for $500 an hour because it figures its cost as $550 an hour, calculated by adding a standard overhead cost of $250 an hour to an incremental operating cost of $300 an hour. The relevant incremental cost of computer usage, however, is only $300, so the firm would forego a $200-per-hour contribution to profit by not selling its excess time. Any firm that adds a standard allocated charge for *fixed* costs and overhead to the true incremental cost of production runs the risk of turning down profitable sales.

On the other hand, care must be exercised to insure against incorrectly assigning a low incremental cost to a decision when a higher cost in fact exists. An example that came to the authors' attention involved a heat-treating plant where metal parts were hardened prior to final assembly in various products. At the time, the economy was depressed and the plant had unused capacity. A major steel company offered the firm a five-year contract to treat certain products, but at a price well below the normal charges. The price offered exceeded operating expenses, but was not sufficient to cover all overhead and provide a normal profit margin. That is, the offered price covered out-of-pocket costs but not full costs plus profits. The heat-treating company accepted the contract, believing that it would cover incremental costs and still have a little left over to contribute to total overhead expenses, which would not be affected by the decision.

A few months later the economy picked up, and other customers, who paid a higher price, began to bring in additional business. The plant was soon operating at full capacity, and the firm faced the prospect of being forced to turn away profitable business. At this point the plant manager realized his mistake—he had misjudged demand and had thereby miscalculated his costs. He had assumed that plant and equipment costs would be unaffected by the new contract, but in fact the contract forced him to expand at some considerable cost. If expansion had not been possible, then the true incremental costs of taking on the steel firm's business would have included the opportunity cost (lost profits) of the foregone regular business.

As another example of the comprehensive nature of the incremental concept, consider the measurement of the incremental revenue resulting from introducing a new product in a firm's product line. Incremental revenue in this case would include not only the revenue received from sale of the new product, but also any change in the revenues generated by the remainder of the firm's product line. Thus, the incremental revenues would include any revenue resulting from increased sales of another product, where that increase was the result of adding the new product to the firm's line. Similarly, if the new item took sales from another of the firm's products, the loss in revenue on sales of those products must be accounted for in measuring the incremental revenue of the new product.

The incremental concept is important for managerial decision making, because it tells us to focus our analysis on changes or differences between the available alternatives. Likewise it tells us that revenues and costs that are unaffected by the decision are irrelevant and should not be included in the analysis. The incremental concept is examined in somewhat greater detail in Chapters 6 and 9.

Summary

Managerial decision making is the process of finding the best solution to a given problem. Managerial economics plays an important role in this process. In this chapter we first introduced a number of methods used to express economic relationships, then proceeded to examine several fundamental principles of economic analysis.

Economic relationships can be expressed as tables, graphs, or equations. The key concepts involve totals, averages, and marginals, which are interrelated in a unique manner. Knowledge of these interrelationships provides valuable insights for managerial decision making.

Frequently, optimality analysis involves locating the maximum value of a function. Values for the function could be calculated and entered in a table or plotted on a graph, and the point where the function is maximized would be observed directly. It is often more convenient, however, to use the marginal concept to locate the optimum point. The total value of a function will be increasing when the marginal is positive and decreasing when the marginal is negative. The marginal value will be zero at the point where the function is maximized.

A similar relationship exists between marginal and average values. When the marginal of a function exceeds the average, the average will increase. Likewise, if the marginal is smaller than the average, the average will decrease. Because the marginal relationship measures changes resulting from a unitary change in the decision variable, its use for managerial decision making is limited. The incremental concept was introduced as a generalized basis for structuring the economic analysis of decision alternatives. The incremental concept stresses the importance in managerial decision making of focusing on an analysis of change or differences. One needs to analyze those factors that are affected by a decision. Factors that do not change, or that are invariant across the alternatives available to the decision maker, will not have any impact on the outcome and are irrelevant to the decision.

Questions

2.1. Describe the relationship between the total and the marginal value of a function, and explain why this relationship is so important for economic analysis.

2.2. Why must a marginal curve always intersect the related average curve at either a maximum or a minimum point?

2.3. Would you expect a firm's total revenue function to be maximized at an output level that is greater or less than the profit maximizing output? Why?

2.4. Explain why marginal profit is zero (and, hence, total profit is maximized) at the output where marginal revenue equals marginal cost.

2.5. Economists have long argued that if you want to tax away excess profits from a firm without affecting the allocative efficiency of market-determined price/output relationships, you should use a lump-sum license tax instead of an excise or sales tax. Use the materials developed in this chapter to support this position.

2.6. Distinguish the incremental concept from the marginal concept.

Solved Problem

2.1. Jim Albright is a student at Southern Technical University. He is preparing for final exams and has decided to devote a total of five hours to the study of finance and managerial economics. Albright's goal is to maximize the average grade earned in the two courses, and he must decide how much time to spend on each. (*Note*: Maximizing the average grade in the two courses is equivalent to maximizing the sum of the grades.) According to his best estimates, Albright's grades will vary according to the schedules shown below.

Finance		Managerial Economics	
Hours of Study	Grade	Hours of Study	Grade
0	25	0	50
1	45	1	62
2	65	2	72
3	75	3	81
4	82	4	88
5	88	5	93

a) Construct a table showing the marginal value of additional hours of study for each subject.

b) How much time should Albright spend studying each subject?

c) In addition to managerial economics and finance, Albright is also taking a marketing course. He estimates that each hour spent studying marketing will result in an eight-point increase on the marketing final examination. He has tentatively decided to spend three hours preparing for the marketing exam. If Albright is attempting to maximize his average grade in all three courses, is this an optimal decision? Why?

Solution

a)

Finance			Managerial Economics		
Hours of Study	Grade	Marginal Value	Hours of Study	Grade	Marginal Value
0	25	——	0	50	——
1	45	20	1	62	12
2	65	20	2	72	10
3	75	10	3	81	9
4	82	7	4	88	7
5	88	6	5	93	5

b) With only five hours to study, Albright will spend three hours on finance and two hours on managerial economics. This solution is found by allocating each hour to the subject with the highest marginal exam score. Thus, the first two hours would be devoted to finance, in which the marginal grades are 20 for each hour. The third hour would be spent studying managerial economics for a marginal return of 12, and the last two hours would be split between finance and managerial economics since each offers a 10-point marginal grade improvement for another hour of study.

c) Albright's decision to spend three hours studying for his marketing exam is incorrect if his objective is to maximize his total grade received in finance, managerial economics, and marketing. Only two hours should be allocated to studying marketing since an additional hour spent on managerial economics would increase his total grade by nine points rather than the eight points gained by the third hour of studying marketing.

2.2. The Janes Manufacturing Company has developed and test-marketed a highly energy-efficient home heating and cooling system. The Janes-Air System is unique, and preliminary indications are that a substantial share of the new home and retrofitting markets can be obtained if Janes acts quickly in expanding its production. Data from independent marketing consultants retained by Janes indicate demand and marginal revenue relationships for the Janes-Air System of

$$P = \$6{,}000 - \$3Q.$$
$$MR = \$6{,}000 - \$6Q.$$

In addition, Janes' accounting department has estimated total variable costs and marginal costs per unit of

$$TVC = \$1{,}000Q + \$2Q^2$$
$$MC = \$1{,}000 \quad + \$4Q.$$

And finally, fixed costs allocated to the Janes-Air System total $800,000 yearly.

a) What are the total revenue (TR) and the profit (π) functions for the Janes-Air System?
b) Determine the sales revenue maximizing price and output levels.
c) Determine the profit maximizing price and output levels.

Solution

a)
$$
\begin{aligned}
TR &= P \cdot Q \\
&= (\$6{,}000 - \$3Q) \cdot Q \\
&= \$6{,}000Q - \$3Q^2. \\
\pi &= TR - TC \\
&= TR - FC - TVC \\
&= \$6{,}000Q - \$3Q^2 - \$800{,}000 - \$1{,}000Q - \$2Q^2.
\end{aligned}
$$

b) Revenue will be maximized at that output level where $MR = 0$. Here:

$$
\begin{aligned}
MR = \$6{,}000 - \$6Q &= 0 \\
\$6Q &= \$6{,}000 \\
Q &= 1{,}000 \text{ units.}
\end{aligned}
$$

Therefore, the revenue maximizing price is

$$
\begin{aligned}
P &= \$6{,}000 - \$3Q \\
&= \$6{,}000 - \$3(1{,}000) \\
&= \$3{,}000.
\end{aligned}
$$

c) Profits will be maximized where $MR = MC$. Here:

$$MR = MC$$
$$\$6,000 - \$6Q = \$1,000 + \$4Q$$
$$\$10Q = \$5,000$$
$$Q = 500 \text{ units.}$$

Therefore, the profit maximizing price is

$$P = \$6,000 - \$3Q$$
$$= \$6,000 - \$3(500)$$
$$= \$4,500.$$

Problem Set

2.1. a) Given the total revenue (TR) and output (Q) data shown in the table below, calculate the related marginal revenue (MR) and average revenue (AR) figures needed to complete the table.

Q	TR	MR	AR
0	$ 0	—	$ 0
1	218	$218	218
2	464	246	232
3	726		242
4	992	266	
5	1250	258	250
6	1488		248
7	1694	206	242
8	1856	162	232
9		106	
10	2000	38	200
11	1958		178
12	1824	(134)	

b) Using a two-part graph, like Figure 2.2, plot the total revenue, marginal revenue, and average revenue curves indicated by the data in the table constructed in part a. (*Note*: The relationships among totals, averages, and marginals are typically more accurately depicted by graphing the marginal values midway between the two output levels to which they relate. For example, the $218 marginal revenue associated with the first unit of output should be plotted at $Q = 0.5$.)

c) Locate on the total revenue curve graphed in Problem 2.1b the points at which marginal, average, and total revenues are maximized.

d) Locate the points of maximum total, average, and marginal revenues, using the average and marginal revenue curves constructed in part b.

e) Compare the relationships between the total, average, and marginal curves on your graph in part b and the table in part a with the relationships indicated in the chapter.

2.2. Jo Walters is a regional sales representative for Dental Metals Inc. Walters offers alloy products created from gold, silver, platinum, and other metals to several dental laboratories in Iowa, Nebraska, and South Dakota. Walters's goal is to maximize her total monthly commission income, which is figured at 8 percent of gross sales. In reviewing her monthly experience over the past year, Walters found the following relationships between days spent in each state and sales generated.

Iowa		Nebraska		South Dakota	
Days	Gross Sales	Days	Gross Sales	Days	Gross Sales
0	5,000	0	5,000	0	4,000
2	8,300	2	10,000	2	6,800
4	10,500	4	14,500	4	8,900
6	12,500	6	17,500	6	10,900
8	14,000	8	19,300	8	11,200
10	15,000	10	20,000	10	11,300

a) Construct a table showing the marginal sales per day in each state.

b) If administrative duties limit Walters to only 16 selling days per month, how should she spend them?

c) An accounting services firm has offered to handle Walters's administrative duties for $100 per month. Would accepting this offer be profitable if Walters would be able to spend an additional three days of selling per month? Explain.

2.3. Steadyride Inc. operates in the highly competitive automotive tire market. Tires are sold at $55 each, and engineering estimates indicate Steadyride's total costs are $TC = \$50{,}000 + \$15Q + \$0.002Q^2$. The related marginal costs per unit are $MC = \$15 + \$0.004Q$.

a) Write an expression for Steadyride's profit function.

b) Calculate the output level that will maximize Steadyride's profit.

c) Calculate this maximum profit.

2.4. Computer World Corporation has recently negotiated a franchise agreement with a Japanese supplier to sell minicomputers in the western region of the United States. Computer World's franchise agreement stipulates a $1,700 supplier price for each minicomputer, and Computer World spends an average of $300 per unit for promotion and servicing. Computer World pays fixed (capital, overhead, and so on) costs of $300,000 per year. Computer World has complete control over product promotion and pricing strategy within its selling area. Furthermore, although Computer World's supplier does not charge a franchise fee, it may unilaterally elect to do so at any time for the remainder of the franchise agreement. Stacy Singleton, marketing manager for Computer World, has been asked to develop a pricing strategy in light of the following sales relations determined by the marketing department:

$$P = \$6{,}000 - \$2Q$$
$$MR = \$6{,}000 - \$4Q,$$

where P is price in dollars, Q is the number of minicomputers sold, and MR is marginal revenue in dollars.

a) Write expressions for Computer World's total revenue, total costs, and profits.

b) Determine profit maximizing price and output levels. Calculate this maximum profit.

c) Determine profit maximizing price and output levels, assuming Computer World's supplier imposes a $1 million per year franchise fee. Calculate this maximum profit.

2.5. Pizza King Inc. has just expanded to a new city and has opened two pizza parlors. Pizza King's owner, Jim Daniels, is considering two short-term strategies. Daniels could continue to operate the two existing pizza parlors and set prices to maximize profit, or he could increase the number of Pizza King pizza parlors and locate them in different parts of the city to develop a pizza delivery service. To increase the number of Pizza King pizza parlors, Daniels is considering setting prices to maximize sales revenue. Recent cost and demand analyses for Pizza King have revealed the following:

$$TC\ (\$000) = \$120 + \$2Q + \$0.05Q^2$$
$$MC = \$2 + \$0.1Q$$
$$P = \$10 - \$0.05Q$$
$$MR = \$10 - \$0.1Q,$$

where Q is in thousands of pizzas.

a) Determine the total revenue function. (Remember that Q is measured in thousands of pizzas.)

b) Determine the total profit function.

c) Calculate the sales maximizing level of output. What price would Daniels set to achieve this level of sales and what profits would be generated?

d) Calculate the profit maximizing level of output. What price would Daniels set to achieve this level of sales and what profits would be generated?

e) The sales maximizing output level calculated in part c should be greater than the profit maximizing output level calculated in part d. Will this always be true? Explain.

2.6. During the past year, California Technical Products Inc. successfully introduced the HS-2, a heat sensor for use in product testing. Estimated revenue and cost relations for the HS-2 are:

$$TR = \$110Q - \$0.006Q^2 \qquad TC = \$196,000 + \$10Q + \$0.004Q^2$$
$$MR = \$110 \quad - \$0.012Q \qquad MC = \$10 + \$0.008Q.$$

a) Calculate quantity, price, and total profits at the profit maximizing output level.

b) Calculate these same values for the average cost minimizing level of output.

c) Discuss any differences between your answers to parts a and b.

References

Albert, Kenneth J., ed. *Handbook of Business Problem Solving*. New York: McGraw-Hill, 1980.

Arrow, Kenneth J., and Michael D. Intriligator, eds. *Handbook of Mathematical Economics*. Amsterdam: North-Holland, 1981.

Barnett, Arnold. "Misapplication Reviews: The Linear Model and Some of Its Friends." *Interfaces* 13 (February 1983): 61–65.

Budnick, Frank S. *Applied Mathematics: for Business, Economics, and the Social Sciences*. New York: McGraw-Hill, 1979.

Cain, Jack, and Robert A. Carman. *Mathematics for Business Careers*. New York: John Wiley & Sons, 1981.

Chiang, Alpha C. *Fundamental Methods of Mathematical Economics*. 3d ed. New York: McGraw-Hill, 1984.

Freund, John E., and Thomas A. Williams. *College Mathematics with Business Applications*. Englewood Cliffs, NJ: Prentice-Hall, 1983.

Funk, Jerry. *Business Mathematics*. Boston: Allyn & Bacon, 1980.

Graham, Robert J. "'Give the Kid a Number': An Essay on the Folly and Consequences of Trusting Your Data." *Interfaces* 12 (June 1982): 40–44.

Haeussler, Ernest F., and Richard S. Paul. *Introductory Mathematical Analysis for Students of Business and Economics*. 3d ed. Reston, Va.: Reston, 1980.

Khoury, Sarkis J., and Torrence D. Parsons. *Mathematical Methods in Finance and Economics*. New York: Elsevier-North Holland, 1981.

Mintzberg, Henry. "A Note on that Dirty Word 'Efficiency.'" *Interfaces* 12 (October 1982): 101–105.

Ostrosky, Anthony L., and James V. Koch. *Introduction to Mathematical Economics*. Boston: Houghton Mifflin, 1979.

Thorn, Richard S. *Business Mathematics*. 2d ed. New York: Harper & Row, 1979.

Weber, Jean E. *Mathematical Analysis: Business and Economic Applications*. 4th ed. New York: Harper & Row, 1982.

Appendix 2.A

Marginal Analysis:
A Mathematical Specification

This appendix will be quite straightforward for all readers, including those who have only limited experience with mathematical studies. The math that is presented here was developed specifically for handling problems such as those found in managerial economics, so some concepts can be understood much more easily when expressed in these terms. Furthermore, the level of math most commonly used in managerial economics is quite elementary and therefore not difficult to learn.

Although tables and graphs are useful for explaining concepts, equations are frequently better suited for problem solving. One reason is that powerful analytical techniques can often be employed to locate maximum or minimum values of an objective function very efficiently through marginal analysis. Additionally, the basic mathematical concepts are easily extended to decision problems where the options available to the decision maker are limited by one or more constraints. Thus, a mathematical approach is especially useful for the constrained optimization problems that characterize much of managerial decision making.

Concept of a Marginal

Earlier, we defined a marginal value as *the change in the value of the dependent variable associated with a one-unit change in an independent variable.* We can specify this relationship more precisely by examining the nature of change in a function. Consider the unspecified function $Y = f(X)$, which is read Y is a function of X. Using Δ (read delta) to denote change, we can express the change in the value of the independent variable, X, by the notation ΔX and the change in the dependent variable, Y, as ΔY.

The ratio $\Delta Y/\Delta X$ provides a very general specification of the marginal concept:

$$\text{Marginal } Y = \frac{\Delta Y}{\Delta X}. \tag{2.A.1}$$

The change in Y, ΔY, divided by the change in X, ΔX, indicates the change in the dependent variable associated with a one-unit change in the value of X.

Figure 2.A.1, which is a graph of a function relating Y to X, illustrates this relationship. For values of X close to the origin, a relatively small change in X provides a large change in Y. Thus, the value of $\Delta Y/\Delta X$, for example $(Y_2 - Y_1)/(X_2 - X_1)$, is relatively large, showing that a small increase in X induces a large increase in Y. The situation is reversed the farther out one moves along the X axis. A large increase in X, say from X_3 to X_4, produces only a small increase in Y, from Y_3 to Y_4, so $\Delta Y/\Delta X$ is small.

It is clear in Figure 2.A.1, that the marginal relationship between X and Y changes at different points on the curve. When the curve is relatively steep, the dependent variable Y is highly responsive to changes in the independent variable; but when the curve is relatively flat, Y

Figure 2.A.1
Illustration of Changing $\Delta Y/\Delta X$ over the Range of a Curve

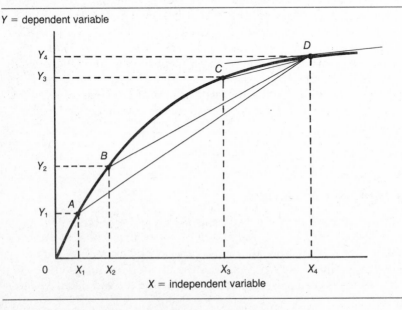

does not respond as significantly to changes in X. Notice, however, that the general expression of the marginal relationship given in Equation 2.A.1 does not necessarily capture this changing marginal relationship. For example, using that equation, one could estimate the marginal relationship as

$$\frac{\Delta Y}{\Delta X} = \frac{Y_4 - Y_1}{X_4 - X_1}$$

This measure of the marginal is shown in Figure 2.A.1 as the slope of the line connecting points A and D. We can see that this measure of the marginal is considerably smaller than the estimate one would obtain looking at the change $(Y_2 - Y_1)/(X_2 - X_1)$, the slope of a straight line connecting points A and B; and it is larger than the marginal found for the change between points C and D, $(Y_4 - Y_3)/(X_4 - X_3)$, the slope of a straight line connecting those points.

The problem is that $(Y_4 - Y_1)/(X_4 - X_1)$ measures the average change in Y for a one-unit change in X between points A and D. Since this "average" marginal value may be significantly different from the actual marginal at a point such as D, it has limited value for decision making and could in fact lead to incorrect decisions.

If a decision maker were interested in knowing how Y varied for changes in X around point D, the relevant marginal would be found as $\Delta Y/\Delta X$ for a very small change in X around X_4. The mathematical concept for measuring the nature of such very small changes is called a *derivative*. A derivative, then, is just a precise specification of the marginal value at a particular point on a function. The mathematical notation for a derivative is:

$$\frac{dY}{dX} = \lim_{\Delta X \to 0} \frac{\Delta Y}{\Delta X},$$

which is read: "The derivative of Y with respect to X equals the limit of the ratio $\Delta Y/\Delta X$, as ΔX approaches zero."[1]

---

[1] A limit can be explained briefly in the following manner: If the value of a function $Y = f(X)$ approaches a constant Y^* as the value of the independent variable X approaches X^*, then Y^* is called the limit of the function as X approaches X^*. This would be written as:

$$\lim_{x \to x^*} f(X) = Y^*.$$

For example, if $Y = X - 4$, then the limit of this function as X approaches 5 is 1; that is:

$$\lim_{x \to 5} (X - 4) = 1.$$

This says that the value of X approaches but does not quite reach 5; the value of the function $Y = X - 4$ comes closer and closer to 1. This concept of a limit is examined in detail in any introductory calculus textbook.

This concept of the derivative as the limit of a ratio is precisely equivalent to the slope of a curve at a point. Figure 2.A.1 also presents this idea. Notice in that figure that the *average* slope of the curve between points A and D is measured as:

$$\frac{\Delta Y}{\Delta X} = \frac{Y_4 - Y_1}{X_4 - X_1},$$

and is shown as the slope of the chord connecting the two points. Similarly, the average slope of the curve can be measured over smaller and smaller intervals of X and shown by other chords, such as those connecting points B and C with D. At the limit, as ΔX approaches zero around point D, the ratio $\Delta Y/\Delta X$ is equal to the slope of a line drawn tangent to the curve at point D. *The slope of this tangent is defined as the derivative, dY/dX, of the function at point D; it measures the marginal change in Y associated with a very small change in X at that point.*

To illustrate the relationship between the mathematical concept of a derivative and the economic concept of a marginal, the dependent variable Y in our example might be total revenue and the independent variable X might be output. The derivative dY/dX then shows precisely how revenue and output are related at a specific output level. Since the change in revenue associated with a change in output is defined as the marginal revenue, the derivative of the total revenue provides a precise measure of marginal revenue at any specific output level. A similar situation exists for total cost: The derivative of the total cost function at any output level indicates the marginal cost at that output.

Derivatives provide much useful information in managerial economics. Other illustrations of their usefulness will be considered later, but first the rules for finding the derivatives of certain frequently encountered functions are provided.

Rules for Differentiating a Function

Determining the derivative of a function is not a particularly difficult task; it simply involves applying a basic formula to the function. The basic formulas or rules for differentiation are presented below. Proofs are omitted here, but they can be found in any introductory calculus textbook.

Constants

The derivative of a constant is always zero; that is, if $Y = $ a constant, then it would not change for different values of X and

$$\frac{dY}{dX} = 0.$$

Figure 2.A.2
Graph of a Constant Function: Y = Constant; $dY/dX = 0$

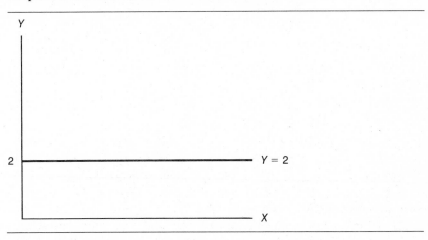

This situation is graphed in Figure 2.A.2 for the example $Y = 2$. Since Y is defined to be a constant, its value is not a function of X and hence dY/dX must be zero.

Powers

The derivative of a power function such as $Y = aX^b$, where a and b are constants, is equal to the exponent b multiplied by the coefficient a times the variable X raised to the $b - 1$ power:

$$Y = aX^b$$

$$\frac{dY}{dX} = b \cdot a \cdot X^{(b-1)}.$$

For example, given the function:

$$Y = 2X^3,$$

then:

$$\frac{dY}{dX} = 3 \cdot 2 \cdot X^{(3-1)}$$

$$= 6X^2.$$

Two further examples of power functions should clarify this rule. The derivative of the function $Y = X^3$ is given as:

$$\frac{dY}{dX} = 3 \cdot X^2.$$

The exponent, 3, is multiplied by the implicit coefficient, 1, and in turn by the variable, X, raised to the second power.

Finally, the derivative of the function $Y = 0.5X$ is:

$$\frac{dY}{dX} = 1 \cdot 0.5 \cdot X^{1-1} = 1 \cdot 0.5 \cdot X^0 = 0.5.$$

The implicit exponent, 1, is multiplied by the coefficient, 0.5, times the variable, X, raised to the zero power. Since any number raised to the zero power equals 1, the result is 0.5.

Examining a graph may help to make the power function concept clear. In Figure 2.A.3, the last two power functions given above, $Y = X^3$ and $Y = 0.5X$, are graphed. Consider first $Y = 0.5X$. The derivative of this function, $dY/dX = 0.5$, is a constant, indicating that the slope of the function is a constant. This can be seen readily from the graph. The derivative measures the *rate of change*. If the rate of change is constant, as it must be if the basic function is linear, then the derivative of the function must be a constant. The second function, $Y = X^3$, rises at an increasing rate as X increases. The derivative of the func-

Figure 2.A.3
Graphs of Power Functions

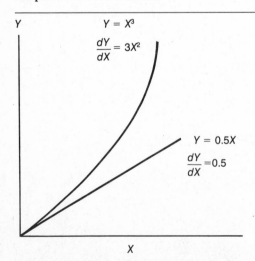

tion, $dY/dX = 3X^2$, also increases as X becomes larger, indicating that the slope of the function is increasing or that the rate of change is increasing.

Sums and Differences

The derivative of a sum (difference) is equal to the sum (difference) of the derivatives of the individual terms. Thus, if $Y = U + V$, then:

$$\frac{dY}{dX} = \frac{dU}{dX} + \frac{dV}{dX}.$$

For example, if $U = 2X^2$, $V = -X^3$, and $Y = U + V = 2X^2 - X^3$, then:

$$\frac{dY}{dX} = 4X - 3X^2.$$

Here the derivative of the first term, $2X^2$, is found to be $4X$ by the power rule; the derivative of the second term, $-X^3$, is found to be $-3X^2$ by that same rule; and the derivative of the total function is the sum of the derivatives of the parts.

Consider a second example of this rule. If $Y = 300 + 5X + 2X^2$, then:

$$\frac{dY}{dX} = 0 + 5 + 4X.$$

The derivative of 300 is 0 by the constant rule; the derivative of $5X$ is 5 by the power rule; and the derivative of $2X^2$ is $4X$ also by the power rule.

The sums and differences rule says that the derivative of a function that is composed of several terms linked together with plus and minus signs is equal to the derivatives of the individual terms linked together in a similar fashion.

Products

The derivative of the product of two expressions is equal to the sum of the first term multiplied by the derivative of the second, *plus* the second term times the derivative of the first. Thus, if $Y = U \cdot V$, then:

$$\frac{dY}{dX} = U \cdot \frac{dV}{dX} + V \cdot \frac{dU}{dX}.$$

For example, if $Y = 3X^2(3 - X)$, then letting $U = 3X^2$ and $V = (3 - X)$:

$$\frac{dY}{dX} = 3X^2 \left(\frac{dV}{dX} \right) + (3 - X) \left(\frac{dU}{dX} \right)$$

$$= 3X^2(-1) + (3 - X)(6X)$$

$$= -3X^2 + 18X - 6X^2$$

$$= 18X - 9X^2.$$

The first factor, $3X^2$, is multiplied by the derivative of the second, -1, and added to the second factor, $3 - X$, times the derivative of the first, $6X$. Simplifying the expression results in the final expression shown.

Quotients

The derivative of the quotient of two expressions is equal to the denominator multiplied by the derivative of the numerator *minus* the numerator times the derivative of the denominator—all divided by the square of the denominator. Thus, if $Y = U/V$, then:

$$\frac{dY}{dX} = \frac{V \cdot \dfrac{dU}{dX} - U \cdot \dfrac{dV}{dX}}{V^2}.$$

For example, if $U = 2X - 3$ and $V = 6X^2$, then:

$$Y = \frac{2X - 3}{6X^2}$$

and

$$\frac{dY}{dX} = \frac{6X^2 \cdot 2 - (2X - 3) \, 12X}{36X^4}$$

$$= \frac{12X^2 - 24X^2 + 36X}{36X^4}$$

$$= \frac{36X - 12X^2}{36X^4}$$

$$= \frac{3 - X}{3X^3}.$$

The denominator, $6X^2$, is multiplied by the derivative of the numerator, 2. Subtracted from this is the numerator, $2X - 3$, times the derivative of the denominator, $12X$. The result is then divided by the square of the denominator, $36X^4$. Algebraic reduction results in the final expression of the derivative.

Although there are additional rules for differentiating functions, these are the ones most often required in economic analysis. Knowledge of them gives one ability to analyze and solve many complex managerial decision problems.

Use of Marginals to Maximize or Minimize Functions

The process of **optimization** frequently requires one to select critical values for decision variables in order to achieve the maximum or minimum value for a function. For a function to be at a maximum or minimum, its slope or marginal value must be zero. The *derivative* of a function is a very precise measure of its slope or marginal value at a particular point. Thus, maximization or minimization of a function occurs where its derivative is equal to zero. To illustrate, consider the following profit function:

$$\pi = -\$10,000 + \$400Q - \$2Q^2. \qquad (2.A.2)$$

Here π = total profit, and Q is output in units. As shown in Figure 2.A.4, if output is zero, the firm incurs a $10,000 loss (fixed costs are $10,000); but as output rises, profit also rises. A breakeven point (the output level where profit is zero) is reached at approximately 29 units of output; profit is maximized at 100 units and declines thereafter.

The profit maximizing output could be found by calculating the value of the function at a number of outputs, then plotting these as is done in Figure 2.A.4. The maximum can also be located by finding the derivative, or marginal, of the function, then determining the value of Q that makes the derivative (marginal) equal to zero.

$$\text{Marginal Profit } (M\pi) = \frac{d\pi}{dQ} = \$400 - \$4Q.$$

Setting the derivative equal to zero results in:

$$\$400 - \$4Q = 0$$

$$\$4Q = \$400$$

$$Q = 100 \text{ units}$$

Therefore, when $Q = 100$, marginal profit is zero and total profit is at a maximum. Even in this simple illustration it is easier to locate the profit

Figure 2.A.4
Profit as a Function of Output

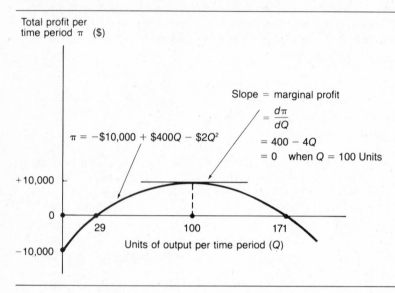

Total profit per
time period π ($)

Slope = marginal profit

$$= \frac{d\pi}{dQ}$$

$\pi = -\$10,000 + \$400Q - \$2Q^2$

$= 400 - 4Q$

$= 0$ when $Q = 100$ Units

+10,000

0

29   100   171

$-10,000$

Units of output per time period (Q)

maximizing value by finding the marginal profit as the derivative of
total profit and determining the output at which marginal profit is zero,
than by graphic analysis; had the function been more complex, the use
of the derivative might have been the only efficient means of determining the profit maximizing output level.

Distinguishing Maximums from Minimums

A problem can arise when marginals are used to locate maximums or
minimums. The first derivative of the total function provides a measure of whether the function is rising or falling at any point. To be maximized or minimized, the function must be neither rising nor falling;
that is, the slope as measured by the first derivative must be zero.
However, the marginal value or derivative will be zero for both maximum and minimum values of a function, so further analysis is necessary to determine whether a maximum or a minimum has been
located.

   This point is illustrated in Figure 2.A.5, where we see that the slope
of the total profit curve is zero at both points A and B. Point A, how-

ever, locates an output that minimizes profits, while *B* locates the profit-maximizing output.

Points of maximization can be distinguished from points of minimization by a more detailed examination of the marginal relationship. Notice in Figure 2.A.5 that the marginal profit curve is rising at output level Q_A and falling at output Q_B. At point *A*, marginal profit, which has been negative and thereby causing total profit to decline, is rising through zero on its way to becoming positive, which will cause total profit to increase. Thus, if a marginal curve has a positive slope as it passes through the horizontal axis, the local extreme found at that point will be a minimum.

Figure 2.A.5
Locating Maximum and Minimum Values of a Function

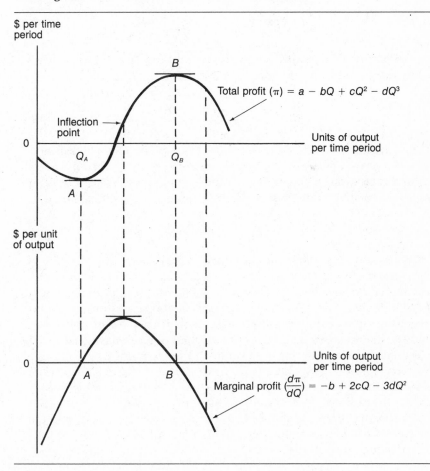

The opposite relationship holds for points that are maximums. Consider point B. Here the marginal profit curve is falling as it passes through the axis. Although declining, it has, up to point B, been positive and total profit is increasing. As it passes through zero, the total function ceases to increase and turns down. Thus, at points of local maximization, the marginal curve will have a negative slope and will be declining.

The slope of a marginal curve is just its own marginal value, and one can use the derivative concepts developed above to find these marginals. This relationship is called a *second-order derivative* since it relates to finding the derivative of a marginal (or derivative) function. For example, if total profit is given by the equation $\pi = a - bQ + cQ^2 - dQ^3$, as in Figure 2.A.5, then the first-order derivative that defines the marginal profit function is:

$$\frac{d\pi}{dQ} = M\pi = -b + 2cQ - 3dQ^2. \qquad \text{(2.A.3)}$$

The second-order derivative of the total profit function is the derivative of the marginal profit function, Equation 2.A.3:

$$\frac{d^2\pi}{dQ^2} = \frac{dM\pi}{dQ} = 2c - 6dQ.$$

Just as the first derivative measures the slope of the total profit function, the second derivative measures the slope of the first derivative or, in this case, the slope of the marginal profit curve. We can use the second derivative to distinguish between points of maximization and minimization because the second derivative of a function is always *negative* when evaluated at a point of *maximization* and *positive* at a point of *minimization*.

The reason for this inverse relationship can be seen in Figure 2.A.5. Note that profits reach a local minimum at point A because marginal profits, which have been negative and therefore causing total profits to fall, suddenly become positive. Marginal profits pass through the zero level from below at point A and hence are increasing, or positively sloped. The reverse situation holds at a point of local maximization; the marginal value is positive but declining up to the point where the total function is maximized, and it is negative after that point. Thus, the marginal function is negatively sloped (that is, *its* derivative is negative) at the point of maximization of the total function.

A numerical example should help clarify this concept. Assume that the total profit function illustrated in Figure 2.A.5 is given by the following equation:

$$\text{Total Profit} = \pi = -\$3,000 - \$2,400Q + \$350Q^2 - \$8.333Q^3. \quad \text{(2.A.4)}$$

Marginal profit is given by the first derivative of the total profit function:

$$\text{Marginal Profit} = \frac{d\pi}{dQ} = -\$2{,}400 + \$700Q - \$25Q^2. \qquad \text{(2.A.5)}$$

Total profit is either maximized or minimized at the points where the first derivative (marginal profit) is zero; that is, where:

$$\frac{d\pi}{dQ} = -\$2{,}400 + \$700Q - \$25Q^2 = 0. \qquad \text{(2.A.6)}$$

Output quantities of 4 and 24 units satisfy Equation 2.A.6 and are therefore points of either maximum or minimum profits.[2]
   Evaluation of the second derivative of the total profit function at each of these output levels will indicate whether they are minimums or maximums. The second derivative of the total profit function is found by taking the derivative of the marginal profit function, Equation 2.A.5:

$$\frac{d^2\pi}{dQ^2} = \frac{dM\pi}{dQ} = \$700 - \$50Q.$$

At output quantity $Q = 4$:

$$\frac{d^2\pi}{dQ^2} = \$700 - \$50 \cdot 4 = \$500.$$

Since the second derivative is positive, indicating that marginal profits are increasing, total profit is *minimized* at 4 units of output. In other words, total profit at 4 units of output corresponds to point A in Figure 2.A.5.
   Evaluating the second derivative at 24 units of output, we obtain:

$$\frac{d^2\pi}{dQ^2} = \$700 - \$50 \cdot 24 = -\$500.$$

---

[2] Any equation of the form $Y = aX^2 + bX + c$ is a quadratic, and its two roots can be found by the general quadratic equation:

$$X = \frac{-b \pm \sqrt{b^2 - 4ac}}{2a}.$$

Substituting the values from Equation 2.A.6 into the quadratic equation, we obtain:

$$X = \frac{-700 \pm \sqrt{700^2 - 4(-25)(-2{,}400)}}{2(-25)} = \frac{-700 \pm \sqrt{490{,}000 - 240{,}000}}{-50}$$

$$X = \frac{-700 \pm \sqrt{250{,}000}}{-50} = \frac{-700 \pm 500}{-50} = 4 \text{ or } 24.$$

Since the second derivative is negative at 24 units, indicating that marginal profit is decreasing, the total profit function has reached a *maximum* at that point. This output level corresponds to point B in Figure 2.A.5.

Multivariate Optimization

Since many managerial decision problems involve more than one decision variable, it is useful to extend the concepts of optimization to equations with three or more variables. Consider the demand function for a product where the quantity demanded, Q, is determined by the price charged, P, and the level of advertising expenditure, A. Such a function would be written as:

$$Q = f(P,A). \qquad (2.A.7)$$

When analyzing multivariable relationships, such as the one in Equation 2.A.7, we need to know the marginal effect of each independent variable on the dependent variable. In other words, optimization in this case requires an analysis of how a change in each independent variable affects the dependent variable, *holding constant the effect of all other independent variables*. The partial derivative is the concept used for this type of marginal analysis. In oral and written treatments of this concept, the word derivative is frequently omitted. That is, reference is typically made to the *partial* of Q rather than the *partial derivative* of Q.

Using the symbol ∂, called delta, we can examine two partial derivatives for the demand function of Equation 2.A.7.

1. The partial of Q with respect to price, $\partial Q/\partial P$.

2. The partial of Q with respect to advertising expenditure, $\partial Q/\partial A$.

The rules for determining partial derivatives are essentially the same as those for simple derivatives. Since the concept of a partial derivative involves an assumption that all variables except the one with respect to which the derivative is being taken remain unchanged, those variables are treated as constants in the differentiation process. Consider the equation $Y = 10 - 4X + 3XZ - Z^2$. In this function there are two independent variables, X and Z, so two partial derivatives can be evaluated. To determine the partial with respect to X, note that the function can be rewritten as:

$$Y = 10 - 4X + (3Z)X - Z^2.$$

Since Z is treated as a constant, the partial derivative of Y with respect to X is:

$$\frac{\partial Y}{\partial X} = 0 - 4 + 3Z - 0$$

$$= -4 + 3Z.$$

The change in Y resulting from a one-unit change in X is equal to -4 plus 3 times the *unchanged* value of Z. In determining the partial of Y with respect to Z, X is treated as a constant, so we can write:

$$Y = 10 - 4X + (3X)Z - Z^2,$$

and the partial with respect to Z is:

$$\frac{\partial Y}{\partial Z} = 0 - 0 + 3X - 2Z$$

$$= 3X - 2Z.$$

A one-unit change in Z, holding X constant, results in a change in Y equal to 3 times the unchanged value of X minus 2 times the initial value of Z. Another example should help clarify the technique of partial differentiation. Let $Y = 2X + 4X^2Z - 3XZ^2 - 2Z^3$. Then, the partial with respect to X is:

$$\frac{\partial Y}{\partial X} = 2 + 8XZ - 3Z^2 - 0,$$

and the partial with respect to Z is:

$$\frac{\partial Y}{\partial Z} = 0 + 4X^2 - 6XZ - 6Z^2.$$

Maximizing Multivariable Functions

The requirement for maximization (or minimization) of a multivariate function is a straightforward extension of that for single variable functions. All first-order partial derivatives must equal zero.[3] Thus, maximization of the function $Y = f(X, Z)$ requires:

---

[3]The second-order requirements for determining maxima and minima of multivariate functions are somewhat complex and are beyond the requirements of our basic treatment of this topic. A full discussion of these requirements can be found in any elementary calculus text.

$$\frac{\partial Y}{\partial X} = 0,$$

and

$$\frac{\partial Y}{\partial Z} = 0.$$

To illustrate this procedure, consider the function:

$$Y = 4X + Z - X^2 + XZ - Z^2, \qquad \text{(2.A.8)}$$

whose partial derivatives are

$$\frac{\partial Y}{\partial X} = 4 - 2X + Z,$$

and

$$\frac{\partial Y}{\partial Z} = 1 + X - 2Z.$$

To maximize Equation 2.A.8, the partials must be set equal to zero:

$$\frac{\partial Y}{\partial X} = 4 - 2X + Z = 0, \qquad \text{(2.A.9)}$$

and

$$\frac{\partial Y}{\partial Z} = 1 + X - 2Z = 0. \qquad \text{(2.A.10)}$$

Here we have two equations in two unknowns. Solving them simultaneously, we find the values for X and Z that maximize the function.

	$4 - 2X + Z = 0$	(2.A.9)
plus	$\underline{2 + 2X - 4Z = 0}$	
	$6 \phantom{{}+2X} - 3Z = 0$	$2 \times$ (2.A.10)
	$3Z = 6$	
	$Z = 2$	

$$4 - 2X + 2 = 0 \qquad \text{(2.A.9)}$$
$$2X = 6$$
$$X = 3.$$

Inserting these values for X and Z into Equation 2.A.8, we find the value of Y to be 7; therefore, the maximum value of Y is 7.

Summary

Frequently, optimality analysis involves locating the maximum or the minimum value of a function. Values for the function can be calculated and entered in a table or plotted on a graph, and the point where the function is maximized (minimized) can be observed directly. It is frequently more convenient, however, to use calculus to locate the optimum point, simply calculating the derivative of the total function and setting it equal to zero; that is, $dY/dX = 0$. Accordingly, the use of derivatives for determining points of maximization and minimization was explained in some detail.

A function may have several values at which the derivative is zero, with some points representing maximums and others minimums. To determine whether a maximum or a minimum has been found, the second derivative is calculated. If d^2Y/dX^2 is negative, a maximum has been found; if it is positive, a minimum has been located.

If a function contains more than two variables, partial differentiation is used; therefore, the process of finding partials was examined. To maximize a function of two or more variables, the partial with respect to each variable must be calculated, and these partials must simultaneously be set equal to zero.

Chapter 3

Demand Analysis

Key Terms

Complements   Income elasticity
Cross-price elasticity   Price elasticity
Demand curve   Regression analysis
Demand function   Substitutes
Elasticity

In many respects the most important determinant of a firm's profitability is the demand for its products. No matter how efficient its production processes and regardless of the astuteness of its financial manager, personnel director, or other officers, the firm cannot operate profitably unless a demand for its products exists or can be created, or unless it can find a new set of products for which a demand exists.

Because of the critical role of demand as a determinant of profitability, estimates of expected future demand constitute a key element in all planning activities. Production decisions are profoundly influenced by the firm's underlying demand function. For example, if demand is relatively stable, then long, continuous production runs may be scheduled; if demand fluctuates, either flexible production processes must be employed or sizable inventories must be carried. Demand conditions in the product market also affect the firm's labor and capital requirements. If product demand is strong and growing, the financial manager must arrange to finance the firm's growing capital requirements, and the personnel director must arrange to recruit and train a sufficiently large work force to produce and sell the firm's products.

The demand function also interacts with the set of possible production technologies to determine the market structure the firm will operate in and, hence, the level of competition it will face. Where these demand and production factors would lead to monopoly or oligopoly, direct regulation or antitrust actions may be used to secure the public interest. In Chapters 8, 9, and 10—where market structure, pricing practices, and regulation and antitrust policy are discussed—the importance of demand as a determinant of public policy will become quite apparent.

Demand is a complex subject, but it must be thoroughly understood because this helps managers to achieve their goals. Accordingly, in this chapter we examine the theory of demand, emphasizing the major determinants of demand for goods and services, the methods of analyzing the strength of demand for a product, and the effect of changing conditions on that demand. We also use the relationships developed here to formulate models that can actually be used to estimate demand functions.

The Basis for Demand

The term *demand* refers to the number of units of a particular good or service that customers are willing and able to purchase during a specified period and under a given set of conditions. The time period might be a year, and the conditions that must be specified would include the price of the good in question, prices and availability of competitive goods, expectations of price changes, consumer incomes, consumer tastes and preferences, advertising expenditures, and so on. The amount of the product that consumers wish to purchase, the *demand* for the product, is dependent on all these factors.

For managerial decision making, the primary focus is on market demand. Market demand, however, is merely the aggregate of individual, or personal, demand, and much insight into market demand relationships is gained by understanding the nature of individual demand.

At the level of the individual, demand is determined by two factors: (1) the value associated with acquiring and using the good or service, and (2) the ability to acquire. Both are required for effective individual demand. Desire without purchasing power may lead to wants, but not to demand.

There are two basic models of individual demand. One, known as the theory of consumer behavior, relates to the demand for personal consumption products. This model is appropriate for analyzing individual demand for goods and services that directly satisfy consumer desires. In this model the value or worth of a good or service, its *util-*

ity, is the prime determinant of individual demand. Individuals are viewed as attempting to maximize the total utility or satisfaction provided by the goods and services they acquire and consume. This optimization process requires them to examine such relationships as the marginal utility of acquiring additional units of a product and the relative value of acquiring and consuming one product as opposed to another. Characteristics of both the product and the individual are important determinants of personal demand for consumer products.

Many goods and services are acquired not for their direct consumption value but rather because they are important inputs in the manufacture and distribution of other products. The demand for production workers, salespersons, managers, office business machines, production equipment, bank loans, and equity capital are all examples of goods and services whose individual demand is not directly related to final personal consumption but rather is derived indirectly from it. For products whose demand is derived rather than direct, the theory of the firm provides the basis for analyzing individual demand. This is because demand for those goods stems from the value they provide to the firm—value in terms of their impact on the maximization of value objective of the firm. As with all managerial decisions, the key components in this demand determination are the marginal benefits and marginal costs associated with employing the good or service.

Regardless of whether a good or service is in demand at the individual level as a final consumption product (direct demand) or as a factor in providing other goods and services (derived demand), the fundamentals of economic analysis provide a basis for investigating the characteristics of that demand. In both situations individual demand arises from an attempt to maximize an objective. For final consumption products it is utility maximization as developed by the theory of consumer behavior. For goods and services used in the production of other products, the theory of the firm provides the framework for the optimization problem. Since both demand models are based on optimization (only the nature of the objective differs), it should come as no surprise that while specific product and individual characteristics affecting demand may differ, the fundamental relationships are essentially the same. This means that the principles of managerial economics, and particularly the principles of optimal resource utilization provide a basis for understanding individual demand by both firms and final consumers.[1] With this brief introduction to individual demand we now turn attention to the market demand relationship.

---

[1] In Chapter 5, where production is examined, the economics of resource employment by the firm, and hence, demand for its inputs, is more fully developed. The concepts introduced there provide the foundation for the derived demand of goods and services used by firms.

The Market Demand Function

Although an understanding of individual demand provides important insight into the characteristics of demand and enables one to analyze important demand relationships more thoroughly, it is the aggregate of individual demand that a firm faces in the market. The market **demand function** for a product is a statement of the relationship between the quantity of the product demanded and all the factors that affect this quantity. Written in general functional form, the demand function may be expressed as:

$$\left.\begin{array}{l}\text{Quantity of}\\\text{Product } X\\\text{Demanded}\end{array}\right\} = Q_x = \left\{\begin{array}{l} f \text{ (Price of } X\text{, Prices of Competitive Goods,}\\ \text{Expectations of Price Changes, Consumer}\\ \text{Incomes, Tastes and Preferences, Adver-}\\ \text{tising Expenditures, and so on).}\end{array}\right. \tag{3.1}$$

The generalized demand function expressed in Equation 3.1 is really just a listing of the variables that influence demand; for use in managerial decision making, the demand function must be made explicit. That is, the relationship between quantity demanded and each of the demand-determining variables must be specified. To illustrate what is involved, let us assume that we are analyzing the demand for automobiles, and the demand function has been specified as follows:

$$Q_t = a_1 P_t + a_2 Y_t + a_3 Pop_t + a_4 C_t + a_5 A_t. \tag{3.2}$$

This equation states that the number of automobiles demanded during a given year, Q_t, is a linear function of the average price of cars, P_t; average per capita disposable income, Y_t; population, Pop_t; an index of credit availability, C_t; and advertising expenditures, A_t. The terms $a_1, a_2, \ldots, a_5$ are called the *parameters* of the demand function. They indicate how the quantity demanded for a product is related to the value of each variable in the demand function. We shall examine procedures for estimating parameter values, together with indicators of how confident we are in these estimates later in the chapter. For now, we shall simply assume that we know the parameters and that the demand function does accurately predict the quantity of the product demanded.[2]

---

[2]If all the variables that influence demand are not included in the demand function, or if the parameters are not correctly specified, the equation will not predict demand accurately, sales forecasts will be in error, and incorrect expansion and operating decisions will be made. Obviously, the more accurate the firm's demand estimates, the lower its risk. Thus, a close relationship exists between risk and the ability to accurately estimate the demand function.

Table 3.1

**Estimating Industry Demand for Automobiles
by Using a Hypothetical Demand Function**

Independent Variable (1)	Estimated Value of the Independent Variable for Coming Year (2)	Parameter (3)	Estimated Total Demand (2) × (3) (4)
Average price	$9,000	−3,000	−27,000,000
Disposable income	$17,000	1,000	17,000,000
Population	220,000,000	0.05	11,000,000
Index of credit terms	3.00	1,500,000	4,500,000
Advertising expenditures	$100,000,000	0.05	5,000,000
		Total demand	10,500,000

Substituting a set of assumed parameter values into Equation 3.2, we obtain:

$$Q = -3,000P + 1,000Y + 0.05Pop + 1,500,000C + 0.05A. \quad (3.3)$$

Equation 3.3 indicates that automobile demand falls by 3,000 units for each $1 increase in the average price charged; it increases by 1,000 units for each $1 increase in per capita disposable income; it increases by 0.05 units for each additional person in the population; it increases by 1.5 million units if the index of credit availability increases 1 unit; and it increases by 0.05 units for each $1 spent on advertising.

If we multiply each parameter in Equation 3.3 by the value of its respective variable and then sum these products, we will have the estimated demand for automobiles during the coming year. Table 3.1 illustrates this process, showing that the estimated demand for autos, assuming the stated values of the independent variables, will be approximately 10.5 million units.

Industry Demand versus Firm Demand

Demand functions can be specified either for an entire industry or for an individual firm. Somewhat different independent variables would typically be used in industry, as compared to firm, demand equations; most importantly the variables representing competitors' actions would be stressed in firm demand functions. For example, a firm's demand function would include the competitor's price and the competitors' advertising expenditures. Demand for the firm's product would be negatively related to its own price, but positively related to the price charged by competing firms. Similarly, demand for its products would increase with its own advertising expenditures, but could increase or decrease with additional advertising by other firms.

Moreover, the parameters for specific variables would differ in the two functions. To illustrate, population would influence the demand for Ford's automobiles and for all producers' autos, but the parameter value in Ford's demand function would be smaller than that in the industry demand function. Only if Ford had 100 percent of the market—that is, if Ford were the industry—would the parameters for the firm and the industry demand functions be identical.

Since firm and industry demand functions differ, different models, or equations, must be estimated for analyzing the two levels of demand. This matter need not concern us at present, however, because the demand concepts developed here are applicable to both firm and industry demand functions.

The Demand Curve

The *demand function* specifies the relationship between quantity demanded and *all* the variables that determine demand. The **demand curve** is that part of the demand function that expresses the relation between the price charged for a product and the quantity demanded, *holding constant the effects of all other demand-determining variables*. Frequently, a demand curve is shown in the form of a graph, and all independent variables in the demand function, except the price of the product, are assumed to be fixed. In the automobile demand function given in Equation 3.3 and Table 3.1, for example, we could hold constant income, population, credit policies, and advertising expenditures, to examine the relationship between price and quantity demanded.

To illustrate the process, consider the relationship depicted in Equation 3.3 and Table 3.1. Assuming that income, population, credit conditions, and advertising expenditures are all held constant at their Table 3.1 values, we can express the relationship between changes in price and changes in quantity demanded as:

$$Q = -3{,}000\,(P) + 1{,}000\,(17{,}000) + 0.05\,(220{,}000{,}000)$$

$$+\ 1{,}500{,}000\,(3) + 0.05\,(100{,}000{,}000)$$

$$= -3{,}000P + 17{,}000{,}000 + 11{,}000{,}000 + 4{,}500{,}000 + 5{,}000{,}000$$

$$= 37{,}500{,}000 - 3{,}000P.$$

(3.4)

Equation 3.4, which represents the demand curve for automobiles, given the specified values of all of the other variables in the demand

Figure 3.1
A Hypothetical Automobile Demand Curve

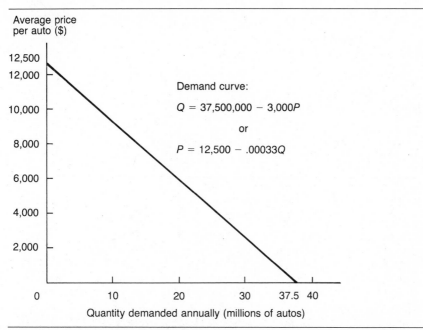

Average price
per auto ($)

Demand curve:

$Q = 37,500,000 - 3,000P$

or

$P = 12,500 - .00033Q$

Quantity demanded annually (millions of autos)

Note: The dependent variable (quantity demanded) is plotted on the horizontal axis and the independent variable (price) on the vertical axis. Ordinarily, we would expect to see the dependent variable on the vertical scale and the independent variable on the horizontal scale. This point can be confusing, because it is easy to write a demand equation as in Equation 4.4, then *incorrectly* graph it by treating the 37,500,000 as the Y-axis intercept instead of the X-axis intercept, and similarly misspecify the slope of the curve.

The practice of plotting price on the vertical axis and quantity on the horizontal axis originated many years ago with the theory of competitive markets. Here firms have no control over price, but they can control output, and output in turn determines market price. Hence, in the original model, price was the dependent variable and quantity (supplied, not demanded) was the independent variable. For that reason, price/quantity graphs appear as they do.

function for automobiles, is presented graphically in Figure 3.1. As is typical for most products, we see that a reduction in price increases the quantity demanded, and, conversely, an increase in price decreases the quantity demanded.

Relationship between Demand Function and Demand Curve

The interrelationship between the demand function and the demand curve can be demonstrated graphically. Figure 3.2 shows three demand curves for automobiles: D_1, D_2, and D_3. Each curve is constructed in a manner similar to Figure 3.1, and each represents the relationship between price and quantity, holding the values of all the other variables in the demand function constant at some specific level. If D_1 is the

Figure 3.2
Hypothetical Automobile Demand Curves

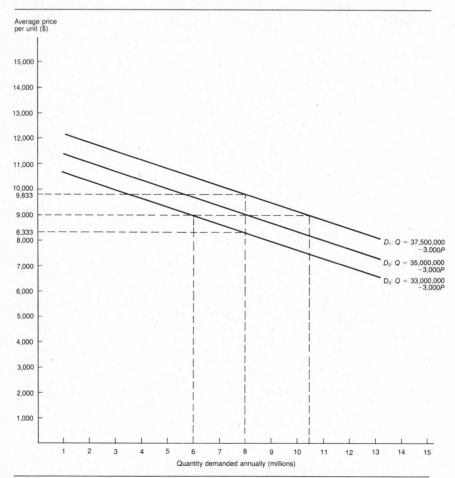

demand curve that relates to the expected values for the nonprice variables in the demand function, then 10.5 million automobiles can be sold if the average price is $9,000, while only 7.5 million autos will be demanded if the average price is raised to $10,000. Changes in price such as illustrated in this example result in *movements along a demand curve* and are said to describe changes in the quantity demanded of a product.

A *demand curve shift*—a movement from one demand curve to another—indicates a change in one or more of the nonprice variables in the product's demand function. For example, a shift from D_1 to D_2 might be caused by a decrease in incomes or advertising expenditures, by more restrictive credit terms, or by a combination of these and other changes.

Consider the effect of shifts in the demand curve from D_1 to D_2 to D_3. At an average price of \$9,000 per car, the demand for autos falls from 10.5 million to 8 million to 6 million. Alternatively, if the number of units is fixed at a constant amount, say 8 million, these cars could be sold only at successively lower prices, ranging from \$9,833 to \$8,333 as the demand curve shifts from D_1 to D_3. The result of the shift is a lower level of demand at each sales price; the cause of the shift could be lower disposable incomes, tighter credit, less aggressive advertising campaigns, or a combination of these and other factors. If we were considering the demand curve for a *firm*, rather than for an *industry*, this shift might also occur because of competitors' price cuts, more aggressive promotional activities, and so on.

Demand Relationships and Managerial Decisions

A firm must have good information about its demand function to make effective long-run planning decisions and short-run operating decisions. For example, one must know the effect of changing prices on demand to establish or alter price policy. Similarly, one must know the effects of credit terms on demand to appraise the desirability of a new credit program. In long-run planning, good estimates of the sensitivity of demand to both population and income changes enable a firm to predict future growth potential and, thus, to establish effective long-range programs.

Measuring Responsiveness: Elasticity

The firm must know how sensitive demand is to changes in the demand determining variables in its demand function. Some variables such as price and advertising can be controlled by the firm, and it is important for management to know the effects of altering them in order to make good price and advertising decisions. Although other variables are outside the control of the firm—consumer incomes and competitors' prices, for example—the effect of changes in these variables must also be known if the firm is to respond effectively to changes in the economic environment within which it operates. Indeed, anticipating the values of variables outside the firm's control and estimating the response of demand to changes in these variables are major elements in demand analysis.

One measure of responsiveness employed not only in demand analysis but throughout managerial decision making is **elasticity**, defined as *the percentage change in a dependent variable*, Y, *resulting from a 1 percent change in the value of an independent variable*, X. The equation for calculating elasticity is:

$$\text{Elasticity} = \frac{\text{Percentage Change in } Y}{\text{Percentage Change in } X} = \frac{\Delta Y/Y}{\Delta X/X}$$

(3.5)

$$= \frac{\Delta Y}{\Delta X} \cdot \frac{X}{Y}.$$

Here Y is the dependent variable, X is an independent variable that affects Y, and Δ designates a change in the variable. The term $\Delta Y/\Delta X$ in the elasticity equation measures the actual change in Y for a one unit change in X. Multiplying this absolute relationship by the ratio X/Y converts it to a relative measure, i.e., to the percentage change in Y for a one percent change in X.

The concept of elasticity is quite general; it involves simply the percentage change in one variable associated with a given percentage change in another variable. In addition to use in demand analysis, the concept is used in finance, where the impact of changes in sales on earnings under different production levels (operating leverage) and different financial structures (financial leverage) is measured by an elasticity factor. Elasticities are also used in production analysis to compare the effects of output changes on costs.

Point Elasticity and Arc Elasticity

Elasticity can be measured in two different ways, called point elasticity and arc elasticity. *Point elasticity* measures the elasticity at a given point; *arc elasticity* measures the average elasticity over some range of a function.

Note that the first term in Equation 3.5, $\Delta Y/\Delta X$, is a measure of the marginal relationship between X and Y. This term, when multiplied by the second term in the equation, X/Y, equals elasticity. Thus, using the Greek letter ε (epsilon) as the symbol for point elasticity, we have:

$$\text{Point Elasticity} = \varepsilon_x = \frac{\Delta Y}{\Delta X} \cdot \frac{X}{Y}.$$

(3.6)

In words, point elasticity is determined by multiplying the ratio $\Delta Y/\Delta X$ by the ratio X/Y at the point being analyzed.

An example using the demand relationship described by Equation 3.3 and the variable values given in Table 3.1 will illustrate how point elasticity can be calculated, and how managers can incorporate this information in the decision-making process. Assume we are interested in analyzing the responsiveness of automobile demand to changes in advertising expenditures. The point advertising elasticity at the 10.5 million unit demand level shown in Table 3.1 is calculated as:

$$\text{Point Advertising Elasticity} = \varepsilon_A = \frac{\Delta Q}{\Delta A} \cdot \frac{A}{Q}.$$

In Equation 3.3 the parameter for advertising is 0.05. If advertising is increased by one unit, Q will increase by 0.05 units. Hence, the ratio $\Delta Q/\Delta A$ is 0.05 (0.05/1.0 = 0.05). Advertising expenditures at the 10.5 million unit demand level are $100 million. Thus, the point advertising elasticity is

$$\varepsilon_A = 0.05 \cdot \frac{100,000,000}{10,500,000}$$

$$\approx 0.48.$$

A 1 percent change in advertising expenditures results in approximately a 0.48 percent change in the number of automobiles demanded. The elasticity is positive, indicating a direct relationship between advertising outlays and automobile demand; that is, an increase in advertising expenditures leads to an increase in demand, and, conversely, a decrease in advertising expenditures leads to a decrease in demand.

For many business decisions, managers are concerned with the impact of substantial changes in a demand-determining factor, such as advertising, rather than with the impact of a small change. In these instances the point-elasticity concept suffers a significant shortcoming. To see the nature of the problem, consider the calculation of the advertising elasticity of demand for automobiles when advertising changes from $100 million to $50 million. Assume for this example that all the other demand-influencing variables retain their Table 3.1 values. With advertising at $100 million, demand is 10.5 million units. Changing advertising to $50 million results in a 2.5-million-unit decline in automobile demand (−$50 million × 0.05 = 2.5 million), so total demand at that level is 8 million units.[3] Using Equation 3.5 to calculate the point price elasticity for the change from $100 million in advertising to $50 million, we find that:

$$\text{Advertising Elasticity} = \frac{-2.5 \text{ million}}{-50 \text{ million}} \cdot \frac{100 \text{ million}}{10.5 \text{ million}} = 0.48.$$

---

[3] This change in demand is illustrated graphically by Figure 3.2. Assuming population, income, credit availability, and all other factors that influence the level of automobile sales, *except advertising*, remain unchanged from their Table 3.1 values, the shift from demand curve D_1 to demand curve D_2 reflects the impact of reducing advertising to $50 million. At a $9,000 price, automobile demand along demand schedule D_2 is 8 million units.

The advertising elasticity is 0.48, just as we found above using the point elasticity equation. Consider, however, the indicated elasticity if we move in the opposite direction, that is, the advertising elasticity associated with increasing advertising from $50 million to $100 million. The indicated elasticity is:

$$\text{Advertising Elasticity} = \frac{+2.5 \text{ million}}{+50 \text{ million}} \cdot \frac{50 \text{ million}}{8 \text{ million}} = 0.31.$$

We see that the indicated elasticity is quite different. The problem stems from the fact that elasticity relationships are typically not constant but change with different levels of the variables. The advertising elasticity of 0.31 is the point elasticity where advertising is $50 million and the quantity demanded is 8 million. (This can be verified by calculating the point advertising elasticity at the $50 million level, as was done above at the $100 million level.)

To overcome this problem of changing elasticities, an arc elasticity equation has been formulated to calculate an average elasticity for an interval. The arc elasticity equation is:

$$\text{Arc Elasticity} = E_x = \frac{\dfrac{\text{Change in } Y}{\text{Average } Y}}{\dfrac{\text{Change in } X}{\text{Average } X}} = \frac{\dfrac{Y_2 - Y_1}{(Y_2 + Y_1)/2}}{\dfrac{X_2 - X_1}{(X_2 + X_1)/2}} \qquad (3.7)$$

$$= \frac{\dfrac{\Delta Y}{(Y_2 + Y_1)/2}}{\dfrac{\Delta X}{(X_2 + X_1)/2}} = \frac{\Delta Y}{\Delta X} \cdot \frac{X_2 + X_1}{Y_2 + Y_1}.$$

Again we divide the percentage change in a dependent variable Y by the percentage change in an independent X variable, but here the bases used to calculate the percentage changes are averages of the two data points rather than the initially observed value. The arc elasticity equation reflects the *average* relative relationship between the dependent and independent variables over the range of the data points. It is independent of which end of the range is viewed as the initial point and results in a more accurate measure of the average relative relationship between the two variables over the range indicated by the data. This averaging is important when large changes in the data are being considered.

The arc advertising elasticity over the $50 million to $100 million range can be calculated as:

$$\text{Arc Advertising Elasticity} = \frac{\Delta Q}{\Delta A} \cdot \frac{A_2 + A_1}{Q_2 + Q_1}$$

$$= \frac{-2,500,000}{-50,000,000} \left(\frac{50,000,000 + 100,000,000}{8,000,000 + 10,500,000} \right)$$

$$= \frac{-2,500,000}{-50,000,000} \cdot \frac{150,000,000}{18,500,000} \approx 0.41.$$

Thus, *on average* a 1 percent change in the level of advertising expenditures in the range of $50 million to $100 million will result in a 0.41 percent change in automobile demand.

We can summarize by noting that point elasticity is a marginal concept. It measures the elasticity at a specific point on a function. Proper use of point elasticity is limited to analysis of very small (unitary) changes in variables. Arc elasticity is a better concept for measuring the average elasticity over an extended range. It is the appropriate tool for incremental or interval analysis.

We turn now to an examination of several important demand elasticities.

Price Elasticity of Demand

One of the most widely used elasticity measures in managerial economics is the **price elasticity** *of demand*, which provides a measure of the responsiveness of the quantity demanded to changes in the price of the product, holding constant the values of all other variables in the demand function.

Using the formula for point elasticity, price elasticity of demand is found as:

$$\text{Point Price Elasticity} = \varepsilon_p = \frac{\text{Percentage Change in Quantity } (Q)}{\text{Percentage Change in Price } (P)}$$

(3.8)

$$= \frac{\Delta Q}{\Delta P} \cdot \frac{P}{Q}$$

where $\Delta Q / \Delta P$ is the change in quantity demanded following a one unit change in price, and P and Q are the price and quantity at a point on the demand curve.

The concept of point price elasticity can be illustrated by referring to Equation 3.3, which was used to construct demand curve D_1 in Figure 3.2.

$$Q = -3,000P + 1,000Y + 0.05Pop + 1,500,000C + 0.05A. \qquad \text{(3.3)}$$

In Equation 3.3 the parameter for price is $-3,000$. If price is increased 1 unit, Q will fall by 3,000 units. Hence, the ratio

$$\frac{\Delta Q}{\Delta P} = -3,000.$$

Now let us calculate ε_p at two points on the demand curve: (1) where $P_1 = \$9,000$ and $Q_1 = 10,500,000$, and (2) where $P_2 = \$9,500$ and $Q_2 = 9,000,000$:

$$(1)\ \varepsilon_{p1} = (-3,000) \frac{9,000}{10,500,000} = -2.57,$$

$$(2)\ \varepsilon_{p2} = (-3,000) \frac{9,500}{9,000,000} = -3.17.$$

Thus, on demand curve D_1 in Figure 3.2 a 1 percent increase in price from the $9,000 level results in a 2.57 percent reduction in the quantity demanded; but at a $9,500 price a 1 percent increase results in a 3.17 percent reduction in the quantity demanded. This example illustrates that price elasticity can vary along a demand curve, with ε_p increasing in absolute value at higher prices and lower quantities. As we will show in a later section, price elasticity always varies along a linear demand curve. It can, however, under certain conditions, be constant along a curvilinear demand curve.

Note also that the price elasticities are negative. This follows from the fact that the quantity demanded for most goods and services is inversely related to price. Thus, in the example, at a $9,000 price, a 1 percent *increase (decrease)* in price leads to a 2.57 percent *decrease (increase)* in the quantity demanded. In some texts the equation for price elasticity is multiplied by -1 to change price elasticities to positive numbers. We do not follow this convention, although it creates no problem so long as one remembers the inverse relationship between price and quantity. We alert the reader to this possible construction because price elasticities are sometimes reported as positive numbers.

Using the arc elasticity concept, the equation for price elasticity is:

$$\text{Arc Price Elasticity} = E_p = \frac{\text{Percentage Change in Quantity } (Q)}{\text{Percentage Change in Price } (P)}$$

$$= \frac{\Delta Q}{\Delta P} \cdot \frac{P_2 + P_1}{Q_2 + Q_1}$$

$$= \frac{Q_2 - Q_1}{P_2 - P_1} \cdot \frac{P_2 + P_1}{Q_2 + Q_1}.$$

This form is especially useful for analyzing the average sensitivity of quantity demanded to price changes over an extended range. For example, the average price elasticity in the automobile demand example for a price between \$9,000 and \$9,500 is:

$$E_p = \frac{9,000,000 - 10,500,000}{9,500 - 9,000} \cdot \frac{9,500 + 9,000}{9,000,000 + 10,500,000}$$

$$= \frac{-1,500,000}{500} \cdot \frac{18,500}{19,500,000} = -3.0.$$

This means that on average, a 1 percent change in price leads to a 3.0 percent change in quantity demanded when price is between \$9,000 and \$9,500.

Elastic and Inelastic Demand

One of the most important aspects of the price elasticity concept lies in the fact that it provides a useful summary measure of the effect of a price change on revenues. Depending on the degree of price elasticity, a price reduction will increase, decrease, or leave total revenue unchanged. If we have a good estimate of price elasticity, we can estimate the change in total revenues that will follow a price change.

Elastic, Unitary, and Inelastic Demand. For decision-making purposes, three specific ranges of price elasticity have been identified. Using $|\varepsilon_p|$ to denote the absolute value of the price elasticity, the three ranges can be denoted as:

1. $|\varepsilon_p| > 1.0$, defined as elastic demand.
   Example: $\varepsilon_p = -3.2$ and $|\varepsilon_p| = 3.2$
2. $|\varepsilon_p| = 1.0$, defined as unitary elasticity.
   Example: $\varepsilon_p = -1.0$ and $|\varepsilon_p| = 1.0$
3. $|\varepsilon_p| < 1.0$, defined as inelastic demand.
   Example: $\varepsilon_p = -0.5$ and $|\varepsilon_p| = 0.5$

If demand is *elastic* (that is, $|\varepsilon_p| > 1$), the relative change in quantity is larger than that of price, so a given percentage increase in price causes quantity to decrease by a larger percentage, decreasing total revenue. Thus, if demand is elastic, a price increase will lower total revenue, and a decrease in price will raise total revenue. Now consider *unitary elasticity*, the situation where the percentage change in quantity divided by the percentage change in price equals -1. Since price and quantity are inversely related, a price elasticity of -1 means that the effect of a price change is *exactly* offset by the change in quantity demanded, with the result that total revenue, the product of price times quantity, *remains* constant. Finally, if demand is inelastic, a price increase will produce a less than proportionate decline in the quantity

demanded, so total revenues will rise. These relationships are summarized below:

1. Elastic demand: $|\varepsilon_p| > 1.0$. Total revenue declines with price in-
creases; rises with price decreases.

2. Unitary elasticity: $|\varepsilon_p| = 1.0$. Total revenue is unaffected by changes
in price.

3. Inelastic demand: $|\varepsilon_p| < 1.0$. Total revenue rises with price increases;
declines with price decreases.

The Limiting Cases. Price elasticity can range from 0 (completely inelastic) to $-\infty$ (perfectly elastic). To illustrate, consider first the case
where the quantity demanded is independent of price, so that some
fixed amount, Q^*, will be demanded regardless of price. The demand
curve of such a good is shown in Figure 3.3. Price elasticity is defined
(using the point elasticity definition) as the change in quantity demanded
resulting from a unitary change in price, $\Delta Q / \Delta P$, multiplied by the ratio P/Q. That is:

$$\varepsilon_p = \frac{\Delta Q}{\Delta P} \cdot \frac{P}{Q}.$$

Since quantity demanded as illustrated in Figure 3.3 remains constant
regardless of price, the ratio $\Delta Q / \Delta P$ is equal to zero; hence, price elasticity for the product will be equal to zero. This can be confusing if one

Figure 3.3
Completely Inelastic Demand Curve: $\varepsilon_p = 0$

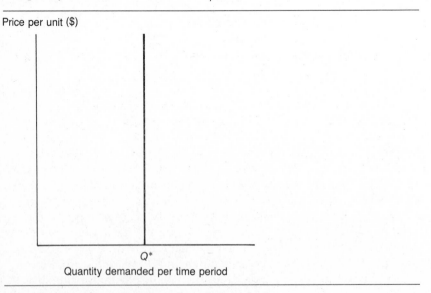

Price per unit ($)

Q^*
Quantity demanded per time period

Figure 3.4
Perfectly Elastic Demand Curve: $\varepsilon_p = -\infty$

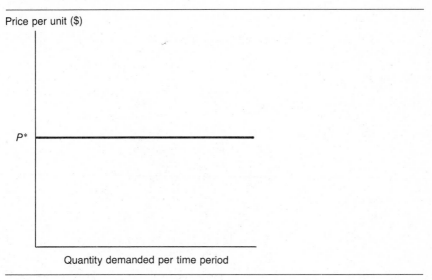

Price per unit ($)

P^*

Quantity demanded per time period

does not remember that the axes of Figure 3.3 are reversed in the sense that the dependent variable, Q, is plotted on the X axis. One must remember that $Q = Q^* =$ a constant. In other words, $Q = Q^* + 0 \cdot P$, so $\Delta Q / \Delta P$ is zero.

The other limiting case, that of infinite elasticity where $\varepsilon_p = -\infty$, is shown in Figure 3.4. Here the ratio $\Delta Q / \Delta P$, is $-\infty$, so the value of ε_p in Equation 3.8 must be $-\infty$ regardless of the P/Q ratio.

The economic properties of these limiting cases should be understood. A firm faced with the vertical, perfectly inelastic demand curve could charge any price and still sell Q^* units. Conversely, a firm facing a horizontal, perfectly elastic demand curve can sell an unlimited amount of output at the price P^*, and thus has no reason to offer its product at a lower price, but would lose all of its customers if it raised the price by even a small amount. Vertical and horizontal demand curves are rare in the real world, but monopolistic firms selling necessities (for example, water companies) have relatively inelastic demand curves, while firms in very competitive industries (for example, grain producers) face highly elastic demand curves.

Varying Elasticity at Different Points
on a Demand Curve

All linear demand curves, except perfectly elastic or perfectly inelastic ones, are subject to varying elasticities at different points on the curve.

Figure 3.5
Elasticities along a Linear Demand Curve

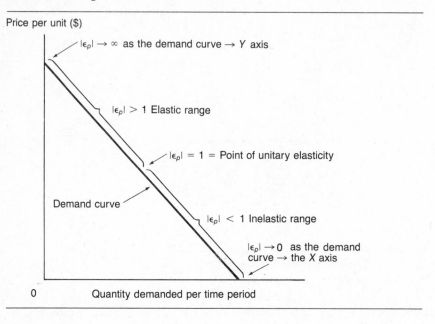

In other words, a linear demand curve will be price elastic at some output levels but inelastic at others. To see this, recall again the definition of point price elasticity:

$$\varepsilon_p = \frac{\Delta Q}{\Delta P} \cdot \frac{P}{Q}. \tag{3.8}$$

The slope of a linear demand curve, $\Delta P/\Delta Q$, is constant, and thus so is its reciprocal, $1/(\Delta P/\Delta Q) = \Delta Q/\Delta P$. However, the ratio P/Q varies from 0 at the point where the demand curve intersects the horizontal axis (where price $= 0$) to $+\infty$ at the vertical (price) axis intercept (where quantity $= 0$). Since we are multiplying a negative constant by a ratio that varies between 0 and $+\infty$, the price elasticity of a linear curve must range from 0 to $-\infty$.

Figure 3.5 illustrates this relationship. As we move along the demand curve and approach the vertical axis, the ratio P/Q approaches infinity, and ε_p approaches minus infinity. As we approach the horizontal axis, the ratio P/Q approaches 0, causing ε_p also to approach 0. At the midpoint of the demand curve $(\Delta Q/\Delta P)\,(P/Q) = -1.0$; this is the point of unitary elasticity.

Relationships among Price Elasticity and Average, Marginal, and Total Revenue

We can further clarify the relationship between price elasticity and revenue developed above and emphasize its importance in demand analysis by examining Figure 3.6 and Table 3.2. Figure 3.6a reproduces the demand curve shown in Figure 3.5 but adds the associated marginal revenue curve. We see in Figure 3.6a that marginal revenue is positive in the range where demand is price elastic, zero where $\varepsilon_p = -1$, and negative in the inelastic range. Thus, there is an obvious relationship between price elasticity and both average and marginal revenue. This important relationship is generalized by the equation:[4]

$$MR = P \left(1 + \frac{1}{\varepsilon_p} \right).$$

(3.9)

---

[4]Equation 3.9 follows directly from the precise mathematical definition of marginal relationships developed in Appendix 2.A. Using these relationships, marginal revenue is the derivative of the total revenue function. That is, $MR = dTR/dQ$. Since total revenue equals price times quantity ($TR = P \cdot Q$), marginal revenue is found by taking the derivative of the function $P \cdot Q$ with respect to Q:

$$MR = \frac{d(P \cdot Q)}{dQ}.$$

(3.10)

Because price and quantity are interdependent in the typical demand situation, the rule for differentiating a product must be employed in taking the derivative of Equation 3.10:

$$MR = \frac{dTR}{dQ} = \frac{dP \cdot Q}{dQ} = P \cdot \frac{dQ}{dQ} + Q \cdot \frac{dP}{dQ}$$

(3.11)

$$= P \cdot 1 + Q \cdot \frac{dP}{dQ}$$

$$= P + Q \cdot \frac{dP}{dQ}.$$

Equation 3.11 is a completely general specification of marginal revenue, which, if P is factored out from the right-hand side, can be rewritten as:

$$MR = P \left(1 + \frac{Q}{P} \cdot \frac{dP}{dQ} \right).$$

(3.11A)

Note now that the term $Q/P \cdot dP/dQ$ in Equation 3.11A is the reciprocal of the definition for point price elasticity ($\varepsilon_p = dQ/dP \cdot P/Q$):

$$\frac{Q}{P} \cdot \frac{dP}{dQ} = \frac{1}{\dfrac{dQ}{dP} \cdot \dfrac{P}{Q}} = \frac{1}{\varepsilon_p}$$

Thus, Equation 3.11A can be rewritten as Equation 3.9:

$$MR = P \left(1 + \frac{1}{\varepsilon_p} \right).$$

(3.9)

Figure 3.6
Relationships among Price Elasticity and Marginal, Average, and Total Revenue: (a) Demand (Average Revenue) and Marginal Revenue Curves (b) Total Revenue

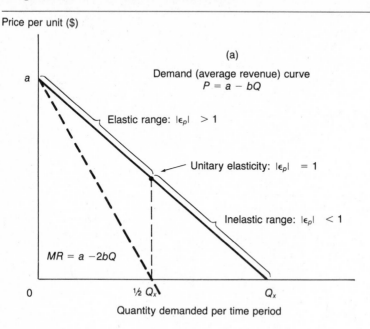

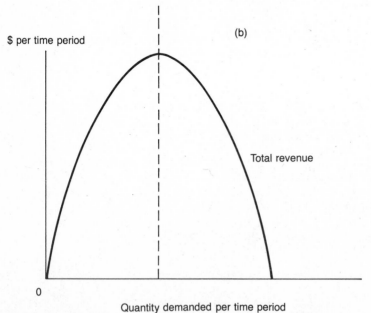

Table 3.2
Elasticity and Revenue Relationships

Price P	Quantity Q	Total Revenue $TR = P \cdot Q$	Marginal Revenue $MR = \Delta TR/\Delta Q$	Elasticity[a] E_p
100	1	100		
			80	−6.33
90	2	180		
			60	−3.40
80	3	240		
			40	−2.14
70	4	280		
			20	−1.44
60	5	300		
			0	−1.00
50	6	300		
			−20	−0.69
40	7	280		
			−40	−0.47
30	8	240		
			−60	−0.29
20	9	180		
			−80	−0.16
10	10	100		

[a] Since the price and quantity data in the table are discrete numbers, the price elasticities have been calculated by using the arc elasticity equation:

$$E_p = \frac{\Delta Q}{\Delta P} \cdot \frac{P_2 + P_1}{Q_2 + Q_1}.$$

Because price elasticity, ε_p, is a negative number, it is clear from Equation 3.9 that when demand is elastic ($|\varepsilon_p| > 1$) marginal revenue will be positive as indicated in Figure 3.6. With unitary elastic demand ($\varepsilon_p = -1$), marginal revenue must be zero and when demand is inelastic ($|\varepsilon_p| < 1$), marginal revenue will be negative. The value of this simple relationship between price elasticity and marginal revenue as a pricing tool is examined in Chapter 9 where mark-up, or margin, pricing is presented.

As shown in Figure 3.6b, price elasticity is also closely related to total revenue. Total revenue increases with price reductions in the elastic range (where $MR > 0$) because the increase in quantity demanded at the new lower price more than offsets the lower revenue per unit received at that reduced price. Total revenue peaks at the point of unitary elasticity (where $MR = 0$), since the increase in quantity associated with the price reduction exactly offsets the lower revenue per unit. Finally, total revenue declines when price is reduced in the inelastic range (where $MR < 0$), because although the quantity demanded continues to increase with reductions in price, the relative increase in quantity is less than the percentage decrease in price, and thus it is not large enough to offset the reduction in revenue per unit sold.

The numerical example in Table 3.2 illustrates these relationships. It can be seen that for one to five units of output demand is elastic, $|\varepsilon_p| > 1$, and a reduction in price leads to an increase in total revenue. For example, decreasing price from \$80 to \$70 results in output increasing from three units to four units. Marginal revenue is positive over this range of output, and total revenue increases from $240 to $280. For output above six units (price below $50) demand is inelastic, $|\varepsilon_p| < 1$. Here price reductions result in less total revenue, because the increase in quantity demanded is not large enough to offset the lower price per unit. With total revenue decreasing as output expands, marginal revenue must be negative. For example, reducing price from $30 to $20 results in revenue declining from $240 to $180 even though output increases from eight to nine units. Marginal revenue is $-$60$.

Determinants of Price Elasticity

Industry Demand. Why is the price elasticity of demand high for one product and low for another? In general, there are three major causes for differential price elasticities: (1) the extent to which a good is considered to be a necessity, (2) the availability of substitute goods that satisfy a given need, and (3) the proportion of income spent on the product. A relatively constant quantity of such necessities as salt and electricity for residential lighting purposes will be purchased almost irrespective of price, at least within the price ranges customarily encountered. For these goods there are no close substitutes. Other goods— grapes, for example—while desirable, face considerably more competition, and the demand for them will depend more on price.

Similarly, the demand for high-priced goods that account for a large portion of purchasers' incomes will be relatively more sensitive to price. Demand for less expensive products, on the other hand, will not be so sensitive to price; the small percentage of income spent on these goods means that it simply will not be worthwhile to expend time and effort worrying about their prices. Accordingly, the elasticity of demand will typically be higher for major items than for minor ones. Thus, the price elasticity of demand for automobiles is higher than that for automobile tires. The fact that automobiles are durable goods whose purchase can be more readily postponed when prices are high also tends to make them more price elastic.

Firm Demand. Are the price elasticities of an individual firm's demand curve the same as its respective industry demand curve? In general, the answer is an emphatic no. The reason for this is discussed in detail in Chapter 8, which deals with market structure, but an intuitive explanation can be given here.

In pure monopoly the firm's demand curve is also the industry's demand curve, so obviously the firm's elasticity at any output is the same as that of the industry. Consider the other extreme: pure competition, as approximated by wheat farming. The industry demand curve for wheat is downward sloping: the lower its price, the greater the quantity of wheat that will be demanded. However, the demand curve facing any individual wheat farmer is virtually horizontal. Farmers can sell any amount of wheat at the going price, but if they raise the price the smallest fraction of a cent they can sell nothing. The wheat farmer's demand curve—or that of any firm operating under pure competition—is therefore perfectly elastic. Figure 3.4 illustrated such a demand curve.

Uses of Price Elasticity

Price elasticity is useful for a number of purposes. First, firms need to be aware of the price elasticity of demand when they price their products. For example, a profit-maximizing firm would typically never choose to lower its prices into the inelastic range of its demand curve; such a price decrease would decrease total revenue and at the same time increase costs, since output would be rising. The result would be a dramatic decrease in profits. Even over the range where demand is elastic, a firm will not necessarily find it profitable to cut price; the profitability of such an action depends on whether the marginal revenues generated by the price reduction exceed the marginal cost of the added production. Price elasticities can be used to answer such questions as these:

1. What will be the impact on sales of a 5 percent price increase?

2. How great a price reduction is necessary to increase sales by 20 percent?

The energy crisis that developed following the 1973–1974 Arab oil embargo illustrates the importance of price elasticity. First, electric utility companies were forced to raise prices dramatically because of rapid increases in fuel costs. The question immediately arose: How much of a cutback in quantity demanded and, hence, reduction in future capacity needs would these price increases cause; that is, what is the price elasticity of electricity? In view of the long lead times required to build electric generating capacity and the major economic dislocations that arise from power outages, this was a most critical question for both the consumers and producers of electricity.

Similarly, price elasticity has played a major role in the debate on a national energy policy. Some industry and government economists believed that the price elasticities for petroleum products were sufficiently large that the rather substantial oil price increases that occurred in late 1973 and early 1974 would reduce the quantity demanded sufficiently to remove the imbalance between supply and demand. Others argued that the price elasticities were so low that only unconscionable price increases could reduce the quantity demanded sufficiently to overcome the supply shortfall, and therefore a rationing system was needed as a replacement for market allocation of petroleum products. These same issues have been a focal point of the controversy concerning deregulation of natural gas prices in the United States. (In the debate on energy policy the relationship between price and quantity supplied—the price elasticity of supply—is also an important component for determining an appropriate policy. As with most economic issues, both sides of the marketplace demand and supply must be analyzed to arrive at a rational decision.)

Yet another current example of the importance of price elasticity in managerial decision making relates to the widespread discounting, or reduced fares, introduced in the airline industry following price deregulation. Many of the discounts were in the range of 30 to 40 percent off the standard fare. The question of whether the reduced fares would attract enough additional travelers to offset the lower revenues per passenger was directly related to the question of the price elasticity of demand for air travel. The large increase in passenger traffic that airlines experienced following the introduction of reduced fares suggests that demand for air travel is highly price elastic.

Price Elasticity for Derived Demand Products

The demand functions of some goods contain as one of the independent variables the demand for a second product. This relationship indicates that the quantity of the good purchased is derived from the demand for the other good, so we use the term *derived demand* to denote this kind of relationship. The demand for mortgage money is an example. The quantity of mortgage credit demanded is not determined autonomously or directly; rather, it is derived from the more fundamental demand for housing. Similarly, the demand for air transportation to major resort areas is not a direct demand but rather is derived from the demand for recreation. Although the demand for consumer goods (or final products) may or may not be derived, the demand for all producers' goods (those products used in the production of goods and services) is derived; the aggregate demand for consumption goods determines in large part the demand for the capital equipment, materials, labor, and energy used to manufacture them. For example, the demands for steel, aluminum, and plastics are all derived demands, as are the demands for machine tools and labor. None of these producers' goods is demanded because of its direct value to consumers but rather because of the role they play in the production of goods and services.

As one would expect, the demand for producers' goods is related to the demand for the final products they are used to make; therefore, an examination of the final product's demand is an important part of the demand analysis for the intermediate, or producers', good. This relationship is not always a direct one. For example, the demand for intermediate goods is often less price elastic than is the demand for the resulting final product. This is because the intermediate good represents only one input in the production process; and unless its cost represents a major part of the total cost of the final product, any given percentage price change for the intermediate good will result in a smaller percentage change in the cost (and price) of the final product.

This relationship can be illustrated by looking at the demand for a specially formulated epoxy paint used in the finish of a sailboat. The total cost to manufacture the boat is $5,000, and $100 of this is the cost of the paint. Assume the price of the paint is doubled (a 100 percent increase) so that it now requires $200 of this input for each sailboat produced. In this situation the cost increase of the final product—and the price increase necessary to recover this added cost—will be only 2 percent (100/5,000 = 0.02). If the price elasticity of demand for the sailboat is −3.0, this 2 percent increase in its price would result in a 6 percent reduction in the quantity of sailboats demanded. Assuming the amount of the epoxy paint required to finish each boat were fixed and that no good substitutes were available so that it continued to be used in the manufacturing process, the 100 percent increase in the price of the paint would result in only a 6 percent reduction in the quantity demanded. That implies a price elasticity of −0.06 percent (−6/100 = −0.06 = ε_p). In other words, a 1 percent increase in the price of the paint would cause demand for it to decline by only six hundredths of 1 percent. The demand for the epoxy paint is extremely price inelastic even though the demand for the final product is quite elastic.

Additional uses of the price elasticity concept are explored in later chapters. We now shift to an introduction of several additional key demand relationships.

Income Elasticity of Demand

For many goods, income is a major determinant of demand; it is frequently as important as price, advertising expenditures, credit terms, or any other variable in the demand function. This is particularly true of luxury items such as foreign sports cars, country club memberships, art treasures, and the like. On the other hand, the demand for such basic commodities as salt, bread, and milk is not very responsive to income changes. These goods are bought in fairly constant amounts regardless of changes in income.

Income can be measured in many ways—for example, on a per capita, per household, or aggregate basis. Gross national product, national income, personal income, and disposable personal income are all used as income measures in demand studies.

The **income elasticity** of demand provides a measure of the responsiveness of quantity demanded to changes in income, holding constant the impact of all other variables that influence demand. Letting I represent income, point income elasticity is defined as:

$$\varepsilon_I = \frac{\text{Percentage Change in Quantity } (Q)}{\text{Percentage Change in Income } (I)} \, .$$

(3.12)

$$= \frac{\Delta Q}{\Delta I} \cdot \frac{I}{Q} \, .$$

Income and the quantity purchased typically move in the same direction. That is, income and sales are directly rather than inversely related, so $\Delta Q/\Delta I$ and hence ε_I are positive. For a limited number of products, termed *inferior goods*, this does not hold. For such products as beans and potatoes, for example, demand declines as income increases, because consumers replace them with more expensive alternatives. More typical products, whose demand is positively related to income, are defined as *normal goods*.

To examine income elasticity over a range of income rather than at a single income level, we use the arc elasticity relationship:

$$E_I = \frac{\text{Percentage Change in Quantity } (Q)}{\text{Percentage Change in Income } (I)}$$

$$= \frac{\Delta Q}{\Delta I} \cdot \frac{I_2 + I_1}{Q_2 + Q_1}$$

$$= \frac{Q_2 - Q_1}{I_2 - I_1} \cdot \frac{I_2 + I_1}{Q_2 + Q_1}$$

Again, this provides a measure of the average relative responsiveness of demand for the product to a change in income in the range from I_1 to I_2.

For most products income elasticity is positive, indicating that as the economy expands and national income increases, demand for the product will also rise. However, the actual size of the elasticity coefficient is also important. Suppose, for example, that ε_I for a particular product is 0.3. This means that a 1 percent increase in income will cause demand for this product to increase by only $3/10$ of 1 percent—the product would thus not be maintaining its relative importance in the economy. Another product might have an income elasticity of 2.5; for this product, demand will increase 2½ times as fast as income. *We see, then, that if $\varepsilon_1 < 1.0$ for a particular good, producers of the good will not share proportionately in increases in national income. On the other hand, if $\varepsilon_1 > 1.0$, the industry will gain more than a proportionate share of increases in income.*

These relationships have important policy implications for both firms and governmental agencies. Firms whose demand functions have high income elasticities will have good growth opportunities in an expanding economy, so forecasts of aggregate economic activity will figure importantly in their plans. Companies faced with low income elasticities, on the other hand, are not so sensitive to the level of business activity. This may be good in that such a business is harmed relatively little by economic downturns, but since the company cannot expect to share fully in a growing economy, it may seek entry into industries that provide better growth opportunities.

Income elasticity can also play an important role in the marketing activities of a firm. If per capita or household income is found to be an important determinant of the demand for a particular product, this can affect the location and nature of sales outlets. It can also have an impact on advertising and other promotional activities. For example, many firms providing products or services with high income elasticities direct significant promotional efforts at young professionals in such areas as business, law, and medicine, primarily because of the potential for substantially increased future business from them as their incomes increase.

At the national level the question of income elasticity has figured importantly in several key areas. Agriculture, for example, has had problems for many years partly because the income elasticity of many food products is less than 1.0. This fact has made it difficult for farmers' incomes to keep up with those of urban workers, a problem that, in turn, has caused much concern in Washington, D.C., and national capitals throughout the world.

A somewhat similar problem arises in housing. Congress and all presidents since the end of World War II have stated that improving the United States housing stock is a primary national goal. If, on the one hand, the income elasticity for housing is high, something in excess of 1.0, an improvement of the housing stock will be a natural by-product of a prosperous economy. On the other hand, if housing income elasticity is low, a relatively small percentage of additional income will be spent on houses; as a result, the housing stock will not improve much even if the economy is booming and incomes are increasing. In this case direct government actions, such as public housing or rent and interest subsidies, are necessary to bring the housing stock up to the prescribed level. In any event, not only has the income elasticity of housing been an important issue in debates on national housing policy, but these very debates have also stimulated a great deal of research into the theory and measurement of income elasticities.

Cross-Price Elasticity of Demand

The demand for many goods is influenced by the prices of other goods. For example, the demand for beef is related to the price of a close substitute, pork. As the price of pork increases, so does the demand for beef; consumers substitute beef for the now relatively more expensive pork.

This direct relationship between the price of one good and the quantity of a second good purchased holds for all **substitute** products. Other goods (for example, video recorders and video tapes or computers and computer software) exhibit a completely different relationship. Here, price reductions in one product typically lead to an increase in demand for the other. Goods that are inversely related in this manner are known as **complements**; they are used together rather than in place of each other.

The concept of **cross-price elasticity** is utilized to examine the responsiveness of demand for one product to changes in the price of another. Point cross-price elasticity is given by the equation

$$\varepsilon_{PX} = \frac{\text{Percentage Change in } Q_Y}{\text{Percentage Change in } P_X}$$

$$= \frac{\Delta Q_Y}{\Delta P_X} \cdot \frac{P_X}{Q_Y},$$

(3.13)

where Y and X are two different goods. The arc cross-price elasticity relationship is

$$\varepsilon_{PX} = \frac{\text{Percentage Change in } Q_Y}{\text{Percentage Change in } P_X}$$

$$= \frac{\Delta Q_Y}{\Delta P_X} \cdot \frac{P_{X2} + P_{X1}}{Q_{Y2} + Q_{Y1}}$$

$$= \frac{Q_{Y2} - Q_{Y1}}{P_{X2} - P_{X1}} \cdot \frac{P_{X2} - P_{X1}}{Q_{Y2} - Q_{Y1}}$$

The cross-price elasticity for substitutes is positive: The price of one good and the demand for the other always move in the same direction.

Cross-price elasticity is negative for complements; price and quantity move in opposite directions. Finally, cross-price elasticity is zero, or nearly zero, for unrelated goods; variations in the price of one good have no effect on demand for the second.

We can illustrate the concept of cross-price elasticity by considering the following unspecified demand function for Product Y:

$$Q_Y = f(P_W, P_X, P_Y, P_Z, I).$$

Here Q_Y is the quantity of Y demanded; P_W, P_X, P_Y, and P_Z are the prices of goods W, X, Y, and Z; and I is disposable income. For simplicity, assume that these are the only variables that affect Q_Y, and that the parameters of the demand equation have been estimated as follows:

$$Q_Y = 5{,}000 - 0.3P_W + 0.2P_X - 0.5P_Y + 0.000001P_Z + 0.0037I. \quad \text{(3.14)}$$

Each parameter estimate in Equation 3.17 gives the ΔQ caused by a unit change in each independent variable. Thus,

$$\frac{\Delta Q_Y}{\Delta P_W} = -0.3$$

$$\frac{\Delta Q_Y}{\Delta P_X} = +0.2$$

$$\frac{\Delta Q_Y}{\Delta P_Z} = 0.000001 \approx 0.$$

Since both P and Q are always positive, the ratios P_W/Q_Y, P_X/Q_Y, and P_Z/Q_Y are also positive. Therefore, the signs of the three cross-price elasticities in the example are determined by the sign on each parameter estimate:

$\varepsilon_{PW} = (-0.3)(P_W/Q_Y) < 0$. Accordingly, W and Y are complements.

$\varepsilon_{PX} = (0.2)(P_X/Q_Y) > 0$. Accordingly, X and Y are substitutes.

$\varepsilon_{PZ} = (0.000001)(P_Z/Q_Y) \approx 0$, so long as the ratio P_Z/Q_Y is not extremely large. Accordingly, Z and Y are independent.

The concept of cross-price elasticity is used for two main purposes. First, it is obviously important for the firm to be aware of how the demand for its product is likely to respond to changes in the prices of other goods; this information is necessary for formulating the firm's own pricing strategy and for analyzing the risk associated with various products. This is particularly important for firms with extensive product lines, where significant substitution or complementary interrelationships exist between the various products. Second, cross-price elasticity is used to measure the interrelationships among industries. To illustrate, one firm may appear to dominate a particular market completely; it is the only supplier of a particular product in the market. If, however, the cross-price elasticity between this firm's product and products in related industries is large and positive, the firm, even though it may be a monopolist in a narrow sense, will not be able to raise its prices without losing sales to other firms in related industries. This argument has been raised in connection with antitrust actions. In banking, for example, even though relatively few banks may exist in a given market, banks compete with savings and loan associations, credit unions, commercial finance companies, and the like. The extent of this competition has been gauged in terms of cross-elasticities of demand between the various financial services of competing institutions.

Other Demand Elasticities

The elasticity concept is simply a way of measuring the effect of a change in an independent variable on the dependent variable in any functional relationship. The dependent variable in this chapter is the demand for a product, and the demand elasticity of any variable in the demand function may be calculated. We have emphasized the three most common demand elasticities (price elasticity, income elasticity, and cross-price elasticity), but examples of other demand elasticities will reinforce the generality of the concept.

In the housing market mortgage interest rates are an important determinant of demand; accordingly, the interest rate elasticity has been used in analyzing and forecasting the demand for housing construction and building materials. Studies indicate that the interest rate elasticity of residential housing demand is about -0.15. This indicates that a 10 percent rise in interest rates decreases the demand for housing by 1.5 percent, provided all the other variables remain unchanged. If Federal Reserve policy is expected to cause interest rates to rise from 10 to 12 percent, a 20 percent increase, we can project a 3 percent decrease $(-0.15 \times 20 = -3)$ in housing demand as the result of this change in interest rates.

Public utilities calculate the weather elasticity of demand for their services. They measure the sensitivity of demand for gas and electricity for heating and air conditioning to changes in temperature. This elasticity factor is used, in conjunction with weather forecasts, to anticipate service demand and peak-load conditions.

Time Impact on Elasticity

Time is an important factor in demand analysis. One of the important time characteristics of demand relates to the lack of an instantaneous response in the marketplace.

Consumers often react slowly to changes in prices and other conditions in the marketplace. To illustrate this delayed or lagged effect, consider the demand for electric power. Suppose an electric utility raises its rates by 30 percent. What effect will this have on the quantity of electric power demanded? In the very short run the effect will be slight. Customers may be more careful to turn off unneeded lights, but total demand, which is highly dependent on the appliances owned by the utility's residential customers and the equipment operated by their industrial and commercial customers, will probably not be greatly affected. Prices will go up and quantity demanded will not fall very much, so total revenue will increase substantially. In other words, the short-run demand for electric power is relatively *inelastic*.

Over the longer run, however, the increase in power rates has more substantial effects. Residential users will reduce their purchases of air conditioners, electric heating units, and other appliances, and those appliances that are purchased will be more energy-efficient. These actions will reduce the demand for power. Similarly, industrial users will tend to switch to other energy sources, will employ less energy-intensive production methods, or will relocate in areas where electric costs are lower. Thus, the ultimate effect of the price increase on demand may be substantial, but it will take a number of years before the full impact is felt. This phenomenon of long-run elasticity exceeding short-run elasticity is typical for most demand determining factors.

Demand Estimation

We have introduced several concepts useful in demand analysis and indicated the key role that product demand plays in most business decisions. To use these important demand relationships in decision analysis, one must be able to estimate the structural form and parameters of the demand function empirically.

In some cases it is relatively easy to obtain accurate estimates of demand relationships, especially those necessary for short-run demand or sales forecasting. In other situations it is exceedingly difficult to obtain even the information needed to make short-run demand forecasts and still more difficult to make long-run forecasts or to determine how changes in specific demand variables (price, advertising expenditures, credit terms, prices of competing products, and so on) will affect the quantity of a product demanded. These demand relationships are sufficiently important that we should consider procedures used to estimate them.

There are three primary methods used to estimate the parameters of demand functions: the interview (or survey) method, market experimentation, and regression analysis. Each of these techniques is sufficiently complex to warrant more extensive study than can be provided in an introductory managerial economics course. Here, we can only introduce the techniques and show how they are used to obtain important demand information.

Consumer Interviews

The consumer interview, or survey procedure, requires the questioning of a firm's customers or potential customers in an attempt to estimate the relationship between the demand for its products and a variety of variables perceived to be important for the marketing and profit planning functions. The technique can be applied naïvely by simply stopping shoppers and asking questions about the quantity of the product they would purchase at different prices. At the other extreme, trained interviewers may present sophisticated questions to a carefully selected sample to elicit the desired information.

Theoretically, consumer surveys can provide excellent information on a number of important demand relationships. The firm might question each of its customers (or take a statistical sample if the number of customers is large) about projected purchases under a variety of different conditions relating to price, advertising expenditures, prices of substitutes and complements, income, and any number of other variables in the demand function. Then, by aggregating data, the firm could forecast the total quantity of its product demanded and estimate some of the important parameters in the demand function for its product.

Unfortunately, this procedure does not always work smoothly in practice. The quantity and quality of information obtainable by this technique are likely to be limited. Consumers are often unable, and in many cases unwilling, to provide accurate answers to hypothetical questions about how they would react to changes in the key demand variables.

Consider the problem of attempting to determine the effect of just two variables, price and advertising expenditures, on the demand for automobiles. If an interviewer asked how you would react to a 1, 2, or 3 percent increase (or decrease) in the price of a specific model of car, could you respond accurately? What if the question relates to the effect of shifting the emphasis in the firm's advertising campaign from fuel efficiency to safety or to changing advertising media? Could you tell how this action would affect your demand for the car? Because most people are unable to answer such questions—even for major items such as automobiles, appliances, and housing—it is obviously difficult to use such a technique to estimate the demand relationships for most consumer goods.

We do not wish to imply that consumer survey techniques have no merit in demand analysis. Using subtle inquiries, a trained interviewer can extract a good deal of useful information from consumers. For example, an interviewer might ask questions about the relative prices of several competing goods and learn that most people are unaware of existing price differentials. This is a good indication that demand is not highly responsive to price changes, so a producer would not attempt to increase quantity demanded by reducing price; consumers would probably not even notice the reduction. Similar questions can be used to determine whether consumers are aware of advertising programs and to what extent they are aware, what their reaction is to the ads, and so on. Thus, some useful information is obtainable by surveys, and the quality of the results is adequate for some decision purposes.

Also, for certain kinds of demand information there is no substitute for the consumer interview. For example, in short-term demand or sales forecasting, consumer attitudes and expectations about future business conditions frequently make the difference between an accurate estimate and one that misses by a wide margin. Such subjective information can typically be obtained only through interview methods.

Market Studies and Experimentation

A second technique for obtaining useful information about a product's demand function involves market experiments. One market experiment technique entails examining consumer behavior in actual markets. The firm locates one or more markets with specific characteristics, then varies prices, packaging, advertising, and other controllable variables in the demand function, with the variations occurring either over time or between markets. For example, Del Monte Corporation may have determined that uncontrollable consumer characteristics are quite similar in Denver and Salt Lake City. Del Monte could raise the price of sliced pineapple in Salt Lake City vis-à-vis that in Denver, then compare pineapple sales in the two markets. Alternatively, Del Monte could make a series of weekly or monthly price changes in one market, then determine how these changes affected quantity demanded. With several segregated markets, the firm may also be able to use census or survey data to determine how such demographic characteristics as income, family size, educational level, and ethnic background affect demand. Market experiments have several serious shortcomings. They are expensive and are therefore usually undertaken on a scale too small to allow high levels of confidence in the results. Related to this problem is the one of short-run versus long-run effects. Market experiments are seldom run for sufficiently long periods to indicate the long-run effects of various price, advertising, or packaging strategies. The experimenter is thus forced to examine short-run data and attempt to extend it to a longer period.

Difficulties associated with the uncontrolled parts of the market experiment also reduce its value as an estimating tool. A change in economic conditions during the experiment is likely to invalidate the results, especially if the experiment includes the use of several separated markets; a local strike or layoffs by a major employer in one of the market areas, a severe snowstorm, or the like might well ruin the experiment. Likewise, a change in a competing product's promotion, price, or packaging might distort the results. There is also the danger that customers lost during the experiment as a result of price manipulations cannot be regained when the experiment ends.

A second market experimentation procedure utilizes a controlled laboratory experiment wherein consumers are given funds with which to shop in a simulated store. By varying prices, product packaging, displays, and other factors, the experimenter can often learn a great deal about consumer behavior. The laboratory experiment, while providing similar information to field experiments, has the advantage of greater control of extraneous factors.

The consumer clinic or laboratory experiment technique is not without shortcomings, however. The primary difficulty is that the subjects invariably know that they are part of an experiment, and this knowledge may well distort their shopping habits. They may, for example, exhibit considerably more price consciousness than is typical in their everyday shopping. Moreover, the high cost of such experiments necessarily limits the sample size, which makes inference from the sample to the general population tenuous at best.

Demand for Oranges: An Illustrative Market Experiment

During 1962 researchers from the University of Florida conducted a market experiment in Grand Rapids, Michigan, to examine the competition between California and Florida Valencia oranges. The experiment was designed to provide estimates of the price elasticities of demand for the various oranges included in the study, as well as to measure the cross-price elasticities of demand among varieties of oranges.[5]

---

[5]This section is adapted from Marshall B. Godwin, W. Fred Chapman, Jr., and William T. Hanley, *Competition between Florida and California Valencia Oranges in the Fruit Market*, Bulletin 704, December 1965, Agricultural Experiment Stations, Institute of Food and Agricultural Services, University of Florida, Gainesville, Florida, in cooperation with the U.S. Department of Agriculture, Florida Citrus Commission.

The researchers chose Grand Rapids because its size, economic base, and demographic characteristics are representative of the Midwest market for oranges. Nine supermarkets located throughout the city cooperated in the experiment, which consisted of varying the prices charged for Florida and California Valencia oranges daily for 31 days and recording the quantities of each variety sold. The price variations for each variety of orange covered a range of 32¢ a dozen (±16¢ around the price per dozen that existed in the market at the time the study began). More than 9,250 dozen oranges were sold during the experiment.

The price and quantity data obtained in this study enabled the researchers to examine the relationship between sales of each variety of orange and its price, as well as the relationship between sales and the price charged for competing varieties. The results of the study are summarized in Table 3.3, where the elasticities of these price variables are reported. The numbers along the diagonal represent the price elasticities of the three varieties of oranges, while the off-diagonal figures estimate the cross-price elasticities of demand.

The price elasticity for all three varieties was quite large. The −3.07 price elasticity for Florida Indian River oranges means that a 1 percent decrease in their price resulted in a 3.07 percent increase in their sales. The other Florida oranges had a similar price elasticity, while the price elasticity of the California oranges was somewhat lower, indicating that demand for California oranges is less responsive to price changes than is demand for the Florida varieties.

The cross-price elasticities of demand reveal some interesting demand relationships among these three varieties of oranges. First, note that cross-price elasticities of demand between the two Florida varieties are positive and relatively large. This indicates that consumers view these two varieties as close substitutes and therefore switch readily between them when price differentials exist. The cross-price elasticities of demand between the Florida and California oranges, on the other hand, are all very small, indicating that consumers do not view them as close substitutes. That is, the market for California oranges in Grand Rapids is quite distinct from the market for Florida varieties.

Table 3.3
Demand Relationships for California and Florida Valencia Oranges

A 1 Percent Change in the Price of	Percentage Change in the Sales of		
	Florida Indian River	Florida Interior	California
Florida Indian River	−3.07	+1.56	+0.01
Florida Interior	+1.16	−3.01	+0.14
California	+0.18	+0.09	−2.76

This market study provided estimates of two important demand relationships, the price elasticity of demand for Florida and California oranges and their cross-price elasticities of demand. The researchers were able to identify and measure these relationships because the 31-day study period was brief enough to prevent changes in incomes, tastes, population, and other variables that would influence the demand for oranges; and they were able to insure that adequate supply quantities of the various Valencia oranges were available to consumers at each experimental price.

Regression Analysis

A third approach to estimating demand relationships is through the use of statistical procedures. The statistical method most frequently employed in demand estimation is regression analysis. With **regression analysis** one attempts to estimate the parameters of the demand function by fitting an equation to a set of observed data. There are limitations to this technique, but regression analysis can frequently provide good estimates of demand relationships at a relatively low cost.

We analyze the regression analysis approach to demand estimation in somewhat more detail than consumer interviews and market experiments for two reasons. First, in many instances, regression analysis is the best inexpensive means available for estimating demand relationships. And second, regression analysis is not only valuable in demand estimation, but it also has many uses in the study of production and cost relationships. Regression analysis may be the single most important estimating technique used in managerial decision making. In later chapters we will draw on this tool extensively.

Specifying the Variables

The first step in regression analysis is to specify the variables that are expected to influence demand. Product demand, measured in physical units, is the dependent variable. The list of independent variables, or those that influence demand, always includes the price of the product and generally includes such factors as the prices of complementary and competitive products, advertising expenditures, consumer incomes, and population of the consuming group. Demand functions for expensive durable goods, such as automobiles and houses, include interest rates and other credit terms; those for ski equipment, beverages, or air conditioners include weather conditions. Demand determinants for capital goods, such as industrial machinery, include corporate profitability, output/capacity ratios, and wage rate trends.

Obtaining Data on the Variables

The second step in regression analysis is to obtain accurate estimates of the variables: measures of price, credit terms, output/capacity ratios, advertising expenditures, incomes, and the like. Obtaining estimates of these variables is not always easy, especially if the study involves data for past years. Further, some key variables, such as consumer attitudes toward quality and their expectations about future business conditions (which are quite important in demand functions for many consumer goods) may have to be obtained by survey (questionnaire and interview) techniques, which introduce an element of subjectivity into the analysis, or by market or laboratory experiments, which may produce biased data.

Specifying the Regression Equation

Once the variables have been specified and the data gathered, the next step is to specify the form of the regression equation or the manner in which the independent variables are assumed to interact to determine the level of demand. The most common specification is a linear relationship such as the following:

$$Q = a + bP + cA + dY. \qquad \text{(3.15)}$$

Here Q represents the quantity of a particular product demanded, P is the price charged, A represents advertising expenditures, and Y is per capita disposable income. The quantity demanded is assumed to change linearly with changes in each of the independent variables. For example, if $b = -1.5$, quantity demanded will decline by 1½ units for each 1-unit increase in the price of the product. The demand curve for a demand function such as that shown in Equation 3.15 is linear; that is, it is a straight line.

Linear demand functions have great appeal in empirical work for two reasons. First, experience has shown that many demand relationships are in fact approximately linear over the range for which data are typically encountered. Second, the parameters (b, c, and d in Equation 3.15) provide a direct measure of the marginal relationships in the demand function. That is, they indicate the change in quantity demanded associated with a one-unit change in the related variable.

There are numerous other structural forms that can be used as the basis for regression analysis of demand; logarithmic and exponential equations are both frequently employed.[6] The algebraic form of the de-

---

[6]See Chapter 5 in J. L. Pappas, E. F. Brigham, and M. Hirschey, *Managerial Economics*, 4th ed., Hinsdale, Ill.: The Dryden Press, 1983, for a more detailed discussion of other structural forms used in demand analysis.

Table 3.4
Sales and Advertising Data for XYZ Corporation

	1978	1979	1980	1981	1982	1983	1984	Mean
Sales (thousands of units)	37	48	45	36	25	55	63	$\bar{Y} = 44$
Advertising expenditures (millions of dollars)	$4.5	$6.5	$3.5	$3.0	$2.5	$8.5	$7.5	$\bar{A} = \$5.1$

mand function (linear, multiplicative, or other form) should always be chosen to reflect the true relationships among variables in the system being studied. That is, care should be taken to insure that the structural form chosen for an empirical demand function is consistent with the underlying theory of demand. In practice, however, there is often no a priori basis for specifying the form of the relationship. In such cases several theoretically appropriate forms may be tested, and the one that best fits the data should be selected as being most likely to reflect the true relationship. Methods of fitting regression equations are described in the following section.

Estimating the Regression Parameters

Regression equations are typically fitted (that is, the coefficients a, b, c, and d of Equation 3.15 are estimated) by the method of least squares. Usually one need not worry about actually performing the calculations necessary to estimate the coefficients since business and personal computers (and even some calculators) can do so rapidly and at minimal cost. However, a brief discussion of the estimation procedure will be valuable for developing a basic understanding of the technique. Using a very simple two-variable case, we can demonstrate the method as follows. Assume that data on XYZ Corporation's sales of Product Y and the advertising expenditures on this product have been collected over the past seven years. (The data are given in Table 3.4.) If a linear relationship between sales of Y and advertising expenditures, A, is hypothesized, the regression equation would take the following form:

$$\text{Sales } Y = a + bA. \tag{3.16}$$

The method of least squares is then applied to select the values of a and b that best fit the data in Table 3.4 to the regression equation. The procedure is presented graphically in Figure 3.7. Here each point represents the advertising expenditure and sales of Y in a given year. In terms of Equation 3.16, each point can be specified by the relationship:

$$\text{Sales}_t = Y_t = a + bA_t + u_t, \tag{3.17}$$

Figure 3.7
Relationship between Sales and Advertising
Expenditures for XYZ Corporation

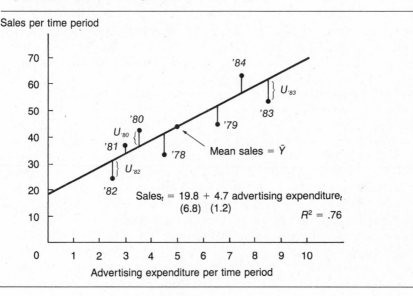

where u is a residual term that measures the unexplained variation of each data point and includes the effects of all determinants of sales that have been omitted from the regression equation, as well as a stochastic, or random, element, and t is used to denote the year of the observation. Notice that in this regression equation, a is the intercept of the regression line with the sales axis, b is the slope of the line, and u_t is the error term, or residual, which measures the vertical deviation of each tth data point from the fitted regression line. The sum of the squares of these error terms is minimized by the choice of a and b through the least squares technique.[7] The linear regression equation that best fits the XYZ data to Equation 3.17 is

$$\text{Sales}_t = Y_t = 19.8 + 4.7A_t. \tag{3.18}$$

Notice that we have dropped the error term, u_t, at this point since its expected value is always zero.

---

[7] The error terms are squared because the deviations are both positive and negative and, hence, many different lines can be fitted that will result in the sum of the actual deviations being zero. That is, the *sum* of the deviations can be zero even though substantial positive and negative deviations exist. By squaring the deviations we are summing a set of positive numbers, and the line that minimizes this sum most accurately depicts the relationship between the dependent and the independent variables.

Interpreting the Regression Equation

Once we have estimates of the regression equation, how do we interpret the values of the coefficients? First, a, the intercept term, frequently has no economic meaning. Caution must always be exercised when interpreting points outside the range of the observed data, and typically the intercept lies far outside this range. In our present example the intercept cannot be interpreted as the expected level of sales if advertising is completely eliminated. It *might* be true that the level of sales with zero advertising would equal the intercept term, a, but since the current example includes no observations of sales at zero advertising expenditures, we cannot safely assume that 19,800 units can be sold with no advertising. Similarly, it would be hazardous to extend the sales/advertising curve very far upward from the range of observed values. For example, we could not extrapolate the sales curve out to advertising expenditures of $15 or $20 million and have much confidence in the predicted level of sales (consider the possible saturation of advertising's effect on demand). In summary, it is very important that we restrict our interpretation of regression relationships to within the range of data observations.

The slope coefficient, b, gives us an estimate of the change in sales associated with a 1-unit change in advertising expenditures. Since advertising expenditures were measured in millions of dollars for the regression estimation, while sales were in thousands of units, a $1-million increase in advertising will lead to a 4,700-unit expected increase in sales; a $2-million advertising increase to 9,400 additional units sold; and so on. Again, caution must be used when extending the analysis beyond the range of observed values in the data used to estimate the regression coefficients.

The results of this simple two-variable regression model can easily be extended to multiple-variable models. To illustrate the extension, suppose that we also have information on the average price, P, charged for Product Y in each of the seven years. This new information can be added to the linear model given in Equation 3.17, resulting in the following regression equation:

$$\text{Sales } Y_t = a + bA_t + cP_t + u_t. \tag{3.19}$$

Computer programs using the method of least squares can be used to fit the data to the model and to estimate the parameters a, b, and c. When this is done, we interpret the coefficients as follows: a is again an intercept term that may or may not have economic significance, depending upon the range of sample values; b is the expected change in sales related to a one-unit change in advertising expenditure, *holding constant the price of* Y; and c is the expected change in sales related to a one-unit change in price, *holding constant advertising expenditures.*

Graphic representations of multiple regression models are not generally feasible, but Figure 3.7 can be used to gain insights into the process. Note that actual sales in 1983 were well below the value predicted by the regression line, so u_{83} was large and negative. Similarly, note that actual sales exceeded the predicted level in 1980, so u_{80} was large and positive. Now suppose that our new information on prices reveals that the average price of Y was relatively low in 1980 but high in 1983. Further, high prices prevailed in 1982, 1978, and 1979, while prices were low in 1981 and 1984 as well as in 1980. Thus, the price data seem to explain the deviations in the graph. Accordingly, we would expect that when price data are added to the regression equation, the error terms, u_t, will be reduced; that is, the average absolute value of u in Equation 3.19 should be less than that of u in Equation 3.17, since more of the variation in sales can be explained by variables included in the model and, therefore, less need be impounded in the error terms. Given that the sum of the squared error terms will be lower, Equation 3.19 is said to provide a better fit or explanation of the observed data.

To illustrate the use of regression analysis for demand estimation we present the following example.

Frozen Fruit Pie Demand: An Illustrative Regression Analysis Problem

In late 1984 Wisco Foods Inc., a regional processor located in the upper Midwest, undertook an empirical estimation of the demand relationships for its Mrs. Smyth's frozen fruit pies. The firm was attempting to formulate its pricing and promotional plans for the following year, and management was interested in learning how certain decisions would affect sales of the frozen pies.

An analysis of earlier demand studies for its other prepared foods led Wisco to hypothesize that demand for the fruit pies was a linear function of the price charged, advertising and promotional activities, the price of a competing brand of frozen pies, per capita income, and population in the market area. It was decided that a trend term should also be included in the hypothesized demand function to account both for the continuing shift to prepared foods and for the growth in sales resulting from increased consumer awareness of the product.

Wisco had been processing these frozen pies for about three years, and its market research department had two years of quarterly data for six regions on sales quantities, on the retail price charged for its pies, on local advertising and promotional expenditures, and on the price charged for the major competing brand of frozen pies. Statistical data published by *Sales Management* magazine on population and disposable incomes in each of the six locations were also available for the analysis; it was thus possible to include all the hypothesized demand determinants in the empirical estimation.

The following regression equation was fitted to the data:

$$Q_{it} = a + bP_{it} + cA_{it} + dPX_{it} + eY_{it} + fPop_{it} + gT_{it} + u_{it}. \qquad (3.20)$$

Here, Q is the quantity of pies sold during the tth quarter; P is the retail price in cents of Wisco's frozen pies; A represents the dollars spent for advertising and promotional activities; PX is the price, measured in cents, charged for competing pies; Y is dollars of per capita disposable income; Pop is the population of the market area; and T is the trend factor. The subscript i indicates the regional market from which the observation was taken, while the subscript t represents the quarter during which the observation occurred.

Least squares estimation of the regression equation on the basis of the 48 data observations (eight quarters of data for each of the six areas) resulted in the estimated regression coefficients and statistics given in Table 3.5.

The terms in parentheses are the standard errors of the coefficients. An analysis of the error terms, or residuals, indicated that all the required assumptions regarding their distribution were met; hence the least squares regression procedure is a valid technique for estimating the parameters of this demand function.

The coefficients of the regression equation can be interpreted as follows: The intercept term, -500, has no economic meaning in this instance; it lies far outside the range of observed data and obviously cannot be interpreted as the demand for Mrs. Smyth's frozen fruit pies when all the independent variables take on zero values. The coefficient for each independent variable indicates the marginal relationship between that variable and sales of the pies, holding constant the effect of all the other variables in the demand function. For example, -275, the coefficient of P, the price charged for Mrs. Smyth's pies, indicates that when we hold constant the effects of all other demand variables, each 1¢ increase in price will cause quarterly sales to decline by 275 pies. Similarly, the coefficient of A, the advertising and promotional variable, indicates that for each dollar spent on advertising during the quarter, 5 additional pies will be sold, and the coefficient of the disposable income variable, $+7.25$, indicates that an added dollar of disposable per

Table 3.5
Estimated Demand Function for Frozen Pies

$$Q = -500 - 275P_{it} + 5A_{it} + 150PX_{it} + 7.25Y_{it} + 0.25Pop_{it} + 875T. \qquad (3.19)$$
$$\quad\;\;(52)\quad\;(1.1)\quad\;\;(66)\quad\;\;(3.2)\quad\;\;(0.09)\quad\;\;(230)$$

Coefficient of determination = R^2 = 0.92.

Standard error of the estimate = 775.

capita income leads on average to an increase of 7.25 pies demanded quarterly.

The coefficient of determination, typically indicated by the symbol R^2, is a statistic that indicates how well the regression model explains variation in the value of the dependent variable. It is defined as *the proportion of total variation in the dependent variable that is explained by the full set of independent variables included in the model*. Accordingly, R^2 can take on values ranging from 0, indicating that the model provides absolutely no explanation of variation in the dependent variable, to 1.0, indicating that all the variation has been explained by the independent variables. The coefficient of determination in this equation ($R^2 = .92$) indicates that 92 percent of the total variation in pie sales has been explained by the regression model, a very satisfactory level of explanation for the model as a whole.

In the regression equation, each parameter estimate (the coefficients associated with each independent variable) is over twice as large as its standard error, which means that the estimates are all statistically significant. This conclusion is derived as follows. In a regression equation there is a 68 percent probability that b^*, the true marginal relationship between an independent variable X and the dependent variable Y_b, lies in the interval $\hat{b} \pm$ one standard error of the coefficient b, where b is the relationship between X and Y estimated by the regression technique. There is a 95 percent probability that b^* lies in the interval $\hat{b} \pm$ two standard errors of the coefficient; and a 99 percent probability that b^* is in the interval $\hat{b} \pm$ three standard errors of the coefficient. Thus, to test whether a regression coefficient is significantly different from zero, we hypothesize that $b^* = 0$ and test for a $\hat{b}$ value far enough away from zero to reject the hypothesis. A parameter estimate, twice as large as its standard error of the coefficient, means that one can reject the hypothesis that the true parameter value is zero at a 95 percent confidence level (i.e., with only a 5 percent chance of being wrong).[8] In the equation for

---

[8] A parameter estimate twice as large as its standard error is equivalent to observing a t value of 2 for the regression coefficient since the t-statistic for this test is merely the regression coefficient divided by its standard error.

$$t = \frac{\hat{b}}{\text{Standard error of } b}$$

Thus, the t-statistic is a measure of the number of standard errors between $\hat{b}$ and the hypothesized value $b^* = 0$. If the sample used to estimate the regression parameters is large (for example, > 30), the t-statistic follows a normal distribution and properties of a normal distribution can be used to make confidence statements concerning the relationship between $\hat{b}$ and b^* as is done in the text above. (The properties of a normal distribution are more fully developed in Chapter 11.) For small sample sizes (for example, < 30), the t-distribution deviates from a normal distribution, and a t-table should be used for testing the significance of estimated regression parameters.

Mrs. Smyth's frozen fruit pies we can reject at the 95 percent confidence level the hypothesis that each of the independent variables is unrelated to the demand for the pies.

Note also that the standard errors of the coefficients of the two key controllable decision variables, price and advertising, are very small in relation to their respective coefficients. With a small standard error of the coefficient, the true parameter value relating an independent variable to the dependent variable will lie in a narrow band around the estimated value, i.e., there is a 95 percent probability that the true value lies in the range of $\hat{b} \pm 2$ times the standard error of the coefficient. The small standard errors of the coefficients for price and advertising mean that the regression coefficients for these two variables are probably very good estimates of the true relationship between them and the demand for Mrs. Smyth's pies, so they can be used for decision-making purposes with a great deal of confidence.

The standard error of the estimate provides a means of estimating a confidence interval for predicting values of the dependent variable in a regression equation, *given* values for the independent variables. That is, the standard error of the estimate is used to determine a range within which we can predict the dependent variable with varying degrees of statistical confidence. Thus, although our best estimate of the value for the dependent variable is $\hat{Y}$, the value predicted by the regression equation, we must use the standard error of the estimate to determine just how accurate a prediction $\hat{Y}$ is likely to be.

Assuming the standard errors are normally distributed about the regression equation, there is a 68 percent probability that future observations of the dependent variable will lie within the range $\hat{Y} \pm$ one standard error of the estimate. The probability that some future observation of Y will lie within two standard errors of its predicted value increases to 95 percent, and there is a 99 percent chance that an actual observed value for Y will lie in the range $\hat{Y} \pm$ three standard errors.[9] It is clear, then, that greater predictive accuracy is associated with smaller standard errors of the estimate.

To examine the use of the standard error of the estimate, assume that Wisco wishes to project the next quarter's sales of Mrs. Smyth's frozen fruit pies in Market Area B. It has set the price of its pies at $2.75 (or 275 cents) and promotional expenditures at $1,000. The prices of the competing pies are expected to remain at their current level of $2.40; population in the market area is 50,000; per capita disposable income

---

[9]The standard error is essentially equivalent to a standard deviation; it is the standard deviation of the dependent variable *about the regression line.*

is \$8,000; and the quarter being forecast is the ninth quarter in the model. Inserting these values into the demand equation results in an estimated demand of 43,250 pies:

$$Q = -500 - 275(275) + 5(1,000) + 150(240) + 7.25(8,000)$$
$$+ 0.25(50,000) + 875(9) = 43,250.$$

While 43,250 is the best point estimate of demand, the standard error of the estimate allows us to construct a confidence interval for sales projection. For example, sales can be projected to fall within an interval of ± 2 standard errors of the estimate about the expected sales level, with a confidence level of 95 percent. The standard error of the estimate for Mrs. Smyth's pies is 775. Thus, an interval of $\pm 1,550$ pies about the expected sales of 43,250 pies represents the 95 percent confidence interval. This means that one can predict with a 95 percent probability of being correct that the sales of Mrs. Smyth's pies during the next quarter in Market Area B will lie in the range of 41,700 to 44,800 pies. The company could use Equation 3.24 to forecast sales in each of the six areas, then sum these area forecasts to obtain the estimated demand for the product line as a whole.

Summary

The demand for a firm's products is a critical determinant of its profitability, and demand forecasts enter as key elements in virtually all managerial planning. To make a reliable demand forecast, one must have a thorough understanding of certain concepts and relationships. These concepts were introduced in this chapter, and they were used extensively as we examined ways of actually estimating demand functions.

Several general points were noted. First, product demand is usually a function of several variables, such as price, income, and advertising expenditures. The explicit statement of these relationships is the *demand function*. The partial relationship between *the quantity demanded* and price is expressed by the *demand curve*. *Shifts in the demand curve* represent changes in variables other than price in the demand function; *movements along a demand curve* imply that factors other than price in the demand function are held constant.

A key concept introduced in the chapter is *elasticity*, the percentage change in quantity demanded associated with a percentage change in one of the determinants of demand. *Price* elasticity, ε_p and E_p, denoting *point* and *arc* elasticity respectively, relates changes in the quantity demanded to changes in the product's own price. If $|\varepsilon_p| > 1.0$, this is defined as *elastic* demand, and a price reduction leads to an increase in total revenue. If $|\varepsilon_p| < 1.0$, we have *inelastic* demand, and a price reduction decreases total revenue. If $|\varepsilon_p| = 1.0$, demand is unitary elastic and price and quantity changes exactly offset each other, resulting in no change in total revenue.

Income elasticity, ε_I or E_I, relates demand to a measure of income. Ordinarily, ε_I is positive, signifying that higher incomes cause greater demand, but the size of the elasticity coefficient is also important. If $\varepsilon_I > 1.0$, demand increases more than in proportion to income increases; if $\varepsilon_I < 1.0$, the converse holds. This has important implications for the growth and variability of a product's demand.

Cross-price elasticity, ε_{PX} or E_{PX}, relates the demand for Product Y to the price of Product X. If $\varepsilon_{PX} > 0$, an increase in P_X causes an increase in Q_Y, and the goods are *substitutes*. If $\varepsilon_{PX} < 0$, the goods are *complements*; if $\varepsilon_{PX} \approx 0$, the goods are *independent*.

Other kinds of elasticity can be calculated and used in demand analysis: Interest rate elasticity and advertising elasticity are two examples.

Another important point in demand analysis concerns the concept of *derived demand*: The demand for one product may be derived from a more fundamental demand for another. It was shown that the demand for capital goods is derived from the demand for consumer products.

Time has an impact on demand relationships in numerous ways. The frictions in the marketplace typically cause short-run demand impacts to be smaller than the impact over an extended period where the full influence of a change has run its course.

And finally, we examined a variety of techniques for empirically analyzing demand relationships. We considered the use of consumer interview and market experiment techniques for demand estimation in situations where the data necessary for statistical analysis are not available. These techniques can provide valuable information about some important demand relationships. However, because of high costs and severe limits on the information that can be obtained from them, statistical demand estimation is frequently employed for empirical demand studies.

Because least squares regression analysis is by far the most widely used statistical estimating procedure in demand analysis, this technique was examined in somewhat greater detail. The emphasis was on the specification of the regression model and the interpretation and use of the estimated parameters and associated regression statistics. We concluded with an example of the use of a regression model for empirically estimating a product's demand function.

Questions

3.1. Explain the rationale for each of the demand variables in Equation 3.1.

3.2. Distinguish between a demand function and a demand curve. What is the difference between a change in the quantity demanded and a shift in the demand curve?

3.3. What is the relationship between a demand function and a total revenue function? Explain how one would construct the total revenue function corresponding to a given demand function.

3.4. Define each of the following terms, giving both a verbal explanation and an equation.
   a) Point elasticity
   b) Arc elasticity
   c) Price elasticity
   d) Cross-price elasticity
   e) Income elasticity

3.5. What is likely to be the sign of the cross-price elasticities of demand between the following:
   a) Movie cameras and video recorders? Why?
   b) Movie cameras and film? Why?
   c) Movie cameras and milk? Why?

3.6. What relationship do you think would exist between the shape of a firm's demand curve and the degree of competition in its industry (that is, whether the industry is highly competitive or is monopolistic)?

3.7. How could the cross-price elasticity concept be used in an analysis of the degree of competition in the industry?

3.8. Do you think that the price elasticity of demand would be greater if computed for an industry or for one firm in the industry? Why?

Solved Problems

3.1. KROM-FM is currently contemplating a T-shirt advertising promotion. Limited sales data from a few T-shirt shops marketing a prototype of the KROM design indicate that

$$Q = 1,200 - 200P,$$

where Q is T-shirt sales and P is price.
   a) How many T-shirts could KROM sell at $4.50 each?
   b) What price would KROM have to charge to sell 900 T-shirts?
   c) At what price would T-shirt sales equal zero?
   d) How many T-shirts could be given away?
   e) Calculate the point price elasticity of demand at a price of $3.00.

Solution

3.1.

  a)

$$Q = 1{,}200 - 200P$$
$$Q = 1{,}200 - 200(4.50)$$
$$Q = 300.$$

  b)

$$Q = 1{,}200 - 200P$$
$$900 = 1{,}200 - 200P$$
$$200P = 300$$
$$P = \$1.50.$$

  c)

$$Q = 1{,}200 - 200P$$
$$0 = 1{,}200 - 200P$$
$$200P = 1{,}200$$
$$P = \$6.$$

  d)

$$Q = 1{,}200 - 200P$$
$$Q = 1{,}200 - 200(0)$$
$$Q = 1{,}200.$$

e) The point price elasticity of demand at a price of $3.00 is calculated as follows:

$$\varepsilon_P = \frac{\Delta Q}{\Delta P} \cdot \frac{P}{Q}$$

$$= -200 \times \frac{3}{1{,}200 - 200(3)}$$

$$= -200 \times \frac{3}{600} = -1, \text{ indicating unitary elasticity.}$$

3.2. Recently, Jayhawk Cinema reduced its ticket prices for afternoon "early bird" shows from $4 to $2 and enjoyed an increase in theater traffic, Q, from 50 to 250 persons.

  a) Calculate the price arc elasticity for theater tickets.

  b) Cost pressures are forcing Jayhawk management to consider an increase in ticket prices. What is the implied advertising elasticity if an increase in advertising from $100 to $125 is necessary in order to offset the effect on Q of an increase in ticket prices from $2 to $3?

  c) Holding all else equal, would further price increases result in higher or lower total revenues?

Solution

   a)

$$E_p = \frac{Q_2 - Q_1}{P_2 - P_1} \cdot \frac{P_2 + P_1}{Q_2 + Q_1}$$

$$= \frac{250 - 50}{2 - 4} \cdot \frac{2 + 4}{250 + 50}$$

$$= \frac{200}{-2} \cdot \frac{6}{300}$$

$$= -2.$$

b) In order to determine the implied advertising elasticity, we must first calculate the effect on Q due to a ticket price increase from $2 to $3.

$$E_p = \frac{Q_2 - Q_1}{P_2 - P_1} \cdot \frac{P_2 + P_1}{Q_2 + Q_1}$$

$$-2 = \frac{Q_2 - 250}{3 - 2} \cdot \frac{3 + 2}{Q_2 + 250} .$$

$$-2 = \frac{(Q_2 - 250)(5)}{Q_2 + 250}$$

$$-2Q_2 + 500 = 5Q_2 - 1250$$

$$7Q_2 = 750$$

$$Q_2 = 107.$$

Now, the offsetting advertising effect can be used to calculate the implied advertising elasticity.

$$E_A = \frac{Q_2 - Q_1}{A_2 - A_1} \cdot \frac{A_2 + A_1}{Q_2 + Q_1}$$

$$= \frac{250 - 107}{125 - 100} \cdot \frac{125 + 100}{250 + 107}$$

$$= \frac{143}{25} \cdot \frac{225}{357}$$

$$= 3.6$$

c) Since demand is *elastic* in this range, $|E_p| = 2$, price increases will decrease total revenues.

Problem Set

3.1. Allied Electric Company is developing a new design for its porta-
ble electric hair dryer. Accurately pricing the new product is essential
for success in this highly competitive market. Test market data indicated a demand for the new hair dryer of

$$Q = 30{,}000 - 1\,000P,$$

where Q is hair dryer sales and P is price.

    a) How many hair dryers could Allied sell at $22.50 each?

    b) What price would Allied have to charge to sell 12,000 hair
dryers?

    c) At what price would hair dryer sales equal zero?

    d) Calculate the point price elasticity of demand at a price of $20.

3.2. The demand for personal computers is characterized by the following elasticities: Price elasticity $= -1.9$, cross-price elasticity with software (programs) $= -1.1$, income elasticity $= +2.1$. Indicate whether
each of the following statements is true or false and why.

    a) A price reduction for personal computers will increase *both* the
number of units demanded and the total revenue received by
sellers.

    b) The cross-price elasticity indicates that a 10 percent reduction in
the price of personal computers results in an 11 percent increase in
the demand for software.

    c) Demand for personal computers is price elastic *and* they are su-
perior goods.

    d) Falling prices for software will definitely increase *both* the num-
ber of computers bought and the revenues from software sales.

    e) A 2 percent reduction in the price of personal computers would
result in a 3.8 percent increase in their demand.

3.3. Dan Marshall, owner of the Wilmington Tigers minor league base-
ball team, is trying to determine the best ticket-pricing strategy for
home games. Historical ticket-sales data reveal the following ticket demand point elasticities:

$$\text{"Own" Price} = -0.08$$
$$\text{Refreshment Price} = -0.14$$
$$\text{Wilmington Population} = +0.75.$$

    a) Marshall is contemplating a "moderate" increase in ticket prices
in order to increase revenue. Is this a good idea? Why or why not?

    b) How would you characterize the relationship between tickets
and refreshments?

    c) If the Wilmington population increased from 140,000 to 145,600, what would be the resulting effect on ticket demand? Assume all else is unchanged.

3.4. The manager of Wilson's Grocery Store has noticed that over the past several months sales of potato chips have typically been close to 90 cases per week. On two occasions, however, sales declined to 60 cases per week. The manager notes that during these two periods the store was running a special on pretzels and had reduced the price of a bag of pretzels from $1.00 to 80¢.

a) What is the arc cross-price elasticity between potato chips and pretzels?

b) What level of sales for potato chips would you predict if the price of pretzels is increased from $1.00 to $1.20?

3.5. Rachel's Hair Salon cuts and styles hair for men and women. During 1984 the salon grossed $187,500 in revenue on an average hair styling fee of $12.50. Rachel Stevens, the owner of Rachel's Hair Salon, believes that a price increase to $14.50 will not result in any reduction in the number of customers during 1985 because of increases in consumer personal income. Industry studies have shown that salons of this type have an arc price elasticity of −1.5.

a) If consumer personal income is expected to rise from $14,000 in 1984 to $16,000 in 1985, what arc elasticity is Stevens assuming in her statement?

b) What 1985 gross revenue would you predict for Rachel's Hair Salon if your elasticity estimate in part a is correct?

3.6. Modern Motors is a car dealership that primarily sells compact cars. The list price of an average model is approximately $8,000. During 1984 its sales volume was 36 cars per month. In January 1985 a competitor, Smart Motors, cut the average list price of its compact cars from $8,200 to $7,600. The following month Modern Motors sold only 30 cars.

a) Determine the arc cross-price elasticity of demand betweeen Modern Motors' cars and Smart Motors' cars. (Assume that Modern Motors' price is held constant.)

b) Assume that the arc price elasticity for Modern Motors' cars is −2.0. Assume also that Smart Motors keeps the price of its cars at $7,600. What price cut must be made by Modern Motors to increase its sales volume back to 36 cars per month?

3.7. As a means for increasing sales of a slow-moving product line, Walt's Sport Shop offered a coupon worth $2 toward the purchase of Zebko fishing reels during the month of June. During May, Walt's sold 50 reels at an average price of $40. Due to the success of the coupon promotion, June sales totaled 60 reels.

a) Calculate the point price elasticity for the Zebko reels.

b) If Walt's buys Zebko reels from a local distributor for $27, calculate the price Walt's would charge its customers in order to maximize profits. (Assume the $27 represents marginal cost and recall that profits are maximized at the output where $MR = MC$.)

c) Calculate expected unit sales, revenues, and profits at the profit maximizing activity level.

3.8. Norton Soap Company produces two brands of laundry detergent. Dazzle is a boxed powder detergent and Sparkle is a liquid detergent. A Norton study using sales data from the past 36 months has revealed a demand function for Sparkle that is

$$Q = 500 - 5.0P + 4.0A + 2.0P_D - 1.5A_D,$$

where:

Q = Cases of Sparkle Sold.
P = Price of a Case of Sparkle ($).
A = Advertising Expenditures for Sparkle ($000).
P_D = Price of a Case of Dazzle ($).
A_D = Advertising Expenditures for Dazzle ($000).

During the past month the price of Sparkle was $20, advertising expenditures for Sparkle were $50,000, the price of Dazzle was $30, and advertising expenditures for Dazzle were $40,000.

a) Estimate the monthly cases of Sparkle sold.
b) Calculate the point own price elasticity for Sparkle.
c) Would raising the price of Sparkle result in an increase or decrease in total revenue?
d) Calculate the point cross-price elasticity with Dazzle.
e) Are Sparkle and Dazzle complements, substitutes, or independent goods?

3.9. Frontier and JBC are competitors in the home stereo industry. Each company produces complete home stereo units that have the demand curves:

Frontier $P_F = \$1,000 - \$0.05Q_F$.
JBC $P_J = \$1,400 - \$0.04Q_J$.

The firms are currently selling 10,000 and 20,000 home stereo units, respectively.

a) What are the point price elasticities currently faced by the firms?
b) Assume that JBC reduces its price and increases its sales to 25,000 units and that this action results in a reduction in Frontier's sales to 7,000 units. What is the indicated cross-price elasticity between Frontier and JBC home stereos?

c) Does the hypothesized price reduction by JBC make sense economically, assuming that JBC's managers operate so as to maximize profits? Why or why not?

d) Is the cross-price elasticity calculated in part b intuitively sound? Why or why not?

3.10. Kettle Grills Inc. has retained you to aid the firm in an evaluation of its marketing strategy. KGI's grills, used in outdoor cookouts, are marketed through retail outlets in the eastern United States. A move to extend KGI's market to midwestern and western states is currently being contemplated.

A marketing research group conducted an empirical analysis of demand for KGI's standard model grill in 66 markets and found the following (standard errors in parentheses):

$$Q = -518 - 10P + 12.5I + 5T - 0.5\tilde{A} + 5A$$
$$ (240) \quad (1.3) \quad (8.6) \quad (3.8) \quad (0.4) \quad (2.3)$$

$$R^2 = 0.74$$

Standard Error of the Estimate = 200,

where:

Q = Quantity Sold (Units)
P = Price ($)
I = Disposable Income in Relevant Market ($000,000)
T = Average Annual Temperature (Degrees)
$\tilde{A}$ = Competitor Advertising ($000)
A = KGI's "Own" Advertising ($000)

a) Fully evaluate and interpret the empirical results reported above. Include in your analysis a discussion of the coefficient of determination (R^2), the standard error of the estimate, and the standard errors of the parameter estimates.

b) Can you be certain at the 95 percent confidence level that the quantity sold depends on KGI's "own" advertising?

c) Will a recession hurt sales?

d) Is demand significantly dependent upon average temperature?

e) Champaign-Urbana, Illinois, is a potential midwestern market with economic characteristics typical of those eastern markets included in the empirical analysis. Given that disposable income in the Champaign-Urbana market is $180,000,000, average temperature is 54°F, total competitor advertising is $64,000, and KGI's own advertising expenditure is $6,000, derive the demand curve for the Champaign-Urbana market.

3.11. Kalamazoo Electronics produces wrist watches in two models, standard and deluxe. In early 1985, the marketing manager decided to evaluate sales of the deluxe watches with respect to the sales volume during the preceding 12 years. The following data are available for analysis:

Year	Number of Deluxe Watches Sold Q	Advertising Expenditures A	Price of Deluxe Watches P	Price of Standard Watches P_s
1973	5,000	$60,000	$60	$25
1974	4,900	60,000	65	25
1975	5,000	65,000	65	30
1976	5,100	65,000	65	35
1977	5,000	65,000	60	25
1978	5,100	65,000	60	30
1979	5,000	60,000	60	30
1980	5,100	65,000	70	30
1981	4,900	65,000	70	25
1982	4,800	65,000	75	25
1983	5,000	75,000	75	30
1984	5,100	80,000	75	30

You are to prepare data that will aid the sales manager in the analysis. Remember that in order to determine the required elasticities, you should only use years when other factors are held constant. Note also that by using only consecutive years, changes in factors that are not explicitly accounted for in the data are less likely to affect the estimated elasticities.

a) What is the arc price elasticity of demand for the deluxe model? (Average your individual estimates.)

b) What is the arc advertising elasticity of demand for the deluxe model? (Average your individual estimates.)

c) What is the arc cross-price elasticity of demand between the standard and deluxe models? Are the standard and deluxe models close substitutes?

d) On the basis of a linear regression model, the demand function for the deluxe model is estimated to be:

$$Q = 4,589 + 0.010A - 10.829P + 16.403P_s$$

i. Calculate the *point* price, advertising, and cross-price elasticities for 1981 and 1984, using the regression model.

ii. Compare the results in part d(i) to the results in parts a, b, and c. Which elasticity figures do you feel provide better estimates of the true relationships? Why?

iii. The following standard errors of the coefficients apply: $(A) = 0.004$, $(P) = 3.778$, $(P_s) = 5.357$. For each independent variable, determine whether you can reject at a 95 percent confidence level the hypothesis that no relationship exists between the independent variables and the dependent variable (Q).

iv. The coefficient of determination, R^2, is 0.775. What proportion of total variation in the dependent variable (Q) is explained by the full set of independent variables included in the model? What other independent variables might be added to the equation to obtain a better explanation of variation in the dependent variable (Q)?

References

Callasch, H. Frederick. "Price Elasticities of Demand at Retail and Wholesale Levels: An Automotive Example." *Business Economics* 19 (January 1984): 61–62.

Crafton, Steven M., and George E. Hoffer. "Estimating a Transaction Price for New Automobiles." *Journal of Business* 54 (October 1981): 611–621.

Dwyer, Gerald P., and Cotton M. Lindsay. "Robert Giffen and the Irish Potato." *American Economic Review* 74 (March 1984): 188–192.

Eilon, Samuel. "Three Price Elasticities of Demand." *Omega* 11 (1983): 479–490.

Freedman, David. "Some Pitfalls in Large Econometric Models: A Case Study." *Journal of Business* 54 (July 1981): 479–500.

Hanushek, Eric A., and John M. Quigley. "What is the Price Elasticity of Housing Demand?" *Review of Economics and Statistics* 62 (August 1980): 449–454.

Healey, John S., and Harold H. Kassarjian. "Advertising Substantiation and Advertiser Response: A Content Analysis of Magazine Advertisements." *Journal of Marketing* 47 (Winter 1983): 107–117.

Hirschey, Mark. "Intangible Capital Aspects of Advertising and R&D Expenditures." *Journal of Industrial Economics* 30 (June 1982): 375–390.

Knight, Frank H. "Realism and Relevance in the Theory of Demand." *Journal of Political Economy* 50 (1944): 289–318.

Lancaster, Kelvin J. *Consumer Demand: A New Approach.* New York: Columbia University Press, 1971.

Leamer, Edward E. "Let's Take the Con out of Econometrics." *American Economic Review* 73 (March 1983): 31–43.

Mark, John, Frank Brown, and B. J. Pierson. "Consumer Demand Theory, Goods and Characteristics: Breathing Empirical Content into the Lancastrian Approach." *Managerial and Decision Economics* 2 (March 1981): 32–39.

Morgan, James N. "Multiple Motives, Group Decisions, Uncertainty, Ignorance and Confusion: A Realistic Economics of the Consumer Requires Some Psychology." *American Economic Review* 68 (May 1978): 58–63.

Neslin, Scott A., and Robert W. Shoemaker. "Using a Natural Experiment to Estimate Price Elasticity: The 1974 Sugar Shortage and the Ready-to-Eat Cereal Market." *Journal of Marketing* 47 (Winter 1983): 44–57.

Reddy, Jack, and Abe Berger. "Three Essentials of Product Quality." *Harvard Business Review* 61 (July–August 1983): 153–159.

Chapter 4

Forecasting

Two key functions of management for any organization are *planning* and *control*. The firm must plan for the future. Planning for the future involves the following steps:

1. Determine the product and geographic markets where the firm can earn the highest returns.

2. Forecast the level of demand in these markets under different conditions of price, promotional activities, competition, and general economic activity.

3. Forecast the cost of producing different levels of output under conditions of changing technology, wage rates, and raw materials prices.

4. Decide on the optimum operating plan, that is, the value maximizing plan.

5. Engage in capital acquisition programs, labor training programs, and so forth, in order to implement the general corporate plan.

Once the plan has been determined, it must be carried out in the *control*, or *operating*, phase of activity of the enterprise. Planning and control are closely related; in practice, they are often inseparable. Operating procedures, or the process of control, must be geared to the firm's plans. If the forecasts about demand or about the cost of the input factors of production, technology, and the like that go into the plan are seriously in error, then the plan will be useless and the control phase will also break down.

In view of the key role of forecasting in managerial decisions, it is not surprising that forecasting per se is emphasized in managerial economics. In this chapter we describe and illustrate several useful techniques employed in forecasting.

Forecasting Methodologies

Many techniques are available for use in forecasting economic variables. They range from simple, often somewhat naïve, and relatively inexpensive procedures to methods that are quite complex and very expensive. Some forecasting techniques are basically quantitative; others are qualitative. Forecasting techniques can be divided into the following three broad categories:

1. Qualitative Analyses
2. Time Series Analysis and Projection
3. Econometric Methods

It is impossible to state unequivocally that one or another of these basic forecasting approaches is superior to all others. The best one for a particular task depends in large part on a number of factors in each specific forecasting problem. Some of the important factors that must be considered include the following:

1. The distance into the future that one must forecast
2. The lead time available for making decisions
3. The level of accuracy required
4. The quality of data available for analysis
5. The nature of relationships included in the forecasting problem
6. The cost and benefits associated with the forecasting problem

Some techniques—for example, certain time series, barometric, and survey methodologies—are well suited for short-term projections. Others require more lead time and are therefore more useful for long-run forecasting. Within each class of forecasting techniques, the level of sophistication also varies. Typically, the greater the level of sophistication required for a given level of forecast accuracy, the higher the cost.

If the level of accuracy required in projection is low, less sophisticated methods may provide adequate results at minimal cost. Therefore, the choice of an appropriate forecasting methodology depends upon both the underlying characteristics of the forecasting problem and the level of accuracy required.

In order to determine an appropriate level of forecast accuracy, one must compare the costs and benefits of increased forecast accuracy. When forecast accuracy is low, the probability of significant forecasting error is high, as is the chance of making erroneous managerial decisions. Conversely, when forecast accuracy is high, the probability of substantial forecasting error is reduced and the chance of making erroneous managerial decisions is low. Thus, it is reasonable to require a relatively high level of forecast accuracy when the dollar costs of forecast error are high. When only minor costs result from forecast error, only inexpensive and typically less precise methods can be justified.

In the material that follows, we examine both the advantages and limitations of various forecasting techniques. By understanding the strengths and weaknesses of various forecasting methodologies, managers can select an appropriate method or combination of methods to generate required forecast values.

Qualitative Analyses

When quantitative information is unavailable, **qualitative analysis** must be relied upon to prepare required forecasts. Qualitative analysis can be a highly useful forecasting technique if the approach adopted allows for the systematic collection and organization of data derived from unbiased informed opinion. However, qualitative methods can produce biased results in instances where specific individuals dominate the forecasting process through reputation, force of personality, or strategic position within the organization.

Expert Opinion

The most basic form of qualitative analysis used in forecasting is *personal insight*. Here an informed individual uses personal or organizational experience as a basis for projecting future expectations. While this approach is highly subjective and nonscientific, it cannot be rejected out-of-hand since the reasoned judgment of informed individuals often provides invaluable insight. Because this approach is highly subjective, it is important that the underlying assumptions involved in various forecast scenarios be stated explicitly so that changes in basic conditions can be accounted for in the analysis. When the informed opinion of several individuals is relied upon, the approach is called forecasting through use of *panel consensus*. The panel consensus method assumes that several experts can arrive at forecasts that are superior to those that individuals generate. Direct interaction among experts is used in the panel consensus method, with the hope that resulting forecasts embody all available objective and subjective evidence.

While the panel consensus method often results in forecasts that embody the collective wisdom of consulted experts, it can sometimes be unfavorably affected by the force of personality of one or a few key individuals. A related approach, the *delphi method*, has been developed to counter this disadvantage of the panel consensus method. In the delphi method a panel of experts is individually presented a series of questions relating to the underlying forecasting problem. Responses are analyzed by an independent party, who then tries to elicit the apparent consensus opinion by providing feedback to the panel members in a manner that prevents direct identification of individual positions. This method can prove useful in limiting the possible steamroller or bandwagon problems of the panel consensus approach.

Survey Techniques

Survey techniques constitute another important forecasting tool, especially for short-term projections. Surveys generally involve use of interviews or mailed questionnaires asking business firms, government agencies, and individuals about their future plans. Business firms plan and budget virtually all their expenditures in advance of actual purchases or production. Surveys asking about capital budgets, sales budgets, and operating budgets can thus provide much useful information for forecasting. Government units also prepare formal budgets well before the actual spending is done, and surveys of budget material, congressional appropriations hearings, and the like can provide a wealth of information to the forecaster. Finally, even individual consumers usually plan expenditures for such major items as automobiles, furniture, housing, vacations, and education well ahead of the purchase date, so surveys of consumer intentions can sometimes accurately predict future spending on consumer goods.

While surveys do provide an alternative to quantitative forecasting techniques, they are frequently used to supplement rather than replace quantitative analysis. (Survey information may be all that is obtainable in certain forecasting situations, for example, when a firm is attempting to project the demand for a new product.) The value of survey techniques as a supplement to quantitative methods stems from two factors. First, a nonquantifiable psychological element is inherent in most economic behavior, and surveys and other qualitative methods are especially well suited to picking up this phenomenon. Second, econometric models generally assume stable consumer tastes and the like, and if these factors are actually changing, survey data may reveal such changes.

Surveys for Forecasting Various Classes of Expenditures

Many useful surveys for forecasting business activity in various sectors of the U.S. economy are published periodically by private and government units. Some of these are:

Plant and Equipment Expenditures. Surveys of businesses' intentions to expand plant and equipment are conducted by the U.S. Department of Commerce, the Securities and Exchange Commission, the National Industrial Conference Board, McGraw-Hill Inc., *Fortune* magazine, and various trade associations such as the Edison Electric Institute and the American Gas Association.

Inventory Changes and Sales Expectations. The U.S. Commerce Department, *Fortune* magazine, McGraw-Hill Inc., Dun and Bradstreet, and the National Association of Purchasing Agents all survey businesspeople's expectations about future sales levels and their plans for inventory changes. These surveys, while not nearly so accurate as those for long-term investment, provide a useful check on other forecasting methods.

Consumer Expenditures. The consumer intentions surveys of the Census Bureau, the University of Michigan Research Center, and the Sindlinger-National Industrial Conference Board all provide information on planned purchases of specific products, such as automobiles, housing, and appliances. In addition, these surveys often indicate consumer confidence in the economy and, thereby, spending expectations in general. Attempts are being made to quantify all aspects of survey data and to incorporate this information directly into econometric models. Although some success is being achieved with these attempts, a great deal of judgment is still required. Forecasting is becoming a science, but it still contains elements of art.

Time-Series Analysis and Projection

Probably the most frequently employed forecasting methodology is one variously known as *trend projection, extrapolation,* or *curve fitting*. **Time series methods** are based on the assumption that future events will follow along an established path or, alternatively, that past patterns of economic behavior prevail sufficiently to justify using historical data to predict the future. The economic forecaster who uses this technique looks at the historical pattern of the variable of interest and then projects, or forecasts, that it will continue moving along the path described by its past movement.

The many variations of forecasting by trend projection are all predicated on the assumption of a continuing relationship between the variable being projected and the passage of time, so all of them employ time-series data. An economic time series is a sequential array of the values of an economic variable. Weekly, monthly, or annual series of sales and cost data, income statistics, population, labor force participation rates, and gross national product (GNP) are all examples of economic time series.

All time series, regardless of the nature of the economic variable involved, can be described by the following four characteristics:

1. *Secular trend*, or the long-run increase or decrease in the series

2. *Cyclical fluctuations*, or rhythmic variations in the economic series

3. *Seasonal variation*, or variations caused by weather patterns and/or social habits that produce an *annual* pattern in the time series

4. *Irregular or random influences*, or unpredictable shocks to the system—such as wars, strikes, natural catastrophes, and so on

These four patterns are illustrated in Figure 4.1, where (a) shows secular and cyclical trends in sales of women's clothing and (b) shows (1) the seasonal pattern superimposed over the long-run trend (which, in this case, is a composite of the secular and cyclical trends) and (2) random fluctuations around the seasonal curve.

Time-series analysis can be as simple as projecting or extrapolating the unadjusted trend. Applying either graphic analysis (by *eye* fitting) or least squares regression techniques, one can use historical data to determine the average increase or decrease in the series during each time period and then project this rate of change into the future.

Time-series analysis can also be considerably more complex and sophisticated, allowing examination of seasonal and cyclical patterns as well as the basic trend. The X-11 procedure developed by the U.S. Census Bureau and the Box-Jenkins method are two of the more useful and used of these techniques.

Since extrapolation techniques assume that a variable will follow its established path, the problem is to determine accurately the appropriate trend curve. In theory, one could fit any complex mathematical function to the historical data and extrapolate to estimate future values. In practice, however, one typically finds linear, simple power, or exponential curves used for economic forecasting.

Selection of the appropriate curve is guided by both empirical and theoretical considerations. Empirically, it is a question of finding the curve that best fits the historical movement in the data. Theoretical considerations intervene when logic dictates that a particular pattern of future events must prevail. For example, output in a particular industry may have been expanding at a constant rate historically, but be-

Figure 4.1
Time-Series Characteristics: (a) Secular Trend and Cyclical Variation in Women's Clothing Sales (b) Seasonal Pattern and Random Fluctuations

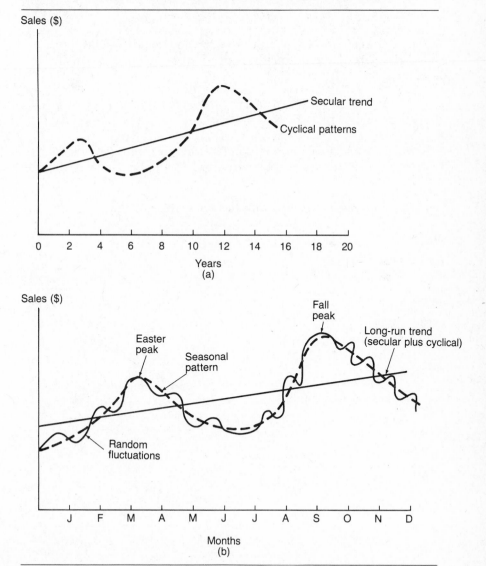

cause of known resource limitations, one might use a declining growth rate model to reflect the slowdown in growth that must ultimately prevail.

A simple trending procedure is illustrated in Figure 4.2. There the total sales data for General Mills Inc. given in Table 4.1 are displayed, along with a curve representing a linear relationship between sales and time over the 1974–1983 period.

The general linear relationship between firm sales and time illustrated in Figure 4.2 can be written as:

$$S_T = a + b \cdot t. \qquad (4.1)$$

The coefficients of this equation were estimated using General Mills' sales data and least squares regression as (standard errors in parentheses):

$$S_T = 1397.02 + 413.94t \qquad R^2 = .986 \qquad (4.2)$$
$$ (109.14) \qquad (17.59)$$

Although a linear trend projection for firm sales is relatively naïve, it is obvious that there is an important trend element in General Mills'

Figure 4.2
Total Sales Revenue for General Mills Inc. (1974–1983)

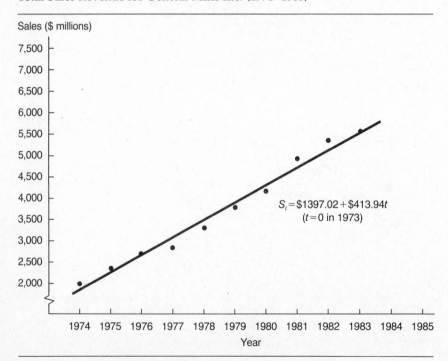

Sales ($ millions)

$S_t = \$1397.02 + \$413.94t$
($t = 0$ in 1973)

Year

Table 4.1
Total Sales Revenue for General Mills Inc. (1974–1983)

Year	Sales ($Millions)
1983	$5,550.8
1982	5,312.1
1981	4,852.4
1980	4,170.3
1979	3,745.0
1978	3,243.0
1977	2,909.4
1976	2,645.0
1975	2,308.9
1974	2,000.1

Source: General Mills 1983 Annual Report, for period ending May 29, 1983.

sales data. Using the linear trend equation estimated over the 1974–1983 period, we can forecast firm sales for future time periods. To do so it is important to realize that in the above model $t = 1$ for 1974, $t = 2$ for 1975, and so on. This means that $t = 0$ in the 1973 base period. To forecast sales in any future period we simply subtract 1973 from the year in question to determine a relevant value for t.

For example, a sales forecast for 1990 using Equation 4.2 would be

$$t = 1990 - 1973 = 17$$

$$S_{1990} = 1397.02 + 413.94(17)$$

$$= \$8,434 \text{ million.}$$

Similarly, a sales forecast for 1995 would be calculated as:

$$t = 1995 - 1973 = 22$$

$$S_{1995} = 1397.02 + 413.94(22)$$

$$= \$10,503.7 \text{ million.}$$

Note that these sales projections are based upon a *linear* trend line, which implies that sales are increasing by a constant dollar amount each year. However, there are important reasons for believing that the underlying trend relationship for General Mills' sales is nonlinear and that the forecasts generated above will be relatively poor estimates of actual values. To see why a linear trend relationship may not be accurate, consider the relationship between actual sales data and the linear trend shown in Figure 4.2. Remember that the least squares regression

line is the line that minimizes the sum of squared residuals between actual and fitted values over the sample period. As is typical, actual data
points lie both above and below the fitted regression line. Note, however, that the pattern of the differences between actual and fitted values
varies dramatically over the sample period. Differences between actual
and fitted values are generally positive in both early (1974–1976) and
late (1981–1983) periods, while negative in the intervening period. This
suggests that the slope of the regression is not constant, but rather increases over the sample period.

Although an assumption of constant absolute annual change is
quite appropriate in some situations, there are several alternative assumptions that more accurately describe the way many economic series
change over time. One widely used alternative model is the constant
growth rate, or constant rate of change, model. Sales revenues for many
products appear to change over time in a proportional rather than constant absolute amount.

The constant *rate* of change, or proportional change model, involves
determining the average historical rate of change in a variable and projecting that rate into the future. This is essentially identical to the compounding of value model used in finance.[1] For example, if a firm is projecting its sales for five years into the future and if it has determined that
sales are increasing at an annual rate of 10 percent, the projection would
simply involve multiplying the 10 percent compound value interest factor for five years times current sales. Assuming current sales are $1 mil-
lion, the forecast of sales five years from now would be:

$$\text{Sales in Year 5} = \text{Current Sales} \times (1 + \text{Growth Rate})^5$$

$$= \$1{,}000{,}000 \times (1.10)^5$$

$$= \$1{,}000{,}000 \times 1.61$$

$$= \$1{,}610{,}000.$$

More generally, the constant rate of change projection model can be
stated as follows:

$$\text{Value } t \text{ Years in the Future} = \text{Current Value} \times (1 + \text{Rate of Change})^t.$$

Just as one can estimate the constant annual change in an economic
time series by fitting historical data to a linear regression model of the
form $Y = a + bT$, so, too, can one estimate the annual growth rate in
a constant rate of change projection model by using the same technique. In this case the growth rate is estimated using linear regression

---

[1]The section entitled "Future Value (or Compound Value)" in Appendix A at the back of
the text provides more material on proportional growth models.

by fitting historical data to the logarithmic transformation of the basic model. For example, if one were to formulate a constant growth rate model for firm sales it would take the form:

$$S_t = S_0 \cdot (1 + g)^t. \tag{4.3}$$

Here sales t years in the future is assumed to be equal to current sales, S_0, compounded at a growth rate, g, for a period of t years. Taking logarithms of both sides of Equation 4.3 results in the expression:

$$ln\ S_t = ln\ S_0 + ln\ (1 + g) \cdot t. \tag{4.4}$$

Note that Equation 4.4 is an expression of the form:

$$Y_t = a + bt,$$

where $Y_t = ln\ S_t$, $a = ln\ S_0$, and $b = ln\ (1 + g)$; hence, its coefficients, $ln\ S_0$ and $ln\ (1 + g)$, can be estimated using the least squares regression technique.

Applying this technique to the sales data in Table 4.1 results in the regression (standard errors in parentheses)

$$ln\ S_t = 7.51 + 0.117t \qquad R^2 = .994, \tag{4.5}$$
$$(0.023)\ \ (0.003)$$

or, equivalently, by transforming this estimated equation back to its original form:

$$S_t = [\text{Antilog } 7.51] \times [\text{Antilog } 0.117]^t = 1{,}826.21\,(1.124)^t \tag{4.6}$$

In this model, \$1,826.21 million is the adjusted sales for $t = 0$ (which would be 1973, since the first year of data used in the regression estimation [$t = 1$] was 1974); and 1.124 is equal to one plus the average annual rate of growth, meaning that General Mills' sales have been increasing by 12.4 percent annually over the 1974–1983 period.[2]

---

[2] Another frequently used form of the constant growth rate model is based on a *continuous* (as opposed to annual) compounding assumption. This model is expressed by the exponential equation

$$Y_t = Y_0 e^{gt},$$

and its logarithmic equivalent is:

$$ln\ Y_t = ln\ Y_0 + gt.$$

Thus, with the exponential growth assumption, the regression model's estimate of the slope coefficient, g, is a direct estimate of the continuous rate of growth. For example, in the General Mills' sales regression model, Equation 4.5, the coefficient 0.117 (= 11.7 percent) is a direct estimate of a continuous compounding growth rate for General Mills' sales.

As before, to forecast sales in any future year using this model, we subtract 1973 from the year being forecast to determine t. Thus, a constant growth model forecast of sales in 1990 is:

$$t = 1990 - 1973 = 17$$

$$S_{1990} = 1,826.21 (1.124)^{17}$$

$$= \$13,322.26 \text{ million.}$$

Similarly, a constant growth model forecast of General Mills' sales in 1995 is:

$$t = 1995 - 1973 = 22$$

$$S_{1995} = 1,826.21 (1.124)^{22}$$

$$= \$23,900.61 \text{ million.}$$

The importance of selecting the correct structural form for a trending model can be demonstrated by comparing the sales projections that result from the two models we have examined. Recall that with the constant absolute annual change model, sales were projected to be \$8.4 billion and \$10.5 billion in 1990 and 1995, respectively. These projections compare with the \$13.3 billion sales projection for 1990 and \$23.9 billion forecast for 1995 obtained with the constant growth rate model. Notice the difference in the near-term forecasts (1990) is small relative to the difference in the 1995 projections. This points up the fact that if an economic time series is growing at a constant rate rather than increasing by a constant absolute amount—and General Mills' sales appear to exhibit this characteristic—then forecasts based on a linear trend model will tend to become less and less accurate the further out into the future one projects.

Although trend projections can provide very adequate estimates for some forecasting purposes, a number of serious shortcomings in the technique limit its usefulness for many purposes. First, trend projections are typically more useful for intermediate- to long-term forecasting than for short-run estimation. The reason lies in the inability of the technique to predict cyclical turning points or fluctuations. Second, trend projections implicitly assume that the historical relationships involved in the time series will continue into the future. This is not always the case. There are many examples of the disastrous effects of using this forecasting method just prior to economic recessions in 1975, 1980, and 1982. Finally, trend analysis entails no analysis of causal relationships and hence offers no help in analyzing either why a particular series moves as it does or what the impact of a particular policy decision would be on the future movement of the series.

Seasonal and Cyclical Variations

Many important economic time series are regularly influenced by seasonal and cyclical variations. Figure 4.1 illustrated how such variations can influence demand patterns for a typical consumer product. It is worthwhile to consider these influences further since the treatment of seasonal and cyclical variations plays an important role in time-series analysis and projection.

New housing starts constitute an important economic time series that is regularly influenced by seasonal and cyclical variations. Table 4.2 provides data on the number of new privately owned housing units started in the United States during a recent fifteen-year period, 1967– 1981. Thousands of housing units started are reported in Table 4.2a, and seasonally adjusted annual rates are shown in Table 4.2b. From 4.2a it is clear that there is an important seasonal element in the total variation of housing starts. Quite understandably, housing starts tend to be high in the months of May, June, and July and relatively low in November, December, and January. The obvious source of such variations is the weather. In many northern states it is difficult if not impossible to maintain a high level of housing starts during colder winter months. After adjusting for the seasonal element in housing starts, a regular pattern of cyclical variations becomes apparent. Seasonally adjusted annual data provided in Table 4.2b show that housing starts declined precipitously in 1974, 1979, and 1981. Because these declines preceded the economic downturns of 1975, 1980, and 1982, respectively, housing starts are considered a leading economic indicator.

Although housing starts are an obvious and classic example of economic data subject to seasonal and cyclical variations, they are by no means a unique case. For example, economic activity in the clothing, recreation, travel, automobile, and related industries are all affected by such variations. As a result, controlling for seasonal and cyclical variations is an important aspect of time-series analysis and projection. For many economic projections an analysis of seasonal and cyclical fluctuations can vastly improve forecasting results, especially short-run forecasting results.

There are several techniques for estimating seasonal variations. A simple one examines the ratio of actual monthly data to the trend projection. For example, if monthly sales data for a product indicate that, on the average, December sales are 20 percent above the trend line, a seasonal adjustment factor of 1.20 can be applied to that trend projection to forecast sales in that month. Likewise, if it is found that February sales had on average been 15 percent below the trend, an adjustment factor of 0.85 would be applied in projecting February sales. To illustrate, annual sales might be forecast at $1.2 million, or $100,000 a month. When the seasonal factor is introduced, however, December sales would be projected at $120,000 (= $100,000 × 1.20) and February

Table 4.2

New Privately Owned Housing Units Started, 1967–1981

(a)   Unadjusted Monthly Data
                                             Thousands

	Jan.	Feb.	Mar.	Apr.	May	June	July	Aug.	Sept.	Oct.	Nov.	Dec.	Total
1981	84.5	65.5	95.3	109.5	97.9	93.0	87.7	74.3	71.5	75.9	55.0	52.7	962.8
1980	68.0	72.7	78.0	85.6	80.7	103.4	107.0	113.0	121.4	152.7	112.9	95.7	1,191.1
1979	73.9	84.5	152.9	142.3	170.5	173.1	144.5	145.4	144.7	152.6	106.9	91.6	1582.9
1978	75.6	84.7	141.9	163.9	174.6	172.8	154.6	156.0	149.2	158.0	158.6	102.5	1692.4
1977	81.3	112.5	173.5	182.2	201.3	197.6	189.8	194.0	177.7	193.1	154.8	129.2	1987.1
1976	72.5	89.9	118.4	137.2	147.9	154.2	136.6	145.9	151.8	148.4	128.1	108.6	1539.7
1975	56.1	54.7	80.2	97.9	116.1	110.3	119.3	117.3	111.9	123.6	96.2	76.1	1160.4
1974	84.5	109.4	124.8	159.5	149.0	147.6	126.6	111.1	98.3	96.7	75.1	55.1	1337.7
1973	146.6	138.0	200.0	205.0	234.0	202.6	202.6	197.2	148.4	147.1	133.3	90.4	2045.3
1972	149.1	152.2	203.9	211.6	225.8	223.1	206.5	228.6	203.0	216.5	185.7	150.5	2356.6
1971	110.6	102.2	167.9	201.1	198.5	193.8	194.3	204.5	173.8	179.7	173.7	152.1	2052.2
1970	66.4	74.3	114.7	128.4	125.0	135.2	140.8	128.7	130.9	140.9	126.9	121.4	1433.6
1969	101.5	90.1	131.9	159.0	155.5	147.3	125.2	124.9	129.3	123.4	94.6	84.1	1466.8
1968	80.5	84.6	126.6	162.0	140.9	137.9	139.8	136.6	134.3	140.8	127.1	96.4	1507.6
1967	59.1	61.4	91.5	113.7	132.0	125.4	125.3	127.4	121.9	135.4	118.4	80.1	1291.6

(b)   Seasonally Adjusted Annual Rates
                                             Thousands

	Jan.	Feb.	Mar.	Apr.	May	June	July	Aug.	Sept.	Oct.	Nov.	Dec.
1981	1,585	1,294	1,318	1,301	1,172	1,046	1,040	946	899	854	860	882
1980	1,389	1,273	1,040	1,044	938	1,184	1,277	1,411	1,482	1,519	1,550	1,532
1979	1,727	1,469	1,800	1,750	1,801	1,910	1,764	1,788	1,874	1,710	1,522	1,548
1978	1,779	1,762	2,028	2,182	2,018	2,092	2,090	1,983	2,014	2,001	2,111	2,052
1977	1,527	1,943	2,063	1,892	1,971	1,893	2,058	2,020	1,949	2,042	2,042	2,142
1976	1,262	1,452	1,427	1,405	1,468	1,508	1,410	1,546	1,753	1,662	1,680	1,824
1975	1,032	904	993	1,005	1,121	1,087	1,226	1,260	1,264	1,344	1,360	1,321
1974	1,453	1,784	1,553	1,571	1,415	1,526	1,290	1,145	1,180	1,100	1,028	940
1973	2,481	2,289	2,365	2,084	2,266	2,067	2,123	2,051	1,874	1,677	1,724	1,526
1972	2,494	2,390	2,334	2,249	2,221	2,254	2,252	2,382	2,481	2,485	2,421	2,366
1971	1,828	1,741	1,910	1,986	2,049	2,026	2,083	2,158	2,041	2,128	2,182	2,295
1970	1,108	1,322	1,364	1,230	1,280	1,396	1,506	1,401	1,531	1,589	1,621	1,944
1969	1,769	1,705	1,561	1,524	1,583	1,528	1,368	1,358	1,507	1,381	1,229	1,327
1968	1,344	1,498	1,472	1,532	1,384	1,393	1,561	1,501	1,527	1,579	1,690	1,618
1967	1,111	1,149	1,094	1,116	1,274	1,233	1,369	1,407	1,445	1,496	1,569	1,354

Source: Standard and Poor's Industry Surveys, *Basic Statistics, Building and Building Materials*. New York: Standard and Poor's Corporation, 1982, p. 137.

sales at $85,000 (= $100,000 × 0.85). Production, inventory, and financing requirements could be scheduled accordingly.

Determination of cyclical patterns is very similar to that for seasonal patterns. Here the interest is on rhythmic patterns that occur over a period of years. Although a few industries appear to have rhythmic oscillations that repeat with enough regularity to be considered cycles (home construction is frequently cited) these are probably the exception rather than the rule. Further, statistical problems make any breakdown of a time series into trend and cycle components tenuous at best. Most analysts today recognize that both secular trends and cycles are typically generated by a common causal mechanism, and therefore separation of the two does not lead to unambiguous forecasts. Moreover, the timing, size, and duration of cycles change over time, making cyclical adjustments difficult.

The Box-Jenkins technique for time-series analysis provides one very sophisticated approach to analyzing the various components—trend, seasonal, cyclical, and random—that make up an economic time series. This technique enables one to analyze complex patterns that exist in an ordered data set. For many forecasting purposes it provides a very substantial improvement over simpler extrapolation procedures.

Barometric Methods

Although cyclical patterns in most economic time series are so erratic as to make simple projection a hazardous short-term forecasting technique, there is evidence that a relatively consistent relationship exists between the movements of *different* economic variables over time. In other words, even though an economic series may not exhibit a consistent pattern over time, it is often possible to find a second series (or group of series) whose movement is closely correlated to that of the first. Should the forecaster have the good fortune to discover an economic series that *leads* the one he or she is attempting to forecast, the leading series can be used as a barometer for forecasting short-term change, just as a meteorologist uses changes in a mercury barometer to forecast changes in the weather.

There is evidence that the barometric, or leading indicator, approach to business forecasting is nearly as old as business itself. More than 2,000 years ago merchants used the arrival of trading ships as indicators of business activity. Over 100 years ago Andrew Carnegie is reported to have used the number of smoking industrial chimneys to forecast business activity and hence the demand for steel. Today, the barometric approach to forecasting has been refined considerably, primarily through the work of the National Bureau of Economic Research and the U.S. Department of Commerce. *Business Conditions Digest*, a monthly publication of the Department of Commerce, provides extensive data on a large number of business indicators. Table 4.3 lists 12 leading, 4 coincident, and 6 lagging economic indicators of business cycle peaks that are contained in that data.

Table 4.3
Leading, Coincident, and Lagging Economic
Indicators of Business Cycle Peaks

Leading Indicators
Average workweek for production, manufacturing workers (hours)
Average weekly initial claims for state unemployment insurance (thousands)
New orders for consumer goods and materials ($billions)
Vendor performance: companies receiving slower deliveries (percentage)
Index of net business formations (1967 = 100)
Contracts and orders for plant and equipment ($billions)
Index of new building permits for private housing units (1967 = 100)
Change in inventories on hand and on order (annual rate, $billions)
Change in sensitive materials prices (percentage)
Index of stock prices for 500 common stocks (1941–1943 = 10)
Money supply (M_2) ($billions)
Change in credit: business and consumer borrowing (annual rate, percentage)

Coincident Indicators
Employees on nonagricultural payrolls (thousands)
Personal income less transfer payments (annual rate, $billions)
Index of total industrial production (1967 = 100)
Manufacturing and trade sales ($millions)

Lagging Indicators
Average duration of unemployment (weeks)
Ratio of constant-dollar inventories to sales for manufacturing and trade (ratio)
Labor cost per unit of manufacturing output: actual data as a percentage of trend
  (percentage)
Average prime rate charged by banks (percentage)
Commercial and industrial loans outstanding ($millions)
Ratio of consumer installment credit to personal income (percentage)

Barometric Forecasting

As indicated above, barometric, or indicator, forecasting is based on
the observation that there are relationships among many economic
time series. Changes in some series appear to be consistently related to
changes in one or more other series. The theoretical basis for some of
these leads and lags is obvious. For example, building permits issued
precede housing starts, and orders for plant and equipment lead production in durable goods industries. The reason is that each of these
indicators refers to plans or commitments for the activity that follows.
Other barometers are not so directly related to the economic variables
they forecast. An index of common stock prices, for example, is a good
leading indicator of general business activity. Although the causal relationship here is not readily apparent, stock prices reflect aggregate
profit expectations by business managers and others and hence a composite expectation of the level of business activity.

Barometric methods of forecasting require the identification of an economic time series that consistently leads the series being forecast. Once this relationship is established, forecasting directional changes in the lagged series is simply a matter of keeping track of movement in the leading indicator. In practice, several problems prevent such an easy solution to the forecasting problem. First, few series *always* correctly indicate changes in another economic variable. Even the best leading indicators of general business conditions forecast with only 80 to 90 percent accuracy. Second, even the indicators that have good records of forecasting directional changes generally fail to lead by a consistent period. If a series is to be an adequate barometer, it not only must indicate directional changes but, must also provide a constant lead time. Few series meet the test of lead time consistency. Finally, barometric forecasting suffers in that, even when leading indicators prove to be satisfactory from the standpoint of consistently indicating directional change with a stable lead time, they provide very little information about the magnitude of change in the forecast variable.

Composite and Diffusion Indexes

Two techniques that have been used with some success in partially overcoming the difficulties in barometric forecasting are composite indexes and diffusion indexes. *Composite indexes* are weighted averages of several leading indicators. The combining of individual series into a composite index results in a series with less random fluctuation, or *noise*. The smoother composite series has a lesser tendency to produce false signals of change in the predicted variable.

Diffusion indexes are similar to composite indexes. Here, instead of combining a number of leading indicators into a single standardized index, the methodology consists of noting the percentage of the total number of leading indicators that are rising at a given point in time. For example, if twelve individual indicators have all proved to be relatively reliable leading indicators of steel sales, a diffusion, or *pressure*, index would show the percentage of those indicators that are increasing at the present time. If seven are rising, the diffusion index would be seven-twelfths, or 58 percent; with only three rising, the index would register 25 percent. Forecasting with diffusion indexes typically involves projecting an increase in the economic variable if the index is above fifty (that is, when over one half of the individual leading indicators are rising) and a decline when it is below fifty.

Even with the use of composite and diffusion indexes, the barometric forecasting technique is a relatively poor tool for estimating the magnitude of change in an economic variable. Thus, although it represents a significant improvement over simple extrapolation techniques for short-term forecasting, where calling the turning points is necessary, the barometric methodology is not the solution to all forecasting problems.

Econometric Methods

Econometric methods of forecasting combine economic theory with mathematical and statistical tools to analyze economic relationships. The use of econometric forecasting techniques has several distinct advantages over alternative methods. For one, it forces the forecaster to make explicit assumptions about the interrelationships among the variables in the economic system being examined. In other words, the forecaster must deal with *causal* relationships. This process reduces the probability of logical inconsistencies in the model and thus increases the reliability and acceptability of the results.

A second advantage of econometric methods lies in the consistency of the technique from period to period. The forecaster can compare forecasts with actual results and use the insights gained from this comparison to improve the model. That is, by feeding past forecasting errors back into the model, the forecaster can obtain new parameter estimates that should improve future forecasting results.

The type of output provided by econometric forecasts is another major advantage of this technique. Since econometric models provide estimates of actual values for forecasted variables, these models indicate not only the direction of change but also the magnitude of change. This is a significant improvement over the barometric approach, which provides little information about the magnitude of expected changes.

Perhaps the most important advantage of econometric models relates to their basic characteristic of *explaining* economic phenomena. In the vast majority of business forecasting problems, management has some degree of control over many of the variables present in the relationship being examined. For example, in forecasting sales of a product, the firm must take into account the price it will charge, the amount it has spent and will spend on advertising, and many other variables over which it may or may not have any influence. Only by thoroughly understanding the interrelationships involved can management hope to forecast accurately and to make optimal decisions as it selects values for controllable variables.

Single Equation Models

Many of the firm's forecasting problems can be adequately addressed with single equation econometric models. The first step in developing an econometric model is to express the hypothesized economic relationship in the form of an equation. For example, in constructing a model for forecasting regional demand for new personal computers, one might hypothesize that demand (Q) is determined by price (P), disposable income (Y_d), population (Pop), availability of credit (C), and advertising expenditures (AD). A linear model expressing this relationship could be written as follows:

$$Q = a_0 + a_1P + a_2Y_d + a_3Pop + a_4C + a_5AD. \qquad \text{(4.7)}$$

Once the economic relationship has been expressed in equation form, the next step in econometric modeling is to estimate the parameters of the system, or values of the a's in Equation 4.7. The most frequently used technique for parameter estimation is the application of least squares regression analysis with either time-series or cross-section data.

Once the coefficients of the model have been estimated, forecasting with a single equation model consists of obtaining values for the independent variables in the equation and then evaluating the equation for those values. This means that an econometric model used for forecasting purposes must contain independent or explanatory variables whose values for the forecast period can be readily obtained.

Multiple Equation Systems

Although forecasting problems can often be analyzed adequately with a single equation model, in many cases the interrelationships involved are so complex that they require the use of multiple equation systems. In these systems we refer to the variables whose values are determined within the model as *endogenous*, meaning originating from within, and to those determined outside, or external to, the system as *exogenous*. The values of endogenous variables are determined with the model; the values of exogenous variables are given externally. Endogenous variables are equivalent to the dependent variable in a single equation system; exogenous and predetermined variables are equivalent to the independent variables.

Multiple equation econometric models are composed of two basic kinds of equations, identities and behavioral equations. Identities, or definitional, equations express relationships that are true by definition. The statement that profits (π) are equal to total revenue (TR) minus cost (TC) is an example of an identity:

$$\pi = TR - TC. \qquad \text{(4.8)}$$

Profits are *defined* by the relationship expressed in Equation 4.8; the equation is true by definition.

The second group of equations encountered in econometric models, behavioral equations, reflects hypotheses about how the variables in a system interact with one another. Behavioral equations may indicate how individuals and institutions are expected to react to various stimuli, or they may be technical as, for example, a production function that indicates the technical relationships in the production system.

Perhaps the easiest way to illustrate the use of multiple equation systems is to examine a simple three-equation model of equipment and related sales for a personal computer retailer. As you recall, in Equation 4.7 we expressed a single equation model that might be used to forecast regional demand for new personal computers. However, total revenues for a typical retailer would not only include sales of personal computers, but also sales of software programs (including computer games) and sales of peripheral equipment (video display terminals, printers, and so on). Although actual econometric models used to forecast total sales revenue from these items might include several equations and a large number of important economic variables, the simple system described next should suffice to provide insight into the multiple equation approach without being so complex as to become confusing. The three equations are:

$$S_t = b_0 + b_1 TR_t + u_1 \tag{4.9}$$

$$P_t = c_0 + c_1 C_{t-1} + u_2 \tag{4.10}$$

$$TR_t = S_t + P_t + C_t, \tag{4.11}$$

where S is software sales, TR is total revenue, P is peripheral sales, C is personal computer sales, t is the current time period, $t - 1$ is the previous time period, and u_1 and u_2 are error, or residual terms.

Equations 4.9 and 4.10 are behavioral hypotheses. The first hypothesizes that current period software sales is a function of the current level of total revenues; the second, that peripheral sales depend on previous period personal computer sales. The last equation in the system is an identity. It defines total revenue as being equal to the sum of software, peripheral, and personal computer sales.

The stochastic disturbance terms in the behavioral equations, the u's, are included because the hypothesized relationships are not exact. In other words, other factors that can affect software and peripheral sales are not accounted for in the system. So long as these stochastic elements are truly random and their net effects are cancelled (that is, the expected value of each stochastic term is zero), they do not present a barrier to empirical estimation of system parameters. However, if the error terms are not randomly distributed, parameter estimates will be biased and the reliability of model forecasts will be questionable. Furthermore, large error terms, even if they are distributed randomly, will tend to reduce forecast accuracy.

Empirical estimation of the parameters, that is, the b's and c's in Equations 4.9 and 4.10, for multiple equation systems often requires the use of statistical techniques that go beyond the scope of an introductory text. We can, however, illustrate the use of such a system for forecasting purposes after parameters have been estimated.

To forecast next year's software and peripheral sales and total revenue for the firm represented by our illustrative model, we must express S, P, and TR in terms of those variables whose values are known (or can be estimated) at the moment the forecast is generated. In other words, each endogenous variable (S_t, P_t and TR_t) must be expressed in terms of the exogenous and predetermined variables (C_{t-1} and C_t). Such relationships are called reduced-form equations, because they reduce complex simultaneous relations to their most basic and simple form. Consider the manipulations of equations in the system necessary to solve for TR via its reduced form equation.

Substituting Equation 4.9 into 4.11, that is, replacing S_t with Equation 4.9, results in[3]

$$TR_t = b_0 + b_1 TR_t + P_t + C_t. \tag{4.12}$$

A similar substitution of Equation 4.10 for P_t produces:

$$TR_t = b_0 + b_1 TR_t + c_0 + c_1 C_{t-1} + C_t. \tag{4.13}$$

Collecting terms and isolating TR in Equation 4.13 gives

$$(1 - b_1) TR_t = b_0 + c_0 + c_1 C_{t-1} + C_t,$$

or alternately:

$$TR_t = \frac{b_0 + c_0 + c_1 C_{t-1} + C_t}{(1 - b_1)} \tag{4.14}$$

$$= \frac{b_0 + c_0}{(1 - b_1)} + \frac{c_1}{(1 - b_1)} C_{t-1} + \frac{1}{(1 - b_1)} C_t.$$

Equation 4.14 now relates current total revenues to previous and current period personal computer sales. Assuming that data on previous period personal computer sales can be obtained, and that current period personal computer sales can be estimated using Equation 4.7, Equation 4.14 provides us with a forecasting model that takes into ac-

---

[3] The stochastic disturbance terms (u's) have been dropped from the illustration since their expected values are zero. The final equation for TR, however, is stochastic in nature.

count the simultaneous relations expressed in our simplified multiple equation system. Of course, in real-life situations, it is possible, perhaps even likely, that personal computer sales depend upon the price, quantity, and quality of available software and peripheral equipment. Then S, P, and C, along with other important factors, may all be endogenous, involving a large number of relations in a highly complex multiple equation system. Untangling the important, but often subtle, relations involved in such a system makes forecasting with multiple equation systems one of the most challenging and intriguing subjects in managerial economics.

Input-Output Analysis

A forecasting method known as **input-output analysis** provides perhaps the most complete examination of all the complex interrelationships within an economic system. Input-output analysis shows how an increase or a decrease in the demand for one industry's output will affect other industries. For example, an increase in the demand for trucks will lead to increased production of steel, plastics, tires, glass, and other materials. The increase in the demand for these materials will have secondary effects. The increase in the demand for glass will lead to a further increase in the demand for steel, as well as for trucks used in the manufacture of glass, steel, and so on. Input-output analysis traces through all these interindustry relationships to provide information about the total impact on all industries of the original increase in the demand for trucks.

Input-output forecasting is based on a set of tables that describe the interrelationships among all the component parts of the economy. The construction of input-output tables is a formidable task; fortunately, such tables are available for the United States from the Office of Business Economics, U.S. Department of Commerce. To use the tables effectively, one must understand their construction. Accordingly, the construction of these tables, as well as the use of input-output tables, is examined in this section.

Input-Output Tables

The starting point for constructing input-output tables is the set of accounts on which the nation's GNP is based; the basic accounts are listed in Table 4.4. The table shows that GNP is equal to the sum of the national income accounts, items 1–9, or, alternatively, to the sum of final product flows to consuming sectors, items 10–13.

Table 4.4

List of National Income and Product Accounts Used to Construct GNP

National Income Accounts

1. Compensation of Employees
2. Proprietors' Income
3. Rental Income of Persons
4. Corporate Profits and Inventory Valuation Adjustment
5. Net Interest
6. Business Transfer Payments   } Gross National Product
7. Indirect Business Tax and Nontax Liability
8. Less: Subsidies Less Current Surplus of Government
   Enterprises
9. Capital Consumption Allowances

Final Product Accounts

10. Personal Consumption Expenditures
11. Gross Private Domestic Investment   } Gross National Product
12. Net Export of Goods and Services
13. Government Purchases of Goods and Services

Input-output tables break down the income and the product account data and provide information about interindustry transactions. Table 4.5 is an example of a simplified input-output table. It is a matrix of the same gross national product data contained in Table 4.4, but with the addition of a (shaded) section showing interindustry transactions as well. Although the illustrated input-output table has only eight industry classifications, actual U.S. input-output tables are far more complex, containing roughly 500 separate industry classifications. The industry-to-industry flows in the shaded area depict the input-output structure of the economy. For example, the manufacturing row, row 4, shows the sales by manufacturing firms to other manufacturing firms, to other industries, and also to final users. Thus, cell 4, 2 shows sales from manufacturers to mining companies; cell 4, 4 from manufacturers to other manufacturers; and cell 4, 7 from manufacturers to service firms such as banks, entertainment companies, and the like. The manufacturing column, column 4, shows the sources of goods and services purchased by manufacturers for production, as well as the value added in their production of output. For example, cell 2, 4 shows manufacturing firms' purchases from mining companies; cell 6, 4 shows manufacturing firms' purchases from the transportation industry.

Since interindustry sales are included in the value of products sold to various final consumers, they must be omitted from the measurement of total gross national product. That is, to avoid double counting, producer-to-producer sales must be excluded from the determination

Table 4.5
Input-Output Flow Table

| | Interindustry transactions | | | | | | | | Final Markets (National Product Accounts) | | | |
	Agri-culture (1)	Mining (2)	Construc-tion (3)	Manufac-turing (4)	Trade (5)	Transpor-tation (6)	Services (7)	Other (8)	Persons (9)	Investors (10)	For-eigners (11)	Govern-ment (12)
Agriculture (1)									Personal consumption expenditures (Account 10)	Gross private domestic investment (Account 11)	Net exports of goods and services (Account 12)	Government purchases of goods and services (Account 13)
Mining (2)				2, 4								
Construction (3)												
Manufacturing (4)		4, 2		4, 4			4, 7					
Trade (5)												
Transportation (6)				6, 4								
Services (7)												
Other (8)												
Employees (9)	Compensation of employees (Account 1)											
Owners of business and capital (10)	Profit-type income and capital consumption allowances (Accounts 2, 3, 4, 5, 6, 9)*											
Government (11)	Indirect business taxes and current surplus of government enterprises, and so forth (Accounts 7, 8)											

Interindustry transactions

Value added (National Income Accounts)

Gross national product

of GNP. The same is true when calculating GNP by use of the national income accounts; interindustry transactions must be eliminated to avoid redundancy. Accordingly, the entire shaded area of Table 4.5 is ignored when GNP is determined: GNP is calculated either as the total of all the cells shown in the Final Markets columns or as the total of cells in the Value Added rows.

Uses of Input-Output Analysis

Input-output analysis has a variety of applications, ranging from forecasting the sales of an individual firm to probing the implications of national economic policies. The major contribution of input-output analysis is that it facilitates measurement of the effects on all industrial sectors of changes in the activity of any one sector.

The usefulness of input-output analysis can be illustrated by the following example, which shows the effect of an increase in consumer demand for passenger cars. The first effect of the change in demand is an increase in the output of the automobile industry; there are further effects, however. The increase in auto output requires more steel production, which in turn requires more chemicals, more iron ore, more limestone, and more coal. Auto production also requires other products, and demand will increase for upholstery fabrics, synthetic fibers, plastics, and glass. There will be still further reactions; for example, the production of synthetic fibers and other chemicals will lead to increased demand for electricity, containers, and transportation services. Input-output analysis traces this intricate chain reaction through all industrial sectors and measures the effects, both direct and indirect, on the output of each of the industries.

The industry outputs derived in this way can be used for estimating related industry requirements. For example, with supplementary data the estimated output of each industry can be translated into requirements for employment or for additional plant and equipment. Or, bolstered by information on the geographic distribution of industries, input-output analysis can also shed light on the regional implications of changes in national GNP.

Recognizing the unique ability of input-output analysis to account completely for the complex interaction among industries, many businesses have been guided in their decision making by this analysis. For example, input-output has been used to evaluate market prospects for established products, to identify potential markets for new products, to spot prospective shortages in supplies, to add new dimensions and greater depth to the analysis of the economic environment in which the firms can expect to operate, and to evaluate investment prospects in various industries.

Input-output analysis has also been employed in the decision-making processes of government agencies at every level. A notable federal application has been in the study of the long-term growth of the economy and its implications for labor force requirements. Input-output analysis has also been used to calculate the impact of U.S. exports and imports on employment in various industries and regions. A number of state and local governments have sponsored the construction of input-output tables for use in evaluating the effects of different types of economic development. Others have used input-output analysis to study the industrial impact of alternative tax programs. In some states input-output analysis is a central element in large-scale systems for forecasting demographic and economic variables and also serves as an aid in planning land use, expenditure and revenue programs, industrial development, and so on.

Moreover, many regions throughout the country have been increasingly concerned about the adequacy of water resources. Input-output analysis is being used as part of a total system to measure industrial requirements for water. The analysis is particularly helpful in identifying activities that generate important demands for water, not only as direct users but also because their suppliers of materials, power, and other inputs also require water.

Judging Forecast Reliability

One of the most important aspects of forecasting is judging **forecast reliability**. How well do various methodologies deal with specific forecasting problems? In comparing forecast and actual values, how close is close enough? Is forecast reliability over one sample or time period necessarily transferable to other samples and time periods? Each of these questions is fundamentally important and must be adequately addressed prior to the implementation of any successful forecasting program.

Ideally, to test predictive capability, a model generated from data of one sample or period is used to forecast data for some alternate sample or period. Thus, the reliability of a model for predicting firm sales, such as that shown in Equation 4.5, can be tested by examining the relationship between forecast and actual data for years beyond 1983, given that the model was generated by using data from the 1974–1983 period. At times, it may be desirable to test a model without waiting for new data to become available. In such instances one can divide the available data into two subsamples, called a test group and a forecast group. The forecaster then estimates a forecasting model, using data from the test group, and uses the resulting model to forecast the data of interest in the forecast group. A comparison of forecast and actual values can then be conducted to test the stability of the underlying cost or demand relationship.

One method of evaluating a model's predictive capability is through consideration of the average amount of forecast error, the root mean squared forecast error. The root mean squared forecast error, denoted by the symbol U, is calculated as:

$$U = \sqrt{\frac{1}{n} \sum_{i=1}^{n} (f_i - x_i)^2},$$ (4.15)

where n is the number of sample observations, f_i is a forecast value, and x_i is the corresponding actual value. A small average forecast error is desirable and increases the likelihood of accurate forecasts.

In analyzing a model's forecast capability the correlation between forecast and actual values is also of substantial interest. The formula for the simple correlation coefficient, r, for forecast and actual values, f and x, respectively, is:

$$r = \frac{\sigma_{fx}}{\sigma_f \sigma_x},$$ (4.16)

where σ_{fx} is the covariance between the forecast and actual series, and σ_f and σ_x are the sample standard deviations of the forecast and actual series, respectively. It is seldom necessary to calculate r since most computer statistical packages and many hand-held calculators can readily calculate such coefficients. Generally speaking, correlations between forecast and actual values in excess of 0.99 (99 percent) are highly desirable and indicate that the forecast model being considered constitutes an effective tool for analysis. However, in cross-section analysis, where the important trend element in most economic data is held constant, a correlation of 99 percent between forecast and actual values would be quite rare. In instances where unusually difficult forecasting problems are being addressed, correlations between forecast and actual data of 90 percent or 95 percent may prove satisfactory. On the other hand, in critical decision situations forecast values may have to be estimated at very precise levels. In such instances, forecast and actual data may have to exhibit an extremely high level of correlation, 99.5 percent or 99.75 percent, in order to generate a high level of confidence in forecast reliability. In summary, the correlation between forecast and actual values necessary to reach a threshold reliability acceptance level depends, in large part, upon the difficulty of the forecasting problem being analyzed and the cost of forecast error.

Forecasting Average Hourly Wages
for the Metal Mining Industry:
An Illustrative Forecasting Example

Troka Mining Ltd. is a large and profitable multinational with interests
in coal and iron ore mining. One of the key functions of Troka's planning department is to identify important trends in demand and production costs so that funds available for investment can be efficiently
allocated. Currently, Troka's North American subsidiary is contemplating the introduction of labor-saving equipment to be used in its large
Wyoming coal strip-mine operations. A key element involved in calculating the return on investment for this machinery is the future trend
in labor costs. Therefore, the company has a need to generate accurate
forecasts of average hourly earnings for the metal mining industry.

Predicting the future trend in wage costs is made difficult by the fact
that both industry-specific and economy-wide influences must be considered. Accurate forecasting may require a multiple equation system
approach involving complex relations among several important economic variables. For illustrative purposes, however, it would be interesting to compare the accuracy of a simple trend projection reflecting a
linear relation between wage rates and time, a constant change model,
a constant growth model, and a simple single equation econometric
model. Although obviously naïve, these simple forecasting models can
be used to provide the forecaster with a starting point for more comprehensive analyses. In addition, these models offer an opportunity
to illustrate the methodology for judging forecast accuracy.

Table 4.6 shows data on average hourly wage rates for the metal
mining industry and the cost of living index for the 1956–1980 period.
Whereas trend forecasts of average wage rates would simply involve
using wage rate and time period data, a comprehensive econometric
forecasting approach would involve using cost of living data, among
other important economic variables. There are, of course, good economic reasons for expecting wage rates to be related to the cost of living index. In some instances, unionized workers have received automatic increases in wages following rises in the cost of living index. As
was seen during the recession of 1982, however, negotiated automatic
wage escalator clauses will be set aside if weak industry demand threat-
ens wide-scale layoffs in the face of high and increasing wage rates.
Under extremely serious conditions, wage rates may be frozen or even
scaled back in order to save jobs. Thus, we expect a close but imperfect
relation between wage rates and the cost of living index.

Table 4.7 shows ordinary least squares regression results for two
simple trend models relating wage rates and time, and a simple econometric model relating wage rates to the cost of living index. Results for

Table 4.6

Average Hourly Wage Rates for the Metal Mining Industry 1956–1980

Year	Average Hourly Wage (W) (in Dollars)	Cost of Living Index (COL) (1967 = 100)	Time Period (T)
1980	$9.18	246.8	25
1979	8.50	217.4	24
1978	7.67	195.4	23
1977	6.94	181.5	22
1976	6.76	170.5	21
1975	6.13	161.2	20
1974	5.44	147.7	19
1973	4.83	133.1	18
1972	4.56	125.3	17
1971	4.12	121.3	16
1970	3.88	116.3	15
1969	3.64	109.8	14
1968	3.42	104.2	13
1967	3.24	100.0	12
1966	3.17	97.2	11
1965	3.06	94.5	10
1964	2.96	92.9	9
1963	2.88	91.7	8
1962	2.83	90.6	7
1961	2.74	89.6	6
1960	2.66	88.7	5
1959	2.55	87.3	4
1958	2.46	86.6	3
1957	2.39	84.3	2
1956	2.27	81.4	1

Sources: *Standard and Poor's Industry Surveys, Production Indexes and Labor Statistics*, New York: Standard and Poor's Corporation, 1982, p. 72, 76.

Table 4.7

Descriptive and Forecast Models for Average Wage Rates (Standard Errors in Parentheses)

Descriptive Models (entire 1956–1980 period, $n = 25$)

(1) $W = 0.980 + 0.258T$ $R^2 = .851$ Constant Change Model
     (0.334)   (0.022)

(2) $\ln W = 0.633 + 0.057T$ $R^2 = .944$ Constant Growth Model
     (0.043)   (0.003)

(3) $W = -1.212 + 0.044COL$ $R^2 = .993$ Simple Econometric Model
     (0.106)   (0.001)

Forecast Models (1956–1975 subperiod, $n = 20$)

(1) $W = 1.705 + 0.167T$ $R^2 = .862$ Constant Change Model
     (0.189)   (0.016)

(2) $\ln W = 0.717 + 0.046T$ $R^2 = .940$ Constant Growth Model
     (0.033)   (0.003)

(3) $W = -1.551 + 0.048COL$ $R^2 = .995$ Simple Econometric Model
     (0.087)   (0.001)

Notes: W = Average Wage Rate.
      T = Time Period (1956 = 1, . . . , 1980 = 25).
    COL = Cost of Living Index.

Table 4.8

Average Wage Rate Forecast Analysis

Year	Actual Wage Rate, x_i	Constant Change Forecast, f_i	Squared Forecast Error $(f_{1i} - x_i)^2$	Constant Growth Forecast, f_{2i}	Squared Forecast Error $(f_{2i} - x_i)^2$	Econometric Forecast, f_{3i}	Squared Forecast Error $(f_{3i} - x_i)^2$
1980	$9.18	$5.88	$10.89	$6.47	$7.35	$10.30	$1.24
1979	8.50	5.71	7.77	6.18	5.39	8.88	0.15
1978	7.67	5.55	4.51	5.90	3.13	7.83	0.03
1977	6.94	5.38	2.44	5.64	1.70	7.16	0.05
1976	6.76	5.21	2.40	5.38	1.90	6.63	0.02
Average:	$\bar{x}_i = \$7.81$	$\bar{f}_1 = \$5.55$	$U_1^2 = \$ 5.60$	$\bar{f}_2 = \$5.91$	$U_2^2 = \$3.90$	$\bar{f}_3 = \$ 8.16$	$U_3^2 = \$0.30$
Average Forecast Error:			$U_1 = \$ 2.37$		$U_2 = \$1.97$		$U_3 = \$0.55$
Correlation between Forecast and Actual Wage:			$r_{x,f_1} = 0.984$		$r_{x,f_2} = 0.987$		$r_{x,f_3} = 0.990$

the entire 1956–1980 period provide an interesting *description* of the wage-time and wage–cost of living relation. On the other hand, results for the 1956–1975 subperiod provide a useful test model that can be used to *forecast* wage rates over the 1976–1980 period.

On an overall basis, a more stable relation between wage rates and time, and between wage rates and the cost of living index, is evident for the subperiod 1956–1975. This undoubtedly reflects the fact that large unanticipated rates of inflation characterized the 1976–1980 period and suggests that forecasting wages over the 1976–1980 period will prove difficult. Among the three forecast models shown in Table 4.7, we would anticipate that the simple econometric model would forecast most accurately, given its high R^2 (= .995), which reflects an ability to explain 99.5 percent of the variation in wage rates over the 1956–1975 subperiod. On the other hand, the constant change model reflecting a linear relation between wages and time is only able to explain 86.2 percent of the total variation in wages and should thus provide a relatively poor tool for forecasting.

For exploratory purposes, the estimation results for the 1956–1975 subperiod reported in Table 4.7 were used to generate wage forecasts for the 1976–1980 period. Table 4.8 presents these forecasts and related information. Of particular interest is the fact that despite high correlations between forecast and actual wage levels ($r = .84$ and $r = .987$), both the constant change and constant growth trend projection forecast models systematically forecast below actual wage levels, and by substantial amounts.

The average forecast error, *the root mean squared forecast error*, is $2.37 for the constant change model and $1.97 for the constant growth model. These are large, and probably unacceptable, average wage forecast errors. In contrast, the simple econometric forecasting model not only results in a high correlation ($r = .99$) between the forecast and actual wage data series, but the root mean squared forecast error is a relatively modest $0.55, or only 7 percent of average actual wages. For most forecasting purposes, this would be an acceptable level of forecast error.

The lessons from this illustrative average wage forecasting example are quite simple. First, although trend projection methods of forecasting are sometimes successful in forecasting firm sales, wages, GNP, and other aggregate economic variables, econometric models have the potential for increasing forecast accuracy in many instances. In the above wage forecasting example, the link between wages and the cost of living index is much stronger than the simple trend element in average wage rates over time. And second, as this simple example illustrates, an exceedingly high share of historical variation in an important economic variable (such as wages) must be explained by a descriptive model if a high level of forecast accuracy is to be achieved. Requiring

regression models to explain 99 percent or more of historical variation
($R^2 \geqq .99$) is a common requirement before such models will be relied
upon for forecasting purposes.

Summary

Managerial decision making requires forecasts of many future events.
In this chapter we examined several techniques that are used for economic forecasting. These included qualitative analysis, time-series analysis and projection, econometric models, and input-output methods.

All of these forecasting procedures have their particular strengths
and shortcomings. The appropriate method for a given forecasting
problem will depend on such factors as the distance into the future being forecast, available lead time, the required accuracy, the quality of
data available for analysis, and the nature of relationships involved in
the forecasting problem. When little quantitative information is available, qualitative analysis must be relied upon to form the basis for forecasts. Time-series approaches are appropriate for forecasting in those
situations when it is thought that the historical pattern of the economic
series being analyzed provides the best clues about future movement of
the variable. Barometric methods make use of consistent lead and lag
relationships between economic variables to project directional changes
in the time series. Although it is difficult to forecast the magnitude of a
change using these procedures, they have proven useful for calling turning points in economic activity. Composite and diffusion indexes combine various leading indicators, thereby reducing random fluctuations
and providing a smoother series, which reduces the generation of false
signals.

Econometric methods move beyond pure forecasting to provide estimates of important relationships that affect an economic system. This
explanatory characteristic of econometric methods allows them to be
used to determine the impact on the economic variable being examined
of changes in specific key variables, such as product price, advertising,
consumer incomes, and so on. Specification of these important interrelationships allows econometric methods to forecast economic conditions under a variety of assumptions. Input-output analysis is another
forecasting tool that focuses on the interrelationships in an economic
system. By tracing out flows between sectors, input-output analysis
provides a basis for examining how changes in one sector of the economy will affect other sectors. It is also useful for examining aggregate
requirements for such various key resources as energy, labor, water,
and so on.

An important aspect of forecasting is testing the reliability of fore-casts obtained from various basic forecasting techniques. Two statistics used in reliability analysis are the simple correlation between forecast and actual values and the average amount of forecasting error (root mean squared error).

Questions

4.1 What is the delphi method? Describe its main advantages.

4.2 Describe the main advantages and limitations of survey data.

4.3 What is the basic shortcoming of trend projection that barometric approaches improve on?

4.4 What advantage do diffusion and composite indices provide in the barometric approach to forecasting?

4.5 What forecasting methods would one employ to develop a model that could be used to examine various "what if" questions about the future?

4.6 Cite some examples of forecasting problems that might be ad-dressed by using input-output analysis.

4.7 What are the main characteristics of accurate forecasts?

Solved Problem

4.1 The change in the quantity demanded of Product A in any given week is inversely proportional to the change in sales of Product B in the previous week; that is, if sales of B rose by X percent last week, sales of A can be expected to fall by X percent this week.

    a) Write the equation for next week's sales of A, using the symbols A = sales of Product A, B = sales of Product B, t = time. Assume there will be no shortages of either product.

    b) Two weeks ago, 200 units of Product A and 150 units of Product B were sold. Last week 160 units of A and 180 units of B were sold. What would you predict the sales of A to be this week?

Solution

    a)

$$A_t = A_{t-1} + \Delta A_{t-1} + u$$

$$= A_{t-1} - \left(\frac{B_{t-1}}{B_{t-2}} - 1 \right) A_{t-1} + u.$$

b) For A_t we find:

$$A_t = A_{t-1}\left(\frac{B_{t-1}}{B_{t-2}} - 1\right)A_{t-1} + u$$

$$= 160 - \left(\frac{180}{150} - 1\right)160 + u$$

$$= 160 - 32 + u$$

$$= 128 + u.$$

Solved Problem

4.2 To convince the loan officer at a local bank of the viability of your new store, Life Styles Ltd., you would like to generate a sales forecast. Based on your assumption that next period sales are a function of current period local disposable income, own advertising, and competitor advertising (i.e., advertising by a competing retailer):

  a) Write an equation for predicting sales if you assume that the percentage change in sales is twice as large as the percentage change in local disposable income and own advertising, but only one half as large and of the opposite sign of the percentage change in competitor advertising. Use the symbols S = sales, Y = disposable income, A = own advertising, and Ax = competitor advertising.

  b) Forecast sales if, during the current period, sales total $300,000, disposable income is $204 million, own advertising is $24,000, and competitor advertising is $66,000. Previous period levels were $200 million (disposable income), $30,000 (own advertising), and $60,000 (competitor advertising).

Solution

  a)

$$S_{t+1} = S_t + 2(Y_t/Y_{t-1} - 1)S_t + 2\left(\frac{A_t}{A_{t-1}} - 1\right)S_t - \frac{1}{2}\left(\frac{Ax_t}{Ax_{t-1}} - 1\right)S_t + u$$

$$= S_t + 2S_t(Y_t/Y_{t-1}) - 2S_t + 2S_t(A_t/A_{t-1}) - 2S_t - \frac{1}{2}S_t\left(\frac{Ax_t}{Ax_{t-1}}\right) + \frac{1}{2}S_t + u$$

$$= 2S_t(Y_t/Y_{t-1}) + 2S_t(A_t/A_{t-1}) - \frac{1}{2}S_t\left(\frac{Ax_t}{Ax_{t-1}}\right) - 2.5S_t + u.$$

b)

$$S_{t+1} = 2(\$300{,}000)(1.02) + 2(\$300{,}000)(0.80) - \frac{1}{2}(\$300{,}000)(1.10)$$
$$- 2.5(\$300{,}000) + u$$

$$= \$612{,}000 + \$480{,}000 - \$165{,}000 - \$750{,}000 + u$$

$$= \$177{,}000 + u.$$

Problem Set

4.1 The following figures constitute annual sales for Gino's Restaurant:

Year	Sales
1975	$239,000
1976	287,000
1977	315,000
1978	353,000
1979	384,000
1980	427,000
1981	462,000
1982	520,000
1983	575,000
1984	628,000

a) Calculate the growth rate in sales for 1975 to 1984, using the constant rate of change model with annual compounding.

b) Forecast sales for 1985 and 1990.

4.2 Luke Andrews, controller for Technical Systems Ltd., is concerned about assembly division unit labor cost increases from $16 to $23.20 during the past three years. Andrews feels that importing components from foreign suppliers at a (labor plus transportation) cost equivalent of $30 may soon be desirable.

a) Calculate unit labor cost growth rate using the constant rate of change model with continuous compounding.

b) Forecast when unit labor costs will equal the current cost of importing.

4.3 Phil Maguire, manager of product packaging at Hayward Chemicals, is evaluating the cost effectiveness of the preventive maintenance program in his department. He believes that the monthly downtime of the packaging line, due to equipment breakdown, is related to the hours spent each month on preventive maintenance.

a) Write an equation for next month's downtime, using the symbols D = downtime, M = preventive maintenance, t = time, a_0 = constant term, a_1 = regression slope coefficient, and u = random disturbance, assuming that downtime in the forecast month decreases by the same percentage as preventive maintenance increased during the preceding month.

b) If eight hours were spent last month on preventive maintenance and this month's downtime were 20 hours, what should downtime be next month if preventive maintenance this month is ten hours? Use the equation developed in part a.

4.4 Cathy Boulger, manager of Toyland Ltd., must forecast sales for a popular adult game named Dungens and Dragoons in order to avoid stockouts or excessive inventory charges during the coming Christmas season. By analyzing recent data Boulger discovers that game sales seem to fall because of price increases, but rise as store traffic increases. In percentage terms, Boulger estimates that game sales fall at double the rate of price increases and grow at triple the rate of customer traffic increases. Furthermore, these effects seem to be independent.

a) Write an equation for estimating the Christmas season sales, using the symbols S = sales, P = price, T = traffic, t = time, and u = a random disturbance term.

b) Forecast this season's sales if Toyland sold 2,000 games last season at $15 each, this season's price is anticipated to be $16.50, and customer traffic is expected to rise by 15 percent over previous levels.

4.5 American Cinema, Inc. runs a chain of movie theaters and has found

$$Q = 800 - 400\,P + 20\,Y + 15\,Pop + 100\,AD + 100\,S$$

where Q is weekly ticket sales, P is price in $, Y is disposable income per capita in $000, Pop is population in thousands, AD is advertising expenditures in $00, and S is a binary or dummy variable equal to one in summertime, zero otherwise (on average, weekly ticket sales increase by 100 during the summer). In addition, popcorn (PC) and other concessions (OC) revenues are described by the equations:

$$PC = .25\,TR$$

$$OC = .5\ \ PC$$

where TR is total ticket plus popcorn plus other concession revenue.

a) Show the relation describing total ticket (T), plus popcorn plus other concession revenue.

b) Forecast weekly summer (that is, $S = 1$) ticket revenue (R) for

Stillwater, Oklahoma, assuming an average ticket price of $3.50, disposable income of $8,000, population of 36,000 persons, and advertising expenditures of $400.

c) Forecast total ticket plus popcorn plus other concession revenue for Stillwater.

4.6 The management of McKean Industries is evaluating the merits of building a new plant in order to fulfill a new contract with the federal government. The alternative to expansion is to use additional overtime, reduce other production, or a combination of both. The company manufactures a wide range of parts for aircraft, automotive, and agricultural equipment industries and will want to add new capacity only if the economy appears to be expanding. Forecasting the general economic activity of the United States, therefore, is of obvious interest to the company as an input to the decision process.

The firm has collected the data and has estimated the relationship for the United States economy shown below:

Last year's total profits (all corporations) P_{t-1} = $600 billion.
This year's government expenditures G = $1,000 billion.
Annual consumption expenditures C = $120 billion + 0.70($Y$) + u.
Annual investment expenditures I = $8 billion + 0.85 ($P_{t-1}$) + u.
Annual tax receipts T = 0.25 GNP.
National income Y = $GNP - T$.
Gross national product GNP = $C + I + G$.

Assume that all random disturbances average out to zero. Forecast each of the above variables through the simultaneous relationships expressed in the multiple equation system.

References

Ang, James S.; Chua, Jess H. and Fatemi, Ali M. "A Comparison of Econometric, Time Series, and Composite Forecasting Methods in Predicting Accounting Variables." *Journal of Economics and Business* 35 (August 1983): 301–312.

Armstrong, J. Scott. "Forecasting with Econometric Methods: Folklore Versus Fact." *Journal of Business* 51 (October 1978): 549–564.

Bails, Dale G. and Peppers, Larry C. *Business Fluxuations: Forecasting Techniques and Applications*. Englewood Cliffs, NJ: Prentice-Hall, 1982.

Beardsley, George and Mansfield, Edwin. "A Note on the Accuracy of Industrial Forecasts of the Profitability of New Products and Processes." *Journal of Business* 51 (January 1978): 127–135.

Box, G. E. P., and Jenkins, G. M. *Times Series Analysis, Forecasting and Control*, 2d ed. San Francisco: Holden-Day, 1976.

Chambers, John C.; Mullick, Satinder K. and Smith, Donald D. "How to Choose the Right Forecasting Technique." *Harvard Business Review* 49 (July–August 1971): 45–74.

Chow, Gregory C. "Are Econometric Models Useful for Forecasting?" *Journal of Business* 51 (October 1978): 565–571.

Francis, Jack Clark. "Financial Planning and Forecasting Models: An Overview." *Journal of Economics and Business* 35 (August 1983): 285–300.

Freedman, David. "Some Pitfalls in Large Econometric Models: A Case Study." *Journal of Business* 54 (July 1981): 479–500.

Granger, C. W. J. *Forecasting in Business and Economics*. New York: Academic Press, 1980.

Gross, Charles W. and Peterson, Robin T. *Business Forecasting*. 2d ed. Boston: Houghton Mifflin, 1983.

Hirschey, Mark. "Incentive Contracting for Railroad Subsidies: A Statistical Approach to Cost Control." *Land Economics* 56 (August 1980): 366–379.

Sobek, Robert S. "A Manager's Primer on Forecasting." *Harvard Business Review* 51 (May–June 1973): 1–9.

Valentine, Lloyd M. and Dauten, Carl A. *Business Cycles and Forecasting*. 6th ed. Cincinnati: South-Western, 1983.

Zarnowitz, Victor. "An Analysis of Annual and Multiperiod Quarterly Forecasts of Aggregate Income, Output, and the Price Level." *Journal of Business* 52 (January 1979): 1–33.

Zarnowitz, Victor and Moore, Geoffrey H. "Sequential Signals of Recession and Recovery." *Journal of Business* 55 (January 1982): 57–85.

Chapter 5

Production

Key Terms

Isoquant	*Marginal revenue*
Marginal product	* product*
Marginal rate of	*Production function*
* technical*	*Returns to a factor*
* substitution*	*Returns to scale*

Given the demand for its product, how does a firm determine the optimal level of output? Given several alternative production methods, which one should the firm choose? If the firm undertakes an expansion program to increase productive capacity, will the cost per unit be higher or lower after the expansion? These questions are critically important to the firm, and answers, or at least insights useful in analyzing the questions, are provided by the study of production.

Production is concerned with the way in which resources (inputs) are employed to produce a firm's products (outputs). The concept of production is quite broad and encompasses both the manufacture of physical goods and the provision of services. In both cases, production theory focuses on the efficient use of inputs to create outputs. In other words, production analysis examines the technical and economic characteristics of systems used to provide goods and services, with the aim of determining the optimal manner of combining inputs so as to minimize costs.

It is worth emphasizing that the term *production* refers to more than the physical transformation of resources. Production involves all the activities associated with providing goods and services. Thus, the hiring of workers (from unskilled labor to top management), personnel training, and the organizational structure used to maximize productivity are all part of the production process. The acquisition of capital resources and their efficient employment are also parts of production, as are the design and use of appropriate accounting control systems.

Thus, in addition to providing an important foundation for the understanding of costs and cost/output relationships, production theory enhances one's comprehension of the integrated nature of the firm. Perhaps no other single topic in managerial economics so clearly lays out the interrelationships among the various factors employed by the firm and among the functional components (for example, the output/revenue and output/cost components) in our valuation model of the firm.

Production Function

A **production function** relates inputs to outputs. It specifies the maximum possible output that can be produced for a given amount of inputs or, alternatively, the minimum quantity of inputs necessary to produce a given level of output. Production functions are determined by the technology available to the firm. That is, the input/output relationship for any production system is a function of the technological characteristics of the plant, equipment, labor, materials, and so on employed by the firm. Any improvement in technology, such as the addition of a process control computer which permits a manufacturing company to produce a given quantity of output with fewer raw materials and less energy and labor, or a training program which increases the productivity of labor, results in a new production function.

The basic properties of production functions can be illustrated by examining a simple two-input, one-output system. Consider a production process in which various quantities of two inputs, X and Y, can be used to produce a product, Q. The inputs X and Y might represent resources such as labor and capital or energy and raw materials. The product Q could be a physical item such as television sets, cargo ships, or breakfast cereal, but it could also be a service such as medical care, education, or banking services.

The production function for this system can be written as the following general relationship:

$$Q = f(X, Y). \qquad (5.1)$$

Table 5.1 is a tabular representation of such a two-input, single-output production system. Each element in the table shows the maximum

Table 5.1
Representative Production Table

Units of Y Employed	Output Quantity									
10	52	71	87	101	113	122	127	129	130	131
9	56	74	89	102	111	120	125	127	128	129
8	59	75	91	99	108	117	122	124	125 ·	126
7	61	77	87	96	104	112	117	120	121	122
6	62	72	82	91	99	107	111	114	116	117
5	55	66	75	84	92	99	104	107	109	110
4	47	58	68	77	85	91	97	100	102	103
3	35	49	59	68	76	83	89	91	90	89
2	15	31	48	59	68	72	73	72	70	67
1	5	12	35	48	56	55	53	50	46	40
	1	2	3	4	5	6	7	8	9	10

Units of X Employed

quantity of Q that can be produced with a specific combination of X and Y. The table shows, for example, that 2 units of X and 3 units of Y can be combined to produce 49 units of output; 5 units of X coupled with 5 units of Y results in 92 units of output; 4 units of X and 10 units of Y produce 101 units of Q; and so on. The units of input could represent *hours* of labor, *dollars* of capital, *cubic feet* of natural gas, *tons* of raw materials, and so on. Similarly, units of Q could be *numbers* of television sets or cargo ships, *boxes* of cereal, *patient days* of hospital care, customer *transactions* of a banking facility, and so on.

The production relationships in Table 5.1 can also be displayed graphically as in Figure 5.1. There the height of the bars associated with each input combination indicates the output produced. The tops of the output bars map the production surface for the system.

The discrete production data shown in Table 5.1 and Figure 5.1 can be generalized by assuming that the underlying production function is continuous. This generalization will aid us in our examination of production concepts.

A continuous production function means the inputs can be varied in a continuous fashion rather than incrementally, as in the preceding example. For a continuous production function, all possible combinations of the inputs can be represented by the graph of the input surface, as shown in Figure 5.2. Each point in the XY plane represents a combination of Inputs X and Y that will result in some level of output, Q, determined by the relationship expressed in Equation 5.1.

The three-dimensional diagram in Figure 5.3 is a graphic illustration of a continuous production function for a two-input, single-output sys-

Figure 5.1
Representative Production Surface

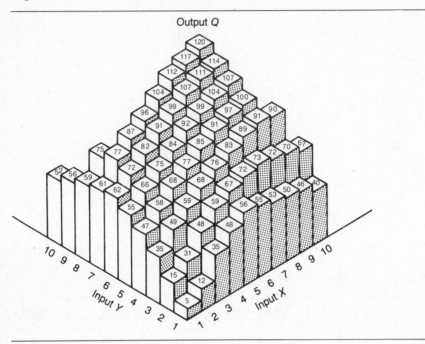

Figure 5.2
Input Surface for the Production Function: $Q = f(X, Y)$

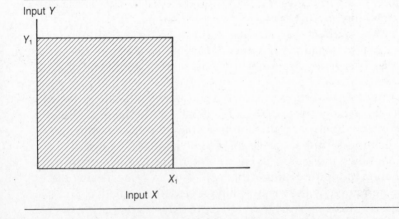

Figure 5.3
Production Surface

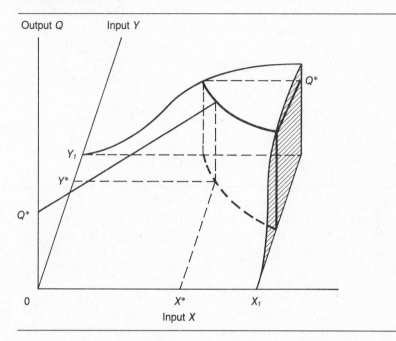

tem. Following the X axis outward indicates that increasing amounts of Input X are being used; going out the Y axis represents an increasing usage of Y; and moving up the Q axis means that larger amounts of output are being produced. The maximum amount of Q that can be produced with each combination of Inputs X and Y is represented by the height of the production surface erected above the input plane. Q^*, for example, is the maximum amount of Q that can be produced using the combination X^*, Y^* of the inputs.

In studying production functions, there are two types of relationships between inputs and outputs that are of interest for managerial decision making. One is the relationship between output and variation in all inputs. This type of production relationship is known as the **returns to scale** of a production system. Returns to scale play an important role in managerial decisions. They affect the optimal scale of a firm or its production facilities. They also affect the nature of competition in an industry and thus are factors in determining the profitability of investment in a particular economic sector.

The second important relationship in a production system is that between output and variation in only one of the inputs employed. The terms *factor productivity* and **returns to a factor** are used to denote this relationship between the quantity of an individual input (or factor of production) employed and the output produced. Factor productivity is the key to determining the optimal combination, or proportions of inputs, that should be used to produce a product. That is, factor productivity provides the basis for efficient resource employment in a production system. Because an understanding of factor productivity will aid in our comprehension of returns to scale, we examine this relationship first.

Total, Average, and Marginal Product

We have noted that the economic concept known as factor productivity or returns to a factor is important in the process of determining optimal input combinations for a production system. Because the process of optimization entails an analysis of the relationship between the total and marginal values of a function, it will prove useful to introduce the concepts of total, average, and marginal products for the resources employed in a production system.

The term *total product* is used to denote the total output from a production system. It is in fact synonymous with Q in Equation 5.1. Total product is a measure of the total output or product that results from employing a specific quantity of resources in a production system.

The concept of total product is used to describe the relationship between output and variation in only one input in a production function. For example, suppose that Table 5.1 represents a production system in which Y is a capital resource and X represents a labor input. If a firm is operating with a given level of capital (say, $Y = 2$), then the relevant production function for the firm in the short run is represented by the row in Table 5.1 corresponding to that level of fixed capital. (In economic terminology the *short-run* corresponds to a period of time during which at least one resource in a production system is fixed; that is, the quantity of that resource is constant regardless of the quantity of output produced.) Operating with 2 units of capital, the output (total product) from the system will depend upon the quantity of labor (X) employed. This total product of X can be read from the $Y = 2$ row in Table 5.1. It is also shown in column 2 of Table 5.2 and is illustrated graphically in Figure 5.4a.

More generally, the total product of a production factor can be expressed as a function relating output to the quantity of the resource employed. Continuing the example, the total product of X is given by the production function:

$$Q = f(X|Y = 2).$$

Table 5.2

Total Product, Marginal Product, and Average Product
of Factor X, Holding $Y = 2$

Input Quantity (X)	Total Product of the Input (Q)	Marginal Product of the Input $MP_X = \Delta Q/\Delta X$	Average Product of the Input $AP_X = Q/X$
1	15	+15	15.0
2	31	+16	15.5
3	48	+17	16.0
4	59	+11	14.7
5	68	+ 9	13.6
6	72	+ 4	12.0
7	73	+ 1	10.4
8	72	− 1	9.0
9	70	− 2	7.8
10	67	− 3	6.7

This equation relates the output quantity Q (the total product of X) to the quantity of Input X employed, fixing the quantity of Y used at 2 units. One would of course obtain other total product functions for X if the factor Y were fixed at levels other than 2 units.

Figure 5.5 illustrates the general concept of the total product of an input as the schedule of output obtained as that input increases, *holding constant the amounts of the other inputs employed*. (In Figure 5.5 we are once again assuming a continuous production function where inputs can be varied in a continuous fashion rather than discretely, as in the preceding example.) Suppose we fix, or hold constant, the amount of Input Y at the level Y_1. The total product curve of Input X, holding Input Y constant at Y_1, originates at Y_1 and rises along the production surface as the use of Input X is increased. Four other total product curves are shown in the figure: another for X, holding Y constant at Y_2, and three for Input Y, holding X fixed at X_1, X_2, and X_3, respectively.

Total product curves from Figure 5.5 can also be drawn in two-dimensional space. A total product curve for Input X, holding Y constant at Y_1, is shown in Figure 5.6a. This curve is developed directly from Figure 5.5, and a series of such curves can be drawn for various levels of Y. Similarly, total product curves can be drawn for Input Y, holding X constant at various levels.

Given the total product function for an input, the marginal and average products can easily be derived. First, recognize that the **marginal product** of a factor, MP_X, is the change in output associated with a unit change in the factor, holding other inputs constant. Accordingly, for a discrete total product function (such as is shown in Table 5.2 and

Figure 5.4
Total, Average, and Marginal Product for Input X: Given $Y = 2$

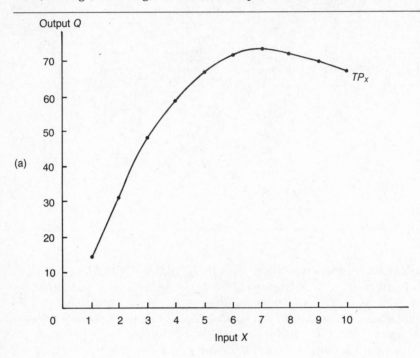

(a)

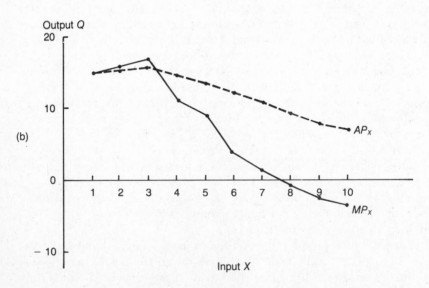

(b)

Figure 5.5
Total Product Curves for X and Y

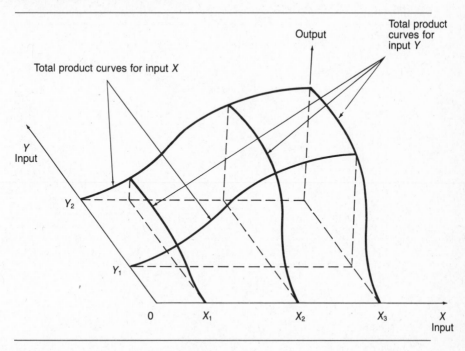

Figure 5.4), the marginal product is expressed by the relationship:

$$MP_X = \frac{\Delta Q}{\Delta X},$$

where ΔQ is the change in output resulting from a change of ΔX units in the variable input factor. Again this expression assumes that the quantity of the other input, Y, remains unchanged.

A factor's *average product* is the total product divided by the units of the input employed, or:

$$AP_X = \frac{Q}{X}.$$

The average product for X, given $Y = 2$ units, in the discrete production example is shown in the last column of Table 5.2.

For a continuous total product function, as illustrated in Figure 5.6a, the marginal product is equal to the slope of the total product curve, and the average product is equal to the slope of a line drawn from the origin to a point on the total product curve. The average and marginal products for Input X can be determined in this manner, and these points are plotted to form the average and marginal product curves shown in Figure 5.6b.

Figure 5.6

Total, Marginal, and Average Product Curves: (a) Total Product Curve for *X*,
Holding *Y* = *Y₁* (b) Marginal Product Curve for *X*, Holding *Y* = *Y₁*

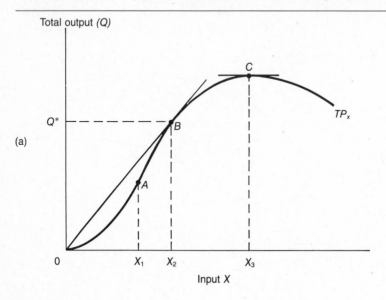

(a)

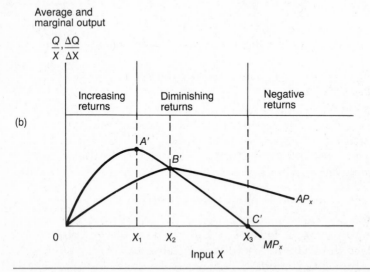

(b)

Three points of interest, *A*, *B*, and *C*, may be identified on the total
product curve in Figure 5.6a, and each has a corresponding location on
the average or marginal product curves. Point *A* is the inflection point
of the total product curve. The marginal product of *X* (the slope of the
total product curve) increases until this point is reached, after which it

begins to decrease. This phenomenon can be seen in Figure 5.6b, as MP_X is at a maximum at A'.

The second point on the total product curve, B, indicates the output at which the average and the marginal products are equal. The slope of a line from the origin to any point on the total product curve measures the average product of X at that point, while the marginal product is equal to the slope of the total product curve. At Point B, where X_2 units of Input X are employed, such a line from the origin is tangent to the total product curve, so $MP_X = AP_X$. Note also that the slopes of successive lines drawn from the origin to the total product curve increase until Point B, after which their slopes decline. Thus, the average product curve rises until it reaches B, then declines; this feature is also shown in Figure 5.6b as Point B'. Here we see again that $MP_X = AP_X$, and that AP_X is at a maximum.

The third point, C, indicates where the slope of the total product curve is zero and the curve is at a maximum. Beyond C the marginal product of X is negative, indicating that an increase in the usage of Input X results in a *reduction* of total product. The corresponding point in Figure 5.6b is C', the point where the marginal product curve intersects the X axis.

The Law of Diminishing Returns to a Factor

The total and the marginal product curves in Figure 5.6 demonstrate the property known as the *law of diminishing returns*. This law states that as the quantity of a variable input increases, with the quantities of all other factors being held constant, resulting *increases* in output eventually diminish. Alternatively stated, the law of diminishing returns states that the marginal product of the variable factor must eventually decline if enough of it is combined with some fixed quantity of one or more other factors in a production system. Because the law of diminishing returns deals specifically with the *marginal* product of an input factor, it is sometimes called the law of diminishing *marginal* returns to emphasize the point.

The law of diminishing returns is not a law that can be derived deductively. Rather, it is a generalization of an empirical phenomenon that has been observed to be true in every known production system. The basis for this relationship is easily demonstrated for the labor input in a production process where a fixed amount of capital is employed.

Consider a factory with an assembly line for the production of automobiles. If one employee is put to work manufacturing automobiles, that individual must perform each of the activities necessary to construct a car. Output from such a combination of labor and capital is likely to be quite small. (In fact, it may be less than could be achieved with a smaller amount of capital because of the inefficiency of having one employee accompany the car down the assembly line rather than building the car at a single station.)

As additional units of labor are added to this production system, holding constant the capital input, output is likely to expand rapidly. The intensity with which the capital resource is used increases with the additional labor input, and an increasingly efficient input combination results. The improvement in capital utilization resulting from the increased labor employment could result in the marginal product (increase in output) of each successive employee actually increasing over some range of labor additions. This increasing marginal productivity might result from each unit of labor using a more manageable quantity of capital than is possible with less total labor input (for example, working at a single assembly station). The specialization of activity that could accompany increased labor employment is another factor that might lead to an increasing marginal product for labor as successive units are employed.

An illustration of a production situation where the marginal product of an input increases over some range was presented in Table 5.2. There, the first unit of labor (Input X) resulted in 15 units of production. With 2 units of labor 31 units were produced—the marginal product of the second unit of labor (16) exceeded that of the first (15). Similarly, addition of another unit of labor resulted in output increasing to 48 units, indicating a marginal product of 17 for the third unit of labor.

Eventually, enough labor will be combined with the fixed capital input that the benefits of further labor additions will not be as large as the benefits achieved earlier. When this occurs, the rate of increase in output per additional unit of labor (the marginal product of labor) will drop. Although total output will continue to increase as added units of labor are employed (the marginal product of labor is positive), the rate of increase in output will decline (the marginal product will decrease). This diminishing marginal productivity is exhibited by the fourth, fifth, sixth, and seventh units of Input X in Table 5.2.

Finally, a point may be reached where the quantity of the variable input factor is so large that total output actually begins to decline with additional employment of that factor. In the automobile assembly example this would occur when the labor force became so large that employees were getting in each other's way and hindering the manufacturing process. This happened in Table 5.2 when more than 7 units of Input X were combined with 2 units of Input Y. The eighth unit of X resulted in a 1-unit reduction in total output (its marginal product was -1), while units 9 and 10 caused output to fall by 2 and 3 units respectively.

In Figure 5.6b the regions where the variable input factor X exhibited increasing, diminishing, and negative returns have been labeled. Although the information provided by these return or productivity relationships is insufficient to enable one to determine the optimal quantities of the inputs to use in a production system, it does enable one to eliminate a set of input combinations that would be irrational under realistic economic conditions.

This concept of irrational stages of production, as well as the underlying factor, productivity relationships, can be more fully explored using isoquant analysis, which explicitly recognizes the potential variability of both factors in a two-input, one-output production system. This technique is introduced in the following section, where it is used to examine the role of input substitutability in determining optimal input combinations.

Production Isoquants

Although one can examine the properties of production functions graphically using three-dimensional production surfaces like the one shown in Figure 5.3, a two-dimensional representation using isoquants is often equally instructive and simpler to use. The term **isoquant** (derived from *iso*, meaning "equal," and *quant*, meaning "quantity") denotes a curve that represents all the different combinations of inputs which, when combined efficiently, produce a specified quantity of output. For example, we see in Table 5.1 that 91 units of output can be efficiently produced by four input combinations: $X = 3$, $Y = 8$; $X = 4$, $Y = 6$; $X = 6$, $Y = 4$; and $X = 8$, $Y = 3$. Therefore, those four input combinations would all lie on the $Q = 91$ isoquant. Similarly, the combinations $X = 6$, $Y = 10$; $X = 7$, $Y = 8$; $X = 10$, $Y = 7$ all result in 122 units of production and, hence, lie on the $Q = 122$ isoquant.

These two isoquants are illustrated in Figure 5.7. Each point on the $Q = 91$ isoquant indicates a different combination of X and Y that can be used to produce 91 units of output. For example, 91 units can be produced with 3 units of X and 8 units of Y, with 4 units of X and 6 units of Y, or with any other combination of X and Y on the isoquant $Q = 91$. A similar interpretation can be given the isoquant for $Q = 122$ units of output.

The isoquants for the continuous production function displayed in Figure 5.3 can be located by passing a series of planes through the production surface, horizontal to the XY plane, at various heights. Each plane represents a different level of output. Two such planes have been passed through the production surface shown in Figure 5.8 at heights Q_1 and Q_2. Every point on the production surface with a height of Q_1

Figure 5.7
Representative Isoquants from Table 6.1

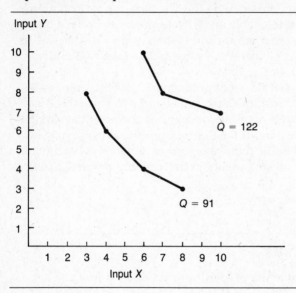

Figure 5.8
Isoquant Determination

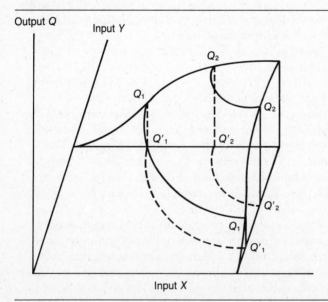

Figure 5.9
Production Isoquants

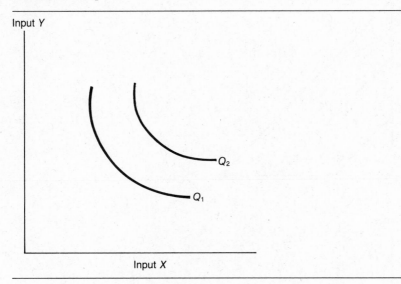

above the input plane (that is, all points along curve Q_1) represents an equal quantity, or isoquant, of Q_1 units of output. The curve Q_2 maps out the locus of all input combinations that result in Q_2 units of production.

These isoquant curves can be transferred to the input surface, as indicated by the dashed curves Q'_1 and Q'_2 in Figure 5.8, then further transferred to the two-dimensional graph shown in Figure 5.9. These latter curves represent the standard form of an isoquant.

Substituting Input Factors

The shapes of the isoquants reveal a great deal about the substitutability of the input factors; that is, the ability to substitute one input for another in the production process. This point is illustrated in Figure 5.10a, b, and c.

In some production systems certain inputs can be easily substituted for one another. In the production of electricity, for example, the fuels used to power the generators might represent readily substitutable inputs. Figure 5.10a shows isoquants for such an electric power generation system. The technology, a power plant with a bank of boilers equipped to burn either oil or gas, is given; various amounts of electric power can be produced by burning gas only, oil only, or varying amounts of each. Gas and oil are perfect substitutes here, and the isoquants are straight lines. Other examples of readily substitutable inputs include

Figure 5.10
Isoquants for Inputs with Varying Degrees of Substitutability: (a) Electric Power Generation (b) Bicycle Production (c) Dresses

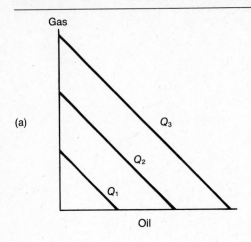

(a)

Gas

Q_3

Q_2

Q_1

Oil

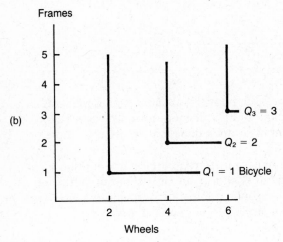

(b)

Frames

5

4

3

2

1

$Q_3 = 3$

$Q_2 = 2$

$Q_1 = 1$ Bicycle

2   4   6

Wheels

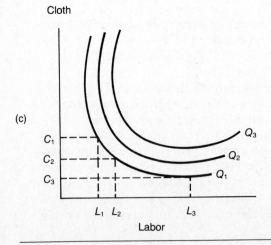

(c)

Cloth

Q_3

Q_2

Q_1

C_1

C_2

C_3

L_1 L_2 L_3

Labor

fish meal and soybeans to provide protein in a feed mix; energy and time in a drying process; United Parcel Service and the U.S. Postal Service for delivery of packages. In each of these cases one would expect to find linear production isoquants.

At the other extreme of input substitutability are production systems where inputs are perfect complements for each other. In these situations exact amounts of each input are required to produce a given quantity of output. Figure 5.10b, illustrating the isoquants for bicycles, represents this case of complete nonsubstitutability. Exactly two wheels and one frame are required to produce a bicycle, and wheels cannot be substituted for frames, or vice versa. Pants and coats for suits, engines and bodies for trucks, barbers and shears for haircuts, and chemicals in compounds for prescription drugs are further examples of complementary inputs. Production isoquants in the case of complementary inputs take the shape of right angles as indicated in Figure 5.10b.

Figure 5.10c shows an intermediate situation, that of a production process where inputs can be substituted for each other, but the substitutability is not perfect. A dress can be made with a relatively small amount of labor (L_1) and a large amount of cloth (C_1). The same dress can also be made with less cloth (C_2) if more labor (L_2) is used because the worker can cut the material more carefully and reduce waste. Finally, the dress can be made with still less cloth (C_3), but the worker must be so extremely painstaking that the labor input requirement increases substantially (L_3). Note that while a relatively small addition of labor, from L_1 to L_2, allows the input of cloth to be reduced from C_1 to C_2, a very large increase in labor, from L_2 to L_3, is required to obtain a similar reduction in cloth from C_2 to C_3. The substitutability of labor for cloth diminishes from L_1 to L_2 to L_3. The substitutability of cloth for labor in the manufacture of dresses also diminishes, as can be seen by considering the quantity of cloth that must be added to replace each unit of reduced labor in moving from L_3 to L_1.

Most labor-capital substitutions in production systems exhibit this diminishing substitutability. Energy and insulation used in providing heating services exhibit diminishing substitutability, as do doctors and medical technicians in providing health care services.

Marginal Rate of Technical Substitution

The slope of the isoquant provides the key to the substitutability of input factors. In Figure 5.10c, the slope of the isoquant is simply the change in Input Y (cloth) divided by the change in Input X (labor). This relationship, known as the **marginal rate of technical substitution** ($MRTS$) of factor inputs, provides a measure of the amount of one input factor that must be substituted for one unit of the other input factor if output is to remain unchanged. This can be stated algebraically:

$$MRTS = \frac{\Delta Y}{\Delta X} = \text{Slope of an Isoquant.} \tag{5.2}$$

The marginal rate of technical substitution is usually not constant, but diminishes as the amount of substitution increases. In Figure 5.10c, for example, as more and more labor is substituted for cloth, the increment of labor necessary to replace cloth is increasing. Finally, at the extremes, the isoquant may even become positively sloped, indicating that there is a limit to the range over which the input factors may be substituted for each other while the level of production is held constant. The classic example of this case is the use of land and labor to produce a given output of wheat. As labor is substituted for land, at some point the farmers trample the wheat. As more labor is added, more land must also be added, if wheat output is to be maintained. The new workers must have some place to stand.

The input substitution relationship indicated by the slope of a production isoquant follows directly from the concept of diminishing marginal productivity introduced in the section entitled "The Law of Diminishing Returns to a Factor." To see this, it can be shown that the marginal rate of technical substitution is equal to minus one times the ratio of the marginal products of the input factors. Since output is held constant along an isoquant, if Input Y is reduced, causing output to decline, Input X must be increased sufficiently to return output to the original level. The loss in output resulting from a small reduction in Y is equal to the marginal product of Y, MP_Y, multiplied by the change in Y, ΔY. That is:

$$\Delta Q = MP_Y \cdot \Delta Y. \tag{5.3}$$

Similarly, the change in Q associated with the increased use of Input X is given by the expression:

$$\Delta Q = MP_X \cdot \Delta X. \tag{5.4}$$

For substitution of X for Y along an isoquant, the absolute value of ΔQ in Equations 5.3 and 5.4 must be the same. That is, the change in output associated with the reduction in Input Y must be exactly offset by the change in output resulting from the increase in Input X if we are to remain on the same isoquant. Therefore, ΔQ in Equations 5.3 and 5.4 must be equal in size and have the opposite signs. From this it follows that:

$$-MP_Y \cdot \Delta Y = MP_X \cdot \Delta X. \tag{5.5}$$

Transposing the variables in Equation 5.5 produces the relationship

$$MRTS = -\frac{MP_X}{MP_Y} = \frac{\Delta Y}{\Delta X} = \text{Slope of an Isoquant.} \qquad (5.6)$$

Thus, the slope of a production isoquant, shown in Equation 5.2 to be equal to $\Delta Y/\Delta X$, is determined by the ratio of the marginal products of the inputs. Looking at Figure 5.10c we can see that the isoquant Q has a very steep negative slope at the point L_1C_1. This means that when cloth is relatively abundant, the marginal product of labor is high as compared with the marginal product of cloth. On the other hand, when labor is relatively abundant at, say, point L_3C_3, the marginal product of labor is low relative to the marginal product of cloth.

Equation 5.6 provides a basis for examining the concept of irrational input combinations. It is irrational for a firm to combine resources in such a way that the marginal product of any input is negative, since this implies that output could be increased by using less of that resource. Alternatively stated, it is irrational for a firm to increase resource usage, and therefore input costs, when the result is a decline in output. Note from Equation 5.6 that if the inputs X and Y are combined in proportions such that the marginal product of either factor is negative, then the slope of the production isoquant will be positive. That is, in order for a production isoquant to be positively sloped, one of the input factors must have a negative marginal product. From this it follows that input combinations lying along a positively sloped portion of a production isoquant are irrational and would be avoided by the firm.

In Figure 5.11 the rational limits of input substitution are indicated by the points where the isoquants become positively sloped. The limits to the range of substitutability of X for Y are indicated by the tangencies between the isoquants and a set of lines drawn perpendicular to the Y axis. Similarly, the limits of substitutability of Y for X are shown by the tangencies of lines perpendicular to the X axis. The maximum and the minimum proportions of Y and X that would be combined to produce each level of output are determined by the tangencies of these lines with the production isoquants.

It is irrational for a firm to use any input combination outside these tangencies, or *ridge lines*, as they are called. The reason such combinations are irrational lies in the fact that the marginal product (the change in output resulting from an incremental increase in an input factor) of the relatively more abundant input is negative outside the ridge lines. This means that addition of the last unit of the excessive input factor actually reduces the output of the production system. Obviously, if the input factor has a positive cost, it would be irrational for a firm to buy and employ additional units that caused production to decrease. To il-

Figure 5.11
Maximum Variable Proportions for Inputs X and Y

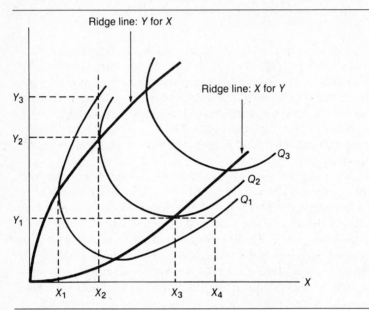

lustrate, suppose a firm is currently operating with a fixed quantity of Input Y equal to Y_1 units, as shown in Figure 5.11. In such a situation the firm would never employ more than X_3 units of Input X because employment of additional units of X results in successively lower output quantities being produced. For example, if the firm combines Y_1 and X_4, output is equal to Q_1 units. By reducing usage of X from X_4 to X_3, output can be increased from Q_1 to Q_2.

A similar relationship is shown for Input Y. We see that in the area above the upper ridge line the relative amount of Y is excessive. In this area it is possible to increase production (move to a higher isoquant) by reducing the amount of Y employed. For example, the input combination X_2Y_3 results in Q_1 units of output. However, by reducing to Y_2 the amount of Y employed while holding X constant at X_2, the firm produces a higher level of output, Q_2. This means that the marginal product of Y is negative, since reducing its usage increases production. Thus, in the area above the upper ridge line Input Y is excessive relative to Input X, and here Y's marginal product is negative. For combinations below the lower ridge line Input X is excessive relative to the amount of Input Y employed, and here X's marginal product is negative. Only for input combinations lying between the ridge lines will *both* inputs have positive marginal products, and it is here (along the negatively sloped portion of the isoquant) that we must look for optimal input combinations.

The Role of Revenue and Cost in Production

To answer the question of what constitutes an optimal input combination in a production system we must move beyond technological relationships and introduce revenues and costs. In an advanced economy productive activity results in goods that are sold rather than *consumed* by the producer, so we must be concerned with returns to the owners of the various input factors—labor, materials, and capital—that result from those sales. Therefore, to gain an understanding of how the factors of production should be combined for maximum efficiency, it is necessary that we shift from an analysis of *physical* productivity of inputs to an examination of their *economic* productivity, or revenue generating capability. The conversion from physical to economic relationships is accomplished by multiplying the marginal product of the input factors by the marginal revenue resulting from the sale of the goods or services produced, to obtain a quantity known as the **marginal revenue product** of the input:

$$\text{Marginal Revenue Product of Input } X\ (MRP_x) = MP_x \cdot MR_Q. \tag{5.7}$$

The marginal revenue product of an input is the value of the output produced as a result of employing one additional unit of that input. Alternatively stated, a factor's marginal revenue product is the change in total revenue resulting from the sale of products produced by adding another unit of the input to the production system. For example, if the addition of one more hour of labor to a work force would result in the production of two incremental units of a product that can be sold for $5 per unit, the marginal product of labor is 2, and its marginal revenue product is $10 (2 × $5). Table 5.3 illustrates the marginal revenue product concept for a simple one-factor production system. The marginal revenue product values shown in column 4 of that table assume each unit X employed equals the 3 units of output produced times the $5 revenue received per output can be sold for $5. Thus, the marginal revenue product of the first unit of X employed equals the 3 units of output produced times the $5 revenue received per unit, or $MRP_{X=1} =$ $15. The second unit of X adds 4 units of production (that is, $MP_{X=2} =$ 4); hence, the *MRP* of the second unit of X is $20 (4 × $5). The marginal revenue products of the other quantities of X are all determined in this manner.

Table 5.3
Marginal Revenue Product for a Single Input

Units of Input (X)	Total Product of X (Q)	Marginal Product of X (ΔQ)	Marginal Revenue Product of X ($MP_X \times \$5$)
1	3	3	$15
2	7	4	$20
3	10	3	$15
4	12	2	$10
5	13	1	$5

Optimal Employment of a Single Input

To see how the economic productivity of an input, as defined by its marginal revenue product, is related to the use of the factor for productive purposes, one need only consider the simple question: If the price of input X in the production system depicted in Table 5.3 is $12, how many units of X would a firm use? The answer is that 3 units of X would be employed, because the value of adding each of the first three units, as measured by their marginal revenue products, exceeds the added cost. The fourth unit of X would not be used, because the value of the marginal product produced by the fourth unit of X ($10) is less than the cost of that factor ($12).

The relationship between resource productivity as measured by the marginal revenue product and optimal employment or factor use can be generalized by referring to the basic marginal principles of profit maximization (developed in Chapter 2). Recall that so long as marginal revenue exceeds marginal cost, profits must increase. In the context of production decisions this means that if the marginal revenue product of an input, that is, the marginal revenue generated by its employment in a production system, exceeds its marginal cost, then profits are increased as input employment increases. Similarly, when the marginal revenue product is less than the cost of the factor, marginal profit is negative, so the firm would reduce employment of that factor.

This concept of optimal resource use can be clarified by examining a very simple production system in which a single variable input, L, is used to produce a single product, Q. Profit maximization requires that production be at a level such that marginal revenue equals marginal cost. Since the only variable factor in the system is Input L, the marginal cost of production can be expressed as:

$$MC_Q = \frac{\Delta Cost}{\Delta Quantity}$$

$$= \frac{P_L}{MP_L}.$$

(5.8)

That is, dividing P_L, the price of a marginal unit of L, by MP_L, the number of units of output gained by the employment of an added unit of L, provides a measure of the marginal cost of producing each additional unit of the product.

Since marginal revenue must equal marginal cost at the profit maximizing output level, we can substitute for MC_Q from Equation 5.8 and derive the expression,

Marginal Revenue$_Q$ = Marginal Cost$_Q$

$$MR_Q = \frac{P_L}{MP_L}.$$

(5.9)

Equation 5.9 must hold for profit maximization since it was demonstrated that the right-hand side of Equation 5.9 is just another expression for marginal cost. Solving Equation 5.9 for P_L results in:

$$P_L = MR_Q \cdot MP_L,$$

or, since $MR_Q \cdot MP_L$ is by definition the marginal revenue product of L:

$$P_L = MRP_L.$$

(5.10)

Equation 5.10 states the general result that a profit maximizing firm will always employ an input up to the point where its marginal revenue product is equal to its price. If the marginal revenue product exceeds the cost of the input, profits are increased by employing additional units of the factor. Similarly, when the resource's price is greater than its marginal revenue product, profit is increased by using less of the factor. Only at the level of usage where $MRP = P$ are profits maximized.

It follows from the above analysis that the demand curve for a factor of production is defined by its MRP. Figure 5.12 illustrates this point. There the marginal revenue product for an input, L, is shown along with its market price, P_L^*. Over the range 0 to L^*, expanding usage of L will increase total profits, since the marginal revenue product gained from employing each unit of L exceeds its price. Beyond L^*, increased usage of L will reduce profits, since the benefits gained (MRP_L) are less

Figure 5.12
The MRP Curve Is an Input Demand Curve

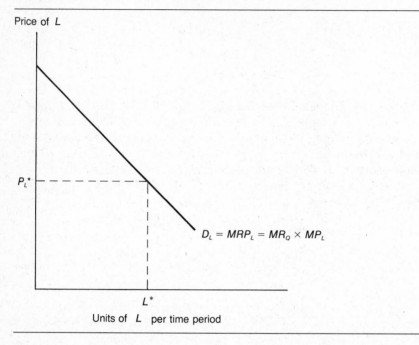

Price of L

P_L^*

$D_L = MRP_L = MR_Q \times MP_L$

L^*

Units of L per time period

than the costs incurred (P_L). Only at L^*, where $P_L^* = MRP_L$, will total profits be maximized. Of course, if P_L^* were higher the quantity of L demanded would be reduced. Similarly, if P_L^* were lower the quantity of L purchased would be greater.

Optimal Proportions of Multiple Inputs

The results of the preceding section can be extended to production systems employing several input factors. Although there are several possible approaches to this extension, one of the simplest involves combining technological and market relationships through the use of isoquant and isocost curves. That is, the optimal input proportions can be found graphically for a two-input, single-output system by adding an "isocost curve" (a line of constant costs) to the diagram of production isoquants. Each point on an isocost curve represents some combination of inputs, say X and Y, whose cost is equal to a constant expenditure. Isocost curves, which are illustrated in Figure 5.13, are constructed in the following manner: Let $P_X = \$500$ and $P_Y = \$250$; these are the prices of X and Y. For a given expenditure, say, $E_1 = \$1,000$, the firm can purchase 4 units of Y ($\$1,000/\$250 = 4$ units) and no units of X, or 2 units

Figure 5.13
Isocost Curves

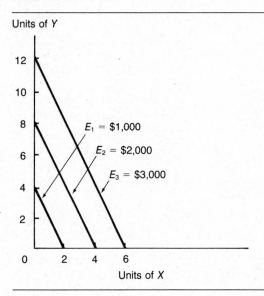

Units of Y

$E_1 = \$1,000$

$E_2 = \$2,000$

$E_3 = \$3,000$

Units of X

of X ($1,000/$500 = 2 units) but none of Y. These two quantities represent the X and Y intercepts of an isocost curve, and a straight line connecting them provides the locus of all combinations of X and Y that can be purchased for $1,000.

The equation for an isocost curve is merely a statement of the various combinations of the inputs that can be purchased for a given expenditure. For example, the various combinations of X and Y that can be purchased for a fixed expenditure, E, are given by the expression:

$$E = P_X \cdot X + P_Y \cdot Y.$$

Solving this expression for Y so that it can be graphed, as in Figure 5.13, results in:

$$Y = \frac{E}{P_Y} - \frac{P_X}{P_Y} X. \tag{5.11}$$

Note that the first term in Equation 5.11 is the Y-axis intercept of the isocost curve. It indicates the quantity of Input Y that can be purchased with a given budget or expenditure limit, *assuming zero units of Input X are bought*. The slope of an isocost curve $\Delta Y/\Delta X$ is equal to $-P_X/P_Y$ and, therefore, is a measure of the relative prices of the inputs. From this, it follows that a change in the expenditure level, E, leads to a parallel

Figure 5.14
Optimal Input Combination

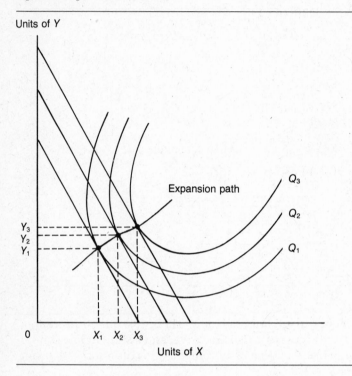

Units of Y

Q_3

Expansion path

Q_2

Y_3
Y_2
Y_1

Q_1

0   X_1 X_2 X_3

Units of X

shift of an isocost curve, while changes in the prices of the inputs result in changes in the slope of the curve.

Extending the example introduced above and illustrated in Figure 5.13 will clarify these relationships. With a $1,000 expenditure level, the Y-axis intercept of the isocost curve has already been shown to be 4 units. The slope of the isocost curve is determined by the relative prices. Thus, in Figure 5.13 the slope of the isocost curves is given by the expression:

$$\text{Slope} = -\frac{P_x}{P_Y} = -\frac{\$500}{\$250} = -2.$$

Suppose a firm has only $3,000 to spend on inputs for the production of Q. Combining a set of production isoquants with the isocost curve, E_3, of Figure 5.13 to form Figure 5.14, we find that the optimal input combination occurs at the point of tangency between the isocost curve and a production isoquant. At that point, X and Y are combined in proportions that maximize the output attainable for expenditure E_3. No other combination of X and Y that can be purchased for $3,000 will produce as much output. Alternatively stated, the combination X_1Y_1 is the least-cost input combination that can be used to produce output Q_1. Similarly, X_2Y_2 is the least-cost input combination for producing Q_2, X_3Y_3 is the least-cost input combination for producing Q_3, and so on. All other possible combinations for producing Q_1, Q_2, and Q_3 are intersected by higher isocost curves. The line connecting points of tangency between isoquant and isocost curves constitutes what economists call an *expansion path* since it depicts optimal input combinations as the scale of production expands.

The fact that optimal input combinations occur at a point of tangency between a production isoquant and an isocost curve leads to a very important economic principle. The slope of an isocost curve was shown above to be equal to $-P_X/P_Y$. Recall that the slope of an isoquant curve is equal to the marginal rate of technical substitution of one input factor for the other when production is held constant at some level. The marginal rate of technical substitution was shown in Equation 5.6 to be given by the ratio of the marginal products of the input factors. That is, the slope of a production isoquant equals $-MP_X/MP_Y$.

At the point where inputs are combined optimally, there is a tangency between the isocost and isoquant curves, and, hence, their slopes are equal. Therefore, for optimal input combinations the ratio of the prices of the inputs must be equal to the ratio of their marginal products, as is shown in Equation 5.12:

$$-\frac{P_X}{P_Y} = -\frac{MP_X}{MP_Y}. \tag{5.12}$$

Or, alternatively, the ratios of marginal product to price must be equal for each input:

$$\frac{MP_X}{P_X} = \frac{MP_Y}{P_Y}. \tag{5.13}$$

The economic principle for least-cost combinations of inputs, as given in Equation 5.13, implies that the optimal proportions are such that an additional dollar spent on a given input adds as much to total output as would a dollar spent on any other input. Any combination violating this rule is suboptimal in the sense that a change of inputs could result in the same quantity of output being produced for a lower cost. Consider the case of a firm combining X and Y in such a way that the marginal product of X equals 10, while that of Y equals 9. Assuming that X costs \$2 a unit and Y costs \$3, the marginal product per dollar spent is found to be:

$$\frac{MP_X}{P_X} = \frac{10}{2} = 5 \text{ and } \frac{MP_Y}{P_Y} = \frac{9}{3} = 3.$$

This combination violates the optimal proportions rule: The ratios of the marginal products to prices are not equal. In this situation the firm can reduce its use of Y by 1 unit, reducing total output by 9 units and total costs by \$3. Then, by employing an additional nine-tenths of 1 unit of X at a cost of \$1.80, the 9 units of lost production may be regained. The result is production of the 9 units of output at a cost which is less than in the original situation—the \$3 saved on Y is offset by only an additional \$1.80 spent on X for a net cost reduction of \$1.20. This new input combination may still be suboptimal; that is, the example merely indicates that an alternative combination of inputs can lower production costs. It would be necessary to examine the new marginal product/price ratios for an input combination of 10.9 units of X and 8 units of Y to determine if further savings are possible.

Optimal Level of Multiple Inputs

Combining a production system's inputs in proportions that meet the conditions of Equation 5.13 insures that *any* output quantity will be produced at minimum cost. That is, cost minimization requires only that the ratios of marginal product to price be equal for each input, i.e., that inputs be combined in optimal proportions. Profit maximization, however, requires that a firm employ optimal input proportions *and* produce an optimal quantity of output. Thus, *cost minimization (optimal input proportions) is a necessary but not sufficient condition for profit maximization.*

At the optimal (profit maximizing) output level, meeting the conditions of Equation 5.13 is equivalent to employing each input up to the point where its marginal revenue product is equal to its price, the optimality condition developed in Equation 5.10. To see this, note that by the same reasoning that led to the development of Equation 5.8, the inverse of the ratios expressed in Equation 5.13 must necessarily measure the marginal cost of producing goods at any output level. That is, dividing the price of an input by the marginal product of that input is by definition the marginal cost ($MC = \Delta\text{cost}/\Delta\text{output}$) of producing the output that results from use of an additional unit of the input.

$$\frac{P_X}{MP_X} = \frac{P_Y}{MP_Y} = MC_Q. \qquad (5.14)$$

Since marginal cost will equal marginal revenue at the optimal output level, $MC_Q = MR_Q$, Equation 5.14 can be written as the following system of equations:

$$\frac{P_X}{MP_X} = MR_Q,$$

and

$$\frac{P_Y}{MP_Y} = MR_Q.$$

Rearranging produces:

$$P_X = MP_X \cdot MR_Q = MRP_X \tag{5.15}$$

and

$$P_Y = MP_Y \cdot MR_Q = MRP_Y. \tag{5.16}$$

Thus, a firm's profits will be maximized when price equals marginal revenue product for each input. The difference between cost minimization and profit maximization is that cost minimization (optimal input proportions) requires considering only supply-related factors of input prices and marginal productivity, whereas profit maximization requires consideration of these supply-related factors *and* demand-related marginal revenue of output. When a firm employs each input in a production system so that its MRP = Price, it insures that inputs are being combined in optimal proportions *and* that the total level of resource employment is optimal.

Returns to Scale

Thus far our discussion of production has focused on the productivity of an individual input. A closely related topic is the question of how a proportionate increase in *all* the inputs will affect total production. This is a question of *returns to scale,* and there are three possible situations. First, if the proportional increase in output is equal to the proportional increase in all inputs, *returns to scale are constant.* For example, if doubling of all inputs leads to a doubling of output, then returns to scale are constant. Second, the proportional increase in output may be larger than that of the inputs, which is termed *increasing returns to scale.* Third, if output increases less than proportionally with input increases, we have *decreasing returns to scale.*

The returns to scale concept can be clarified by reexamining the production data in Table 5.1. Assume the production system represented by that data is currently operating with 1 unit of Input X and 3 units of Input Y. Production from such an input combination would be 35 units. Suppose we are interested in determining the effect on the quantity of output produced of a 100 percent increase in the quantity of the two

Figure 5.15
Returns to Scale

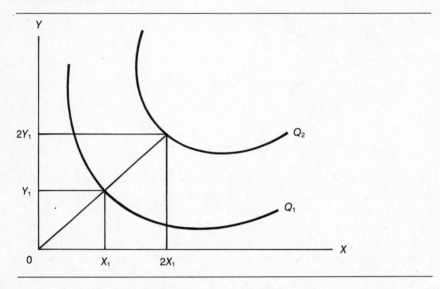

input factors used in the production process. Doubling X and Y results in an input combination where $X = 2$ and $Y = 6$. Output from this input combination would be 72 units. A 100 percent increase in both X and Y increases output by 37 units $(72 - 35)$, a 106 percent increase $(37/35 = 1.06)$. Thus, output increases more than proportionately with the increase in the productive factors. The production system exhibits increasing returns to scale over this range.

The returns to scale of a production system can vary over different levels of input use. Consider, for example, the effect of a 50 percent increase in X and Y from the combination $X = 2$, $Y = 6$. Increasing X by 50 percent results in an employment of 3 units of that factor $(2 \times 1.5 = 3)$, while a 50 percent increase in Y leads to 9 units $(6 \times 1.5 = 9)$ of that input being used. The new input combination results in 89 units of production, and we see that a 50 percent increase in input factors produces only a 24 percent $[(89 - 72)/72 = 0.24]$ increase in output. Since the output increase is less than proportionate to the increase in inputs, the production system exhibits decreasing returns to scale over this range of input use.

Isoquant analysis can be used to examine returns to scale for a two-input, single-output production system. Consider in Figure 5.15 the production of Q_1 units of output using the input combination of $X_1 Y_1$. Doubling both inputs shifts production to Q_2. If Q_2 is precisely twice as large as Q_1, the system is said to exhibit constant returns to scale over the range $X_1 Y_1$ to $X_2 Y_2$. If Q_2 is greater than twice Q_1, returns to scale are increasing, and if Q_2 is less than double Q_1, the system exhibits decreasing returns to scale.

The returns to scale implicit in a given production function can also be examined in terms of two- and three-dimensional graphs such as those drawn in Figures 5.16 through 5.19. In these graphs the slope of a curve drawn from the origin up the production surface indicates whether returns to scale are constant, increasing, or decreasing. In the production system illustrated in Figure 5.16a, for example, a curve drawn from the origin will have a constant slope, indicating that returns to scale are constant. Accordingly, the outputs for given (optimal) combinations of X and Y shown in Figure 5.16b are increasing in exact proportion to increases in X and Y. In Figure 5.17, the backward bending curve from the origin exhibits a constantly increasing slope, indicating increasing returns to scale. The situation is reversed in Figure 5.18, where the production surface is increasing at a decreasing rate, indicating that decreasing returns to scale are present.

A more general specification is for a production function to have first increasing, then decreasing, returns to scale, as is shown in Figure 5.19. The region of increasing returns is attributable to specialization: As output increases, specialized labor can be used and efficient, large scale machinery can be employed in the production process. Beyond some scale of operations, however, not only are further gains from specialization limited but also problems of coordination may begin to in-

Figure 5.16
Constant Returns to Scale

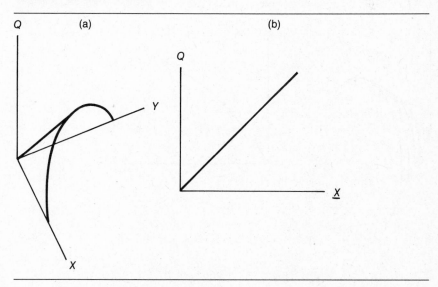

Figure 5.17
Increasing Returns to Scale

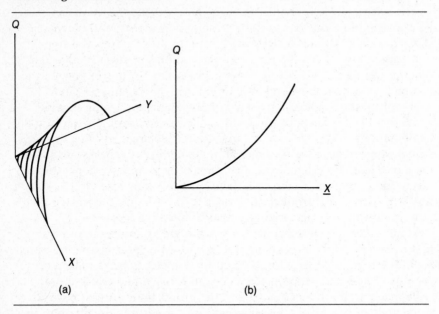

(a)   (b)

Figure 5.18
Decreasing Returns to Scale

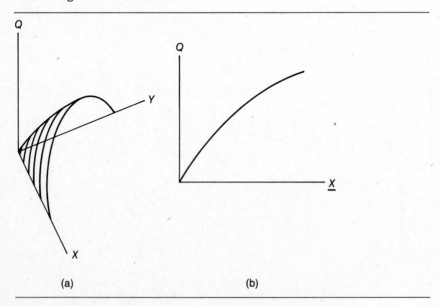

(a)   (b)

Figure 5.19
Variable Returns to Scale

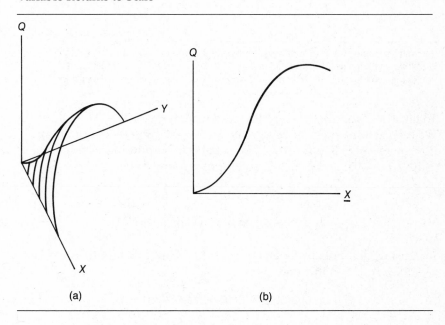

(a)   (b)

crease costs substantially. When coordination expenses more than off-set additional benefits of specialization, decreasing returns to scale set in.

Output Elasticity and Returns to Scale

Whereas graphic representations of returns to scale such as those provided in Figures 5.16, 5.17, and 5.18 are intuitively appealing, returns to scale can be more accurately determined for production functions through an analysis of output elasticities. *Output elasticity, ε_Q, is defined as the percentage change in output associated with a one percent change in all inputs.* Letting $\underline{X}$ represent the entire set of input factors,

$$\varepsilon_Q = \frac{\text{Percentage Change in Output } (Q)}{\text{Percentage Change in All Inputs } (\underline{X})}$$

$$= \frac{\Delta Q/Q}{\Delta \underline{X}/\underline{X}}$$

$$= \frac{\Delta Q}{\Delta \underline{X}} \cdot \frac{\underline{X}}{Q}$$

If we remember that $\underline{X}$ refers to a complete set of input factors, i.e., $\underline{X}$ = capital, labor, energy, etc., then it becomes clear that:

If	then	returns to scale are
Percentage change in Q > Percentage change in $\underline{X}$	$\varepsilon_Q > 1$	increasing
Percentage change in Q = Percentage change in $\underline{X}$	$\varepsilon_Q = 1$	constant
Percentage change in Q < Percentage change in $\underline{X}$	$\varepsilon_Q < 1$	diminishing

To illustrate, consider the production function $Q = 2X + 3Y + 1.5Z$. We can examine the returns to scale for this function by determining how increasing all inputs by 2 percent affects output. Initially, let X = 100, Y = 100, and Z = 100, so output is found to be:

$$Q_1 = 2(100) + 3(100) + 1.5(100)$$

$$= 200 + 300 + 150 = 650 \text{ units.}$$

Increasing all inputs by 2 percent leads to the input quantities $X = 102$, $Y = 102$, and $Z = 102$, and:

$$Q_2 = 2(102) + 3(102) + 1.5(102)$$

$$= 204 + 306 + 153 = 663 \text{ units.}$$

Since a 2 percent increase in all inputs leads to a 2 percent increase in output ($Q_2/Q_1 = 663/650 = 1.02$), the system exhibits constant returns to scale.

Empirical Production Functions

From a theoretical standpoint, the most appealing form of a production function might be a cubic, such as the equation:

$$Q = a + bXY + cX^2Y + dXY^2 - eX^3Y - fXY^3.$$

This form, graphed in Figure 5.19, is general in that it exhibits stages of first increasing and then decreasing returns to scale. Similarly, the marginal products of the input factors also exhibit this pattern of first increasing and then decreasing returns, as was illustrated in Figure 5.6.

Given enough input/output observations, either over time for a single firm or at a point in time for a number of firms in an industry, regression techniques can be used to estimate the parameters of the production function. Frequently, however, the data observations do not exhibit enough dispersion to indicate the full range of increasing and then decreasing returns. In these cases simpler functional specifications can be used to estimate the production function within the range of data available. In other words, the generality of a cubic function may be unnecessary, and an alternative model specification can be used for empirical estimation. The power function described below is one approximation for production functions that has proven extremely useful in empirical studies.

Power Functions

One function commonly employed in production studies is the power function, which indicates a multiplicative relationship between the various inputs and takes the form:

$$Q = aX^b Y^c. \tag{5.17}$$

Power functions have several properties useful in empirical research. First, power functions allow the marginal productivity of a given input to depend upon the levels of all inputs employed, a condition that often holds in actual production systems. Second, they are linear in logarithms and thus can be easily analyzed using linear regression analysis. That is, Equation 5.17 is equivalent to:

$$ln\ Q = ln\ a + b\ ln\ X + c\ ln\ Y. \tag{5.18}$$

The least squares technique can be used to estimate the coefficients of Equation 5.18 and thereby the parameters of Equation 5.17.

Third, power functions facilitate returns to scale estimation. Returns to scale are easily calculated by summing the exponents of the power function (or alternately by summing the loglinear model coefficient estimates). If the sum of the exponents is less than one, diminishing returns are indicated. A sum greater than one indicates increasing returns. If the sum of the exponents is exactly one, returns to scale are constant and the powerful tool of linear programming, described in Chapter 7, can be used to determine the optimal input/output relationships for the firm.

Power functions have been employed in a large number of empirical production studies, particularly since Charles W. Cobb and Paul H. Douglas's pioneering work in the late 1920s. The impact of this work was so great that power production functions are now frequently referred to as Cobb-Douglas production functions.

Selection of a Functional Form
for Empirical Studies

Many other alternative functional forms are available for empirical analysis of production functions. As with empirical demand estimation, the primary determinant of the form of function to use in the empirical model should depend on the relationship hypothesized by the researcher. Selection of the functional form on this basis is difficult, however, and in many instances several alternative model specifications must be fitted to the data to determine which form seems most representative of actual conditions.

Summary

In this chapter we learned that a firm's production function is determined by the technical characteristics of the plant and equipment it employs. It relates inputs to outputs, showing the maximum product obtainable from a given set of inputs.

Several important properties of production systems were examined, including the substitutability of inputs, a characteristic expressed by the marginal rate of substitution, and diminishing returns to factor inputs. The production function was also used to demonstrate that only those input combinations where the marginal products of all input factors are positive need be analyzed to determine the optimal input proportions.

Adding prices to the analysis enabled us to specify the necessary conditions for optimality in input combination. The *least-cost* combination of inputs requires input proportions such that an additional dollar's worth of each input adds as much to total output as does a dollar's worth of any other input. Algebraically, this relationship is given by the expression:

$$\frac{MP_X}{P_X} = \frac{MP_Y}{P_Y}.$$

It was also demonstrated that employment of resources up to the point where the marginal revenue products equaled price resulted not only in least-cost-input combinations but also in *profit maximizing* activity levels. Algebraically this relationship is given by the expressions:

$$MRP_X = P_X,$$

and

$$MRP_Y = P_Y.$$

The question of returns to scale was also examined, and several methods of measuring this property were illustrated. Returns to scale in production plays a major role in determining market structures, a topic examined in Chapters 8, 9, and 10.

Empirical estimation of production functions frequently makes use of regression analysis. While theoretical considerations indicate that cubic equations, with their greater generality, might be preferred for estimation purposes, it was shown that simpler functional forms are often quite adequate for estimation of production relationships over the range of data available. In fact, the power function, or the Cobb-Douglas production function, is by far the most frequently encountered form in empirical work.

Questions

5.1 Given the isoquant diagram illustrated below (in which K^* and L^* indicate the optimal combination for producing Output Q^* as determined by a tangency between an isocost curve and an isoquant curve):

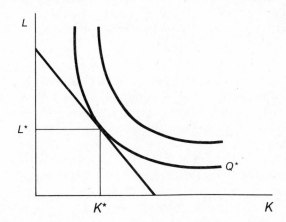

a) What would be the effect of an increase in the relative productivity of labor, L, in this production system on the isocost and the isoquant curves and on the optimal input combination?
b) What would be the effect of a technological change which increased the productivity of capital, K, on the curves and on the combination referred to in part a?
c) What would be the effect of a change that proportionally increases the effectiveness of both capital and labor simultaneously?

5.2 Using a diagram of isoquant and isocost curves like those shown in question 5.1, demonstrate that *both* relative input prices and factor productivity play roles in determining optimal input combinations.

5.3 Is the use of least-cost input combinations a necessary condition for profit maximization? Is it a sufficient condition? Explain.

5.4 A labor economist discussing productivity once argued: "If you worked 2,000 hours last year at a $3.50 per hour wage rate and produced 10,000 widgets, your output per hour was five widgets: total output divided by total hours worked. If you are averaging six widgets an hour this year, your productivity (output per hour) has gone up 20 percent. Assuming a widget sells for $2, the same as last year, and you still get paid $3.50 per hour, your employer's labor cost per widget has gone down from 70¢ to 58¢. The employer gets added profits on each widget and therefore can afford to share the extra profits with the workers."

    a) Under what circumstances would this reasoning be correct?

    b) Assume that last year the firm employed $30,000 in capital equipment per employee and also spent $1 per unit on materials used in the production of widgets. This year the firm has expanded its investment in capital equipment per employee to $40,000 and is now paying $1.083 for materials going into a widget because the supplier of those materials is doing more finishing work, reducing the labor effort necessary to assemble a widget. Does the labor economist's argument hold in this case if one assumes that capital investment has a 10 percent cost? Explain why or why not, and use the data provided to prove your point.

5.5 In our analysis of production relationships, we developed the requirement that marginal product to price ratios must be equal for all inputs in efficient input combinations. Although this is a necessary condition for the optimal employment of input factors, it is not sufficient for determination of the most profitable quantity of a resource to use in a production system.

    a) Explain the above statement. (That is, explain why the MP/P relationship is deficient as a mechanism for determining optimal resource employment levels.)

    b) Develop the appropriate relationship for determining the quantities of all inputs to employ in a production system, and explain its rationale.

5.6 Suppose labor, capital, and energy inputs must be combined in fixed proportions. Does this mean returns to scale will be constant?

Solved Problem

5.1 North Slope Oil Ltd. has designed a pipeline that provides a throughput of 80,000 barrels of oil per 24-hour period. If the diameter of the pipeline were increased by one inch, throughput would increase 5,000 barrels per day. Alternatively, throughput could be increased by 6,000 barrels per day if the original pipe diameter were used with pumps that were 100 horsepower larger.

a) Estimate the marginal rate of technical substitution between pump horsepower and pipe diameter.
b) Assuming the cost of additional pump size is $500 per horse-power and the cost of larger diameter pipe is $100,000 per inch, does the original design exhibit the property required for optimal input combinations? If so, why? If not, why not?

Solution

5.1

a) The marginal rate of technical substitution is calculated by comparing the marginal products of "diameter," MP_D, and "horse-power," MP_H:

$$MP_D = \Delta Q/\Delta D = 5,000/1 = 5,000 \text{ bls.}$$

$$MP_H = \Delta Q/\Delta H = 6,000/100 = 60 \text{ bls.}$$

So,

$$MRTS_{DH} = -\frac{MP_D}{MP_H} = -\frac{5,000}{60}$$

$$\frac{\Delta Q/\Delta D}{\Delta Q/\Delta H} = -83.33$$

$$\frac{\Delta H}{\Delta D} = -83.33,$$

or $\Delta H = -83.33\Delta D$ or $\Delta D = -0.012\Delta H$. This means, for example, that output would remain constant following a one inch reduction in pipe diameter provided horsepower were increased by 83.3.

b) The rule for optimal input proportions is:

$$\frac{MP_D}{P_D} = \frac{MP_H}{P_H}$$

In this instance the question is:

$$\frac{MP_D}{P_D} \overset{?}{=} \frac{MP_H}{P_H}$$

$$\frac{5,000}{\$100,000} \overset{?}{=} \frac{60}{\$500}$$

$$.05 \neq .12$$

Here the additional throughput provided by the last dollar spent on more horsepower (.12 barrels/day) is more than twice the gain in production resulting from the last dollar spent to increase the pipe diameter (.05 barrels/day). Thus, horsepower and pipe diameter are not being employed in optimal proportions in this situation.

Solved Problem

5.2 In 1984, Thermo Insulation Inc. employed 2,500 workers and used 1,000,000 tons of cellulose fiber in its production of insulation products. Its short-run production and marginal product functions relating labor (L) and fiber (F) inputs to insulation are:

$$Q = 2L^{0.5}F^{0.5}$$

$$MP_L = F^{0.5}/L^{0.5}$$

$$MP_F = L^{0.5}/F^{0.5},$$

where insulation output (Q) is measured in tons, labor is measured in number of workers, and fiber is measured in tons. During 1984 the annual wage was $16,000.

a) Determine and interpret returns to scale.

b) Assuming that Thermo employed labor and fiber in optimal cost minimizing proportions, what was the price of fiber during 1984?

c) What is the marginal revenue of Thermo's product if the quantities of labor and energy employed were profit maximizing?

d) How many workers would Thermo employ if a fiber shortage reduced the amount available from 1,000,000 to 810,000 tons? Assume factor and output prices remain constant and that Thermo continues to employ a profit maximizing level of labor. (Assume also that the price of the output is constant so that price and marginal revenue are equal.)

Solution

5.2

a) Initially, let $L = F = 100$ so output is found to be

$$Q = 2(100)^{0.5}(100)^{0.5}$$

$$= 200 \text{ units}$$

Increasing all inputs by 5 percent leads to input quantities

$$L = F = 105$$

and

$$Q = 2(105)^{0.5}(105)^{0.5}$$

$$= 210 \text{ units.}$$

Since a 5 percent increase in all inputs leads to a 5 percent increase in output ($Q2/Q1 = 210/200 = 1.05$), the output elasticity is 1 and the production system exhibits constant returns to scale.

b) If Thermo Insulation employs labor and fiber in optimal proportions, then:

$$\frac{MP_L}{MP_F} = \frac{P_L}{P_F}$$

$$\frac{F^{0.5}/L^{0.5}}{L^{0.5}/F^{0.5}} = \frac{P_L}{P_F}$$

$$\frac{F}{L} = \frac{P_L}{P_F}$$

$$\frac{1,000,000}{2,500} = \frac{16,000}{P_F}$$

$$1,000,000 P_F = 40,000,000$$

$$P_F = \$40 \text{ (per ton)}.$$

c) If the quantities of labor and fiber employed by Thermo Insulation Inc. were optimal (profit maximizing), then the marginal revenue product (MRP) for each input should be equal to its price. Using the fiber input we have

$$MRP_F = P_F$$

$$MP_F \cdot MR = P_F.$$

Since

$$MP_F = L^{0.5}/F^{0.5}$$

$$= 50/1,000$$

$$= 0.05.$$

Then,

$$0.05 \cdot MR = \$40$$

$$MR = \$800.$$

One could find this same result by setting $MRP_L = P_L$.

d) With constant input and output prices, we know that Thermo will use all of the fiber it has available (recall they used one million tons in the unconstrained previous period). The labor input will be used up to the point where its marginal revenue product (MRP)

is equal to its price. With fiber at a 810,000-ton level, the MP of labor is

$$MP_L = F^{0.5}/L^{0.5}$$

$$= (810,000)^{0.5}/L^{0.5}$$

$$= 900/L^{0.5},$$

and

$$MRP_L = MP_L \cdot MR$$

$$= \left(\frac{900}{L^{0.5}}\right) \$800,$$

setting $MRP_L = P_L$ we have

$$\left(\frac{900}{L^{0.5}}\right) \$800 = \$16,000$$

$$\$720,000 = \$16,000 L^{0.5}$$

$$45 = L^{0.5}$$

$$L = 2,025.$$

In this instance, we see that a shortage of fiber input would result in a loss of 475 jobs $(2,500 - 2,025)$.

Problem Set

5.1 The following production table provides estimates of the maximum amounts of output possible with different combinations of two input factors, X and Y. (Assume that these are just illustrative points on a spectrum of continuous input combinations.)

Units of Y Used	Estimated Output per Day				
5	210	305	360	421	470
4	188	272	324	376	421
3	162	234	282	324	360
2	130	188	234	272	305
1	94	130	162	188	210
	1	2	3	4	5
			Units of X Used		

a) Do the two inputs exhibit the characteristics of constant, increasing, or decreasing marginal rates of technical substitution? How do you know?

b) Assuming output sells for $3 per unit, complete the following tables:

	X Fixed at Two Units			
Units of Y Used	Total Product of Y	Marginal Product of Y	Average Product of Y	Marginal Revenue Product of Y
1				
2				
3				
4				
5				

	Y Fixed at Three Units			
Units of X Used	Total Product of X	Marginal Product of X	Average Product of X	Marginal Revenue Product of X
1				
2				
3				
4				
5				

c) Assume the quantity of X is fixed at two units. If the output of the production system sells for $3.00 and the cost of Y is $120 per day, how many units of Y will be employed?

d) Assume that the company is currently producing 162 units of output per day, using 1 unit of X and 3 units of Y. The daily cost per unit of X is $120 and that of Y is also $120. Would you recommend a change in the present input combination? Why or why not?

e) What is the nature of the returns to scale for this production system if the optimal input combination requires that $X = Y$?

5.2 Determine whether the following production functions exhibit constant, increasing, or decreasing returns to scale.

    a) $Q = 0.5X + 2Y + 40Z$.

    b) $Q = 3L + 10K + 500$.

    c) $Q = 4A + 6B + 8AB$.

(continued)

d) $Q = 7L^2 + 5LK + 2K^2.$

e) $Q = 10L^{0.5}K^{0.3}$

5.3 Long Beach Brewery has just introduced a new low-alcoholic beer called LB. Vice President of Marketing Jim Meyer is attempting to determine the optimal level of television advertising for the product. Television ads cost $250,000 per minute and Meyer estimates that the television ad-sales relationship is given by the expression:

$$\text{Sales (Units)} = -5,000 + 130,000A - 5A^2$$

and

$$\Delta \text{ Sales}/\Delta A = 130,000 - 10A.$$

Here A represents a one-minute television ad, and sales are measured in cases of product.

In thinking about this problem, Meyer noted its resemblance to the optimal resource employment problem he had just studied in a managerial economics course that is part of his executive MBA program. The advertising-sales relationship could be thought of as a production function where advertising was an input and "sales" the output. The problem is to determine the profit maximizing level of "employment" for the "input" advertising in this "production" system. Meyer recognized that to solve the problem he needed a measure of output value and he requested a figure for the net marginal revenue of LB. The financial services group told Meyer that sales could be expected to provide a $2 per case net marginal revenue (price minus all marginal costs except advertising).

a) Continuing with Meyer's production analogy, what is the "marginal product" of advertising?

b) What is the rule for determining the optimal amount of a resource to employ in a production system? Explain the logic underlying this rule.

c) Using the rule for optimal resource employment, determine the profit maximizing number of television ads for LB.

5.4 The Big Northern Railway (BNR) is in the process of establishing a natural resource division to develop its vast coal holdings. A preliminary engineering analysis suggests the following production and marginal product functions:

$$Q = 3,000L^{0.5}K^{0.5}$$

$$MP_L = 1,500L^{-0.5}K^{0.5}$$

$$MP_K = 1,500L^{0.5}K^{-0.5},$$

where

$$Q = \text{Coal Output in Tons}$$

$$L = \text{Labor in Number of Employees}$$

$$K = \text{Capital in Millions of Dollars.}$$

At peak production, the natural resources division is expected to employ 10,000 workers and require a $900 million capital investment. Coal output is to be sold in competitive markets at an expected price of $50 per ton.

a) Determine and interpret returns to scale.

b) What is the maximum annual salary the BNR would be willing to pay in order to attract a labor force of 10,000 employees? (Assume a capital investment of $900 million.)

c) Assume BNR makes the capital investment of $900 million and that following the opening of the plant an employee union is successful in forcing the labor wage rate to $25,000. Assuming a constant capital investment level and the firm operates so as to maximize profits, how many jobs would you expect BNR to eliminate?

5.5 Jake Barnes, production manager for the Wayne, New Jersey, operations of Harvestone Cooperatives, has authorized an engineering analysis of the planting, cultivating, and harvesting (PCH) division in order to learn whether or not additional increases in operating efficiency might be possible. In this analysis, production relationships for the PHC division were estimated as:

$$Q = 600L^{0.1}K^{0.1}N^{0.8}$$

$$MP_L = 60L^{-0.9}K^{0.1}N^{0.8}$$

$$MP_K = 60L^{0.1}K^{-0.9}N^{0.8}$$

$$MP_N = 480L^{0.1}K^{0.1}N^{-0.2},$$

where

$$Q = \text{Corn output (in hundreds of bushels)}$$

$$L = \text{Labor input (in worker years)}$$

$$K = \text{Capital investment input (in dollars)}$$

$$N = \text{Land input (in sections, where one section} = 640 \text{ acres).}$$

a) During the coming period, PCH plans to work 24 sections of land and employ 10 workers. Workers earn $19,200 per year and land is leased at an annual rate of $100 per acre. If PCH has a required rate of return on capital of 24 percent, what level of capital investment (in machinery, buildings, and so on) is implied, assuming a profit maximization objective?

b) Would a fall in PCH's required rate of return from 24 to 18 percent have an effect on the number of workers who would be employed in the short run, assuming levels of both K and N remain constant?

5.6 Financial Planning Services advises individuals on investment and tax matters. The primary resources employed by FPS are skilled financial planners and computers. FPS financial planners cost the firm $50 per hour. Computer time is purchased on a time-sharing basis for $200 per hour.

Currently FPS employs ten financial planners and purchases an average of 100 hours of computer time each week. Each financial planner works a 40-hour week. This level of employment allows FPS to complete 100 financial analyses per week. The firm receives $600 for each analysis.

FPS is operating at capacity, and the president of the firm is considering using financial planners on an overtime basis to increase output. Overtime will cost FPS $100 per employee hour, but additional computer time is available at an off-peak rate of $100 per hour. The president estimates that rather than the standard 4 hours of labor (financial planner time) and 1 hour of computer time currently being used, it would be possible to process additional financial evaluations, using 3 hours of labor and 2.5 hours of computer support.

a) Assuming that both returns to factors and returns to scale are constant, what are the marginal products for (1) financial planners and (2) computer time (up to the full capacity level)?

b) Is FPS employing financial planners and computers in an optimal ratio, assuming that substitution of the resources is possible? Explain.

c) Determine the marginal revenue products for financial planners and for the computer services employed by FPS. (Use the assumption of constant returns to factors in part a.)

d) Is FPS employing an optimal (profit maximizing) quantity of labor and computer time? Explain.

e) Assuming that financial planner time and computer time are continuously substitutable and that the combination being considered for overtime work is just one of many possible combinations, is the overtime input ratio a cost minimizing combination or is there a better one? Explain.

f) Assuming now that the overtime combination being considered, i.e., 3 hours of labor and 2.5 hours of computer time for each individual financial analysis, is the *only* possible overtime combination, would it be profitable for the firm to use overtime to conduct more financial analyses? Explain.

g) Assuming additional financial planners were available for employment during the day at the current wage of $50 per hour and additional computer time could be purchased for $200 per hour, would you still recommend the overtime option?

References

Balke, Thomas R. "Some Applications of Productivity Analysis to the Petroleum Industry." *Omega* 11 (1983): 329–341.

Christiansen, Gregory B. and Haveman, Robert H. "Public Regulations and the Slowdown in Productivity Growth." *American Economic Review* 71 (May 1981): 320–325.

Comitini, Salvatore and Huang, David S. "A Study of Production and Factor Shares in the Halibut Fishing Industry." *Journal of Political Economy* 75 (August 1967): 366–372.

Doll, John P. and Orazem, Frank. *Production Economics.* 2d ed. New York: John Wiley, 1984.

Douglas, Paul H. "Are There Laws of Production?" *American Economic Review* 38 (March 1948): 1–41.

Griliches, Zvi. "R&D and the Productivity Slowdown." *American Economic Review* 70 (May 1980): 343–348.

Kendrick, John W. *Improving Company Productivity.* Baltimore: Johns Hopkins University, 1983.

Kendrick, John W. and Vaccara, Beatrice N., eds. *New Developments in Productivity Measurement and Analysis.* Chicago: University of Chicago Press, 1980.

Levitan, Sar A. and Werneke, Diane. *Productivity: Problems, Prospects and Policies.* Baltimore: Johns Hopkins University, 1984.

Lloyd, P. J. "Why Do Firms Produce Multiple Outputs?" *Journal of Economic Behavior and Organization* 4 (March 1983): 41–51.

Nadiri, M. Ishaq and Schankerman, M. A. "Technical Change, Returns to Scale, and the Productivity Slowdown." *American Economic Review* 71 (May 1981): 314–319.

Rees, Albert. "Improving Productivity Measurement." *American Economic Review* 70 (May 1980): 340–342.

Scherer, F. M.; Beckenstein, Alan; Kaufer, Erich; Murphy, R. Dennis and Bougeon-Maassen, Francine. *The Economics of Multi-Plant Operation.* Cambridge: Harvard University Press, 1975.

Teece, David J. "Towards an Economic Theory of the Multiproduct Firm." *Journal of Economic Behavior and Organization* 3 (March 1982): 39–63.

Walters, A. A. "Production and Cost Functions: An Econometric Survey." *Econometrica* 31 (January–April 1963): 1–66.

Chapter 6

Cost Analysis

Key Terms

Cost-volume-profit
    analysis
Economies of scale
Explicit cost
Implicit cost
Incremental cost
Learning curve

Long-run cost
Minimum efficient
    scale
Opportunity cost
Relevant cost
Short-run cost

Cost analysis plays a central role in managerial economics because every managerial decision requires a comparison between costs and benefits. For example, a decision to expand output requires that the increased revenues derived from added sales be compared with the higher production costs incurred. Likewise, a decision to expand capital assets requires a comparison between the revenues expected from the investment and the cost of funds to acquire the new assets. The expected benefits of an advertising program must be compared with the costs of the program. A decision to pave the employees' parking lot or refurbish the company lunchroom requires a comparison between the project costs and the benefits expected to result from improved morale and productivity. In each case, appropriate decision analysis requires a comparison between the costs and benefits resulting from the decision.

In this chapter we examine a number of cost concepts, including alternative (or opportunity) costs, explicit versus implicit costs, marginal costs, incremental costs, and sunk costs. Further, we relate production costs to production functions and develop long-run and short-run cost functions suitable for empirical measurement. The materials in this chapter are useful for managerial decisions; they also help one to understand how various industry structures develop and to see some of the implications of public policy designed to alter the structure of industry.

Relevant Cost Concept

The term *cost* can be defined in a number of ways, and the correct definition varies from situation to situation, depending upon how the cost figure is to be used. Cost generally refers to the price that must be paid for an item. If we buy a product for cash and use it immediately, no problems arise in defining and measuring its cost. However, if the item is purchased, stored for a time, and then used, complications will arise. The problem is even more acute if the item is a long-lived asset that will be used at varying rates for some indeterminate period. What then is the cost of using the asset during any given period?

The cost figure that should be used in a specific application is defined as the **relevant cost**. When calculating costs for use in completing a firm's income tax returns, accountants are required by law to list the actual dollar amounts spent to purchase the labor, raw materials, and capital equipment used in production. Thus, for tax purposes actual historical dollar outlays are the relevant costs. This is also true for Securities and Exchange Commission reports and for reports of profits to stockholders.

For managerial decisions, however, historical costs may not be appropriate; generally, current and projected future costs are more relevant than historical outlays. For example, consider a construction firm that has an inventory of 1,000 tons of steel purchased at a price of $250 a ton. Steel prices now double to $500 a ton. If the firm is asked to bid on a project, what cost should it assign to the steel used in the job, the $250 historical cost or the $500 current cost? The answer is the current cost. The firm must pay $500 to replace the steel it uses, and it can sell the steel for $500 if it elects not to use it on the proposed job. Therefore, $500 is the *relevant cost* of steel for purposes of bidding on the job. Note, however, that the cost of steel for tax purposes is still the $250 historical cost.

Similarly, if a firm owns a piece of equipment that has been fully depreciated (that is, its accounting book value is zero), it cannot assume that the cost of using the machine is zero. If the machine could be sold for $1,000 now, but its market value is expected to be only $200 one year from now, the relevant cost of using the machine for one additional year is $800.[1] Again, there is little relationship between the $800 true cost of using the machine and the zero cost that would be reported on the firm's income statement.

Opportunity Costs

The preceding discussion of relevant costs is based upon an alternative-use concept. Economic resources have value because they can be used to produce goods and services for consumption. When a firm uses a resource for producing a particular product, it bids against alternative users. Thus, the firm must offer a price at least as great as the resource's value in an alternative use. The cost of aluminum used in the manufacture of airplanes, for example, is determined by its value in alternative uses. An airplane manufacturer must pay a price equal to this value or the aluminum will be used to produce alternative goods, such as cookware, automobiles, building materials, and so on. Similarly, if a firm owns capital equipment that can be used to produce either Product A or Product B, the relevant cost of producing A includes the profit of the alternative Product B that cannot be produced because the equipment is tied up manufacturing Product A.

The **opportunity cost** concept, then, reflects the fact that all decisions are based on choices between alternative actions. The cost of a resource is determined by its value in its best alternative use.

Explicit and Implicit Costs

Typically, the costs of using resources in production involve both out-of-pocket or **explicit costs** plus other noncash costs called **implicit costs**. Wages paid, utility expenses, payment for raw materials, interest paid to the holders of the firm's bonds, and rent on a building are all examples of explicit expenses. The implicit costs associated with any decision are much more difficult to compute. These costs do not involve cash expenditures and are therefore often overlooked in decision analysis. The rent a farmer could receive on buildings and fields if he did

---

[1] This statement contains a slight oversimplification. Actually, the cost of using the machine for one year is the current value minus the discounted present value of its value one year hence. This adjustment is necessary to account for the fact that dollars received in the future have a lower *present* worth than dollars received today.

not use them is an implicit cost of his own farming activities, as is the salary he could receive by working for someone else instead of operating his own farming enterprise.

An example should clarify these cost distinctions. Consider the costs associated with the purchase and operation of a Mother Baker's Pie Shop. The franchise can be bought for $25,000, and an additional $25,000 working capital is needed for operating purposes. Jones has personal savings of $50,000 that he can invest in such an enterprise; Smith, another possible franchisee, must borrow the entire $50,000 at a cost of 15 percent, or $7,500 a year. Assume that operating costs are the same no matter who owns the shop, and that Smith and Jones are equally competent to manage it. Does Smith's $7,500 annual interest expense mean that her costs of operating the shop are greater than those of Jones? For managerial decision purposes the answer is no. Even though Smith has higher explicit costs because of the interest on the loan, the true financing cost, implicit as well as explicit, might well be the same for both individuals. Jones has an implicit cost equal to the amount he can earn on his $50,000 in some alternative use. If he can obtain a 15 percent return by investing in other assets of equal risk, then Jones's opportunity cost of putting his own $50,000 in the pie shop is $7,500 a year. In this case, Smith and Jones each have a financing cost of $7,500 a year, with Smith's cost being explicit and Jones's implicit.

Can we then say that the total cost of operating the shop will be identical for both individuals? Not necessarily. Just as the implicit cost of Jones's capital must be included in the analysis, so, too, must be the implicit cost of management. If Jones is a journeyman baker earning $18,000 a year and Smith is a master baker earning $25,000 annually, the implicit cost of management will not be equal for the two. The implicit management expense for Smith is equal to her value in her best alternative use, the $25,000 she would earn as a master baker. Jones, on the other hand, has an opportunity cost of only $18,000. Thus, Smith's relevant total costs of owning and operating the shop will be $7,000 greater than those of Jones.

Incremental and Sunk Costs in Decision Analysis

The relevant-cost concept also entails the idea of incremental cost. This means that for any decision the relevant costs are limited to those that are affected by the decision. This definition of **incremental costs** as costs that vary with the decision is very much like the marginal concept, which was introduced as a key component in the optimization process. One must take care to recognize, however, that these two concepts, while related, have significant differences. The primary distinction is that marginal costs are always defined in terms of unitary changes in output. The incremental cost concept is considerably broader, encompassing not only the marginal cost concept but also cost variations that arise from any aspect of the decision problem. For example, we can speak of the incremental costs of introducing a new product line or changing the production system used to produce the current product(s) of a firm.

The incremental cost concept means that fixed costs which will not be affected by a decision are irrelevant and should not be included in the analysis. Consider, for example, a firm that refuses to sell excess computer time for $300 an hour because it figures its cost as $350 per hour, calculated by adding a standard overhead cost of $150 an hour to an incremental operating cost of $200 an hour. The relevant cost is only $200, so the firm foregoes a $100 per hour contribution to profit by not selling its excess time. Adding a standard allocated charge for fixed costs and overhead which are not affected by a decision entails the risk of rejecting profitable opportunities or choosing a less satisfactory alternative.

Care must also be exercised to insure against incorrectly assigning a low incremental cost to a decision when in fact a higher cost prevails. This frequently happens to firms faced with temporary reductions in demand resulting in excess production capacity. Such firms often accept contracts with prices that are sufficient to cover operating expenses, but do not fully cover all overhead and provide a normal profit margin. The firm accepts on the grounds that the contract price appears to exceed incremental costs and thus provides a contribution to total overhead and profit. After accepting, other business picks up. Soon the firm is faced with turning away more profitable business or incurring higher production costs, perhaps increasing fixed costs. In this situation the true incremental costs include the increased production costs of other business or perhaps the forgone profit of business that must be turned down due to capacity constraints. It is important to remember that incremental costs include *all* costs that are affected by the decision. This means that future costs as well as current costs must be considered and opportunity costs cannot be ignored.

Inherent in the incremental cost concept is the principle that any cost which is not affected by the decision is an irrelevant cost for purposes of that decision. Costs which are invariant across the alternatives are labeled *sunk costs*, as they play no role in determining the optimal course of action. For example, if a firm has unused warehouse space that will otherwise stand idle, the cost of storing a new product in it will be will be zero, and zero is the incremental storage cost that should be considered in deciding whether to produce the new product. Similarly, a firm may have spent $5,000 on an option which permits it to purchase land for a new factory at a price of $100,000. Later it may be offered another equally usable site for $98,000. The $5,000 is a sunk cost which will not be affected by the decision as to which piece of property is acquired, and it should not enter into the analysis.

To understand this, consider the alternatives available at the time the firm is faced with the decision to purchase the original property or to acquire the second property. If the firm proceeds with the purchase of the first property, it will have to pay a price of $100,000. The newly offered property will require an expenditure of $98,000. These are the relevant costs for the decision, and, obviously, purchase of the $98,000 property results in a $2,000 savings as compared to the original property. The $5,000 paid for the original option is an expense that will not be affected by the decision at this time. It is a sunk cost which is invariant regardless of which property is actually acquired.

Because of the frequency with which sunk costs are incorrectly treated in managerial decision making, another example should prove worthwhile. Assume that a firm is offered a contract for $10,000 to construct the heating and air-conditioning ducts in a new building. The labor and other operating expenses for the job are estimated to be $7,000. The firm has all the materials required to complete the work in its inventory. Assume that the materials (primarily sheet metal) originally cost the firm $4,000 but that price declines have resulted in a current market value of $2,500. The market for sheet metal is not likely to change in the near future, so no gains are expected from holding the materials in inventory. Should the firm accept the contract?

Correct analysis of this contract proposal requires that one recognize that the $4,000 original cost for the materials in inventory is a sunk cost; it will not be affected by the decision. The firm has suffered a $1,500 loss in inventory value regardless of whether or not it accepts the contract. The relevant materials cost is the current market value of the sheet metal ($2,500). Including this cost in the analysis leads one to the correct decision, which is to accept the contract since it results in a $500 gain for the firm.

In managerial decision making, care must be exercised to insure that only costs that are actually affected by the decision are included in the analysis. The incremental costs associated with a given course of action can include both implicit and explicit costs. If a decision entails long-run commitments, any future costs stemming from those commitments must be accounted for. Any cost that is not affected by the decision alternatives available to a manager is a sunk cost and is irrelevant for purposes of that decision.

Short-Run and Long-Run Costs

Proper use of the relevant-cost concept for output and pricing decisions requires an understanding of the relationship between a firm's cost and output, or its *cost function*. Cost functions are dependent (1) on the firm's production function and (2) on the market supply function for its inputs. The production function specifies the technical relationship between inputs and the output, and when, combined with the prices of inputs, determines the cost function. Two basic cost functions are used in managerial decision making: **short-run cost** functions, used in most day-to-day operating decisions, and **long-run cost** functions, typically used for long-range planning.

How does one distinguish the short run from the long run? The short run is defined as a period during which some inputs of a firm are fixed. In the long run the firm can increase, decrease, or otherwise alter *all* factors of production without restriction. Thus, in the short-run period the firm's decisions are constrained by prior capital expenditures and other commitments; in the long run no such restrictions exist. For a public accounting firm operating out of a rented office, this period of constraint might be as short as several weeks, the time remaining on the office lease. A steel company, on the other hand, has a substantial investment in long-lived fixed assets, and until existing assets wear out and are replaced, its production and cost functions will be constrained.

In addition to the economic life of a firm's assets, their degree of specialization will also affect the period during which decisions are constrained. Consider, for example, a drugstore's purchase of an automobile for making deliveries. If the car is a standard model without modifications, it is essentially an unspecialized input factor; the car has a resale market consisting of the used-car market in general, and the pharmacy can sell it readily without an undue price reduction. If, however, the pharmacy has modified the car by adding refrigeration equipment for transporting perishable drugs, the car is a more specialized resource and its resale market is limited to those individuals and firms who need a vehicle containing refrigeration equipment. In this case, the market price of the car might not equal its value in use to the pharmacy; hence, the short run is extended. We see, then, that at one extreme a firm operating with perfectly unspecialized factors has a very brief short run; it can adjust to changes almost immediately by disposing of or purchasing assets in well-established markets. At the other extreme, when a firm employs highly specialized factors, no ready market exists; and the firm's short run extends for the entire economic life of the resources it currently owns.

The length of time required to order, receive, and install new assets also influences the duration of the short run. Electric utilities, for example, frequently require eight or more years to bring new generating plants on line, and this obviously extends their short-run time horizon.

In summary, the long run is a period of sufficient length to permit a company to change its productive facilities completely by adding, subtracting, or modifying assets. The short run is the period during which at least some of the firm's productive inputs cannot be altered. From this it is easy to see why long-run cost curves are often called *planning curves* and short-run curves *operating curves*. In the long run, plant and equipment are variable, so management can plan the most efficient physical plant, given an estimate of the firm's demand function. Once the optimal plant has been determined and the resulting investment in equipment has been made, operating decisions will be constrained by these prior decisions.

Fixed and Variable Costs

Costs that are invariant with respect to output are defined as *fixed costs*. Included are interest on borrowed capital, rental expense on leased plant and equipment, depreciation charges associated with the passage of time, property taxes, and salaries of employees who would not be laid off during periods of reduced activity. Since all costs are variable in the long run, the fixed-cost concept is limited to short-run analysis.

Variable costs vary with changes in output; they are a function of the output level. Included are such costs as raw materials expense, depreciation associated with the use of equipment, the variable portion of utility charges, some labor costs, sales commissions, and the costs of all other inputs that vary with output. In the long run, all costs are variable.

Such a sharp distinction between fixed and variable costs is not always realistic. A president's salary may be fixed for most purposes, but if a firm went into a really severe downturn this so-called fixed cost could certainly be reduced. Similarly, supervisors' wages might be fixed within a certain range of outputs, but below a lower limit supervisors might be laid off, and above an upper limit additional supervisors would be hired. Also, the longer the duration of abnormal demand, the greater the likelihood that some "fixed" costs will actually be varied.

This recognition that certain costs are fixed only if output stays within prescribed limits, and that other costs can and will be varied if changed conditions are expected to persist, led to the development of the *semivariable cost* concept. In incremental cost analysis, it is essential that one consider the possibility of semivariable costs, which are fixed if incremental output does not exceed certain limits, but are variable outside these bounds.

Short-Run Cost Curves

Short-run total cost curves are constructed to reflect optimal, or least cost, input combinations for producing output *given a specific plant size*. For a currently existing plant, the short-run cost curve illustrates the minimum costs required to produce at various output levels and, therefore, can be used to guide the current operating decisions of the firm.

Both fixed and variable costs affect the short-run costs of a firm. Total cost at each output level is the sum of total fixed costs (a constant) and total variable costs. Using *TC* to represent total cost, *TFC* for total fixed cost, *TVC* for total variable cost, and *Q* for the quantity of output produced, various unit costs are calculated as follows:

$$\text{Average Fixed Cost} = AFC = \frac{TFC}{Q}$$

$$\text{Average Variable Cost} = AVC = \frac{TVC}{Q}$$

$$\text{Average Total Cost} = ATC = \frac{TC}{Q} = AFC + AVC$$

$$\text{Marginal Cost} = MC = \frac{\Delta TC}{\Delta Q} = \frac{\Delta TVC}{\Delta Q}.$$

These cost relationships are illustrated in Table 6.1 and Figure 6.1. Using the data in Table 6.1, one can both verify the various cost relationships defined above, and examine some important cost behavior. For example, note that *TFC* is invariant with increases in output and that *TVC* at each output is equal to the sum of the *MC* up to that output.

Table 6.1
Short-Run Cost Relationships

Q	TC	TFC	TVC	ATC	AFC	AVC	MC
1	120	100	20	120	100	20	20
2	138	100	38	69	50	19	18
3	151	100	51	50.3	33.3	17	13
4	162	100	62	40.5	25	15.5	11
5	175	100	75	35	20	15	13
6	190	100	90	31.7	16.7	15	15
7	210	100	110	30	14.3	15.7	20
8	234	100	134	29.2	12.5	16.7	24
9	263	100	163	29.2	11.1	18.1	29
10	300	100	200	30	10	20	37

Figure 6.1
Short-Run Cost Curves

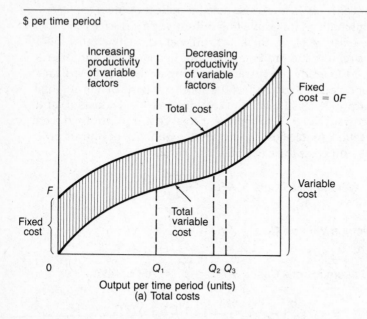

$ per time period

Increasing productivity of variable factors

Decreasing productivity of variable factors

Fixed cost = 0F

Total cost

F

Variable cost

Fixed cost

Total variable cost

0   Q_1 Q_2 Q_3

Output per time period (units)
(a) Total costs

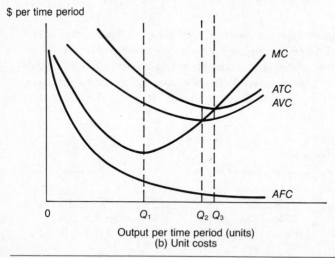

$ per time period

MC

ATC
AVC

AFC

0   Q_1 Q_2 Q_3

Output per time period (units)
(b) Unit costs

Marginal cost is the change in cost associated with a *change* in output and because fixed costs are invariant with respect to output, fixed costs do not affect marginal costs. The data also show that *AFC* decline continuously with increases in output and that *ATC* and *AVC* decline so long as they exceed *MC*, but increase when they are less than *MC*.

These cost relationships are also shown in Figure 6.1. In Figure 6.1a total cost and total variable cost curves are illustrated. The corresponding unit curves are shown in Figure 6.1b. Again, several important cost relationships are illustrated in the figure. First, the shape of the total cost curve is determined entirely by the total variable cost curve. That is, the slope of the total cost curve at each output level is identical to the slope of the total variable cost curve; fixed costs merely shift the total cost curve to a higher level. This means that marginal costs are totally independent of fixed cost.

Second, the shape of the total variable cost curve, and hence the total cost curve, is largely determined by the productivity of the variable input factors employed. Note that the variable cost curve in Figure 6.1 increases first at a decreasing rate, up to output level Q_1, and then at an increasing rate. Assuming constant input factor prices, this implies that the marginal productivity of variable production inputs is first increasing, then decreasing. In other words, the variable input factors exhibit increasing returns in the range of 0 to Q_1 units and diminishing returns thereafter. This relationship is not unexpected. A firm's fixed factors, its plant and equipment, are designed to operate at some specific production level. Operating below that output level requires input combinations in which fixed factors are underutilized. In this output range, production can be increased more than proportionately to increases in variable inputs. At higher than planned output levels, however, fixed factors are being more intensively utilized, the law of diminishing returns takes over, and a given percentage increase in the variable inputs will result in a smaller relative increase in output.

This relationship between short-run costs and the productivity of variable input factors is also revealed by the unit cost curves. Marginal cost declines initially, over the range of increasing productivity, and rises thereafter. This imparts the familiar U shape to the average variable cost and average total cost curves. Notice also that the marginal cost curve first declines rapidly in relation to the average variable cost curve and the average total cost curve, then turns up and intersects each of these curves at its respective minimum point.[2]

Long-Run Cost Curves

In the long run the firm has no fixed commitments and, accordingly, all long-run costs are variable. Additionally, just as short-run cost curves

---

[2]The relationships among total, average, and marginal curves were discussed in Chapter 2, where we explained why the marginal cost curve intersects the average variable cost curve and the average total cost curve at their minimum points.

assume optimal, or least-cost, input combinations for producing any level of output, *given a specific scale of plant*, long-run cost curves are constructed on the assumption that an optimal plant, *given existing technology*, is used to produce any given output level. *Existing technology* refers to the state of knowledge and abilities in the industry. If technological improvements occur, as in the development of more efficient smelting processes in a foundry, the old production and cost functions no longer exist; they are replaced by new functions, which can be quite different from the old ones.

Long-run cost curves reveal both the nature of returns to scale and optimal, or preferred, plant sizes. Thus, long-run cost curves are used to guide a firm's planning decisions.

Long-Run Total Costs

If the prices of a firm's inputs are not affected by the amount of the resource purchased, a *direct* relationship exists between cost and production. Consider a production function that exhibits constant returns to scale, as was illustrated in Figure 5.16. Such a production function is linear, and a doubling of inputs leads to a doubling of output. With constant input prices, a doubling of inputs doubles their total cost, producing a linear total cost function, as is illustrated in Figure 6.2.

Figure 6.2
Total Cost Function for a Production System Exhibiting
***Constant* Returns to Scale**

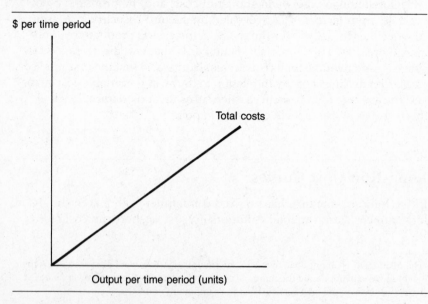

Figure 6.3
Total Cost Function for a Production System Exhibiting
Decreasing **Returns to Scale**

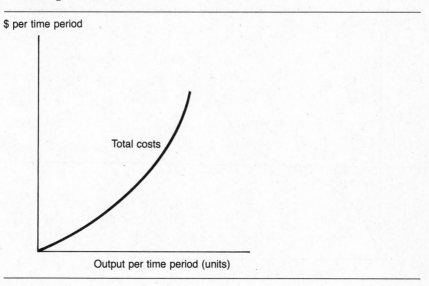

If a firm's production function is subject to decreasing returns to scale, as was illustrated in Figure 5.18, inputs must more than double in order to double output. Again, assuming constant input prices, the cost function associated with a production system of this kind will rise at an increasing rate, as is shown in Figure 6.3.

A production function exhibiting first increasing and then decreasing returns to scale was shown in Figure 5.19. This production function is shown again along with its implied cubic cost function in Figure 6.4. Here costs increase less than proportionately with output over the range where returns to scale are increasing, but more than proportionately after decreasing returns set in.

All the direct relationships between production and cost functions described above are based on constant input prices. If input prices are a function of output, owing to such factors as discounts for volume purchases or, alternatively, to higher prices with greater usage because of a limited supply of inputs, the cost function will reflect this fact. For example, the cost function of a firm with constant returns to scale, but whose input prices increase with quantity purchased, will take the shape shown in Figure 6.3. Costs will rise more than proportionately as output increases. Quantity discounts, on the other hand, will produce a cost function that increases at a decreasing rate, as in the increasing returns section of Figure 6.4.

Figure 6.4
Total Cost Function for a Production System Exhibiting
Increasing **Then** *Decreasing* **Returns to Scale**

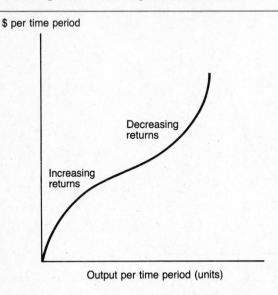

Output per time period (units)

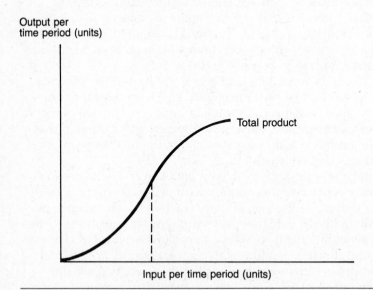

We see, then, that while cost and production are related, the nature of input prices must be examined before we attempt to relate a cost function to the underlying production function. Input prices and productivity jointly determine the total cost function.

Returns to Scale

Many factors combine to produce this pattern of first increasing, then decreasing returns to scale.[3] **Economies of scale**, which cause long-run average costs to decline, result from both production and market relationships. Specialization in the use of labor is one important factor that results in economies of scale. In the small firm workers will probably have several jobs, and their proficiency at any of them is likely to be less than that of employees who specialize in a single task. Thus, labor productivity is frequently greater in the large firm, where individuals can be hired to perform specialized tasks. This reduces the unit cost of production for large-scale operation.

Technological factors also lead to economies of scale. As with labor, large-scale operations typically permit the use of highly specialized equipment, as opposed to the more versatile but less efficient machines used in smaller firms. Also, the productivity of equipment frequently increases with size much faster than does its cost. For example, a 500,000-kilowatt electricity generator costs considerably less than twice as much as a 250,000-kilowatt generator, and it also requires less than twice the fuel and labor inputs when operated at capacity.

The existence of quantity discounts also leads to economies through large-scale purchasing of raw materials, supplies, and other inputs. These economies extend to the cost of capital, as large firms typically have greater access to capital markets and can acquire funds at lower rates. These factors and many more lead to increasing returns to scale and thus to decreasing average costs. At some output level economies of scale typically no longer hold, and average costs level out or begin to rise. Increasing average costs at high output levels are often attributed to limitations in the ability of management to coordinate an organization after it reaches a very large size. This means both that staffs tend to grow more than proportionately with output, causing unit costs to rise, and that managements become less efficient as size increases, again raising the cost of producing a product. While the existence of such diseconomies of scale is questioned by some researchers, the evidence indicates that diseconomies may be significant in certain industries.

Cost Elasticities. Although Figures 6.2, 6.3, and 6.4 are useful for illustrating the total cost and output relation to returns to scale, it is often

---

[3]The terms *economies of scale* and *returns to scale* are often used interchangeably.

easier to calculate scale economies for a given production system by considering cost elasticities. *Cost elasticity, ε_c, measures the percentage change in total costs associated with a 1 percent change in output.*

Algebraically the elasticity of cost with respect to output is:

$$\varepsilon_c = \frac{\text{Percentage Change in Cost } (C)}{\text{Percentage Change in Output } (Q)}$$

$$= \frac{\Delta C/C}{\Delta Q/Q}$$

$$= \frac{\Delta C}{\Delta Q} \cdot \frac{Q}{C}.$$

Cost elasticity is related to economies of scale as follows:

If	then	returns to scale are
Percentage Change in C < Percentage Change in Q	$\varepsilon_c < 1$	Increasing
Percentage Change in C = Percentage Change in Q	$\varepsilon_c = 1$	Constant
Percentage Change in C > Percentage Change in Q	$\varepsilon_c > 1$	Decreasing

With a cost elasticity of less than one ($\varepsilon_c < 1$), costs increase at a slower rate than output. Given constant input prices, this would imply a higher output-to-input ratio and increasing returns to scale. If $\varepsilon_c = 1$, then output and costs increase proportionately, and constant returns to scale are implied. And finally, if $\varepsilon_c > 1$, then for any increase in output, costs increase by a greater relative amount, implying decreasing returns to scale.[4]

Long-Run Average Costs

Additional insight into both scale economies and the relationship between long-run and short-run costs can be obtained by examining long-run average cost (LRAC) curves. Since short-run cost curves relate costs and output for a specific scale of plant and long-run cost curves identify optimal scales of plant for each production level, LRAC curves can be thought of as an envelope of the short-run average cost curves (SRAC). This concept is illustrated in Figure 6.5, where four short-

---

[4]To prevent confusion concerning the relationship between cost elasticity and returns to scale we remind the reader that there is an *inverse* relationship between costs and scale economies and a *direct* relationship between resource usage and scale economies. Thus, although $\varepsilon_C < 1$ implies increasing returns to scale, recall from Chapter 5 that an output elasticity *greater* than one ($\varepsilon_Q > 1$) also implies increasing returns to scale. Similarly, decreasing returns to scale are implied by $\varepsilon_C > 1$ and by $\varepsilon_Q < 1$.

Figure 6.5
Short-Run Cost Curves for Four Scales of Plant

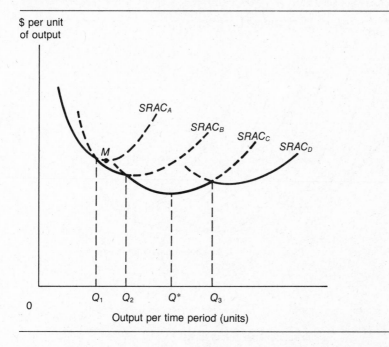

run average cost curves representing four different scales of plant are shown. The four plants each have a range of output for which they are most efficient. Plant A, for example, provides the least-cost production system for output in the range 0 to Q_1 units; Plant B provides the least-cost system for output in the range Q_1 to Q_2; Plant C is most efficient for output quantities Q_2 to Q_3; Plant D provides the least-cost production process for output above Q_3.

The solid portion of each curve in Figure 6.5 indicates the minimum long-run average cost for producing each level of output, assuming only four possible scales of plant. We can generalize this by assuming that plants of many sizes, each one only slightly larger than the preceding one, are possible. As shown in Figure 6.6, the long-run average cost curve is then constructed so that it is tangent to each short-run average cost curve. At each tangency, the related scale of the plant is optimal; no other plant will produce that particular level of output at so low a total cost. The cost systems illustrated in Figures 6.5 and 6.6 display first increasing, then decreasing returns to scale. Over the range of output produced by Plants A, B, and C in Figure 6.5, average costs are declining; these declining costs mean that total costs are increasing less than proportionately with output. Since Plant D's minimum cost is

Figure 6.6
Long-Run Average Cost Curve as the Envelope of
Short-Run Average Cost Curves

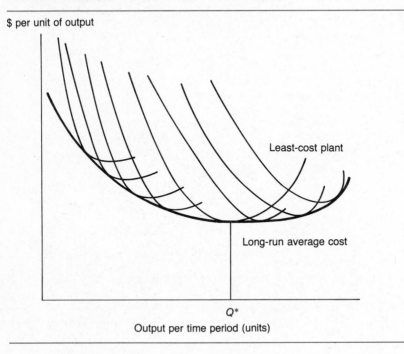

$ per unit of output

Least-cost plant

Long-run average cost

Q^*

Output per time period (units)

greater than that for Plant C, the system exhibits decreasing returns to scale at this higher output level.

Production systems that reflect first increasing, then constant, then diminishing returns to scale result in U-shaped long-run average cost curves such as that illustrated in Figure 6.6. Notice that with a U-shaped long-run average cost curve, the most efficient plant for each output level will typically not be operating where its short-run average costs are minimized, as can be seen by referring to Figure 6.5. Plant A's short-run average cost curve is minimized at Point M, but at that output Plant B is more efficient; that is, B's short-run average costs are lower. In general, where increasing returns to scale exist, the least-cost plant for an output level will operate at less than full capacity.[5] Only for that single output level at which long-run average cost is minimized, Out-

---

[5] We define *capacity* not as a physical limitation on output but rather as the point where short-run average costs are minimized. We should note that businesspersons and business writers use the term in many different ways, so its economic interpretation is not always obvious.

put Q^* in Figures 6.5 and 6.6, will the optimal plant be operating at the minimum point on its short-run average cost curve. At all outputs in the range where decreasing returns to scale exist, that is, at any output greater than Q^*, the most efficient plant will be operating at an output slightly greater than its capacity.

Minimum Efficient Scale

The shape of long-run average cost curves is important not only because of its implications for plant scale decisions, but also because it affects the potential level of competition that will emerge in an industry. Although U-shaped cost relationships are quite common, they are not universal. In some industries, first increasing, then constant returns to scale are encountered. In such industries, an L-shaped long-run average cost curve emerges, and larger plants are at no relative cost disadvantage vis-a-vis smaller plants. Typically, the number of competitors and ease of entry will be greater within industries with U-shaped long-run average cost curves than where L-shaped or downward sloping long-run average cost curves exist. Insight in this area is gained by examining the concept of the **minimum efficient scale** (MES) of plant. *MES is defined as the output level where long-run average costs are first minimized.* Thus, MES will be found at the minimum point on a U-shaped long-run average cost curve (output Q^* in Figures 6.5 and 6.6), and at the corner of an L-shaped long-run average cost curve.

Generally speaking, the number of competitors will be large and competition will tend to be most vigorous within industries where MES is small relative to total industry demand because of correspondingly minor barriers to entry such as those relating to capital investment and skilled labor requirements. Competition can be less vigorous when MES is large because barriers to entry tend to be correspondingly substantial, limiting the number of potential competitors. In considering the competitive impact of a given MES level, we must always consider the overall size of the industry. Some industries are large enough that substantial numbers of very large and efficient competitors can be present. In such instances, even though MES is large in an absolute sense, it can be quite small in a relative sense, and vigorous competition can still be possible. Furthermore, when the cost disadvantage of operating less than MES-size plants is relatively small, there will seldom be serious anticompetitive consequences. In summary, the barriers to entry effects of MES depend upon the size of the MES plant relative to total industry demand as well as the slope of the long-run average cost curve at points of less than MES size operations.

Transportation Costs and MES

Transportation costs play an important role in determining the efficient scale of operation. Transportation costs include terminal, line-haul, and inventory charges associated with moving output from production facilities to customers. Terminal charges consist of handling expenses necessary for loading and unloading of shipped materials. Since terminal charges do not vary with the distance of shipment, they are as high for short hauls as for long hauls. Line-haul expenses include the equipment, labor, and fuel costs associated with moving a given commodity a specified distance. They tend to vary directly with the distance goods are shipped. Although line-haul expenses are relatively constant on a per mile basis, they vary widely from one commodity to another. For example, it costs more to ship a ton of fresh fruit 500 miles than to ship a ton of steel a similar distance. Fresh fruit comes in odd shapes and sizes and requires more container space than a product like steel, which can be compactly loaded. Similarly, any product that is perishable, fragile, or particularly susceptible to pilfering (e.g., personal computers, cigarettes) will tend to have high line-haul expenses due to greater equipment insurance, and labor expenses. And finally, there is an inventory cost component to transportation costs because of the time element involved in shipping goods. The time involved in transit is extremely important because slower forms of transport such as railroads or barges delay receipt of sale proceeds from customers. Even though out-of-pocket expenses will be greater, air cargo or motor carrier shipments can sometimes reduce the total economic costs of transportation because of their greater speed in delivery.

The relative magnitude of transportation costs can play an important role in determining optimal plant sizes. As more output is produced at a given plant, it becomes necessary to reach out to more distant customers. This can lead to increased transportation costs per unit sold. To illustrate, consider Figure 6.7. Here an L-shaped long-run average cost curve is shown reflecting average production costs which first decline and then become nearly constant. Assuming relatively modest terminal and inventory costs, greater line-haul expenses will cause transportation costs per unit to increase at a relatively constant rate. Before considering transportation costs, Q_A^* would represent the MES plant size. Including transportation expenses, however, reduces the MES plant size to Q_B^*. In general, as transportation costs become increasingly important, MES will fall. In the extreme, when transportation costs are large in relation to production costs, as is the case with milk, gravel, cement, and many other products with high weight, or bulk, to value ratios, even small, relatively inefficient production facilities can be profitable when located near important product markets. On the other hand, when transportation costs are relatively insignificant (i.e., for

Figure 6.7
Effect of Transportation Costs on Optimal Plant Size

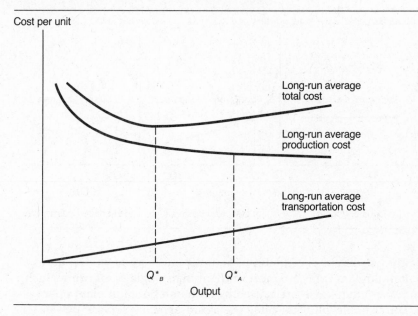

relatively low-weight, compact, and high-value products), markets will be national or international in scope, and increasing returns to scale will cause output to be produced in only a few large plants.

Firm Size and Plant Size

Production and cost functions exist both at the level of the individual plant and, for multiplant firms, at the level of the entire firm. The cost function of a multiplant (or multiproduct) firm can be simply the sum of the cost functions of the individual plants, or it can be greater or smaller than this figure. To illustrate, suppose that the situation as shown in Figure 6.6 holds; that is, there is a U-shaped long-run average cost curve at the plant level. If demand is sufficiently large, the firm will employ N plants, each of the optimal size and each producing Q^* units of input.

In this case what will be the shape of the firm's long-run average cost curve? Figure 6.8 shows three possibilities. Each possible long-run average cost curve has important implications for the minimum efficient firm size, Q_F^*. First, the long-run average cost curve can be L-shaped, as in a, if there are no economies or diseconomies of combining plants.

Figure 6.8
Three Possible Long-Run Average Cost Curves for a Multiplant Firm

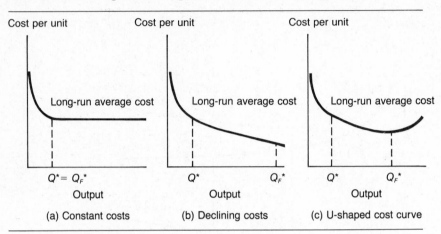

(a) Constant costs   (b) Declining costs   (c) U-shaped cost curve

Second, costs might decline throughout the entire range of output, as in b, if multiplant firms are more efficient than single-plant firms. Such cases, where they exist, are caused by economies of multiplant operation. For example, all plants may use a central billing service; purchasing or distribution economies may be obtained; centralized staffs of various types may serve all plants; and so on. The third possibility, shown in c, is that costs will first decline (beyond Q^*, the output of the most efficient plant), and then rise. Here economies of scale for multiplant costs dominate initially, but later the cost of coordinating many operating units more than offsets these multiplant cost advantages.

All three shapes of cost curves shown in Figure 6.8 have been found in the United States economy, with different ones holding in different industries. Since optimal plant and firm sizes will be identical only when multiplant economies are negligible, the magnitude of such influences must be carefully considered in evaluating the effect of scale economies on entry conditions. Both intraplant and multiplant economies can have an important effect on the minimum efficient firm size.

Plant Size and Flexibility

Is the plant that can produce a given output at the lowest possible cost necessarily the optimal plant for producing that expected level of output? Not necessarily. Consider the following situation. Although actual demand for a product is uncertain, it is expected to be 5,000 units a year. Two possible probability distributions for this demand are given in Fig-

Figure 6.9
Probability Distributions of Demand

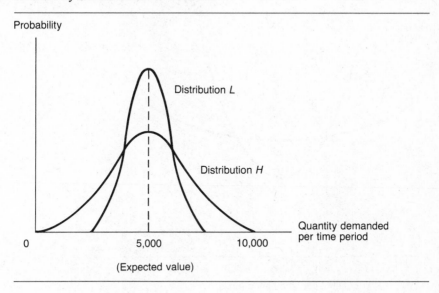

Probability

Distribution *L*

Distribution *H*

Quantity demanded
per time period

0   5,000   10,000

(Expected value)

ure 6.9. Distribution *L* exhibits a low degree of variability in demand, and Distribution *H* indicates substantially higher variation in possible demand levels.

Now suppose two plants can be employed to produce the required output. Plant *A* is quite specialized and is geared to produce a specified output at a low cost per unit. If, however, more or less than the specified output is produced (in this case 5,000 units), unit production costs rise rapidly. Plant *B*, on the other hand, is more flexible. Output can be expanded or contracted without excessive cost penalties, but unit costs are not so low as those of Plant *A* at the optimal output level. These two cases are shown in Figure 6.10.

Plant *A* is more efficient than Plant *B* between 4,500 and 5,500 units of output, but outside this range *B* has lower costs. Which plant should be selected? The answer depends on the relative cost differentials at different output levels and the probability distribution for demand. The firm should make its plant size decision on the basis of the expected average total cost and the variability of that cost. In the example, if the demand probability distribution with the low variation, Distribution *L*, is correct, the more specialized facility will be optimal. If probability Distribution *H* more correctly describes the demand situation, the lower minimum cost of the more specialized facilities will be more than offset by the possibility of very high costs of producing outside the 4,500 to 5,500 unit range; and Plant *B* could have lower expected costs or a more attractive combination of expected costs and potential variation in cost.

Figure 6.10
Alternative Plants for Production of Expected 5,000 Units of Output

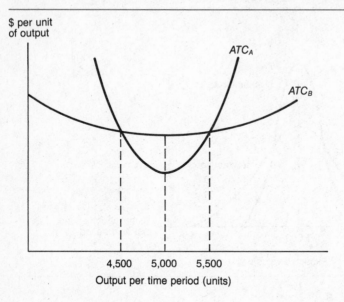

Learning Curves

For many manufacturing processes average costs decline substantially as *cumulative* total output increases. This results from both management and labor becoming more knowledgeable about production techniques as their experience levels increase. Improvements in production equipment and procedures are important in this process, as are reduced waste from defects and reduced labor requirements as workers become more proficient in their jobs.

When knowledge gained from manufacturing experience is used to improve production methods so that output is produced with increasing efficiency, the resulting decline in average costs is said to reflect the effects of the firm's learning curve. The **learning curve** (also known as an *experience curve*) phenomenon has an effect on average costs similar to that for any technological advance that provides an improvement in productive efficiency. Both involve a downward shift in the long-run average cost curve at all levels of output. That is, learning through production experience permits the firm to produce output more efficiently at each and every output level.

Figure 6.11
The Long-Run Average Cost Curve Effects of Learning

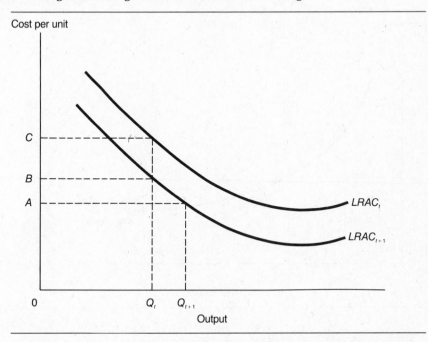

To illustrate, consider Figure 6.11, which shows hypothetical long-run average cost curves for periods t and $t + 1$. With increased knowledge about production methods, gained through the experience of producing Q_t units in period t, long-run average costs have declined for every output level in period $t + 1$. This means that Q_t units could be produced during period $t + 1$ at an average cost of OB rather than the earlier OC. The learning curve cost savings is BC. If output were expanded from Q_t to Q_{t+1} between the periods, average costs would fall from OC to OA. This decline in average costs reflects both the learning curve effect, BC, and effect of economies of scale, AB.

In order to evaluate the average cost effect of learning experience, it is necessary to identify carefully that portion of average cost changes over time that is due to other factors. One of the most important of these is the effect of economies of scale. As seen above, the change in average costs experienced between periods t and $t + 1$ reflects the effects of both learning and economies of scale. This is a typical situation. Similarly, the effects of important technological breakthroughs, causing a downward shift in LRAC curves, and input cost inflation, causing an upward shift in LRAC curves, must be constrained in order to examine learning curve characteristics. Only when output scale, technology,

Figure 6.12
Learning Curve on an Arithmetic Scale

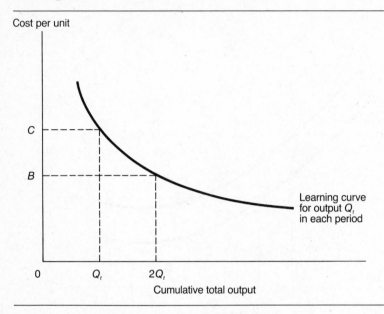

Cost per unit

C

B

Learning curve
for output Q_t
in each period

0   Q_t $2Q_t$

Cumulative total output

and input prices are all held constant can the learning curve relation
be accurately represented.

Figure 6.12 depicts the learning curve relation suggested by Figure
6.11. Note that learning results in dramatic average cost reductions at
low total production levels but increasingly modest savings at higher
cumulative production levels. This is a typical situation since many
improvements in production methods become quickly obvious and
are readily adopted. Later gains often come more slowly and are less
substantial.

Given this typical shape of the learning curve relation, the learning
or experience curve phenomenon is often characterized as a constant
percentage decline in average costs as cumulative output increases. This
percentage represents the proportion by which unit costs decline as the
cumulative quantity of total output doubles. Suppose, for example, average costs per unit for a new product were $100 during 1985 but fell to
$90 during 1986. Furthermore, assume these average costs are in con-
stant dollars reflecting an accurate adjustment for input price inflation,
and that an identical technology was used in production. Given equal
output in each period, to insure that economies of scale are not incorporated in the data, the learning or experience rate, defined as the percentage by which average cost falls as output doubles, is:

$$\text{Learning rate} = \left(1 - \frac{AC_2}{AC_1}\right) \times 100$$

$$= \left(1 - \frac{90}{100}\right) \times 100$$

$$= 10 \text{ percent.}$$

Thus, as cumulative total output doubles, average costs would be expected to fall by 10 percent. Continuing the example, if annual production is projected to remain constant, it will take two additional years of production for output to double again. Thus, one would project that average unit costs will decline to $81.90 (90 percent of $91) in 1989. Since the cumulative total output at that time will equal four years' production at the constant annual rate, output will again double by 1993. At that time, the learning curve will have reduced average unit costs to $73.71 (90 percent of $81.90).

The learning curve concept is useful for a variety of managerial decisions. Research in a number of industries ranging from aircraft manufacture to semiconductor memory chip production has shown that constant percentage learning experience is a widespread phenomenon. Learning or experience rates of 20 to 30 percent are often reported. These high learning rates imply a rapid decline in manufacturing costs as cumulative total output increases. (It should be noted that many learning curve studies fail to account for the expansion of annual production levels adequately, meaning that reported learning or experience rates include an economies-of-scale component. In spite of this, actual learning rates are quite significant.) Managers have found that use of the learning curve concept significantly improves their ability to forecast production costs based on projected cumulative output totals. This in turn improves pricing decisions and even entire product strategies. Managers in electronics industries have used their knowledge of the learning curve to price new products from emergent technologies. These pricing strategies take explicit account of the cost reductions expected to accompany rapid increases in total production, often resulting in attempts to maximize both market size and market share. In other instances managers have analyzed their cost position relative to major competitors and concluded that, because of significant differences in total production levels, they are just chasing the competition down the experience curve and are unlikely ever to be cost competitive. This has led to decisions to drop a product line or to concentrate on a narrower segment of the market in hopes of accelerating the rate of production for one specific product, thereby increasing specialized learning and the rate at which unit costs will decline.

Because of the frequency with which one finds the learning curve concept described as a cause of economies of scale, it is worth repeating that although related, the two are quite distinct. Scale economies relate to cost differences associated with different output levels during a single production period. They are specified in terms of the cost-output relation measured *along* a single LRAC curve. Learning curves relate cost differences to total cumulative output levels for a single product. They are measured in terms of *shifts* in LRAC curves. These shifts result from improved production efficiencies stemming from knowledge gained through production experience. Care must be exercised to separate learning and scale effects in cost analysis.

Cost-Volume-Profit Analysis

Cost-volume-profit analysis is an important analytical technique used to study the relationships among costs, revenues, and profits. The nature of this analysis is depicted in Figure 6.13, a basic cost-volume-profit chart, composed of a firm's total cost and total revenue curves.

Figure 6.13
A Linear Cost-Volume-Profit Chart

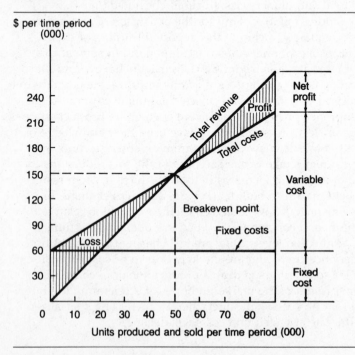

The volume of output is measured on the horizontal axis, and revenue and cost are shown on the vertical axis. Since fixed costs are constant regardless of the output produced, they are indicated by a horizontal line. Variable costs at each output level are measured by the distance between the total cost curve and the constant fixed costs. The total revenue curve indicates the price/demand relationship for the firm's product, and profits (or losses) at each output are shown by the distance between the total revenue curve and the total cost curve.

In the example depicted in Figure 6.13, fixed costs of $60,000 are represented by a horizontal line. Variable costs are assumed to be $1.80 per unit, so total costs rise by $1.80, the variable cost per unit, for each additional unit of output produced. The product is assumed to be sold for $3 per unit, so total revenue is a straight line through the origin. The slope of the total revenue line is steeper than that of the total cost line; this follows from the fact that the firm receives $3 in revenue for every unit produced and sold, but spends only $1.80 on labor, materials, and other variable input factors.

Up to the breakeven point, found at the intersection of the total revenue line and the total cost line, the firm suffers losses. After that point, it begins to make profits. Figure 6.13 indicates a breakeven point at a sales and cost level of $150,000, which occurs at a production level of 50,000 units.

Algebraic Cost-Volume-Profit Analysis

Although cost-volume-profit charts provide a useful means of illustrating profit/output relationships, algebraic techniques are typically a more efficient means for analyzing decision problems. The algebraic relationships in cost-volume-profit analysis can be developed as follows. First, let:

$$P = \text{Price per Unit Sold}$$

$$Q = \text{Quantity Produced and Sold}$$

$$TFC = \text{Total Fixed Costs}$$

$$AVC = \text{Average Variable Cost}$$

$$\pi_c = \text{Profit Contribution}$$

Profit contribution, π_c is defined as the difference between revenues and variable cost. It is equal to price minus average variable cost on a per unit basis ($\pi_c = P - AVC$). Profit contribution can be applied to cover fixed costs and then to provide profits. It is the foundation of cost-volume-profit analysis.

One useful application of cost-volume-profit is in the determining of breakeven activity levels for a product. The breakeven quantity, defined as that volume of output at which total revenue ($P \cdot Q$) is exactly equal to total costs ($TFC + AVC \cdot Q$), is found as follows:

$$P \cdot Q = TFC + AVC \cdot Q$$

$$(P - AVC)Q = TFC$$

$$Q = \frac{TFC}{P - AVC} \tag{6.1}$$

$$= \frac{TFC}{\pi_c}.$$

The breakeven quantity is found by dividing the per unit profit contribution into total fixed costs. In the example illustrated in Figure 6.13, $P = \$3$, $AVC = \$1.80$, and $TFC = \$60,000$. Profit contribution is \$1.20 (\$3.00–\$1.80) and the breakeven quantity is found as follows:

$$Q = \frac{\$60,000}{\$1.20}$$

$$= 50,000 \text{ Units.}$$

A more extensive example will indicate additional uses of the concept in managerial decision making. The textbook publishing business provides a good illustration of the effective use of breakeven analysis for new product decisions. Consider the following hypothetical analysis for a college textbook:

Fixed Costs

Copy editing and other editorial costs	$ 6,000
Illustrations	16,000
Typesetting	28,000
Total fixed costs	$50,000

Variable Costs per Copy

Printing, binding, and paper	$3.20
Bookstore discounts	4.80
Commissions	.50
Author's royalties	3.20
General and administrative costs	2.30
Total variable costs per copy	$14.00

List Price per Copy	$24.00

The fixed costs can be estimated quite accurately; the variable costs, which are linear and which for the most part are set by contracts, can also be estimated with little error. The list price is variable, but competition keeps prices within a sufficiently narrow range to make a linear total revenue curve reasonable. The variable costs of the proposed book are $14 a copy, and the price is $24. This means that each copy sold provides $10 in profit contribution. Applying the formula of Equation 6.1, we find the breakeven sales volume to be 5,000 units:

$$Q = \frac{\$50,000}{\$10}$$

$$= 5,000 \text{ Units.}$$

Publishers can estimate the size of the total market for a given book, the competition, and other factors. With these data as a base, they can estimate the possibilities that a given book will reach or exceed the breakeven point. If the estimate is that it will do neither, the publisher may consider cutting production costs by reducing the number of illustrations, doing only light copy editing, using a lower grade of paper, negotiating with the author to reduce the royalty rate, and so on.

Assume now that the publisher is interested in determining how many copies must be sold in order to earn a $20,000 profit on the text. Because profit contribution is the amount available to cover fixed costs and provide profit, the answer is found by adding the profit requirement to the book's fixed costs, then dividing by the per-unit profit contribution. The sales volume required in this case is 7,000 books, found as follows:

$$Q = \frac{\text{Fixed Costs} + \text{Profit Requirement}}{\text{Profit Contribution}}$$

$$= \frac{\$50,000 + \$20,000}{\$10}$$

$$= 7,000 \text{ Units.}[6]$$

---

[6]To see that 7,000 units will indeed produce a profit of $20,000, note the following calculations:

Sales Revenue = $24 × 7,000 =	$168,000
Total Cost = FC + VC = $50,000 + $14(7,000) = $50,000 + $98,000 =	148,000
Profit = Sales Revenue − Total Cost =	$ 20,000

Consider yet another decision problem that might confront the publisher. Assume that a book club has indicated an interest in purchasing the textbook for its members and has offered to buy 3,000 copies at $12 per copy. Cost-volume-profit analysis can be used to determine the incremental effect of such a sale on the publisher's profits.

Since fixed costs are invariant with respect to changes in the number of textbooks sold, they should be ignored in the analysis. Variable costs per copy are $14, but note that $4.80 of this cost represents bookstore discounts. Since the 3,000 copies are being sold directly to the club, this cost will not be incurred, and hence the relevant variable cost is $9.20. Profit contribution per book sold to the book club then is $2.80 (= $12 − $9.20), and $2.80 times the 3,000 copies sold indicates that the order will result in a total profit contribution of $8,400. Assuming that these 3,000 copies would not have been sold through normal sales channels, the $8,400 profit contribution indicates the increase in profits to the publisher from accepting this order.

Cost-Volume-Profit Analysis and Operating Leverage

Cost-volume-profit analysis is also a useful tool for analyzing the financial characteristics of alternative production systems. Here the analysis focuses on how total costs and profits vary with output as the firm operates in a more mechanized or automated manner and thus substitutes fixed costs for variable costs.

Operating leverage reflects the extent to which fixed production facilities, as opposed to variable production facilities, are used in operations. The relationship between operating leverage and profit variation is clearly indicated in Figure 6.14, in which three firms, A, B, and C, with differing degrees of leverage, are contrasted. The fixed costs of operations in Firm B are considered typical. It uses equipment, with which one operator can turn out a few or many units at the same labor cost, to about the same extent as the average firm in the industry. Firm A uses less capital equipment in its production process and has lower fixed costs, but note the steeper rate of increase in variable costs of A over B. Firm A breaks even at a lower level of operations than does Firm B. For example, at a production level of 40,000 units, B is losing $8,000, but A breaks even.

Firm C has the highest fixed costs. It is highly automated, using expensive, high-speed machines that require very little labor per unit produced. With such an operation, its variable costs rise slowly. Because of the high overhead resulting from charges associated with the expensive machinery, C's breakeven point is higher than that of either A or B. Once Firm C reaches its breakeven point, however, its profits rise faster than do those of the other two firms.

Figure 6.14
Breakeven and Operating Leverage

Firm *A*

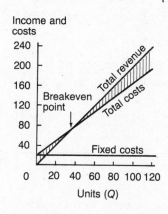

Selling price = $2.00
Fixed costs = $20,000
Variable costs = $1.50Q

Units sold (*Q*)	Sales	Costs	Profit
20,000	$40,000	$50,000	− $10,000
40,000	80,000	80,000	0
60,000	120,000	110,000	10,000
80,000	160,000	140,000	20,000
100,000	200,000	170,000	30,000
120,000	240,000	200,000	40,000

Firm *B*

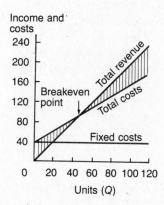

Selling price = $2.00
Fixed costs = $40,000
Variable costs = $1.20Q

Units sold (*Q*)	Sales	Costs	Profit
20,000	$40,000	$64,000	− $24,000
40,000	80,000	88,000	− 8,000
60,000	120,000	112,000	8,000
80,000	160,000	136,000	24,000
100,000	200,000	160,000	40,000
120,000	240,000	184,000	56,000

Firm *C*

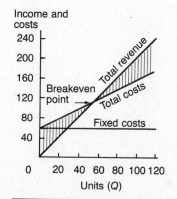

Selling price = $2.00
Fixed costs = $60,000
Variable costs = $1.00Q

Units sold (*Q*)	Sales	Costs	Profit
20,000	$40,000	$80,000	− $40,000
40,000	80,000	100,000	− 20,000
60,000	120,000	120,000	0
80,000	160,000	140,000	20,000
100,000	200,000	160,000	40,000
120,000	240,000	180,000	60,000

Degree of Operating Leverage. Operating leverage can be defined more precisely in terms of how a given change in volume affects profits. For this purpose we use the degree of operating leverage concept. *The degree of operating leverage is defined as the percentage change in profit that results from a one percent change in units sold.* Algebraically, this may be expressed as:

$$\text{Degree of Operating Leverage} = \frac{\text{Percentage Change in Profit}}{\text{Percentage Change in Sales}}$$

$$= \frac{\Delta\pi/\pi}{\Delta Q/Q} \tag{6.2}$$

$$= \frac{\Delta\pi}{\Delta Q} \cdot \frac{Q}{\pi}.$$

The degree of operating leverage is an elasticity concept, so we could call this measure the *operating leverage elasticity of profits.* When based upon linear cost and revenue curves, this elasticity measure will vary depending on the particular part of the breakeven graph that is being considered. For example, the degree of operating leverage is always greatest close to the breakeven point, where a very small change in volume can produce a very large percentage increase in profits, simply because the base profits are close to zero near the breakeven point.

For Firm *B* in Figure 6.14, the degree of operating leverage at 100,000 units of output is 2.0, calculated as follows:[7]

$$DOL_B = \frac{\Delta\pi/\pi}{\Delta Q/Q}$$

$$= \frac{(\$41,600 - \$40,000)/\$40,000}{(102,000 - 100,000)/100,000} = \frac{1,600/40,000}{2,000/100,000}$$

$$= \frac{4\%}{2\%} = 2.$$

Here π is profit and Q is the quantity of output in units.

---

[7]To show the calculation, we arbitrarily assume that the change in Q (ΔQ) = 2,000. If we assume any other ΔQ—for example, $\Delta Q = 1,000$ or $\Delta Q = 4,000$—the degree of operating leverage will still turn out to be 2.0, because we are using linear cost and revenue curves. But if we choose a base different from 100,000 units, we will find the degree of operating leverage to be different from 2.0.

For linear relationships, a formula has been developed to aid in calculating the degree of operating leverage at any level of Output Q:[8]

$$\text{Degree of Operating Leverage at Point } Q = \frac{Q(P - AVC)}{Q(P - AVC) - TFC} . \quad (6.3)$$

Here P is the price per unit, AVC is the variable cost per unit, and TFC is total fixed costs. Using Equation 6.3 we find Firm B's degree of operating leverage at 100,000 units of output to be:

$$DOL_B \text{ at 100,000 Units} = \frac{100,000(\$2.00 - \$1.20)}{100,000(\$2.00 - \$1.20) - \$40,000}$$

$$= \frac{\$80,000}{\$40,000} = 2.$$

Equations 6.2 or 6.3 can also be applied to Firms A and C. When this is done, we find A's degree of operating leverage at 100,000 units to be 1.67; C's is 2.5. Thus, with a 10 percent increase in volume, C (the firm with the most operating leverage) will experience a profit increase of 25 percent. For the same 10 percent volume gain A, the firm with the least leverage, will have only a 16.7 percent profit gain.

The calculation of the degree of operating leverage shows algebraically the same pattern that Figure 6.12 shows graphically: that the profits of Firm C, the company with the most operating leverage, are most sensitive to changes in sales volume, while those of Firm A, which has only a small amount of operating leverage, are relatively insensitive to volume changes. Firm B, with an intermediate degree of leverage, lies between the two extremes.

---

[8] Equation 6.3 is developed as follows: The change in output is defined as ΔQ. Fixed costs are constant, so the change in profit is $\Delta Q(P - AVC)$, where P = Price per Unit and AVC = Average Variable Cost.

The initial profit is $Q(P - AVC) - TFC$, so the percentage change in profit is:

$$\frac{\Delta Q(P - AVC)}{Q(P - AVC) - TFC} .$$

The percentage change in output is $\Delta Q/Q$, so the ratio of the percentage change in profits to the percentage change in output is:

$$\frac{\Delta Q(P - AVC)/[Q(P - AVC) - TFC]}{\Delta Q/Q} = \frac{\Delta Q(P - AVC)}{Q(P - AVC) - TFC} \cdot \frac{Q}{\Delta Q}$$

$$= \frac{Q(P - AVC)}{Q(P - AVC) - TFC} .$$

Limitations of Linear
Cost-Volume-Profit Analysis

Cost-volume-profit analysis helps one understand the relationships among volume, prices, and cost structure; and it is useful in pricing, cost control, and other financial decisions. However, the analysis has limitations as a guide to managerial actions.

Linear cost-volume-profit analysis is especially weak in what it implies about the sales possibilities for the firm. Any given linear cost-volume-profit chart is based on a constant selling price. Therefore, in order to study profit possibilities under different prices, a whole series of charts is necessary, one chart for each price. Nonlinear cost-volume-profit analysis can be used as an alternative method.

Linear cost-volume-profit analysis is also deficient with regard to costs. The linear relationships indicated by the chart do not hold at all output levels. As sales increase, existing plant and equipment are worked beyond capacity, thus reducing their productivity. This situation results in a need for additional workers and frequently longer work periods, which require the payment of overtime wage rates. All of these tend to cause variable costs to rise sharply. Additional equipment and plant may be required, thus increasing fixed costs. Finally, over a time the products sold by the firm change in quality and quantity. Such changes in product mix influence both the level and the slope of the cost function.

Although linear cost-volume-profit analysis has proved to be a useful tool for managerial decision making, care must be taken to insure that it is not used in situations where its assumptions are violated so that the results are misleading. In short, this decision tool is like all others in that it must be employed with a good deal of judgment.

Summary

Cost relationships play a key role in most managerial decisions. In this chapter we introduced a number of cost concepts, showed the relationship between cost functions and production functions, and examined several short-run and long-run cost relationships.

Although the definition of relevant costs varies from one decision to another, several important relationships are common in all cost analyses. First, relevant costs are typically based on the alternative-use concept: the relevant cost of a resource is determined by its value in its best alternative use. Second, the relevant cost of a decision includes only those costs which are affected by the action being contemplated. This is the incremental-cost concept. If a particular cost is unchanged by an action, the relevant incremental cost for decision purposes is zero. Finally, care must be taken to insure that all costs, both explicit and implicit, which are affected by a decision are included in the analysis.

Proper use of the relevant-cost concept requires an understanding of a firm's cost/output relationship or its cost function. Cost functions are determined by the production function and the market-supply function for its inputs, with the production function specifying the technical relationship between inputs and output and the prices of inputs converting this physical relationship to a cost/output function.

Two basic cost functions are used in managerial decision making: short-run cost functions, used in most day-to-day operating decisions, and long-run cost functions, used for planning purposes. The short run is the period during which some of the firm's productive facilities are unalterable; the long run is a period of sufficient length to permit the company to change its production system completely by adding, subtracting, or completely modifying its assets.

In the short run the shape of a firm's cost curves will be determined largely by the productivity of its variable input factors. Over that range of output where the marginal productivity of the variable inputs is increasing, costs will be increasing less than proportionately to output, so unit costs will be declining. Once diminishing returns to the variable factors set in, costs begin to increase faster than output, and unit costs will begin to rise.

A similar relationship holds for long-run cost curves. Here all inputs are variable, and the shape of the cost curve is determined by the presence of economies or diseconomies of scale. If economies of scale are present, the cost elasticity of output will be less than one ($\varepsilon_c < 1$), and unit costs will decline as output increases. Once diseconomies of scale begin to dominate, however, $\varepsilon_c > 1$, and average cost curves will turn up.

The output level at which economies of scale cease to significantly affect costs defines the minimum efficient scale (MES) of operation. MES has important implications for both plant and firm scale decisions and for industry competition.

Although a firm desires to produce its output at the minimum possible cost, the existence of uncertainty often dictates a trade-off between lower costs and production flexibility. In these cases, the firm must examine the probability distribution of demand and the relative cost differentials of alternative production techniques, then select as the optimal system the one which maximizes the value of the firm.

Learning curves describe the decline in average costs that typically results from increased production experience. This phenomenon is an important factor in projecting future manufacturing costs.

Finally, cost-volume-profit analysis was shown to be an important tool for analyzing relationships among fixed costs, variable costs, revenues, and profits. Its uses include analysis of the effects of varying the degree of operating leverage that a firm employs and analysis of incremental profit using the profit contribution concept.

Questions

6.1 The relevant cost for most managerial decision purposes is the *current* cost of an input. The relevant cost for computing income for taxes and stockholder reporting is the *historical* cost. Would it be preferable to use current costs for tax and stockholder reporting purposes?

6.2 What are the relationships among historical costs, current costs, and alternative opportunity costs?

6.3 Are implicit costs reflected in income-tax calculations?

6.4 What is the difference between the marginal and incremental cost concepts?

6.5 What is a sunk cost, and how is it related to a decision problem?

6.6 Explain in some detail the relationship between production functions and cost functions. Be sure to include in your discussion the impact of conditions in input factor markets.

6.7 The president of a small firm has been complaining to the controller about rising labor and material costs. However, the controller notes that a just completed cost study indicates that average costs have not increased during the past year. Is this possible? What factors might you examine to analyze this phenomenon?

6.8 How is it possible for a multiplant firm to have either higher or lower unit costs than a single-plant firm?

Solved Problem

6.1 Charlotte Instruments manufactures a single precision measuring instrument, which it sells to other manufacturers, who process it further for ultimate sales to university laboratories. The yearly volume of output is 5,000 units produced and sold. The selling price and cost per unit are shown below:

Selling Price.		$250
Costs:		
Direct material	$40	
Direct labor	60	
Variable overhead	30	
Variable selling expenses	25	
Fixed selling expenses	20	175
Unit profit before tax.		$ 75

Management is evaluating the alternative of performing the necessary processing to allow Charlotte to sell its entire output directly to university laboratories for $300 per unit. Although no added investment is required in productive facilities, there are additional processing costs estimated as:

Direct labor	$20 per unit
Variable overhead	$ 5 per unit
Variable selling expenses	$ 2 per unit
Fixed selling expenses	$20,000 per year

Should Charlotte process the product further?

Solution
This problem should be answered by using incremental profit analysis. The analysis deals only with the incremental revenues and costs associated with the decision to engage in further processing.

Incremental revenue per unit ($300 − $250)	$50
Incremental variable cost per unit ($20 + $5 + $2)	− 27
Incremental profit contribution per unit	$23
Yearly output volume in units	× 5,000
Incremental variable profit per year	$115,000
Incremental fixed cost per year	20,000
Yearly incremental profit	$ 95,000

Since the incremental profit is positive, the decision to engage in further processing would be more profitable than continuing the present operating policy.

Solved Problem

6.2 Colonial Furniture produces medium-priced home furniture. It is contemplating an expansion into the office furniture market by producing an office desk that it would sell at a price of $800. The production of each desk would require $310 in materials and 35 hours of labor at the rate of $8 per hour. Energy, supervisory and other variable overhead costs would amount to $60 for each desk produced. Colonial's fixed costs would be affected by the introduction of the new desk, and the accounting department has derived an allocated fixed overhead charge of $75 per desk (at a projected volume of 2,000 units) to account for the increased fixed costs.

(continued)

a) What is Colonial Furniture's breakeven sales volume for office desks?

b) Calculate the degree of operating leverage for the production of office desks at a projected production volume of 2,000 units and explain what the DOL means.

Solution

a) The breakeven level of output is

$$Q = \frac{TFC}{P - AVC}$$

$$= \frac{75 \cdot 2,000}{800 - [310 + 60 + (8 \cdot 35)]}$$

$$= \frac{150,000}{800 - 650}$$

$$= 1,000 \text{ Units.}$$

b) The equation for calculating the degree of operating leverage is

$$DOL = \frac{Q(P - AVC)}{Q(P - AVC) - TFC},$$

where DOL is the degree of operating leverage, Q is output, and all other variables are as before. Therefore, DOL at $Q = 2,000$ is:

$$DOL = \frac{2,000(800 - 650)}{2,000(800 - 650) - 150,000}$$

$$= \frac{300,000}{300,000 - 150,000}$$

$$= 2.$$

The DOL of 2 means that for a 1 percent change in output, profits would be expected to change 2 percent.

Problem Set

6.1 Manhattan Couriers Inc. (MCI) provides same-day package delivery service to Wall Street brokerage firms at a price of $5 for each package delivered. Of this amount, $1.25 is profit contribution. MCI is considering an attempt to differentiate its service from several other competitors by insuring each delivery up to $5,000 against loss due to fire, theft, and so on. If offered, insured delivery would increase MCI's unit cost by $0.25 per package delivery. Current monthly profits are $5,000 on 12,000 package deliveries.

a) Assuming average variable costs are constant at all output levels, what is MCI's total cost function before the proposed change?

b) What will the total cost function be if insured package delivery is offered?

c) Assume delivery prices remain stable at $5; what percentage increase in deliveries would be necessary to maintain current profit levels?

6.2 Manchester Shoes manufactures and sells a line of high-quality products to retail shoe stores in the northeastern United States. Last month, Manchester sold 10,000 pairs of shoes at an average variable manufacturing cost of $30 per pair. Each pair of shoes contributes one third of its revenue to fixed costs and profits.

a) If Manchester reduces the average price of its products by 5 percent, how many pairs of shoes will it have to sell this month in order to obtain the same profits as earned last month?

b) Manchester's primary competition comes from the Greenville Shoe Company, whose product sells for an average $42 per pair. If Greenville's average profit contribution is 30 percent, what are that company's average variable costs?

6.3 Management of the Blacksburg Beverage Company, a regional bottler operating in the southeastern United States, is considering two alternative proposals for expansion into midwestern states.

Alternative 1: Construct a single plant in Chicago, Illinois, with a monthly production capacity of 30,000 cases per month, a monthly fixed cost of $25,000, and a variable cost of $2.80 per case.

Alternative 2: Construct three plants, one each in Muncie, Indiana; Normal, Illinois, and Dayton, Ohio, with capacities of 12,000, 10,000, and 8,000 respectively and monthly fixed costs of $12,000, $11,000, and $10,000 each. Variable costs would be only $2.50 per case because of lower distribution costs. To achieve these costs, sales from each plant would be limited to demand within its state. The total estimated monthly sales volume of 20,000 cases in these three midwestern states is distributed as follows: 8,000 cases in Indiana, 7,000 cases in Illinois, and 5,000 cases in Ohio.

a) Assuming a wholesale price of $4.50 per case, calculate the break-even output quantities for each alternative.

b) At a wholesale price of $4.50 per case in all states, and assuming sales at the projected levels, which alternative expansion scheme provides Blacksburg with the highest profit?

c) If sales increase to production capacities, which alternative would prove to be more profitable?

6.4 Alberta Industries is currently considering production of a new product called the "Scoop." The Scoop is a new type of snow shovel with a design that significantly reduces the stress of lifting and throwing. The Scoop would be marketed at a price of $32 and could be produced by a labor- or a capital-intensive technology. Unit costs using each technology would be:

	Technology	
	Labor-Intensive	Capital-Intensive
Raw materials	10	10
Direct labor	9	5
Variable overhead	5	7
Allocated fixed overhead	3	2
Total cost	27	24

Use of the labor-intensive technology would require a capital investment of $100,000; the capital-intensive technology would require a capital investment of $150,000.

    a) What sales level (in dollars) would be required for breakeven operations under each technology?

    b) Calculate the degree of operating leverage under each technology at a sales level of 18,000 units.

    c) What would be the profits or losses under each technology for the production of the Scoop, assuming a sales level of 14,000 units?

6.5 The Clairmont Ice Cream Company is a producer of assorted flavors of ice cream. The firm's current production capacity is 500,000 gallons per month, and this capacity cannot be increased in the short run. Sales for next month have been forecast at 460,000 gallons, but Clairmont has just received a purchase offer for 80,000 gallons from a large chain of grocery stores. The chain offered to pay $2.20 per gallon, which is below Clairmont's standard selling price of $2.50. The per gallon costs associated with the production of ice cream are:

Raw materials	$0.90
Direct labor	0.60
Variable overhead	0.30
Fixed overhead (allocated over 460,000 units)	0.20
Total cost per gallon	$2.00

    a) What is the breakeven output level for Clairmont, assuming all sales are through standard distribution channels?

    b) Assuming that Clairmont must either reject the grocery chain offer or supply the entire 80,000 gallons, what are the relevant costs for the decision? (Assume that the new offer is from outside Clair-mont's normal channels of distribution.)

c) Using the profit contribution analysis concept, determine whether Clairmont would increase or decrease its profits by accepting the offer.

6.6 Distinctive Products Inc. is a large manufacturer of soaps and detergents. To remain competitive with other soap manufacturers, the management at Distinctive Products has decided to offer its popular brand of hand soap, Ventura, in a liquid form. The product will be sold to wholesalers in cases of 12 bottles for $8.50 per case. Since Distinctive Products already has the capacity necessary to produce the new product, no additional fixed charges will be incurred. However, a $300,000 fixed charge has been allocated to the product as a share of the company's present fixed costs.

Using the estimated sales and production level of 200,000 cases of Ventura as the standard volume, the accounting department has developed the following costs per case:

Direct labor	$2.50
Direct materials	$3.00
Total overhead	
(Fixed and variable)	$2.00

Although Distinctive Products produces plastic bottles for many of its other soap products, it has approached a container manufacturer to discuss the possibility of purchasing the plastic bottles for Ventura. The empty bottle purchase price would be $1.60 for 12 bottles. If Distinctive Products accepts the proposal to purchase the plastic bottles, it is estimated that direct labor and variable overhead costs would be reduced by 20 percent, and direct material costs would be reduced by 30 percent.

a) Should Distinctive Products produce or buy the plastic bottles for Ventura?

b) What would be the maximum purchase price acceptable to Distinctive Products for the plastic bottles?

c) Rather than the initial estimate of 200,000 cases, revised estimates predict a sales volume of 250,000 cases. At this new volume, additional bottle manufacturing equipment must be rented at an annual cost of $25,000. However, this incremental cost would be the only additional fixed cost required, even if sales increased to the future production goal of 450,000 cases. If the company has the option to produce and buy bottles at the same time, how should Distinctive Products acquire the additional 50,000 plastic bottles required?

Appendix 6.A

Empirical Cost Analysis

In Chapter 6, we demonstrated the importance of a detailed knowledge of both long-run and short-run cost functions for many managerial decision purposes. The short-run cost curve provides useful information for short-run pricing and output decisions; with the long-run curve, the firm can do a better job of planning its capacity requirements and future plant configurations.

Public officials are also interested in long-run and short-run cost functions. As will be shown in Chapters 8 and 10, regulatory authorities (including the Antitrust Division of the Justice Department) can influence the size of business enterprises. If the size of a firm is held down below the least-cost level, economic efficiency suffers. On the other hand, if economies of scale are not important, regulators create fewer problems with policies that limit firm size in order to stimulate competition.

A number of analytical techniques have proved useful in the empirical estimation of cost functions. In this appendix we examine several of these techniques, illustrating their particular strengths and noting some of their weaknesses and limitations.

Short-Run Cost Estimation

By assuming that the firm has been operating efficiently, or at least that inefficiencies can be isolated and accounted for, it is possible to estimate cost functions by statistical analysis. Time-series and cross-sectional regression analyses are the most popular methods used for estimating a firm's short-run variable cost function.[1] In such regression studies, cost is regressed on output, typically in a model that includes a number of other variables whose effects on cost we wish to analyze or at least to account for. For estimating short-run cost relationships, the total variable cost function rather than the total cost function is estimated in order to remove the very difficult problem of allocating fixed costs to a particular production quantity. Since these allocated costs are invariant with respect to output, they cannot affect the important average variable cost function and the marginal cost function that are used for short-run decision making purposes and can therefore be safely eliminated from the analysis.

Cost Specification and Data Preparation

Most difficulties encountered in statistical cost analysis arise from two causes: (1) errors in the specification of the cost characteristics that are relevant for decision making purposes and (2) problems in the collection and modification of the data to be analyzed. Thus, before examining the types of regression models actually used to estimate short-run cost functions, we should consider several caveats regarding specification, collection, and modification of cost data.

Conceptual Problems. Managerial decision making pertains to future activities and events, so the relevant costs for managerial decisions are future costs, as opposed to current or historical costs. Cost estimates based on accounting data, which record actual current or past costs and are thus historical, must therefore be considered as only first approximations to the relevant costs in managerial economics. These accounting costs must be modified before they are used for decision making purposes. The most typical adjustment involves setting prices of input factors such as labor, materials, and energy at their current or projected levels.

A second conceptual problem that occurs when accounting data are used for cost analysis stems from the failure of accounting systems to record opportunity costs. Since opportunity costs are frequently the largest and the most important costs in a short-run decision problem, cost functions derived from accounting data are often inappropriate. As Joel Dean, a pioneer in the development of managerial economics, has so aptly stated: "In business problems the message of opportunity costs is that it is dangerous to confine cost knowledge to what the firm

---

[1] See Chapter 3 for a discussion of the least squares regression technique.

is doing. What the firm is not doing but could do is frequently the critical cost consideration which it is perilous but easy to ignore."[2]

Cost/Output Matching. A problem may arise in the attempt to relate certain costs to output. In short-run cost analysis, only costs that vary with output should be included, but it is often difficult to distinguish between those costs which are and are not related to output. Economic depreciation of capital equipment is perhaps the best example of this difficulty. For most depreciable assets, both time and usage determine the rate of decline in value, but only the component related to usage should be included in short-run cost estimation. Both components, however, are generally embodied in accounting data on depreciation costs, and it is often impossible to separate use costs from obsolescence or time-related costs.

Semivariable costs also present a problem in cost/output matching. Some costs may not vary with output changes over certain ranges but may vary with output once a critical level has been exceeded for a long-enough period. These cost/output relationships must be accounted for if accurate short-run cost functions are to be estimated.

Timing of Costs. Another problem that arises from the use of accounting data is that of relating costs to the corresponding output. Care must be taken to adjust the data for leads and lags between cost reporting and output production. Maintenance expense provides a typical example of this problem: Production in one period causes additional maintenance expenses not in that period but, rather, in subsequent periods. During a period of high production, recorded maintenance expenses will be unusually low because the firm's equipment is being used at full capacity, and maintenance is postponed if possible. Repairs that are made will usually be temporary in nature, aimed at getting the equipment back into production rapidly until a period when some slack exists in the production system. Without careful adjustment, this problem can cause gross errors in statistically estimated cost functions.

Inflation. Price level changes present still another problem. In time-series analysis, recorded historical data are generally used for statistical cost analysis, and during most of the period for which data are available the costs of labor, raw materials, and other items have been rising. At the same time, an expanding population and greater affluence have caused the output of most firms to increase. The more recent output is therefore large and has a relatively high cost (in nominal or current dollar terms), so a naïve cost study might suggest that costs rise rapidly

---

[2]Joel Dean, *Managerial Economics* (Englewood Cliffs, N.J.: Prentice-Hall, 1951), p. 260.

with increases in output when this is not the case. To remove this bias, cost data must be deflated for price level changes. Because factor prices increase at different rates, the use of composite price indexes for this deflation often will not provide satisfactory results. Rather, an index for each category of inputs must be used. The problem of adjusting for price variation is further compounded by the fact that input price changes related to increases in demand for the input when the firm's output rate increases must not be removed. Only price changes that are independent of the production system under examination should be eliminated; otherwise, the statistically estimated cost function will understate the true cost of high-level production.

A further difficulty encountered in statistical cost studies results from the substitution among input factors that takes place when their relative prices change. Price level changes rarely result in proportional changes in the prices of all goods and services and, as was shown in Chapter 5, optimal input combinations depend in part on the relative prices of resources. Changes in optimal input combinations will affect the cost projections that are relevant for managerial decision analysis.

Observation-Period Problems. Short-run cost curves are, by definition, cost/output relationships for a plant of specific scale and technology. If the short-run curve is to be accurately estimated, the period of examination must be one during which the product remains essentially unchanged and the plant facilities remain fixed. It should be noted that even though a firm's book value of assets remains relatively constant during the observation period, the plant may have actually changed significantly. Consider, for example, a firm that replaces a number of obsolete manual milling machines, which have been fully depreciated, with a single automated machine that it leases. The firm's production function, and hence its total cost function, could have changed substantially even though the book value of assets remains constant. The problem of changing plant and product can be minimized by limiting the length of the period over which data are analyzed. For satisfactory statistical estimation, however, the cost analyst needs an adequate sample size with a fairly broad range of outputs, and this requirement tends to lengthen the necessary period of data observations; this in turn necessitates a careful examination of a firm's total activities over the period of a cost study if accurate results are to be achieved.

Given the need for numerous data observations over a relatively short period, it is apparent that frequent data observations covering short production periods can improve the statistical results in empirical cost studies. Likewise, it is theoretically more satisfying to use frequent data observation points (for example, daily or weekly) so that output rates will be fairly constant *within* the observation period. At odds with this, however, is the fact that data collection and correction problems are magnified as the length of the observation period is shortened. Although the best length for the observation period will vary from situation to situation, one month is the period most frequently used. In other words, the various elements of variable costs incurred during each month are collected and compared with output produced during the month. A total period of perhaps two to three years (24 to 36 months) can provide enough observations for statistical analysis, yet still be short enough that the plant and product will have remained relatively unchanged. Still it is not possible to generalize about the best period of study for all cases as the facts of the individual case must always be taken into account.

This brief examination of some of the major data problems encountered in short-run statistical cost analysis points up the importance of proper data collection within the firm. That is, the value of statistical cost analysis to a firm is in large part a function of its cost accounting records. With this in mind, many firms are developing computerized management information systems in which cost and output data are recorded in sufficient detail to allow statistical analysis of their cost/ output relations. It must be emphasized that, to be useful for managerial decision making purposes, these management information systems must go well beyond the collecting and reporting of data found in standard accounting systems. Thus, careful planning and a clear understanding of the relevant cost concepts used for various business decisions are required for establishing an information system that will provide the necessary inputs for proper decision analysis.

Statistical Short-Run Cost Functions

Once the data problems have been solved, cost analysts are faced with the problem of determining the proper functional form of the cost curve. A variety of linear and nonlinear models suitable for least squares regression analysis are available. If there are good theoretical or engineering reasons for using a particular model, that model will be selected. Often, however, there is no a priori reason for choosing one model over another, and in such cases the typical procedure is to fit several models to the cost/output data, then use the one that seems to fit best in terms of the statistical results, especially R^2, the coefficient of determination. In other words, if one model has an R^2 of 0.80, indicating that the model explains 80 percent of the variation in total variable costs, and another model has an R^2 of 0.90, the second model will be relied upon for operating decisions.[3]

---

[3]This assumes that the independent variables in each model are the same; only the model structure is different. Without this proviso it would be possible to artificially inflate the R^2 for one model merely by adding additional explanatory variables.

Linear Short-Run Cost Functions. For a great many production systems, a linear statistical cost curve of the form shown below provides an adequate fit of the cost/output data:

$$C = a + bQ + \sum_{i=1}^{n} c_i X_i.$$

Here, C refers to the total variable cost during an observation period; Q is the quantity of output produced during that period; X_i designates all other independent variables whose cost effects the analyst wants to account for; and a, b, and c_i are the coefficients of the model as determined by the least squares regression technique. The other independent variables to be accounted for include such items as wage rates, fuel and materials costs, weather, input quality, production lot size, product mix, and changes in product design. Including them in the model enables the analyst to obtain a better estimate of the relationship between cost and output.

The intercept coefficient a in this model is typically irrelevant. It cannot be interpreted as the firm's fixed costs because such costs are not included in the data. Even if total costs, as opposed to total variable costs, are used as the dependent variable, the intercept coefficient a may still not reflect the firm's fixed costs. This coefficient is simply the intercept of the estimated cost curve with the vertical axis. This intersection occurs where output is zero and usually lies far outside the range of cost/output data observation points.

In those limited instances where observations with very small levels of output are being considered and the measured costs are total costs, the a coefficient can be taken as an estimate, albeit an imperfect one, of fixed costs. In all instances, the interpretation of individual coefficient estimates must be restricted to the relevant range of observations.

Although a linear form for the cost/output relationship may be accurate for the range of available data, extrapolation far outside this range can lead to serious misstatements of the true relationship. The problem of extrapolation outside the observation range is illustrated in Figure 6.A.1. Within the observed output range, Q_1 to Q_2, a linear function closely approximates the true cost/output relationship. Extrapolation beyond these limits, however, leads to inaccurate estimates of the firm's variable costs.

Coefficient b is very important in a linear model of this type. As shown in both Figures 6.A.1 and 6.A.2, b provides an approximation to both marginal costs and average variable costs within the relevant output range.

Quadratic and Cubic Cost Functions. Two other forms, the quadratic and the cubic, are also widely used in empirical cost studies. Figures

Figure 6.A.1
Linear Approximation of the Cost/Output Function

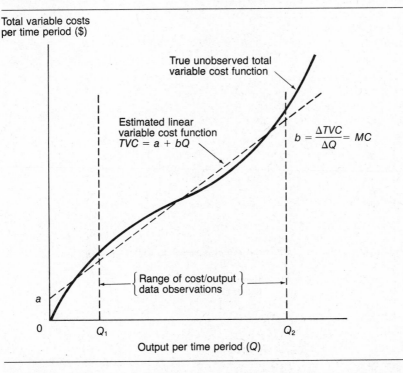

Total variable costs
per time period ($)

True unobserved total
variable cost function

Estimated linear
variable cost function
$TVC = a + bQ$

$b = \dfrac{\Delta TVC}{\Delta Q} = MC$

$\left\{ \begin{array}{c} \text{Range of cost/output} \\ \text{data observations} \end{array} \right\}$

a

0 Q_1 Q_2

Output per time period (Q)

6.A.3 and 6.A.4 illustrate the average variable cost and marginal cost curves associated with quadratic and cubic cost functions. Again, it should be emphasized that costs that are invariant with respect to output (fixed costs) are not typically included in the empirical estimates of short-run cost curves, so these curves are representative of variable costs only. An estimate of fixed costs must be added to determine the firm's short-run total cost function.

Empirically Estimated Short-Run Cost Functions. Many empirical studies have been undertaken in attempts to ascertain the nature of cost/output relationships in the short run. Joel Dean's pioneering studies of short-run costs in a furniture factory, a hosiery mill, and a leather belt shop in the late 1930s and early 1940s all indicated that costs and output were linearly related and hence that marginal costs were constant over the observed output ranges. In another cost study Dean estimated that marginal costs were constant in the hosiery and the shoe departments of a large department store, and slightly declining in the coat department. Dean concluded his report of the latter study by noting

Figure 6.A.2
Average Variable Cost and Marginal Cost for a
Linear Cost Function: $TVC = a + bQ$

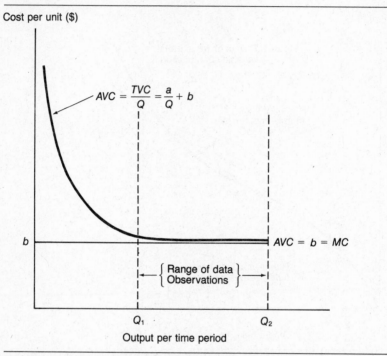

Cost per unit ($)

$AVC = \dfrac{TVC}{Q} = \dfrac{a}{Q} + b$

b $AVC = b = MC$

$\left\{ \begin{array}{l} \text{Range of data} \\ \text{Observations} \end{array} \right\}$

Q_1 Q_2

Output per time period

Note: If $a = 0$, $AVC = b$, a constant. However, if $a > 0$, AVC declines continuously, but at a decreasing rate as output increases, because as Q becomes larger, a/Q becomes smaller and smaller.

that while the regression results indicated a linear cost function for two of the three departments, "the unexplained scatter of observations is great enough to permit a cubic of the traditional form to be fitted in each case. However, the curvature would be so slight as to be insignificant from a managerial viewpoint, so that it could scarcely affect any economic conclusions which might be derived from the linear functions."[4]

Another early cost study was that conducted by T. O. Yntema on costs at United States Steel Corporation.[5] The statistical cost function he estimated was:

$$\text{Total Cost} = \$132,100,000 + \$55.73Q,$$

---

[4]Dean, *Managerial Economics*, p. 254.

[5]T. O. Yntema, "Steel Prices, Volume and Costs," *United States Steel Corporation Temporary National Economic Committee Papers*, 2 (New York: U.S. Steel, 1940): 53.

Figure 6.A.3
**Average Variable Cost and Marginal Cost Curves for Quadratic Total
Variable Cost Function:** $TVC = a + bQ + cQ^2$

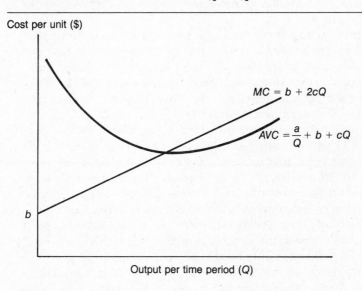

Cost per unit ($)

$MC = b + 2cQ$

$AVC = \dfrac{a}{Q} + b + cQ$

b

Output per time period (Q)

Figure 6.A.4
**Average Variable Cost and Marginal Cost Curves for a Cubic
Variable Function:** $TVC = a + bQ - cQ^2 + dQ^3$

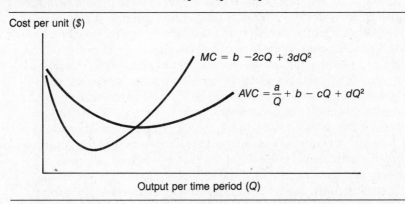

Cost per unit ($)

$MC = b - 2cQ + 3dQ^2$

$AVC = \dfrac{a}{Q} + b - cQ + dQ^2$

Output per time period (Q)

where Q was a measure of output in tons of steel. Thus, Yntema found
that the company's cost function was linear and that the marginal cost
of producing an additional ton of steel was $55.73.

These early findings that short-run costs could be accurately estimated for many kinds of businesses by a linear function have been supported by more recent cost studies for both manufacturing and service

firms. This confirmation of the generality of the linear relationships reported earlier by Dean and by Yntema lends support to the hypothesis that marginal costs for many firms remain fairly constant over a substantial output range.

The empirical finding of constant marginal cost over a wide variety of production systems raises an interesting question. The law of diminishing productivity in microeconomic theory leads one to expect that short-run marginal costs would be increasing, imparting the traditional U shape to the average variable cost curve. Why is it that this relationship is not observed in empirical studies?

Although a number of explanations for this phenomenon have been hypothesized, one of the most satisfying relates to the way input factors are utilized in a modern production system. In microeconomic theory, the quantity of the fixed factor *employed* in the production process is held constant in the short run, and varying quantities of the variable factor are used in conjunction with that fixed factor. In practice, the quantity of the fixed factor *actually used* often varies with output in some relatively constant ratio to the variable factor(s). Thus, only in theory is the fixed production factor truly fixed. The theory states that once a certain minimum level of production has been reached, additional units of the variable inputs exhibit diminishing productivity because of limitations imposed by the fixed factor. In actual production systems, however, capital equipment (the fixed factor) is frequently fixed with respect to cost (that is, costs are invariant with respect to output level) but quite variable with respect to actual usage. For example, a firm producing electronics devices may vary output by changing the number of assembly stations it operates, keeping the ratio of capital (fixed factor) to labor (variable factor) *actually employed* fixed over short-run production periods. Textile mills, where the number of spindles in operation varies with output, and electricity generation plants, where the number of generators in actual use is varied to increase or decrease output, provide other examples of variable employment of the "fixed" factor. Negotiated work rules also add to the fixity of capital and labor input ratios. Many labor contracts specify within narrow ranges the combinations of labor and capital equipment that can be utilized in a production system and the rate at which the capital equipment is operated.

In these situations, the rate of utilization of each unit of the capital factor is nearly constant regardless of the production level. Since fixed and variable inputs are being used in constant proportions over wide ranges of production output, the law of diminishing productivity does not hold, and the marginal cost of production remains constant. For these reasons the empirical findings are not particularly surprising.

Long-Run Statistical Cost Estimation

Statistical estimation of long-run cost curves, although similar in many respects to short-run cost estimation, is typically somewhat more complex. In the long run, all costs are variable, and the problem is to determine the shape of the least-cost production curve for plants of different size. Total cost curves must be estimated, and this, in turn, introduces a number of additional difficulties.

As with short-run analysis, one can analyze the long-run cost/output relationship by examining a single firm over a long period. In this case the assumption that plant size is held constant during the examination period is removed, and total costs are regressed against output. The basic problem with this approach is that it is almost impossible to find a situation where the scale of a firm has been variable enough to allow statistical estimation of a long-run cost curve while, at the same time, technology and other important factors have remained constant. Without constant technology, the function estimated in this manner will bear little resemblance to the relevant long-run cost function necessary for planning purposes.

Because of difficulties encountered in using time-series data to estimate long-run cost functions, a different procedure, cross-sectional regression analysis, is frequently employed. This procedure involves a comparison of different size firms (or plants) at one point in time by regressing their total costs against a set of independent variables. The key independent variable is again a measure of output, and other independent variables (such as regional wage rates, fuel costs, and the like) are included to account for the effect on cost of factors other than the level of output.

The use of cross-sectional analysis, as opposed to time-series analysis, for estimating long-run cost functions reduces some estimation problems and magnifies others. For example, since the data all represent factor prices at the same point in time, the problem of price inflation (or deflation) is removed. A new problem arises, however, because factor input prices vary in different regions of the country; unless all firms in the sample are located in the same region, interregional price variations may distort the analysis.

A second difficulty in cross-sectional studies can be traced to variations in accounting procedures. Differing depreciation policies among firms and varying techniques for amortizing major expenses such as planning and development costs can substantially distort the true cost/output relationship.

Finally, even if all these data problems are solved so that the effects on costs of all factors other than output are held constant, a last requirement must also be met if we are to estimate accurately the long-run cost

Figure 6.A.5
Estimating Long-Run Average Cost Curves with Cross-sectional Data

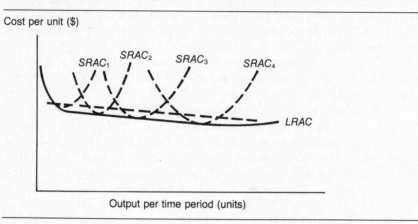

function. A basic assumption in the use of cross-sectional data is that all firms are operating at the point along the long-run curve at which costs are minimized. That is, the cross-sectional technique assumes that all firms are operating in an efficient manner and are using the most efficient plant available for producing whatever level of output they are producing. If this assumption holds, the cost/output relationship found in the analysis does trace a long-run cost curve, such as that shown as *LRAC* in Figure 6.A.5. If this assumption is violated, however, the least squares regression line will lie above the true *LRAC* curve, and costs will be overstated.

Even more troublesome than the uniform overstatement of average cost is the possibility that the true curvature in the long-run average cost curve may be distorted and may thereby either under- or overstate any economies or diseconomies of scale in the industry being examined. For example, if the smaller firms in Figure 6.A.5 are operating well to the right of their optimal output (as they might in a rapidly expanding industry), the estimated *LRAC* curve will have a downward slope much steeper than the true *LRAC* curve, and this bias will cause one to overestimate the extent of economies of scale in the industry. Similarly, scale economies may be underestimated due to a selection bias which results if small high-cost firms fail to compete successfully, go bankrupt, and thus fail to get included in the cost study.

A majority of empirically estimated long-run cost functions exhibit sharply increasing returns to scale at low output levels, but these scale economies decline as output increases and constant returns often appear to hold at high output levels. This means that the long-run average cost curve decreases at a decreasing rate as output increases, finally becoming horizontal. Very few studies have found evidence of decreasing returns to scale, an upturn in the average cost curve, at high output levels. These results have caused researchers to hypothesize that typical long-run average cost curves are L-shaped rather than U-shaped.

Alternative Cost Estimation Techniques

Because of the difficulty of obtaining satisfactory statistical estimates of long-run cost/output relationships, several alternative means of empirically examining cost functions have been developed. Two of these, the survivor technique and the engineering technique, have proven useful in certain situations where statistical cost estimation is tenuous or impossible because of the absence of adequate data, or where checks on statistical cost estimates are sought. These techniques are discussed below.

Survivor Technique. The survivor principle was developed by George Stigler.[6] The basic idea behind this technique is that more efficient firms, that is, those with lower average costs, will survive and prosper over time. Therefore, by examining the size makeup of an industry over time, one can determine the nature of its cost/output relations.

More specifically, Stigler proposes that one classify the firms in an industry by size and calculate the share of industry output or capacity provided by each size class. If the share of one class declines over time, that size production facility is assumed to be relatively inefficient. If the relative output share increases, however, firms of that size are presumed to be relatively efficient and thus to have lower average costs.

The survivor technique has been applied to several industries to examine the question of returns to scale. Stigler examined the distribution of steel production among firms of varying size in 1930, 1938, and 1951.[7] He found that over this period the percentage of industry output accounted for by the smallest- and largest-size classes declined, while the output share of medium-size firms increased. These findings indicate a U-shaped long-run average cost curve. Returns to scale are increasing at low output levels, are nearly constant over a wide range of intermediate output, and are decreasing at higher output levels.

Stigler also applied the technique to the automobile industry. Again, he found that the smallest firms showed a continual decline in their

---

[6] George J. Stigler, "The Economies of Scale," *Journal of Law and Economics* 1 (October 1958), pp. 54–71.
[7] Ibid.

Table 6.A.1
Economies of Scale in the Portland Cement Industry, 1973–1980

Plant Capacity (thousand short tons per year)	Percentage of Total Capacity	
	1973	1980
100– 299	7.21	4.22
300– 399	12.14	6.92
400– 499	13.36	13.02
500– 599	14.82	12.38
600– 699	12.71	11.92
700– 799	8.30	13.33
800– 899	5.55	6.98
900– 999	7.28	3.91
1000–1099	1.15	5.33
1100–1199	3.74	8.22
1200–1299	5.41	5.17
1300–1499	0.00	2.86
1500–1699	3.38	3.26
1700–1899	2.06	0.00
over 2000	2.88	2.47

Source: Reprinted by permission of the author from Bruce T. Allen, "Economies of Scale in the Portland Cement Industry, 1973–1980," working paper, Michigan State University, 1971, Revised, April 8, 1981.

share of total industry output; he concluded from this that average costs decline with size. The small firms' losses were distributed equally among medium-size and larger firms, indicating first increasing, then constant, returns to scale. Since there was no indication of diseconomies of scale at very high output levels, the conclusion was that the automobile industry's long-run average cost curve is L-shaped.

In a continuing study of economies of scale in the Portland cement industry Bruce T. Allen also finds an L-shaped long-run average cost curve.[8] Table 6.A.1 provides data on the composition of cement production by plant size for the years 1973 and 1980. The data indicate that plant-size classes of less than 700,000 tons a year accounted for smaller shares of industry capacity in 1980 than in 1973 and that plant-size classes between 700,000 and 1.5 million tons accounted for larger shares of industry capacity in 1980 than in 1973.

Allen's study does not reveal the conventional U-shaped long-run average cost curve; rather, it suggests that long-run average cost de-

---

[8]Bruce T. Allen, "Economies of Scale in the Portland Cement Industry, 1973–1980," working paper, Michigan State University, 1971, revised April 8, 1981; and "Vertical Integration and Market Foreclosure: The Case of Cement and Concrete," *Journal of Law and Economics* 14 (April 1971), pp. 251–274.

creases as plant capacity increases to about 700,000 tons and that they are then flat at least up to a capacity of 1.5 million tons. Beyond 1.5 million tons there is slight evidence of diseconomies of scale. However, in these large capacity classes the data are dominated by single-firm activities and may be explained by area market conditions rather than scale economies. Thus, it appears that the minimum efficient scale in the Portland cement industry is about 700,000 tons per year and that any diseconomies are weak and exist only for plants above 1.5 million tons.

Although the survivor technique is a valuable tool for examining cost/output relations, it too has limitations. First, its premise is the notion that survival is directly related to minimization of long-run average costs. As is demonstrated in more detail in Chapter 8, this premise implicitly assumes that the firms examined are operating in a highly competitive market structure. If markets are protected by regulation or various barriers to entry, even inefficient firms can survive for extended periods. Second, high transportation costs can make survival possible for strategically located firms despite productive inefficiencies. Third, in many industries inefficient smaller firms survive by emphasizing personalized service or customized production. Successful product differentiation often makes it possible for smaller firms to not only survive but flourish in the face of competition from larger, more efficient rivals.

Finally, because of the very long-run nature of the analysis, the survivor technique is particularly susceptible to the problem of distorted results arising from inflation and changing technology. In many instances inventions or innovations over time favor firms in specific-size classes. Resulting changes in the distribution of industry output may reveal little about the shape of industry long-run average cost curves (i.e., economies of scale), reflecting instead shifts in cost/output relationships.

Engineering Technique. The engineering method of cost analysis is based directly on the physical relationship expressed in the production function for a particular product or firm. On the basis of a knowledge of the production technology involved, the optimal input combination for producing any given output quantity is determined. The cost curve is then formulated by multiplying each input in these least-cost combinations by its price and summing to develop the cost function.

The engineering technique comes the closest of any of the estimation procedures to reflecting the timeless nature of theoretical cost functions. It is based on currently available technology, and it alleviates the possibility of confounding the results through improper data observations. That is, while cost observations used for statistical cost estimation may be contaminated by any number of extraneous factors, engineering estimation abstracts from these complications by coupling current price quotations from suppliers with estimates of required quantities of various inputs.

The engineering method of cost estimation has proven useful for examining cost/output relationships in such areas as oil refining, chemical production, and nuclear power generation. Leslie Cookenboo, Jr., for example, used the technique to estimate cost functions for oil pipeline systems.[9] Cookenboo first analyzed input/output relationships for the three main factors in the system—pipe diameter, horsepower of pumps, and number of pumping stations—in order to determine the production function for the system. By adding input prices to the analysis, he was able to determine the least-cost combination of inputs for each production level and to develop the long-run cost curve for oil pipelines. His results showed that long-run costs decline continuously over the range of output levels examined.

The engineering method of cost estimation is not without pitfalls, and care must be exercised in using the method if accurate cost functions are to be developed. The difficulty often comes in trying to extend engineering production functions beyond the range of existing systems, or in going from pilot plant operations to full-scale production facilities. These problems are illustrated by the difficulties encountered by a major chemical company in developing a facility that made use of a new production technology. The firm completed an engineering cost study based on projected input/output relationships developed from a small pilot facility. The estimated cost of constructing the new plant was $100 million; and it was projected that output would have a marginal cost of approximately $100 a ton, substantially below the costs in existing facilities. Once construction got underway, however, it became clear that the projection of production relations beyond the pilot plant's size were woefully inadequate. A planned two-year construction period dragged on for five years, and construction costs ballooned to $300 million. After completion of the plant, actual marginal costs of production were $150 a ton, a 50 percent increase over the estimated level. Although this is an extreme case, it does illustrate that while the engineering method can provide a useful alternative to statistical cost estimation, it too must be applied with great care if accurate cost projection is to result.

---

[9]Leslie Cookenboo, Jr. *Crude Oil Pipelines and Competition in the Oil Industry* (Cambridge, Mass.: Harvard University Press 1955).

Summary

Empirical determination of a firm's cost function is a necessary requirement for optimal decision making. In this appendix a variety of techniques for analyzing both short-run and long-run cost/output relationships were examined.

The primary statistical methodology used for cost estimation is least squares regression analysis. Properly conducted time-series analysis of a single firm's cost/output relationship can provide an excellent estimate of the firm's short-run variable cost function. This function indicates the nature of marginal costs and average variable costs, the relevant-cost concepts for short-run decision making.

Statistical estimation of long-run costs typically involves cross-section analysis as opposed to time-series regression analysis. Here cost/output relationships for many firms of varying size are analyzed to determine the nature of the total cost function for firms of different scale.

Two major findings dominate the work of researchers in the area of cost analysis. In the short run the relationship between cost and output appears to be best approximated in most cases by a linear function. This means that marginal costs are constant over a significant range of output for most firms. Long-run estimation has typically indicated that sharply increasing returns to scale (decreasing average cost) are available over low output ranges in most industries, giving way to constant returns (constant average cost) at higher output levels. Decreasing returns to scale (increasing average costs), even at very high output quantities, appear to be the exception rather than the rule for most long-run cost functions.

Because of difficulties encountered in statistical cost estimation, alternative techniques of empirical analysis are frequently employed. The survivor technique and the engineering technique are two methods commonly used for this purpose.

The survivor technique is based on the assumption that more efficient firms, those with lower average costs, will have a greater probability of survival over time. Therefore, by examining the size makeup of an industry over time, one can determine the nature of cost/output relationships.

The engineering technique is based on the physical relationships expressed in the production function for a firm. Using engineering estimates of input/output relationships, one determines the optimal production system and multiplies each required input by its cost to determine the cost function. This method is particularly useful for estimating cost relationships for new products or plants involving new technologies where historical data necessary for statistical cost analysis are unavailable.

Questions

6.A.1 The law of diminishing productivity in microeconomic theory leads one to expect that short-run marginal (and average variable) cost curves would be U-shaped. What factors might lead to the empirical finding of constant marginal costs for most firms?

6.A.2 Name and briefly elaborate on three common problems encountered in short-run cost analysis.

6.A.3 Short-run statistical cost studies have been reported for a wide variety of industries, ranging from autos to Xerox machines. Long-run cost studies, on the other hand, have been restricted to a few industries, such as steel manufacturing, banks, savings and loans, insurance, and utilities. Why do you suppose so many more short-run than long-run studies have been conducted?

6.A.4 What conditions are necessary in order to estimate a long-run cost function?

6.A.5 For long-run statistical cost estimation, cross-sectional analysis, as opposed to time-series analysis, is typically used at least partly to overcome the problem of changing technology. Does the use of cross-sectional data necessarily eliminate this problem? Why or why not?

6.A.6 Does the survivor technique for estimating long-run cost/output relations overcome the problem of changing technology?

Problem Set

6.A.1 A steel manufacturer is considering a plan to reduce production costs by switching some of its steel production to a new minimill. Minimills convert steel scrap into products such as bars, rods, and light structural steel products. Their production costs are roughly one third lower than those of the large integrated plants. Using industry and trade association data, engineering analyses of cost/output relations for similar minimills have been calculated as

$$C = 9{,}375 + 70Q - 0.04Q^2 \qquad R^2 = 0.98$$
$$(1{,}650) \quad (9.5) \quad (0.006) \qquad SEE = 20$$

C = Total Costs (in Thousands of Dollars)

Q = Output (in Thousands of Tons).

In the above cost function, \$9,375 (000) represents fixed costs, which do not include capital costs of \$6 million, reflecting an average 12 percent cost of capital. The market price for the steel is predicted to be \$60 per ton.

a) What is the business profit breakeven output level for the proposed minimill?

b) What is the economic profit breakeven output level?

c) Calculate estimated average cost at the anticipated production level of 800,000 tons.

d) What is the degree of operating leverage at 800,000 tons of production?

e) Would you have a high level of confidence in the breakeven, estimated cost, and DOL levels calculated above? Why or why not?

References

Anthony, Robert N. "What Should 'Cost' Mean?" *Harvard Business Review* 48 (May–June 1970): 121–131.

Bain, Joe S. "Survival-Ability as a Test of Efficiency." *American Economic Review* 59 (May 1969): 99–104.

Berndt, Ernst R. and Morrison, Catherine J. "Capacity Utilization Measures: Underlying Economic Theory and an Alternative Approach." *American Economic Review* 71 (May 1981): 48–52.

Duetsch, Larry L. "Geographic Market Size and the Extent of Multiplant Operations." *Review of Economics and Statistics* 64 (February 1982): 165–167.

Hirschey, Mark. "Economies of Scale in Advertising." *Managerial and Decision Economics* 3 (March 1982): 24–29.

Hirschey, Mark. "Estimation of Cost Elasticities for Light Density Railroad Freight Service." *Land Economics* 55 (August 1979): 366–378.

Hirshleifer, Jack. "The Firm's Cost Function: A Successful Reconstruction." *Journal of Business* (July 1962): 235–255.

Longbrake, William A. "Statistical Cost Analysis." *Financial Management* 2 (Spring 1973): 48–56.

Miller, Edward M. "The Extent of Economies of Scale: The Effect of Firm Size on Labor Productivity and Wage Rates." *Southern Economic Journal* 44 (January 1978): 470–487.

Oi, Walter Y. "Slack Capacity: Productive or Wasteful?" *American Economic Review* 71 (May 1981): 64–69.

Peterson, R. D. "The Survivor Principle and Small-Firm Entry Decisions." *Journal of Small Business Management* 20 (October 1982): 13–21.

Stigler, George J. "The Economies of Scale." *Journal of Law and Economics* 1 (October 1958): 54–71.

Thompson, Arthur A. "Strategies for Staying Cost Competitive." *Harvard Business Review* 62 (January–February 1984): 110–117.

Tucker, Irvin B. and Wilder, Ronald P. "Trends in Vertical Integration in the U.S. Manufacturing Sector." *Journal of Industrial Economics* 26 (September 1977): 81–94.

Walters, A. A. "Production and Cost Functions: An Econometric Survey." *Econometrica* 31 (January–April 1963): 1–66.

Chapter 7

Linear Programming

Key Terms
Constraints
Feasible space
Objective function
Slack variables

Linear programming is an analytical technique used to determine the optimal solution to a decision problem. It is particularly powerful in solving problems when constraints limit or restrict the course of action available to the decision maker. Since most managerial problems are of this nature, linear programming is a useful analytical technique for managerial decision making.

The value of linear programming in managerial decision making can be seen by considering a few of the many types of constrained optimization problems to which it has been applied. Applications cover such diverse managerial problems as product design and product mix specification, input allocation in production systems (including job assignment of key personnel), product distribution analysis (including plant location and delivery routing), promotional mix in marketing activities, inventory and cash management, and capital budgeting (investment) decisions. Although quite different in terms of their focus, each of these problem structures involves the allocation of scarce resources to achieve some specific goal.

In the area of production related decisions, firms are often faced with a variety of capacity limitations. Limited availability of skilled labor and

271

specialized equipment, fixed plant size, and limits on raw materials or energy inputs can all constrain production. When such capacity constraints exist, managers must exercise careful judgment to insure that scarce resources are used in the most efficient manner possible to produce only the products that provide the greatest returns or profits.

For example, an oil company has a specified quantity of crude oil and a fixed refinery capacity. It can produce gasoline of different octane ratings, diesel fuel, heating oil, kerosene, or lubricants. Given its crude oil supplies and refinery capacity, what mix of outputs should it produce? Integrated forest products companies face a similar problem. Because they have a limited supply of logs and limited mill capacity, their problem is to determine the optimum output mix of lumber, plywood, paper, and other wood products.

A related production problem involves determining the best way of producing a given output. A firm owns two plants that can be used to produce its products. The plants employ somewhat different technologies, so their cost functions are different. How should production be allocated between the two plants to minimize the total cost of production, subject to these constraints: (1) Both plants must, because of a union contract, operate at least thirty hours a week; and (2) at least 100,000 units of output must be produced each week to satisfy the firm's supply contracts.

In marketing, a frequently encountered issue is: What is the optimal advertising mix among various media, where *optimal* is defined as that mix that minimizes the cost of reaching a specified number of potential customers with certain characteristics of age, income, education, and other factors?

In finance, firms may have a large number of investment opportunities but be limited in the funds available for investment. What set of projects will maximize the value of new long-term investments, subject to the constraint that the total capital budget not exceed some specified maximum? Moreover, firms must hold balances of cash, a nonearning asset. What is the minimum amount of cash that can be held, subject to bank compensating balance and payment schedule constraints?

In none of these problem situations is there a simple rule-of-thumb solution. The interrelationships involved are complex, and arriving at optimal solutions requires careful analysis of the alternatives. The fact that linear programming has proved useful in solving such a broad range of constrained decision problems indicates its value as a managerial decision tool. Linear programming is indeed a powerful technique, one that promises to be applied to business problems with ever greater frequency in future years.

Assumption of Linearity

The basic relationship involved in linear programming problems in business and economics revolves around revenue functions, production and cost functions, and their composite, the profit function. Each of these must be linear; that is, as output increases, revenues, costs, and profits must increase linearly. For revenues to increase linearly with output, product prices must be constant. For costs to rise linearly with output, two conditions are required: (1) The firm's production function must be linear, meaning that returns to scale are constant; and (2) input prices must be constant. Constant returns to scale, when coupled with constant input price, result in a linear total cost function.

Under what conditions are product and factor prices likely to be constant? In other words, when can a firm buy unlimited quantities of its inputs, and sell unlimited amounts of its products, without having to change prices? The answer is, under conditions of pure competition. Does this mean that linear programming is applicable only for purely competitive industries and, further, only for competitive industries where returns to scale are constant? The answer is no, because linear programming is used for decision making over limited output ranges. Because input and product prices are approximately constant over these ranges, the profit function can be approximated by a linear relationship.

To illustrate, consider an oil company deciding the optimal output mix for a refinery with a capacity of 150,000 barrels of oil per day. It may be perfectly valid to assume that crude oil costs $30 a barrel, regardless of how much is purchased, and that products can be sold at constant prices, regardless of the quantities offered. The firm may have to pay more for crude oil and may have to sell its output at lower prices if it tries to expand the refinery by a factor of 10, but within the range of feasible outputs (up to 150,000 barrels a day) prices are approximately constant. Further, up to its capacity limits, it is reasonable to expect that a doubling of crude oil inputs leads to a doubling of output; therefore, returns to scale are also constant. Roughly the same conditions hold for forest-product companies, office-equipment manufacturers, automobile producers, and many other firms.

We see, then, that in many instances the linearity assumptions are valid. Further, in other cases, when the assumption does not hold precisely, linear approximations will not seriously distort the analysis.

Linear Programming and Production Planning: One Product

Although linear programming has been applied in almost all aspects of business management, it has been developed most fully and is used most frequently in production decisions. Often the decision problem is to determine the least cost combination of inputs needed to produce a particular product. In other cases, the problem may be concerned with obtaining the maximum level of output from a fixed quantity of resources. Both problems can be readily solved by linear programming. To see this more clearly, we start with a simple case and examine the problem faced by a firm that can use two inputs in various combinations to produce a single product. Then, in later sections, we examine more realistic but necessarily more complex cases.

Production Processes

Assume that a firm produces a single product, Q, using two inputs, L and K, which might represent labor and capital. Further, instead of the possibility of continuous substitution between L and K, as was hypothesized in Chapter 5, assume that there are only four possible input combinations with which the firm can produce Q. In other words, four different production processes are available to the firm for making Q, each of which uses a different but fixed combination of the two inputs, L and K. In most industries, this is an entirely reasonable assumption, much more reasonable than continuous substitution. The four production processes discussed here, for example, might be thought of as being four different plants, each with its fixed asset configuration and each requiring a specific amount of labor to operate the equipment. Alternatively, they could be four different assembly stations or assembly lines, each using a slightly different combination of equipment and labor.

The four production processes are illustrated in Figure 7.1. Process A requires the combination of 15 units of L and 1 unit of K for each unit of Q produced. Process B uses 10 units of L and 2 units of K for each unit of output; Processes C and D use 7.5 units of L with 3 units of K, and 5 units of L with 5 units of K, respectively, for each unit of Q produced. The four production processes are illustrated as rays in the figure. Each point along the production ray for Process A combines L and K in the ratio 15 to 1; and Process Rays B, C, and D are developed in the same way. Each point along a single production ray combines the two inputs in a fixed ratio, with the ratios differing from one production process to another. If we assume that L and K represent labor and capital inputs, we can view the four production processes as different

Figure 7.1
Production Process Rays in Linear Programming

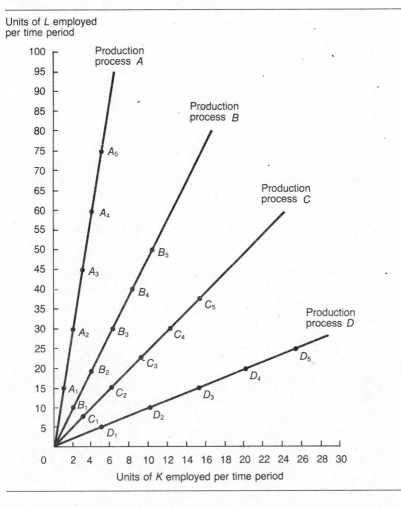

Units of L employed
per time period

Units of K employed per time period

plants employing different production techniques. Process A, for example, is very labor intensive in relation to the other production systems, while B, C, and D are based on increasingly capital intensive technologies.

Examining Process A, we see that Point A_1 indicates the combination of L and K required to produce 1 unit of output using that production system. Doubling the quantities of both L and K doubles the quantity of Q produced; this is indicated by the distance moved along Ray A from A_1 to A_2. In other words, the line segment $0A_2$ is exactly twice the length of line segment $0A_1$ and thus represents twice as much output. Further, along Production Process Ray A, the distance $0A_1 = A_1A_2 = A_2A_3 = A_3A_4 = A_4A_5$. Each of these line segments indicates the addition of 1 unit of output, using increased quantities of L and K in the fixed ratio of 15 to 1.

Output along the ray increases proportionately with increases in the input factors. Thus, if each input is doubled, output is doubled; or if inputs are increased by a factor of 10 percent, output increases in the same proportion. This follows from the linearity assumption noted above: Each production process must exhibit constant returns to scale.

Output is measured in the same way along the other three production process rays in Figure 7.1. For example, Point C_1 indicates the combination of L and K required to produce 1 unit of Q using Process C. The production of 2 units of Q by that process requires the combination of L and K indicated at Point C_2, and the same is true for Points C_3, C_4, and C_5. Note that although the production of additional units by Process C is indicated by line segments of equal length, just as for Process A, the line segments are of different lengths between the various production systems. That is, although each production process exhibits constant returns to scale, allowing us to determine output quantities by measuring the length of the process ray in question, equal distances along *different* process rays do *not* ordinarily indicate equal output quantities.

Production Isoquants

Joining points of equal output on the four production process rays provides us with a set of isoquant curves, as illustrated in Figure 7.2, where isoquants for $Q = 1, 2, 3, 4$, and 5 are shown. These curves have precisely the same interpretation as the isoquants developed in Chapter 5. They represent all possible combinations of Input Factors L and K that can be used to produce a given quantity of output. The production isoquants in linear programming are composed of linear segments connecting the various production processes, and the segments of the various isoquants are always parallel to one another. For example, Line Segment A_1B_1 is parallel to Segment A_2B_2; similarly, Isoquant Segment B_3C_3 is parallel to B_2C_2.

The points along each segment of an isoquant between two process rays represent a combination of output from each of the two adjoining production processes. Consider Point X in Figure 7.2, which represents production of a total of 4 units of Q using 25 units of L and 16 units of K. None of the available production processes can be used to manufacture Q using L and K in the ratio 25 to 16, but that combination is possible by producing part of the output with Process C and part with Pro-

Figure 7.2
Production Isoquants in Linear Programming

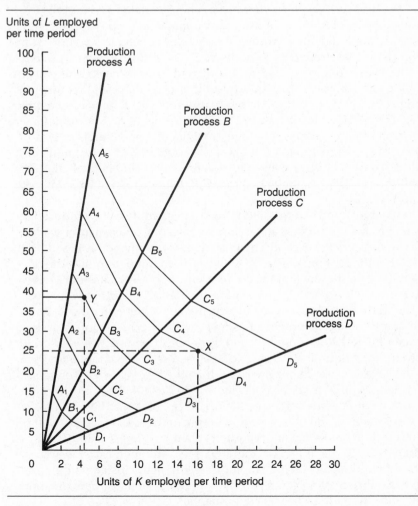

cess D. In this case, 2 units of Q can be produced using Process C and 2 units using Process D. Production of 2 units of Q with Process C utilizes 15 units of L and 6 units of K. For the production of 2 units of Q with Process D, 10 units each of L and K are necessary. Thus, although no single production system is available with which the firm can produce 4 units of Q using 25 units of L and 16 units of K, Processes C and D together can produce in that combination.

All points lying on the production isoquant segments can be interpreted in a similar manner. Each point represents a linear combination of output using the production process systems that bound the particular segment. Point Y in Figure 7.2 provides another illustration of this. At Y, 3 units of Q are being produced, using a total of 38.5 units of L and 4.3 units of K.[1] That input/output combination is possible through a linear combination of Processes A and B. The reader can verify from Figure 7.2 that producing 1.7 units of Q using Process A and 1.3 units with Process B requires 38.5 units of L and 4.3 units of K. This can also be seen algebraically. To produce 1 unit of Q by Process A requires 15 units of L and 1 unit of K. Therefore, to produce 1.7 units of Q requires 25.5 (1.7 × 15) units of L and 1.7 (1.7 × 1) units of K. To produce a single unit of Q by Process B requires 10 units of L and 2 units of K, so 1.3 units of Q requires 13 (10 × 1.3) units of L and 2.6 (2 × 1.3) units of K. Thus, Point Y calls for the production of 3 units of Q in total, 1.7 units by Process A and 1.3 units by Process B, using a total of 38.5 units of L and 4.3 units of K.

One easy approach for determining the quantity to be produced by each production process at varying points along an isoquant is called the *relative distance method*. The relative distance method is based on the fact that the location of a point along an isoquant determines the relative shares of production for the adjacent processes. Consider Point X in Figure 7.2. If Point X were on Process Ray C, all output would be produced using Process C. Similarly, if Point X were on Process Ray D, all output would be produced using Process D. Since Point X lies between Process Rays C and D, both Processes C and D will be used to produce the output. Process C will be used relatively more than Process D if X is closer to Process Ray C than to Process Ray D. Conversely, Process D will be used relatively more than Process C if X is closer to Process Ray D than to Process Ray C. Since Point X in Figure 7.2 lies at the midpoint of the $Q = 4$ isoquant segment between C_4 and D_4, it implies production of equal proportions using Processes C and D. Thus, at Point X, $Q = 4$ and $Q_C = 2$ and $Q_D = 2$. Although extreme accuracy would require painstaking graphic detail, in many instances the relative distance method can be used to provide adequate approximations of production intensities along isoquants.

---

[1] In linear programming we also assume that fractional variables are permissible. In many applications this assumption is not important. For example, in the present illustration we might be talking about labor-hours and machine-hours for the inputs. The solution value calling for $L = 38.5$ merely states that 38.5 hours of labor are required.

In some cases, however, where inputs are large (whole plants, for example), the fact that linear programming assumes divisible variables is important. In such cases linear programming as described herein may be inappropriate, and a more complex technique, integer programming, may be required.

Figure 7.3
Determination of Least-Cost Production Process

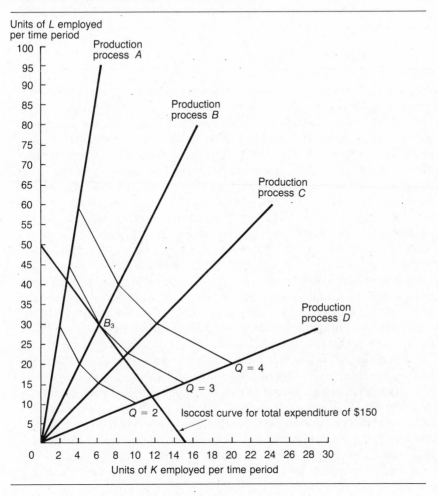

Least-Cost Input Combinations

Adding isocost curves to the set of isoquants permits one to determine least cost input combinations for the production of Product Q. This is shown in Figure 7.3, under the assumption that each unit of L costs $3 and each unit of K costs $10. The isocost curve illustrated indicates a total expenditure of $150.

The tangency between the isocost curve and the isoquant curve for $Q = 3$, at Point B_3, indicates that Production Process B, which combines Inputs L and K in the ratio 5 to 1, is the least cost method of producing Q. For any expenditure level, production is maximized by using Process B. Alternatively, Production Process B is the least cost method for producing any quantity of Q, given the assumed prices for L and K.

Optimal Input Combinations with Limited Resources

Frequently, firms are faced with limited inputs during specific production periods and because of this may find it optimal to use inputs in proportions other than the least-cost combination. Examples of such resource **constraints** include limitations on the hours of skilled labor available, shortages of a particular type of equipment, insufficient raw materials, limited warehouse space, and so on. In these cases the linear programming problem must be stated in terms of physical constraints on inputs rather than in terms of constraints on total expenditures.

To illustrate, consider the effect of limits on the quantities of L and K available in our example. Assume that only 20 units of L and 11 units of K are available during the current production period and that the firm seeks to maximize production of Q. These constraints are shown in Figure 7.4. The horizontal line drawn at $L = 20$ indicates the upper limit on the quantity of L that can be employed during the production period; the vertical line at $K = 11$ indicates a similar limit on the quantity of K.

We can determine the production possibilities for this problem by noting that, in addition to the limitations on Inputs L and K, the firm must operate within the area bounded by Production Process Rays A and D. In other words, the firm is unable to combine L and K in ratios that lie either above Production Process Ray A or below Production Process Ray D. Thus, we see that combining the production possibilities with the input constraints restricts the firm to operations within the shaded area $0PRS$ in Figure 7.4. This area is known as the **feasible space** in the programming problem. Any point within the space combines L and K in a technically feasible ratio, and availability limits on L and K are not exceeded.

Since the firm is trying to maximize the production of Q, subject to constraints on the use of L and K, it should operate at that point in the feasible space that touches the highest possible isoquant. This is Point R in Figure 7.4, where $Q = 3$.

Although it is possible to solve problems like the foregoing example by using carefully constructed graphs, it is typically more useful to combine graphic analysis with algebraic manipulations to obtain accurate solutions efficiently. For example, consider again Figure 7.4. Even if the isoquant for $Q = 3$ were not drawn, it would be apparent from the slopes of the isoquants for 2 or 4 units of output that the optimal solution to the problem must be at Point R. That is, it is readily apparent

Figure 7.4
Optimal Input Combination with Limited Resources

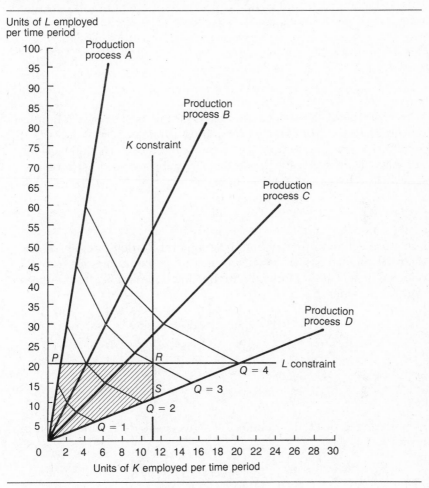

Units of L employed
per time period

from the graph that the maximum production will be obtained by operating at the point where both inputs are fully employed. Since Point R
lies at the intersection of the two input constraints, this means that all
20 units of L and 11 units of K will be employed. Because R lies between
Production Processes C and D, we also know that the output-maximiz-
ing production combination will make use of only these two production processes.

With this information from the graph we can solve algebraically for
the optimal quantities to be produced using Processes C and D. Recall

that each unit of output produced using Process C requires 7.5 units of L. Thus, the total L required in Process C will be equal to $7.5Q_C$. Similarly, each unit produced using Process D requires 5 units of L so that total L used in Process D equals $5Q_D$. At Point R, 20 units of L are being used in Processes C and D together, and thus the following relationship must hold:

$$7.5Q_C + 5Q_D = 20. \tag{7.1}$$

A similar relationship can be developed for the use of K. Each unit of output produced from Process C requires 3 units of K; in Process D, 5 units of K are used to produce each unit of output. The total use of K equals 11 units at Point R, and these 11 units are used in Processes C and D such that

$$3Q_C + 5Q_D = 11. \tag{7.2}$$

Equations 7.1 and 7.2 must both hold at Point R; therefore, by solving them simultaneously we can determine the output quantities from Processes C and D at that location. Subtracting Equation 7.2 from Equation 7.1 provides

$$7.5Q_C + 5Q_D = 20 \tag{7.1}$$
$$\text{minus}\ \underline{3.0Q_C + 5Q_D = 11} \tag{7.2}$$
$$4.5Q_C \qquad\quad = 9$$
$$Q_C \qquad\quad = 2 .$$

Substituting 2 for Q_C in Equation 7.2 allows us to determine the output from Process D:

$$3(2) + 5Q_D = 11$$
$$5Q_D = 5$$
$$Q_D = 1 .$$

Therefore, total output at Point R is 3 units, composed of 2 units from Process C and 1 unit from Process D.

The ability to combine graphic and algebraic representations of the relationships in a linear programming problem allows one to obtain precise solutions in many cases with relative ease. This combined approach to solving linear programming problems is developed more fully in the following section.

Linear Programming and Production Planning: Multiple Products

Most production decisions, as well as decisions in other areas, are considerably more complex than the preceding example. Accordingly, we expand our discussion, moving first to the problem of the optimal output mix for a multiproduct firm facing restrictions on productive facilities and other inputs. This problem, which is precisely the one faced by oil refineries, cereal processing firms, and forest-products companies, among others, is readily solved by linear programming, as the following example reveals.

Consider a firm that produces Products X and Y and uses Inputs A, B, and C. To maximize its total profits, the firm must determine the optimal quantities of each product to produce, subject to the constraints imposed by limitations on input availability.

Specification of the Objective Function

We assume that the firm wishes to maximize total profits from the two products, X and Y, during each time period. If the unit profit contribution, or excess of price over average variable cost, is \$12 for Product X and \$9 for Product Y, we can write the **objective function** as:

Maximize

$$\pi = 12Q_x + 9Q_Y. \tag{7.3}$$

Here Q_X and Q_Y represent the quantities of each product produced. The unit profit contribution of X times the units of X produced and sold, plus the unit contribution of Y times Q_Y, is the total profit contribution, π, earned by the firm. It is this total profit contribution that the firm wishes to maximize, since by maximizing profit contribution the firm also maximizes its net profit.[2]

Specification of the Constraint Equations

Table 7.1, which specifies the available quantities of each input, as well as their usage in the production of X and Y, provides all the information necessary to construct the constraint relationships for this problem.

---

[2] Fixed costs must be subtracted from the profit contribution to determine net profits. However, since fixed costs are constant, regardless of how much or how little output is produced, maximizing profit contribution is tantamount to maximizing profit, and the output mix that maximizes profit contribution also maximizes net profit. This concept of profit contribution was developed more fully in Chapter 6.

Table 7.1
Inputs Available for Production of X and Y

Input	Quantity Required per Unit of Output		Quantity Available per Time Period
	X	Y	
A	4	2	32
B	1	1	10
C	0	3	21

From the table we see that 32 units of Input A are available in each period, and that 4 units of A are required in the production of each unit of X, while 2 units of A are necessary to produce 1 unit of Y.

Since 4 units of A are required for the production of a single unit of X, the total amount of A used to manufacture X can be written as $4Q_X$. Similarly, 2 units of A are required to produce each unit of Y, so $2Q_Y$ represents the total quantity of A used in the production of Product Y. Summing the quantities of A used in the production of X and Y provides an expression for the total usage of A, and since this total cannot exceed the 32 units available, we can write the constraint condition for Input A as:

$$4Q_X + 2Q_Y \leq 32. \qquad (7.4)$$

The constraint for Input B can be determined in a like manner. One unit of Input B is necessary for the production of each unit of either X or Y, so the total amount of B that will be expended is $1Q_X + 1Q_Y$. The maximum quantity of B available for production in each time period is 10 units; thus, the constraint requirement associated with Input B is:

$$1Q_X + 1Q_Y \leq 10. \qquad (7.5)$$

Finally, there is the constraint relationship for Input C, which is used only in the production of Y. Each unit of Y requires an input of 3 units of C, and 21 units of Input C are available. Total usage of C, then, is given by the expression $3Q_Y$, and the constraint can be written as:

$$3Q_Y \leq 21. \qquad (7.6)$$

Constraint equations play major roles in solving linear programming problems. One further concept must be introduced, however, before we can completely specify the linear programming problem and examine how the constraints are used to obtain its solution.

Nonnegativity Requirement

Because linear programming is nothing more than a mathematical tool for solving constrained optimization problems, nothing in the technique itself insures that an answer will make economic sense. For example, in a production problem, for some very unprofitable product the mathematically optimal output level may be a *negative* quantity, clearly an impossible solution. Likewise, in a distribution problem, an optimal solution might include negative shipments from one point to another, again an impossible act.

To prevent such nonsense results, we must include a nonnegativity requirement. This is a statement that all variables in the problem must be equal to or greater than zero. Thus, for the production problem we are examining, we must add the expressions:

$$Q_X \geq 0$$

and

$$Q_Y \geq 0.$$

Graphic Specification and Solution of the Linear Programming Problem

Having specified the component parts of the firm's linear programming problem, we first examine this problem graphically, then analyze it algebraically. Let us begin by restating the decision problem in terms of the system of expressions for the objective function and input constraints. The firm wishes to maximize its total profit contribution, π, subject to constraints imposed by limitations on its resources. This can be expressed as:

Maximize

$$\pi = 12Q_X + 9Q_Y, \tag{7.3}$$

subject to the following constraints:

$$\text{Input } A: 4Q_X + 2Q_Y \leq 32, \tag{7.4}$$

$$\text{Input } B: 1Q_X + 1Q_Y \leq 10, \tag{7.5}$$

$$\text{Input } C: \qquad 3Q_Y \leq 21, \tag{7.6}$$

where

$$Q_X \geq 0 \text{ and } Q_Y \geq 0.$$

Figure 7.5
Constraint Imposed by Limitations in Input A

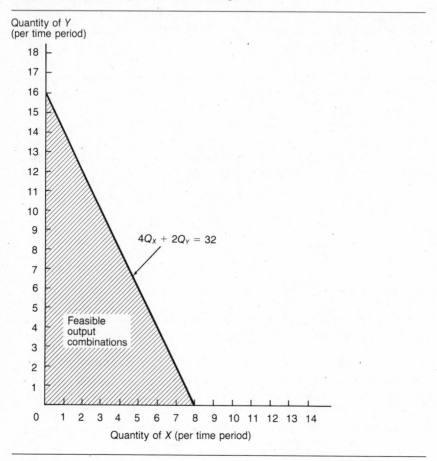

Quantity of Y
(per time period)

$4Q_X + 2Q_Y = 32$

Feasible
output
combinations

Quantity of X (per time period)

Determining the Feasible Space

Figure 7.5 is a graph of the constraint equation for Input A, $4Q_X + 2Q_Y$ $= 32$, which indicates the maximum quantities of X and Y that can be produced, given the limitation on the availability of Input A. A maximum of 16 units of Y can be produced if no X is manufactured; 8 units of X can be produced if the output of Y is zero. Any point along the line connecting these two outputs represents the maximum combination of X and Y that can be produced using no more than 32 units of A.

This constraint equation divides the XY plane into two half-spaces. Every point lying on the line or to the left of it satisfies the constraint expressed by the equation $4Q_X + 2Q_Y \le 32$; every point to the right of this line violates these conditions. Thus, only points on the constraint

Figure 7.6
Feasible Space

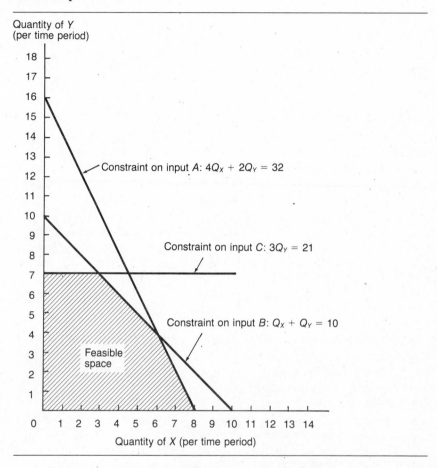

Quantity of Y
(per time period)

Constraint on input A: $4Q_X + 2Q_Y = 32$

Constraint on input C: $3Q_Y = 21$

Constraint on input B: $Q_X + Q_Y = 10$

Feasible
space

Quantity of X (per time period)

line or to the left of it can be in the feasible space. The shaded area of Figure 7.5 represents the feasible area as bounded by the constraint on Input A along with the nonnegativity requirements on the variables Q_X and Q_Y.

In Figure 7.6 we have further limited the feasible space by adding the constraints for Inputs B and C. The constraint on Input B can be expressed as $Q_X + Q_Y = 10$. Thus, if no Y is produced, a maximum of 10 units of X can be produced; if output of X is zero, 10 units of Y can be manufactured. All combinations of X and Y lying on, or to the left of, the line connecting these two points are feasible with respect to utilization of Input B.

The horizontal line at $Q_Y = 7$ in Figure 7.6 represents the constraint imposed by Input C. Since C is used only in the production of Y, it does not constrain the production of X at all. Seven units of Y, however, are the maximum quantity that can be produced with the 21 units of C available.

The three input constraints, together with the nonnegativity requirement, completely delimit the feasible space of our linear programming problem, which is the shaded area of Figure 7.6. Only those points within this area meet all the constraints.

Graphing the Objective Function

The objective function in our example, $\pi = 12Q_X + 9Q_Y$, can be graphed in the $Q_X Q_Y$ space as a series of isoprofit curves. This is illustrated in Figure 7.7, where isoprofit curves for $36, $72, $108, and $144 are shown. Each isoprofit curve illustrates all possible combinations of X and Y that result in a constant total profit contribution. For example, the isoprofit curve labeled $\pi = 36 is the locus of all points that satisfy the equation $\pi = 36 = 12Q_X + 9Q_Y$. Alternatively stated, each *combination* of X and Y lying along that curve results in a total profit contribution of $36. Similarly, all output combinations along the $\pi = 72 curve satisfy the equation $72 = 12Q_X + 9Q_Y$ and thus provide a total profit contribution of $72. It is clear from Figure 7.7 that the isoprofit curves are a series of parallel lines that take on higher values as we move upward and to the right.

Isoprofit curves are identical in form to the isocost curves developed in Chapter 5. Here, the profit function $\pi = aQ_X + bQ_Y$, where a and b are the profit contributions of Products X and Y respectively, is solved for Q_Y, resulting in an equation of the form:

$$Q_Y = \frac{\pi}{b} - \frac{a}{b} Q_X.$$

Given the individual profit contributions, a and b, the Q_Y intercept is determined by the profit level of the isoprofit curve, while the slope is given by the relative profitabilities of the products. Since the relative profitability of the products is unaffected by the output level, isoprofit curves in a linear programming problem will always be a series of parallel lines. In the example, all the isoprofit curves have a slope of $-12/9$, or -1.33.

Graphic Solution of the Linear Programming Problem

Since the firm's objective is to maximize total profit, it should operate on the highest isoprofit curve obtainable. Combining the feasible space limitations shown in Figure 7.6 with the family of isoprofit curves from

Figure 7.7
Isoprofit Contribution Curves

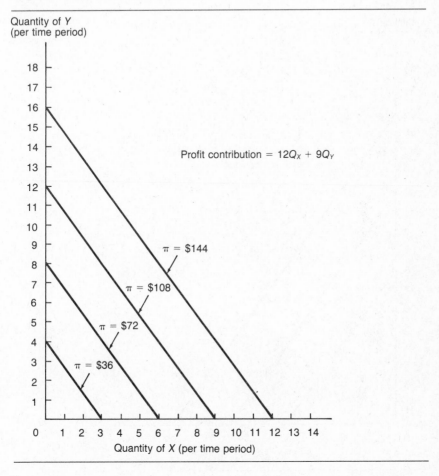

Quantity of Y
(per time period)

Profit contribution = $12Q_X + 9Q_Y$

$\pi = \$144$

$\pi = \$108$

$\pi = \$72$

$\pi = \$36$

Quantity of X (per time period)

Figure 7.7 allows us to obtain the graphic solution to our linear programming problem. The combined graph is illustrated in Figure 7.8.

Point *M* in the figure indicates the solution to the problem. Here,
the firm produces 6 units of *X* and 4 units of *Y*, and the total profit contribution is $108 [(12 × 6) + (9 × 4)], which is the maximum available
under the conditions stated in the problem. No other point within the
feasible space touches as high an isoprofit curve.

We can also obtain this result by using the combined graphic and
analytical procedure introduced in the preceding section. From the
graph we see that the highest possible isoprofit curve is reached at Point
M. This is apparent even if we do not know the actual level of profit
contribution at that point. At *M* the constraints on Inputs *A* and *B* are

Figure 7.8
Graphic Solution to the Linear Programming Problem

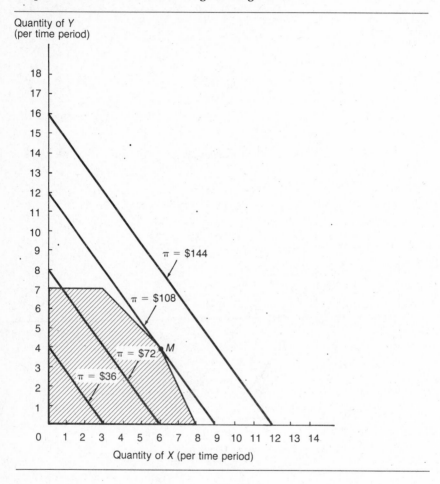

Quantity of Y
(per time period)

Quantity of X (per time period)

both binding. That is, at M the 32 units of Input A and 10 units of Input B are being completely utilized in the production of X and Y. Thus, Expressions 7.4 and 7.5 can be written as equations and solved simultaneously for Q_X and Q_Y:

$$4Q_X + 2Q_Y = 32 \qquad (7.4)$$

$$\text{minus} \underline{\quad 2Q_X + 2Q_Y = 20 \quad} \qquad 2 \times (7.5)$$

$$2Q_X \qquad\quad = 12$$

$$Q_X \qquad\quad = 6.$$

Substituting 6 for Q_X in Equation 7.5 results in

$$6 + Q_Y = 10 \qquad (7.5)$$

$$Q_Y = 4.$$

Inserting these values for Q_X and Q_Y in the objective function (Equation 7.3) allows us to determine the actual profit contribution at Point M

$$= 12(6) + 9(4)$$

$$= \$108.$$

Notice that the optimal solution to the linear programming problem occurs at a corner of the feasible space. This is not a chance result; rather, it is a feature of the linearity assumptions underlying the linear programming technique. When the objective function and all constraint relationships are specified in linear form, there must be constant returns to scale. Because input and output prices do not change as production expands, it will always prove optimal to move as far as possible in the direction of higher outputs, provided that sales prices exceed variable costs per unit. This means that the firm will always move to a point where some capacity limit is reached; that is, to a boundary of the feasible space.

A final step is necessary to show that an optimal solution to any linear programming problem always lies at a corner of the feasible space. Since all the relationships in a linear programming problem must be linear by definition, every boundary of the feasible space is linear. Furthermore, the objective function is linear. Thus, the constrained optimization of the objective function takes place either at a corner of the feasible space, as in Figure 7.8, or at one boundary face, as is illustrated by Figure 7.9.

In Figure 7.9 we have modified the linear programming example by assuming that each unit of either X or Y produced yields a profit of \$5. In this case, the optimal solution to the problem includes any of the combinations of X and Y found along Line Segment LM, since all these combinations are feasible and all result in a total profit of \$50. If all points along Line LM provide optimal combinations of output, the combinations found at Corners L and M are also optimal. That is, since the firm is indifferent to whether it produces the combination of X and Y indicated at Point L or at Point M, or at any point between them, either corner location provides an optimal solution to the production problem. Thus, even when the highest obtainable isoprofit curve lies along a bounding face of the feasible space, it is possible to achieve an optimal solution to the problem at a corner of the feasible space.

Figure 7.9

Graphic Solution of a Linear Programming Problem Where the Objective Function Coincides with a Boundary of the Feasible Space

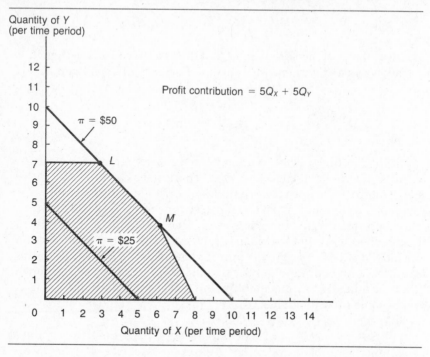

From this result it follows that in linear programming problems we can limit our analysis to just the corners of the feasible space. In other words, we can ignore the infinite number of points lying within the feasible space and concentrate our efforts solely on the corner solutions. This greatly reduces the computations necessary to solve linear programming problems that are too complex to solve by graphic methods.

Algebraic Specification and Solution of the Linear Programming Problem

The graphic technique described above is useful to illustrate the nature of linear programming, but it can be applied only in the two-output case. Since most linear programming problems contain far too many variables and constraints to allow solution by graphic analysis, we must use algebraic methods. These algebraic techniques are especially valuable in that they permit us to solve large, complex linear programming problems using computers, and this greatly extends the usefulness of the linear programming method.

Slack Variables

In order to specify a linear programming problem algebraically we must introduce one additional concept, that of **slack variables**. These variables are added to a linear programming problem to account for the amount of any input that is *unused* at a solution point. One slack variable is introduced for each constraint in the problem. In our illustrative problem, the firm is faced with capacity constraints on Input Factors A, B, and C, so the algebraic specification of the problem contains three slack variables: S_A, indicating the units of Input A that are not used in any given solution; S_B, representing unused units of B; and S_C, which measures the unused units of C.

The introduction of these slack variables allows us to write each constraint relationship as an equation rather than as an inequality. Thus, the constraint on Input A, $4Q_X + 2Q_Y \leq 32$, can be written as:

$$4Q_X + 2Q_Y + S_A = 32. \tag{7.7}$$

Here $S_A = 32 - 4Q_X - 2Q_Y$, which is the amount of Input A not used in the production of X or Y. Similar equality constraints can be specified for Inputs B and C. Specifically, the equality form of the constraint on Input B is:

$$1Q_X + 1Q_Y + S_B = 10, \tag{7.8}$$

while for C the constraint equation is:

$$3Q_Y + S_C = 21. \tag{7.9}$$

Note that the slack variables not only allow us to state the constraint conditions in equality form, thus simplifying algebraic analysis, but also provide us with valuable information. In the production problem, for example, slack variables whose values are *zero* at the optimal solution indicate inputs that cause bottlenecks or are limiting factors. Slack variables with *positive* values, on the other hand, provide measures of excess capacity in the related factor. In either case, the information provided by slack variables is important. Slack variables obviously can never take on negative values, since this would imply that the amount of the resource used exceeds the amount available. Thus, slack variables are included in the general nonnegativity requirements for all variables.

Algebraic Solution

The complete specification of our illustrative programming problem can now be stated as follows:

Maximize

$$\pi = 12Q_X + 9Q_Y, \tag{7.3}$$

subject to these constraints:

$$4Q_X + 2Q_Y + S_A = 32, \tag{7.7}$$

$$1Q_X + 1Q_Y + S_B = 10, \tag{7.8}$$

$$3Q_Y + S_C = 21, \tag{7.9}$$

where

$$Q_X, Q_Y, S_A, S_B, S_C \geq 0.$$

In words, the problem is to find the set of values for Variables Q_X, Q_Y, S_A, S_B, and S_C that maximizes Equation 7.3 and at the same time satisfies the constraints imposed by Equations 7.7, 7.8, and 7.9 and the nonnegativity requirements.

The problem stated in this form is underdetermined: We must obtain a simultaneous solution to the constraint equations, but there are more unknowns (five) than constraint equations (three), so we cannot solve the system for unique values of the variables. However, the requirement that the solution to any linear programming problem must occur at a corner of the feasible space provides enough information to allow one to obtain the solution. To see how, let us first state the following facts:

1. The optimal output occurs at a corner point. Accordingly, we need examine only the corner locations of the feasible space.

2. There are a total of $M + N$ variables in the system, where M equals the number of products and N equals the number of constraints. Thus, in our example, $M = X + Y = 2$, and $N = A + B + C = 3$, so we have a total of five variables.

3. Each variable must be equal to or greater than zero.

4. At each corner point the number of non-zero-valued variables is no greater than the number of constraint equations.

Consider Figure 7.10, where the feasible space for our illustrative problem has been regraphed. At the origin, where neither X nor Y is produced, Q_X and Q_Y both equal zero. Slack exists in all inputs, however, so S_A, S_B, and S_C are all greater than zero. Now move up the ver-

Figure 7.10
Determination of Zero-Valued Variables at Corners of the Feasible Space

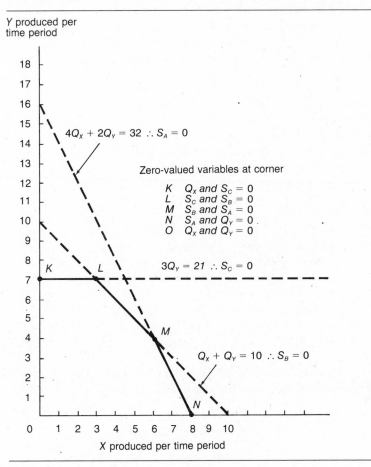

Y produced per
time period

4Q_X + 2Q_Y = 32 ∴ S_A = 0

Zero-valued variables at corner

	Zero-valued variables at corner
K	Q_X and $S_C = 0$
L	S_C and $S_B = 0$
M	S_B and $S_A = 0$
N	S_A and $Q_Y = 0$
O	Q_X and $Q_Y = 0$

$3Q_Y = 21 \therefore S_C = 0$

$Q_X + Q_Y = 10 \therefore S_B = 0$

X produced per time period

tical axis to Point K. Here Q_X and S_C both equal zero, because no X is being produced and Input C is being used to the fullest possible extent. However, Q_Y, S_A, and S_B all exceed zero. At Point L, Q_X, Q_Y, and S_A are all positive; but S_B and S_C are equal to zero. The remaining corners, M and N, can be examined similarly, and at each of them the number of non-zero-valued variables is exactly equal to the number of constraints.

We see then that the optimal solution to a linear programming problem occurs at a corner of the feasible space, and that at each corner the number of non-zero variables is equal to the number of constraints. These properties enable us to rewrite the constraints as a system with three equations and three unknowns for each corner point; such a system can be solved.

Solving the constraint equations at each corner point provides values for Q_X and Q_Y as well as for S_A, S_B, and S_C. The profit contribution at each corner can be determined by inserting the values for Q_X and Q_Y into the objective function (Equation 7.3). The corner solution that produces the maximum profit is the constrained profit maximizing output, the solution to the linear programming problem.

The procedure described above is followed in actual applications of linear programming. Computer programs are available that find solution values of the variables at a corner point, evaluate profits at that point, and then iterate to an adjacent corner point with a higher profit, continuing until the optimal corner point is located.

We can illustrate the technique somewhat more fully by examining the algebraic determination of the corner solutions in our present example. Although we could set any two of the variables equal to zero, it is convenient to begin by setting Q_X and Q_Y equal to zero and examining the solution to the programming problem at the origin. Substituting those values into the three constraint equations (7.7, 7.8, and 7.9) indicates that the three slack variables are equal to the total units of their respective inputs available to the firm; that is, $S_A = 32$, $S_B = 10$, and $S_C = 21$. This result is not unexpected, because at the origin neither X nor Y is produced, and, therefore, none of the inputs is expended for production. The total profit contribution at the origin corner of the feasible space is zero.

Now let us examine the solution at a second corner, N in Figure 7.10, where Q_Y and S_A equal zero. Substituting into Constraint Equation 7.7 permits us to solve for Q_X:

$$4Q_X + 2Q_Y + S_A = 32 \qquad (7.7)$$

$$4Q_X + 2 \cdot 0 + 0 = 32$$

$$4Q_X = 32$$

$$Q_X = 8.$$

With the value of Q_X determined, we can substitute into Equations 7.8 and 7.9 to determine values S_B and S_C:

$$Q_X + Q_Y + S_B = 10 \qquad (7.8)$$

$$8 + 0 + S_B = 10$$

$$S_B = 2,$$

and

$$3Q_Y + S_C = 21 \tag{7.9}$$

$$3 \cdot 0 + S_C = 21$$

$$S_C = 21.$$

The total profit contribution is:

$$\pi = 12Q_X + 9Q_Y \tag{7.3}$$

$$= 12 \cdot 8 + 9 \cdot 0$$

$$= \$96.$$

Next, we assign zero values to S_B and S_A, which permits us to reach solution values for Point M. Substituting zero values for S_A and S_B in Equations 7.7 and 7.8 gives us two equations in two unknowns:

$$4Q_X + 2Q_Y + 0 = 32. \tag{7.7}$$

$$Q_X + Q_Y + 0 = 10. \tag{7.8}$$

Multiplying Equation 7.8 by two and subtracting the result from Equation 7.7 provides the value for Q_X:

$$4Q_X + 2Q_Y = 32 \tag{7.7}$$
$$\text{minus } \underline{2Q_X + 2Q_Y = 20} \qquad 2 \times \text{(7.8)}$$
$$2Q_X \qquad\quad = 12$$
$$Q_X \qquad\quad = 6$$

Then, substituting 6 for Q_X in Equation 7.8, we find that $Q_Y = 4$. Total profit contribution in this case is $108 [(\$12 \cdot 6) + (\$9 \cdot 4)]$.

Similar algebraic manipulation would provide the solution for the remaining two corners of the feasible space. However, rather than work through those corner solutions, we present the results in Table 7.2. Here it is apparent, just as we illustrated in the earlier graphic analysis, that the optimal solution occurs at Point M, where 6 units of X and 4 units of Y are produced. Total profit is $108, which exceeds the profit at any other corner of the feasible space.

Slack Variables at the Solution Point

At each corner solution the values of the slack variables are determined by the linear programming process. For example, at the optimal solution (Corner M) reached in the preceding section, S_A and S_B are both equal

Table 7.2
Algebraic Solution to a Linear Programming Problem

Solution of Corner	Q_X	Q_Y	Value of Variable S_A	S_B	S_C	Total Profit Contribution
O	0	0	32	10	21	$ 0
N	8	0	0	2	21	96
M	6	4	0	0	9	108
L	3	7	6	0	0	99
K	0	7	18	3	0	63

to zero, meaning that Inputs A and B are used to the fullest extent possible, but the value of S_C is determined as follows. First, note that Q_Y = 4 at the optimal corner. Substituting this value into Constraint Equation 7.9, we find the solution value of S_C:

$$3Q_Y + S_C = 21$$

$$3 \cdot 4 + S_C = 21$$

$$S_C = 9.$$

Production of the optimal combination of X and Y completely exhausts the available quantities of Inputs A and B, but 9 units of Input C remain unused. Thus, because Inputs A and B impose effective constraints on the firm's profit level, it may wish to acquire more of one or both of them in order to expand output. Input C, on the other hand, is in excess supply, so the firm would certainly not want more C; it might even attempt to reduce its purchases of C during future production periods. Alternatively, if C is a fixed facility, such as a computer, the firm might attempt to sell some of that excess capacity to other computer users.

Constrained Cost Minimization: An Additional Linear Programming Problem Example

The use of linear programming to solve constrained optimization problems is relatively complex, as is developing an understanding of the economic significance of the results. Gaining facility with the use of the technique requires substantial exposure and practice. Accordingly, in this section we provide an additional example of a typical managerial problem that can be solved with linear programming.

Constrained cost-minimization problems are frequently encountered in managerial decision making. One interesting example associated with

Table 7.3
Advertising Media Characteristics

	Radio	Television
Cost per ad	$ 6,000	$10,000
Total audience per ad	10,000	20,000
Audience per ad with income $\geq$ $25,000	10,000	10,000
Audience per ad single	8,000	4,000

a firm's marketing activities is the problem of minimizing advertising expenditures subject to meeting certain audience exposure requirements. Consider, for example, a firm that is planning an advertising campaign for a new product. The goals that have been set for the campaign include exposure to at least 100,000 individuals, with no fewer than 80,000 of those individuals having incomes of at least $25,000 annually and no fewer than 40,000 of them being unmarried. For simplicity we will assume that the firm has only two media, radio and television, available for this campaign. One television ad costs $10,000 and is estimated to reach an audience numbering, on average, 20,000 persons. Ten thousand of these individuals will have incomes of $25,000 or more, while 4,000 of them will be single. A radio ad, on the other hand, costs $6,000 and reaches a total audience of 10,000 individuals, all of whom have at least $25,000 in income. Eight thousand of those exposed to a radio ad will be unmarried. Table 7.3 summarizes these data.

The Linear Programming Problem

The linear programming problem the firm would use to solve this constrained-optimization problem is developed as follows. The objective is to minimize the cost of the advertising campaign. Since total cost is merely the sum of the amounts spent on radio and television ads, the objective function is given by the expression:

Minimize

$$\text{Cost} = \$6{,}000R + \$10{,}000TV,$$

where R and TV represent the number of radio and television ads, respectively, that are to be employed in the advertising campaign.

The linear programming problem will have a total of three constraint equations: (1) the requirement for total audience exposure, (2) the income-related exposure requirement, and (3) the requirement that at least 40,000 single persons be among those exposed to the advertising campaign.

Assuming that individuals are exposed only once to a radio or television ad, the restriction on the minimum number of individuals that must be reached by the ad campaign can be expressed as:

$$10,000R + 20,000TV \geq 100,000.$$

This equation states that the number of persons exposed to radio ads (10,000 times the number of radio ads) plus the number exposed to television ads (20,000 times the number of television ads) must be equal to or greater than 100,000.

The remaining two constraints can be constructed similarly from the data in Table 7.3. The constraint on exposures to individuals with incomes of at least \$25,000 is written:

$$10,000R + 10,000TV \geq 80,000,$$

and the marital status constraint is given by:

$$8,000R + 4,000TV \geq 40,000.$$

Combining the cost minimization objective function with the three constraints, written in their equality form through the introduction of slack variables, allows us to write the programming problem as:

Minimize

$$\text{Cost} = \$6,000R + \$10,000TV, \tag{7.10}$$

subject to:

$$10,000R + 20,000TV - S_A = 100,000, \tag{7.11}$$

$$10,000R + 10,000TV - S_I = 80,000, \tag{7.12}$$

and

$$8,000R + 4,000TV - S_S = 40,000, \tag{7.13}$$

where

$$R, TV, S_A, S_I, S_S \geq 0.$$

Here S_A, S_I, and S_S are slack variables indicating the extent to which the minimums on total audience exposure, on exposure to individuals with

Figure 7.11
Advertising Cost-Minimization Linear Programming Problem

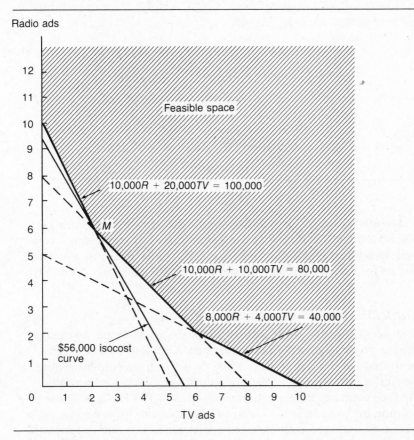

incomes of at least $25,000, and on exposure to single individuals, re-
spectively, have been exceeded. Note that the slack variables are *subtracted* from the constraint equations in this situation since we are dealing with equal-to or greater-than inequalities. That is, excess capacity
or slack in any of the constraints implies that the audience exposure is
greater than required. Thus, in order to make the exposures exactly
equal to the required quantity, one must subtract the slack from the
total.

The solution to this linear programming problem is easily obtained
graphically. Figure 7.11 illustrates that solution. There the feasible space
for the programming problem is determined by the three constraint
equations and the nonnegativity requirements. Addition of an isocost
curve allows one to determine that costs are minimized at Point M,
where the constraints on total audience exposure and exposures to in-

dividuals meeting the income requirement are binding. This means that the slack variables in those two constraints will both be zero. Using this information we can solve constraints 7.11 and 7.12 for the optimal number of radio and television ads

$$10,000R + 20,000TV - 0 = 100,000 \qquad (7.11)$$

$$\text{minus } 10,000R + 10,000TV - 0 = 80,000$$

$$10,000TV = 20,000$$

$$TV = 2$$

$$10,000R + 20,000(2) - 0 = 100,000 \qquad (7.11)$$

$$10,000R = 60,000$$

$$R = 6$$

The solution to the problem indicates that the firm should employ 6 radio and 2 television ads in its campaign in order to minimize its expenditure while meeting the audience goals set for the program. The total cost for such a campaign would be \$56,000 [6,000(6) + 10,000(2)].

Complex Linear Programming Problems

Our illustrative linear programming problems were simple by design: We chose problems that could be solved both graphically and algebraically so that we could first explain the theory of linear programming through the use of graphs, then rework the problems algebraically to show the symmetry between the two methods. The kinds of linear programming problems encountered in the real world, however, are quite complex, frequently involving very many constraints and output variables. Such problems are obviously too complex to solve graphically; the geometry is messy if we have three decision variables, impossible for four or more. However, computer programs, which use algebraic techniques, can handle very large numbers of variables and constraints. While it is not necessary for our purposes to extend the discussion to use of these computer based solution algorithms, we call attention to them to indicate the potential problem solving capability of the technique.

Summary

Linear programming is a technique for solving maximization or minimization problems in which inequality constraints are imposed on the decision maker. This kind of problem occurs frequently in both business and government, so linear programming is rapidly becoming one of the most widely used methods in the sophisticated decision maker's tool kit.

Although linear programming has been applied to a wide variety of business problems, it has been developed most fully, and is used most frequently, in production problems. Accordingly, we used two production problems to explain the basic elements of the theory of linear programming. First, we presented the theory in graphic form, and then showed that the same solution can be reached by an algebraic technique. The graphic method is useful to explain the theory; but the algebraic method is often used in actual practice, because it can be adapted for solution by computers and used to solve the large, complex problems actually faced by managers.

Questions

7.1 Give some illustrations of situations where you think the linear programming technique would be useful.

7.2 Why can linear programming *not* be used in each of the following situations?
   a) Strong economies of scale exist.
   b) As the firm expands output, the prices of variable factors of production increase.
   c) As output increases, product prices decline.

7.3 Assume output can only be produced by using processes A and B. If Process A requires $2L:4K$ and Process B requires $4L:2K$, how is it possible to produce output efficiently using $3L$ and $3K$?

7.4 Describe the relative distance method.

7.5 How many isocost, isorevenue, or isoprofit lines can be drawn in a typical two-input bounded feasible space?

7.6 Why is the fact that, at corners of the feasible space, the number of non-zero-valued variables exactly equals the number of constraints so critical in linear programming?

7.7 When will maximizing the profit contribution *not* also result in maximizing total net profits?

Solved Problem

7.1 Utah Mining Company (UMC) has two mines with different production capacities for producing the same type of ore. After mining and crushing, the ore is graded into three classes: high, medium, and low. The company has contracted to provide a smelter with 24 tons of high-grade, 16 tons of medium-grade, and 48 tons of low-grade ore each week. It costs UMC $2,000 per day to operate Mine A and $1,600 per day to run Mine B. In a day's time, Mine A produces 6 tons of high-grade, 2 tons of medium-grade, and 4 tons of low-grade ore. Mine B produces 2, 2, and 12 tons per day of each grade, respectively. The problem faced by UMC's management is to determine how many days a week to operate each mine.

a) Use a linear programming approach to solve this problem. Set up the problem algebraically, using both the inequality and equality forms of the constraint equations. Use a graph to determine the optimal solution (corner point) and then check your solution algebraically. (*Hint*: Find the correct corner point by constructing an isocost curve for an arbitrary cost level and using the fact that all isocost curves are parallel).

b) How much must the daily cost to operate Mine B increase before UMC would change the operating decision arrived at in part A?

Solution

a) Minimize:

$$\text{Total Cost} = 2{,}000A + 1{,}600B.$$

Subject to:

$$6A + 2B \geq 24. \text{ (High-grade ore constraint)} \qquad (1)$$

$$2A + 2B \geq 16. \text{ (Medium-grade ore constraint)} \qquad (2)$$

$$4A + 12B \geq 48. \text{ (Low-grade ore constraint)} \qquad (3)$$

$$A \leq 7. \text{ (Operation of Mine } A \text{ (day) constraint)} \qquad (4)$$

$$B \leq 7. \text{ (Operation of Mine } B \text{ (day) constraint)} \qquad (5)$$

Or, in their equality form

$$6A + 2B - S_H = 24. \quad (1)$$

$$2A + 2B - S_M = 16. \quad (2)$$

$$4A + 12B - S_L = 48. \quad (3)$$

$$A + S_A = 7. \quad (4)$$

$$B + S_B = 7. \quad (5)$$

$$A, B, S_H, S_M, S_L, S_A, \text{ and } S_B \geq 0.$$

Here, A and B represent the days of operation per week for the two mines; S_H, S_M, and S_L represent excess production of high-, medium-, and low-grade ore, respectively; S_A and S_B are days per week the mines are not operated.

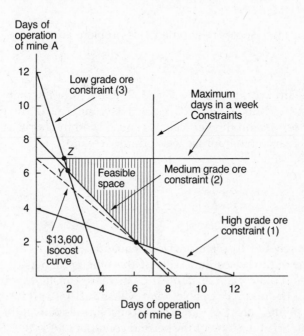

The graph indicates that the optimal solution occurs at point X, where constraints (1) and (2) are binding. Thus, $S_H = S_M = 0$ and

$$6A + 2B - 0 = 24 \tag{1}$$

$$\text{minus } \underline{2A + 2B - 0 = 16} \tag{2}$$

$$4A \qquad\qquad = \ 8$$

$$A = \ 2 \text{ days per week.}$$

Substitute $A = 2$ in (1):

$$6(2) + 2B = 24 \tag{1}$$

$$12 + 2B = 24$$

$$2B = 12$$

$$B = \ 6 \text{ days per week.}$$

(continued)

Then,

$$\text{Total Cost} = \$2,000\,A + \$1,600B$$
$$= \$2,000(2) + \$1,600(6)$$
$$= \$13,600.$$

b) In general, the isocost relation for this problem is:

$$C_0 = C_A A + C_B B,$$

where C_0 is any weekly cost level, and C_A and C_B are the daily operating costs for Mines A and B, respectively. In terms of the graph shown above, A is on the vertical axis and B is on the horizontal axis. Thus, rearranging our isocost formula we find:

$$C_A A = C_0 - C_B B$$

$$A = \frac{C_0}{C_A} - \frac{C_B}{C_A}\,B,$$

with an intercept of C_0/C_A and a slope equal to $-C_B/C_A$.

The slope of the isocost line will rise (become more negative) as C_B increases, holding C_A constant. If C_B increases to slightly more than \$2,000, the optimal feasible point will shift from point X ($6B,2A$) to point Y ($2B,6A$), since the isocost line slope will then be steeper than -1, the slope of the second constraint ($A = 8 - B$). Thus, an increase in C_B from \$1,600 to at least \$2,000, or an increase of at least \$400, is necessary before the optimal operating decision arrived at in part a will change.

It is interesting to note that an increase in C_B to slightly more than \$6,000 would be necessary before point Z ($1.\overline{6}B,7A$) becomes optimal. With $C_B \geq \$6,000$ and $C_A = \$2,000$ the isocost slope will be steeper than -3, the slope of the third constraint: $A = 12 - 3B$. Thus, if $C_A = \$2,000$, point Y ($2B,6A$) will be optimal so long as $\$2,000 \leq C_B \leq \$6,000$.

Problem Set

7.1 Atlanta Medical Laboratory (AML) provides a variety of medical testing services to doctors and hospitals in the southeastern United States. AML has just received a large order for blood tests to detect a virus that has caused a major epidemic among school children. Because of concern about the spread of the disease, AML has been offered a substantial premium for rapid processing of the samples. To receive the premium, AML must complete the tests at a rate of at least 1,800 per day.

AML uses two primary inputs in its testing operation, medical technicians and a special centrifuge. The quantities of these resources cannot be increased in time to assist with this job, so AML is limited to 55 hours of medical technician and 14 hours of centrifuge input per day. AML does, however, have the ability to use three different test procedures, each of which uses a different combination of technician and centrifuge time. The input ratios are fixed for each test procedure, and each exhibits constant returns to scale. The input requirements for each procedure are provided below.

Resource	Input Requirements for Test Procedure		
	A	B	C
Medical technician hours	0.040	0.030	0.020
Centrifuge hours	0.004	0.006	0.010

a) The optimal usage of inputs for the tests can be determined by using linear programming methods. Set up the appropriate linear programming problem. (Define Q_A, Q_B, and Q_C as the quantity of tests performed by procedures A, B, and C, respectively. Use the equality form for expressing the constraint conditions.)

b) Given the constraints on the availability of inputs, what is the maximum number of tests that can be completed each day? (*Hint*: Draw an isoquant for tests performed, and then use the fact that all isoquants are parallel to one another in order to determine the corner solution.)

c) At the optimal output level, how many tests are performed using each technique?

d) Interpret all variables *and* equations in the linear programming problem.

e) Carefully examine the graph you constructed for part b, and then answer the following questions:

   i. Will test procedure B or C be used more intensively if more medical technician time is made available?

   ii. How many additional medical technician hours are required to cause AML to cease using test procedure C?

7.2 Philip's Arms Company (PAC) is a specialized producer of small arms (shotguns) for use in small-game hunting, as well as target (skeet) competition. Currently, two shotgun models are produced. The hunting, H, model retails for $1,000; the target, T, model retails for $1,600. Both are offered to consumers by retailers at a 100 percent markup on their cost from PAC. PAC's variable production costs are $300 for the H model and $600 for the T model.

Each model uses scarce woodworking, W, and metalworking, M, capacity. The H model requires four hours for woodworking and two hours for metalworking; the T model requires three hours for wood-working and three hours for metalworking. In addition, each T model requires two hours of hand finishing, F. PAC currently has a monthly capacity of 2,400 hours for woodworking, 1,500 hours for metalworking, and 800 hours for hand finishing.

    a) Set up the linear programming problem that PAC might use to determine optimal output levels for the H and T models in light of an operating philosophy of profit maximization.

    b) Solve and interpret the solution values for the linear programming problem.

    c) Would the output levels determined be optimal if PAC had an operating philosophy of sales rather than profit maximization? Explain.

7.3 Western Technical Services is a small engineering firm in Fort Collins, Colorado, that provides a variety of technical and drafting services. Western employs three engineers, five drafters, and three secretaries. Western has developed a leading reputation in the design of low- and medium-capacity heat exchangers for electrical equipment. A large backlog of jobs has accumulated, and the firm has decided it must complete the back orders. The firm wants to maximize the number of jobs finished each day in order to eliminate its backlog. The average time required to design a medium capacity heat exchanger is 4 hours of engineer time, 3 hours of time by a drafter, and 3 hours of secretarial work. Designing a low-capacity heat exchanger requires an average 1.5 hours of work from an engineer, 4 hours of work from a drafter, and 1.5 hours of secretarial effort.

    a) Formulate a linear programming problem that Western could use to determine how best to employ its resources. Assume that the engineers and drafters each work 10-hour days, and the secretaries work 8 hours per day.

    b) Solve the linear programming problem and interpret the solution values.

7.4 Readymix Concrete Company produces concrete for road construction and mortar for bricklaying. The production and sale of these products are independent of each other, except that they make use of the same inputs in production. The production functions for both products exhibit constant returns to scale. Four inputs are used to produce the concrete and mortar. The inputs are cement, sand, gravel, and water. The production of a unit of concrete requires 300 pounds of gravel, 200 pounds of sand, 100 pounds of cement, and 20 gallons of water. Each unit of mortar requires 100 pounds of sand, 100 pounds of cement, and 10 gallons of water. The water needed to produce the two products is available in unlimited quantities, but a rail strike has left Readymix with only 60,000 pounds of gravel, 60,000 pounds of sand, and 50,000 pounds of cement mix available for production. Profit contributions from the sale of concrete and mortar are $11 and $8 per batch, respectively, regardless of the output levels.

   a) Formulate the linear programming problem that Readymix would use to maximize short-run profits, assuming that all the concrete and mortar that was produced could be sold.

   b) Solve the linear programming problem and interpret all variables.

   c) Assume Readymix is offered $12 per 100 pounds of gravel because of the shortage of this material. How much gravel will Readymix sell?

7.5 Madison Power and Light (MP&L) is a small electric utility, located in the upper midwest, serving approximately 200,000 customers. MP&L currently uses coal-fired capacity to satisfy its "base load" electricity demand. Base load electricity demand is a minimum level of electricity demand that is present 24 hours per day, 365 days per year.

   MP&L currently burns both high-sulfur eastern coal and low-sulfur western coal. Each type of coal has its advantages. Eastern coal is more expensive ($45 per ton) but has higher heat-generating capabilities. Although western coal doesn't generate as much heat as eastern coal, western coal is less expensive ($30 per ton) and doesn't cause as much sulfur dioxide pollution. MP&L's base load requirements are such that at least 1,200 million BTUs must be generated per hour. Each ton of eastern coal burned generates 24 million BTUs, and each ton of western coal burned generates 20 million BTUs. In order to limit sulfur dioxide emissions, the state Environmental Protection Agency (EPA) requires MP&L to limit its total burning of sulfur to no more than 1.5 tons per hour. This affects MP&L's coal usage since eastern coal contains 3 percent sulfur, and western coal contains 2 percent sulfur. The EPA also limits MP&L particulate emissions to no more than 600 pounds per hour. MP&L emits 6 pounds of particulates per ton of eastern coal burned, and 12 pounds of particulates per ton of western coal burned.

   a) Set up and interpret the linear program MP&L would use to minimize hourly coal usage costs.

   b) Calculate and interpret all relevant solution values.

   c) Holding all else equal, how much would the price of western coal have to rise before only eastern coal would be used? Explain.

7.6 The Pequot Explorer Fund is an open-end investment company (mutual fund) with an objective of maximizing the expected return to shareholders. The fund has a policy of remaining largely invested in common stocks but can hold cash from time to time for defensive purposes. Its prospectus states that non–dividend-paying small company stocks are emphasized, representing at least two-thirds of stock investments. To reduce downside risk during bear markets, at least 20 percent of the portfolio is invested in stocks of dividend-paying bigger companies, and borrowing is prohibited. The expected return is 15 percent on small company stocks (S) and 12 percent on big company stocks (B).

a) Set up and interpret the linear programming problem Pequot would use to determine the optimal percentage holdings of small company stocks (S) and big company stocks (B). Use both the inequality and equality forms of the constraint equations.

b) Use a graph to determine the optimal solution, and check your solution algebraically. Interpret the solution.

c) How much would the expected return on small stocks have to fall before the optimal investment policy determined in part a would change?

References

Boquist, John A. and Moore, William T. "Estimating the Systematic Risk of an Industry Segment: A Mathematical Programming Approach." *Financial Management* 12 (Winter 1983): 11–18.

Chiang, Alpha C. *Fundamental Methods of Mathematical Economics*. 3d ed. New York: McGraw-Hill, 1984.

Deininger, Rolf A. "Teaching Linear Programming on a Microcomputer." *Interfaces* 13 (August 1983): 30–33.

Dorfman, Robert. "Mathematical, or Linear, Programming: A Nonmathematical Approach." *American Economic Review* 43 (December 1953): 797–825.

Dorfman, Robert; Samuelson, Paul A.; and Solow, Robert M. *Linear Programming and Economic Analysis*. New York: McGraw-Hill, 1958.

Eldredge, David L. "A Cost Minimization Model for Warehouse Distribution Systems." *Interfaces* 12 (August 1982): 113–119.

Harvey, Charles M. *An Introduction to Linear Optimization*. New York: North-Holland, 1979.

Hayes, James W. "Discount Rates in Linear Programming Formulations of the Capital Budgeting Problem." *Engineering Economist* 29 (Winter 1984): 113–126.

Heiner, Karl W.; Kupperschmid, Michael and Ecker, J. G. "Maximizing Restitution for Erroneous Medical Payments When Auditing Samples from More than One Provider." *Interfaces* 13 (October 1983): 12–17.

Lee, Sang M. and Schniederjans, Marc J. "A Multicriteria Assignment Problem: A Goal Programming Approach." *Interfaces* 13 (August 1983): 75–81.

Markland, Robert E. and Nauss, Robert M. "Improving Transit Check Clearing Operations at Maryland National Bank." *Interfaces* 13 (February 1983): 1–9.

Peiser, Richard B. and Andrus, Scot G. "Phasing of Income-Producing Real Estate." *Interfaces* 13 (October 1983): 1–9.

Rau, Nicholas. *Matrices and Mathematical Programming: An Introduction for Economists*. New York: St. Martin's Press, 1981.

Rothenberg, Ronald I. *Linear Programming*. New York: North-Holland, 1980.

Wu, Yuan-Li, and Kwang, Ching-Wen. "An Analytical Comparison of Marginal Analysis and Mathematical Programming in the Theory of the Firm," in *Linear Programming and the Theory of the Firm*, eds. Kenneth E. Boulding and W. Allen Spivey. New York: McGraw-Hill, 1960.

Chapter 8

Market Structure and the Theory of Competition

Key Terms

Barriers to entry
Concentration
Monopolistic
   competition

Natural monopoly
Oligopoly
Perfect (pure)
   competition

Perfect (pure)
   monopoly
Price takers

We began our study of managerial economics by examining the microeconomic model of the firm. That model assumes maximization of value—subject to constraints imposed by technology, resource limitations, and the economic and political environments in which the firm operates—to be the primary objective of management. This maximization process is extremely complex, involving the full range of business functions. Thus far, we have (1) examined the principles of economic analysis, (2) studied the characteristics of demand and ways of estimating the demand function, (3) analyzed the process of production, (4) investigated the nature of cost/output relationships and the role of costs in managerial decision making, (5) developed an understanding of optimal resource employment, and (6) considered how constraints can be incorporated into managerial decision making.

Having examined these components of managerial economics, we are now in a position to integrate these topics to show how demand, production, and cost characteristics interact to determine both the market structure within which a firm operates and the nature of the price/output decision faced by the firm. In this chapter we develop the basic models of market structure and the theory of competition.

Classification of Market Structures

Market structure refers to the number and size distribution of buyers and sellers in the market for a good or service. A market consists of all firms and individuals who are willing and able to buy or sell a particular product. This includes firms and individuals currently engaged in buying and selling, and potential entrants. Markets are traditionally divided into four basic classifications; these four structures are first defined and then elaborated in the remainder of the chapter.

Perfect (pure).competition is a market structure characterized by a large number of buyers and sellers of an essentially identical product, where each participant's transactions are so small in relation to total industry output that they cannot affect the price of the product. Individual buyers and sellers are **price takers**. Perfectly competitive markets are characterized by complete freedom of entry and exit. No firm earns above-normal profits in the long run.

Perfect (pure) monopoly is a market structure characterized by the existence of a single producer. A monopolistic firm simultaneously determines product price and output. Output is differentiated and substantial barriers to entry are present. As a result, it is possible for a monopoly to earn above-normal profits, even in the long run.

Monopolistic competition is a market structure quite similar to pure competition but distinguished from it by the fact that consumers perceive differences among the products of different firms. Firms have some control over the prices at which they sell their products. As in pure competition, above-normal profits are attainable only in the short run.

Oligopoly is a market structure in which a small number of firms produce most of an industry's output. Under oligopoly, price/output decisions of firms are interdependent in the sense that if one firm changes its price, the other firms may react, and this knowledge is incorporated into the price/output decision problem. In oligopoly, as in the case of monopoly, barriers to entry can be substantial and it may be possible for firms to earn above-normal profits, even in the long run. In other instances, competition among a few firms can be vigorous, and above-normal profits may only be observed in the short run.

Factors Determining the Level of Competition

Two key elements are involved in determining the level of competition in a given market: the number and relative size of buyers and sellers in the market, and the extent to which the product is standardized. These factors, in turn, are influenced by the nature of the product and production systems, the scope of potential entry, and buyer characteristics. These relationships are described in the following sections.

Effect of Product Characteristics on Market Structure

If other products are good substitutes for the one in question, this will increase the degree of competition in the market for that product. To illustrate, rail service between two points is typically supplied by only one railroad. Transportation service is available from several sources, however, and railroads now compete with bus lines, truck companies, barges, airlines, and private autos. The substitutability of these other modes of transportation for rail service increases the degree of competition in the transportation service market.

It is important to realize that market structures are not static. In the 1800s and early 1900s—before the introduction of trucks, buses, autos, and airplanes—railroads faced very little competition. Railroads could therefore charge excessive prices and earn monopoly profits. Because of this exploitation, laws were passed giving public authorities permission to regulate the prices railroads charge (a topic discussed in detail in Chapter 10). Additionally, other firms were enticed by the railroads' profits to develop competing transportation service systems, which led ultimately to a much more competitive market structure. Today, few would argue that railroads retain significant monopoly power, and public regulation of the railroads is being reduced in recognition of this fact.

The physical characteristics of a product can also influence the competitive structure of its market. A low ratio of distribution cost to total cost, for example, tends to increase competition by widening the geographic area over which any particular producer can compete. Rapid perishability of a product produces the opposite effect. Thus, in considering the level of competition for a product, the national, regional, or local nature of the market must be considered.

Effect of Production Characteristics on Competition

When minimum efficient scale is large in relation to overall industry output, only a few firms will be able to attain the output size necessary for productive efficiency. In such instances, competitive pressures will result in only a few firms' surviving in an industry. On the other hand, when minimum efficient scale is small in relation to overall industry output, many firms will be able to attain the size necessary for efficient operations. Holding all else equal, competition tends to be most vigorous when many, as opposed to only a few, efficient competitors are present in the market. This is especially true when firms smaller than minimum efficient scale face significantly higher production costs, and when the construction of minimum efficient scale plants involves the commitment of substantial capital, skilled labor, and material resources. When construction of minimum efficient scale plants involves the commitment of only modest resources, or when smaller firms face no important production cost disadvantages, economies of scale will have little or no effect on the competitive potential of new or entrant firms.

Effect of Entry Conditions on Competition

An economic market for a particular good or service consists of those firms or individuals willing and able to buy or sell. Importantly, this includes established businesses and individuals actively engaged in buying and selling, along with so-called *potential entrants*.

Potential entrants are those firms or individuals who have both the economic resources and motivation to enter a particular market, given sufficient economic incentives. For example, car manufacturers often purchase key components from independent suppliers. Typically, only a few suppliers produce any given part. One might think that such a situation would place suppliers in a relatively advantaged position, and that suppliers of specialty parts would often enjoy above-normal profits. However, this is seldom the case. Suppliers realize that charging excessive prices leading to above-normal profits in the short run would cause automobile manufacturers to increase their own component manufacturing in order to reduce, if not eliminate, reliance on outside suppliers. In the case of the auto component parts business, General Motors, Ford, and other large auto manufacturers are potential entrants who can affect market prices by simply presenting a credible threat of entry.

The above-normal profits and/or productive inefficiency of some oligopolistic or monopolistic industries are only possible in the long run when substantial barriers to entry are present. A **barrier to entry** can be defined as any factor or industry characteristic that creates an advantage for incumbents over new rivals. Legal rights such as patents and local, state, or federal licenses can present formidable barriers to new entry in pharmaceutical, cable television, broadcasting, and other industries. Additional factors that sometimes create barriers to entry include substantial economies of scale, large capital requirements, and ties of customer loyalty created through advertising or other means.

It is important to note, however, that factors that create barriers to entry can sometimes result in compensating advantages for consumers. As discussed in Chapter 10, although patents can lead to monopoly profits for inventing firms, they also spur new product and process development. Similarly, an extremely efficient or innovative firm will make new entry into an industry difficult but can have the favorable effect of lowering industry prices or increasing product quality.

Effect of Buyers on Competition

The degree of competition in a market is affected by buyers as well as sellers. If there are only a few buyers, there will be less competition than if there are many buyers. This situation, which is defined as *monopsony* (only one buyer) or *oligopsony* (a few large buyers), sometimes exists in local labor markets dominated by a single firm, in local agricultural markets dominated by a few large processors, in governmental purchases of complex defense systems, and in markets for certain consumer durable goods, such as appliances sold by major retail chains.

Monopsony and oligopsony are more common in factor input markets rather than in markets for final demand. In terms of economic efficiency, they tend to be least harmful, and can sometimes even be beneficial, in markets where monopsony or oligopsony buyers face monopoly or oligopoly sellers. For example, consider the case of a one-mill town where the mill is the sole employer of unskilled labor. The mill is a monopsony since it is a single buyer of labor and it may be able to use its power to reduce wage rates below competitive levels. However, if workers organize a union to bargain with their employer, a single monopoly seller of labor would be created that could offset the employer's monopsony power and increase wages toward competitive market norms. Monopsony and oligopsony are accepted and sometimes even encouraged if buyer market power can be seen as a useful offset to seller market power (monopoly and oligopoly).

Pure Competition

The market characteristics described in the preceding section determine, to a large extent, the level of competition in the market for any good or service. In this section we discuss pure competition in some detail; other market structures defined above are discussed in subsequent sections.

Pure competition exists when the individual producers in a market have no influence on prices: They are price takers as opposed to price makers. This lack of influence on price requires the following conditions:

Large numbers of buyers and sellers. Each firm in the industry produces a small portion of industry output, and each customer buys only a small part of the total.

Product homogeneity. The output of each firm is perceived by customers to be essentially equivalent to the output of any other firm in the industry.

Free entry and exit. Firms are not restricted from entering or leaving the industry.

Perfect dissemination of information. Cost, price, and quality information is known by all buyers and all sellers in the market.

These four basic conditions, which are necessary for the existence of a purely competitive market structure, are far too restrictive for pure competition to be commonplace in the real world. Although security and commodity exchanges approach the requirements, imperfections occur even there. For example, the sale by AT&T of $1.5 billion of new securities clearly affects the price of its stocks and bonds. Nonetheless, for some firms, pricing decisions must be made under circumstances in which they have no control over price, and an examination of a purely competitive market structure provides insights into pricing decisions in these cases. More importantly, a clear understanding of pure competition provides a reference point from which to analyze the more typically encountered market structures—and monopolistic competition and oligopoly.

Market Price Determination

Market price for a competitive industry is determined by supply and demand; individual firms have no control over price. There is a total industry demand curve for the product—an aggregation of the quantities that individual purchasers will buy at each price—and an industry supply curve—the summation of the quantities that individual firms are willing to supply at different prices. The intersection of the industry supply and demand curves determines market price.

The data in Table 8.1 illustrate the process by which an industry supply curve is constructed. First, suppose there are five firms in an industry and that each firm is willing to supply varying quantities of the product at different prices. The summing of the individual supply quantities of these five firms for each price determines their combined supply schedule, shown in the Partial Market Supply column. For example, at a price of $2 the output quantities supplied by the five firms are 15, 0, 5, 25, and 45 units, respectively, resulting in a combined supply of 90 units at that price. With a product price of $8, the supply quantities become 45, 115, 40, 55, and 75 for a total supply by the five firms of 330 units.

Now assume that the five firms, while representative of firms in the industry, account for only a small portion of the industry's total output.

Table 8.1
Market Supply Schedule Determination

Price ($)	Quantity Supplied by Firm					Partial Market Supply	× 1,000 =	Total Market Supply
	1 +	2 +	3 +	4 +	5 =			
1	5	0	5	10	30	50		50,000
2	15	0	5	25	45	90		90,000
3	20	20	10	30	50	130		130,000
4	25	35	20	35	55	170		170,000
5	30	55	25	40	60	210		210,000
6	35	75	30	45	65	250		250,000
7	40	95	35	50	70	290		290,000
8	45	115	40	55	75	330		330,000
9	50	130	45	65	80	370		370,000
10	55	145	50	75	85	410		410,000

Assume specifically that there are actually 5,000 firms in the industry, each with an individual supply schedule identical to one of the five firms illustrated in the table. That is, there are 1,000 firms just like each one illustrated in Table 8.1, so the total market supply, the total quantity supplied at each price, will be 1,000 times that shown under the Partial Market Supply schedule. This supply schedule is illustrated in Figure 8.1, and adding the market demand curve to the industry supply curve, as in Figure 8.2, allows us to determine the equilibrium market price.[1]

Although it is apparent from Figure 8.2 that both the quantity demanded and total supplied are dependent on price, a simple example should demonstrate the inability of an individual firm to affect price. Assume that the total demand function in Figure 8.2, which again represents the summation at each price of the quantities demanded by individual purchasers, can be described by the equation:

$$\text{Quantity Demanded} = Q = 400,000 - 10,000P, \qquad (8.1)$$

---

[1]The market price is found by first equating the market supply and demand to find the equilibrium activity level, and then substituting that quantity into either the demand or supply curve to find the market clearing price. Using the curves in Figure 8.2 we have:

$$\text{Demand} = \text{Supply}$$
$$40 - .0001Q = -0.254 + .000025Q$$
$$.000125Q = 40.254$$
$$Q = 322,032$$
$$P = 40 - .0001(322,032)$$
$$= 40 - 32.20$$
$$= \$7.80.$$

Figure 8.1
Hypothetical Industry Supply Curve

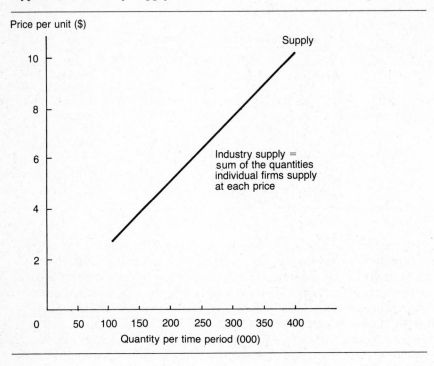

or, solving for price:

$$\$10,000P = \$400,000 - Q$$

(8.1a)

$$P = \$40 - 0.0001Q.$$

According to Equation 8.1a, a 100-unit change in output would cause only a $0.01 change in price, or, alternatively, a $0.01 price increase (reduction) would lead to a decrease (increase) in total market demand of 100 units.

The demand curve shown in Figure 8.2 is redrawn for an individual firm in Figure 8.3. The slope of the curve is −0.0001, the same as in Figure 8.2; only the scales have been changed. The intercept $7.80 is the going market price as determined by the intersection of the market supply and demand curves in Figure 8.2.

At the scale shown in Figure 8.3, the firm's demand curve is seen to be, for all practical purposes, a horizontal line. An output change of even 100 units by the individual firm results in only a $0.01 change

Figure 8.2
Market Price Determination in Perfect Competition

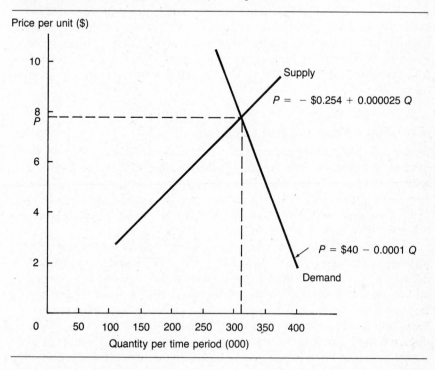

Figure 8.3
Demand Curve Faced by a Single Firm in Perfect Competition

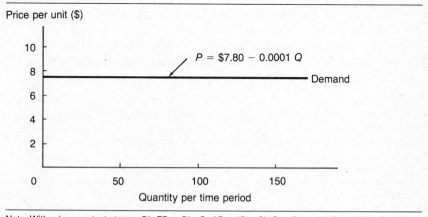

Note: With price constant at, say, P^*, $TR = P^* \cdot Q$, $AR = (P^* \cdot Q)/Q = P^*$, and $MR = \Delta TR/\Delta Q = P^*$.

in market price, and the data in Table 8.1 indicate that the typical firm would not vary output by this amount unless the market price changed by more than $10 a unit. Thus, it is clear that under pure competition the individual firm's output decisions do not affect price in any meaningful way, and for pricing decisions the demand curve is taken to be perfectly horizontal. That is, price is assumed to be constant irrespective of the output level at which the firm chooses to operate.

The Firm's Price/Output Decision

Figure 8.4 illustrates the firm's price/output decision in a competitive market. We assume for simplicity in this section on pure competition and later in the section on monopolistic competition that the firm whose curves are graphed is a representative firm. Thus, the cost curves in Figure 8.4 are representative of an average firm in a perfectly competitive industry.

Profit maximization was shown in Chapter 2 to require that a firm operate at an output level where marginal revenue and marginal cost are equal to each other. With price a constant, average revenue, or price, and marginal revenue must always be equal, so the profit maximization requirement for a firm operating in a perfectly competitive market is that market price must be equal to marginal cost. In the example depicted in Figure 8.4, the firm chooses to operate at output level Q^*, where price (and hence marginal revenue) equals marginal cost and profits are maximized.

Notice from the illustration that above-normal profits may exist in the short run even under conditions of pure competition.[2] For example, in Figure 8.4 the firm produces and sells Q^* units of output at an average cost of C dollars; and with a market price P, the firm earns economic profits of $P - C$ dollars per unit. Total economic profit, $(P - C)Q^*$, is shown by the shaded rectangle $PMNC$.

Over the long run, positive economic profits will attract additional firms into the industry, lead to increased output by existing firms, or

---

[2] A normal profit, defined as a rate of return on capital just sufficient to attract the capital investment necessary to develop and operate a firm (see Chapter 1), is included as a part of economic costs. Therefore, any profit shown in a graph such as Figure 8.4 or 8.5 is defined as economic profit, and it represents an above-normal profit. Notice also that economic losses are incurred whenever the firm fails to earn a normal profit. Thus, a firm might show a small accounting profit but be suffering economic losses because these profits are insufficient to provide an adequate return to the firm's stockholders. In such instances, firms will not replace plant and equipment and will exit the industry in the long run.

Figure 8.4
Competitive Firm's Optimal Price/Output Combination

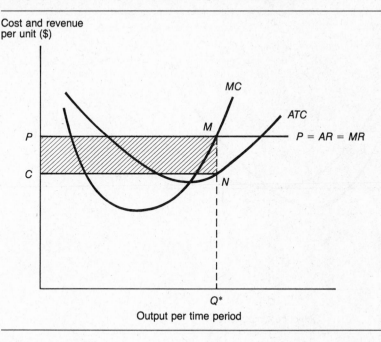

Cost and revenue
per unit ($)

MC

ATC

M

P — P = AR = MR

C

N

Q*

Output per time period

both. As industry supply is expanded, there will be downward pressure on the market price for the industry as a whole (output for the industry can be expanded only by offering the product at a lower price) and simultaneously upward pressure on cost, because of increased demand for factors of production. Long-run equilibrium will be reached when all economic profits and losses have been eliminated and each firm in the industry is operating at an output that minimizes average cost. The long-run equilibrium for a firm under pure competition is graphed in Figure 8.5. At the profit maximizing output, price, or average revenue, equals average cost, so the firm neither earns economic profits nor incurs economic losses. When this condition exists for all firms in the industry, new firms are not encouraged to enter the industry nor are existing ones pressured into leaving it. Prices are stable, and each firm is operating at the minimum point on its short-run average cost curve. All firms must also be operating at the minimum cost point on the long-run average cost curve; otherwise firms would make production changes, decrease costs, and affect industry output and prices. Accordingly, a stable equilibrium requires that firms be operating with optimally sized plants.

Figure 8.5
Long-Run Equilibrium in a Competitive Market

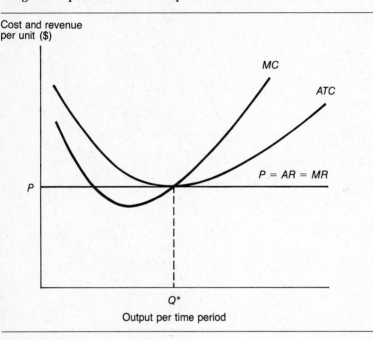

Output per time period

The Firm's Supply Curve

Market supply curves were seen above to be the summation of supply quantities of individual firms at various prices. We are now in a position to examine how supply schedules for individual firms are determined.

In Figure 8.6 we add the firm's average variable cost curve to the average total cost and marginal cost curves of Figure 8.4. *In the short run the competitive firm's supply schedule will correspond to that portion of the marginal cost curve that lies above the average variable cost curve, that is, the solid portion of the marginal cost curve in Figure 8.6.*

To understand the reason for this, consider the options available to the firm. Profit maximization under pure competition requires that the firm operate at the output where marginal revenue equals marginal cost, if it produces any output at all. That is, the firm will either (1) produce nothing and incur a loss equal to its fixed costs, or (2) produce an output determined by the intersection of the horizontal demand curve and the marginal cost curve. It will choose the alternative that maximizes

Figure 8.6
The Competitive Firm's Short-Run Supply Curve

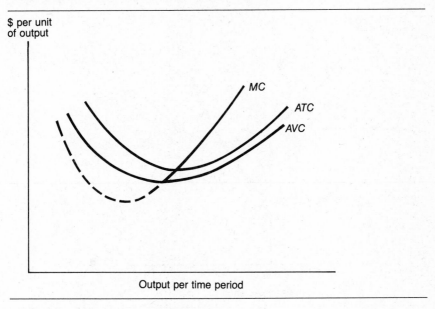

$ per unit
of output

Output per time period

profits or, if losses must be incurred, minimizes losses. If the price is less than average variable costs, the firm should produce nothing and incur a loss equal to its total fixed cost; if the firm produces any product under this condition, its losses will increase. But if price exceeds average variable costs, then each unit of output provides some profit contribution which can be applied to cover fixed costs and provide profit; the firm should produce and sell its product, because this production reduces losses or leads to profits. Accordingly, the minimum point on the firm's average variable cost curve determines the cutoff point, or the lower limit, of its supply schedule. This conclusion is illustrated in Figure 8.7. At a very low price such as $1, $MR = MC$ at 100 units of output. But notice that at 100 units the firm has a total cost per unit of $2 and a price of only $1, so it is incurring a loss of $1 a unit.

Since the difference between the ATC and the AVC curves represents the fixed cost per unit of output, the total loss consists of a fixed cost component, $2.00 − $1.40 = $0.60, and a variable cost component, $1.40 − $1.00 = $0.40. Thus, the total loss is:

$$\text{Total Loss} = (100 \text{ Units}) \cdot (\$0.60 \text{ Fixed Cost Loss} + \$0.40 \text{ Variable Cost Loss})$$

$$= \$100.$$

Figure 8.7

Prices, Cost, and Optimal Supply Decisions for a Firm under Pure Competition

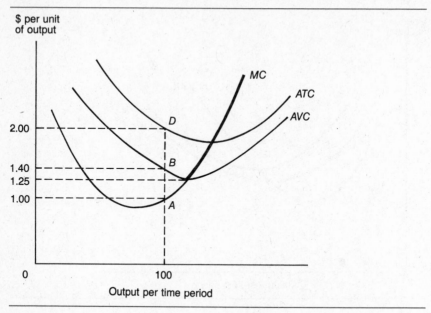

If the firm simply shuts down and terminates production, it would cease to incur variable costs, and its loss would be reduced to the level of the fixed cost loss, that is, to 100($0.60) = $60.

Variable cost losses will occur at any price less than $1.25, the minimum point on the AVC curve, so this is the lowest price at which the firm will operate. Above $1.25, the price more than covers variable costs. Therefore, even though total costs are not covered, it is preferable to operate and provide some contribution to cover a portion of fixed costs rather than to shut down and incur losses equal to total fixed costs.

To recapitulate, *the firm's short-run supply curve is that portion of the marginal cost curve which lies above the AVC curve.* Where marginal cost is below average cost, but above average variable cost, the firm will incur losses but will produce, nonetheless. Positive economic profits occur over that part of the supply function where price (and marginal cost) is greater than average total cost.

The firm's long-run supply function is similarly determined. Since all costs are variable in the long run, a firm will choose to shut down unless total costs are completely covered. Accordingly, that portion of the firm's long-run marginal cost curve which lies above its long-run average total cost curve represents its long-run supply schedule.

Monopoly

Pure monopoly lies at the opposite extreme from pure competition on the market structure continuum. Monopoly exists when a single firm is the sole producer of a good that has no close substitutes, in other words, a single firm is the industry. Pure monopoly, like pure competition, exists primarily in economic theory; few goods are produced by a single producer, and fewer still are free from competition of a close substitute. Even public utilities are imperfect monopolists in most of their markets. Electric companies, for example, typically approach a pure monopoly in their residential lighting market, but they face strong competition from gas and oil suppliers in the heating market. Further, in all phases of the industrial and commercial power markets, electric utilities face competition from gas- and oil-powered private generators.

Even though pure monopoly rarely exists, it is still worthy of careful examination. Many of the economic relationships found under monopoly can be used to estimate optimal firm behavior in the less precise, but more prevalent, partly competitive and partly monopolistic market structures that dominate the real world. In addition, an understanding of monopoly market relationships provides the background necessary to examine the economics of regulation, a topic of prime importance to business managers.

Price/Output Decision under Monopoly

Under monopoly, the industry demand curve is identical to the demand curve of the firm, and because industry demand curves typically slope downward, monopolists also face downward-sloping demand curves. In Figure 8.8, for example, 100 units can be sold at a price of $10 a unit. At an $8 price, 150 units will be demanded. If the firm decides to sell 100 units, it will receive $10 a unit; if it wishes to sell 150 units, it must accept an $8 price. We see then that the monopolist can set either price or quantity, but not both. Given one, the value of the other is determined by the relationship expressed in the demand curve.

A monopolistic firm uses the same profit maximization rule as a firm in a competitive industry; it operates at the output where marginal revenue equals marginal cost. The demand curve facing the monopolistic firm, however, is not horizontal, or perfectly elastic, so marginal revenue will not coincide with price at any but the first unit of output. Marginal revenue is always less than price for output quantities greater than one. Marginal revenue is less than price because of the negatively sloped demand curve. Since the demand (average revenue) curve is negatively sloped and hence declining, the marginal revenue curve

Figure 8.8
The Firm's Demand Curve under Monopoly

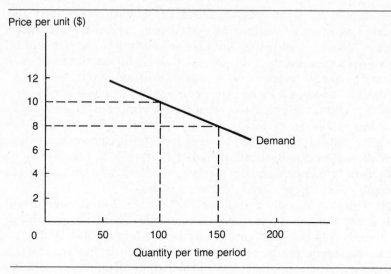

must lie below it. (This relationship was examined earlier in Chapters 2 and 3.)

When the monopolistic firm equates marginal revenue and marginal cost, it simultaneously determines the output level and the market price for its product. This decision is illustrated in Figure 8.9. Here the firm produces Q units of output at a cost of C per unit, and it sells this output at price, P. Profits, which are equal to $(P - C)$ times (Q), are represented by the area $PP'C'C$, and are at a maximum.

While Q is the optimal short-run output, the firm will engage in production only if average revenue, or price, is greater than average variable cost. This condition holds in Figure 8.9, but if the price had been below the average variable cost, losses would have been minimized by shutting down.

Long-Run Equilibrium under Monopoly

In the long run a monopoly firm will operate only if its price exceeds its long-run average cost. Because all costs are variable in the long run, the firm will not operate unless all costs are covered. No firm, monopolistic or competitive, will operate in the long run if it is suffering losses.

As was shown earlier, purely competitive firms must, in the long run, operate at the minimum point on the *LRAC* curve. This condition does not necessarily hold under monopoly. For example, consider again Figure 8.9 and assume that the *ATC* curve represents the long-run aver-

Figure 8.9
Price/Output Decision under Monopoly

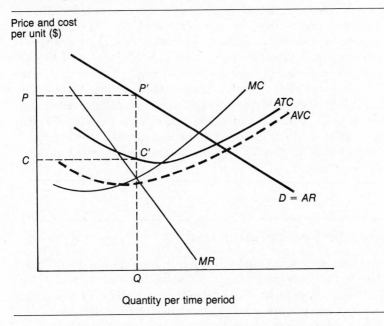

Price and cost
per unit ($)

Quantity per time period

age total cost curve of the firm. Here the firm will produce Q units of output at an average cost of C per unit, somewhat above the minimum point on the ATC curve. This firm is called a **natural monopoly**, since the profit maximizing output occurs at a point where *long-run* average costs are declining. A single firm can produce the total market supply at a lower total cost than could any number of smaller firms, hence the term *natural*. Utility companies are the classic examples of natural monopoly, as the duplication of production and distribution facilities would greatly increase costs if more than one firm served a given area. The case of natural monopoly is discussed in greater detail in Chapter 10.

Regulation of Monopoly

The existence of natural monopolies presents something of a dilemma. On the one hand, economic efficiency could be enhanced by restricting the number of producing firms to one; on the other hand, monopolistic firms have an incentive to underproduce and can earn excessive profits. *Underproduction* is defined as a situation where the firm curtails production to a level where the value of the resources needed to produce an additional unit of output, as measured by the marginal cost of production, is less than the social benefit derived from the additional unit, which is measured by the price someone is willing to pay for the additional unit. Under monopoly, marginal cost is clearly less than price at the firm's profit maximizing output level.

The term *excessive profits* is defined as business profits larger than needed to allow the firm to earn its required rate of return on invested capital. Profits serve a useful function in providing incentives and in allocating resources, but it is difficult to justify above-normal profits that are the result of market power, as opposed to exceptional performance.

How can we escape from the dilemma posed by the twin facts (1) that monopoly can be efficient but (2) that monopoly can lead to excessive profits and underproduction? The answer lies in regulation, a topic discussed in Chapter 10.

Monopolistic Competition

Pure competition and pure monopoly rarely exist in the real world; most firms are subject to some competition, but not to the extent that would exist under pure competition. Even though most firms are faced with a large number of competitors producing highly substitutable products, firms still have some control over the price of their output—they cannot sell all they want at a fixed price, nor would they lose all their sales if they raised prices slightly. In other words, most firms face downward-sloping demand curves, signifying less than perfect competition.

The theory of monopolistic competition provides a more realistic explanation of the actual market structure faced by many firms. The theory retains two assumptions of a purely competitive market structure: (1) Each firm makes its decisions independently of all others; that is, each producer assumes that competitors' prices, advertising, and so on are invariant with respect to its own actions. Thus, price changes by one firm are assumed not to cause other firms to react by changing their prices. (If reactions occur, then the market structure is called oligopoly, a market structure examined in the next section of this chapter.) (2) There are a large number of firms in the industry all producing the same basic product. The assumption of completely homogeneous products is removed, however, so each firm is assumed to be able to differentiate its product, at least to some degree, from those of rival firms.

The assumption of no direct reactions by competitors should not be misconstrued as implying an independence among firms in a monopolistically competitive market. There is an assumed independence in decision making, just as in a perfectly competitive market. However, the demand function faced by each firm in such an industry is significantly affected by: (1) the existence of numerous firms all producing goods that consumers view as reasonably close substitutes and (2) the fact that many demand and cost factors have a simultaneous impact on all firms, leading frequently to similar price movements by them. This latter phenomenon causes each firm's demand to be more price inelastic than would be the case if total interfirm independence prevailed.

Product differentiation takes many forms. A tube of Crest toothpaste at a nearby drugstore is different from an identical tube available at a distant store. Since consumers evaluate products on the basis of their ability to satisfy specific wants they have, as well as *when* and *where* they have them, products involve not only quantity, quality, and price characteristics, but time and place attributes as well. Quality differentials, packaging, credit terms, or superior maintenance service, such as IBM is reputed to supply, can lead to product differentiation, as can advertising which leads to brand-name identification. The important factor in all these forms of product differentiation, however, is that some consumers prefer the product of one seller to those of others.

The effect of product differentiation is to remove the perfect elasticity of the firm's demand curve. Instead of being a price taker facing a horizontal demand curve, the firm determines its optimal price/output combination. The degree of price flexibility depends on the strength of a firm's product differentiation. Strong differentiation results in greater consumer loyalty and hence in more control over price. Alternatively stated, the more differentiated a firm's product, the lower the substitutability of other products for it. This is illustrated in Figure 8.10, which

Figure 8.10
Relationship between Product Differentiation and Elasticity of Demand

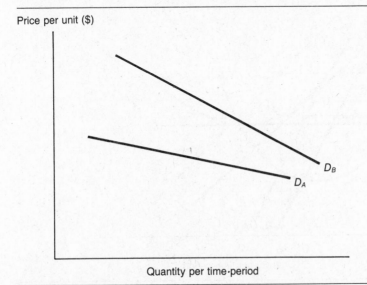

Price per unit ($)

D_B

D_A

Quantity per time-period

shows the demand curves of Firms A and B. Consumers view Firm A's product as being only slightly differentiated from the bulk of the industry's output, and since many other brands are suitable replacements for its own output, Firm A is close to being a price taker. Firm B, on the other hand, has successfully differentiated its product, and consumers are therefore less willing to substitute for B's output. Accordingly, B's demand is not so sensitive to changes in price.

Price/Output Decisions under Monopolistic Competition

As its name suggests, monopolistic competition embodies elements of both monopoly and perfect competition. The monopoly aspect of monopolistic competition is observed in the short run. Consider Figure 8.11. There, with the demand curve, D_1, and its related marginal revenue curve, MR_1, the optimum output, Q_1, is found at the point where $MR_1 = MC$. Here, short-run monopoly profits equal to the area P_1LMATC_1 are earned. These profits may be the result of the introduction of a patented invention, an unpatented but valuable innovation, or other factors such as an unexpected rise in demand.

Figure 8.11
Price/Output Combinations under Monopolistic Competition

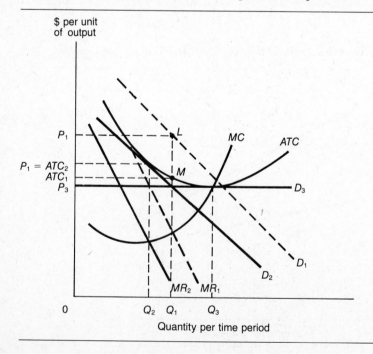

With time, however, competition is attracted by these short-run monopoly profits, and entry into the industry is observed. Therefore, the competitive aspect of monopolistic competition is seen in the long run. As more firms enter and offer close (but imperfect) substitutes, the market share of the initial firm is reduced. This means that firm demand and marginal revenue curves will shift to the left, as for example to D_2 and MR_2 in Figure 8.11. The firm's optimal output (the point where $MR_2 = MC$) shifts to Q_2; and since price, P_2, is equal to ATC_2, economic profits are zero.[3] If perfect rather than close substitutes were offered by new entrants, firm demand in the long-run would become more nearly horizontal, and the perfectly competitive situation, D_3 with P_3 and Q_3, would be approached.

Note that in equilibrium a monopolistically competitive firm will never be operating at the minimum point on its average cost curve. The firm's demand curve is downward sloping, so it can be tangent to the ATC curve only at a point above the minimum of the ATC curve. Does this mean that a monopolistically competitive industry is inefficient? The answer is no, except in a superficial sense. The very existence of the downward-sloping demand curve implies that some consumers value the firm's products more highly than they do products of other producers. If the number of producers were reduced, perhaps by government edict, so that all the remaining firms could operate at their minimum cost point, some consumers would clearly suffer a loss in welfare, *because the product variety they desired would no longer be available*. The higher prices and costs of monopolistically competitive industries, as opposed to perfectly competitive industries, can be seen as the economic cost of product variety. If consumers are willing to bear such costs, and often they are, then they must not be excessive. The success of many branded products in the face of generic competition is powerful testimony in favor of this presumption.

Although the perfectly competitive and pure monopoly settings are comparatively rare in real-world markets, monopolistic competition is frequently observed. It often develops from the competitive forces that continually shape markets. For example, in 1960 a small ($37 million in sales) office-machine company, Haloid Xerox Inc., revolutionized the copy industry with the introduction of the Xerox 914 copier. Xerography was a tremendous improvement on electrofax and other coated paper copiers. It permitted the use of untreated paper, which not only resulted in a more desirable copy product but one that was less expensive on a cost-per-copy basis as well. Invention of the dry copier established what is now Xerox Corporation at the forefront of a rapidly growing office-

---

[3] Recall that the term *cost* includes a normal profit sufficient to compensate the owners of the firm for their capital investment.

copier industry and propelled the firm to a position of virtual monopoly by 1970. However, between 1970 and 1980 the industry's market structure changed dramatically due to an influx of competition as many of Xerox's original patents expired. IBM entered the copier market in April of 1970 with its Copier I model and expanded its participation in November 1972 with Copier II. Eastman Kodak made its entry into the market in 1975 with its Ektaprint model. Of course, Minnesota Mining and Manufacturing (3M) has long been a factor in the electrofax copier segment of the market. A partial list of smaller domestic firms with rapidly growing participation in the industry would include Addressograph-Multigraph, Nashua, and Savin Business Machines Company. A more complete list of Xerox's recent domestic and international competitors would include at least 30 firms. The effect of this entry on Xerox's market share and profitability was dramatic. Between 1970 and 1978, for example, Xerox's share of the domestic copier market fell from 98 to 56 percent, and its return on stockholders' equity fell from 23.6 to 18.2 percent.

Therefore, the monopolistic dry-copier market of 1970 evolved into a much more competitive industry as we entered the 1980s. Because IBM, Kodak, 3M, and Savin copiers are only close rather than perfect substitutes for Xerox machines, each company retains some price discretion, and the industry can be described as monopolistically rather than perfectly competitive.

Oligopoly

The theory of monopolistic competition, while borrowing heavily from those of pure competition and pure monopoly, provides a more accurate picture of the actual markets in which many businesses operate by recognizing that firms often have some control over price, but their actions are limited by the large number of close substitutes for their products. The theory assumes, however, that firms make decisions without explicitly taking into account competitive reactions. Such a behavioral assumption is appropriate for some industries but inappropriate for others. When an individual firm's actions will in fact produce reactions on the part of its competitors, *oligopoly* exists.

In the United States, aluminum, automobiles, cigarettes, electrical equipment, glass, and steel are all produced and sold under conditions of oligopoly. Notice that in each of these industries a small number of firms produce all, or at least a very large percentage of, the total output. In the automobile industry, for example, General Motors, Ford, Chrysler, Volkswagen, and Renault-American Motors account for almost all auto production in the United States. Even the primary competition from imported automobiles is limited to a relatively small number of firms. Aluminum production is also highly concentrated, with Alcoa, Reynolds, and Kaiser producing almost all domestic output.

Oligopoly market structures also exist in a number of other industries where the market area for a single firm is quite small. Examples of this type of local oligopolistic structure include the retail markets for gasoline and food. Here, only a few sellers (service stations and grocery stores) compete within a small geographic area.

It is the fewness of sellers that introduces interactions into the price/output decision problem under oligopoly. Consider *duopoly*, a special form of oligopoly, under which only two firms produce a particular product. For simplicity, assume that the product is homogeneous and customers choose between the firms solely on the basis of price. Assume also that both firms charge the same price and that each has an equal share of the market. Now suppose Firm A attempts to increase its sales by lowering its price. All buyers will attempt to switch to Firm A, and Firm B will lose a substantial share of its market. To retain customers, B will react by lowering its price. Thus, neither firm is free to act independently; actions taken by one will lead to reactions by the other.

Price/Output Decisions under Oligopoly

Demand curves relate the quantity of a product demanded to its price, *holding constant the effect of all other variables*. One variable that is assumed to remain fixed is the price charged by competing firms. In an oligopolistic market structure, however, if one firm changes the price it charges, other firms will react by changing their prices. The demand curve for the initial firm shifts position, so that instead of moving along a single demand curve as it changes price, the firm moves to an entirely new demand curve.

This phenomenon of shifting demand curves is illustrated in Figure 8.12a. Firm A is initially producing Q_1 units of output and selling them at a price, P_1. Demand Curve D_1 applies here, *assuming* prices charged by other firms remain fixed. Under this assumption, a price cut from P_1 to P_2 would increase demand to Q_2. Assume, however, that only a few firms operate in the market and that each has a fairly large share of total sales. Therefore, if one firm cuts its price and obtains a substantial increase in volume, the other firms must lose a large part of their business. Further, they know exactly why their sales have fallen, and they react by cutting their own prices. This action shifts Firm A down to the second demand curve, D_2, which causes a reduction in Firm A's demand at P_2 from Q_2 to Q_3 units. The new curve is just as unstable as the old one, so a knowledge of its shape is useless to Firm A; if it tries to move along D_2, competitors will react, forcing the company to yet another curve.

Figure 8.12
Shifting Demand under Oligopoly

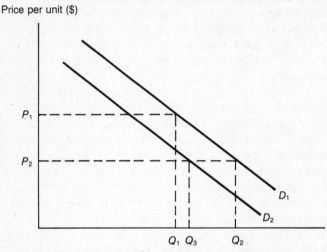

(a) Demand curves that do not explicitly recognize reactions

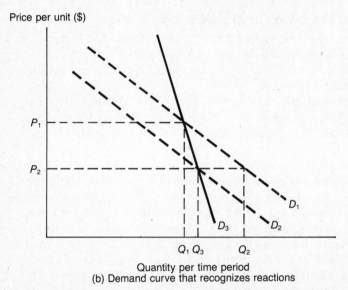

(b) Demand curve that recognizes reactions

Shifting demand curves would present no real difficulty in making price/output decisions *if Firm A knew for sure how its rivals would react to price changes*. The reactions would just be built into the price/demand relationship, and a new demand curve could be constructed to include interactions among firms. Curve D_3 in Figure 8.12b represents such a reaction-based demand curve; it shows how price reductions affect quantity demanded after competitive reactions have been taken into account. The problem with this approach, however, lies in the fact that there are many different theories about interfirm behavior, and each theory leads to a different pricing model and thereby to different decision rules.

Cartel Arrangements

In an oligopolistic market it would benefit all the firms in an industry if they got together and set prices so as to maximize total industry profits. The firms could reach an agreement whereby they set the same prices as would a monopolist and thereby extract the maximum amount of profits from consumers. If such a formal, overt agreement were made, the group would be defined as a *cartel*; if a covert, informal agreement were reached, the firms would be operating in collusion. Both practices are generally illegal in the United States. Cartels are legal, however, in many parts of the world, and multinational United States corporations often become involved in them in foreign markets. Additionally, several important domestic markets are in effect cartels, through producer associations, and appear to operate without interference from the government. Certain farm products, including milk, are prime examples of products marketed under cartel-like arrangements.

If a cartel has absolute control over all the firms in the industry, it can operate as a monopoly. To illustrate, consider the situation shown in Figure 8.13. The marginal cost curves of each firm are summed horizontally to arrive at an industry marginal cost curve. Equating the cartel's total marginal cost with the industry marginal revenue curve determines the profit maximizing output and, simultaneously, the price, P^*,

Figure 8.13
Price/Output Determination for a Cartel

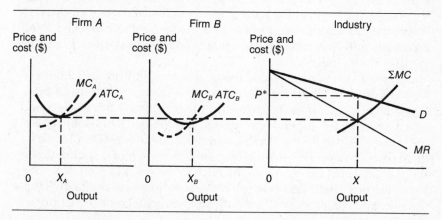

to be charged. Once this profit maximizing price/output level has been determined, each individual firm finds its output by equating its own marginal cost to the previously determined industry profit maximizing marginal cost level.

While profits are often divided among firms on the basis of their individual outputs, other allocating techniques can be used. Historical market shares, capacity as determined in a number of ways, and a bargained solution based on economic power have all been used in the past.

For numerous reasons cartels have typically been rather short-lived. In addition to the long-run problems of changing products and of entry into the market by new producers, cartels are subject to disagreements among the members. While firms usually agree that maximizing joint profits is mutually beneficial, they seldom agree on the equity of various profit allocation schemes, a problem leading to attempts to subvert the cartel agreement.

Subversion of the cartel by an individual firm can be extremely profitable to that firm. With the industry operating at the monopoly price/output level, the demand curve facing an individual firm is highly elastic, provided it can lower its price without other cartel members learning of this action and retaliating. The availability of significant profits to a firm that cheats on the cartel, coupled with the ease with which secret price concessions can be made, makes policing cartel agreements extremely difficult. These problems combine to make cartel survival difficult.

Price Leadership

A less formal but nonetheless effective means of reducing oligopolistic uncertainty is through price leadership. Price leadership results when one firm establishes itself as the industry leader and all other firms in the industry accept its pricing policy. This leadership may result from the size and strength of the leader firm, from cost efficiency, or as a result of the recognized ability of the leader to forecast market conditions accurately and to establish a price that produces satisfactory profits for all firms in the industry.

A typical case is price leadership by a dominant firm, usually the largest firm in the industry. Here the leader faces a price/output problem similar to a monopolist, while the other firms are price takers and face essentially a competitive price/output problem. This is illustrated in Figure 8.14, where the total market demand curve is D_T, the marginal cost curve of the leader is MC_L, and the horizontal summation of the marginal cost curves for all the price followers is labeled MC_f. Because the price followers take prices as given, they choose to operate at that output level at which their individual marginal costs equal price,

Figure 8.14
Oligopoly Pricing with Dominant Firm Price Leadership

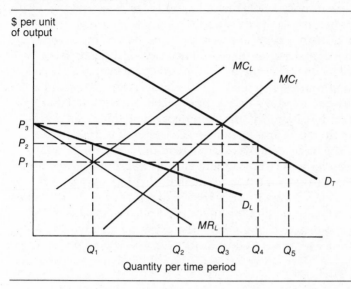

just as they would in a purely competitive market structure. Accordingly, the MC_f curve represents the supply curve for the follower firms. This means that at price P_3, the followers would supply the entire market, leaving nothing for the dominant firm. At all prices below P_3, however, the horizontal distance between the summed MC_f curve and the market demand curve represents the demand faced by the price leader. At a price of P_1, for example, the price followers will provide Q_2 units of output, leaving a demand of $Q_5 - Q_2$ for the price leader. Plotting of all the residual demand quantities for prices below P_3 results in the demand curve faced by the price leader, D_L in Figure 8.14, and the related marginal revenue curve, MR_L.[4]

Since the price leader faces the monopoly demand curve D_L, it maximizes profit by operating where marginal revenue equals marginal cost; that is, where $MR_L = MC_L$. At this output for the leader, Q_1, the market price is established to be P_2. The price followers will supply a com-

---

[4]More generally, the leader faces a demand curve of the form:

$$D_L = D_T - S_f,$$

where D_L is the leader's demand, D_T is total demand, and S_f is the followers' supply curve found by setting price = MC_f and solving for Q_f, the quantity that will be supplied by the price followers. Since D_T and S_f are both functions of price, D_L is likewise determined by price.

bined output of $Q_4 - Q_1$ units. If no one challenges the price leader, a stable short-run equilibrium has been reached.

A second type of price leadership is *barometric price leadership*. In this case one firm announces a price change in response to what it perceives as a change in industry supply and demand conditions. This change could stem from cost increases that result from a new industry labor agreement, higher energy or material input prices, or changes in taxes, or it might result from a substantial increase or decrease in demand. With barometric price leadership the price leader will not necessarily be the largest or dominant firm in the industry. The price leader role may even vary from one firm to another over time. It is important, however, that the price leader accurately read the prevailing industry view of the need for a price adjustment and the appropriate new price level. If a firm is incorrect in its assessment of the desire for a price change by other firms, then its price move may not be followed, and it may have to rescind or modify the announced price change in order to retain its market share or perhaps, if the price change involved a reduction, in order to prevent other firms from retaliating with even lower prices.

Kinked Demand Curve

An often-noted characteristic of oligopolistic markets is that once a general price level has been established, whether through a cartel or through some less formal arrangement, it tends to remain fixed for an extended period. This rigidity of prices is typically explained by yet another set of assumptions about firm behavior under conditions of price interdependence, known as the *kinked demand curve theory of oligopoly prices*.

The kinked demand curve theory describes a behavior pattern in which rival firms are assumed to follow any decrease in price in order to maintain their respective market shares but to refrain from following price increases, thereby allowing their market shares to increase at the expense of the price raiser. Thus, the demand curve facing an individual firm is kinked at the current price/output combination as illustrated in Figure 8.15. The firm is producing Q units of output and selling them at a price of P per unit; if it lowers its price, competing firms will retaliate by lowering their prices. The result of a price cut, therefore, is a relatively small increase in sales; that is, the demand curve associated with price reductions has very low elasticity.[5] Price increases, on the other hand, result in significant reductions in quantities demanded and

---

[5]The reader is referred to Figure 8.12, where the shift in demand curves which results from a price cut was explained. The curve D_3 in Figure 8.12 is the counterpart of the steeper segment of D in Figure 8.15.

Figure 8.15
Kinked Demand Curve

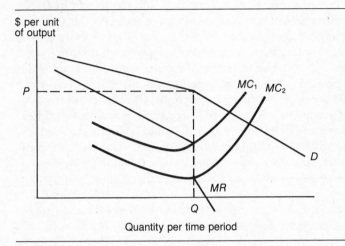

in related decreases in total revenue, because customers will shift to competing firms that do not follow the price increases.

Associated with the kink in the demand curve is a point of discontinuity in the marginal revenue curve. That is, the firm's marginal revenue curve has a gap at the current price/output level, and it is this gap in the marginal revenue curve that explains the rigidity of price. The profit maximizing firm always chooses to operate at the point where marginal cost equals marginal revenue, and because of this gap in the marginal revenue curve, the price/output combination at the kink can remain optimal even though marginal cost fluctuates. Thus, as illustrated in Figure 8.15, the firm's marginal cost curve can fluctuate between MC_1 and MC_2 without causing a change in the firm's profit maximizing price/output combination.

Nonprice Competition

Because rival firms are likely to retaliate against price cuts, oligopolists often emphasize nonprice competitive techniques to boost demand. What does nonprice competition mean? To explain the concept, let us first assume that a firm's demand function is given by Equation 8.2:

$$Q_A = f(P_A, P_X, Ad_A, Ad_X, SQ_A, SQ_X, I, Pop, \ldots)$$

$$= a - bP_A + cP_X + dAd_A - eAd_X + fSQ_A \quad \text{(8.2)}$$
$$- gSQ_X + hI + iPop + \ldots,$$

where Q_A is the quantity of output demanded from Firm A, P_A is A's price, P_X is the average price charged by other firms in the industry, Ad

is advertising expenditures, SQ denotes an index of styling and quality, I represents income, and Pop is population. The firm can control three of the variables in Equation 8.2: P_A, Ad_A, and SQ_A. If it reduces P_A in an effort to stimulate demand, it will probably cause a reduction in P_X, offsetting the hoped-for effects of the initial price cut. Rather than get a substantial boost in sales, Firm A may have simply started a price war.

Now consider the effects of changing the other controllable variables in the demand function, Ad_A and SQ_A. Increased advertising could be expected to shift the demand curve to the right, thus enabling the firm to increase sales at a given price or to sell a constant quantity at a higher price. An improvement in styling or quality would have the same effect as a boost in the advertising budget; similar results would follow from easing credit terms, training salespersons to be more courteous, providing more convenient retail locations, or any other improvement in the product. Competitors can be expected to react to changes in nonprice variables, but the reaction rate is likely to be slower than for price changes. For one thing, these changes are generally less obvious, at least initially, to rival firms, so it will take them longer to recognize that changes have occurred. Then, too, advertising campaigns have to be designed, and media time and space must be purchased. Styling and quality changes frequently require long lead times, as do training programs for salespeople, the opening of new facilities, and the like. Further, all these nonprice activities tend to differentiate the firm's products in the minds of consumers from those of other firms in the industry, and rivals may therefore find it difficult to regain lost customers even after they have reacted. Although it may take longer to build up a reputation through the use of nonprice competition, once the demand curve has been shifted outward, it often takes rivals longer to counteract that shift. Thus, the advantageous effects of nonprice competition are likely to be more persistent than the fleeting benefits of a price cut.

How far should nonprice competition be carried? The answer is that such activities should be carried to the point where the marginal cost of the action is just equal to the marginal profit produced by it. For example, suppose widgets sell for $10 per unit and the variable cost per unit is $8. If less than $2 of additional advertising expenditures will boost sales by 1 unit, the additional expenditure should be made.

Concentration and Market Structure

Markets fall along the continuum from perfect competition to monopoly. Where an industry falls along this continuum is important both for firms currently in the industry and those contemplating entry. Price-output strategies will vary markedly depending on the market structure encountered. In addition, profit rates are affected by the level of competitive pressures. Among the attributes describing market structure, perhaps the number and size distribution of competitors are most important and therefore must be carefully considered in managerial decision making.

Market Concentration

In addition to those directly engaged in business, both government and the public share an interest in the size distribution of firms. As described in Chapter 10, a small number of competitors can sometimes have direct implications for regulation and antitrust policy. Thus, significant public resources are devoted to monitoring both the size distribution of firms and economic performance in several important sectors of the economy. Data that describe these characteristics of the U.S. economy are regularly compiled and published in economic census reports published by the Department of Commerce. Among those sectors covered by the economic censuses, manufacturing is clearly the largest, accounting for approximately 20 percent of aggregate economic activity in the United States. Firm sizes are much larger in manufacturing than in other major sectors such as retail and wholesale trade, construction, services (legal, medical, etc.), and so on. While there are over 16 million business enterprises in the U.S., manufacturing is the domain of the large corporation and provides an interesting case study for considering data which are available on the size distribution of firms.

Every five years the U.S. Bureau of the Census publishes data describing the number and size distribution of firms in manufacturing, along with a wealth of related information. In reporting these data, the Bureau disaggregates domestic industrial activity into various levels of distinction. These levels proceed from very general two-digit product groups to very specific seven-digit product classifications. (See Chapter 13 for a discussion of this classification system.) Most economists agree that the four-digit level classifications correspond quite closely with the economic definition of a market and therefore use four-digit data in analyses of industrial competition.

Table 8.2 shows numbers of competitors, industry sales, and leading firm market share data for a small sample of four-digit industries taken from the 1977 *Census of Manufacturers*, the most recent census year available. Here, as is generally the case, leading firm market shares are calculated using sales data for the top four or top eight firms in an industry. These market share data are called *concentration ratios* because they measure the percentage market share held by (concentrated in) an industry's top four (CR_4) or eight firms (CR_8). When concentration ratios are low, industries tend to be made up of many firms and competi-

Table 8.2
A Representative Sample of Four-Digit Census Industries, 1977

Standard Industrial Classification (SIC Code)	Description	Number of Firms	Industry Sales (millions of dollars)	Market Share (Percent)	
				Top Four Firms (CR_4)	Top Eight Firms (CR_8)
2043	Cereal Breakfast Foods	32	$ 2,497.5	89	98
2047	Dog, Cat, and Other Pet Food	218 133	3,086.7	58	74
2095	Roasted Coffee		5,616.4	61	73
2371	Fur Goods	620	383.4	11	19
2387	Apparel Belts	281	286.9	21	32
2621	Paper Mills	171	12,613.3	23	42
3425	Handsaws and Saw Blades	105	363.3	53	69
3711	Motor Vehicles and Car Bodies	254	76,517.8	93	99
3721	Aircraft	151	14,834.2	59	81
3732	Boat Building and Repairing	2,148	1,822.6	11	19

tion will be vigorous. Industries where the four leading firms are responsible for less than 20 percent of total industry sales, i.e., $CR_4 < 20$, are highly competitive and approximate the pure competition model. On the other hand, when concentration ratios are high, leading firms dominate following firms in terms of size, and leading firms may have the potential for both pricing flexibility and excess profits. Industries where the four leading firms control more than 80 percent of total industry sales, i.e., $CR_4 > 80$, are highly concentrated and market structure can tend toward monopoly. However, industries where $CR_4 < 20$, or $CR_4 > 80$ are quite rare. Fully 75.9 percent of all manufacturing industries (representing 73.3 of total industry sales) fall in a range where $20 \leq CR_4 \leq 80$. In terms of relative importance, market structures which can be described as monopolistically competitive or oligopolistic are much more common than pure competition or monopoly.

Despite their obvious attraction as a useful source of information on the number and size distribution of current competitors, it is prudent to remain cautious in the use and interpretation of concentration data. Perhaps four specific limitations are most important in terms of both business and public policy. By not recognizing these limitations, one might make incorrect judgments concerning market structure.

A first serious limitation of concentration data relates to their coverage. Concentration data ignore domestic sales by foreign competitors (imports) as well as exports by domestic firms. Only data on domestic sales from *domestic production*, not total domestic sales, are reported. This means, for example, that if foreign car manufacturers have a market share of 25 percent, the four leading domestic car manufacturers account for 70 percent (= 93 percent of 75 percent) rather than the 93 percent of total U.S. foreign plus domestic car sales shown in Table 8.2. Therefore, in industries where import competition is significant, concentration ratios significantly overstate the relative importance of large domestic leading firms. Furthermore, while falling concentration is evident in many sectors, rising concentration is often apparent in industries where increasing foreign competition has been responsible for the liquidation or merger of many smaller domestic firms with older, less efficient production facilities. Despite a reduction in the number of domestic firms and a consequent rise in concentration, the increase in foreign competition may actually be responsible for making industries such as apparel and fabricated metal products more efficient and more competitive rather than less so. The effect of foreign competition is important in many industries, but is particularly so in manufacturing industries such as: apparel, steel, automobiles, television sets, cameras, copiers, and motorcycles.

A second limitation of concentration data is that they are *national totals* whereas the relevant economic market may be national, regional or local in scope. If high transportation costs or other product characteristics cause markets to be regional or local rather than national in scope, concentration ratios can significantly understate the relative importance of leading firms. For example, the leading firm in many metropolitan newspaper markets often accounts for 80 percent or more of total market advertising and subscription revenues. Thus, a national CR_4 level for newspapers of 19 percent in 1977 significantly understates localized market power in that industry. Whereas national concentration ratios in the 20 percent range usually suggest a highly competitive market structure, the local or regional character of some markets can make national concentration figures meaningless. Other examples of products with local or regional rather than national markets include: milk, bread and bakery products, commercial printing, and ready mix concrete.

Another problem relates to the fact that concentration data provide an imperfect view of market structure by including only firms which are *currently active* in a particular industry. Recall that an economic market includes all firms willing and able to sell an identifiable product. This not only includes firms currently active in an industry, but also those which can be regarded as likely potential entrants. Often the mere presence of one or more potential entrants constitutes a sufficient threat to force competitive market behavior in industries with only a handful of established competitors. Major retailers such as K-Mart and Sears, for example, use their positions as potential entrants into manufacturing to obtain attractive prices on a wide range of private label merchandise, such as clothing, lawn mowers, washing machines, and so on.

Finally, considering concentration data in isolation may result in misleading conclusions regarding the vigor of competition in an industry because the degree of competitiveness appears in more than one dimension. Concentration ratios measure only one element of market structure; other elements include the market shares of individual firms, barriers to entry or exit, vertical integration, and so on. Under certain circumstances, even a very few large competitors can compete vigorously. Thus, while concentration ratios are helpful indicators of the relative importance of leading firms and perhaps the potential for market power, it must be remembered that a high level of concentration does not necessarily imply a lack of competition. In some instances, *competition among the few can be vigorous*. In addition to considering the number and size distribution of competitors as measured by concentration, firms must judge the competitive environment in light of foreign competition, transportation costs, regional product differences, likely potential entrants, advertising, customer loyalty, research and development, demand growth, and economies of scale in production, among other factors, if accurate pricing and output decisions are to be made. All of the above features of markets constitute important elements of market structure.

Summary

Demand functions and cost functions interact to determine market structures, and this chapter has explained the process by which this determination is made. If average cost curves become constant or rise at an output that is small in relation to total demand, then a large number of firms will operate, and a *competitive* market structure will emerge. However, if unit costs decline throughout the entire range of outputs, then in the absence of external controls (such as antitrust legislation) the industry is likely to consist of but one firm, a *natural monopoly*.

If a large number of firms exist in the industry and if a homogeneous product is produced, the result is likely to be *pure competition*, in which firms face horizontal demand curves. On the other hand, if the product is somewhat differentiated, each firm will face a downward-sloping demand curve, and a market structure called *monopolistic competition* will be observed.

Under competition, either pure or monopolistic, no individual firm is enough of a factor in the market so that its actions affect other firms seriously enough to cause them to respond. Accordingly, competitive firms do not take into account reactions of other firms when making their price and output decisions. However, if only a few firms operate in the market, each of them will have a sizable share of the total market, and an action by one firm will have a noticeable effect on other firms. Therefore, other firms will react to the actions of any individual firm, and all firms will recognize this fact and will take such reactions into consideration in their pricing decisions. This situation is defined as *oligopoly*.

The profit maximizing decision rules are relatively simple and straightforward under monopoly, pure competition, and monopolistic competition. Under oligopoly, however, the rules become complex, almost to the point of being indeterminate. Firms recognize that profits could be maximized by some form of cooperative behavior, so *cartels*, *price leadership arrangements*, and stable prices as explained by the *kinked demand curve* may develop. Also, because reactions may be delayed, oligopolistic firms are likely to engage in such forms of nonprice competition as advertising, styling and quality changes, and service improvements as much as or more than firms in direct price competition.

Knowledge concerning the size distribution of firms is important for both managerial and public policy decisions. Thus, significant public resources are devoted to regularly collecting and publishing these data in economic census reports. Market *concentration ratios* measure the share of industry output concentrated among small groups of leading firms, an important aspect of market structure. Relatively high levels of concentration do not necessarily imply a lack of competition. Competition among the few is often vigorous.

Questions

8.1 Explain the process through which above-normal profits are eliminated in a purely competitive industry and in a monopolistically competitive industry.

8.2 Would the demand curve for a firm in a monopolistically competitive industry be more or less elastic after any above-normal profits have been eliminated?

8.3 "One might expect firms in a competitive industry to experience greater swings in the price of their products over the business cycle than those in an oligopolistic industry. However, fluctuations in profits will not necessarily follow the same pattern." Do you agree with this statement? Why, or why not?

8.4 When a single buyer faces many sellers, a condition known as *monopsony* exists. Describe the relationship between this form of market structure and the development of labor laws.

8.5 When a single seller faces a large number of buyers, a condition known as *monopoly* exists.

  a) Give an illustration of this form of market structure in U.S. labor markets.

  b) Discuss the impact of such a structure on inflation.

  c) Discuss the feasibility of modifying the antitrust laws to deal with such situations.

8.6 Why is the four-firm concentration ratio only an imperfect measure of market power?

8.7 Will revenue-maximizing firms have profits as large or larger than profit maximizing firms? If so, when? If not, why not?

8.8 Is a revenue maximizing firm necessarily inconsistent with the more traditional long-run profit maximizing model of firm behavior? Why, or why not?

Solved Problem

8.1 Wind Sail Inc. is a small firm in the water recreation equipment industry, which is purely competitive. The market price of each wind sail is $640 and the company's total and marginal cost functions are:

$$TC = \$240Q - \$20Q^2 + \$1Q^3$$

$$MC = \$240 \ \ - \$40Q \ + \$3Q^2.$$

A normal profit is included in the cost functions.

  a) Determine the following:

  i. Output at which profit is maximized

  ii. Average cost per unit at this output

  iii. Total profits

  b) If this firm is typical of all firms in the industry, is the industry in equilibrium? How do you know?

  c) Assume that this firm's input factors are perfectly unspecialized, such that there is no difference between short-run and long-run cost curves. If the firm and the industry are not now in equilibrium, when they do reach an equilibrium what will be the

  i. Output per firm?

  ii. Cost per unit of output?

  iii. Price per unit of output?

  d) Describe the process that will drive the industry to equilibrium.

Solution

a) i. Profits will be maximized when $MR = MC$. In this case,

$$MR = MC$$

$$640 = 240 - 40Q + 3Q^2$$

$$3Q^2 - 40Q - 400 = 0.$$

Using the quadratic formula to find Q:

$$Q = \frac{40 \pm \sqrt{(-40)^2 - 4(3)(-400)}}{2(3)}$$

$$Q = \frac{40 \pm 80}{6}$$

$Q_1 = -6.67$ (not feasible).

$Q_2 = 20$ units of output.

ii. Average costs are determined as follows:

$$AC = TC/Q = 240 - 20Q + Q^2$$

$$= 240 - 20(20) + 20^2$$

$$= \$240.$$

iii. Total profits are:

$$\pi = TR - TC$$

$$= 640(20) - [240(20) - 20(20)^2 + 1(20)^3]$$

$$= \$8,000.$$

b) No. The industry is defined to be a competitive one and costs are stated to include a normal profit, so the firm is earning above-normal or *economic* profits. Thus, the industry is not in equilibrium.
c) In equilibrium, firms must be earning only normal profits, and $P = MR = MC = AC$. Using these relationships, we can determine output, cost, and price.

    i. In competitive equilibrium, firms operate at the minimum point on their average cost curves. This point is reached where $MC = AC$. In this instance,

$$MC = AC$$

$$240 - 40Q + 3Q^2 = \frac{240Q - 20Q^2 + 1Q^3}{Q}$$

$$240 - 40Q + 3Q^2 = 240 - 20Q + Q^2$$

$$2Q^2 = 20Q$$

$$2Q = 20$$

$$Q = 10 \text{ units of output in equilibrium.}$$

In competitive long-run equilibrium, the firm will produce 10 units of output.

ii. Costs per unit of output at the optimum output level are:

$$AC = 240 - 20Q + Q^2 = 240 - 20(10) + (10)^2 = \$140$$

$$MC = 240 - 40Q + 3Q^2 = 240 - 40(10) + 3(10)^2 = \$140 .$$

iii. In competitive long-run equilibrium, $P = MC = AC$, so $P = \$140$.

d) In the current disequilibrium there is insufficient capacity in the industry. Each firm is producing on the rising part of its cost curve rather than at its minimum cost point. However, price still substantially exceeds average cost per unit of output, so firms are making excess profits. These above-normal profits will attract new firms, and as new firms enter and make their output available, the price of wind sails will decline. As price declines, firms will reduce their output, moving down their MC curves (which are their supply curves), until $P = MR = MC = AC$, at which point equilibrium is attained.

Solved Problem

8.2 Consider an industry where there are one large firm and a number of small firms. The large firm acts as a price leader and sets the industry price. The small firms are price followers and can sell all they want at the industry price. The demand curve for the industry is:

$$Q_I = 2,000 - 0.1P.$$

The total and marginal cost curves for the large firm and the aggregate curves for the smaller firms are as follows:

$$TC_L = 10,000 + 2,000Q_L. \qquad MC_L = 2,000.$$

$$TC_S = 1,000Q_S + 20Q_S^2. \qquad MC_S = 1,000 + 40Q.$$

a) What is the aggregate supply curve of the price followers?
b) Determine the relevant demand curve for the large firm.
c) Determine the price and output combination that maximizes the price leader's profit.
(*Note*: If $TR_L = 16,200Q_L - 8Q_L^2$ then $MR_L = 16,200 - 16Q_L$).
d) What output would be supplied by the smaller firms?

Solution

a) Since price followers take prices as given, they operate at the output level at which their marginal costs equal price. Therefore,

$$P = MC_S$$

$$= 1,000 + 40Q_S.$$

or

$$Q_S = -25 + 0.025P.$$

b) The demand curve for the large firm can be calculated algebraically by subtracting the supply curve of the price-following firms from the total industry demand, i.e., $Q_L = Q_I - Q_S$. Since the supply curve for the price followers is $Q_S = -25 + 0.025P$,

$$Q_L = Q_I - Q_S$$

$$= 2,000 - 0.1P - (-25 + 0.025P)$$

$$= 2,025 - 0.0125P,$$

or

$$P = 16,200 - 8Q_L.$$

c) Set

$$MR_L = MC_L$$

$$16,200 - 16Q_L = 2,000$$

$$16Q_L = 14,200$$

$$Q_L = 887.5$$

$$P = 16,200 - 8(887.5)$$

$$= \$9,100.$$

d) The total quantity supplied by both the large and small firms can be found by substituting the price of $9,100 into the industry demand equation.

$$Q_I = 2,000 - 0.1P$$

$$= 2,000 - 0.10(9,100)$$

$$= 2,000 - 910$$

$$= 1,090 \text{ Units.}$$

The total quantity supplied will be 1,090 units. The small firms should supply $1,090 - 887.5 = 202.5$ units. At this quantity, their marginal costs will equal their marginal revenue.

Proof:

$$MR_S = P = \$9,100$$

$$MC_S = 1,000 + 40Q$$

$$MC_S = MR_S.$$

$$1,000 + 40Q = 9,100$$

$$40Q = 8,100$$

$$Q = 202.5.$$

Problem Set

8.1 Tempe Manufacturing is considering introducing a new measurement device. The market is expected to be highly competitive, and Tempe forecasts industry supply and demand curves to be

$$Q_S = 80P_X$$

$$Q_D = 60,000 - 240P_X.$$

Accurately estimating the market price for this product is critical to Tempe's decision.
a) Graph the supply and demand curves.
b) Determine both graphically and algebraically the equilibrium price for this market.

8.2 Fayetteville Foundry Inc. is a medium-sized foundry, specializing in heavy duty pipe for industrial uses. Fayetteville's total revenue and marginal revenue functions are estimated as $TR = 600Q - 0.01Q^2$ and $MR = 600 - 0.02Q$, respectively. The company's accounting department, after consulting with production and marketing managers, has reported the following total cost function for the near future: $TC = \$250,000 + \$80Q$. This total cost function includes a normal return of 14 percent on capital resources. In the demand and total cost relations specified above, Q is output (in hundreds of feet of heavy gauge pipe), P is price, and TC is total costs. The marginal cost for 100 feet of pipe is estimated at $80.

a) Determine the profit maximizing output level.

b) What is the profit at this level of output?

c) What price will be charged under profit maximization?

d) What price will be charged under the assumption that the company seeks to maximize dollar sales volume? Compute profits under this assumption.

e) Assume that Fayetteville operates in a monopolistically competitive industry. If Fayetteville is typical of other firms in the industry, and if normal profits are implicit in the cost function, is the industry in equilibrium? If not, describe the process that will lead to equilibrium. What changes in prices, costs, firm output levels, and profits would you expect to result from the move to equilibrium? (Describe the direction of these changes, rather than attempting to calculate their magnitude).

8.3 Orange County Printing Ltd. is a pure monopolist and has the following revenue and cost equations:

$$TR = 5,500Q - 2Q^2. \qquad TC = 30,000 + 1,500Q.$$

$$MR = 5,500 - 4Q. \qquad MC = 1,500.$$

a) What would be the selling price and quantity supplied by the monopolist?

b) Assuming a "normal" profit level is included in the total cost function, what would be the level of "supernormal" or "economic" profits for the firm?

c) Graph the demand, marginal revenue, and marginal cost curves.

d) It has been said that a monopolist charges a higher price and supplies a smaller quantity than would a purely competitive firm. Using the example above, show this to be true.

e) What would the monopolist's profits be if it decided to maximize total revenue instead of total profits?

8.4 Athens Pharmaceutical is a leading manufacturer of drugs used to treat digestive disorders and is the sole producer of XO-Hydrolyzien, a medication used in the treatment of peptic ulcers. XO-Hydrolyzien has long been one of Athens's most successful products. The total market demand curve for XO-Hydrolyzien is $P = \$20 - \$0.00001Q$, where Q is ounces of the drug demanded. Athens's costs of manufacture, including capital costs, are $8Q$. The firm operates so as to maximize profits.

a) Athens has been selling XO-Hydrolyzien at a price of $14 per ounce. Calculate the sales level and the profits Athens obtains at this price.

b) Now assume that the patents covering XO-Hydrolyzien expire, several competitors begin offering generic equivalents, and the market becomes perfectly competitive. Calculate the new equilibrium market price for the product. (Assume the additional producers of XO-Hydrolyzien have the same costs as Athens.)

c) What are the benefits to Athens of patent protection? Are there any benefits to society in general?

8.5 Safety Service Products (SSP) faces the following segmented demand and marginal revenue curves for its new infant safety seat:

$$P = 60 - Q$$
$$MR = 60 - 2Q$$

over the range of 0–10,000 units of output.

$$P = 80 - 3Q$$
$$MR = 80 - 6Q$$

when output exceeds 10,000 units.

The company's total and marginal cost functions are as follows:

$$TC = 100 + 20Q + 0.5Q^2.$$

$$MC = 20 + Q,$$

where P is price (in dollars), Q is output (in thousands), and TC is total cost (in thousands of dollars).

a) Graph the demand, marginal revenue, and marginal cost curves.

b) How would you describe the market structure of the industry in which SSP operates? Explain why the demand curve takes the shape indicated above.

c) What is the firm's optimal price and quantity, and what will its profits be at this output?

d) How much could marginal costs rise before the optimal price would increase? How much could they fall before the optimal price would decrease?

8.6 Following the air traffic controllers' strike, the Federal Aviation Administration (FAA) required airlines to reduce traffic into various airports temporarily. As a result, airlines cut the number of flights and laid off pilots, crews, and maintenance personnel at a substantial savings in variable costs. Fixed costs related to the leasing of aircraft were unaffected, at least in the short run.

a) When would short-run industry profits fall after the FAA order?

b) When would they rise?

c) Describe the likely long-run implications of the FAA order.

8.7 IBM produces a wide variety of computer equipment and user software programs. Given the tremendous success of its personal computers, a number of independent firms have begun to offer compatible computer programs and peripheral equipment.

a) Discuss the optimal long-run pricing strategy for IBM if:

i. IBM's profit maximizing price on software and peripheral equipment is below the independents' minimum attainable average total costs (including a normal profit).

ii. IBM's profit maximizing price is above the independents' minimum ATC.

b) Explain why IBM might enjoy a large share of the market for computing equipment but a much smaller share of the software and peripherals markets.

c) Could IBM use a superior capability in the production of computing equipment to dominate the software and peripherals markets?

8.8 Laguna Software Inc. offers computer software for use in computer-assisted primary and secondary education programs. Laguna is a dominant price-leading firm in many of its markets. Recently, Basic Programs Ltd. and Danbury Software Inc. have begun to offer products with the same essential characteristics as Laguna's "Readyeasy" software. The total and marginal cost functions for the Basic and Danbury products are:

$$TC_B = 75,000 - 7Q + 0.0025Q_B^2$$

$$MC_B = -7 + 0.005Q_B$$

$$TC_D = 50,000 + 3Q_D + 0.0025Q_D^2$$

$$MC_D = 3 + 0.005Q_D.$$

Laguna's total and marginal costs for "Readyeasy" are:

$$TC_L = 300,000 + 5Q_L + 0.0002Q_L^2$$

$$MC_L = 5 + 0.0004Q_L.$$

The industry demand curve for this product is:

$$Q_I = 500,800 - 19,600P.$$

a) Determine the supply curves for the Basic and Danbury products, assuming the firms operate as price takers.

b) What is the demand curve faced by Laguna for its "Readyeasy" software? Assume here and throughout the problem that the Basic and Danbury products are perfect substitutes for "Readyeasy."

c) Calculate Laguna's profit maximizing price and output levels for "Readyeasy." (*Hint*: Laguna's total marginal revenue functions are $TR = 25Q_S - 0.00005Q_S^2$ and $MR = 25 - 0.0001Q_S$).

d) Calculate the profit maximizing output levels for the Basic and Danbury products.

e) Is the market for the products from these three firms in short-run equilibrium?

References

Baumol, William J. "Contestable Markets: An Uprising in the Theory of Industry Structure." *American Economic Review* 72 (March 1982): 1–15.

Demsetz, Harold. "Barriers to Entry." *American Economic Review* 72 (March 1982): 47–57.

Dixit, Avinash. "Recent Developments in Oligopoly Theory." *American Economic Review* 72 (May 1982): 12–17.

Henderson, Bruce D. "The Anatomy of Competition." *Journal of Marketing* 47 (Spring 1983): 7–11.

Hirschey, Mark. "The Effect of Advertising on Industrial Mobility, 1947–1972." *Journal of Business* 54 (April 1981): 329–339.

Hirschey, Mark and Pappas, James L. "Market Power and Manufacturer Leasing." *Journal of Industrial Economics* 30 (September 1980): 39–47.

Lindenberg, Eric B. and Ross, Stephen A. "Tobin's *q* Ratio and Industrial Organization." *Journal of Business* 54 (January 1981): 1–32.

Mansfield, Edwin. "Technological Change and Market Structure: An Empirical Study." *American Economic Review* 73 (May 1983): 205–209.

Means, Gardner C. "Corporate Power in the Marketplace." *Journal of Law and Economics* 26 (June 1983): 467–485.

Peltzman, Sam. "The Gains and Losses from Industrial Concentration." *Journal of Law and Economics* 20 (October 1977): 229–263.

Qualls, P. David. "Market Structure and the Cyclical Flexibility of Price-Cost Margins." *Journal of Business* 52 (April 1979): 305–325.

Ravenscraft, David J. "Structure-Profit Relationships at the Line of Business and Industry Level." *Review of Economics and Statistics* 64 (November 1982): 22–31.

Shepherd, William G. "Causes of Increased Competition in the U.S. Economy, 1939–1980." *Review of Economics and Statistics* 64 (November 1982): 613–626.

Shepherd, William G. "Contestability vs. Competition." *American Economic Review* 74 (September 1984): 572–587.

Weiss, Leonard W. "The Extent and Effects of Aggregate Concentration." *Journal of Law and Economics* 26 (June 1983): 429–455.

Chapter 9

Pricing Practices

Key Terms

Cost-plus pricing

Incremental analysis

Joint products

Margin

Mark up on cost

Multiple-product
  pricing

Price discrimination

Chapter 8 demonstrated that regardless of the market structure within which the firm operates, pricing for profit maximization is based on a careful analysis of the relationship between marginal cost and marginal revenue. Research into the question of actual pricing practices, however, indicates that many firms set prices without an explicit analysis of marginal relationships. The evidence shows that most firms use **cost-plus pricing**, setting prices to cover all direct costs plus a percentage markup for overhead and profit instead of determining the specific price at which $MR = MC$. How can this conflict between economic theory and observed pricing practices be reconciled? We believe that if one thoroughly understands the procedures used in actual pricing decisions, there is no real conflict between theory and practice. In this chapter we examine a variety of pricing practices, indicate their value to firms, and demonstrate the economic rationale for their use.

Cost-Plus Pricing

Surveys of actual business pricing indicate that cost-plus pricing, or markup pricing as it is sometimes called, is by far the most prevalent pricing method employed by business firms. There are many varieties of cost-plus pricing, but a typical one involves estimating the average variable costs of producing and marketing a product, adding a charge for overhead, and then adding a percentage markup, or margin, for profits. The charge for indirect costs, or overhead, is usually determined by allocating these costs among the firm's products on the basis of their average variable costs. For example, if a firm's total overhead for a year was projected to be $1.3 million, and the estimated total variable costs of its planned production was $1.0 million, then overhead would be allocated to products at the rate of 130 percent of variable cost. Thus, if the average variable costs of a product are estimated to be $1, the firm would add a charge of 130 percent of that variable cost, or $1.30, for overhead, obtaining an estimated fully allocated average cost of $2.30. To this figure the firm might add a 30 percent markup for profits, or $0.69, to obtain a price of $2.99 per unit.

In general, the **markup on cost** formula is given by the expression:

$$\text{Markup on cost} = \frac{\text{Price} - \text{Cost}}{\text{Cost}}. \tag{9.1}$$

The numerator of this expression is called the markup on cost, or **margin**. In the example cited above, the 30 percent markup on cost is calculated as:

$$\text{Markup on cost} = \frac{\text{Price} - \text{Cost}}{\text{Cost}}$$

$$= \frac{\$2.99 - \$2.30}{\$2.30}$$

$$= 0.30 \text{ or } 30 \text{ percent.}$$

Solving Equation 9.1 for price provides the expression used to determine price in a cost plus pricing system:

$$\text{Price} = \text{Cost} (1 + \text{Markup}). \tag{9.2}$$

Continuing with the example developed above, the selling price for the product is found as:

$$\text{Price} = \text{Cost} (1 + \text{Markup})$$

$$= \$2.30(1.30)$$

$$= \$2.99.$$

Cost-plus pricing is sometimes criticized as a naïve pricing technique based solely on cost considerations—and the wrong costs at that. The failure of the technique to examine demand conditions, coupled with its emphasis on fully allocated accounting costs rather than marginal costs, is said to lead to suboptimal price decisions. Although it is true that firms that use cost-plus pricing naïvely may fail to make optimal decisions, the widespread use of the technique by many successful firms causes one to question the charge that it has no place in managerial decision making. In fact, a closer examination of the technique indicates both its value and its limitations in pricing analysis.

Role of Costs in Cost-Plus Pricing

Although several different cost concepts are employed in cost-plus pricing, most firms use a standard, or normal, cost concept. These fully allocated costs are determined by first estimating direct costs per-unit, then allocating the firm's expected indirect expenses, or overhead, assuming a standard or normal output level. The resulting standard cost per unit is then used for price determination, irrespective of short-term variations in actual unit costs.

The standard cost concept is sometimes based on historical accounting costs, and this can give rise to several problems. First, firms may fail to properly adjust the historical cost data to reflect recent or *expected* price changes for key input factors. Unadjusted historical accounting costs have little relevance for decision making. The firm should use estimates of future costs; that is, costs that will be incurred during the period for which prices are being set. A further problem is that accounting costs may not reflect true economic costs. The concept of opportunity, or alternative, costs must be employed for optimal decision making.

The use of fully allocated costs as opposed to incremental costs also causes errors in some pricing decisions. The use of fully allocated costs is appropriate when the firm is operating at capacity. Under these conditions, an increase in production is likely to result in an increase in all plant, equipment, labor, materials, and other expenditures, and fully allocated costs per unit are relevant for pricing. If a firm has excess capacity, only those costs that actually rise with production, the incremental costs per unit, should be the basis for setting prices. Successful firms that employ cost plus pricing typically set prices using fully allocated prices under normal conditions, but offer substantial price discounts or use lower margins during periods of excess capacity.

Role of Demand in Cost-Plus Pricing

The variability in margins among different products sold by firms using cost-plus pricing methods provides clear evidence that demand analysis does, in fact, play an important role in price determination. Studies indicate that most firms differentiate their markups for different product lines on the basis of competitive pressure and demand elasticities. While companies have always been willing to adjust prices or profit margins on specific products as market conditions varied, flexibility is now commonplace and often a key element of competitive strategy. For example, both foreign and domestic automobile companies regularly offer rebates or special equipment packages for slow moving models. Similarly, airlines promote different pricing schedules for various types of peak and off-peak travel demand. Clearly, the airline and automobile industries are examples of industries for which competitive conditions require a careful and thorough analysis of demand conditions for pricing. Efforts to assess the competitive relationships of products and the costs of making them is by no means limited to these industries. In both goods and service producing sectors, successful firms are judged by their ability to adjust prices to different market conditions.

An examination of the margins set by a successful regional grocery store chain provides additional evidence that demand conditions play an important role in cost plus pricing. Table 9.1 shows the typical

Table 9.1
Markup on Cost for a Variety of Grocery Items

Item	Markup on Cost
Bread—private label	0–5%
Bread—brand name	30–40
Breakfast cereals (dry)	5–15
Cake mixes	15–20
Coffee	0–10
Cold cuts (processed meats)	20–45
Cookies	20–30
Delicatessen items	35–45
Fresh fruit—in season	40–50
Fresh fruit—out of season	15–20
Fresh vegetables—in season	40–50
Fresh vegetables—out of season	15–20
Ground beef	0–10
Ice cream	15–20
Laundry detergent	5–10
Milk	0–5
Nonprescription drugs	35–55
Pastry (cakes, pies, etc.)	20–30
Pet foods	15–20
Snack foods	20–25
Soft drinks	0–10
Spices	30–40
Soup	0–15
Steak	15–35
Toilet tissue	10–15
Toothpaste	15–20

markup on cost set by the firm for a variety of products sold in its stores. Note the wide range of margins applied to different items.

A field manager with over twenty years experience in the grocery business provided some useful insight into the firm's pricing practices. He stated that the "price sensitivity" of an item is the primary consideration in setting margins. Staple products like bread, coffee, ground beef, milk, and soup are highly price sensitive and the margins applied are relatively low. Products with high margins tend to be those for which demand is less price sensitive.

We see this retail grocery store pricing example as a particularly insightful case of how cost plus pricing rules are used in setting an efficient pricing policy. Although the words "price elasticity" were never used in our discussions, it is clear that this concept plays a key role in the firm's cost plus pricing decisions. To examine those decisions further it is necessary to develop the basis for determining optimal markups in cost plus pricing.

Cost Plus Pricing and Profit Maximization.

That demand analysis plays an important role in cost plus pricing is clear. An unanswered question, however, is: How does one determine the optimal markup for products with differing demand elasticities? The answer lies in two previously examined relationships. Recall from our analysis of demand in Chapter 3 that there is a direct relation among marginal revenue, price elasticity of demand, and the price charged for a product. This was expressed in Equation 3.10 as:

$$MR = P\left(1 + \frac{1}{\varepsilon_P}\right) \tag{9.3}$$

For profit maximization a firm must operate at the activity level where marginal revenue equals marginal cost. But since marginal revenue is always equal to the right-hand side of Equation 9.3, at the profit maximizing output level we have:

$$P\left(1 + \frac{1}{\varepsilon_P}\right) = MC \tag{9.4}$$

or,

$$P = MC\left(\frac{1}{1 + \frac{1}{\varepsilon_P}}\right). \tag{9.5}$$

Equation 9.5 provides a formula for the profit maximizing markup on a product in terms of its price elasticity. Equation 9.5 states that the profit maximizing price is found by multiplying marginal cost by the term

$$\left(\frac{1}{1 + \dfrac{1}{\varepsilon_P}} \right).$$

Recall from Equation 9.2 that the price established under a cost plus system is equal to "cost" multiplied by the expression (1 + markup). The implication of Equation 9.5 is that marginal cost is the appropriate "cost" basis for cost plus pricing and that

$$MC\,(1 + \text{Markup}) = MC \left(\frac{1}{1 + \dfrac{1}{\varepsilon_P}} \right).$$

Thus, the profit maximizing margin or markup is

$$\text{Markup} = \left(\frac{1}{1 + \dfrac{1}{\varepsilon_P}} \right) - 1. \tag{9.6}$$

Table 9.2 shows the optimal markup on marginal cost for products with varying price elasticity of demand. As demonstrated in the table, the more elastic the demand for a product (the more "price sensitive" it is), the *smaller* the optimal margin. Products with relatively less elastic demand will be optimally priced with higher markups. In the retail grocery data, the very low markup on milk is consistent with a high price elasticity of demand for that product. Demand for fruits and vegetables during their primary seasons is considerably less price elastic and the markups reflect this lower price sensitivity of demand. We see that far from being a naive rule-of-thumb, cost plus pricing can, if carefully applied, allow a firm to arrive at optimal prices for its

Table 9.2
Optimal Markup on Cost at Various Price Elasticity Levels

Price Elasticity of Demand, ε_P	Optimal Markup on Cost
− 1.5	200%
− 2.0	100
− 2.5	67
− 5.0	25
−10.0	11
−25.0	4

products in a relatively efficient manner. In fact, cost plus pricing might well be an optimal technique for implementing marginal analysis for pricing in a world of uncertainty. An attempt to reduce uncertainty and to estimate more completely the marginal revenue and marginal cost relations for a product will itself result in added costs. Marginal analysis concepts indicate that the firm must weigh the added expense against the possible gain and act accordingly. That is, the firm must determine whether the added expense associated with obtaining more complete estimates of marginal relationships in order to apply a full marginal revenue–marginal cost analysis is more than offset by the expected gain in profits. It follows that cost plus pricing may in many instances result in maximum profits when full consideration is given to the added expense of obtaining the data necessary for a more complete analysis of marginal revenue and cost.

Incremental Analysis in Pricing

For many pricing decisions the correct approach involves *incremental profit analysis*, which deals with the relationship between the *changes* in revenues and costs associated with managerial decisions. The emphasis on only the costs or revenues that are actually affected by the decision insures proper economic reasoning in decision analysis. That is, proper use of incremental profit analysis results in accepting any action that increases net profits and in rejecting any action that reduces profits. (This statement abstracts from the possibility of changing the firm's risk posture such as undertaking an action that might increase expected profits but be so risky that it would raise the firm's capitalization rate to a point where the value of the firm might decline.)

The fact that **incremental analysis** involves only those factors that are affected by a particular decision does not mean that the concept is easy to apply. Proper use of incremental analysis requires a wide-ranging examination of the *total* effect of the decision. Consider, for example, a firm's decision to introduce a new product. Incremental analysis requires that the decision be based on the net effect of changes in revenues and costs. An analysis of the effect on revenues involves an estimate of the net revenues to be received for the product and, additionally, a study of how sales of the new product will affect the firm's other products. It may well be that the new product will, in fact, compete with the firm's existing products; if so, even though the new product has a high individual revenue potential, the net effect on revenue might not justify the added expense. At the other extreme, although a new product may not be expected to produce much profit on its own, if it is complementary to the firm's other products, the expected gain in sales of these other products could result in a large incremental increase in total profit. Kodak's Instamatic camera series is an example of a product introduced, in part at least, because of the complementarity between it and a major component of the firm's existing product line, photographic film.

Incremental cost analysis is just as far-reaching. In addition to the direct incremental costs associated with the new product, the firm must consider any impact on the costs of existing products. For example, introduction of a new product might cause production bottlenecks that would raise the cost of other products.

Incremental analysis involves long-run as well as short-run effects. A new product may appear to be profitable in an incremental sense in the short run because the firm has excess capacity in its existing plant and equipment. Over the long run, however, the commitment to produce the new item may require a substantial investment when the necessary equipment wears out and must be replaced. There may also be high opportunity costs associated with future production if either expansion of other product lines or development of future alternative products is restricted by the decision to produce the new product.

It is important to stress once again that incremental analysis is based on the changes associated with the decision. For short-run analysis, fixed cost (overhead) is irrelevant and must not be included in incremental analysis. If the impact of the decision extends into the long run, however, fixed costs are indeed relevant and must be considered.

An Illustration of Incremental Analysis

There are numerous examples which reflect the use of incremental logic by firms. The value of the approach can be demonstrated by an example of how Continental Airlines has used incremental analysis in its flight service decisions.[1] When considering adding a new flight (or dropping an existing one that appeared to be doing poorly), Continental engaged in an incremental analysis along the lines of Table 9.3. The corporate philosophy was clear: "If revenues exceed out-of-pocket costs, put the flight on." In other words, Continental compared the out-of-pocket, or incremental, costs associated with each proposed flight to the total revenues generated by that flight. An excess of revenues over incremental costs led to a decision to add the flight to Continental's schedule.

---

[1] Adapted from the April 20, 1963, issue of *BusinessWeek* by special permission. © 1963 by McGraw-Hill, Inc., New York, N.Y. 10020. All rights reserved.

Table 9.3
Incremental Analysis as Employed by Continental Airlines

Problem: Shall Continental run an extra daily flight from City X to City Y?

Facts:	Fully allocated costs of this flight	$4,500
	Out-of-pocket costs of this flight	$2,000
	Flight should gross	$3,100

Decision: Run the flight. It will add $1,100 to net profit by adding $3,100 to revenues and only $2,000 to costs. Overhead and other costs totaling $2,500 ($4,500 minus $2,000) would be incurred whether the flight is run or not. Therefore, fully allocated or average costs of $4,500 are not relevant to this business decision. It is the out-of-pocket, or incremental, costs that count.

The out-of-pocket cost figures used by Continental were obtained by circulating a proposed schedule for the new flight to every operating department concerned and finding out what added expenses would be incurred by each of them. Here, an alternative cost concept was used. If a ground crew was on duty and between work on other flights, the proposed flight was not charged a penny of their salary. Some costs may even have been reduced by the additional flight. For example, on a late-night round trip flight between Colorado Springs and Denver, Continental often flew without any passengers and with only a small amount of freight. Even without passenger revenues, these flights were profitable because their net costs were less than the rent for overnight hangar space at Colorado Springs.

On the revenue side, Continental considered not only the projected revenues for the flight but also the effect on revenues of competing and connecting flights on the Continental schedule. Several Continental flights that failed to cover their out-of-pocket costs directly brought in passengers for connecting long-haul service. When the excess of additional revenue over cost on the long-haul flight was considered, Continental earned a positive net profit on the feeder service.

Continental's use of incremental analysis extended to its scheduling of airport arrival and departure times. A proposed schedule for the Kansas City Municipal Airport, for example, had two planes landing at the same time. This was expensive for Continental, because its facilities in Kansas City at that time were not sufficient to service two planes simultaneously. Continental would have been forced to lease an extra fuel truck and to hire three new employees at an additional monthly cost of $1,800. However, when Continental began shifting around proposed departure times in other cities to avoid the congestion at Kansas

City, it appeared that the company might lose as much as $10,000 in monthly revenues if passengers switched to competing flights leaving at more convenient hours. Needless to say, the two flights were scheduled to be on the ground in Kansas City at the same time.

The Time Factor in Incremental Analysis

Although microeconomic theory is based on an assumed goal of value maximization, much of it is developed around a static construct in which the firm is assumed to operate so as to maximize *short-run* profits. Implicit in this is the assumption that continual maximization of short-run profits, coupled with proper adjustments to the physical plant as technology, factor prices, and demand change, will lead to long-run profit and value maximization.

The real world is more complicated than this model suggests. Actions taken at one time affect results in subsequent times, and wise business managers recognize this fact. Accordingly, because short-run profit maximization is seldom entirely consistent with long-run wealth maximization, firms do not focus solely on short-run profit maximization.

An illustration will help to clarify the point. Consider a firm that sets the current price of its product below the short-run profit maximizing level in order to expand its market rapidly. Such a policy can lead to long-run profit maximization if the firm is able to secure a larger permanent market share by its action. A similar policy might also be used to forestall competitive entry into the market. From a legal standpoint, a policy of accepting less than maximum short-run profits could reduce the threat of antitrust suits or government regulation, thereby again leading to long-run profit and wealth maximization.

The pricing practices of U.S. automobile manufacturers in the years just after World War II provide an example of this kind of behavior. Prices on most models were maintained well below the short-run profit maximizing level. Automobile manufacturers felt that the rapid expansion of both private automobile ownership and their dealership networks that would result from this policy would lead to higher long-run profits. Further, there was some fear of alienating customers by charging high prices during this period of extremely heavy demand; moreover, the possibility of antitrust action also affected automobile-pricing decisions.

The correct application of incremental analysis in pricing practice requires that both short-run and long-run effects on costs and revenues be considered. More often than not, apparent conflicts between pricing practice and economic theory can be reconciled when the long-run implications of pricing decisions are understood.

Price Discrimination

Additional complexities are introduced into the pricing decision when the firm sells its products in multiple markets. The existence of more than one market, or customer group, gives rise to the possibility of price discrimination, or differential pricing.

In a general sense **price discrimination** can be said to exist whenever different classes of customers are charged different prices for the same product, or when a multiproduct firm prices closely related products in such a manner that the differences in their prices are not proportional to the differences in their costs. In other words, price discrimination occurs whenever a given firm's prices in different markets are not related to differentials in production and distribution costs. For example, a practice of nationwide uniform pricing for fountain pens by the Parker Pen Company of Janesville, Wisconsin, would be a form of price discrimination. The transportation cost of selling these pens in Chicago is lower than transportation cost to the Los Angeles market; thus a uniform price for the product reflects a lower markup in Los Angeles than in Chicago.

Price discrimination does not carry an evil connotation in a moral sense. It is merely a term used in economics to describe a pricing practice that must be judged good or bad on other grounds. In some situations price discrimination can actually lead to lower costs and prices and to the provision of more goods and services than would otherwise be available. For example, a theater company that charges lower prices for students than for nonstudents may not only provide students who could not afford the usual price an opportunity to attend performances but also, because of the incremental revenues provided by students, be able to stage productions that could not be supported by ticket sales to nonstudents alone. Of course, price discrimination can also be used by a predatory monopolist to increase already excessive profits, in which case most would agree with antitrust laws designed to thwart such behavior.

Requirements for Profitable Price Discrimination

There are two necessary conditions for profitable price discrimination. First, the firm must be able to segment the market for a product; that is, to identify submarkets and to prevent transfers among customers in different submarkets. When markets are segmented, the firm can isolate one group of buyers from another. If this is possible, the firm can sell at one price to some buyers and at a different price to others without the possibility of intermarket leakages.

Second, different price elasticities of demand for the product must exist in the various submarkets. Unless price elasticities differ among submarkets, there is no point in segmenting the market. With identical elasticities, the profit maximizing price policy calls for charging the same price in all segments. This point is elaborated in a later section.

Types of Price Discrimination

The extent, or *degree*, to which a firm can engage in price discrimination has been classified into three major categories. Under *first-degree price discrimination* the firm extracts the maximum amount each and every purchaser is willing to pay for its product. The firm prices each unit of output separately at the level indicated at successive quantities along a demand curve. (In effect, the demand curve becomes the firm's marginal revenue curve.) Although there are some cases where first degree price discrimination actually occurs—primarily in the provision of personal services, such as legal services, medical care, and personal financial advising—the formidable demand information requirements (the seller must know the maximum price each buyer will pay for each unit of output) and problems of market segmentation associated with this type of price discrimination prevent its use in most situations.

Second-degree price discrimination, a more frequently employed type of price discrimination, involves the setting of prices on the basis of quantity purchased. Typically, prices are *blocked*, with a high price set for the first unit or block of units purchased by each consumer and lower prices set for successive units or blocks. Public utilities, such as electric companies, gas companies, and water companies, frequently use block rates that are discriminatory. (Remember that in order for differential prices to be discriminatory in an economic sense, they cannot be related to cost differences. Therefore, block rates based strictly on different costs of service would not be classified as price discrimination.) The use of second-degree price discrimination is also somewhat limited, since it can be applied only to products whose use is metered in some fashion, which explains its use by electric, gas, and water utilities. Office equipment such as copiers or time-sharing computer systems, which lend themselves to such metering, are other examples of products where second-degree price discrimination is practiced.

The most commonly observed form of price discrimination is *third-degree price discrimination*; this results when a firm separates its customers into several classes and sets a different price for each class. These customer classifications can be based on a variety of factors. Geographical differentials may be used when a product's supplier feels that regional markets can be isolated through control of the product distribution system. For example, in 1978 General Motors set a lower price on its Chevette model in the western United States than in the rest of the country, because Japanese competition made the West Coast small-car automobile market more price-elastic than the markets in other parts of the United States. (Price differentials among geographically separated markets that are proportional to transportation costs are not classified as discriminatory.)

Product use provides another basis for third-degree price discrimination. Local newspapers, for example, typically charge different rates for classified advertising based on the value of the item or service being advertised. Electric, gas, water, and telephone utilities' rate differentials between commercial and private consumers are another example of price discrimination based on product use. The utilities face very different demand elasticities in the residential and industrial sectors of their markets. The demand for electricity from residential users is inelastic, because these customers have no good substitutes for the electricity supplied by the power utility. Industrial buyers, on the other hand, have a much more elastic demand, because many of them could generate their own power if electricity prices should rise above the cost of operating in-plant generating equipment.

Time, either clock or calendar, provides another common basis for this form of price discrimination. Segmenting the day for long-distance telephone rates is one example of such price discrimination; rates are higher during periods of the day when demand is greatest, for example, during business hours. Theater pricing provides another example of price discrimination based on clock time. Calendar-time price discrimination is often reflected in peak-season and off-season pricing for resort facilities.

Age, sex, and income provide still other bases of discrimination, particularly for services as opposed to physical products. For example, lower prices for children's haircuts and movie tickets are discriminatory practices based on age; ladies'-day admission prices for sports events illustrate price discrimination based on sex. Discrimination on the bases of age, sex, and income is controversial, both popularly and legally, so this pricing practice should be closely monitored for changes.

An Illustration of Price Discrimination

Just as the airline industry provided an interesting illustration of incremental analysis in pricing practice, it also provides an interesting basis for discussing price discrimination. That airlines charge different prices to a wide variety of customer classes is obvious to all air travelers. What is less clear, however, is the extent to which these price differences reflect differences in the cost of service, or instead are examples of price discrimination. For example, Table 9.4 shows the range of airfares available on United Airlines for roundtrips between Chicago, Illinois and Denver, Colorado on May 1, 1984. It is perhaps surprising

Table 9.4
Chicago—Denver Roundtrip Airfares Available
on United Airlines, May 1, 1984

Fare	Description	Amount
Discounted Supersaver	Limited number of seats; use between May 1–September 8, 1984	$200.00
Restricted Supersaver—A	Travel Tuesdays or Wednesdays; stay 7–30 days; 14-day advance payment	249.00
Restricted Supersaver—B	No travel Tuesdays or Wednesdays; stay 7–30 days; 14-day advance payment	299.00
Supersaver	Stay over Saturday on 7–60 day trip; 7-day advance payment	349.00
Night Coach	Any day, 9:00 p.m.–6:00 a.m.	422.00
Coach	No restrictions	528.00
First Class Night Coach	Any day, 9:00 p.m.–6:00 a.m.	554.00
First Class	No restrictions	792.00

that the most expensive first class fare is nearly four times the price of the least expensive discounted supersaver fare. In analyzing these price differences between fare classes it is important to realize that airlines such as United serve two broad classes of customers, business and vacation travelers, and that both ticket price sensitivity and service costs are likely to vary between classes.

Important business meetings are often scheduled or cancelled on short notice, and business travelers require a great deal of scheduling flexibility in making travel plans. On the other hand, vacation travelers are able to make plans well in advance, and are often quite flexible as to times for departure and arrival. Vacation travelers also often have more flexibility concerning the length of time involved in travel and can, therefore, consider other modes of transportation. This means that vacation travelers will tend to be more price sensitive than business travelers.

It is tempting to consider the price differences shown in Table 9.4 as a clear example of airline price discrimination between business customers with relatively inelastic demand and vacation customers with more elastic demand. However, it is important to recognize that the costs of serving these two groups of customers can vary widely. Business traffic is particularly heavy on Mondays as these travelers leave home offices to meet with regional office personnel, clients, suppliers, and so on. Since business travelers typically return home for weekends, traffic on Thursdays and Fridays is also heavy. This pattern of business travel often leaves airlines with substantial unused capacity on Tuesdays and Wednesdays, as well as on Saturdays and Sundays. Given this excess capacity, the incremental cost per air traveler can be substantially lower during midweek and weekend periods. The $50 price differential between United's two restricted supersaver fare classes undoubtedly reflects this fact.

Airlines are also better able to schedule their use of airplane capacity when demand is predictable as opposed to erratic, which contributes to lower fares for restricted as opposed to unrestricted travelers. Still, in light of the wide dispersion in fares offered, it seems likely that the price differentials shown in Table 9.4 reflect a combination of the effects of price discrimination and differences in the costs of services.

From this simple illustration it should be clear why price discrimination is such a controversial subject. Even when the conditions for profitable price discrimination are clearly present, determining the magnitude of customer price differences unrelated to product or service cost differentials is often difficult.

Profit Maximization under Price Discrimination

The firm that can segment its market will maximize profits by operating so that marginal revenue equals marginal cost *in each market segment*. This can be demonstrated by an example. Suppose a firm is selling the same product in two separate markets, A and B. The demand curves for the two markets are given by Equations 9.3 and 9.4:

$$\text{Market } A: P_A = 60 - 0.5Q_A. \tag{9.3}$$

$$\text{Market } B: P_B = 110 - 3Q_B. \tag{9.4}$$

P_A and P_B are the prices charged in the two markets, and Q_A and Q_B are the quantities demanded. The firm's total and marginal cost functions for its product are:

$$TC = 1,000 + 9Q + 0.1Q^2. \tag{9.5}$$

$$MC = 9 + 0.2Q. \tag{9.6}$$

Here, Q equals the sum of the quantities sold in Markets A and B; that is, $Q = Q_A + Q_B$.

Figure 9.1 illustrates this pricing situation. The demand curve for Market A is shown in the first panel, that for Market B in the second.

Figure 9.1
Price Discrimination for an Identical Product Sold in Two Markets

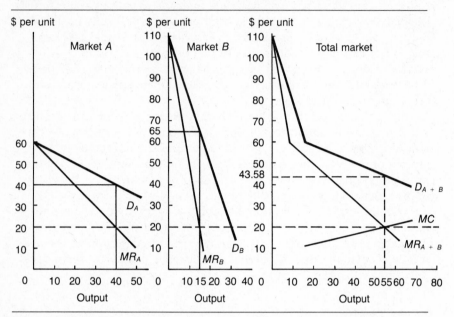

The aggregate demand curve shown in the third panel represents the horizontal sum of the quantities demanded at each price in Markets A and B. The associated marginal revenue curve, MR_{A+B}, has a similar interpretation. For example, marginal revenue equals \$20 at 40 units of output in Market A and \$20 at 15 units of output in Market B. Accordingly, one point on the firm's total marginal revenue curve will have output equal to 55 units and marginal revenue equal to \$20. From a production standpoint it does not matter whether the product is being sold in Market A or Market B; therefore, the single marginal cost curve shown in the third panel is applicable to both markets. If distribution costs differed between the two markets, this fact would have had to be taken into account.

Obtaining the solution to this pricing problem can be thought of as a two-part process. First, the firm must determine the profit maximizing total output level. Profit maximization occurs at that aggregate output level at which marginal cost and marginal revenue are equal. As shown in Figure 9.1, the profit maximizing output is 55 units, where marginal cost and marginal revenue are both equal to \$20. Second, the firm must allocate this output between the two submarkets. Proper allocation of total output between the two submarkets can be determined graphically by drawing a horizontal line through the graphs in the first two panels at \$20 to indicate that \$20 is the marginal cost in *each* market at the indicated aggregate output level. The intersection of this horizontal line with the marginal revenue curve in each submarket indicates the distribution of sales and the optimal pricing structure. According to the figures, our illustrative firm maximizes profits by producing a total of 55 units, then selling 40 units in Market A at a price of $40 and 15 units in Market B at a price of $65.

The price charged in the less elastic Market B is over 50 percent higher than the price charged in Market A, where demand is relatively elastic, and this differential adds significantly to the firm's profits. This can be seen by comparing profits earned with discrimination to profits earned if the firm were unable to segment the market. In the nondiscrimination case the firm acts as though it were facing only the single total market demand curve shown in the third panel of Figure 9.1. Profit maximization requires that the firm operate at the output level where $MR = MC$; that is, at 55 units. Here, however, the single price that would prevail is $43.58, the price determined by the intersection of a vertical line at 55 units of output with the total market demand curve.

Because the optimal output level for the firm is 55 units irrespective of whether or not the firm can engage in price discrimination, total costs are the same in either case, and we need only consider the total revenues to determine the effect of price discrimination on the firm's profits. With price discrimination, the firm's total revenue is equal to $2,575, found as $40 × 40 units = $1,600 revenue in Market A plus $65 × 15 units = $975 revenue in Market B. Without price discrimination total revenue is $2,397 (= $43.58 × 55 units). The difference between these total revenue figures, $178, indicates that the firm gains an additional $178 profit by segmenting its markets and charging a higher price in that segment where demand is relatively inelastic.

Optimal price discrimination in this case, where an identical product is being sold in two markets, requires that the firm operate so that the marginal revenues in both markets are equated not only to marginal costs but also to one another; that is, $MR_A = MR_B = MC$. This is the result of the products being indistinguishable from a production standpoint. If the marginal costs of production and distribution of the product in the two markets were different, profit maximization would have required the equating of marginal revenues to marginal costs in *each separate market*.

Multiple-Product Pricing

The basic microeconomic model of the firm typically assumes that the firm produces a single homogeneous product. Yet most of us would be hard-pressed to name even one firm that does not produce a variety of products. Almost all firms produce at least multiple models, styles, or sizes of their output, and for pricing purposes each of these variations should be considered a separate product. Although **multiple-product pricing** requires the same analysis as for a single product, the analysis is complicated by demand and production interrelationships.

Demand Interrelationships

Demand interrelationships arise because of competition or complementarity among the firm's various products. Consider, for example, a firm that produces two products. If the products are interrelated, either as substitutes or as complements, a change in the price of one will affect the demand for the other. This means that in multiple-product pricing decisions these interrelationships, perhaps among dozens of products, must be taken into account.

Analysis of Demand Interrelationships. Demand interrelationships influence the pricing decision through their effect on marginal revenue. In the case of a two-product firm, the marginal revenue functions for the products can be written as:

$$MR_A = \frac{\Delta TR}{\Delta Q_A} = \frac{\Delta TR_A}{\Delta Q_A} + \frac{\Delta TR_B}{\Delta Q_A}. \tag{9.7}$$

$$MR_B = \frac{\Delta TR}{\Delta Q_B} = \frac{\Delta TR_B}{\Delta Q_B} + \frac{\Delta TR_A}{\Delta Q_B}. \tag{9.8}$$

Equations 9.7 and 9.8 are general statements describing the revenue/output relationships for two products. The first term on the right-hand side of each equation represents the marginal revenue directly associated with each product. The last term illustrates the problem of demand interrelationships. That term indicates the change in total revenues associated with the second product, resulting from a change in the sales of the first. For example, $\Delta TR_B/\Delta Q_A$ in Equation 9.7 shows the effect on the revenues generated by Product B when an additional unit of Product A is sold. Likewise, $\Delta TR_A/\Delta Q_B$ in Equation 9.8 represents the change in revenues received from the sale of Product A when an additional unit of Product B is sold.

These cross-marginal revenue terms showing the demand interrelationships between two products can be positive or negative, depending on the nature of the relationship. For complementary products the net impact will be positive, demonstrating that increased sales of one product will lead to increased revenues associated with the other. For competitive products the reverse is true: Increased sales of one product will reduce demand for the second, and hence the cross-marginal revenue term will be negative.

This brief examination of demand interrelationships demonstrates that proper price determination in the multiple-product case requires a thorough analysis of the total effect of pricing decisions on the firm's revenues. In practice this implies that optimal pricing must be based on a proper application of incremental reasoning so that the total effect of the decision is considered.

Production Interrelationships

Just as the multiple products of a firm can be related through their demand functions, so too are they often interrelated in production. Products may be jointly produced in a fixed ratio, for example in the case of cattle, where hide and beef are obtained from each animal, or in variable proportions as in the refining of crude oil into gasoline and fuel oil. Products may compete with one another for the resources of the firm, as in the case of alternative products; or they may be complementary, as when one product uses wastes generated in the production of another or when increased production of one results in lower costs of another because of economies of scale at the firm level. In each case production interrelationships must be considered if proper pricing decisions are to be made.

Joint Products Produced in Fixed Proportions. The simplest case of joint production is that of **joint products** produced in fixed proportions. In this situation it makes no sense to attempt to separate the products from a production or cost standpoint. That is, if products must be produced in fixed proportions with no possibility of adjusting the ratio of output, they are not really multiple products from a production standpoint but should be considered as a package of output. The reason for this stems from the impossibility of determining the costs for the individual products in the package. Since the products are jointly produced, all costs are incurred in the production of the *package*, and there is no economically sound way of allocating them to the individual products.

Optimal price/output determination requires an analysis of the relationship between the marginal revenue of the output package and its marginal cost of production. So long as the total marginal revenue of the combination, the sum of the marginal revenues obtained from each product in the package, is greater than the marginal cost of producing it, the firm gains by expanding output.

Figure 9.2 illustrates the pricing problem for the case of two joint products produced in fixed proportions. The demand and the marginal revenue curves for the two products and the single marginal cost curve associated with the production of the combined output package are shown. A *vertical* summation of the two marginal revenue curves indicates the total marginal revenue generated by the package of products.

Figure 9.2
Optimal Pricing for Joint Products Produced in Fixed Proportions

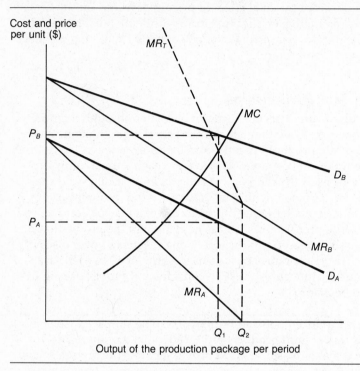

Output of the production package per period

(The marginal revenue curves are summed vertically because each unit of output provides revenues from the sale of both of the joint products.) Thus, it is the intersection of this total marginal revenue curve, MR_T in the figure, with the marginal cost curve that locates the profit maximizing output level.

The optimal price for each product is determined by the intersection of a vertical line at the profit maximizing output quantity with the demand curves for each separate product. Q_1 represents the optimal quantity of the output package to be produced, and P_A and P_B are the prices to be charged for the individual products. To illustrate, if we are dealing with cattle, the joint package would consist of one hide and two sides of beef. Q_1 for the firm in question, a cattle feed lot, might be 3,000 steers, resulting in 6,000 sides of beef sold at a price of P_A and 3,000 hides sold at P_B per unit.

Note that the MR_T curve in Figure 9.2 coincides with the marginal revenue curve for Product B at all output quantities greater than Q_2. This is so because MR_A becomes negative at that point, and hence the firm would not sell more than the quantity of Product A represented

Figure 9.3
Optimal Pricing for Joint Products Produced in Fixed Proportions with Excess Production of One Product

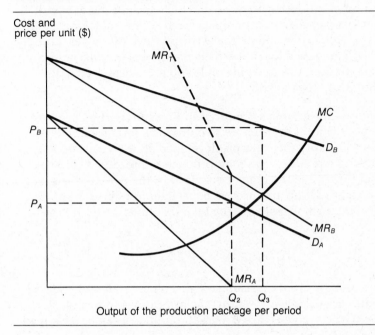

Cost and price per unit ($)

Q_2 Q_3

Output of the production package per period

by Output Package Q_2. That is, the total revenues generated by Product A are maximized at Output Q_2, and, therefore, sales of any larger quantity would reduce revenues and profits.

If the marginal cost curve for producing the package of output intersects the total marginal revenue curve to the right of Q_2, profit maximization requires that the firm raise output up to this point of intersection: price Product B as indicated by its demand curve at that point, and price Product A so as to maximize its total revenue. This pricing situation is illustrated in Figure 9.3, where the same demand and marginal revenue curves presented in Figure 9.2 are shown, along with a new marginal cost curve. The optimal output quantity is Q_3, determined by the intersection of the marginal cost curve and the total marginal revenue curve. Product B is sold in the amount indicated by Output Package Q_3 and is priced at P_B. The sales quantity of Product A is limited to the amount in Output Q_2 and is priced at P_A. The excess quantity of Product A contained in the production, $Q_3 - Q_2$, must be destroyed or otherwise kept out of the market so that its price (and total revenue) is not lowered from that indicated at Q_2.

A case in point involves pineapple, where sliced pineapple and pineapple juice are joint products, the juice being produced as a by-product as pineapples are peeled and sliced. An excessive amount of juice was produced, and rather than put it on the market and depress prices, the excess was destroyed. This did not continue long, however; Dole, Del Monte, and other producers advertised heavily to shift the demand curve for juice and created new products, such as pineapple-grapefruit juice, to bring about a demand for the waste product. Moreover, canning machinery was improved to reduce the percentage of product going into juice. The proportions of sliced pineapple and juice were fixed in the short run but not in the long run.

Pricing Example for Products Produced in Fixed Proportions. An example of a price/output decision for two products produced in fixed proportions will clarify the concepts developed above. Consider a firm that produces two products in a joint production process where we assume output must be in the ratio of $1:1$. That is, the two products, say, A and B, must always be produced in equal quantities because of the nature of the production process. The total cost function for this system is:

$$TC = 500 + 5Q + 2Q^2, \tag{9.9}$$

where Q is a unit of output consisting of one unit of Product A and one unit of Product B. Assume further that the price/demand relationship for the two products, given current market conditions, can be described by the demand curves:

$$P_A = \$395 - Q_A \tag{9.10}$$

and

$$P_B = \$100 - 0.5Q_B. \tag{9.11}$$

The profit maximizing firm would view its price/output decision as being one of determining the optimal quantity of Q (the units of production, composed of equal quantities of A and B) to produce and of setting prices and sales quantities for the individual products, A and B. The problem is most conveniently analyzed by developing the proper profit function for the firm.

Although there are several ways in which one could express the profit function for this pricing problem, the most appropriate is an expression in terms of Q, the unit of production, since the individual products, A and B, must be produced in $1:1$ *fixed* proportions. Consider first the revenues associated with the firm's output. For each unit of Q produced, the firm obtains one unit of Product A and one unit of Product B for sale to its customers. Therefore, the revenue derived from the production and sale of a unit of Q (again the combined product package consisting of one unit each of A and B) is a simple summation of the revenues obtained from the sales of a unit of Product A and a unit of Product B. Similarly, the total revenue function for the firm expressed as a function of Q is merely the summation of the revenue functions for Products A and B. This relationship can be developed algebraically as:

$$TR_{FIRM} = TR_A + TR_B$$

$$= P_A \cdot Q_A + P_B \cdot Q_B.$$

Substituting Equations 9.10 and 9.11 for P_A and P_B, respectively, results in the total revenue function:

$$TR_{FIRM} = (395 - Q_A) Q_A + (100 - 0.5Q_B) Q_B$$

$$= 395Q_A - Q_A^2 + 100Q_B - 0.5Q_B^2.$$

(9.12)

Now, since one unit of Product A and one unit of Product B are contained in each unit of Q produced by the firm, Q_A, Q_B, and Q must all be equal. This means that we can substitute Q for Q_A and Q_B in Equation 9.12 to develop a total revenue function in terms of Q, the unit of production:

$$TR = 395Q - Q^2 + 100Q - 0.5Q^2$$

$$= 495Q - 1.5Q^2.$$

(9.13)

Note that this revenue function is constructed under the assumption that equal quantities of Products A and B are *sold*. That is, it assumes no dumping or other withholding from the market of either product. Thus, it is the appropriate revenue function for use if the solution to the output determination problem is as shown in Figure 9.2, that is, with no excess production of one product. The way to determine whether in fact this condition holds is to solve the problem and then check to ascertain that the marginal revenues of both products are in fact positive at the indicated profit maximizing output level.

Because the firm's total cost function for the production of these joint products was expressed in terms of Q, the unit of production, in Equation 9.9 the profit function can be formed by combining that cost function with the total revenue function, Equation 9.13:

$$\text{Profit} = \pi = TR - TC$$

$$= 495Q - 1.5Q^2 - (500 + 5Q + 2Q^2)$$

$$= 490Q - 3.5Q^2 - 500.$$

The profit maximizing output level is found where marginal profit is zero.

$$\text{Marginal Profit} = \frac{\Delta\pi}{\Delta Q} = 490 - 7Q = 0$$

$$7Q = 490$$

$$Q = 70 \text{ Units.}$$

The optimal solution to the output quantity decision will be 70 units of production, 70 units each of Products A and B, *provided that at a 70-unit output level the marginal revenues of both A and B are nonnegative.* This condition can be checked by determining the marginal revenues for the two products at the 70-unit sales level:

$$TR_A = 395Q_A - Q_A{}^2$$

$$MR_A = \frac{\Delta TR_A}{\Delta Q_A} = 395 - 2Q_A$$

$$= 395 - 2(70) \quad \text{(at 70 Units)}$$

$$= +225.$$

$$TR_B = 100Q_B - 0.5Q_B$$

$$MR_B = \frac{\Delta TR_B}{\Delta Q_B} = 100 - Q_B$$

$$= 100 - 70 \quad \text{(at 70 Units)}$$

$$= +30.$$

Since the marginal revenues are both positive, the solution to the problem is correct and one can then proceed with the determination of the proper prices for the two products.[2] The prices are obtained by substituting into the two demand curves, Equations 9.10 and 9.11:

---

[2] Had one product's marginal revenue been negative at 70 units of output, a problem solution with excess production of one product, as illustrated in Figure 9.3, would have been indicated. In such a situation the firm stops selling additional units of the product with a negative marginal revenue at the point where marginal revenue is zero. Hence, the relevant marginal revenue figure for use in determining the optimal output level is that associated with the other product. This would require use of the revenue function for only the one product being sold at the margin in the profit function used to determine the optimal output level. Equating the marginal revenue of that product to the marginal cost of producing a unit of output results in the optimal output determination.

$$P_A = 395 - Q_A \qquad (9.10)$$

$$P_A = 395 - 70$$

$$= \$325$$

and

$$P_B = 100 - 0.5Q_B \qquad (9.11)$$

$$= 100 - 0.5(70)$$

$$= \$65.$$

Thus, in this example, the firm should produce 70 units of output, selling the resultant 70 units of Product A at $325 per unit and the 70 units of B at a price of $65 per unit.

Joint Products Produced in Variable Proportions. Typically, the firm has the ability to vary the proportions in which joint products are produced. Even the classic example of fixed proportions in the joint production of beef and hides holds only over short periods, because cattle can be bred to provide an output package with differing proportions of these two products.

When the firm can vary the proportions in which the joint output is produced, it is possible to construct separate marginal cost relationships for each of the joint products. This is illustrated in Table 9.4, a matrix of the total cost/output relationships for two joint products, A and B. Since the marginal cost of either product is defined as the increase in total costs associated with a unit increase in that product, *holding constant the quantity of the other product produced*, the marginal costs of producing A can be determined by examining the data in the rows of the table, and the marginal costs of B are obtained from the columns. For example, the marginal cost of the 4th unit of A, holding the production of B at

Table 9.4
Cost/Output Matrix for Two Joint Products

Output of B	1	2	Output of A 3	4	5
1	$ 5	$ 7	$10	$15	$ 22
2	10	13	18	23	31
3	20	25	33	40	50
4	35	43	53	63	75
5	55	67	78	90	105

Figure 9.4
Optimal Price/Output Combinations for Joint Products
Produced in Variable Proportions

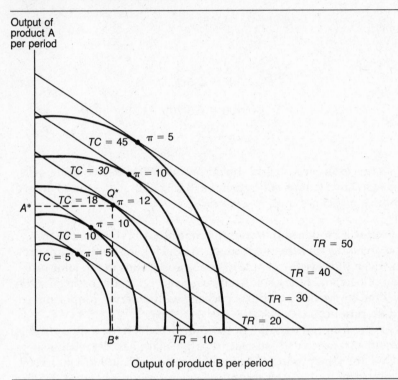

Output of
product A
per period

Output of product B per period

2 units, is \$5(= \$23 − \$18); the marginal cost of the 5th unit of B when output of A is 3 units is \$25(= \$78 − \$53).

Optimal price/output determination for joint products in this case requires a simultaneous solution of their cost and revenue relationships. The procedure can be illustrated graphically through the construction of isorevenue and isocost curves as in Figure 9.4. The isocost curves map out the locus of all production combinations that can be produced for a given total cost; the isorevenue curves indicate all combinations of the products which, when sold, result in a given revenue.[3] At the points of tangency between the isocost and the isorevenue curves, the

---

[3]The isorevenue relationships in Figure 9.4 have been drawn as straight lines for simplicity. This implies that the products are sold in competitive markets; only if the demand curve is horizontal will prices be invariant with respect to changing quantities of the two products. If pure competition does not exist and prices change as output changes, the isorevenue curves will not be straight lines, but the optimum output combinations will still be indicated by tangencies between isocost and isorevenue curves.

marginal costs of producing the products are proportionate to their marginal revenues. The tangencies therefore indicate the optimal proportions in which to produce the products. Since profits are equal to revenue minus cost, the firm maximizes profits by operating at the tangency between the isorevenue and isocost curves whose positive difference is greatest. At that tangency the marginal cost of producing each product is just equal to the marginal revenue it generates.

Point Q^* in Figure 9.4 indicates the profit maximizing combination of Products A and B in the example illustrated in the figure. Production and sale of A^* units of A and B^* units of B result in a profit of 12, the maximum possible under the conditions shown here.

We should note that while the preceding discussion demonstrates the possibility of determining the separate marginal costs of production for goods produced jointly in variable proportions, it is impossible to determine the individual average costs. These individual costs cannot be determined because the common costs of production—costs associated with raw materials and equipment used for both products, management expenses, and other overhead—cannot be allocated to the individual products on any economically sound basis. Therefore, any allocation of common costs that affects the price/output decision is necessarily arbitrary and possibly irrational. This point is stressed because of the frequency with which businesses and government regulatory bodies use fully allocated average costs in pricing problems of this kind.

Optimal multiple-product pricing requires a complete marginal (or incremental) analysis of the total effect of the decision on the firm's profitability. This analysis must include an examination of demand interrelationships to be sure that a complete picture of the marginal revenue to be derived from a decision is drawn. Likewise, complementarity and competition in production must be accounted for in the analysis of marginal costs. For alternative goods produced from a common production facility, this means that opportunity costs of forgone production must be considered in determining the relevant marginal costs of a decision. Linear programming has proven useful for cost/output analysis of this type when common facilities must be allocated among a variety of products.

Summary

In this chapter a number of pricing topics were examined. *Cost-plus pricing*, a pricing technique frequently used in practice, was shown to be closely related to marginal analysis. Proper use of cost-plus pricing requires that close attention be paid to both cost and demand relationships. The wide variation in product margins observed in pricing practice, coupled with the empirical finding of an inverse relationship between the size of a product's margin and the competitiveness of the market in which it is sold, indicates such analysis does, in fact, play a major role in cost-plus pricing as applied by successful managers.

Incremental profit analysis was also shown to be a powerful tool for optimal pricing decisions. Its emphasis on only the costs and revenues associated with the decision under consideration insures proper economic reasoning in decision analysis.

When a firm sells its product in multiple markets, it may be able to increase profits by charging different prices in the various markets, a practice known as *price discrimination*. In order to engage successfully in price discrimination, the firm (1) must be able to segment and isolate its various submarkets to prevent transfers and (2) must face differing price elasticities of demand in the various market segments. Profit maximization under price discrimination requires that the firm operate so as to equate marginal revenue and marginal cost in each separate submarket.

Multiple-product pricing was shown to be based on the same economic concepts used for single-product pricing. The pricing analysis is complicated, however, by demand and production externalities, which arise because of competition or complementarity among the products on either the demand or the production side. Proper use of the incremental profit concept to insure that the total impact of a pricing decision on the firm is analyzed leads to optimal pricing in the multiple-product case, just as with a single product.

Questions

9.1 Develop and explain the relationship between the optimal markup on cost and price elasticity.

9.2 Discuss the role of sunk costs in pricing practice.

9.3 "One of the more opaque suggestions that economists have offered to managers is that they set marginal revenues equal to marginal costs." Discuss this statement.

9.4 "Marginal cost pricing, as well as the use of incremental analysis illustrated by the example of Continental Airlines, is looked upon with favor by economists, especially those on the staffs of regulatory agencies. With this encouragement, regulated industries do indeed employ these 'rational' techniques quite frequently. Unregulated firms, on the other hand, use marginal or incremental cost pricing much less frequently, sticking to cost-plus, or full-cost, pricing except under exceptional circumstances. In my opinion, this goes a long way toward explaining the problems of the regulated firms, especially the airlines, vis-a-vis unregulated industry." Discuss this statement.

9.5 What is price discrimination?

9.6 What conditions are necessary before price discrimination will become both possible and worthwhile? How can price discrimination result in higher profits?

9.7 Why is it possible to determine the marginal costs associated with the production of joint products produced in variable proportions but not joint products produced in fixed proportions?

Solved Problem

9.1 The Cumbersom Equipment Company (CEC) manufactures a battery-powered electric saw. Due to increased demand during the past few years, CEC increased plant capacity for the saw to 300,000 units. The firm's expected output for next year was 250,000 units, but it received a special order for 100,000 units from a firm outside its normal market area. The standard selling price is $50 per unit, but the new firm has offered $40 per unit for the special order. Relevant cost data for the saws are as follows:

	Per Unit Cost
Raw materials	$20.00
Direct labor	10.00
Variable overhead	3.00
Fixed overhead	2.00

Using the incremental profit framework, should CEC accept the special order?

Solution

Incremental revenue from order:	
Price per unit	$40.00
Units	100,000
Total incremental revenue	$4,000,000

Incremental costs of accepting order:	
Raw materials	$2,000,000
Direct labor	1,000,000
Variable overhead	300,000

Opportunity cost:
Capacity is 300,000 units; 50,000 units of next year's expected demand will have to be foregone if the order is accepted:

Sales revenue ($50 per unit)	$2,500,000	
Variable costs ($33 per unit)	−1,650,000	
Profit lost on foregone orders		850,000
Total incremental cost		$4,150,000

$$\text{Incremental Profit} = \text{Incremental Revenue} - \text{Incremental Costs}$$
$$= (\$150,000).$$

The firm should not accept the special order, since the incremental profit is negative.

Solved Problem

9.2 Midcontinental Railroad Company runs a freight train daily between Indianapolis and Chicago. Its two major users of this service are Indiana Steel Corporation and Midwest Agribusiness Inc. The demand for freight cars by each firm is given by the equations:

$$P_1 = 500 - 8Q_1 \quad \text{or} \quad Q_1 = 62.50 - 0.125P_1 \qquad \text{for Indiana.}$$

$$P_2 = 400 - 5Q_2 \quad \text{or} \quad Q_2 = 80 - 0.2P_2 \qquad \text{for Midwest.}$$

P_i is the price charged by Midcontinent for hauling one freight car of materials between Indianapolis and Chicago, and Q_i represents the number of cars demanded by each user. Midcontinent's total and marginal cost function for the daily train service are given by:

$$TC = \$10,000 + \$20Q,$$

$$MC = \$20,$$

where Q is the number of freight cars hauled on a particular trip. Midcontinent's pricing problem can be illustrated graphically as:

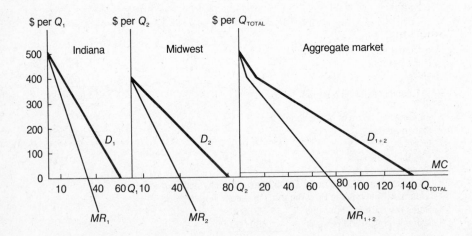

a) What conditions are necessary for profitable price discrimination by Midcontinent?
b) Graphically illustrate the profit maximizing rule Midcontinent will employ to set prices as a price discriminator.

c) The freight-car demand curves for Indiana and Midwest presented imply the following marginal revenue functions:

$$MR_1 = 500 - 16Q_1 \qquad \text{for Indiana.}$$

$$MR_2 = 400 - 10Q_2 \qquad \text{for Midwest.}$$

Given these functions, calculate algebraically the profit maximizing level of output for each market, market prices, and total profits.

d) What is the profit maximizing rule if Midcontinent is unable to engage in price discrimination?

e) Determine market price and sales to Indiana and Midwest without price discrimination. Calculate total profits under this assumption. (*Hint*: Make use of the fact that Midcontinent's total output will be the same as with price discrimination.)

Solution

a) Midcontinent must be able to segment the market and be able to prevent resale from one segment to another in order for price discrimination to be possible. The elasticity of demand in one segment of the market must be lower than in the other if discrimination is to be profitable.

b) The profit maximizing rule is to equate aggregate marginal revenue with marginal cost. Such an equality exists at Point *B*. A horizontal line from *B* intersects MR_1 and MR_2 at points *C* and *D*, respectively. This indicates how total output (68 units) should be allocated between Indiana (30 freight units) and Midwest (38 freight units), and the different prices to be charged each user.

The freight unit price for Indiana is \$260, and that of Midwest is \$210. Marginal revenue in each market is \$20 and is equal to marginal cost.

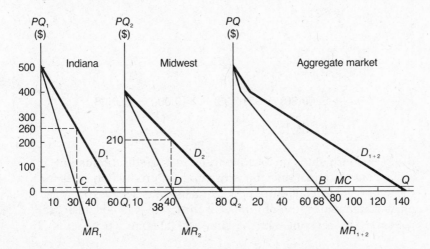

c) Profits will be maximized in each market when $MR = MC$. Since marginal costs equal \$20, optimal output price and profits are:

Indiana

$$MR_1 = MC_1$$

$$500 - 16Q_1 = 20$$

$$16Q_1 = 480$$

$$Q_1 = 30.$$

$$P_1 = 500 - 8Q_1$$

$$= 500 - 8(30)$$

$$= \$260.$$

Midwest

$$MR_2 = MC_2$$

$$400 - 10Q_2 = 20$$

$$10Q_2 = 380$$

$$Q_2 = 38.$$

$$P_2 = 400 - 5Q_2$$

$$= 400 - 5(38)$$

$$= \$210.$$

Profit

$$\pi = P_1Q_1 + P_2Q_2 - TC$$

$$= \$260(30) + \$210(38) - \$10,000 - \$20(68)$$

$$= \$4,420.$$

d) If Midcontinent is unable to engage in price discrimination, it will equate marginal revenue with marginal production costs for the aggregate level of output (i.e., Indiana plus Midwest).
e) As stated above, the profit maximizing rule is to equate aggregate marginal revenue with marginal cost (at Point *B* or 68 units). In

this case, the vertical line from B intersects the aggregate demand curve (Point C), thereby determining an equal price \$229.22 to be charged in each market. A horizontal line at that price level will intersect the individual submarket demand curves (Points E and F) and indicate the quantity of service (33.85 and 34.15 freight units for Indiana and Midwest, respectively) that will be sold to each.

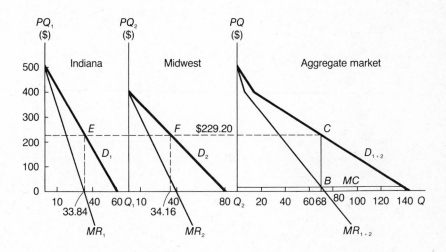

This solution can also be obtained by constructing the aggregate demand curve for rail service under a one price policy. We do this by summing the quantity of service demanded by Indiana and Midwest at each price.

$$Q_1 = 62.5 - 0.125P_1$$

$$Q_2 = 80 - 0.2P_2.$$

Since $P_1 = P_2 = P$, the single market price,

$$Q_{1+2} = Q_1 + Q_2$$

$$= 62.5 - 0.125P + 80 - 0.2P$$

$$= 142.5 - 0.325P$$

$$P = \$438.46 - \$3.077Q_{1+2}.$$

From this aggregate demand curve we can derive the total and marginal revenue functions for freight service under a single price policy:

$$TR = P \cdot Q$$

$$= 438.46Q_{1+2} - 3.077Q_{1+2}^2$$

$$MR = 438.46 - 6.154Q_{1+2}.$$

Setting $MR = MC$ to find the profit maximizing output level, we obtain:

$$438.46 - 6.154Q_{1+2} = 20$$

$$6.154Q_{1+2} = 418.46$$

$$Q_{1+2} = 68.$$

Inserting this quantity into the demand equation for the aggregate market, we see that Midcontinent would operate at this output by setting price at \$229.22:

$$P = \$438.46 - \$3.077Q_{1+2}$$

$$= \$438.46 - \$3.077(68)$$

$$= \$229.22.$$

The quantity demanded by each user is found by inserting the \$229.22 price into each firm's demand curve.

$$Q_1 = 62.5 - 0.125(229.22)$$

$$= 33.85$$

$$Q_2 = 80 - 0.2(229.22)$$

$$= 34.15.$$

Total profit without price discrimination is:

$$\pi = P(Q_1 + Q_2) - TC$$

$$= \$229.20 \, (33.85 + 34.15) - [\$10,000 + \$20(68)]$$

$$= \$15,585 - \$11,360$$

$$= \$4,225.$$

Note that this is less than \$4,420 profit available if price discrimination is possible.

Solved Problem

9.3 Iota Enterprises produces two products in a joint production process. The products are produced in a 1:1 fixed proportion ratio. The total cost function for this production process is: $TC = 50 + 2Q + 2Q^2$, where Q is a unit of output consisting of one unit of Product A and one unit of Product B. The related marginal cost of production is $MC = 2 + 4Q$.

    a) Assume the demand and marginal revenue curves for Iota's two products are:

$$P_A = 352 - Q_A$$

$$MR_A = 352 - 2Q_A,$$

and

$$P_B = 100 - 3Q_B$$

$$MR_B = 100 - 6Q_B.$$

What are the optimal sales quantities and prices for each of the products? (Assume unsold production can be costlessly disposed.)

Solution

    a) We can begin analysis of this problem by examining the optimal activity level of Iota, assuming the firm manufactures and *sells* equal quantities of A and B. In this situation, since each unit of production generates revenues for both Products A and B, the appropriate marginal revenue function is:

$$MR = MR_A + MR_B$$

$$= 352 - 2Q + 100 - 6Q$$

$$= 452 - 8Q.$$

Setting $MR = MC$

$$452 - 8Q = 2 + 4Q$$

$$450 = 12Q$$

$$Q = 37.5.$$

Thus, profit maximization *with equal sales* of each product requires that the firm produce $Q = 37.5$. Under this assumption, marginal revenues for the two products would be

$$MR_A = 352 - 2(37.5) = \$277$$

$$MR_B = 100 - 6(37.5) = (\$125).$$

With the negative marginal revenue of Product B, this solution is incorrect if Iota can dispose of Product B (or otherwise hold it off the market) without incurring additional costs. In this case the firm will want to sell more units of Product A than Product B. Iota would sell Product B only up to the point where its *marginal revenue* equals zero, since given additional production for Product A, the relevant additional marginal cost of B is zero.

$$MR_B = MC$$

$$100 - 6Q_B = 0$$

$$6Q_B = 100$$

$$Q_B = 16.67,$$

and

$$P_B = 100 - 3(Q_B)$$

$$= 100 - 3(16.67)$$

$$= \$49.99.$$

Determination of the optimal production level (and sales level of A) is found by equating the marginal revenue from A (the only product being sold from the marginal production unit) with the marginal cost of production.

$$MR_A = MC_Q$$

$$352 - 2Q = 2 + 4Q$$

$$6Q = 350$$

$$Q_A = 58.33 \qquad (\text{Since } Q_A = Q)$$

and

$$P_A = 352 - Q_A$$

$$= 352 - 58.33$$

$$= \$293.67.$$

Thus, Iota should produce 58.33 units of output, selling all 58.33 units of A at a price of $293.67. Only 16.67 units of B will be sold, with the remaining units being destroyed or otherwise held off the market.

Problem Set

9.1 McCord Ford-Mercury is a large volume dealer and has been pricing its cars using a cost plus system. In calculating cost, McCord combines the invoice price it pays for a car with the variable costs of preparing and delivering it for a customer. A 10 percent markup is added to this cost figure in order to obtain the selling price.

a) Assuming the price elasticity of demand for the cars McCord sells is -5, is its markup policy consistent with short-run profit maximization? Explain.

b) Assume that a new automobile dealership opens in the town where McCord is located, and as a result the demand faced by McCord becomes more elastic. If the new demand elasticity is -15, what price should McCord set for a car that costs the dealership $6,000 and has $200 in variable preparation and delivery costs?

9.2 Following an influx of foreign competition, Donnley Manufacturing recently experienced disappointing sales for its line of specialty high-pressure valves. In order to reduce inventory, Donnley offered customers a 10 percent discount from the list price of $20 per valve. Customer response has been enthusiastic, and units sold have increased by 20 percent.

a) If marginal production costs average $8, calculate Donnley's *current* markup on cost.

b) Calculate the point price elasticity for valves.

c) Calculate the profit maximizing average price for Donnley valves. (*Hint*: Remember from Chapter 3 there is a simple general relation between marginal revenue and price elasticity.)

9.3 Betty's Boutique is a small specialty retailer located in a suburban shopping mall. In setting prices for a new spring line of blouses, Betty's added a standard 100 percent markup on cost. Costs were estimated as the $10 purchase price of each blouse, plus an allocated fixed overhead charge, calculated as 50 percent of variable cost.

Customer response has been so enthusiastic that Betty's fears it will soon sell out its entire stock. Although unsold blouses can be returned to the distributor for a refund less a $2 per item restocking charge, an additional order cannot be filled this season. Thus, Betty's decided to raise prices by 10 percent. Following this increase, weekly blouse sales fell from 80 to 68.

a) Calculate the price of blouses *before* the price increase.

b) Given customer response following the price increase, was Betty's initial price optimal?

c) As the spring season is nearing its close, Betty's still has an inventory of unsold blouses. Estimate the price discount Betty's should feature in their end-of-season sale on blouses.

9.4 Saginaw Meats Inc. is a regional producer of sausage meat products. The company specializes in gourmet bratwurst and polish sausages. Saginaw's polish sausages have proved to be extremely popular, and the company is producing them at peak capacity.

Current production costs per pound are

	Bratwurst	Sausage
Raw materials	$0.75	$0.90
Direct labor	0.30	0.30
Variable overhead	0.20	0.25
Fixed overhead	0.15	0.15
(50% of direct labor)		
Total	$1.40	$1.60

Bratwurst is sold at a 50 percent markup on cost, and Polish sausage is sold at a 75 percent markup on cost.

Saginaw has just received a rush order for 100,000 pounds of Polish sausage for sale at home games of a local NFL football team. To meet this order, an extra $10,000 in overtime costs will be incurred. Production and sales of 40,000 pounds of bratwurst will also have to be foregone. Should Saginaw accept the rush order?

9.5 McFarland Instruments Corporation is a large contractor with the National Aeronautics and Space Administration (NASA). McFarland has received an invitation to submit a bid for construction of a new weather satellite solar energy system. Design and development costs of $500,000 have already been incurred by McFarland in preparation of a bid of $4.25 million for the job. The bid was based on the following projected costs:

Design and development expenses	$ 500,000
Materials	1,190,000
Labor	1,600,000
Overhead (60% of direct labor)	960,000
Total costs and bid	$4,250,000

NASA has just notified McFarland that it is enthusiastic about the design submitted but that budget constraints allow it to pay no more than $4 million for the job. Assuming that McFarland has adequate capacity so that acceptance of the job will not require any increase in fixed expenses, should it accept the $4 million offer? Why or why not?

9.6 The General Appliance Company manufactures an electric toaster. Sales of the toaster have increased steadily during the previous five years and, because of a recently completed expansion program, annual capacity is now 500,000 units. Production and sales during the coming year are forecast at 400,000 units, and standard production costs have been estimated as:

Materials	$ 6.00
Direct labor	4.00
Variable indirect labor	2.00
Fixed overhead	3.00
Allocated cost per unit	$15.00

In addition to production costs, General projects fixed selling expenses and variable warranty repair expenses of $1.50 and $1.20 per unit, respectively. General is currently receiving $20 per unit from its customers (primarily retail department stores) and expects this price to hold during the coming year.

After making these projections, General received an inquiry concerning the purchase of a large number of toasters from a discount department store. The inquiry contained two purchase offers:

Offer 1 The department store would purchase 80,000 units at $14.60 per unit. These units would bear the General label, and the General warranty would be provided.

Offer 2 The department store would purchase 120,000 units at $14.00 per unit. These units would be sold under the buyer's private label and General would not provide warranty service.

a) Evaluate the effect of each offer on pretax net income for next year.

b) What other factors need to be considered in deciding whether to accept one or the other of these offers?

c) Which offer (if either) should General accept. Why?

9.7 The Warriors basketball team has been investigating methods of raising attendance at their home games. It has been observed that the two major groups of Warrior fans are high school and college students below the age of twenty-two, and older adults. An analysis of ticket sales reveals that the average demand per home game for each group is given by the equations:

$$P_1 = \$16 - \$0.004Q_1 \qquad \text{for Adults.}$$

$$P_2 = \$10 - \$0.0025Q_2 \qquad \text{for Students.}$$

P_i is the admission price, and Q_i is the number of tickets demanded by each group. The Warriors' total and marginal cost functions per home game are:

$$TC = \$10,000 + \$2Q$$

$$MC = \$2,$$

where Q is the total number of tickets sold per home game. The Warriors' pricing problem can be illustrated graphically as:

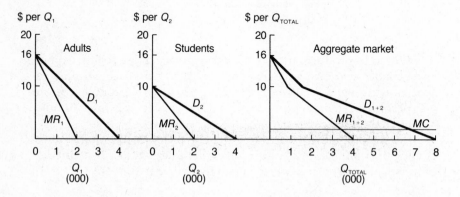

a) What conditions are necessary for profitable price discrimination by the Warriors?
b) Graphically illustrate the profit maximizing rule the Warriors will use to set prices as a price discriminator.
c) The ticket demand curves for adults and students imply the following marginal revenue curves:

$$MR_1 = \$16 - \$0.008Q_1 \quad \text{for Adults.}$$

$$MR_2 = \$10 - \$0.005Q_2 \quad \text{for Students.}$$

Assuming the Warriors keep all revenues from home games and receive no revenue for playing away games, calculate the profit maximizing level of output for each market segment, prices, and total profits.
d) What is the profit maximizing rule if the Warriors are unable to engage in price discrimination?
e) Calculate the market price and total profits without price discrimination.

9.8 Redwood-Olson Corporation (R-O) is a monopolist providing telecommunication service to two firms, Alpha and Beta. The demand and marginal revenue functions for the R-O service are as follows:

Alpha	Beta
$P_A = 6,000 - 20Q_A.$	$P_B = 3,500 - 5Q_B.$
$MR_A = 6,000 - 40Q_A.$	$MR_B = 3,500 - 10Q_B.$

a) If R-O is *unable* to operate as a price discriminating monopolist, what demand curve does it face for the service it provides?

b) Assume now that R-O *can* price discriminate between Alpha and Beta. R-O's total cost function is $TC = 20,000 + Q^2$, and its marginal cost function for providing services to either Alpha or Beta is $MC_A = MC_B = 2Q_A + 2Q_B$. What are the prices it will charge and how many units of service will it offer each customer?

c) Would prohibiting price discrimination have any effect on the likelihood of R-O's acquiring Alpha? Why or why not?

9.9 Montana Refining processes enriched ore to extract gold and copper. Each ton of ore processed results in one ounce of gold and one pound of copper being produced in a fixed ratio. Its marginal processing costs equal \$440 for each ton of ore.

a) Assuming the demand and marginal revenue curves for gold are

$$P_G = \$500 - \$0.025Q_G \qquad MR_G = \$500 - \$0.05Q_G,$$

and for copper are

$$P_C = \$5 - 0.0025Q_C \qquad MR_C = \$5 - 0.005Q_C.$$

Here Q_G is ounces of gold and Q_C is pounds of copper.

What are the optimal sales quantities and prices?

b) Now assume that Montana incurs an added storage and insurance cost of 50¢ for each pound of copper held off the market. What are the optimal sales quantities and prices for gold and copper under these conditions?

References

Aaker, David A. and Ford, Gary T. "Unit Pricing Ten Years Later: A Replication." *Journal of Marketing* 47 (Winter 1983): 118–122.

Carlson, John A. and Pescatrice, Donn R. "Persistent Price Distributions." *Journal of Economics and Business* 33 (Fall 1980): 21–27.

Clarke, Darral and Dolan, Robert J. "A Simulation Analysis of Alternative Pricing Strategies for Dynamic Environments." *Journal of Business* 57 (January 1984): S179–200.

Day, George S. "Assessing the Effects of Information Disclosure Requirements." *Journal of Marketing* 40 (April 1976): 42–52.

Day, R. H.; Morley, S. and Smith, K. R. "Myopic Optimizing and Rules of Thumb in a Micro Model of Industrial Growth." *American Economic Review* 64 (March 1974): 11–23.

Earley, James S. "Marginal Policies of Excellently Managed Companies." *American Economic Review* 46 (March 1956): 44–70.

Isakson, Hans R. and Maurizi, Alex R. "The Consumer Economics of Unit Pricing." *Journal of Marketing Research* 10 (August 1972): 277–285.

Lanzillotti, Robert F. "Pricing Objectives in Large Companies." *American Economic Review* 48 (December 1958): 921–940.

Nagle, Thomas. "Economic Foundations for Pricing." *Journal of Business* 57 (January 1984): S3–26.

Rao, Vithala R. "Pricing Research in Marketing: The State of the Art." *Journal of Business* 57 (January 1984): S39–60.

Russo, J. Edward. "The Value of Unit Price Information." *Journal of Marketing Research* 14 (May 1977): 193–201.

Stigler, George J. "The Economics of Information." *Journal of Political Economy* 64 (June 1961): 213–225.

Scherer, F. M. *Industrial Pricing.* Chicago: Rand-McNally, 1972.

Von Grebmer, Klaus. "International Pharmaceutical Supply Prices: Definitions—Problems—Policy Implications." *Managerial and Decision Economics* 2 (June 1981): 74–81.

Yunker, James A. and Yunker, Penelope J. "Cost-Volume-Profit Analysis Under Uncertainty: An Integration of Economic and Accounting Concepts." *Journal of Economics and Business* 34 (Number 1, 1982): 21–37.

Chapter 10

Regulation and Antitrust: The Role of Government in the Market Economy

---

Key Terms

Antitrust

Deregulation

Efficiency

Equity

Externalities

Market failure

Regulation

The role of government in the market economy is one of the most compelling and controversial topics in managerial economics. A close examination of government's role in the marketplace is crucial to the study of managerial economics because the breadth and depth of government involvement has important implications for the managerial decision making process. It is a controversial subject because government involvement in the marketplace can influence both productive efficiency and the distribution of income. Indeed, public policy often involves some tradeoff between these efficiency and equity considerations.

Although no sector of the U.S. economy can be considered unregulated as we enter the late 1980s, both the scope and the methods of control vary widely. For example, makers of industrial products typically escape price and profit restraint (except during periods of general wage-price control) but are subject to operating regulations governing plant and product pollution emissions, product packaging and labeling, worker safety and health, and so on. On the other hand, many firms, particularly in the financial and the public utility sectors, face financial regulation in addition to such operating controls. Banks, for example, have been subject to both state and federal regulation of prices (interest rates, loan fees, and so on) and financial soundness. Unlike

397

firms in the electric power and telecommunications industries, however, banks face no explicit controls on the level of profits they earn. For this reason, regulation in the financial sector (banking, insurance, securities), although more encompassing than regulation in the industrial sector, is less comprehensive than the regulation of public utilities.

The growing importance of government involvement in the economy makes an examination of its causes, means, and ends an important component of managerial economics. To provide effective leadership, managers must fully understand the nature of government-business interactions in the modern economic environment. In this chapter we analyze the role of government in the market economy by considering (1) the economic and political rationale for regulation; (2) grant policy, which provides firms with positive incentives for "desirable" activity; (3) tax policy, which constrains the nature of goods and services that are marketed and the production processes used to produce them; (4) antitrust policy, designed to maintain a workable level of competition in the economy; (5) direct regulation of firms that possess substantial market power; and (6) the recent trend toward deregulation.

The Rationale for Regulation

Both economic and political considerations enter into decisions of what and how to regulate. Economic considerations relate to cost and efficiency implications of various regulatory methods. From an economic **efficiency** standpoint, a given mode of **regulation**, or change in regulatory policy, is desirable to the extent that benefits exceed costs. Here the question is not so much whether or not to regulate, but rather what type of regulation (market competition or otherwise) is most desirable. On the other hand, **equity**, or fairness, rather than efficiency criteria must be carefully weighed when political considerations bear on the regulatory decision making process. Here the *incidence*, or placement, of costs and benefits of regulatory decisions is considered. For example, if a given change in regulatory policy provides significant benefits to the poor, substantial costs in terms of lost efficiency may be borne willingly by society.

In most decisions regarding regulatory policy the tradeoff between efficiency- and equity-related criteria is a most difficult one. Although we can't hope to resolve the conflict between economic and political rationales for regulation, it is useful to consider more carefully each argument as a basis for regulation. The material that follows addresses the question "Why *should* society regulate?" In later sections we see that some economists suggest far different reasons for why sectors of the private economy actually are regulated.

Economic Considerations

Regulation of production and marketing activities of firms began and perseveres in part because of the public's perception of market imperfections. It is often believed that unregulated market activity could lead to inefficiency and waste or to market failure. **Market failure** can be described as the failure of a system of price-market institutions to sustain "desirable" activities or to eliminate "undesirable" activities.

A first type (or cause) of market failure is called failure by market *structure*. In order for the beneficial results of competition to be attained, there must be many producers (sellers) and consumers (buyers) within each market, or at least the ready potential of many to enter the market. This condition is unfulfilled in some markets. Consider, for example, water, power, and some telecommunications markets. If customers in a given market area can be most efficiently serviced by a single firm (a natural monopoly situation), providers of these services could possess market power and have an ability to achieve excess profits by limiting output and charging high prices. As a result, regulatory control of utility prices and profits was instituted and has continued with the goal of preserving the efficiency of large-scale production while preventing the higher prices and excess profits of monopoly. Where the advantages of large size are not thought to be as great (industrial manufacturing, retailing, and so on), antitrust policy is used to limit the growth and size of large competitors.

A second kind of market failure is failure by *incentive*. In the production and consumption of goods and services, social values and costs often differ significantly from the private costs and values of producers and consumers. Differences between private and social costs, or benefits, are called **externalities**. A negative externality is a cost of producing, marketing, or consuming a product that is not borne by the product's producers or consumers. A positive externality is a benefit of production, marketing, or consumption that is not reflected in the product pricing structure and, hence, does not accrue to the product's producers or consumers.

Environmental pollution is one well-known example of a negative externality. Negative externalities also arise when employees are exposed to hazardous working conditions for which they are not fully compensated. Similarly, if a firm dams a river or builds a solar collector to produce energy, and in so doing limits the access of others to hydropower or solar power, a negative externality is created.

Positive externalities can arise if an increase in a firm's productive activity causes lower costs for its suppliers, thereby reducing costs of a supplier's products to all its customers. The expansion of automobile production by Ford Motor Company conferred this type of external benefit on early users of steel. Economies of scale in steel production, which were achieved through the increased demand for steel brought

about by Ford's mass production of automobiles, resulted in cheaper
steel being available for all firms using steel. Positive externalities in
production also result when a firm trains employees who then are available to work for other firms that incur no training costs. They can also
come from a firm's improvement of production methods that is later
transferred to other firms and industries without compensation. The
dam cited above for its potential negative externalities might also provide positive externalities through flood control or creation of new
recreational facilities.

In sum, externalities lead to differing levels of private and social costs
and benefits. These divergencies have a significant effect on the work-
ings of the economy. Firms that provide substantial positive externalities for which they are not compensated are unlikely to carry their activities out to the socially optimal level. Likewise, consumers whose
consumption activities confer positive externalities may not use as much
of the particular good or service as would be socially optimal. On the
other hand, the existence of negative externalities can result in too many
resources being allocated to a particular activity. This follows from the
fact that producers or consumers generating negative externalities do
not pay the full cost of their activities and will most likely carry them out
beyond the level that maximizes social benefits. These market imperfections, or market failures—situations where the market does not provide
the appropriate cost or benefit signals—give rise to an active government role in the economy.

Political Considerations

Economic considerations play a prominent role in the design of regulatory policies. But political considerations are also important.

From an efficiency standpoint, a most desirable feature of competition is that firms have substantial incentives to produce products consumers want and to produce them in desired quantities. Furthermore,
competitive pressures force each firm to use its resources wisely so
that at least a normal profit will be earned. An important aspect of a
market-based resource allocation system is that it is efficient because
it responds quickly and accurately to consumer preferences. In other
words, the preservation of *consumer choice* or *consumer sovereignty* is an
important aspect of competitive markets. By retaining individual initiative in the market, competition does much to enhance personal freedom. For this reason, reductions in the vigor of competitive pressures
are seen as an indication of lessening consumer sovereignty. Remember:
Firms with market power can limit output and raise prices to earn excess
profits, while firms in competitive markets refer to market prices in order to determine optimal output quantities. In other words, monopolies
have far more discretion as actors than do firms in competitive markets.

Therefore, in cases of monopoly, regulatory policy can be a valuable tool to restore control over the price and quantity decision making process to the public.

A second political purpose for regulatory intervention into the market process is a desire to limit *concentration of economic and political power*. It has long been recognized that economic and political relationships can and do become intertwined. Concentrations of economic power are generally inconsistent with the democratic process. In fact, it has been asserted that one of the most important institutional reforms to characterize the American economic system was the incorporation laws of the 1850s. With these laws it became possible for owners of capital (stockholders) to pool economic resources without also pooling political resources, thereby allowing big business and democracy to coexist. Of course, the large scale of modern corporations has at times diminished the controlling influence of individual stockholders. In these instances, regulatory policy, particularly antitrust policy, has been used to limit the growth or size of large firms in order to avoid undue concentrations of political power.

In conclusion, important political considerations often constitute compelling justification for government intervention in the marketplace. Deciding whether or not a particular reform in regulatory policy is or is not warranted is compounded by the fact that such political considerations can run counter to efficiency considerations. This is not to say that policies where expected benefits are exceeded by expected costs should never be pursued. Costs in the form of lost efficiency may sometimes be borne so that more equitable solutions might be achieved.

Regulatory Response to Incentive Failures

Government intervention in the market economy is designed in part to respond to the problems created by both positive and negative externalities of production, marketing, and consumption. In its effort to limit the frequency of market failure due to incentive problems, government makes frequent use of both grant and tax policies. The granting of patents and operating subsidies, for example, are two frequently used methods by which government recognizes positive externalities and provides compensation to reward activities that provide such externalities. Local, state, and federal governments also use taxes (a form of negative subsidy) along with operating requirements, or controls, to limit the creation of negative externalities. Although grant, tax, and operating-control policies are by no means the only government responses to incentive failures, they are among the most widely employed; and they provide a good introduction to this area of government-business interaction.

Operating Right Grants

The regulation of operating rights is a common, though seldom-discussed, method of providing firms with an incentive to promote service "in the public interest." Common examples would be Federal Communications Commission (FCC) control of local television and radio broadcasting rights; federal and state regulatory bodies that govern national or state chartering of banks and savings institutions; and insurance commissions, which oversee insurance company licensing at the state level. In each of these instances firms must be able to demonstrate fiscal responsibility and to provide evidence that they are meeting the needs of their service areas. Should firms fail to meet these established criteria, public franchises (in the form of broadcasting rights, charters, or licenses) can be withdrawn, or new franchises can be offered to potential competitors. Although such drastic action is rare, the mere threat of such action is often sufficient to compel compliance with prescribed regulations.

Although control of operating rights can be an effective form of regulation, it often falls short of its full potential because of the imprecise nature of many operating criteria. For example, is a television station that broadcasts poorly rated local programming 20 hours per week responding better to the needs of its service area than a station that airs highly popular reruns of hit shows? How progressive in electronic fund-transfer services should a local bank be in order to be sufficiently progressive? Without clear, consistent, and workable standards of performance, policies in the area of operating grant regulation will be hampered by inefficiency and waste. The magnitude of these costs is measured not only by the low quality and limited quantity of desired goods and services, but also by the excessive profits and/or higher costs of producers sheltered by little or no competition.

Patent Grants

Patents are a prime example of a type of limited operating grant that can be conferred by government. Patents are a government grant of the exclusive right to produce, use, or sell an invention or idea for a limited period of time (17 years in the United States). As such, they are a valuable grant of legal monopoly power designed to stimulate research and development. Without patents, firms would be less likely to reap the full benefit of technological breakthroughs, as competitors would quickly exploit and develop close, if not identical, substitutes.

Patent policy is a regulatory attempt to achieve the benefits of both monopoly and competition in the field of research and development. In granting the patent monopoly, the public confers a limited opportunity for monopoly profits in order to stimulate research activity and the economic growth that it creates. By limiting the patent monopoly, competition is encouraged to extend and develop existant bodies of knowledge. These limits on the patent monopoly are not restricted to time period considerations, but include limitations on the use of the patent monopoly as well. Firms may not use patenting as a method of monopolizing or limiting competition. For example, in 1973 the Federal Trade Commission (FTC) charged Xerox with dominating the office-copier industry by engaging in unfair marketing and patent practices. In its complaint the FTC alleged that Xerox, in association with Battelle Memorial Institute, a private research corporation, had created an artificial "patent barrier to competition." A final consent order in 1975 resolved the FTC's monopolization suit against Xerox. The consent order required Xerox to license competitors to use its more than 1700 copier patents on a little or no royalty basis and restricted Xerox's freedom to acquire such rights from its competitors. Partially due to this action, small-firm entry into the copier industry grew rapidly during the late 1970s.

Subsidies

Government also responds to positive externalities by providing subsidies to private business firms. These subsidies can be indirect, as in the case of government construction and highway maintenance grants, which benefit the trucking industry. They can also take the form of direct payments, such as agricultural payment-in-kind (PIK) programs, special tax treatments, and government-provided low-cost financing.

Investment tax credits, allowed for certain types of business investments, and depletion allowances, provided to promote natural resource development, are examples of tax subsidies given in recognition of production externalities that provide benefits to society (e.g., job creation, energy independence). In addition, positive externalities associated with locating a major manufacturing facility in an industrial park have given rise to local government tax incremental or industrial revenue bond financing of such facilities. Such low-cost financing is thought to provide compensation for the external benefits provided.

Tax Policies

Although subsidy policy is a method of providing firms with positive incentives for desirable performance, tax policy is a system of penalties, or negative subsidies, that can be designed to limit undesirable performance. Under tax policy regular and anticipated tax payments are considered, as are fines or penalties that may be assessed on an intermittent or irregular basis.

Local, state, or federal fines for truckers who exceed specified weight limits, pollution taxes, and effluent charges or fines are common examples of tax policies intended to limit negative externalities by shifting external costs of production onto firms and their customers. Determination of an appropriate tax level is extremely difficult because of problems associated with estimating the magnitude of negative externalities. Although determining some of the social costs of air pollution, such as more frequent house painting, may be quite straightforward, calculating the costs of increased discomfort—even death—for emphysema patients is less so. Nevertheless, attempts must be made to consider the full range of consequences associated with negative externalities if appropriate and effective incentives are to be created.

Although tax policy may appear simply as a mirror image of subsidy and other grant policies, an important distinction should not be overlooked. If society wishes to limit the harmful consequences of pollution, for example, either subsidies for pollution reduction or taxes on pollution levels can provide effective incentives. There is, however, a significant difference in implied property rights under the two approaches. Under the subsidy mechanism, a firm's right to pollute is implied, in that society pays to have pollution reduced. In contrast, a system of pollution tax penalties is an assertion of society's right to a clean environment. Here, firms must reimburse society for damage that results from their emissions. The difference is a distinction in who "owns" the environment. Many prefer tax policy as a method for pollution reduction on the simple grounds that it makes explicit recognition of the public's right to a clean environment.

Operating Controls

Operating control regulation, or control by government directive, is an important and growing form of regulation. Operating controls are designed to limit undesirable behavior by compelling certain actions while prohibiting others. If operating control regulation results in 100 percent compliance, a situation is created similar to that resulting when a prohibitive tax policy is instituted. In each instance the undesirable activity in question is completely eliminated, and no tax revenues are collected. When operating controls result in less than full compliance, operating control regulation becomes much like tax policy regulation as fines and levies are instituted to punish violators.

What kinds of operating controls are imposed on business firms? Controls over environmental pollution immediately come to mind, but businesses are also subject to many other kinds of constraints. For example, federal legislation sets limits for automobile emissions, fuel efficiency, and safety standards; firms handling food products, drugs, and other substances that could harm consumers are constrained under the Pure Food and Drug Act. Industrial work conditions are governed under various labor laws and health regulations; included are provisions relating to noise levels, noxious gases and chemicals, and safety standards. Antidiscrimination laws designed to protect minority groups and women also cause some firms to modify their hiring and promotional policies. Wage and price controls, imposed at various times in attempts to reduce high rates of inflation, restrict the freedom of firms in setting prices and affect the usage of resources throughout the economic system.

Like operating grants regulation, the effectiveness of operating control regulations is often limited by statutory specifications that are vague or imprecise. Similarly, if the punitive sanctions taken against violators are overly lenient or poorly defined, effective incentives for compliance are not created. Beyond the difficulties created by poorly defined regulations and sanctions, problems can also result if operating controls that conflict with one another are imposed. For example, mandatory safety standards and pollution control equipment requirements have increased passenger car costs by several hundred dollars. Although such costs were undoubtedly anticipated by those designing auto safety and pollution regulations, it was perhaps less obvious that these regulations would result in important reductions in auto fuel efficiency. Thus, safety and pollution regulations were in direct conflict with other regulations mandating increases in the fuel efficiency of cars in order to reduce U.S. dependence on foreign-produced oil.

Perhaps the clearest difference between operating control regulation and regulation via tax or subsidy policies is the reliance on nonmonetary incentives for compliance. There are no easy alternatives to operating control regulation in those instances where the social costs are prohibitively great (e.g., nuclear disaster, ground water contamination, and so on) or difficult if not impossible to measure (e.g., public health, worker death, or serious injury). In some instances, however, operating control regulations can cause firms to direct their efforts toward being exempted or dismissed from regulation rather than toward reducing the negative externalities of concern to society. It is not clear that operating controls are more effective than tax and subsidy policies in ensuring that the results of regulatory efforts are both effective and equitable.

The "Who Pays?" Issue

The question of who pays for regulations intended to mitigate the problems associated with market failure due to incentive problems is an important one. Although the *incidence* of pollution charges may fall on a heavily polluting foundry, for example, the *burden* of those charges may be passed by the offending firm on to its customers or suppliers. In fact, the question of who pays for specific regulations can seldom be determined by merely considering the fined, taxed, or otherwise regulated party.

In general, who "pays" for operating control regulation depends on the elasticity of demand for the final products of affected firms. Figure 10.1 illustrates this issue by considering the theoretically polar extremes of perfectly elastic demand for final products (Figure 10.1a) and perfectly inelastic demand for final products (Figure 10.1b). Identically upward-sloping *MC* curves are assumed in each instance. Here, as is often the case, regulation is assumed to increase marginal costs by a fixed amount per unit. This amount, *t*, can reflect pollution taxes per unit of output or regulatory induced cost increases.

In Figure 10.1a we see that if good substitutes for a firm's product exist and demand is highly elastic, producers will be incapable of passing taxes or regulation-induced cost increases on to customers. As a result, producers (including investors, employees, and suppliers) will be forced to bear the burden of regulatory costs, at least in the short run. In these instances, falling industry rates of return on invested capital and high rates of industry unemployment will be symptomatic of regulatory influences.

In Figure 10.1b we consider the effect of regulation-induced cost or tax increases in the case of perfectly inelastic final product demand. Without effective substitute products, producers can be successful in passing the burden of regulation on to customers. In contrast to the perfectly elastic demand case, producers may encounter relatively few disadvantages due to regulation-induced cost increases.

Although the above analysis is greatly simplified, it points out that taxes or regulation-induced cost increases can have widely differing effects on industries if demand relationships vary. Similarly, the effect of regulation on industries with similar product demand elasticities will vary to the extent that supply characteristics are different. For example, in industries where marginal costs per unit are constant, per unit taxes will result in output prices rising by an amount greater than in the case of rising marginal costs, but by less than in the instance of falling marginal costs.

In general, regulations that affect the marginal costs of production will usually have some combination of adverse price and output effects for producers and consumers. A realization of this fact has, in some instances, caused policymakers to promote taxes or regulations that result in fixed or "lump sum" charges for producers. (Recall that increases in fixed costs affect neither price nor output levels for profit maximizing firms in the short run.) Even this approach to regulation is far from

Figure 10.1
Regulatory Burden Allocation under Elastic and Inelastic Demand

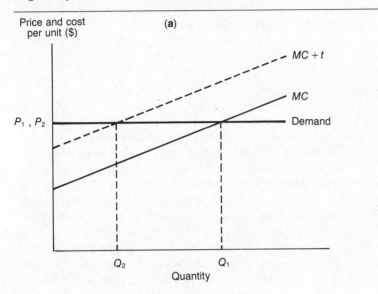

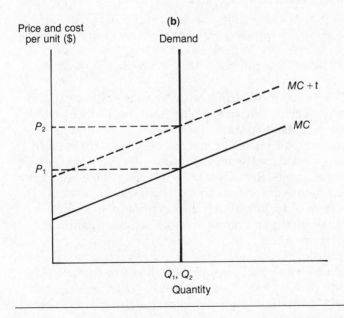

painless, however, since heavily regulated producers may be forced to leave the industry in the long run, should industry profitability be forced below the cost of capital. It is clear that the costs of regulation must be weighed carefully against its benefits.

Regulatory Response to Structural Failures

In Chapter 8 we saw that, under certain conditions, monopoly or oligopoly can develop in an industry and that in these market structures it is possible (but not necessary) that too little output is produced and excess profits are created. Regulatory policies to reduce or eliminate the socially harmful consequences of such structural failures can be aimed at controlling already existant monopoly power or at the prevention of its emergence. Public utility regulation, which controls prices and profits of established monopolies, is an important example of attempts to enjoy the benefits of low-cost production by large firms while avoiding the social costs of unregulated monopoly. Both tax and antitrust policies are used to address the problem of structural failures by attempting to limit not only the abuse of monopoly but also its growth.

The Dilemma of Natural Monopoly

Recall that under perfect competition many firms, perhaps of roughly comparable size, are able to produce with equal efficiency. If many small firms are viable in an industry, large firms can not be more efficient than their smaller rivals. This condition does not necessarily hold in all industries.

Evidence indicates that in some industries average costs of production decline continuously as output expands. That means that a single large firm has the potential to produce total industry output more efficiently than any group of smaller producers. This situation is called *natural monopoly* and is defined as the case where the profit maximizing level of output in an industry occurs at a point where long-run average costs for a single firm are still declining. The term *natural* is used because monopoly would naturally result from the superior efficiency of the single large producer and not necessarily because of anticompetitive or predatory practices.

For example, consider Figure 10.2. Here the firm will produce Q units of output at an average cost of C per unit. Note that this cost level is above the minimum point on the long-run average cost curve, and average costs are still declining. As a monopolist, the firm can earn an economic profit equal to the rectangle $PP'C'C$, or $Q(P - C)$. Local elec-

Figure 10.2
Price/Output Decision under Monopoly

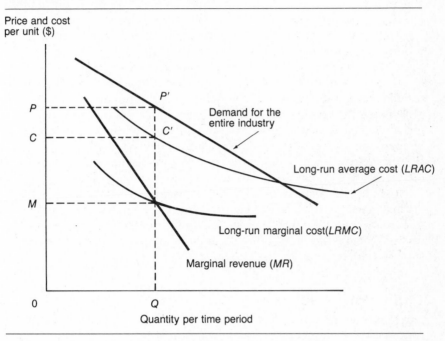

tric, gas, and water companies are the classic examples of natural monopolies, as the duplication of production and distribution facilities
would greatly increase costs if more than one firm served a given area.

This situation presents somewhat of a dilemma. Economic efficiency
could be enhanced by restricting the number of firms to one, but where
only one firm serves a market the possibility of monopolistic inefficiency exists. Specifically, unregulated monopolists tend to earn excessive profits and to underproduce. *Excessive profits* are defined as profits
so large that the firm earns a rate of return on invested capital that exceeds the risk-adjusted normal, or required, rate. Profits are useful both
for allocating resources and as an incentive for efficiency, but it is difficult to justify above-normal profits caused by market power rather
than by exceptional performance.

Underproduction occurs when the firm curtails production to a level
where the marginal value of the resources needed to produce an additional unit of output (marginal cost) is less than the benefit derived
from the additional unit, as measured by the price that consumers are
willing to pay for it. In other words, at outputs just greater than *Q*
in Figure 10.2, consumers are willing to pay approximately *P* dollars

per unit, so the value of additional units is P. However, the marginal cost of producing an additional unit is only slightly greater than M dollars and well below P, so cost is not equal to value. Accordingly, an expansion of output is desirable from society's point of view.

In addition to possibly earning excessive profits and withholding production, an unregulated natural monopolist could be susceptible to operating inefficiency. In competitive markets, firms must operate efficiently to remain in business. Pressure for cost-efficiency from established competitors, however, is absent in the case of natural monopoly. This means that the market power of the natural monopolist would permit some inefficiency and waste in production. While excessive amounts of operating inefficiency would surely attract new competition (entry), significant losses in economic efficiency may persist for extended periods in the case of natural monopoly.

How can we escape from the dilemma posed by the fact that monopoly may have the potential for greatest efficiency, but that unregulated monopoly could lead to excess profits, underproduction, and resource waste? One answer is to permit natural monopolies to persist but to subject them to price and profit regulation.

Utility Price Regulation

The most common method of monopoly regulation is through price controls. Price regulation typically results in (1) a larger quantity of the product being sold than would be the case with an unrestricted monopoly, (2) a reduced dollar profit, and (3) a lower rate of return on investment by the firm's owners. This situation is illustrated in Figure 10.3. A monopolist operating without regulation would produce Q_1 units of output and charge a price, P_1. If regulators set a ceiling on prices at P_2, the firm's effective demand curve would become the kinked curve P_2AD. Since price is a constant from 0 to Q_2 units of output, marginal revenue equals price in this range; that is, P_2A is the marginal revenue curve over the output range $0Q_2$. For output beyond Q_2, marginal revenue is given by the original marginal revenue function, the line LM. Thus, the marginal revenue curve is now discontinuous at Output Q_2, with a gap between Points A and L. This regulated firm will maximize profits by operating at Output Q_2 and by charging the ceiling price, P_2. Marginal revenue is greater than marginal cost up to that output, but less than marginal cost beyond it.

Profits are also reduced by the regulatory action. Without price regulation, price P_1 is charged; a cost of C_1 per unit is incurred; and Output Q_1 is produced. Profit will be $(P_1 - C_1)(Q_1)$, which is equal to the area P_1BFC_1. With price regulation, the price is P_2; the cost is C_2; Q_2 units are sold; and profits are represented by the smaller area P_2AEC_2.

Figure 10.3
Monopoly Price Regulation: Optimal Price/Output Decision Making

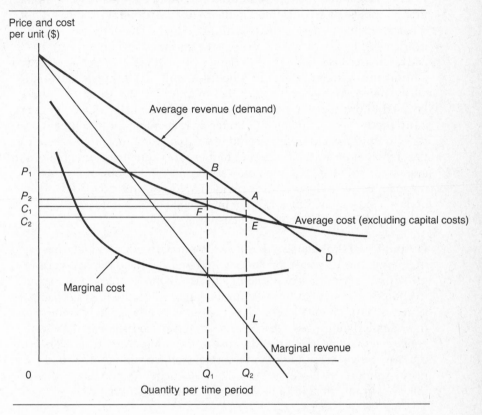

Price and cost per unit ($)

Average revenue (demand)

P_1

P_2
C_1
C_2

B

A

F

E

Average cost (excluding capital costs)

D

Marginal cost

L

Marginal revenue

0   Q_1 Q_2

Quantity per time period

How does the regulatory authority determine a fair price? In essence, the theory is as follows. The regulatory commission has in mind a fair or normal rate of return, given the risk inherent in the enterprise. The regulators also know how much capital investment will be required to produce a given output. The commission then approves prices such that the profits earned, when divided by the required investment at the resultant output level, will produce the target rate of return. In the case illustrated in Figure 10.3, if the profit at Price P_2, when divided by the investment required to produce Q_2, produces a rate of return greater than the target, the price would be reduced until the actual and the target rates of return were equalized. This treatment assumes, of course, that the cost curves in Figures 10.3 and 10.4 do not include equity capital costs. That is, the profit referred to is business profit, not economic profit. This treatment is the norm in public utility regulation.

Problems in Utility Price Regulation

Pricing Problems. Although the concept of price regulation is simple, many problems are confronted in the regulation of public utilities. First, it is impossible to determine cost and the demand schedules, as well as the asset base necessary to support a specified level of output, exactly. Utilities also serve several classes of customers, which means that a number of different demand schedules with varying price elasticities are involved. Therefore, any number of different rate schedules could be used to produce the desired profit level. If local electric power company profits are too low, should rates be raised for summer (peak) or for winter (off-peak) users; should industrial, commercial, or residential customers bear the burden of higher rates equally or unequally? An appeal to cost considerations for a solution to this problem is often of no avail, because the services provided are joint products, a factor that makes it extremely difficult, if not impossible, to separate costs and allocate them to specific classes of customers.

Output Level Problems. A second problem with price regulation is that regulators can make mistakes with regard to the optimal level and growth of service. For example, if a local telephone utility is permitted to charge excessive rates, more funds will be allocated to system expansion, and communication services will grow at a faster than optimal rate. Similarly, if prices allowed to natural gas producers are too low, consumers will be encouraged to use gas at a high rate, producers will not seek new gas supplies, and shortages of gas will occur. Too low a price structure for electricity will likewise encourage the use of power but discourage the addition of new generating equipment.

Inefficiency. Price regulation can also lead to inefficiency. If regulated companies are guaranteed a minimum return on their invested capital, then, provided demand conditions permit, operating inefficiencies can be offset by higher prices. To illustrate, consider the situation depicted in Figure 10.4. A regulated utility faces the demand curve AR and the marginal revenue curve MR. If the utility operates at peak efficiency, the average cost curve AC_1 will apply. At a regulated price, P_1, Q_1 units will be demanded; cost per unit will be C_1; and profits equal to the rectangle $P_1P_1'C_1'C_1$ will be earned. These profits are, let us assume, just sufficient to provide a reasonable return on invested capital.

Now suppose that another company, one with less capable managers, is operating under similar conditions. Because this management is less efficient than that of the first company, its cost curve is represented by AC_2. If its price is set at P_1, it too will sell Q_1 units, but average cost will be C_2; profits will be only $P_1P_1'C_2'C_2$; and the company will be earning less than its required rate of return. In the absence of regulation, inefficiency and low profits go together, but under regulation the ineffi-

Figure 10.4
Efficient and Inefficient Utility Companies

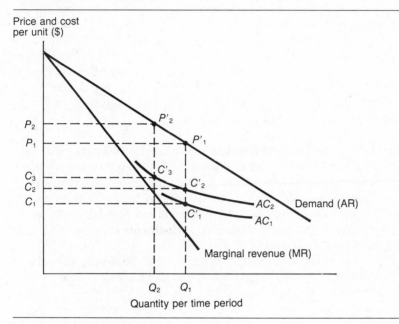

cient company can request—and probably be granted—a rate increase to P_2. Here it can sell Q_2 units of output, incur an average cost of C_3 per unit, and earn profits of $P_2 P_2' C_3' C_3$, resulting in a rate of return on investment approximately equal to that of the efficient company. We see, then, that regulation can reduce the profit incentive for efficiency.

Utility commissions can address this problem by considering efficiency performance when setting rates. For example, a particular commission might feel that 14 percent is a reasonable rate of return but might allow efficient companies within its jurisdiction to earn up to 14.5 percent and penalize inefficient companies by holding them to a return of less than 14 percent. The difficulty with this approach is that each utility operates in a unique setting, so it is extremely difficult to make valid comparisons. One electric company might have a cost of 2 mils per kilowatt hour, and another in the same state might have a cost of 2.5 mils. Is the first company more efficient than the second, or is the cost difference due to fuel cost differences, different plant sizes, labor cost differentials, and differing depreciation charges caused by construction during a more or less inflated period? Because of these difficulties, utility commissions do not frequently make explicit use of efficiency differentials in setting profit rates.

Investment Level. A fourth problem with regulation is that it can lead to overinvestment or underinvestment in fixed assets. Allowed profits are calculated as a percentage of the rate base, which is approximately equal to fixed assets. If the allowed rate of return exceeds the cost of capital, it will benefit the firm to expand fixed assets and to shift to capital-intensive methods of production. Conversely, if the allowed rate of return is less than the cost of capital, the firm will not expand capacity rapidly enough and will produce by methods that require relatively little capital but perhaps excessive amounts of fuel. Thus, regulation can lead to suboptimal input combinations.

Regulatory Lag and Political Problems. A related problem is that of *regulatory lag*, which is defined as the period between the time a price increase (or decrease) is appropriate and the effective date of the allowed price change. Because of the often lengthy legal proceedings involved in these price decisions, long periods can pass between the time when the need for utility rate level adjustments is recognized and when they are implemented.

The problem of regulatory lag is particularly acute during periods of rapidly rising prices. During the late 1960s and the 1970s, for example, inflationary pressures exerted a constant upward thrust on costs. If normal profits and a fair rate of return on capital are to be maintained in such a time, expeditious price increases have to be implemented.

However, public utility commissioners are either political appointees or elected officials, and those who appoint them or the commissioners themselves must periodically stand for reelection. Further, most voters are consumers of utility services and naturally dislike price increases, whether these increases are justified or not. Utility customers can and do exert great pressure on public utility commissioners to deny or at least delay even reasonable rate increases.

At least in part because of regulatory lag, a number of major utility companies experienced severe financial difficulties during the mid-1970s. The largest U.S. electric utility, Consolidated Edison (which serves New York City and the surrounding area), was almost forced into bankruptcy, and many other companies were forced to curtail construction programs because they were unable to obtain the funds necessary to purchase new plants and equipment. Profits were simply inadequate to induce investors to purchase the companies' stocks and bonds.

Cost of Regulation. By this time a sixth problem with price regulation should be obvious. A great deal of careful and costly analysis must be conducted before regulatory decisions can be made. Maintaining public utility commission staffs is expensive, as is maintaining required records and processing rate cases, costs borne directly by companies. Ultimately the cost of both the commissions' and the companies' regulation-related activities are borne by consumers.

Although most economists can see no reasonable alternative to utility regulation for electric, gas, local telephone, and private water companies, serious problems arise from efforts to regulate industry through price determination. If competition is present, the market system is a much more efficient allocator of goods and services, and it is for this reason that efforts are made to maintain a workable level of competition in the economy through tax and antitrust policies.

Excess or Windfall Profit Taxes

In recent years, tax policy has been increasingly used to limit perceived abuses of monopoly power and, to a lesser extent, to encourage the growth of small as opposed to large business. *Excess*, or *windfall profit*, *taxes* are examples of tax policies intended to limit perceived abuses of economic power. *Normal profit* is defined as the risk-adjusted rate of return necessary to maintain investment in an industry. Excess profit, therefore, is profit above and beyond necessary minimums. The term windfall profit is commonly used to distinguish excess profit, which is due to the unexpected and unwarranted good fortune of firms, from economic profits resulting from such factors as superior operating efficiency, innovation, economies of scale, and so on.

Excess profit taxes have been frequently imposed during wartime both to help finance the high level of government expenditure and to reduce the substantial profits accruing to providers of critical goods and services. More recently, in 1980 the United States imposed a windfall profit tax on domestic oil company profits. The intent was to reduce oil company profits resulting from the very rapid increase in crude oil prices.

One of the most serious challenges to a successful excess or windfall profit tax policy is the problem of correctly defining the magnitude of unwarranted profits. This means that prices, operating expenses, and investment policies of affected firms must be carefully scrutinized. Therefore, substantial industry expertise is necessary if potential abuses of a windfall tax policy are to be avoided. If firms perceive that a windfall profits tax policy is only a temporary phenomenon, unnecessary operating expenses may be incurred or unwarranted investments may be undertaken if future benefits from such expenditure are anticipated. For example, the railroad industry substantially rebuilt or replaced its right-of-way (track and related) investments during World War II. Although some reinvestment in plant and equipment was undoubtedly necessary if wartime demands for freight and passenger service were to be met, one can only speculate as to how much investment was undertaken simply to avoid wartime windfall profit taxes. Newer plant and equipment, rather than increased tax payments, were obviously preferable to railroad executives. Quite different problems may result from the windfall taxes on oil company profits. Beyond the obvious problem of defining the magnitude of excess profit, windfall profit taxes can increase the level of risk or uncertainty in doing business. If oil company executives perceive that profits from successful exploration activities will be taxed severely, the risk of obtaining a satisfactory return from the firm's entire drilling program could rise. Higher industry averages for both required profit and product prices would naturally result.

Small Company Tax Preferences

During recent years the corporate income tax has become somewhat more progressive, favoring small as opposed to large business. In 1984 the corporation income tax rate was 15 percent on the first $25,000 in profits; 18 percent between $25,000 and $50,000; 30 percent between $50,000 and $75,000; 40 percent between $75,000 and $100,000; and 46 percent on profits over $100,000. Therefore, firms paid a total of $25,750 in taxes on the first $100,000 of profit, but $46,000 in taxes for each additional $100,000.

The rationale provided for these tax preferences is quite diverse. Growth in small business is seen as consistent with democratic principles of self-determination and individual decision making. Growth in small business is also important because small firms often form a "competitive fringe" in industries, thereby exerting downward pressure on the prices and profits of leading firms. Furthermore, recent evidence suggests that small firms are the source of substantial amounts of invention and technological innovation. To some extent, progressive taxes might also be considered a partial offset to the relatively high costs that regulation and government reporting requirements impose on small businesses.

Whatever the rationale, it is clear that small business plays an important role in the U.S. economy. The extent to which tax and other regulatory preferences enhance the competitive position of small firms is not fully known, but their use to insure the continued success of small business seems likely.

Antitrust Policy

In the late nineteenth century a movement toward industrial consolidation developed in the United States. Industrial growth was rapid, and because of economies of scale or unfair competitive practices, an oligopolistic structure emerged in certain industries. In some instances, pricing decisions were made by industry leaders who concluded that higher profits could be attained through cooperation rather than competition. As a result, voting trusts were formed. In these trusts, voting rights to the stocks of various firms in an industry were consolidated so that a monopoly price/output solution could be achieved. The oil and tobacco trusts of the 1880s are well-known examples.

Although profitable to the firms, the trusts were socially undesirable, and public indignation resulted in the 1890 passage of the Sherman Act, the first significant U.S. antitrust measure. Other important legislation subsequently passed includes the Clayton Act (1914), the Federal Trade Commission Act (1914), the Robinson-Patman Act (1936), and the Celler-Kefauver Act (1950). Each of these acts was designed to prevent anticompetitive actions, whose effects are more likely to reduce competition than to lower costs by increasing operating efficiency. In this section we present an overview of antitrust law, as well as a brief chronology of major antitrust legislation.

Overview of Antitrust Law

As is the case with any major body of law or legal principles, multiple purposes of federal antitrust law are apparent. **Antitrust** law is essentially concerned with facilitating the control of economic and political power through the force of competitive markets. The purpose of such control is not only to improve economic efficiency but to enhance consumer sovereignty and the impartiality of resource allocation while limiting concentrations in both economic and political power.

There is no single antitrust statute in U.S. law. Rather, federal antitrust law is founded on two basic statutes, the Sherman Act and the Clayton Act, and their amendments. An important characteristic of these laws is that they tend to be quite broad and somewhat vague in banning "restraints of trade," "monopolization," "unfair competition," and so on. By never precisely defining the nature of monopolizing, for example, the statutes left it to judicial interpretation to determine prohibited behavior. Because of this, many principles in antitrust law rest on judicial interpretation in key decisions. For this reason, individual court decisions (case law) must be consulted in addition to statutory standards (statutory law) to determine the legality of business practices.

Sherman Act

The Sherman Act of 1890 was the first piece of federal antitrust legislation. In substance, it was brief and to the point. Section 1 forbade contracts, combinations, or conspiracies in restraint of trade (then offenses under common law), and Section 2 forbade monopolization. Both sections could be enforced by civil court decrees or by criminal proceedings, with the guilty liable to fines or jail sentences. In 1974 the Sherman Act was amended to make violations felonies rather than misdemeanors. The act now provides for $1 million maximum fines against corporations and up to $100,000 fines and three years' imprisonment for individuals. In addition to criminal fines and prison sentences, firms and individuals violating the Sherman Act face the possibility of triple-damage civil suits from those injured by the antitrust violation.

Despite some landmark decisions against the tobacco, powder, and Standard Oil trusts, enforcement has proved to be sporadic. Moreover, the Sherman Act is often alleged to be too vague. On the one hand, business people claim not to know what is illegal; on the other, it is sometimes felt that the Justice Department is ignorant of monopoly-creating practices and does not bring suit against them until it is too late and monopoly is already established.

Despite its shortcomings, the Sherman Act remains one of the government's main weapons against anticompetitive behavior. In 1978 a federal judge imposed some of the stiffest penalties in the history of U.S. antitrust actions on eight firms and eleven of their officers who were convicted of violating the Sherman Act. These convictions for price fixing in the electrical wiring devices industry resulted in fines totaling nearly $900,000 and jail terms for nine of the eleven officers charged.

Clayton Act

Congress passed two measures in 1914 designed to overcome weaknesses in the Sherman Act. The most important of these was the Clayton Act, which addressed problems of mergers, interlocking directorships, price discrimination, and tying contracts. Also enacted in 1914 was the Federal Trade Commission Act, which outlawed unfair methods of competition in commerce and established the FTC, an agency intended to enforce the Clayton Act.

Section 2 of the Clayton Act made it illegal for a seller to discriminate in price among its business customers unless (1) cost differentials in serving the various customers justified the price differentials, or (2) the lower prices charged in certain markets were offered to meet competition in the area. The primary concern was that a strong regional or national firm might employ selective price cuts in local markets to drive weak local firms out of business. Once the competitors in one market were eliminated, monopoly prices would be charged in the area, and the excessive profits could be used to subsidize cut-throat competition in other areas. The Robinson-Patman Act was passed in 1936 as an amendment to the section of the Clayton Act dealing with price discrimination. Specific forms of price discrimination, especially related to chain-store purchasing practices, were declared to be illegal.

Section 3 of the Clayton Act forbade tying contracts that reduce competition. A firm, particularly one with the patent on a vital process or a monopoly on a natural resource, could use licensing or other arrangements to restrict competition. One such procedure was the tying contract, through which a firm tied the acquisition of one item to an agreement to purchase other items. For example, the International Business Machines Corporation (IBM) for many years refused to sell its business machines. It rented these machines to customers, who were required to buy IBM punch cards and related materials as well as machine maintenance from the company. This clearly had the effect of reducing competition in the maintenance and service industry, as well as in the punch card and related products industry. After the IBM lease agreement was declared illegal under the Clayton Act, the company was forced to offer its machines for sale and to cease leasing arrangements that tied firms to agreements to purchase other IBM materials and services.

And finally, although voting trusts that lessened competition were prohibited by the Sherman Act, interpretation of the act did not always prevent one corporation from acquiring the stock of competing firms and then merging them into itself. Section 7 of the Clayton Act prohibited such mergers if they were found to reduce competition. Either the Antitrust Division of the Justice Department or the FTC can bring suit under Section 7, and mergers can be prevented. If they have been consummated prior to the suit, divestiture can be ordered. The Clayton Act also prevented individuals from serving on the boards of directors of two competing companies. Two so-called competitors having common directors would obviously not compete very hard. Although the Clayton Act made it illegal for firms to merge through stock transactions when the effect would be to lessen competition, a loophole in the law existed. A firm could purchase the assets of a competing firm, integrate the operations into its own, and effectively reduce competition. The Celler-Kefauver Act closed this loophole, making asset acquisitions illegal when the effect of such purchases was to reduce competition. By a slight change in wording, it made clear that the policy of Congress was to attack all mergers between a buyer and a seller (vertical), between potential competitors (horizontal or product and market extension), and between entirely unrelated firms (pure conglomerate), whenever competition was threatened.

Enforcement

Public enforcement of the antitrust laws is the dual responsibility of the Antitrust Division of the Department of Justice and the FTC. Generally speaking, the Justice Department concerns itself with significant or flagrant offenses against the Sherman Act, as well as with mergers for monopoly covered by Section 7 of the Clayton Act. In most instances, the Justice Department will only bring charges under the Clayton Act when broader Sherman Act violations are also being addressed. In addition to policing law violations, the Sherman Act also charges the Justice Department with the duty of restraining possible future violations. Thus, firms found in violation of the law often receive from the federal courts detailed injunctions regulating future business activity. In fact, "injunctive relief" (e.g., dissolution or divestiture decrees, and so on) is a much more typical outcome of Justice Department suits than are criminal penalties.

Although the Justice Department can institute civil proceedings in addition to the criminal proceedings discussed above, civil proceedings are typically the responsibility of the FTC. The FTC is an administrative agency of the executive branch with quasijudicial powers used to enforce compliance with the Clayton Act. Because the substantive provisions of the Clayton Act do not create criminal offenses, the FTC has no criminal jurisdiction. The FTC holds hearings if law violations are suspected and issues "cease and desist" orders if violations are found. Such "cease and desist" orders under the Clayton Act are subject to review by appellate courts.

Economic Analyses in Antitrust Actions

The various antitrust provisions apply if a particular action would tend to lessen competition substantially. Mergers are attacked if they would alter industry structure in a manner that reduces competition, but they are not illegal if competition is not reduced. When is competition reduced? If two firms merge, each with 1 percent of a market served by 100 competitors, few would argue that the merger reduces competition, for 99 firms would still remain after the merger. However, if each firm had a substantial share of the market and only a few firms would remain after the merger, competition might be affected. The problem lies in defining a "substantial" share of the market and quantifying a "few" remaining firms. Where should these lines be drawn?

Further, if it is judged that a *particular* merger would not itself reduce competition but that a series of similar mergers would do so, should the merger in question be permitted? Suppose 20 firms, each with a 5 percent share of the market, are in competition. A judgment is made, perhaps in a court of law that has heard much economic evidence, that a particular merger will not harm competition. If the merger is approved, however, other firms will also seek to merge, and the ultimate result could be a reduction in competition. When should the trend toward concentration be stopped?

Market concentration is a key element in making judgments about the effect of a merger on the competitive posture of an industry, but how should an industry or a market be determined? To illustrate, suppose two banks in lower Manhattan seek to merge. There are about 14,000 banks in the United States, and the national banking concentration ratio is low. However, the entire United States is not a relevant market for most banking services; a local area is the relevant market. But what local area? Should metropolitan New York be deemed the market? The City of New York? The Borough of Manhattan? Or lower Manhattan only? The answer really depends on the nature of the banks. For certain classes of services, especially loans to major national corporations, the nation as a whole constitutes the market. But for personal checking account and loan services, the local area is the relevant market.

The problem is even more complex when competing products or industries are considered. A particular bank might, for example, be the only one serving a given neighborhood, but the bank might still face intense competition from savings and loan associations, credit unions, and distant banks or money market mutual funds that offer service by mail and toll-free telephone.

Similar problems are found in other aspects of antitrust policy. For example, given the difficulties we have noted in estimating costs for multiproduct firms, determining the presence and magnitude of price discrimination becomes difficult. A comprehensive economic cost analysis is often required before the existence of price discrimination can be detected, and even then the issue is likely to be less than clear-cut.

Antitrust is quite complex, with its complete coverage being well beyond the scope of this text. Additionally, generalizations are difficult. The fact that so many antitrust decisions are made in the courts is testimony to this point. Nevertheless, because antitrust policy does constitute a serious constraint to many business decisions, antitrust considerations are an important, if nebulous, aspect of managerial economics.

The Regulated Environment:
A Second Look

For effective decision making in the regulated environment, managers must be aware of both the causes and the effects of modern regulatory processes. We have briefly addressed this need by considering both economic and political considerations stimulating regulatory responses to perceived market failures caused by incentive or structural problems. Both positive and negative aspects of current regulatory methods were briefly examined. Rather than summarizing this material immediately, we think it will prove useful to look somewhat more closely at both the problems and promise of regulation. Seldom is the issue one of regulation versus complete deregulation; rather it is often one of how much and what kinds of regulation are most appropriate.

Costs of Regulation

Many economists are fond of quoting the phrase "There is no such thing as a free lunch." With respect to regulation, this can be interpreted to mean that every government program and policy has economic costs. The economic costs of regulatory policies are measured in terms of administrative burdens for regulatory agencies, deviations from optimal methods of production, and the general effect that regulation has on the allocation of economic resources.

A first, and most obvious, cost of business regulation is the cost to local, state, and federal governments for supervisory agencies. Estimates for local, state, and federal expenditures for business regulation fall in the $3 to $5 billion per year range. Interestingly, the largest regulatory budgets at the federal level are not those of traditional regulatory agencies, such as the Securities and Exchange Commission (SEC) or Interstate Commerce Commission (ICC), but those devoted to the broader regulatory activities of the Departments of Labor (for employment and job safety standards) and Agriculture (mainly for food inspection).

Although these "direct" costs of regulation are substantial, they may be far less than hidden or "indirect" costs. For example, if the Occupational Safety and Health Administration (OSHA) requires manufacturers to employ safer methods of production, increases in affected product prices will surely occur. Similarly, the cost of Environmental Protection Agency (EPA) mandated reductions in auto emissions will ultimately be borne by consumers. In the case of auto emissions, the National Academy of Sciences and the National Academy of Engineering estimated the annual benefits of the catalytic converter at $5 billion and annual costs at $11 billion. In a social sense, one might ask if the noneconomic advantages of this method of pollution reduction are sufficient to offset what appear to be significant economic disadvantages. Similarly, the economic and noneconomic advantages of regulation must be sufficient to offset annual private costs for pollution control, OSHA-mandated noise reductions, health and safety equipment, FTC-mandated business reports, and so on. Accurately estimating the total direct and indirect costs of regulation involves obvious difficulties, and most recent estimates fall in the area of $100 billion per year. Clearly, a consideration of the total costs of regulation must play a prominent role in the decision of what and how to regulate.

The magnitude of the economic costs of regulation suggests that neither business nor the public may regard them as trivial or unimportant. Where important concerns for the public's health and safety are apparent, for example, business and government can accomplish much through cooperative effort. It is the public's role to supervise this process to insure that government-business interactions yield regulatory policies in the public interest.

The Size-Efficiency Problem

The discussion on the dilemma of natural monopoly suggested that, in some instances, a single seller has the potential for superior cost efficiency. A potentially important negative consequence, however, is that such natural monopolists would have a tendency to restrict output, with resulting higher prices and excess profits. This conflict between the superior efficiency of large firms and the harmful consequences of limited numbers of competitors is one of the oldest controversies in antitrust and regulation. It is clear from public policy initiatives in the area that some, perhaps many, lawmakers believe the sizes reached by the largest firms in our economy cannot be justified on the basis of scale-associated advantages in production. Although such views remain widespread, some counterevidence has emerged in several recent studies that suggest that the commonly observed link between leading firm market shares (industry concentration) and profitability can be explained by the lower costs made possible by superior efficiency, rather than by higher prices due to collusion. These findings are as controversial as they are important and suggest the need to continue research on the size-efficiency problem.

Some of the public policy issues raised by difficulties encountered in tracing the source of above-normal profits can be illustrated by considering recent merger policy initiatives and policies concerning the breakup of long-established firms.

During recent years, federal legislation has been proposed that would prohibit all mergers between firms of a certain size, say, $100 million or more in annual sales. These proposals are a reflection of the belief that such mergers increase monopoly power, with no offsetting advantages in terms of economic efficiency. However, research on the economic causes and consequences of mergers and corporate takeovers indicates that these are the means by which underutilized resources are transferred to more efficient uses. Unfriendly takeovers, for example, are especially unfriendly to inefficient management, which is subsequently replaced. Perhaps one of the greatest dangers to a blanket prohibition on all mergers involving large firms is that inefficient management, or management that is insensitive to stockholder interests, could become insulated against the threat of removal for unsatisfactory performance.

Although questions concerning merger policy are difficult, those related to government policy concerning the breakup of long-established firms are even more complex. The recent Justice Department cases against IBM and AT&T provide classic illustrations.

Even though IBM did not invent the electronic computer, it was one of the first companies to realize the enormous opportunities it presented. IBM's involvement with the computer transformed what was once a modestly successful business machines company into a leader of dominant proportions in various sectors of a rapidly growing industry. Through rapid growth during the 1950s and 1960s, IBM became an industry leader in the mainframe equipment sector of the industry, for example, while playing a lesser role in peripherals and terminal equipment, software services, and other areas. In 1969, the Antitrust Division of the Justice Department, concerned with potentially anticompetitive effects of its market position, filed suit to break up IBM. The case foundered. While all observers, including economists, could agree that IBM was a large and highly profitable company, the sources of this success were a matter of substantial dispute. Was IBM highly profitable merely because of its leadership position, (i.e., monopoly power), or was IBM a highly profitable industry leader by virtue of its ability to offer innovative products at attractive prices (i.e., efficiency)? In the first case, breaking up IBM could be beneficial and lead to lower prices, eliminate monopoly profits, and increase consumer welfare. On the other hand, breaking up IBM would be penalizing the type of efficiency competitive markets are meant to encourage, and innovation and initiative in the industry could be blunted. Determining the sources of IBM's success, and the costs and benefits from a possible dissolution, became a problem with no obvious answer. In 1982, after more than a decade of litigation costing both sides tens of millions of dollars, the Justice Department dismissed its suit. Free from antitrust concerns, IBM clearly became more aggressive in terms of pricing and new product introductions during the early to mid-1980s, with obvious benefits resulting for users of business and personal computer equipment.

An interesting second example of recent antitrust policy in the area is the 1974 Justice Department suit to break up AT&T. The department argued that breaking up AT&T would stimulate competition in the telephone equipment and long-distance phone service sectors of the industry and provide consumers with improved goods and services at lower prices. In order to avoid the expense and uncertainty of a prolonged antitrust case, AT&T agreed to divest itself of its local phone companies. As of January 1, 1984, a "new" AT&T was created, consisting largely of AT&T communications (long-distance phone service), AT&T information systems (computer systems), AT&T international (foreign operations), Bell Labs (research and development), and Western Electric (telephone equipment). The seven local companies created were Ameritech, Bell Atlantic, Bell South, Mynex, Pacific Telesis, Southwestern Bell, and U.S. West. Whether this reorganization of the telecommunications industry will lead to significant benefits for consumers remains to be seen. In the meantime, the enormous costs and risks involved make clear why such "experiments" are so rare.

The "Capture" Problem

In our earlier discussion of the "why regulate" question, we considered both economic and noneconomic factors that influence regulatory decisions. This discussion presented the widely held belief that regulation is in the "public interest" and is used to move firm behavior toward socially desirable ends. This view is not universally held, however, and the compelling nature of counterarguments requires that they be considered.

In a 1971 study, George Stigler presented what may be called the *capture theory* of economic regulation.[1] According to Stigler, the machinery and power of the state are a potential resource to every industry in society. With its power to prohibit or compel, to take or give money, the state can and does selectively help or hurt a vast number of industries. Because of this, regulation may be actively *sought* by an industry. Stigler contends that, as a rule, regulation is acquired by industry and is designed and operated primarily for industry's benefit. Although some regulations are undeniably onerous, these examples are thought to be exceptional rather than usual cases.

Stigler asserts that the types of state favors commonly sought by regulated industries include direct money subsidies, control over entry by new rivals, control over offerings of substitutes and complements, and price-fixing. Therefore, domestic airline "air-mail" subsidies, Federal Deposit Insurance Corporation (FDIC) regulation reducing the rate of entry into commercial banking, suppression of margarine sales by butter producers, price-fixing in motor carrier (trucking) regulation, and American Medical Association control of medical training and licensing can be interpreted as examples of regulatory process control by regulated industries.

In summarizing his views on regulation, Stigler suggests that criticism of the Interstate Commerce Commission's pro-industry policies is as misplaced as would be criticism of the Great Atlantic and Pacific Tea Company (A&P) for selling groceries, or of politicians for seeking popular support. Given current methods of enacting and carrying out regulation, pro-industry policies made by regulatory bodies are to be expected. Stigler contends that the only way to get different results from

---

[1] George J. Stigler, "The Theory of Economic Regulation," *Bell Journal of Economics and Management Science* 2 (Spring 1971): 3–20.

regulation would be to change the political process of regulator selection and to reward regulators on a basis unrelated to their services on behalf of regulated industries.

The Deregulation Movement

Growing concern with the costs and problems of government regulation gave birth to a **deregulation** movement in the early 1970s, a movement that has grown to impressive dimensions as we enter the late 1980s. Although it is difficult to pinpoint a single catalyst for the movement, it is hard to overlook the role played by Stigler and other economists (notably Alfred E. Kahn) who illustrated that the regulatory process can sometimes harm rather than help consumer interests.

Table 10.1 highlights some of the major steps toward deregulation taken since 1970. Although the effects of changing state and local regulation have been felt in many industries, changing federal regulation has been most pronounced in the financial, telecommunications, and transportation sectors. Since 1975, for example, it has been illegal for securities dealers to fix commission rates. This broke a 182-year tradition under which the New York Stock Exchange (NYSE) set minimum rates for each 100-share ("round lot") purchase. Until 1975, everyone charged the minimum rate approved by the NYSE. If 1000 shares were

Table 10.1
Major Steps toward Deregulation since 1970

Year	
1970	Federal Reserve Board frees interest rates on large bank deposits with short maturities ($100,000 or more for six months or less).
1975	Securities and Exchange Commission prohibits fixed commissions on stock sales.
1978	Congress deregulates the airline industry.
1979	Federal Communications Commission allows AT&T to sell unregulated services (e.g., data processing).
1980	Federal Reserve System allows member banks to pay interest on checking.
1980	Congress deregulates trucking and railroads.
1982	Congress deregulates intercity bus services.
1984	AT&T forced to divest itself of its local phone companies.

purchased, the commission was 10 times the minimum, even though the overhead and work involved were roughly the same for small and large stock transactions. This system not only resulted in large profits for NYSE members, but it also sheltered the higher costs of inefficient firms. Following deregulation, commission rates tumbled, and predictably, some of the least efficient brokerage firms merged or otherwise went out of business. Today, more than a decade later, commission rates (prices) have fallen by 50 percent or more, and the industry is noteworthy for its increasing productivity and variety of new product introductions. Also noteworthy is that during the period 1975–1982, the number of sales offices in the industry increased by 80 percent, total employment rose by two thirds, and profits increased to $1.5 billion per year, more than 10 times the 1974 level. All of this leads observers to conclude that deregulation can benefit consumers without causing any lasting damage to industry. In fact, a leaner, more efficient industry may be one of the greatest benefits that deregulation has to offer.

Despite obvious successes following deregulation, the movement has its critics. When airline ticket prices reflect the cost of service, as they must with deregulation, bargain fares will be available on heavily traveled routes between major cities (e.g., New York to Los Angeles, Chicago to Miami), but relatively high fares will result for lightly traveled routes (e.g., Pittsburgh to Buffalo, New York; Kansas City to Omaha). Similarly, deregulation in the telecommunications industry caused rates for long-distance telephone calls to fall but monthly charges for local service to rise. Deregulation in the intercity bus market brought travelers lower prices, but forced Greyhound Corporation to suffer a costly strike in order to convince workers that without regulation its wage levels would have to be reduced. Inefficient firms, consumers who buy goods and services whose cost is partly subsidized by other customers of regulated firms, and workers who take home inflated wages can all be expected to oppose efforts to continue the process of deregulation. Still, the gains from deregulation appear significant, and the process is likely to continue.

Rationalizing the Regulatory Process

Although some feel there is simply a question of regulation versus deregulation, this is seldom the case. Thus, it will prove valuable to consider methods of improving regulation in addition to focusing on the no-regulation alternative.

Our earlier discussion suggested that an important problem of regulation, particularly utility regulation, was that regulators seldom have the information or expertise necessary to specify, for example, the correct level of utility investment, the minimum necessary regulated car-

rier costs, or the optimal method of pollution control accurately. In fact,
because technology is rapidly changing in many industries, often only
those industry personnel currently working at the frontier of technology
have the type of specialized knowledge necessary to deal satisfactorily
with such issues.

One possible method for dealing with the technical expertise problem of current regulation is to have regulators focus on the preferred
outcomes (ends) of regulatory processes, rather than on the technical
means industry adopts in achieving those outcomes. Such an innovation in regulation would allow regulators to specialize in defining the
public interest in regulation, while industry specialized in meeting those
objectives in a least-cost fashion. If regulator rewards and regulated
industry profits were tied to objective output-oriented performance criteria, desirable incentives for minimizing the costs of necessary regulations could be created.

For example, there is a real public interest in safe, reliable, and low-
cost electric power. State and federal regulators who oversee the operations of utilities could develop objective standards for measuring
utility safety, reliability, and cost efficiency. If firm profit rates were tied
to such performance-oriented criteria, real improvements in utility operations could result.

Competitive forces provide a persistent and socially desirable con-
straining influence on firm behavior. In those instances where the vigorous influences of competition are diminished or absent, government
regulation can be justified through both efficiency and equity. Where
regulation is warranted, business, government, and the public must
work together to insure that regulatory processes represent not only
large or special interests, but also those with an individually small but
collectively large stake in regulatory decisions.

Summary

The history of government involvement in the economy is both long
and substantial. In general, government acts to stimulate and assist private enterprise and to regulate or control business practices so that firm
operations are consistent with the public interest. Although we have
discussed some of the interactions between government and business
throughout the text, this chapter provides a more detailed examination.

Both economic and political considerations enter into decisions of
what and how to regulate. Regulation can enhance economic efficiency
when unrestricted market activity fails to provide the types and quantity of goods consumers desire at competitive prices. Market failure

due to *structural* problems occurs when the presence of too few buyers or sellers results in uncompetitive pricing, excess profits, and/or inefficiency. Market failure due to *incentive* problems occurs when some benefits or costs of production are not included in product prices, and inefficient levels of output result. Public utility regulation is intended to limit the effects of market failure due to structural problems by regulating prices and profits in markets where efficiency considerations lead to domination by a single firm. If competition among a large number of firms is feasible, antitrust policy is brought to bear to insure competitive practices. Market failure due to incentive problems can be avoided if, for example, pollution taxes or fines are imposed so that the prices of all goods and services reflect the full costs of production. Beyond these economic advantages, carefully designed regulations can also further the political goals of *maintaining consumer choice or consumer sovereignty* and *limiting concentration of economic and political power*.

The regulatory response to incentive failures includes the supervision of operating rights (licenses), patent grants, government subsidies, taxes or fines, and operating controls. Regulation is costly. Who actually bears the burden of these costs can seldom be determined by merely considering the fined, taxed, or otherwise regulated party. All else equal, producers (including stockholders and employees) bear the burden of regulation when final product demand is highly elastic. In the event demand is inelastic, producers can pass the burden of regulation on to consumers.

The regulatory response to structural failures is twofold. First, when a single firm has the potential to produce output more efficiently than any group of smaller firms, a situation called *natural monopoly*, public utility regulation of prices and profits is instituted to insure that the monopolist acts in the public interest. In essence, the regulator sets a price (lower than the profit maximizing price) designed to give the company only a normal profit. Because public utility regulation presents many problems, it is often thought preferable to limit monopoly by encouraging "workable" levels of competition in markets. Thus, a second approach to limiting structural failures is through antitrust policy, which has the express purpose of maintaining competition. The antitrust laws deal with collusion, price discrimination, mergers, tying contracts, and other practices that threaten competition.

The problems posed by mushrooming costs of regulation, difficulties encountered in learning the sources of high rates of firm profitability, and regulations that seem to serve industry rather than consumer interests all impact on the issues surrounding government-firm interaction. Such problems will continue to shape our decisions on what and how to regulate and thereby define the role of government in the market economy.

Questions

10.1 Define the term *market failure* and cite some causes. Can you also cite some examples of market failure?

10.2 What roles does the price elasticity of demand play in determining the effect of operating controls in an industry if these controls lead to increased fixed costs? What if they lead to increased variable costs?

10.3 Given the difficulties encountered in regulating the various utility industries in the United States, it has been suggested that nationalization might lead to a more socially optimal allocation of resources. Do you agree? Why or why not?

10.4 Antitrust statutes in the United States have been used primarily to attack monopolization by big business. Should monopolization of labor supply by giant unions be as vigorously prosecuted?

10.5 Explain why state tax rates on personal income vary more on a state-by-state basis than do corresponding tax rates on corporate income.

10.6 Do the U.S. antitrust statutes protect competition or competitors? What is the distinction between the two?

10.7 Define price discrimination. When is it legal? When is it illegal? Cite some common examples of price discrimination.

10.8 On January 29, 1973, the federal government charged Xerox Corporation with dominating the office-copier industry by engaging in certain restrictive patent practices while preventing foreign affiliates from competing with it in the United States. In its complaint, the government alleged that Xerox, in association with Battelle Memorial Institute, a private research corporation, had created an artificial "patent barrier to competition."

    a) Carefully describe how creation of an artificial patent barrier to competition could directly violate at least *two* distinct antitrust laws.

    b) Describe and defend an appropriate antitrust remedy. In other words, what should the government do?

10.9 Is the deregulation movement of the 1970s and 1980s consistent or inconsistent with the capture theory of economic regulation?

Solved Problem

10.1 The New England Electric Power Company is under investigation by a state regulatory commission because of recent operating policies. The commission has informed the company it considers 11.5 percent to be the "fair" rate of return on investment that the firm should be earning. However, the firm, according to the commission, had been operating as almost a pure monopolist and earning substantial excess profits. The relevant demand, marginal revenue, and cost curves (the latter curve including a "fair" rate of return) agreed upon by both the firm and commission are as follows:

$$P = 100 - .5Q \qquad \text{(Demand)}$$

$$MR = 100 - Q \qquad \text{(Marginal Revenue)}$$

$$TC = 1{,}000 + 5Q \qquad \text{(Total Cost)}$$

$$MC = 5 \qquad \text{(Marginal Cost)},$$

where P is price (in dollars), Q is output (in thousands of megawatt hours), MR is marginal revenue, TC is total cost (in thousands of dollars), and MC is marginal cost.

a) If the firm were operating as a pure monopolist, what would be its optimal price-output combination and level of economic profits?

b) What price should the commission set if it wishes to eliminate economic profits?

c) Graph the solutions to parts a and b.

Solution

a) Set $MR = MC$ to find profit maximizing output level where

$$MR = MC$$

$$100 - Q = 5$$

$$Q = 95(000), \text{ or } 95{,}000 \text{ Megawatt Hours}$$

$$\text{Price} = P = 100 - 0.5Q$$

$$= 100 - 0.5(95)$$

$$= \$52.50.$$

$$\text{Economic Profit} = \pi$$

$$= TR - TC$$

$$= 100Q - 0.5Q^2 - 1{,}000 - 5Q$$

$$= 100(95) - 0.5(95^2) - 1{,}000 - 5(95)$$

$$= \$3{,}512.50(000) \text{ or } \$3{,}512{,}500.$$

b) To preclude monopoly profits, the commission should set

$$\text{Price} = AR = AC = \frac{TC}{Q}$$

$$100 - .5Q = \frac{(1{,}000 + 5Q)}{Q}$$

$$100Q - .5Q^2 = 1{,}000 + 5Q$$

$$-0.5Q^2 + 95Q - 1{,}000 = 0,$$

which is a quadratic equation of the form

$$aQ^2 + bQ + c = 0,$$

where $a = -.5$, $b = 95$, and $c = -1{,}000$. Its two roots can be obtained by using the *quadratic formula*, where

$$Q = \frac{-b \pm \sqrt{b^2 - 4ac}}{2a}$$

$$= \frac{-95 \pm \sqrt{(95^2) - 4(-.5)(-1{,}000)}}{2(-.5)}$$

$$= \frac{-95 \pm \sqrt{9{,}025 - 2{,}000}}{-1}$$

$$= \frac{-95 \pm 83.82}{-1}$$

$$= 11.18 \text{ or } 178.82,$$

where the "upper" Q is the relevant solution since regulatory commissions generally seek the "largest quantity of service consistent with the public interest."

$$\text{Price} = P = 100 - 0.5Q$$

$$= 100 - .5(178.82)$$

$$= \$10.60.$$

$$\text{Economic Profit} = \pi$$

$$= TR - TC$$

$$= 100Q - 0.5Q^2 - 1{,}000 - 5Q$$

$$= 100(178.82) - 0.5(178.82^2) - 1{,}000 - 5(178.82)$$

$$= \$0.$$

c)

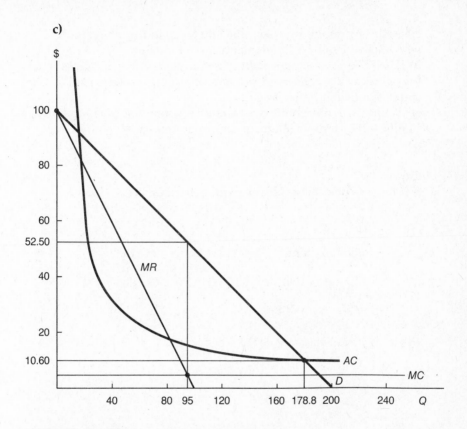

Solved Problem

10.2 Bellville Electronics Inc. assembles electronic components and is a major employer in the Houston, Texas, area. Demand and marginal revenue curves for Bellville are

$$P = 1{,}000 - 0.02Q \quad \text{(Demand)}$$

$$MR = 1{,}000 - 0.04Q \quad \text{(Marginal Revenue)},$$

where Q is the quantity demanded per year. Production of each unit of output requires 100 hours of labor, 0.25 hour of capital equipment time, and $50 of raw materials. Bellville has a total of 5,000 hours of capital equipment time available in its production facility each year and can purchase all the labor and materials it desires. The capital equipment investment by Bellville totals $30 million, and the firm requires a 15 percent return on capital. Assume for simplicity that these are the only costs incurred and that Bellville has a profit maximization objective.

    a) You have been employed by the State Unemployment Service to evaluate the impact on employment at Bellville of a proposed increase in the minimum wage. As a first step in the analysis, develop Bellville's short-run demand curve for labor.

b) If Bellville pays the current minimum wage of, say, $3.35 per hour for labor, calculate the short-run impact on employment of an increase to a $4 minimum wage.

c) Would the long-run impact on unemployment be likely to differ significantly from the short-run impact in this case? Justify your answer.

Solution

a) Bellville's operating rule for profit maximization is

$$MC = MR.$$

To determine the marginal cost function we note that

$$MC = \text{Per Unit Material Cost} + \text{Per Unit Labor Cost}$$

$$= 50 + 100P_L,$$

where P_L is the labor wage rate. Then,

$$MC = MR$$

$$50 + 100P_L = 1,000 - 0.04Q$$

$$100P_L = 950 - 0.04Q$$

$$P_L = 9.5 - 0.0004Q.$$

Since 100 labor hours are required for each unit of Q,

$$L = 100Q \text{ or } Q = \frac{L}{100},$$

and the short-run demand for labor equation can be written

$$P_L = 9.5 - 0.0004Q$$

$$= 9.5 - \frac{0.0004L}{100}$$

$$= 9.5 - 0.000004L,$$

or

$$L = 2,375,000 - 250,000P_L.$$

b) Employment levels at \$3.35 and \$4 per hour can be calculated, using the demand for labor function derived in part a.

$$L_A = 2,375,000 - 250,000P_L$$

$$= 2,375,000 - 250,000(3.35)$$

$$= 1,537,500 \text{ worker hours.}$$

$$L_B = 2,375,000 - 250,000P_L$$

$$= 2,375,000 - 250,000(4)$$

$$= 1,375,000 \text{ worker hours.}$$

Thus, a \$4 minimum wage would reduce labor demand and employment by

$$\text{Employment Loss} = L_A - L_B$$

$$= 1,537,500 - 1,375,000$$

$$= 162,500 \text{ worker hours.}$$

Assuming 2,000 worker hours per year for each employee, this is a reduction of 81.25 ($= 162,500/2,000$) jobs.

c) This question can be addressed by analyzing Bellville's profits at optimal output levels with a \$3.35 and \$4 wage rate, respectively. With $P_L = \$3.35$, output equals $Q = L/(L/Q) = 1,537,500/100 = 15,375$. With $P_L = \$4$, output equals $Q = L/(L/Q) = 1,375,000/100 = 13,750$. Bellville's total revenue function is

$$TR = P \cdot Q$$

$$= (1,000 - 0.02Q)Q$$

$$= 1,000Q - 0.02Q^2.$$

The total cost function is constructed as follows:

$$TC = \text{Fixed Cost} + (\text{Per Unit Material Cost}) \cdot Q$$
$$+ (\text{Per Unit Labor Cost}) \cdot Q$$

$$\text{Fixed Cost} = .15(\$30,000,000)$$

$$= \$4,500,000$$

$$\text{Per Unit Material Cost} = 50$$

(continued)

Per Unit Labor Cost = $100P_L$, where P_L is the labor wage rate

$TC = 4{,}500{,}000 + 50Q + 100P_LQ.$

Therefore,

Profit = $\pi = TR - TC$

$= 1{,}000Q - 0.02Q^2 - 4{,}500{,}000 - 50Q - 100P_LQ.$

With $P_L = \$3.35$, $Q = 15{,}375$, and total profit is

Profit = $1{,}000Q - 0.02Q^2 - 4{,}500{,}000 - 50Q - 100P_LQ$

$= 1{,}000(15{,}375) - 0.02(15{,}375^2) - 4{,}500{,}000 - 50(15{,}375)$
$\qquad - 100(3.35)(15{,}375)$

$= \$227{,}813.$

With $P_L = \$4$, $Q = 13{,}750$, and total profit is

Profit = $1{,}000Q - 0.02Q^2 - 4{,}500{,}000 - 50Q - 100P_LQ$

$= 1{,}000(13{,}750) - 0.02(13{,}750^2) - 4{,}500{,}000 - 50(13{,}750)$
$\qquad - 100(4)(13{,}750)$

$= (\$718{,}750).$

Thus, at the \$3.35 wage rate *economic* profits are positive (recall that the \$4.5 million fixed cost is the required return on capital), and, hence, the firm will operate and will have an incentive to expand in the long run. At $P_L = \$4$, however, economic profits are negative, indicating that the required return on capital is not being made, and, hence, the firm will not be able to attract the capital necessary to continue operating at this level in the long run. This means that the impact of the increase in the minimum wage would be a loss of even more jobs and *could* be a loss of *all* jobs at the firm over the long run.

Solved Problem

10.3 Susquehanna Chemical Corporation (SCC) produces a pesticide called A-pest. During production of A-pest, a byproduct called B-pest is also produced. The two chemicals (*A* and *B*) are produced in the constant ratio of 1:1. SCC has long followed the practice of dumping its excess production into the Susquehanna River and currently incurs no cost from this activity. Total and marginal cost functions for SCC are:

$$TC = 100 + 10Q + 4Q^2,$$

$$MC = 10 + 8Q,$$

where Q represents a unit of production consisting of one unit of A and one unit of B.

a) The demand and marginal revenue curves for the two products are

$$P_A = 600 - Q_A \qquad P_B = 100 - Q_B$$

$$MR_A = 600 - 2Q_A \qquad MR_B = 100 - 2Q_B$$

What would be the optimal price-output combination for the two products, assuming SCC operates as a profit maximizing firm?
b) Determine the smallest fine per unit of B dumped that would cause SCC to stop dumping altogether.

Solution

a) Solution to this problem requires that one look at several production and sales options available to the firm. One option is to produce and sell equal quantities of products A and B. In this case, the firm sets relevant $MC = MR$.

$$MC = MR_A + MR_B = MR$$

$$10 + 8Q = 600 - 2Q + 100 - 2Q$$

$$12Q = 690$$

$$Q = 57.5 \text{ Units.}$$

Thus, the profit maximizing output level for production *and sale* of equal quantities of A and B would be 57.5 units. However, we must check to determine that the marginal revenues of both products are positive at this sales level before claiming that this is an optimal activity pattern.

Evaluated at 57.5 units,

$$MR_A = 600 - 2(57.5) \qquad MR_B = 100 - 2(57.5)$$

$$= \$485. \qquad\qquad = (\$15).$$

Since the marginal revenue for B is negative, and since SCC can costlessly dump excess production, the sale of 57.5 units of product B is suboptimal. This invalidates the entire solution developed

above since output of A is being held down by the negative marginal revenue associated with sales of B. The problem must be set up in a fashion that recognizes that SCC will stop selling B at the point where its marginal revenue becomes zero since, given production for A, the relevant marginal cost of B is zero.
Set

$$MR_B = MC_B$$

$$100 - 2Q_B = 0$$

$$2Q_B = 100$$

$$Q_B = 50 \text{ Units.}$$

Thus, 50 units of B is the maximum that will be sold. Any excess units will be dumped into the Susquehanna River. The price for B at 50 units is

$$P_B = 100 - Q_B$$

$$= 100 - 50$$

$$= \$50.$$

To determine the optimal production level of A, set the marginal revenue of A equal to the marginal cost of producing another unit of the output package. Since $Q_A = Q$,

$$MR_A = MC_A = MC_Q$$

$$600 - 2Q_A = 10 + 8Q_A$$

$$10Q_A = 590$$

$$Q_A = 59$$

and

$$P_A = 600 - Q_A$$

$$= 600 - 59$$

$$= \$541.$$

The firm will maximize profits by producing 59 units of output, selling 59 units of A at a price of $541 and 50 units of B at a price of $50. Nine units of B will be dumped.

b) In part a we saw that the profit maximizing output level for the firm *if* it produced and sold *equal* quantities of the two products was 57.5 units, and that the marginal revenue of B was −$15 at that sales level. Thus, any fine less than $15 will cause the firm to produce added units of the output package since even with dumping of B and paying a fine, the sale of additional units of A is more profitable. A fine greater than $15 would be larger than necessary since all dumping will cease with a fine of that amount.

Thus, a pollution tax of $15 would not raise any tax revenue but would cause SCC to stop dumping B altogether.

Problem Set

10.1 The Gary Steel Works Inc. produces steel at a Gary, Indiana, steel mill. With each ton of steel produced, the firm has been dumping particulate matter (smoke and dust) into the local atmosphere. As a concerned citizen, you are appalled at the aesthetic environmental implications of the company's policies, as well as the potential health hazard to the local population.

a) You cite the occurrence of pollution as a negative production externality and an example of market failure. What might you cite as reasons why markets fail?

b) In analyzing remedies to the current situation, you consider three general types of controls to limit pollution:

Regulations: licenses, permits, compulsory standards, and so on.

Payments: various types of government aid to help companies install pollution control equipment. Aid can be forgiveness of local property taxes, income tax credits, special accelerated depreciation allowances for pollution control equipment, low-cost government loans, and so on.

Charges: excise taxes on polluting fuels (coal, oil, and so forth), pollution discharge taxes, and others.

Review each of these methods of pollution control and

    i. Determine the incentive structure for the polluter under each form of control.

    ii. Decide who pays for a clean environment under each form of control. (*Note*: Each form of control has something definite to say about who owns the property rights to a clean environment.)

    iii. Defend a particular form of control on the basis of your analysis, including both efficiency and equity considerations.

10.2 In a recent hearing before the State Pollution Board, members of the Wilderness Club clashed with representatives of the paper indus-

try over the extent to which the companies should be permitted to discharge wastes into the Catawaba River. The Wilderness Club, whose
representatives were supported by the Resort Owners League, argued
for quite stringent rules, whereas the paper companies sought less severe pollution control regulation and an extended period of time in
which to implement any new rules. The companies were backed by
representatives of Camden and Ridgeway, the two largest towns on the
river and sites of several large paper mills.

There was no argument about the need for *some* controls; everyone
agreed that mercury emissions must cease and also that organic wastes
should be reduced. The arguments were over the *degree* of controls,
with the conservationists calling for a return of the river to its pre-
industrial state and the companies arguing that such tight controls
would cause (a) a severe reduction in production, (b) industry to move
to other states with less severe restrictions, and (c) large losses both to
stockholders and to property owners in the mill towns. Besides, the
companies argued, many other rivers in the state were still unspoiled,
and it made good sense to industrialize some areas, while keeping
others undeveloped.

As the hearings progressed, it became clear that insufficient facts
were available. The companies suggested that the costs of tight pollution controls would be quite high and would drive industry out. The
conservationists argued that the companies were overstating costs and
understating the probability that other states would pass similarly tough
control laws, thus making it impossible for paper mills to escape pollution control laws by relocating. The companies retorted that if all
states passed legislation similar to that backed by the Wilderness Club,
the companies would not be able to pass their cost increases onto customers because of the elastic demand for paper products and because
of foreign imports.

After several days of emotion-packed debate, the Pollution Control
Board adjourned the hearings, commissioned a team of economists
and engineers from State University to develop some facts on the case,
and rescheduled the hearings for a later date when this information
would be available.

As a result of this analysis, the following data were developed:

    i. Demand curve for raw paper facing all United States produc-
ers (Q in millions of tons):

$$P_A = \$650 - \$10Q.$$

    ii. Aggregate total and marginal cost curves (ignoring the re-
quired return on capital) facing all United States producers (dollars in millions, Q in million-unit increments):

$$TC = \$1,800 + \$200Q + \$5Q^2$$

$$MC = \$200 + \$10Q.$$

iii. Total equity investment of all 200 United States paper producers: $5 billion. A normal rate of return is 12 percent. The state in question has 8 percent of the United States paper industry, and all firms operate with similar cost functions.
iv. Demand curve facing each individual producer:

$$P = \$425 - \$0.0Q.$$

v. Increased operating costs of $1 billion a year, excluding any return on the required new investment, would be required to bring the United States paper industry pollution standards up to the level recommended by the Wilderness Club.
a) What price-output solution would be reached in the paper industry, given the above information?
b) What profits would be earned?
c) Would above-normal or below-normal profits be earned? What would economic profits amount to?
d) What would happen to the paper industry if the Wilderness Club recommendation were adopted nationwide, assuming all data given thus far are valid and the firms all continue to operate?
e) In fact, what would be likely to occur? What assumptions in the data would likely be incorrect, causing the result in part d *not* to occur?
f) What market structure would you judge the paper industry to have, assuming the facts given above?
g) What would become of the state paper industry if only this one state put in pollution control restrictions? What bearing has this on *federal* pollution control legislation?

10.3 The Delmarva Water Utility has petitioned the Maryland Public Service Commission (PSC) for rate relief. Delmarva views its current rate structure as inadequate to provide the company with a fair return on its $100 million investment in plant and equipment. In support of its request for higher rates, Delmarva has provided the PSC with the following demand and cost information:

$P = \$10 - \$0.0003Q$	(Demand)
$MR = \$10 - \$0.0006Q$	(Marginal Revenue)
$TC = \$6,000 + \$6Q + \$0.0002Q^2$	(Total Cost)
$MC = \$6 + \$0.0004Q$	(Marginal Cost),

where P is price (in dollars), Q is output (in thousands of gallons), MR

is marginal revenue, *TC* is total cost (in $000), and *MC* is marginal cost. Total costs include allowance for a 12 percent return on investment, a level the PSC has judged fair and commensurate with the Delmarva's risk level.

a) Calculate Delmarva's return on invested capital if its request for a $8.50 rate per 1,000 gallons (0.85¢ per gallon) is granted.

b) Is $8.50 a profit maximizing rate level? If so, explain. If not, explain why not and calculate Delmarva's maximum potential unregulated investment return.

c) Can you explain why Delmarva would submit a rate request that would not maximize short-run profits?

d) Calculate the rate level that would just provide Delmarva with a 12 percent return on invested capital.

10.4 Ken's Flooring Inc. is an independent contractor that installs carpeting sold by large retail outlets in the Seattle, Washington, area. Ken's crews of carpet and pad installers typically include skilled and unskilled laborers. Carpet installation is perfectly competitive in the Seattle market with a standard price of $2.68 per yard for installation. Ken's employs 10 skilled laborers and estimates the marginal product of unskilled labor as $MP = 10L_S/L_U$, where MP = square yards of carpet and pad installed per eight-hour day, L_S = skilled laborers, and L_U = unskilled laborers employed per day.

a) Derive the demand curve for unskilled labor measured in days.

b) Derive the demand curve for unskilled labor *hours*.

c) How many unskilled employees will Ken's employ at a $3.35 minimum wage?

d) Calculate the number of unskilled laborers Ken's will employ, given a $3 minimum wage for teenagers, assuming the entire unskilled labor requirement can be met using teenagers.

e) Would you expect a lower minimum wage for teenagers to expand their employment opportunities without affecting older workers? Why or why not?

10.5 On Monday, December 5, 1977, *The Wall Street Journal* carried a short article titled "Detroit's New Drive against Imported Cars to Be an Uphill Battle." The following is an excerpt from that article.

In the West, where Japanese imports are especially popular, the automakers are pinning their hopes on a new pricing scheme, which puts a lower price tag on their cars. Thus, a two-door Chevette Hatchback will cost $118 less in seven western states than anywhere else in the U.S. Similarly, a Ford Pinto is $122 less than in the rest of the country, and an AMC Gremlin is $120 cheaper.

This two-tier pricing has already raised the ire of some eastern dealers who view it as discriminatory and a violation of antitrust laws.

a) Is this pricing scheme discriminatory in the economic sense? What would be necessary in order for it to be profitable to the automakers?

b) Carefully describe how price discrimination could be a violation of U.S. antitrust laws and be sure to mention which laws in particular might be violated.

10.6 Iowa Pork Inc. processes hogs at a large facility located in Des Moines, Iowa. Each processed hog results in both pork and a render byproduct being produced in a fixed 1:1 ratio. While the byproduct is unfit for human consumption, some can be sold to a local pet food company for further processing. Relevant annual demand and cost relations are:

$P_P = \$110 - \$0.00005Q_P$ (Demand for Pork)

$MR_P = \$110 - \$0.0001Q_P$ (Marginal Revenue from Pork)

$P_B = \$10 - \$0.0001Q_B$ (Demand for Render Byproduct)

$MR_B = \$10 - \$0.0002Q_B$ (Marginal Revenue from Render Byproduct)

$TC = \$10,000,000 + \$60Q$ (Total Cost)

$MC = \$60$ (Marginal Cost).

Here P is price in dollars, Q is the number of hogs processed (average weight of 100 pounds), Q_P and Q_B are pork and render byproduct per hog, respectively; both total and marginal costs are in dollars. Total costs include a risk-adjusted normal return of 15 percent on a $50 million investment in plant and equipment.

Currently, the city allows the company to dump any excess byproduct into its sewage treatment facility at no charge, viewing the service as an attractive means of keeping a valued employer in the area. However, the sewage treatment facility is quickly approaching its peak capacity and must be expanded at an expected operating cost of $3 million per year. This is an impossible burden on an already strained city budget.

a) Calculate the profit maximizing price-output combination and optimal total profit level for Iowa Pork.

b) How much byproduct will be dumped into the Des Moines sewage treatment facility at the profit maximizing activity level?

c) Describe the short-run and long-run effects of a $35 charge per unit of B dumped.

d) Describe the short- and long-run effects of a fixed $3 million per year tax on Iowa Pork to pay for the sewage treatment facility expansion.

e) In your opinion, what should the city of Des Moines do about its sewage treatment problem?

References

Armstrong, Alan G. "Consumer Safety and the Regulation of Industry." *Managerial and Decision Economics* 2 (June 1981): 67–73.

Bailey, Elizabeth E. "Contestability and the Design of Regulatory and Antitrust Policy." *American Economic Review* 71 (May 1981): 178–183.

Bator, Francis M. "The Anatomy of Market Failure." *Quarterly Journal of Economics* 72 (August 1958): 351–379.

Burns, Malcolm R. "An Empirical Analysis of Stockholder Injury Under §2 of the Sherman Act." *Journal of Industrial Economics* 31 (June 1983): 333–362.

Chilton, Kenneth and Weidenbaum, Murray L. "Government Regulation: The Small Business Burden." *Journal of Small Business Management* 20 (January 1982): 4–10.

Hirschey, Mark and Weygandt, Jerry J. "Amortization Policy for Advertising and Research and Development." *Journal of Accounting Research* 23 (Spring 1985).

Kareken, John H. "The First Step in Bank Deregulation: What About the FDIC?" *American Economic Review* 73 (May 1983): 198–203.

LaBarbera, Priscilla A. "The Diffusion of Trade Association Self-Regulation." *Journal of Marketing* 47 (Winter 1983): 58–67.

Neumann, George R. and Nelson, John P. "Safety Regulation and Firm Size: Effects of the Coal Mine Health and Safety Act of 1969." *Journal of Law and Economics* 25 (October 1982): 182–199.

Peltzman, Sam. "The Effects of FTC Advertising Regulation." *Journal of Law and Economics* 24 (December 1981): 403–448.

Piekarz, Rolf, "R&D and Productivity Growth: Policy Studies and Issues." *American Economic Review* 73 (May 1983): 210–214.

Schmalensee, Richard. "Antitrust and the New Industrial Economics." *American Economic Review* 72 (May 1982): 24–28.

Shepherd, William G. "Causes of Increased Competition in the U.S. Economy, 1939–1980." *Review of Economics and Statistics* 64 (November 1982): 613–626.

Stigler, George J. "The Economists and the Problem of Monopoly." *American Economic Review* 72 (May 1982): 1–11.

Stigler, George J. "The Theory of Economic Regulation." *Bell Journal of Economics and Management Science* 2 (Spring 1971): 3–21.

Chapter 11

Decision Making
Under Uncertainty

Key Terms

Certainty equivalent   *Expected value*   *Simulation*

Decision tree   *Probability*   *Standard deviation*

Diminishing   *Risk*   *Utility*
   marginal utility   *Risk-adjusted*
               discount rate

Many simple managerial decisions are made under conditions where the outcomes associated with each possible course of action are known with certainty. A firm with $100,000 in excess cash that can be invested in a thirty-day treasury bill yielding 11 percent ($904 interest for thirty days), or that can be used to prepay a bank loan, saving $936 in interest, can determine with certainty that prepayment of the loan will provide a $32 higher return. Similarly, a manufacturer needing 500,000 units of an industrial fastener that can be purchased from one distributor at 74¢ per unit and from a second at 74½¢ per unit knows with certainty that a cost savings of $2,500 will result by purchasing from the first distributor. Even for decision problems where events and results cannot be exactly predicted, substantial insight into decision-making procedures can be gained by treating the problem as though management had complete information concerning the outcomes of all possible decisions. Understanding the rationale for decisions under certainty conditions provides a strong foundation for the somewhat more complex analysis required for decision making under uncertainty. For these reasons, much of the analysis and many of the optimality conditions developed in managerial economics relate to decision making where perfect information about all events and outcomes is assumed.

In reality, however, virtually all major managerial decisions are made under conditions of uncertainty. Managers must select a course of action from the perceived alternatives with less than perfect knowledge about the occurrence of events affecting the outcome. There is also uncertainty about the effect on the outcome should some particular event occur. In some cases uncertainty also exists about the ultimate consequences of the outcome itself. The pervasiveness of uncertainty in managerial decision situations and the risk entailed by such uncertainty dictate that the concepts of risk and risk analysis be explored in the study of managerial economics.

Risk analysis can be related directly to the basic valuation model underlying the microeconomic theory of the firm. When both risk levels and decision maker attitudes toward risk taking are known, the effects of uncertainty on the basic valuation model can be reflected through adjustments to the model's numerator or denominator. The certainty equivalent method converts expected risky profit streams to their certain sum equivalents in order to eliminate value differences that result from different risk levels. Therefore, the certainty equivalent method adjusts the numerator of the basic valuation model so that present values for projects are risk adjusted and, thereby, comparable. A second method for directly reflecting uncertainty in the basic valuation model is through risk-adjusted discount rates. In this method, the interest rate used in the denominator of the basic valuation model depends upon the level of risk associated with a given cash flow. Thus, discounted expected profit streams once again reflect risk differences among projects and are directly comparable. We begin this chapter by defining risk and discussing methods for measuring it. We then examine the two primary methods for adapting the basic valuation model to account for uncertainty. And finally, we discuss the use of probability theory, decision trees, and simulation as aids to decision making under uncertainty.

Risk in Economic Analysis

Risk is defined as a hazard or peril; as an exposure to harm; and, in commerce, as a chance of loss.[1] Thus, **risk** refers to the possibility that

---

[1]Some writers distinguish between risk and uncertainty, but for our purposes this distinction is unnecessary. Accordingly, we define any decision whose outcome is less than certain as being risky, and we say that such decisions are subject to risk or uncertainty.

some unfavorable event will occur. For example, if one buys a $1 million short-term government bond priced to yield 11 percent, then the return on the investment, 11 percent, can be estimated precisely, and we define the investment as risk free. If, however, the $1 million is invested in the stock of a company being organized to prospect for natural gas in the Gulf of Mexico, the return on the investment cannot be estimated precisely. The return could range from minus 100 percent (a complete loss) to some extremely large figure. Because there is a significant danger of loss, we define the project as relatively risky. Similarly, sales forecasts for different products might exhibit differing degrees of risk. For example, The Dryden Press may be sure that sales of a fifth edition introductory finance text will reach the projected level of 70,000 copies, but the company may be uncertain about the number of copies it will sell of a new first edition statistics text. The greater uncertainty associated with the sales level of the statistics text increases the chance that the firm will not profit from publishing that book. Thus, the risk of that project is greater than that of revising the finance text.

Risk is associated with the chance or probability of undesirable outcomes: The more likely an undesirable outcome, the riskier the decision. It is useful, however, to define risk more precisely. This more precise definition requires a step-by-step development, which constitutes the remainder of this section.

Probability Distributions

The **probability** of an event is defined as the chance, or odds, that the event will occur. For example, a sales manager may state, "There is a 70 percent chance we will get an order from Delta Corporation and a 30 percent chance that we will not." If all possible events or outcomes are listed, and if a probability of occurrence is assigned to each event, then the listing is defined as a *probability distribution*. For our sales example, we could set up the following probability distribution:

Event (1)	Probability of Occurrence (2)
Receive order	0.7 = 70%
Do not receive order	0.3 = 30%
	1.0 = 100%

The possible outcomes are listed in column 1, while the probabilities of each outcome, expressed both as decimals and percentages, are given in column 2. Notice that the probabilities sum to 1.0 or 100 percent, as they must if the probability distribution is complete.

Risk in this very simple example can be read from the probability distribution as a 30 percent chance that the undesirable event (the firm does not receive the order from Delta Corporation) occurs. For most managerial decisions, however, the relative desirability of alternative events or outcomes is not so absolute as indicated here. For this reason, a more general measure of the relationship between risk and the probability distribution is required to incorporate risk into the decision process appropriately. The need for a more general measure of risk can be illustrated by considering the following situation.

Suppose a firm is considering two investments, each calling for an outlay of $1,000. Only one will be chosen. Assume also that the profits on the two projects are related to the level of general economic activity in the coming year as shown in Table 11.1, a table known as a *payoff matrix*. Here we see that both projects will provide a $500 profit in a normal economy, higher profits in a boom economy, and lower profits if a recession occurs. Notice also that the profits from Project B vary far more widely under the different states of the economy than do the profits from Project A. In a normal economy both projects return $500 in profit. Should the economy be in a recession next year, Project A will still provide a $400 profit, substantially more than the $0 profit from Project B in a recession. On the other hand, if the economy is booming next year, Project B's profit will increase to $1,000, while profit for Project A will increase only moderately to $600.

How, then, is one to evaluate these alternatives? Project A is clearly more desirable if the economy is in a recession, while Project B is superior in a boom economy. (In a normal economy the projects offer the same profit potential and we would not favor one over the other.) To answer the question we need to know how likely it is that we will have a boom, a recession, or normal economic conditions. If we have probabilities for the occurrence of these events, we can develop a probability distribution of profits for the two projects and from these obtain measures of both the expected profits and the variability of profits. These measures enable us to evaluate the projects in terms of their expected profit and the risk that the profit will deviate from the expected value.

Table 11.1
Payoff Matrix for Projects A and B

State of the Economy	Profits	
	Project A	Project B
Recession	$400	$ 0
Normal	500	500
Boom	600	1,000

Table 11.2
Calculation of Expected Values

	State of the Economy (1)	Probability of This State Occurring (2)	Outcome if This State Occurs (3)	(4) = (2) × (3)
Project A	Recession	0.2	$ 400	$ 80
	Normal	0.6	500	300
	Boom	0.2	600	120
		1.0	Expected Profit A	$500
Project B	Recession	0.2	$ 0	$ 0
	Normal	0.6	500	300
	Boom	0.2	1,000	200
		1.0	Expected Profit B	$500

To continue the example, assume that economic forecasts indicate that, given current trends in economic indicators, the chances are 2 in 10 that a recession will occur, 6 in 10 that the economy will be normal, and 2 in 10 that there will be a boom. Redefining *chances* as *probability*, we find that the probability of a recession is 0.2, or 20 percent; the probability of normal economic activity is 0.6, or 60 percent; and the probability of a boom is 0.2, or 20 percent. Notice that the probabilities add up to 1.0, or 100 percent: 0.2 + 0.6 + 0.2 = 1.0, or 100 percent. These probabilities have been added to the payoff matrix in Table 11.1 to provide the probability distributions of profit for Projects A and B shown in Table 11.2.

If we multiply each possible outcome by its probability of occurrence and then add these products, we have a weighted average of the outcomes. The weights are the probabilities of occurrence, and the weighted average is defined as the *expected outcome*. Column 4 of Table 11.2 illustrates the calculation of the expected profits for Projects A and B. We multiply each possible profit level (column 3) by its probability of occurrence (column 2) to obtain weighted values of the possible profits. When column 4 of the table is summed for each project, we obtain a weighted average of the profits under various states of the economy; this weighted average is defined as the *expected profit* from the project.[2]

The expected profit calculation can also be expressed by the equation:

$$\text{Expected Profit} = \bar{\pi} = \sum_{i=1}^{N} \pi_i \cdot p_i. \qquad (11.1)$$

---

[2]The weighted average or expected outcome need not be equal to the project's outcome for a normal state of the economy, although it is in this example.

Here π_i is the profit level associated with the ith outcome. p_i is the probability that outcome i will occur, and N is the number of possible outcomes or states of nature. Thus, $\bar{\pi}$ is a weighted average of the possible outcomes (the π_i values), with each outcome's weight being equal to its probability of occurrence.

Using the data for Project A we obtain its expected profit as follows:

$$\bar{\pi}_A = \sum_{i=1}^{3} \pi_i \cdot p_i$$

$$= \pi_1 \cdot p_1 + \pi_2 \cdot p_2 + \pi_3 \cdot p_3$$

$$= \$400(0.2) + \$500(0.6) + \$600(0.2)$$

$$= \$500.$$

We can graph the results shown in Table 11.2 to obtain a picture of the variability of actual outcomes; this is shown as a bar chart in Figure 11.1. The height of each bar signifies the probability that a given outcome will occur. The range of probable outcomes for Project A is from $400 to $600, with an average, or *expected value*, of $500. The expected value for Project B is also $500, but the range of possible outcomes is from $0 to $1,000.

Thus far we have assumed that only three states of the economy can exist: recession, normal, and boom. Actually, the state of the economy could range from a deep depression, as in the early 1930s, to a tremendous boom, with an unlimited number of possibilities in between. Suppose we had the time and the information to assign a probability to each possible state of the economy (with the sum of the probabilities still equaling 1.0) and to assign a monetary outcome to each project for each state of the economy. We would have a table similar to Table 11.2 except that it would have many more entries for "state of the economy," "probability," and "outcome if this state occurs." This table could be used to calculate expected values as shown, and the probabilities and outcomes could be approximated by the continuous curves in Figure 11.2.

Figure 11.2 is a graph of the *probability distribution of returns* on Projects A and B. In general, the tighter the probability distribution, the more likely that the actual outcome will be close to the expected value, or equivalently, the less likely it is that deviations of the actual outcome from the expected value will be large. Since Project A has a relatively tight probability distribution, its *actual* profit is likely to be closer to the *expected* $500 than is that of Project B.

Figure 11.1
Relationship between State of the Economy and Project Returns

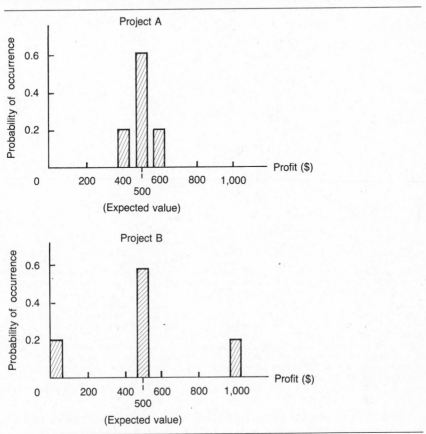

Measuring Risk

Risk is a complex concept and a great deal of controversy has surrounded attempts to define and measure it. However, a common definition and one that is satisfactory for many purposes is stated in terms of probability distributions such as those presented in Figure 11.2. This notion of risk is conveyed by the observation that *the tighter the probability distribution of possible outcomes, the smaller the risk of a given decision,* since there is a lower probability that the actual outcome will deviate significantly from the expected value. According to this definition, Project A is less risky than Project B.

To be most useful, our measure of risk should have some definite value—we need a *measure* of the tightness of the probability distribu-

Figure 11.2
Probability Distributions Showing Relationship between
State of the Economy and Project Returns

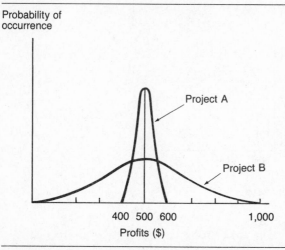

Probability of
occurrence

Profits ($)

Note: The assumptions regarding the probabilities of various outcomes have been changed from those in Figure 11.1. We no longer assume there is a zero probability that Project A will yield less than $400 or more than $600 and that Project B will yield less than $0 or more than $1,000. Rather, we have constructed normal distributions centered at $500 with approximately the same variability of outcome as indicated in Figure 11.1. While the probability of obtaining *exactly* $500 was 60 percent in Figure 11.1, in Figure 11.2 it is *much smaller*, because here there are an infinite number of possible outcomes, instead of just three. With continuous distributions, as in Figure 11.2, it is generally more appropriate to ask what is the cumulative probability of obtaining *at least* some specified value than to ask what the probability is of obtaining exactly that value. (Indeed, with a continuous distribution, the probability of occurrence for any single value is zero.) This cumulative probability is equal to the area under the probability distribution curve up to the point of interest.

tion. One such measure is the **standard deviation**, the symbol for which is σ, read *sigma*. The smaller the standard deviation, the tighter the probability distribution and, accordingly, the lower the riskiness of the alternative.[3] To calculate the standard deviation, we proceed as follows:

1. Calculate the **expected value** or mean of the distribution:

$$\text{Expected Value} = \bar{\pi} = \sum_{i=1}^{n} (\pi_i p_i). \tag{11.2}$$

---

[3]Since we define risk in terms of the chance of an undesirable outcome, it would seem logical to measure risk in terms of the probability of losses, or at least of returns below the expected return, rather than by the entire distribution. Measures of below-expected returns, which are known as semivariance measures, have been developed, but they are difficult to analyze. In addition, such measures are unnecessary if the distribution of future returns is reasonably symmetric about the expected return. For many managerial problems this assumption of symmetry is reasonable, and thus we can use total variability to measure risk.

Here π is the profit or return associated with the ith outcome; p_i is the probability the ith outcome will occur; and $\bar{\pi}$, the expected value, is a weighted average of the various possible outcomes, each weighted by the probability of its occurrence.

2. Subtract the expected value from each possible outcome to obtain a set of deviations about the expected value:

$$\text{Deviation}_i = \pi_i - \bar{\pi}.$$

3. Square each deviation; multiply the squared deviation by the probability of occurrence for its related outcome; and sum these products. This arithmetic mean of the squared deviations is the variance of the probability distribution:

$$\text{Variance} = \sigma^2 = \sum_{i=1}^{n} (\pi_i - \bar{\pi})^2 p_i. \tag{11.3}$$

4. The standard deviation is found by obtaining the square root of the variance:

$$\text{Standard Deviation} = \sigma = \sqrt{\sum_{i=1}^{n} (\pi_i - \bar{\pi})^2 p_i}. \tag{11.4}$$

The calculation of the standard deviation of profit for Project A illustrates this procedure. (The calculation of the expected profit was shown previously and is therefore not repeated.)

Deviation $(\pi_i - \bar{\pi})$	Deviation^2 $(\pi_i - \bar{\pi})^2$	Deviation^2 × Probability $(\pi_i - \bar{\pi})^2 \cdot p_i$
$400 − $500 = −$100	$10,000	$10,000(0.2) = $2,000
$500 − $500 = 0	0	0(0.6) = 0
$600 − $500 = $100	$10,000	$10,000(0.2) = $2,000
		Variance = σ^2 = $4,000

Standard deviation = $\sigma = \sqrt{\sigma^2} = \sqrt{\$4,000} = \$63.25.$

Using the same procedure we can calculate the standard deviation of Project B's profit as $316.23. Since Project B's standard deviation is larger, it is the riskier project.

This relationship between risk and the standard deviation can be clarified by examining the characteristics of a normal distribution as shown in Figure 11.3. If a probability distribution is normal, the actual outcome will lie within ±1 standard deviation of the mean or expected

Figure 11.3
Probability Ranges for a Normal Distribution

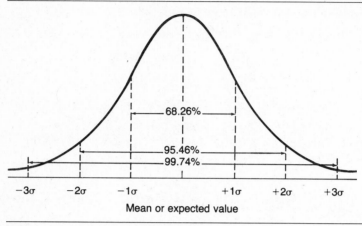

Mean or expected value

Notes:

a. The area under the normal curve equals 1.0 or 100 percent. Thus, the areas under any pair of normal curves drawn on the same scale, whether they are peaked or flat, must be equal.

b. Half the area under a normal curve is to the left of the mean, indicating that there is a 50 percent probability that the actual outcome will be less than the mean and a 50 percent probability that it will be greater than the mean.

c. Of the area under the curve, 68.26 percent is within $\pm 1\sigma$ of the mean, indicating that the odds are 68.26 percent that the actual outcome will be within the range mean -1σ to mean $+1\sigma$.

d. For a normal distribution, the larger the value of σ, the greater the probability that the actual outcome will vary widely from and hence perhaps be far below the most likely outcome. Since the odds on having the actual results turn out to be bad is our definition of risk, and since σ measures these odds, we can use σ as a measure of risk.

value about 68 percent of the time. That is, there is a 68 percent probability that the actual outcome will lie in the range "Expected Outcome $\pm 1\sigma$." Similarly, the probability that the actual outcome will be within two standard deviations of the expected outcome is approximately 95 percent, and there is a better than 99 percent probability that the actual event will occur in the range of three standard deviations about the mean of the distribution. Thus, the smaller the standard deviation, the tighter the distribution about the expected value and the smaller the probability or risk of an outcome that is very far below the mean or expected value of the distribution.

We should note that problems can arise when the standard deviation is used as the measure of risk. Specifically, in an investment problem, if one project is larger than another—that is, if it has a larger cost and larger expected cash flows—it will normally have a larger standard deviation without necessarily being more risky. For example, if a project has expected returns of $1 million and a standard deviation of only $1,000, it is certainly less risky than a project with expected returns of \$1,000 and a standard deviation of \$500, the reason being that the *relative* variation for the larger project is much smaller.

One way of eliminating this problem is to calculate a measure of relative risk, by dividing the standard deviation by the mean expectation, or expected value, $\bar{\pi}$, to obtain the *coefficient of variation*:

$$\text{Coefficient of Variation} = \nu = \frac{\sigma}{\bar{\pi}}. \qquad (11.5)$$

In general, when comparing decision alternatives whose costs and benefits are not of approximately equal size, the coefficient of variation provides better measure of relative risk than does the standard deviation.[4]

Utility Theory and Risk Aversion

The assumption of risk aversion is basic to many decision models used in managerial economics. Because this assumption is so crucial, it is appropriate to examine attitudes toward risk and discuss why risk aversion holds in general.

In theory, we can identify three possible attitudes toward risk: a desire for risk, an aversion to risk, and an indifference to risk. A *risk seeker* is one who prefers risk. Given a choice between more and less risky investments, with identical expected monetary returns, the *risk seeker* will select the riskier investment. Faced with the same choice, the *risk averter* will select the less risky investment. The person who is *indifferent to risk* will be indifferent between two investment projects with identical expected monetary returns regardless of their relative risks. *There undoubtedly are some who prefer risk and others who are indifferent to*

---

[4]Risk is defined here in terms of both the standard deviation and the coefficient of variation based on the *total* variability of a project's outcomes or returns. There are situations, however, when a project's total variability overstates its risk. This is because projects whose returns are less than perfectly correlated with each other can be combined and the variability of the resulting combination, or "portfolio," will be less than the sum of the individual variabilities. Much of the recent work in finance is based on the idea that a project's risk should be measured in terms of its contribution to total return variability on a portfolio of assets. This contribution to overall variation is measured by a concept known as *beta*, which is related to the systematic variability or covariance of one asset's return with returns on other assets. This risk concept, like the two discussed, is based on the variability of returns, and for our purposes it is not necessary that we examine the alternative constructs more closely. The interested reader should consult a basic finance textbook such as E. F. Brigham, *Financial Management*, 3d ed. (Hinsdale, Ill.: The Dryden Press, 1982), Chapter 5 for a more detailed discussion of these alternative risk concepts.

Figure 11.4
Relationships between Money and Its Utility

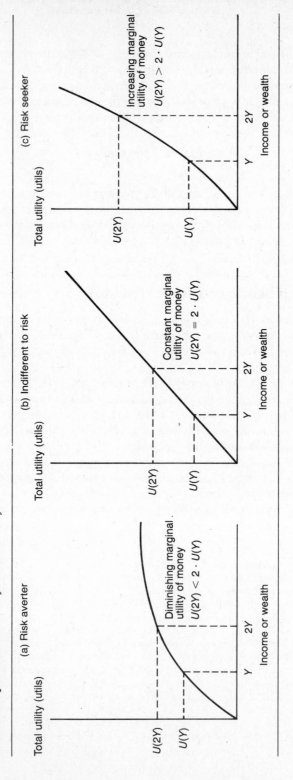

it, but both logic and observation suggest that business managers and investors are predominantly risk averters.

Why should risk aversion generally hold? Given two alternatives, each with the same expected dollar returns, why do most decision makers prefer the less risky one? Several theories have been proposed to answer this question, but perhaps the most logically satisfying one involves *utility theory*.

At the heart of risk aversion is the notion of **diminishing marginal utility** for money. If an individual with no money receives $1,000, it can satisfy his or her most immediate needs. If a second $1,000 is then received, it can be used, but the second $1,000 is not quite so necessary as the first $1,000. Thus, the value, or **utility**, of the second, or *marginal*, $1,000 is less than the utility of the first $1,000, and so on for additional increments of money. We therefore say that the marginal utility of money is diminishing.

Figure 11.4 graphs the relationship between money and its utility, or value, where utility is measured in units called *utils*. This measure of value or satisfaction is an index which is unique to each individual, and thus, the actual numerical values for utils have little interpretive value. Nonetheless, the concept is very important for understanding economic behavior.

Curve 11.4a describes the relationship between utility and money for a risk averter. Here a diminishing marginal utility of money is evident. This means that if the individual's money were to double suddenly, he or she would experience an increase in utility (happiness, or satisfaction) but the new level of total utility would not be twice the previous level. That is, in cases of diminishing marginal utility of money, there is a less than proportional relationship between total utility and money. Accordingly, the utility of a doubled quantity of money is less than twice the utility of the original level. By way of contrast, for those who are indifferent to risk there is a strictly proportional relationship between total utility and money. Such a relationship implies a constant marginal utility of money as illustrated in Figure 11.4b. In cases of a constant marginal utility of money, the utility of a doubled quantity of money is exactly twice the utility of the original level. And finally, for risk seekers there is a more than proportional relationship between total utility and money. In this case the marginal utility of money is increasing. As shown in Figure 11.4c, with increasing marginal utility of money, the utility of a doubling of money is more than twice the utility of the original amount.

Therefore, while total utility increases with increased money for risk averters, risk seekers, and those who are indifferent to risk, the relationship between total utility and money is quite different for each group. These differences lead directly to differences in risk attitudes. Because individuals with a diminishing marginal utility for money will

Figure 11.5
Relationship between Money and Its Utility

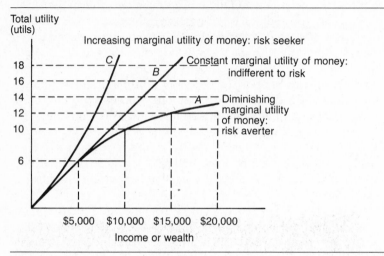

suffer more pain from a dollar lost than they will derive pleasure from a dollar gained, they will be very much opposed to risk. Thus, they will require a very high return on any investment that is subject to much risk. In Figure 11.5, for example, a gain of $5,000 from a base of $10,000 brings 2 utils of additional satisfaction; but a $5,000 loss causes a 4-util satisfaction loss. A person with this utility function and $10,000 would, therefore, be unwilling to make an investment with a 50-50 chance of winning or losing $5,000, the reason being that the 9-util expected utility of such a gamble [$E(u) = 0.5$ times the utility of $5,000 + 0.5$ times the utility of $15,000 = 0.5 \times 6 + 0.5 \times 12 = 9$] is less than the 10 units of utility obtained by forgoing the investment and keeping the $10,000 current wealth with certainty.[5]

A second example should clarify this relationship between utility and risk aversion. Assume that government bonds are riskless securities and that such bonds currently offer a 9 percent rate of return. If an individual buys a $10,000 U.S. Treasury bond and holds it for one year, he or she will end up with $10,900, a gain of $900.

---

[5]For a risk averter the expected utility of a gamble will always be less than the utility of the expected dollar payoff. Since an individual with a constant marginal utility for money will value a dollar gained just as highly as a dollar lost, the expected utility from a fair gamble such as the one offered here will always be exactly equal to the utility of the expected outcome. Because of this, an individual indifferent to risk can make decisions on the basis of expected monetary outcomes and need not be concerned with possible variation in the distribution of outcomes.

Suppose there is an alternative investment opportunity that calls for the $10,000 to back a wildcat oil-drilling venture. If the drilling venture is successful, the investment will be worth $20,000 at the end of the year. If it is unsuccessful, the investors can liquidate their holdings and recover $5,000. There is a 60 percent chance that oil will be discovered, and a 40 percent chance of a dry hole or no oil. If an investor has only $10,000 to invest, should the riskless government bond or the risky drilling operation be chosen?

To analyze this question let us first calculate the expected monetary values of the two investments; this is done in Table 11.3. The calculation in the table is not really necessary for the government bond; the $10,900 outcome will occur regardless of what happens in the oil field. The oil venture calculation, however, shows that the expected value of this venture—$15,000—is higher than that of the bond. Does this mean the investor should invest in the wildcat well? Not necessarily; it depends on the investor's utility function. If an investor's marginal utility for money is sharply diminishing, then the potential loss of utility from a dry hole might not be compensated for by the potential gain in utility from a producing well. If the risk averter utility function shown in Figure 11.5 is applicable, this is precisely the case. Four utils will be lost if no oil is found, and only three will be gained if the well becomes a producer.

Let us modify the expected monetary value calculation to reflect utility considerations. Reading from Figure 11.5, we see that this particular risk averse investor will have 13 utils if he or she invests in the wildcat venture and oil is found and 6 utils if no oil is found. The investor will have 10.7 utils with certainty by choosing the government bond. This information is used in Table 11.4 to calculate the *expected utility* for the oil investment. No calculation is needed for the government bond; its utility is 10.7 (read from Figure 11.5), regardless of the outcome of the oil venture.

Since the expected utility from the wildcat venture is only 10.2 utils, versus 10.7 from the government bond, we see that the government

Table 11.3
Expected Returns from Two Projects

State of Nature	Drilling Operation			Government Bond		
	Probability (1)	Outcome (2)	(1) × (2) (3)	Probability (1)	Outcome (2)	(3) = (1) × (2)
Oil	0.6	$20,000	$12,000	0.6	$10,900	$ 6,540
No oil	0.4	5,000	2,000	0.4	10,900	4,360
		Expected value	$14,000		Expected value	$10,900

Table 11.4
Expected Utility of the Oil-Drilling Project

State of Nature	Probability (1)	Monetary Outcome (2)	Associated Utility (3)	(4) = (1) × (3)
Oil	0.6	$20,000	13.0	7.8
No oil	0.4	5,000	6.0	2.4
			Expected Utility	10.2

bond is the preferred investment. Thus, even though the expected *monetary value* for the oil venture is higher, expected utility is greater for the bond; risk considerations dictate that the investor should buy the government bond.

Adjusting the Valuation Model for Risk

Diminishing marginal utility leads directly to risk aversion, and risk aversion is reflected in the valuation model used by investors to determine the worth of a firm. Thus, if a firm takes an action that increases its risk level, this action affects its value. To illustrate, consider the basic valuation model developed in Chapter 1:

$$V = \sum_{t=1}^{n} \frac{\pi_t}{(1 + i)^t} . \qquad (11.6)$$

This model states that value is the discounted present worth of future profits or income. The stream of profits in the numerator, π, is really the expected value of the profits each year. If the firm must choose between two alternative methods of operation, one with high expected profits and high risk and another with smaller expected profits and lower risk, will the higher expected profits be sufficient to offset the higher risk? If so, the riskier alternative is the preferred one; if not, the low-risk procedure should be adopted.

Certainty Equivalent Adjustments

A number of methods have been proposed to account for risk in the valuation model. One of these, the **certainty equivalent** approach, follows directly from the concept of utility theory developed earlier. Under the certainty equivalent approach, decision makers must specify the amount of money that they would have to be assured of receiving to make them indifferent between this certain sum and the expected value of a risky alternative. To illustrate, suppose you face the following alternatives:

1. Invest $100,000. If the project is successful, you receive $1 million; if it is a failure you receive nothing, i.e., the $100,000 is lost. If the probability of success is 0.5 or 50 percent, the expected payoff of the investment is $500,000 (= 0.5 × $1,000,000 + 0.5 × 0).

2. You do not make the investment, and you retain the $100,000.

If you find yourself indifferent between the two alternatives, $100,000 is your certainty equivalent for the risky $500,000 expected return. In other words, the certain or riskless amount provides exactly the same utility as the risky alternative and, therefore, you are indifferent between them. In this example, a high degree of risk aversion is demonstrated. Indeed, any certainty equivalent less than $500,000 indicates risk aversion. That is, if the maximum amount you would be willing to invest in the first alternative is less than $500,000, you are exhibiting risk averse behavior. In general, any risky investment with a certainty equivalent less than the expected dollar value indicates risk aversion. A certainty equivalent equal to the expected value indicates risk indifference. And finally a certainty equivalent greater than the expected value indicates risk preference. Therefore, an individual's attitude toward risk is directly reflected in the certainty equivalent adjustment factor, calculated as the ratio of the equivalent certain dollar sum (i.e., the certain sum whose utility is equal to the expected utility of the risky alternative) divided by the expected dollar outcome from the risky alternative:

$$\alpha = \frac{\text{Equivalent Certain Sum}}{\text{Expected Risky Sum}} .$$

The following relationships enable one to use the certainty equivalent adjustment factor to analyze risk attitudes:

$$\alpha < 1 \text{ implies risk aversion,}$$

$$\alpha = 1 \text{ implies risk indifference,}$$

$$\text{and } \alpha > 1 \text{ implies risk preference.}$$

The certainty equivalent concept is illustrated in Figures 11.6 and 11.7. Figure 11.6 shows a series of risk-return combinations to which the decision maker is indifferent. For example, Point A represents an investment with a perceived degree of risk ν_A and expected dollar re-

Figure 11.6
Certainty Equivalent Returns

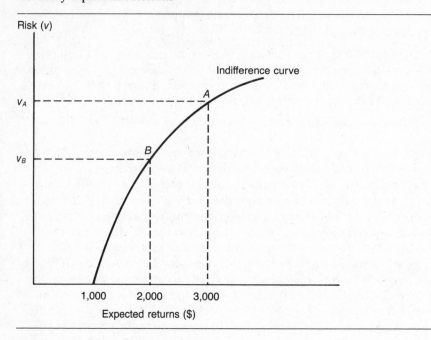

Risk (v)

v_A ----------------------- A

Indifference curve

v_B ------------- B

1,000   2,000   3,000

Expected returns ($)

Figure 11.7
Hypothetical Risk-Aversion Function

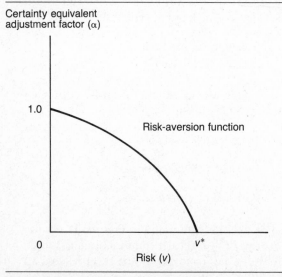

Certainty equivalent
adjustment factor (α)

1.0

Risk-aversion function

0   v^*

Risk (v)

Note: As we have drawn it, the risk-aversion function assumes that $\alpha = 0$ when $v \geq v^*$. Theoretically, α would never actually reach zero; rather, it would approach zero when risk becomes quite high.

turn of $3,000. The risk-return trade-off function or indifference curve shows a person who is indifferent to a certain $1,000, an expected $2,000 with risk v_B, and an expected $3,000 with risk v_A.

The indifference curve shown in Figure 11.6 can be used to construct a risk-aversion function such as the one illustrated in Figure 11.7. This conversion is obtained by dividing each risky return into its certainty equivalent return to obtain a certainty equivalent adjustment factor, α, for each level of risk, v. For example, the certainty equivalent adjustment factor for risk level v_A is:

$$\alpha_A = \frac{\$1,000}{\$3,000} = 0.33.$$

For risk level v_B we have:

$$\alpha_B = \frac{\$1,000}{\$2,000} = 0.50.$$

Conceptually, α values could be developed for all possible levels of v (risk). The range of α would be from 1.0 for $v = 0$ to a value close to 0 for large values of v, assuming risk aversion.

Given the risk-aversion function and the degree of risk inherent in any risky return, the expected risky return could be replaced by its certainty equivalent:

Certainty Equivalent of $\bar{\pi}_t = \alpha\bar{\pi}_t$,

and Equation 11.6 could then be converted to Equation 11.7, a valuation model that explicitly accounts for risk:

$$V = \sum_{t=1}^{n} \frac{\alpha\bar{\pi}_t}{(1 + i)^t}. \tag{11.7}$$

Here expected future profits, $\bar{\pi}_t$, are converted to their certainty equivalents, $\alpha\bar{\pi}_t$, and are discounted at a risk free rate, i, to obtain the present value of a firm or project. With the valuation model in this form, one can appraise the effects of different courses of action with different risks and expected returns.

In order to use Equation 11.7 for real-world decision making, managers must obtain estimates of appropriate α's for various investment opportunities. Deriving such estimates can prove formidable, since α levels vary according to the size and riskiness of investment projects, as well as to the risk attitudes of managers and investors. In many instances, however, the record of past investments can be used as a guide to determine appropriate certainty equivalent adjustment factors.

Use of Certainty Equivalent Adjustments: An Illustration

The following example illustrates how managers use certainty equivalent adjustment factors for decision making. Fitness World Inc. (FWI) has recently opened a number of health clubs in small- to medium-sized midwestern cities. These clubs have been successful in generating attractive rates of return relative to the levels of risk undertaken. FWI managers believe that three health clubs in Ames, Iowa, Bloomington, Indiana, and Columbus, Ohio, are very close to the cutoff point in terms of their acceptability; therefore, they can be used to gain insight into management's risk attitude.

In deciding whether or not to establish these clubs, labeled A, B, and C for simplicity, FWI used the information contained in Table 11.5. In the table we see that the expected profit contribution increases from Project A to B to C. The fact that FWI was only willing to invest some-

Table 11.5

FWI Illustration: Calculation of Certainty Equivalent Adjustment Factors

Outcome (1)	Profit Contribution (2)	Probability (3)	Expected Profit Contribution (Risky Sum) (4)	Annual Investment Cost (Certain Sum) (5)	Coefficient of Variation (6)
Project A					
Failure	$ 90,000	.5	$115,000	$100,000	.217
Success	140,000	.5			

$$\alpha_A = \frac{\$100,000}{\$115,000} = 0.87$$

Project B					
Failure	130,000	.5	175,000	150,000	.257
Success	220,000	.5			

$$\alpha_B = \frac{\$150,000}{\$175,000} = 0.86$$

Project C					
Failure	200,000	.5	275,000	225,000	.273
Success	350,000	.5			

$$\alpha_C = \frac{\$225,000}{\$275,000} = 0.82$$

Note: A project's profit contribution is calculated as total revenues minus total variable costs. To simplify the analysis, we assume that the annual investment cost includes the return required for the use of the funds as measured by the yield available on a riskless security. For example, the $100,000 annual investment cost for Project A is found as the actual investment cost of $90,900 times 1.10 to account for the 10% yield then available on riskless U.S. Treasury bills.

thing less than the level of expected profit contribution for each project suggests that the managers were averse to risk. Examination of the implied certainty equivalent adjustment factors for each project provides further insight into FWI management's risk aversion.

Since FWI management viewed each project as just acceptable, the required investment outlay can be viewed as the certainty equivalent of the project's expected risky return. That is, management was just willing to exchange a certain sum (the annual investment) for a distribution of risky returns (the project) with a given expected return and level of risk. Thus, dividing the investment amount by the expected risky return provides a measure of the implied certainty equivalent adjustment factor, α, for each project. As shown in Table 11.5, α for Project A is 0.87. If FWI's management focuses on the coefficient of variation, ν, for risk considerations, this means that with $\nu = 0.217$, the firm has used (either explicitly or implicitly) a certainty equivalent adjustment factor, $\alpha = 0.87$. Alternatively stated $\alpha_A = 0.87$ means that FWI viewed $0.87 as the certainty equivalent of $1 of expected return on Project A and was willing to pay that amount for each expected risky dollar. Based on the data for Projects B and C, we see that with $\nu_B = 0.257$, $\alpha_B = 0.86$ and with $\nu_C = 0.273$, $\alpha_C = 0.82$. That is, the implicit α's for Projects B and C provide additional measures of the certainty equivalent adjustment factors FWI assigns to various risk levels. Using these observations as well as similar ones for other accepted projects, we could construct for FWI a risk-aversion function of the type shown in Figure 11.7.

This analysis of historical investment decisions provides information that we can use to make future investment decisions. For example, if we know a potential project's required investment and risk level, we can calculate the α implied by a decision to accept the investment, and we can compare it with α's for prior projects that had similar risks. Risk averse individuals should invest in projects if calculated α's are less than or equal to those for accepted historical projects that have the same risk. Further, given an estimate of expected return and risk, the maximum amount the firm should be willing to invest in a given project can also be determined by using the certainty equivalent adjustment factor. Here we can use the expected return and the α on prior projects with similar risk to calculate the maximum that the firm will invest in the project (certainty equivalent amount). Management will accept projects if the level of required investment per dollar of expected return is less than or equal to that for historical projects of similar risk.

Risk-Adjusted Discount Rates

Another way to incorporate risk in the valuation model is to adjust the discount rate, i. Like the certainty equivalent factor, **risk-adjusted discount rates** are based on investors' trade-off between risk and return. For example, suppose investors are willing to trade between risk and

Figure 11.8
Relationship between Risk and Rate of Return

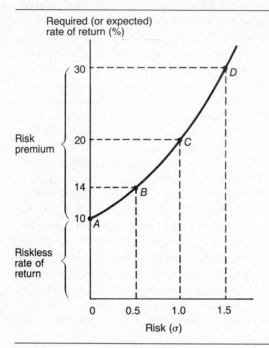

return, as shown in Figure 11.8. The curve is defined as a *market indif-*
ference curve or a *risk-return trade-off function.* The average investor is
indifferent to a riskless asset with a sure 10 percent rate of return, a moderately risky asset with a 20 percent expected return, and a very risky
asset with a 30 percent expected return. As risk increases, higher expected returns on investment are required to compensate investors for
the additional risk.

The difference between the expected rate of return on a particular
risky asset and the rate of return on a riskless asset is defined as the
risk premium on the risky asset. In the hypothetical situation depicted
in Figure 11.8 the riskless rate is assumed to be 10 percent; a 4 percent
risk premium is required to compensate for the level of risk indicated
by $\sigma = 0.5$; and a 20 percent risk premium is attached to an investment
with a risk of $\sigma = 1.5$.

Since required returns are related to the level of risk associated with
a particular investment, we can modify the basic valuation model, Equation 11.6, to account for risk through an adjustment of the discount rate,
i. Such a modification results in the valuation model:

$$V = \sum_{t=1}^{n} \frac{\bar{\pi}_t}{(1 + k)^t} .$$

(11.8)

In Equation 11.8, value is found as the present worth of expected future income or profits, $\overline{\pi}_t$, discounted at a risk-adjusted rate. The risk-adjusted discount rate, k, is determined as the sum of the riskless rate of return and the risk premium required as compensation for the level of risk accepted. Assuming that decision makers use the risk-return trade-off function shown in Figure 11.8, they would evaluate a firm or project with risk level $\sigma = 0.5$ by using a 14 percent discount rate, composed of a 10 percent riskless interest rate and a 4 percent risk premium. Similarly, a riskier project with $\sigma = 1.5$ would require a risk premium of 20 percent and, thus, would be evaluated by using a 30 percent discount rate (30 percent = 10 percent riskless rate + 20 percent risk premium).

Use of Risk-Adjusted Discount Rates: An Illustration

The following example illustrates the use of risk-adjusted discount rates for managerial decision making. Zebec Office Machines Inc. has to decide which of two mutually exclusive computer interfaces to manufacture. These interfaces allow an electronic typewriter to be connected to a computer as an input-output device. One interface is specifically designed for Zebec typewriters and cannot be used with those of other manufacturers; the other adapts to a wide variety of electronic typewriters, both Zebec's and those of competitors. The expected investment outlay for design, engineering, production setup, and so on is $600,000 for each alternative. Expected cash inflows are $220,000 a year for five years if the interface can be used only with Zebec typewriters (Project A) and $260,000 for five years if the interface can be used with a variety of electronic typewriters (Project B). Because of the captive market for Project A, however, the standard deviation of the expected annual returns from the project is only 1.0, while that of Project B is 1.5. In view of this risk differential, Zebec's management decides that Project A should be evaluated with a 20 percent cost of capital, while the appropriate cost of capital for Project B is 30 percent. Which project should be selected?

We can calculate the risk-adjusted value for each project as follows on page 468[6]:

---

[6]The terms

$$\sum_{t=1}^{5} \frac{1}{(1.20)^t} = 2.991$$

and

$$\sum_{t=1}^{5} \frac{1}{(1.30)^t} = 2.436$$

are defined as present value of an annuity interest factors. Appendix A at the end of the text explains how interest factors are calculated. Tables of interest factors for various interest rates and years (t values) are contained in Appendix B at the end of the text.

$$\text{Value}_A = \sum_{t=1}^{5} \frac{\$220,000}{(1.20)^t} - \$600,000$$

$$= \$220,000 \times \left(\sum_{t=1}^{5} \frac{1}{(1.20)^t} \right) - \$600,000$$

$$= \$220,000 \times 2.991 - \$600,000$$

$$= \$58,020.$$

$$\text{Value}_B = \sum_{t=1}^{5} \frac{\$260,000}{(1.30)^t} - \$600,000$$

$$= \$260,000 \times \left(\sum_{t=1}^{5} \frac{1}{(1.30)^t} \right) - \$600,000$$

$$= \$260,000 \times 2.436 - \$600,000$$

$$= \$33,360.$$

Because the risk-adjusted value of the safer Project A is larger than that for Project B, the firm should choose Project A. This choice maximizes the value of the firm.

Techniques for Decision Making under Uncertainty

In many decision situations, the data required for incorporating risk analysis into the decision process are not readily available in a usable form. In such cases *decision trees* and *computer simulation* help one to develop and organize risk data for decision making. We shall now examine these two decision-making techniques and the role that they play in decision making under conditions of uncertainty.

Decision Trees

Many important decisions are not made at one point in time but rather in stages. For example, a petroleum firm considering the possibility of expanding into agricultural chemicals might take the following steps:

1. Spend $100,000 to survey supply and demand conditions in the agricultural chemical industry.

Figure 11.9
Illustrative Decision Tree

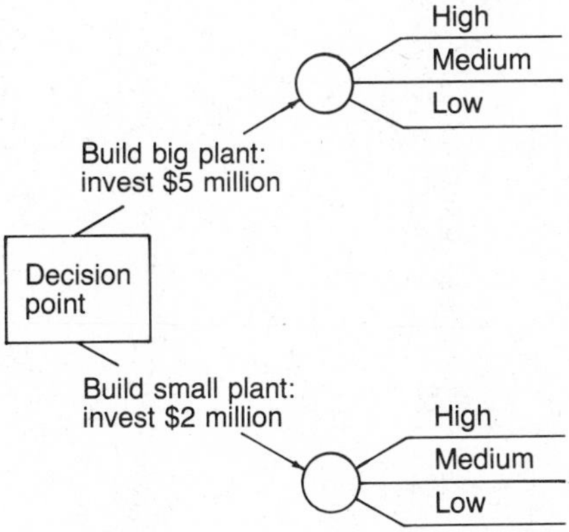

Action (1)	Demand conditions (2)	Probability (3)	Present value of cash flows[a] (4)	(5) = (3) × (4)
	High	0.5	$8,800,000	$4,400,000
	Medium	0.3	$3,500,000	1,050,000
	Low	0.2	$1,400,000	280,000
Build big plant: invest $5 million		Expected value of cash flows		5,730,000
		Cost		5,000,000
		Expected net present value		$ 730,000
Decision point				
Build small plant: invest $2 million	High	0.5	$2,600,000	$1,300,000
	Medium	0.3	$2,400,000	$ 720,000
	Low	0.2	$1,400,000	280,000
		Expected value of cash flows		$2,300,000
		Cost		2,000,000
		Expected net present value		$ 300,000

[a] The figures in column 4 are the annual cash flows from operation—revenues minus cash operating costs—discounted at the firm's cost of capital.

2. If the survey results are favorable, spend $2 million on a pilot plant to investigate production methods.

3. Depending on the costs estimated from the pilot study and the demand potential from the market study, either abandon the project, build a large plant, or build a small one.

Thus, decisions are actually made in stages with subsequent decisions depending on the results of prior decisions.

The sequence of events can be mapped out to resemble the branches of a tree, hence the term **decision tree**. As an example consider Figure 11.9, which assumes that the petroleum company has completed its industry supply and demand analysis and pilot plant study, and has determined that it should develop a full-scale production facility. The firm can build a large plant or a small one. Demand expectations for the plant's products are 50 percent for high demand, 30 percent for medium demand, and 20 percent for low demand. Depending on demand, net cash flows (sales revenues minus operating costs), all discounted to the present, will range from $8.8 million to $1.4 million if a large plant is built, and from $2.6 million to $1.4 million if a small plant is built.

Figure 11.10 Decision Tree with Multiple Decision Points

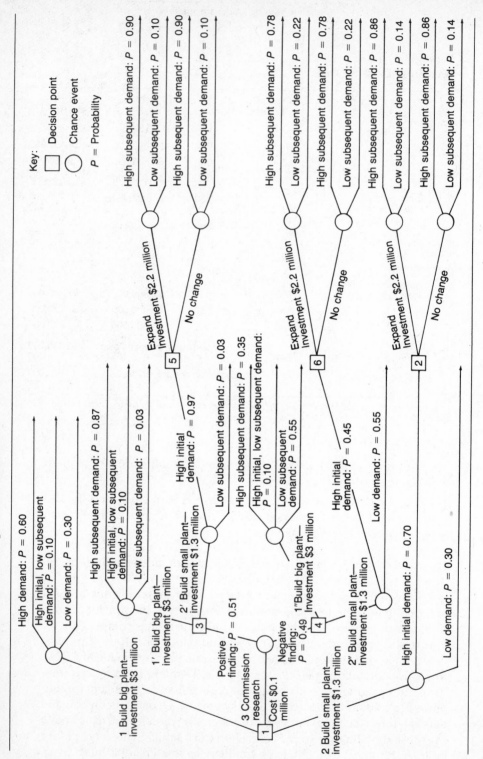

Since the demand probabilities are known, we can find the expected values of cash flows, which are given in column 5 of Figure 11.9. Finally, we can deduct the investment outlays from the expected net revenues to obtain the expected net present value of each decision. In the example, the expected net present value is $730,000 for the large plant and $300,000 for the small one.

Since the net present value of the large plant is higher, should the decision be to construct it? Perhaps, but not necessarily. Notice that the range of outcomes is greater if the large plant is built, with the actual net present values (column 4, present values, in Figure 11.9 minus the investment cost) varying from $3.8 million to *minus* $3.6 million. However, a range of only $600,000 to *minus* $600,000 exists for the small plant. Since the required investment for the two plants is not the same, we must examine the coefficients of variation of the net present value possibilities in order to determine which alternative actually entails the greater risk. The coefficient of variation for the large plant's present value is 4.3, while that for the small plant is only 1.5.[7] Risk is greater for building the large plant.

The decision maker could take account of the risk differentials in a variety of ways. Utility values could be assigned to the cash flows given in column 4 of Figure 11.9, thus stating column 5 in terms of expected utility. The plant size that provided the greatest expected utility could then be chosen. Alternatively, a manager could use the certainty equivalent or risk-adjusted discount rate methods in calculating the present values given in column 4. The plant that offered the larger risk-adjusted net present value would then be the optimal choice.

The decision tree illustrated in Figure 11.9 is quite simple; in actual use, the trees are frequently far more complex and involve a number of sequential decision points. An example of a more complex tree is illustrated in Figure 11.10. The numbered boxes represent *decision points*, instances when the management must choose among several alternatives; the circles represent the *chance events*, indicating outcomes that are possible following the decisions. At Decision Point 1, the firm has three choices: to invest $3 million in a large plant, to invest $1.3 million in a small plant, or to spend $100,000 on market research. If the large plant is built, the firm follows the upper branch, and its position has been fixed: it can only hope that demand will be high. If it builds the small plant, it follows the lower branch. If demand is low, no further action is required; if demand is high, Decision Point 2 is reached, and the firm can either do nothing or expand the plant at a cost of another

---

[7] Using Equation 11.4 and the data on possible returns in Figure 11.9, the standard deviation of return for the large plant is $3.155 million, and for the smaller is $458,260. Dividing each of these standard deviations by the expected returns for their respective plant size, as in Equation 11.5, gives the coefficient of variation.

$2.2 million. (Thus, if it obtains a large plant through expansion, the cost is $500,000 greater than if it had built the large plant in the first place.)

If the decision at Point 1 is to pay $100,000 for more information, the firm moves to the center branch. The research modifies the firm's information about potential demand. Initially, the probabilities were 70 percent for high demand and 30 percent for low demand. The research survey will show either favorable (positive) or unfavorable (negative) demand prospects. If they are positive, we assume that the probability for high final demand will be 87 percent, and that for low demand will be 13 percent; if the research yields negative results, the odds on high final demand are only 35 percent, and those for low demand are 65 percent. These results will influence the firm's decision whether to build a large plant or a small plant.

If the firm builds a large plant and demand is high, sales and profits will be large. If, however, it builds a large plant and there is little demand, sales will be low and they will incur losses. On the other hand, if it builds a small plant and demand is high, sales and profits will be lower than they could have been had a large plant been built, yet they will eliminate the chances of losses in the event of low demand. To build the large plant is therefore riskier than to build the small plant. The cost of the research is, in effect, an expenditure serving to reduce the degree of uncertainty in the decision; the research provides additional information on the probability of high versus low demand, thus reducing the level of risk.

The decision tree in Figure 11.10 is incomplete because no dollar outcomes (or utility values) are assigned to the various situations. If such values are assigned, along the lines shown in the last two columns of Figure 11.9, expected values can be obtained for each of the alternative actions along with measures of the possible variability of outcomes. These values will then help the decision maker to choose among the alternatives.

Simulation

Another technique designed to assist managers in making decisions under uncertainty is computer **simulation**. To illustrate the technique, let us consider the decision to build a new textile plant. The exact cost of the plant is not known. It is expected to be about $150 million. If no difficulties arise in construction, the cost can be as low as $125 million; however, an unfortunate series of events—strikes, unprojected increases in material costs, and technical problems—could result in an investment outlay as high as $225 million.

Revenues from the new facility, which will operate for many years, depend on population growth and personal income in the region, competition, developments in synthetic fabrics, research, and textile import quotas. Operating costs depend on production efficiency, materials, and labor cost trends. Because both sales revenues and operating costs are uncertain, annual profits are also uncertain.

Assuming that probability distributions can be developed for each of the major cost and revenue determinants, a computer program can be constructed to simulate what is likely to occur. In effect, the computer selects one value at random from each of the relevant distributions, combines it with values selected from the other distributions, and produces an estimated profit and net present value, or rate of return, on investment. This particular profit and rate of return occur only for the particular combination of values selected during the trial. The computer proceeds to select other sets of values and to compute other profits and rates of return for perhaps several hundred trials. A count is kept of the number of times each of the various rates of return is computed. When the computer runs are completed, the frequency with which the various rates of return occurred can be plotted as a frequency distribution.

The procedure is illustrated in Figures 11.11 and 11.12. Figure 11.11 is a flow chart outlining the simulation procedure described above; Figure 11.12 illustrates the frequency distribution of rates of return generated by such a simulation for two alternative projects, X and Y, each with an expected cost of $20 million. The expected rate of return on Investment X is 15 percent, and that of Investment Y is 20 percent. However, these are only the average rates of return generated by the computer; simulated rates ranged from -10 percent to $+45$ percent for Investment Y, and from 5 to 25 percent for Investment X. The standard deviation generated for X is only 4 percentage points; that for Y is 12 percentage points. From this we can calculate a coefficient of variation of 0.267 for Project X, and 0.60 for Project Y. On the basis of total variability, Investment Y is riskier than Investment X. The computer simulation has provided an estimate both of the expected returns on the two projects and of their relative risks. A decision about which alternative should be chosen can now be made on the basis of one of the techniques—certainty equivalent, or risk-adjusted discount rate, present value determination, or expected utility—discussed.

One final point should be made about the use of computer simulation for risk analysis. The technique requires obtaining probability distributions about a number of variables such as investment outlays, unit sales, product prices, input prices, and asset lives, all of which involve a fair amount of programming and machine-time costs. Full-scale simulation is expensive and therefore used primarily for large and expensive projects such as major plant expansions or new-product decisions. In these cases, however, when a firm is deciding whether or not to accept a major undertaking involving an outlay of millions of dollars, com-

Figure 11.11
Simulation for Investment Planning

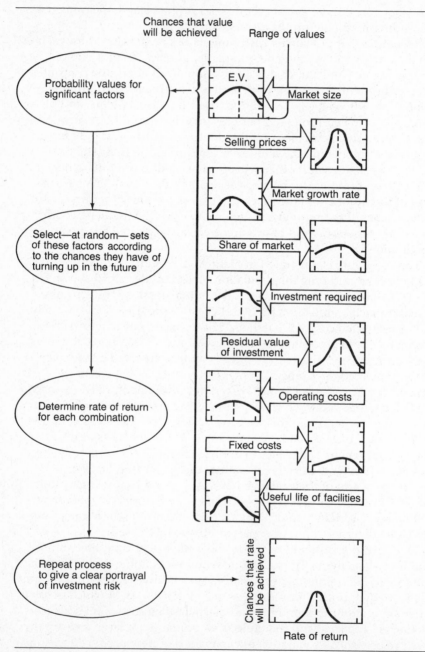

Figure 11.12
Expected Rates of Return on Investments *X* and *Y*

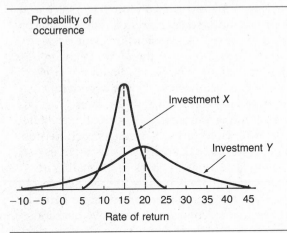

puter simulation can provide valuable insights into the relative merits of alternate strategies.

It should also be noted that a somewhat less expensive simulation technique is available as an alternative method of analyzing the outcomes of various projects or strategies. Instead of using probability distributions for each of the variables in the problem, we can simulate the results by starting with best-guess estimates for each variable and then change the values of the variables (within reasonable limits) to see the effects of such changes on the returns generated by the project. Typically, returns are highly sensitive to some variables, less so to others. Attention is then concentrated on the variables to which profitability is most sensitive. This technique, known as sensitivity analysis, is considerably less expensive than the full-scale simulation and provides similar data for decision-making purposes.

Summary

Risk analysis plays an integral role in the decision process for most business problems. In this chapter we defined the concept of risk, introduced it into the valuation model for the firm, and then examined several techniques for decision making under conditions of uncertainty.

Risk in economic analysis is characterized by variability of outcomes, and it is defined in terms of probability distributions of possible results. The tighter the distribution, the lower the variability, and hence the lower the risk. The standard deviation and coefficient of variation are two frequently used measures of risk in economic analysis.

The assumption of risk aversion by investors and managers is based on utility relationships. For most individuals, marginal utility is sharply diminishing, and this leads directly to risk aversion. Investor risk aversion affects the valuation of the firm and must, therefore, be taken into account for managerial decision making. The basic valuation model can be adjusted to reflect this risk effect through the use of certainty equivalent adjustment factors and risk-adjusted discount rates.

Decision making under conditions of uncertainty is greatly facilitated by decision trees and simulation, two techniques used to structure problems and to generate data necessary for risk analysis. Decision trees map out the sequence of events in a decision problem, providing a means for examining the branching that takes place at each decision point and chance event. Simulation techniques can be used to generate frequency distributions of possible outcomes for alternative decisions and to provide inputs for expected utility, certainty equivalent, or risk-adjusted discount rate analysis.

Questions

11.1 Define the following terms, using graphs to illustrate your answers where feasible:
   a. Probability distribution
   b. Expected value
   c. Standard deviation
   d. Coefficient of variation
   e. Risk
   f. Diminishing marginal utility
   g. Certainty equivalent
   h. Risk-adjusted discount rate
   i. Decision tree
   j. Simulation

11.2 Graphically describe three common attitudes toward money, and mention how each would be consistent with a particular attitude toward risk.

11.3 What is the main difficulty associated with making decisions on the basis of comparisons between expected monetary values of alternative courses of action?

11.4 In this chapter we have defined risk in terms of the variability of possible outcomes, that is, the standard deviation of these outcomes. In constructing this measure of risk, we have implicitly given equal weight to variations on both sides of the expected value. Can you see any problems resulting from this treatment?

11.5 "On reflection, the use of the market indifference curve concept illustrated in Figure 11.8 as a basis for determining risk-adjusted discount rates is all right in theory, but cannot be applied in practice. Market estimates of investors' reactions to risk cannot be measured precisely, so it is impossible to construct a set of risk-adjusted discount rates for the different classes of investment." Comment on this statement.

11.6 Are risk levels of investment alternatives irrelevant to the risk neutral investor?

11.7 What is the value of decision trees in managerial decision making?

Solved Problem

11.1 Jereco Computer has just completed development work on a new line of personal computers. Preliminary market research indicates two feasible marketing strategies: (a) concentration on developing general consumer acceptance by advertising through newspapers, television, and other media; or (b) concentration on distributor acceptance of the computer system through intensive sales calls by company representatives, extensive development of software support (user programs), and so forth. The marketing manager has developed estimates for sales under each alternative plan and has constructed payoff matrices based on an assessment of the likelihood of product acceptance under each plan. These matrices are illustrated below:

Strategy 1: Consumer-Oriented Promotion		Strategy 2: Distributor-Oriented Promotion	
Probability	Outcome (Sales)	Probability	Outcome (Sales)
0.1	$ 500,000	0.3	$1,000,000
0.4	1,500,000	0.4	1,500,000
0.4	2,500,000	0.3	2,000,000
0.1	3,500,000		

a) Assume that the company has a 50 percent profit margin on sales; that is, profits are equal to one-half of sales revenues. Calculate the expected profits for each plan.

b) Construct a simple bar graph of the possible profit outcomes for each plan. On the basis of the appearance of the two graphs, which plan appears to be more risky?

c) Calculate the risk (standard deviation of the profit distribution) associated with each plan.

d) Assume that the management of Jereco has a utility function like the one illustrated below. Which marketing strategy should the marketing manager recommend?

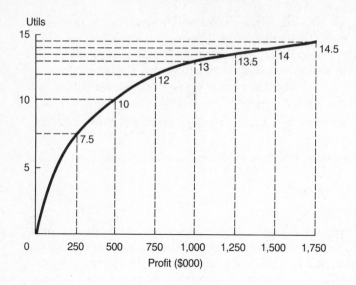

Solution

a)

Strategy 1: Consumer-Oriented Promotion

Probability (1)	Outcomes (Sales) (2)	Profit (3) = (2) × .5	(4) = (3) × (1)
0.1	$ 500,000	$ 250,000	$ 25,000
0.4	1,500,000	750,000	300,000
0.4	2,500,000	1,250,000	500,000
0.1	3,500,000	1,750,000	175,000
1.0			$\overline{\pi}$ = $1,000,000

Strategy 2: Distributor-Oriented Promotion

Probability (1)	Outcomes (Sales) (2)	Profit (3) = (2) × .5	(4) = (3) × (1)
0.3	$1,000,000	$ 500,000	$150,000
0.4	1,500,000	750,000	300,000
0.3	2,000,000	1,000,000	300,000
1.0			$\overline{\pi}$ = $750,000

b)

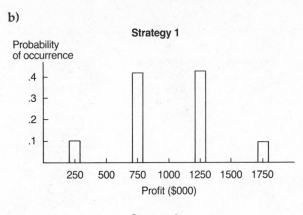

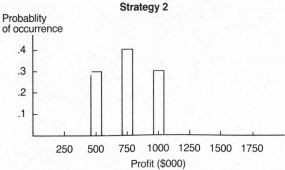

Strategy 1 appears more risky than strategy 2 because of the greater variability of possible outcomes.

c)

Strategy 1

Probability (1)	Deviations (2)	(Deviations)^2 (3)	(4) = (1) × (3)
0.1	−750,000	5.625×10^{11}	5.625×10^{10}
0.4	−250,000	6.250×10^{10}	2.5×10^{10}
0.4	250,000	6.250×10^{10}	2.5×10^{10}
0.1	750,000	5.625×10^{11}	5.625×10^{10}
			$\sigma^2 = 16.25 \times 10^{10}$

$$\text{Standard Deviation} = \sigma = \sqrt{\sigma^2} = \sqrt{16.25 \times 10^{10}}$$
$$= 4.0311 \times 10^5 = \$403{,}110.$$

$$V = \frac{\sigma}{\overline{\pi}} = \frac{\$403{,}110}{\$1{,}000{,}000} = 0.403.$$

Strategy 2

Probability (1)	Deviations (2)	(Deviations)² (3)	(4) = (1) × (3)
0.3	−250,000	6.25×10^{10}	1.875×10^{10}
0.4	0	0	0
0.3	250,000	6.25×10^{10}	1.875×10^{10}
			$\sigma^2 = 3.75 \times 10^{10}$

$$\text{Standard Deviation} = \sigma = \sqrt{\sigma^2} = \sqrt{3.75 \times 10^{10}}$$
$$= 1.9365 \times 10^5 = \$193,650.$$

$$V = \frac{\sigma}{\pi} = \frac{\$193,650}{\$750,000} = 0.258.$$

These calculations make more precise the conclusions reached in part b, i.e., that Strategy 1 is the more risky marketing approach.

d)

Strategy 1

Probability (1)	Profits (2)	Utils (3)	(4) = (3) × (1)
0.1	$ 250,000	7.50	0.75
0.4	750,000	12.00	4.80
0.4	1,250,000	13.50	5.40
0.1	1,750,000	14.50	1.45
1.0		Expected Utility = 12.40	

Strategy 2

Probability (1)	Profits (2)	Utils (3)	(4) = (3) × (1)
0.3	$ 500,000	10	3.0
0.4	750,000	12	4.8
0.3	1,000,000	13	3.9
1.0		Expected Utility = 11.7	

The marketing manager should recommend Strategy 1 because of its higher expected utility. In this instance, the higher expected profit of Strategy 1 more than offsets its greater riskiness.

Solved Problem

11.2 Sport Dynamics Inc. is currently engaged in the production of racketball rackets. An obsolete assembly machine is to be replaced by one of two innovative pieces of equipment. The following cost savings (cash flows) will be generated over the four-year useful lives of the new machines.

	Probability	Cash Flow
Alternative 1	.30	$2,900
	.50	3,500
	.20	4,100
Alternative 2	.30	$ 0
	.50	4,000
	.20	8,000

Whichever piece of equipment is chosen, the total cost will be the same, $4,000. Given that the firm will use a discount rate of 12 percent for the cash flows with a higher degree of dispersion and a 10 percent rate for the less risky cash flows, which machine has the higher expected net present value?

Solution

Expected Values of Cash Flows

	Probability	Cash Flow	Probable Cash Flow
Alternative 1	.3	$2,900	$ 870
	.5	3,500	1,750
	.2	4,100	820
		Expected cash flow	$3,440
Alternative 2	.3	$ 0	$ 0
	.5	4,000	2,000
	.2	8,000	1,600
		Expected cash flow	$3,600

Alternative 2 is riskier because it has the greater variability in its probable cash flows. This is obvious from the inspection of the distributions
of possible returns and could be verified by calculating the standard
deviations of them. Hence, Alternative 2 is evaluated at the 12 percent
cost of capital, while Alternative 1 requires only a 10 percent cost of
capital.

$$NPV_1 = \sum_{t=1}^{4} \left(\frac{\$3,440}{(1.10)^t} \right) - \$4,000$$

= \$3,440 (*PV* Interest Factor of a 4-year annuity at
10 percent) − \$4,000

= \$3,440(3.170) − \$4,000

= \$10,905 − \$4,000 = \$6,905.

$$NPV_2 = \sum_{t=1}^{4} \left(\frac{\$3,600}{(1.12)^t} \right) - \$4,000$$

= \$3,600 (*PV* Interest Factor of a 4-year annuity at
12 percent) − \$4,000

= \$3,600(3.037) − \$4,000

= \$10,933 − \$4,000 = \$6,933.

Alternative 2 has the higher risk-adjusted net present value.

Solved Problem

11.3 Bruce Seifert, the purchasing manager for Lodi Manufacturing
Company, is analyzing a bid he recently received for a contract to supply
electronic control systems for Lodi's stainless steel smokehouses. Altron
Corporation, a nearby firm that has a good record for on-time delivery
and high quality, has been supplying the systems and Lodi is reasonably satisfied with their past performance. The bid just received is from
Betex, a firm that is trying to increase its size and is aggressively seeking to market its products. Betex is known for price aggressiveness,
and the bid received by Lodi reflects this. Betex has offered to supply
the control systems Lodi needs for a price of $120,000. The price for
the systems from Altron is $160,000. Given this 25 percent price differ-
ence, Seifert is carefully examining the offer. He notes that Betex has
included in the offer a money-back guarantee of satisfaction. That is, if
the control systems fail to pass Lodi's quality control inspection when
received, they can be rejected and returned. (The quality control check

is such that if the systems pass they will be no more likely to fail than the Altron controls.) The Altron controls would be purchased in such a situation and Seifert does not believe the service or quality from Altron would decline. Seifert notes that if the units are rejected, a delay costing the firm $60,000 will result.

a) Assume that Seifert places a zero probability of rejection on the Altron system on the basis of his past experience. Construct a decision tree for this problem and determine the maximum probability of rejection Seifert can assign to the Betex controls before he would reject that firm's offer, assuming he makes his decision on the basis of minimizing expected costs.

b) Assume that Seifert assigns a 50 percent probability of rejection to the Betex controls. Would he be willing to pay $15,000 for an insurance policy or assurance bond that would pay Lodi Manufacturing $60,000 if the controls fail the quality check? (Use the same objective as in part a above.) Explain.

Solution

a) The decision tree for this situation is as follows:

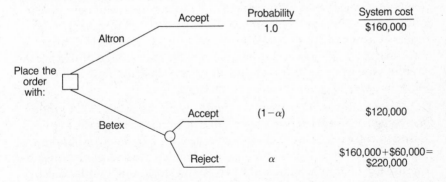

The maximum probability of rejection that could be assigned to the Betex control system is the probability that makes the expected cost equal for the two alternatives.

$$(1 - \alpha)(\$120,000) + \alpha(\$220,000) = \$160,000$$

$$\$120,000\alpha + \$220,000\alpha = \$160,000$$

$$\$100,000\alpha = \$40,000$$

$$\alpha = 0.4.$$

If there is a 40 percent or greater probability of Betex's control systems failing to pass Lodi's quality control inspection, then Lodi would choose the bid from Altron.

b) Solution of this problem requires comparing the lower cost alternatives with and without the insurance policy. Without the insurance policy the expected costs would be:

$$E(Cost_{Altron}) = \$160,000$$

$$E(Cost_{Betex}) = 0.5(\$120,000) + 0.5(\$220,000) = \$170,000.$$

Here purchasing from Altron has the lower expected cost. If the insurance is purchased, only the expected cost of purchase from Betex changes. The expected cost would now be calculated as:

$$E(Cost_{Betex}) = \$15,000 + 0.5(\$120,000) + 0.5(\$160,000) = \$155,000.$$

Thus, we see that ordering the control from Betex with the insurance policy has the lower expected cost.

Problem Set

11.1 Prudent Insurance Company is considering offering a new automobile insurance policy. The advertising campaign for the new policy consists of sending one million brochures in the mail to potential customers at a cost of 50 cents per brochure. If Prudent expects a gross profit margin of $50 for each policy sold, what percentage of the people receiving the advertising brochures must purchase the new insurance policy in order to cover the cost of the campaign?

11.2 Carol Caufield offers free investment seminars to local PTA groups. On average, Caufield expects 1 percent of seminar participants to purchase $10,000 each in tax sheltered investments, and 3 percent to purchase $2,500 each in stocks and bonds. Caufield earns a 4 percent net commission on tax shelters, and 1 percent on stocks and bonds. Calculate Caufield's expected net commissions per seminar if seminar attendance averages 12 persons.

11.3 Bloomington's Department Store is preparing for its annual clearance sale. J. L. Riley, the store's owner and manager, is considering advertising the sale on either television or radio. Riley has estimated the sales for the clearance sale, using each of the following advertising alternatives. Each alternative is expected to cost $10,000.

Alternative 1: Radio		Alternative 2: Television	
Probability	Sales	Probability	Sales
0.4	500,000	0.2	250,000
0.4	750,000	0.3	750,000
0.2	1,000,000	0.3	1,250,000
		0.2	1,750,000

a) Assume that the company has a 40 percent profit margin on sales; that is, profits are equal to 40 percent of sales revenue. Calculate the expected profits for each alternative.

b) Construct a bar graph of the possible outcomes for each plan. On the basis of the appearance of the two graphs, which plan appears to be more risky?

c) Calculate the risk (standard deviation of the profit distribution) associated with each plan.

d) Assume that Riley has a utility function like the one illustrated in the figure below. Which advertising strategy should Riley choose?

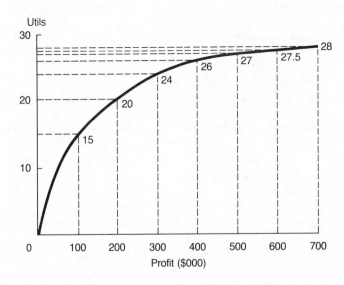

11.4 Classic Gift Shops Inc. is considering the possibility of expanding its 1984 promotional effort to one of three possible "test market" areas. A preliminary analysis has revealed the following returns to a local advertising campaign.

	Market					
	Austin, Tex.		Madison, Wisc.		Sacramento, Calif.	
	Pr.	Revenue	Pr.	Revenue	Pr.	Revenue
Low success	0.2	$400,000	0.4	$500,000	0.4	$300,000
Medium success	0.4	500,000	0.4	600,000	0.2	400,000
High success	0.4	550,000	0.2	800,000	0.4	500,000

a) Calculate the expected revenue from each market.

b) Calculate the standard deviation for each market's returns.

c) Determine the coefficient of variation for each market.

d) On the basis of these findings, can you decide which market Classic Gift Shops should adopt as its test market? Alternatively, can any be eliminated from consideration?

11.5 The Leisure-Time Equipment Company manufactures a line of bowling balls. Part of its production facility is to be replaced by one of two innovative pieces of equipment. The benefits (net cash flows) will be generated over the four-year useful lives of the machines and have the following expectational characteristics:

	Probability	Annual Cash Flow		Probability	Annual Cash Flow
Alternative #1	0.30	$2,900	Alternative #2	0.30	0
	0.50	3,500		0.50	4,000
	0.20	4,100		0.20	8,000

Whichever piece of equipment is chosen, the cost will be the same, $4,000.

a) What are the expected annual net cash flows from each project?
b) The firm currently uses a discount rate of 8% for risk free cash flows and has determined that a 2% risk premium is appropriate for the alternative with the lower risk, while a 4% risk premium should be used for the more risky of the two alternatives. Using the resulting 10% and 12% discount rates, determine which alternative has the higher risk adjusted expected net present value.
c) Suppose we know that the firm is indifferent between a "certain" 4-year annuity of $3,292 per year and the payoff of alternative #1, and would also be indifferent between a "certain" 4-year annuity of $3,300 per year and the return from alternative #2. Thus, for example, in the first case the firm would be indifferent between investing its $4,000 in Alternative 1 or in another investment (e.g. government bonds) that provided a certain payment of $3,292 per year for four years. What certainty equivalent adjustment factors do these figures indicate for each project?
d) Under these circumstances, which piece of equipment should be chosen if the firm uses an *NPV* certainty equivalent approach and an 8 percent riskless discount rate?

11.6 Bradley Manufacturing Inc. produces laundry detergent that it bottles in plastic containers. The existing bottling machine is obsolete and must be replaced. There are two similar, but more economical, bottling machines available to replace the existing machine. The Apex bottling machine operates at a higher speed and thus reduces operating expenses. The Randall bottling machine is somewhat more reliable and has lower expected maintenance expenses. The following yearly cost savings (cash flows) will be generated over the eight-year useful lives of the new machines.

	Probability	Cash Flow (Cost Savings)
Apex Machine (A)	.30	$ 60,000
	.50	90,000
	.20	110,000
Randall Machine (R)	.30	$ 0
	.50	100,000
	.20	200,000

Whichever piece of equipment is chosen, the total cost will be the same, $300,000. Given that the firm uses a discount rate of 12 percent for the cash flows with a higher degree of dispersion and a 10 percent rate for the less risky cash values, which machine has the higher expected net present value?

11.7 Z-Axis Inc. produces a printer compatible with equipment produced by MBI Corporation, a large computer manufacturer. Z-Axis must decide whether or not to discontinue its present line in favor of producing equipment compatible with a new Winesap computer.

If the Winesap is a success, Z-Axis sales will reach $2 million in the first year. A failure would result in $400,000 sales. A 50–50 chance of success or failure is projected. Sales of the current line of printers will be $800,000 if Winesap is a success, and $1.2 million if Winesap is a failure.

 a) Lay out a decision tree illustrating Z-Axis's decision alternatives and associated probabilities.

 b) Assuming Z-Axis wants to maximize expected sales revenue, which printer line should be offered next year?

 c) What probability of Winesap success would make Z-Axis indifferent to the two decision alternatives?

11.8 Garden Fresh Vegetable Company (GF) processes canned vegetables sold under a variety of private labels. The metal cans that GF uses are supplied by Federal Can Company. Federal's employees have been on strike and GF's can supply is expected to be depleted in five days. Although a tentative labor settlement has been reached and Federal Can is expected to be back in operation shortly, it is not certain that shipments will resume in time to prevent a shutdown of GF's production. Such a shutdown would cost GF $20,000 in lost profits. GF has the option of special ordering cans from Alco Can. The cost for this would be $8,000 as compared with $6,000 if Federal Can supplies the cans. Delivery from Alco in time to prevent a shutdown is virtually certain.

a) Lay out a decision tree showing the alternatives faced by GF and their outcomes.

b) Calculate the lowest probability of delivery from Federal Can in time to prevent shutdown that would be necessary to prevent GF from placing the special order with Alco, assuming GF desires to *minimize its total expected costs*.

c) Federal Can has offered to pay a $1,500 penalty for late delivery to prevent GF from placing the special order with Alco. Assuming an 80 percent probability of on-time delivery and the objective stated in part b, should GF accept this offer or place the special order?

References

Ang, James S., and Wilbur C. Lewellen. "Risk Adjustment in Capital Investment Project Evaluations." *Financial Management* 11 (Summer 1982): 5–14.

Bernardo, John J. "A Programming Approach to Measure Attribute Utilities." *Journal of Economics and Business* 33 (Spring–Summer 1981): 239–245.

Bierman, Harold Jr. *Strategic Financial Planning*. New York: Free Press, 1980.

Brown, Rex. "Do Managers Find Decision Theory Useful?" *Harvard Business Review* 48 (May–June 1970): 78–89.

Crum, Roy L., and Frans G. J. Derkinderen, eds. *Capital Budgeting Under Conditions of Uncertainty*. Boston: Martinus Nijhoff Publishers, 1981.

Durand, David. "Comprehensiveness in Capital Budgeting." *Financial Management* 10 (Winter 1981): 7–13.

Green, P. E. "Bayesian Decision Theory in Pricing Strategy." *Journal of Marketing* 27 (January 1963): 5–14.

Grether, David M. "Recent Psychological Studies of Behavior Under Uncertainty." *American Economic Review* 68 (May 1978): 70–74.

Hull, J., P. G. Moore, and H. Thomas. "Utility and Its Measurement." *Journal of the Royal Statistical Society, Series A* 136 (1973): 226–247.

Kihlstrom, Richard E., and Leonard J. Mirman. "Constant, Increasing and Decreasing Risk Aversion with Many Commodities." *Review of Economic Studies* 48 (April 1981): 271–280.

Magee, John F. "How to Use Decision Trees in Capital Budgeting." *Harvard Business Review* 42 (September–October 1964): 79–95.

Morgan, James N. "Multiple Motives, Group Decisions, Uncertainty, Ignorance, and Confusion: A Realistic Economics of the Consumer Requires Some Psychology." *American Economic Review* 68 (May 1978): 58–63.

Pappas, James L., and George P. Huber. "Probabilistic Short-Term Financial Planning." *Financial Management* 2 (Autumn 1973): 36–44.

Shubik, Martin. "The Strategic Audit: A Game Theoretic Approach to Corporate Competitive Strategy." *Managerial and Decision Economics* 4 (September 1983): 160–171.

Singhvi, Surendra S. *Planning for Capital Investments*. Oxford, Oh.: Planning Executives Institute, 1979.

Chapter 12

Long-Term Investment Decisions: Capital Budgeting

Key Terms

Capital budgeting	Net present value
Cash flow	Post-audit
Cost of capital	Profitability index
Internal rate of return	

Management faces two separate but related tasks in working toward its goal of maximizing the value of the firm: (1) It must use existing resources in an optimal manner. (2) It must decide when to increase or reduce the firm's stock of resources. We have not yet explicitly separated these tasks, although our emphasis has been on the first one. Now we explicitly consider the decision to add to the stock of resources, or the decision process known as *investment* or *capital budgeting*.

Capital budgeting consists of the entire process of planning expenditures whose returns are expected to extend beyond one year. The choice of one year is arbitrary, of course, but it is a convenient cutoff for distinguishing between classes of expenditures. Obvious examples of capital outlays are expenditures for land, buildings, and equipment and for permanent additions to working capital (e.g., inventories and receivables) associated with plant expansion. An advertising or promotion campaign or a program of research and development is also likely to have an impact beyond one year and hence to come within the classification of capital budgeting expenditures.

In a very real sense capital budgeting integrates and fuses the various elements of the firm. Although the financial manager generally has administrative control of the capital budgeting process, the effectiveness of the process itself is fundamentally dependent on inputs from all major departments. Because a sales forecast is always required, the marketing department has a key role in the process. Because operating costs must be estimated, the accounting, production, engineering, and purchasing departments are involved. The initial outlay, or investment cost, must be estimated; again engineering and purchasing must supply inputs. Funds must be procured to finance the project, and obtaining these funds and estimating their cost are major tasks of the financial manager. Finally, these various estimates must be drawn together in the form of a project evaluation. Although the finance department generally writes up the evaluation report, top management sets the standards of acceptability and ultimately makes the decision to accept or reject the project.

Our first task in this chapter is to describe the mechanics of the capital budgeting process. Then we discuss in some detail the key roles of the marketing, production, and finance departments in the process.

The Capital Budgeting Process

Capital budgeting is essentially an application of the proposition from the economic theory of the firm that a firm should operate at the point where its marginal revenue is just equal to its marginal cost. When this rule is applied to the capital budgeting decision, marginal revenue is taken to be the rate of return on investments, and marginal cost is the firm's cost of capital.

A graphical presentation of the concept is shown in Figure 12.1a. The horizontal axis measures the dollars of investment during a year; the vertical axis shows both the percentage cost of capital and the rate of return on projects. The projects are denoted by the boxes: Project A, for example, calls for an outlay of $3 million and promises a 17 percent rate of return; Project B requires $1 million and yields about 16 percent; and so on. The last investment, Project E, simply involves buying 9 percent government bonds, which may be purchased in unlimited quantities. In Figure 12.1b the concept is generalized to show a smoothed investment opportunity schedule, the curve labeled IRR.[1]

---

[1] The investment opportunity schedule measures the yield or rate of return on each project. The rate of return on a project is generally called the *internal rate of return* (*IRR*). This is why we label the investment opportunity schedules *IRR*. The process of calculating the *IRR* is explained later in this chapter.

Figure 12.1
Illustrative Capital Budgeting Decision Process

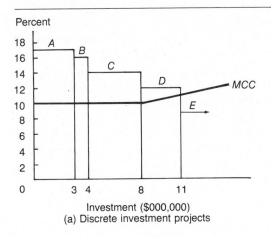

(a) Discrete investment projects

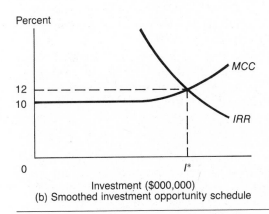

(b) Smoothed investment opportunity schedule

The curve *MCC* designates the marginal cost of capital, or the cost of each additional dollar acquired for purposes of making capital expenditures. As it is drawn in Figure 12.1a, the marginal cost of capital is constant at 10 percent until the firm has raised $8 million, after which the cost of capital begins to rise. To maximize value, the firm should accept Projects *A* through *D*, obtaining and investing $11 million, and reject *E*, the investment in government bonds. The smoothed generalized curves in Figure 12.1b indicate that the firm should invest *I** dollars. Here, the marginal cost of capital, the cost of the last dollar raised, is 12 percent, the same as the rate on the last project accepted.

At the applied level, the capital budgeting process is much more complex than the preceding examples would suggest. Projects do not just appear. A continuing stream of good investment opportunities results from hard thinking, careful planning, and, often, large outlays for research and development. In addition, some very difficult measurement problems are involved: The revenues and costs associated with particular projects must be estimated, frequently for many years into the future, in the face of great uncertainty. Finally, some difficult conceptual and empirical problems arise over the methods of calculating rates of return and the cost of capital. Managers are required to take action, however, even in the face of problems such as these, and the capital budgeting procedure described in this chapter is designed to aid in this decision process.

Investment Proposals

The capital budgeting process begins with the generation of ideas; capital investment proposals must be created. This development of investment proposals is no small task. A firm's growth and development, even its ability to remain competitive and to survive, depend upon a constant flow of new investment ideas. Accordingly, a well-managed firm will go to great lengths to develop good capital budgeting proposals. For example, the executive vice president of one major corporation indicated that his company takes the following steps to generate projects:

Our R & D department is constantly searching for new products, or for ways to improve existing products. In addition, our Executive Committee, which consists of senior executives in marketing, production, and finance, identifies the products and markets in which our company will compete, and the Committee sets long-run targets for each division. These targets, which are formalized in the corporate budget, provide a general guide to the operating executives who must meet them. These executives then seek new products, set expansion plans for existing products, and look for ways to reduce production and distribution costs. Since bonuses and promotions are based in large part on each unit's ability to meet or exceed its targets, these economic incentives encourage our operating executives to seek profitable investment opportunities.

Although our senior executives are judged and rewarded on the basis of how well their units perform, people further down the line are given bonuses for specific suggestions, including ideas that lead to profitable investments. Additionally, a percentage of our corporate profit is set aside for distribution to nonexecutive employees. Our objective is to encourage lower-level workers to keep on the lookout for good ideas, including those that lead to capital investments.

Project Classification

If the firm has capable and imaginative executives and employees, and if its incentive system is working properly, its personnel will advance many ideas for capital investment. Since only some ideas will be good, project-screening procedures must be established. The first step in this screening process is to assemble a list of the proposed new investments, together with the data necessary to evaluate them.

Benefits can be gained from a careful capital expenditure analysis, but such an evaluation is expensive. For certain types of projects, a refined analysis may be warranted; for others, cost-benefit studies will suggest a simpler procedure. Accordingly, firms frequently classify projects into the following categories:

1. *Replacement—Maintenance of Business*: Investments necessary to replace worn-out or damaged equipment

2. *Replacement—Cost Reduction*: Investments to replace working, but obsolete, equipment

3. *Expansion of Existing Products or Markets*: Investments to increase output of existing products or to expand outlets or distribution facilities in markets now being served

4. *Expansion into New Products or Markets*: Investments necessary to produce a new product or to expand into a geographic area not currently served

5. *Safety and/or Environmental*: Investments necessary to comply with government requirements, labor agreements, or insurance policy terms

6. *Other*: A catch-all for investments that do not fall in one of the other categories

Ordinarily, maintenance-type replacement decisions are the simplest to make. Assets wear out and become obsolete, and they must be replaced if production is to continue. The firm has a very good idea of the savings in cost obtained by replacing an old asset, and it knows the consequences of nonreplacement. Relatively simple calculations and only a few supporting documents are required for these investment decisions in profitable plants. More detailed analysis is required for cost reduction replacements, for expansion of existing product lines, and for investments into new products or areas. Also, within each category, projects are broken down by their dollar costs: the larger the required investment, the more detailed the analysis and the higher the level of the officer who must authorize the expenditure. Thus, although a plant manager may be authorized to approve maintenance expenditures up to $10,000 on the basis of a rather unsophisticated analysis, the full board of directors may have to approve decisions that involve

Table 12.1
Estimated Investment Requirements for Project X

Capital Investment	1985	1986	1987	1988	Total
Capital					
1. Land	$ 0	$ 0	$	$	$ 0
2. Land Improvements	0	0			0
3. Buildings	300,000	790,700			1,090,700
4. Process Equipment	900,000	1,602,000			2,502,000
5. Mobile Equipment	0	175,000			175,000
6. Less: Investment Tax Credit	(90,000)	(177,700)			(267,700)
7. Subtotal	$1,110,000	$2,390,000			$3,500,000
Working Capital					
8. Accounts Receivable	$	$ 652,500	$238,500	$ 86,000	$ 977,000
9. Raw Materials Inventory		107,500	52,500	19,000	179,000
10. Goods in Process		170,000	39,000	47,000	256,000
11. Finished Materials Inventory		232,500	45,500	17,000	295,000
12. Operating Materials and Supplies		140,500	12,000	5,000	157,500
13. Payables/Accruals		(270,000)	(72,500)	(22,000)	(364,500)
14. Net Working Capital	$( )	$1,033,000	$315,000	$152,000	$1,500,000
Total Investment (lines 7 + 14)	$				$5,000,000

amounts over $1 million or expansions into new products or markets. A very detailed, refined analysis will be required to support these latter decisions. Investments in the *safety and/or environmental* and *other* categories are frequently treated separately from the regular capital budget because of the complexities involved in their evaluation.

Estimating Cash Flows

The most important and the most difficult step in capital expenditure proposal analysis is the estimation of **cash flow** associated with the project: the outflow associated with building and equipping the new facility and the annual cash inflows the project will produce after it goes into operation. A great many variables are involved in the cash flow forecast, and many individuals and departments participate in developing them. We cannot in this book develop fully the techniques and methodologies used in cash flow analysis, but an examination of Tables 12.1 and 12.2 will provide an idea of what is entailed.

Table 12.1 summarizes the outlay required for an investment project that involves construction of a facility to manufacture a new product. A total outlay of $5 million is necessary: $3.5 million for land, buildings, and equipment, and $1.5 million for the net investment in working capital. These expenditures will be incurred over the four-year period from 1985 to 1988. The plant will be constructed and equipped in 1985 and 1986, and working capital will be built up during 1986, 1987, and 1988.

Table 12.2 shows a series of income statements detailing the expected cash flows during certain years of the project's anticipated 15-year life. Sales in both units and dollars are shown, after which the various types of expenses and taxes are deducted to produce the net income expected from the project as shown on the third line from the bottom. These incremental profits are before all financing charges; the cost of the capital used to finance an investment project is accounted for when the cash flows are evaluated. Depreciation, which is not a cash outlay, is added to profits to produce the bottom line figures, the net cash flows from the project.[2]

The new plant will go into service in 1986, and it is expected to generate a net cash flow of $581,564 in that year. Cash flows are expected to climb during the next two years as the plant is broken in and the market

---

[2]If the treatment of depreciation is not clear, recognize that net sales represent cash received, and that all expenses *except depreciation* represent cash outlays during the year. Thus, the project is expected to generate cash from net sales of $4,275,000 and to incur cash costs for taxes and all expenses shown except depreciation, so that $4,275,000 cash from net sales, minus cash costs totaling $2,898,000 + $662,500 = $3,560,500, minus $132,936 income taxes, equals $581,564. The $581,564 cash flow is, of course, also equal to net income after taxes plus depreciation.

Table 12.2
Cash Flow Analysis for Project X

	1986	1987	1988	1989	Estimated Profits and Cash Flows	1999	2000
Quantity Shipped, Tons	75,000	90,000	100,000	100,000	Years 1990 through 1998 not shown here	100,000	100,000
Gross Sales, Dollars	$4,336,000	$5,203,000	$5,781,000	$5,781,000		$5,781,000	$5,781,000
Less: Freight	(44,000)	(52,000)	(58,000)	(58,000)		(58,000)	(58,000)
Cash Discounts	(17,000)	(21,000)	(23,000)	(23,000)		(23,000)	(23,000)
Total Deductions	(61,000)	(73,000)	(81,000)	(81,000)		(81,000)	(81,000)
Net Sales	$4,275,000	$5,130,000	$5,700,000	$5,700,000		$5,700,000	$5,700,000
Cost of Sales							
Variable	$2,223,000	$2,736,000	$3,078,000	$3,078,000		$3,078,000	$3,078,000
Fixed, Excluding Depreciation and Depletion	342,000	342,000	342,000	342,000		342,000	342,000
Break-in Costs	333,000	137,000	—	—		—	—
Total	2,898,000	3,215,000	3,420,000	3,420,000		3,420,000	3,420,000
Depreciation	437,550	408,380	379,210	350,040		58,290	29,120
Total Cost of Sales	$3,335,550	$3,623,380	$3,799,210	$3,770,040		$3,478,290	$3,449,120
Gross Profit	$1,939,450	$1,506,620	$1,904,790	$1,930,960		$2,222,710	$2,251,880
Selling Expenses	228,000	228,000	228,000	228,000		228,000	228,000
Advertising	124,000	100,000	86,000	86,000		86,000	86,000
Administrative	285,000	285,000	285,000	285,000		285,000	285,000
Provision for Bad Debts	25,500	29,800	32,600	32,600		32,600	32,600
Total: Selling and Administrative	662,500	642,800	631,600	631,600		631,600	631,600
Net Income before Tax	276,950	863,820	1,273,190	1,299,360		1,591,110	1,620,280
Income Tax @ 48%	132,936	414,634	611,131	623,693		763,733	777,734
Net Income	144,014	449,186	662,059	675,667		827,377	842,546
Depreciation	437,550	408,380	379,210	350,040		58,290	29,120
Net Cash Flow	$ 581,564	$ 857,566	$1,041,269	$1,025,707		$ 885,667	$ 871,666

Salvage Value, Buildings and Machines = 0
Recovery of Working Capital = $1,500,000
Net Cash Flow, Year 15 = $2,371,666

developed, but to decline thereafter because of rising taxes caused by declining deductions for depreciation.[3]

Although the estimation of cash flows for capital budgeting analysis is a difficult task, there are a number of key relationships that help insure an appropriate effort in this area of the capital budgeting process. First, cash flows must be constructed on an incremental basis. Only cash flows that will differ with or without acceptance of the project are relevant for inclusion in the analysis. Second, care must be taken to include *all* incremental cash flows, including revenue and cost changes for other activities of the firm that are affected by a particular capital investment. The impact of a new product on the sales revenue of an existing product is an example of a frequently important indirect cash flow. Third, cash flows should be constructed on an aftertax basis. Fourth, depreciation should not be included in the relevant cash flows—except to account for its impact on taxes—as it is a noncash expense.

Net Present Value Analysis

Once cash flow estimates for a proposed investment have been generated, an evaluation must be performed to determine the worth of the project to the firm.[4] Although a number of different methods are used to rank projects and decide whether they should be accepted, the economically sound approaches are all based on the discounted present

---

[3]The firm in our example, like most firms, uses accelerated depreciation for tax calculations. This causes depreciation charges (a noncash expense) to be high early in the project's life and lower later on. The high initial depreciation results in lower tax payments, hence higher cash flows during the early years.

Two other points are worth mentioning here. First, the question of what happens to the cash flows shown at the bottom of Table 12.2 can be raised. The answer is that they are available for payment of dividends and interest on capital and for reinvestment in other projects. The second point has to do with the recovery of working capital. Some amount of working capital—cash, receivables, inventories, less trade credit (accounts payable) and other accruals—must be held to support sales. In the example, $1.5 million is the investment in working capital, and this investment must be maintained as long as the operations continue. Thus the $1.5 million will be needed until 2000, the year the project is expected to end. As operations are phased out during that year, inventories will be worked down; receivables will be collected with no new ones created because sales will cease; and the cash balances to operate the plant will no longer be needed. Thus, during 2000 the $1.5 million of working capital will be recovered and presumably paid to providers of capital (debt and equity) or reinvested elsewhere in the company.

[4]A knowledge of compound interest is necessary for an understanding of this evaluation. Students who have not covered compound interest in other courses or who could use a review should read through the relevant sections of Appendix A.

value concept. Recall from Chapter 1 the basic valuation model of
the firm.

$$\text{Value} = \sum_{t=1}^{n} \frac{\text{Total Revenue}_t - \text{Total Cost}_t}{(1 + k)^t} = \sum_{t=1}^{n} \frac{\text{Net Cash Flow}_t}{(1 + k)^t} . \qquad \text{(12.1)}$$

In this equation Net Cash Flow$_t$ represents the firm's total after-tax profit
plus noncash expenses such as depreciation; and k, which is based on
an appraisal of the firm's overall riskiness, represents the average cost
of capital to the firm. The value of the firm is simply the discounted
present value of the difference between total cash inflows and total cash
outflows. Any investment project would be desirable if by accepting it
the firm's net present value increases, and undesirable if accepting it
causes the firm's net present value to decrease.

The use of net present value analysis in capital budgeting involves
the application of the present value model described in Equation 12.1
to individual projects rather than the firm as a whole. In brief, the procedure is as described below:

1. Estimate project expected net cash flows. Depending on the nature of
the project, these estimates will have a greater or lesser degree of riskiness. For example, the benefits from replacing a piece of equipment
used to produce a stable, established product can be estimated more accurately than those from an investment in equipment to produce a new
and untried product.

2. Estimate the expected cost, or investment outlay, of the project. This
cost estimate will be quite accurate for purchased equipment since cost
is equal to the invoice price plus delivery and installation charges; but
cost estimates for other kinds of projects may be highly uncertain or
speculative.

3. Determine an appropriate discount rate, or **cost of capital**, for the
project. The cost of capital is considered in detail later in this chapter,
but for now it may be thought of as being determined by the riskiness of
the project; that is, by the uncertainty of the expected cash flows and the
investment outlay.

4. Find the present value of the expected cash flows and subtract from
this figure the estimated cost of the project.[5] The resulting figure is de-

---

[5] If costs are spread over several years, this fact must be taken into account. Suppose, for
example, that a firm bought land in 1985, erected a building in 1986, installed equipment
in 1987, and started production in 1988. One could treat 1985 as the base year, comparing the present value of the costs as of 1985 to the present value of the benefit stream as
of that same date. For ease in exposition we shall assume in this chapter that all costs are
incurred immediately and that profits occur annually at the end of each future year.

fined as the **net present value** (*NPV*) of the project. If the *NPV* is greater than zero, the project should be accepted; if it is less than zero, the project should be rejected. In equation form:

$$NPV_i = \sum_{t=1}^{n} \frac{CF_{it}}{(1 + k_i)^t} - C_i, \tag{12.2}$$

where NPV_i is the *NPV* of the *i*th project, CF_{it} represents the expected net cash flows of the *i*th project in the *t*th year, k_i is the risk-adjusted discount rate applicable to the *i*th project, and C_i is the project's investment outlay, or cost.

NPV as an Application of Marginal Analysis

To see that this procedure of accepting only investment projects for which the net present value is positive is in fact an application of the marginal analysis illustrated in Figure 11.1, consider briefly the determination of the yield or internal rate of return on an investment. The **internal rate of return** is defined as that interest or discount rate that equates the present value of the future receipts of a project to the initial cost or outlay. The equation for calculating the internal rate of return is simply the *NPV* formula set equal to zero. That is:

$$NPV_i = \sum_{t=1}^{n} \frac{CF_{it}}{(1 + k_i^*)^t} - C_i = 0. \tag{12.3}$$

Here the equation is solved for the discount rate, k_i^*, which produces a zero net present value or which causes the sum of the discounted future receipts to equal the initial cost. That discount rate is the internal rate of return earned by the project.

Because the net present value equation is a complex polynomial, it is extremely difficult to solve for the actual internal rate of return on an investment. For this reason a trial-and-error method is typically employed. One begins by arbitrarily selecting a discount rate with which to calculate the net present value of the project. If the *NPV* is positive, then the internal rate of return must be greater than the interest or discount rate used, and another *higher* rate is tried. Similarly, if the *NPV* is negative, this implies that the internal rate of return on the project is lower than the discount rate, and the *NPV* calculation must be repeated, using a lower discount rate. This process of changing the discount rate and recalculating the net present value is continued until the discounted present value of the future cash flows is approximately equal to the ini-

Table 12.3
Expected Cash Flows from Projects A and B

Year	A	B
1	$500	$200
2	400	400
3	300	500
4	100	600

tial cost. The interest rate that brings about this equality is the yield, or internal, rate of return on the project.[6]

Now consider again the decision rule, which states that a firm should accept only projects whose net present values are positive when the firm's risk-adjusted cost of capital, k_i, is used as the discount rate. In this model, k_i, the risk-adjusted discount factor, is the firm's marginal cost of capital and is, therefore, the rate of interest that must be paid on the funds invested in a project. As we have seen from the discussion of the calculation of internal rates of return or yields on an investment, if the net present value of a project, calculated using the firm's cost of capital as the discount rate, is positive, this implies that the rate of return on the project is greater than the cost of capital. Likewise, if the NPV is negative, the implication is that the internal rate of return is less than the cost of capital. Thus it is clear that the NPV decision technique, which limits acceptable projects to those whose net present values, using k_i as the discount rate, are positive, is one based essentially on a comparison of the marginal cost of capital and the marginal yield, or return, on the investment.

Illustration of the NPV Technique

To illustrate the NPV evaluation technique, assume that a firm has two investment opportunities, each costing $1,000 and each having the expected profits shown in Table 12.3.

Let us further assume that the cost of each project is known with certainty, but the expected cash flows of Project B are riskier than are those of Project A. After giving due consideration to the risks inherent in each project, management has determined that A should be evaluated with a 10 percent cost of capital, with a 15 percent cost of capital for the riskier Project B.

---

[6]This trial-and-error procedure is a bit tedious if done by hand for a project that extends over a long time horizon. Computers, (and even many hand-held calculators), however, can evaluate numerous trial discount rates very rapidly, and thus the computational side of calculating internal rates of return presents no difficulty for capital budgeting analysis.

Table 12.4
Calculating the Net Present Value (*NPV*) of Projects with $1,000 Cost

| | Project A | | | | Project B | | |
| | Cash | PVIF | PV of Cash | | Cash | PVIF | PV of Cash |
Year	Flow	(10%)	Flow	Year	Flow	(15%)	Flow
1	$500	0.91	$ 455	1	$200	0.87	$ 174
2	400	0.83	332	2	400	0.76	304
3	300	0.75	225	3	500	0.66	330
4	100	0.68	68	4	600	0.57	342
	PV		$1,080		PV		$1,150
	Less Cost		−1,000		Less Cost		−1,000
	NPV_A		$ 80		NPV_B		$ 150

Equation 12.2 can be restated as Equation 12.3, using Project *A* as an example:

$$NPV_A = \sum_{t=1}^{n} \frac{CF_{At}}{(1 + k_A)^t} - C_A \tag{12.4}$$

$$= \left[\frac{CF_{A1}}{(1 + k_A)^1} + \frac{CF_{A2}}{(1 + k_A)^2} + \frac{CF_{A3}}{(1 + k_A)^3} + \frac{CF_{A4}}{(1 + k_A)^4} \right] - C_A$$

$$= \left[(CF_{A1}) \left(\frac{1}{1 + k_A} \right)^1 + (CF_{A2}) \left(\frac{1}{1 + k_A} \right)^2 + (CF_{A3}) \left(\frac{1}{1 + k_A} \right)^3 \right.$$
$$\left. + (CF_{A4}) \left(\frac{1}{1 + k_A} \right)^4 \right] - C_A$$

$$= [CF_{A1} (PVIF_{A1}) + CF_{A2} (PVIF_{A2}) + CF_{A3} (PVIF_{A3})$$
$$+ CF_{A4} (PVIF_{A4})] - C_A.$$

Values for the present value interest factors, the *PVIF* terms, are found in Appendix B. For example, $PVIF_{A1}$, the interest factor for the present value of $1 due in one year discounted at a 10 percent rate, is 0.909; $PVIF_{A2}$, the interest factor for the present value of $1 received in two years discounted at a 10 percent rate, is 0.826; and so on.

Equation 12.3 for both projects is given in tabular form in Table 12.4. Project *A*'s *NPV* is $80 and Project *B*'s is $150. Since both projects have positive *NPV*s, both earn a rate of return in excess of their costs of capital; the marginal rate of return is greater than the marginal cost of capital, in the sense of Figure 12.1. If the two projects are independent, they should both be accepted, because each adds more to the value of the firm than its cost: Project *A* increases the value of the firm by $80 over what it would be if the project is not accepted; Project *B* increases the firm's value by $150. If the projects are mutually exclusive, *B* should be selected, because it adds more to the firm's value than does *A*.[7]

Other Issues in Project Evaluation

Ordinarily, firms operate as illustrated in Figure 12.1; that is, they take on investments to the point where the marginal returns from investment are just equal to their marginal cost of capital. For firms operating in this way the decision process is as described above: They make investments having positive net present values, reject those whose net present values are negative, and choose between mutually exclusive investments on the basis of the higher net present value. For many capital budgeting problems, however, the use of the *NPV* concept for analyzing capital budgeting decisions is far more complex than the illustration suggests. For example, the capital budgeting problem may require analysis of mutually exclusive projects with different expected lives or with substantially different initial costs. When these conditions exist, the net present value criterion as discussed above may not result in the selection of projects that maximize the value of the firm.

A similar complication arises when the firm sets an absolute limit on the size of its capital budget that is less than the level of investment that would be undertaken on the basis of the criteria described above. The rationale behind such *capital rationing*, as it is called, stems from a number of factors. First, it is sometimes a fallacy to consider that what is true of the individual parts will be true of the whole. Although individual projects appear to promise a relatively attractive yield, when

---

[7]Some firms use the internal rate of return (*IRR*) approach for selecting capital investment projects rather than the *NPV* method. Under the *IRR* criterion, projects are ranked according to their *IRR*; and projects whose *IRR* exceeds the appropriate risk-adjusted discount rate (cost of capital) are accepted. Although the *IRR* and *NPV* methods will lead to the same accept-reject decisions for an individual project, they can provide contradictory signals concerning the choice between mutually exclusive projects. That is, one project can have a higher *IRR* but lower *NPV* when discounted at the firm's cost of capital. This problem arises because the *IRR* is the implied reinvestment rate for cash flows under the *IRR* method and the discount rate used in the *NPV* model is the implicit reinvestment rate with that methodology. In most situations the reinvestment of cash flows at a rate close to the cost of capital is more realistic; therefore, the *NPV* method is generally superior.

they are taken together unforeseen difficulties can prevent the achievement of all the favorable results. One problem is that, although individual projects promise favorable yields, to undertake a large number of
projects simultaneously might involve a very high rate of expansion by
the firm. Such substantial additional personnel requirements and organizational problems may be involved that overall rates of return will be
diminished. Top management, at some point in the capital budgeting
process, must therefore make a decision regarding the total volume of
favorable projects that can be successfully undertaken without causing a significant reduction in the prospective returns from individual
projects.

Another reason for limiting the capital budget, and one that perhaps
better meets the strict definition of capital rationing, is the reluctance
of some managements to engage in external financing (borrowing or
selling stock). One management, recalling the plight of firms with substantial amounts of debt in the 1930s, may simply refuse to use debt.
Another management, which has no objection to selling debt, may not
wish to sell equity capital for fear of losing some measure of voting control. Still others may refuse to use any form of outside financing, considering safety and control to be more important than additional profits.
The existence of such capital rationing complicates the capital budgeting
process and requires the use of more complex tools and techniques of
analysis.

Profitability Index or Benefit-Cost Ratio Analysis

A variant of *NPV* analysis that is often used in complex capital budgeting situations is called the **profitability index**, or the benefit-cost ratio
method. The profitability index (*PI*) is calculated as:

$$PI = \frac{\text{PV of Cash Flows}}{\text{Cost}} = \frac{\sum\limits_{t=1}^{n} [CF_{it}/(1 + k_i)^t]}{C_i} \qquad (12.5)$$

The *PI* shows the *relative* profitability of any project, or the present value
of benefits per dollar of cost.

In *PI* analysis, a project with $PI > 1$ should be accepted, and a project with $PI < 1$ should be rejected. This means that projects will be accepted provided they return more than a dollar of discounted benefits
for each dollar of cost. Thus, the *PI* and *NPV* methods always indicate
the same accept-reject decision for independent projects since $PI > 1$ implies $NPV > 0$ and $PI < 1$ implies $NPV < 0$. However, when alternative

Table 12.5

Comparison of *PI* and *NPV* Rankings of Projects with Unequal Costs

	Project B	Project C
PV Cash Flow @ k = 15%	$1,150	$1,700
Cost	$1,000	$1,500
$PI = \dfrac{PV\ \text{Cash Flow}}{\text{Cost}}$	1.15	1.13
$NPV = PV$ Cash Flow $-$ Cost	$ 150	$ 200

projects of unequal size are being considered, *PI* and *NPV* can give different project *rankings*. This can sometimes cause problems when mutually exclusive projects are being evaluated.

Table 12.5 shows *PI* and *NPV* values for two mutually exclusive projects of unequal size. The present value of cash flow calculation for Project *B* was shown earlier in Table 12.4, and a similar calculation for Project *C* was performed. Note that the investment cost of *B* is $1,000, whereas the investment cost for *C* is $1,500. Since each project has *PI* > 1 and *NPV* > 0, they would both be acceptable under either criterion. However, the ranking of these projects will be different, depending upon whether the *PI* or *NPV* method is used. Using the *PI* criterion, we would select Project *B* first. If we compute the ratio of the present value of the returns (or benefits) of each project to its cost, we find *B*'s *PI* ratio to be $1,150/$1,000 = 1.15 and *C*'s ratio to be $1,700/$1,500 = 1.13. Thus, using the *PI* for our ranking, we would select Project *B* because it produces higher discounted net returns per dollar invested. On the other hand, a ranking using *NPV* would suggest selection of Project *C* before Project *B*. The *NPV* of *C* is $1,700 − $1,500 = $200, and the *NPV* of *B* is $1,150 − $1,000 = $150. Project *C* is to be preferred according to the *NPV* criterion since it provides the larger discounted net benefit.

Given this conflict, which project ranking method should be adopted? Alternatively stated: Is it better to use the net present value approach on an absolute basis (*NPV*) or on a relative basis (*PI*)? For a firm with substantial investment resources and a goal of maximizing shareholder wealth, the *NPV* method is better. For a firm with more limited resources, however, the *PI* approach results in scarce funds available for investment being used where their relative impact on value is greatest. In some cases, this leads to a better combination of investment projects and higher firm value. The *PI*, or benefit-cost ratio, approach has also proved to be a useful tool in public sector decision making, where allocating scarce public resources among competing projects is a typical problem.

Steps in the Capital Budgeting Process

The information requirements of the capital budgeting decision process are very extensive. In fact, almost all the topics covered in this book must be brought to bear on important capital budgeting decisions. Demand functions, production functions, and cost functions must all be estimated and analyzed. Market structures may have to be appraised, both for use in determining how competitors are likely to react to major decisions and for the antitrust implications of particular courses of action; antitrust analysis is especially important if the action involves an investment in another firm or a joint venture with another company. Regulated firms are subject to special problems in their long-term investment programs, and almost all manufacturing companies are undergoing appraisals of the costs of and benefits accruing from pollution-control, and worker health and safety investments.

Demand Forecasts

The first step in most capital budgeting decisions is estimating future demand. The need for this step is obvious in expansion decisions, but it is also a vital part of replacement, modernization, and pollution-control investments. A worn-out machine should not be replaced unless demand for its output will continue for some time into the future; a plant should be closed rather than equipped with pollution-control equipment if demand for the plant's output is weak.

Cost Forecasts

Once the demand function has been estimated, the next step is to determine the operating cost function. This procedure frequently involves a knowledge of production theory, input factor markets, and statistical cost estimation. And, although we do not take up these considerations in this chapter, accurate cost analysis is also heavily dependent on such accounting-based topics as depreciation, inventory valuation procedures, and tax considerations.

Cash Flow Forecasts

The third step in the process is to integrate demand and cost relationships to determine the optimal output level and the expected annual cash flows resulting from operation at this output. Many firms have set up systems to generate the data necessary for thorough analyses of options, and many of them construct simulation models, with demand and cost functions as key components, to appraise major investment proposals.

Cost of Capital

Determining the firm's cost of capital for use as the appropriate discount rate is an essential part of the capital budgeting process. The cost of capital is a complex subject, which is discussed in detail in finance courses, and a thorough treatment of the topic is beyond the scope of this book. Accordingly, we shall merely summarize some of the important elements of the cost of capital theory as it is developed in finance.

Firms raise funds in many forms, including long-term and short-term debt, preferred and common stock, retained earnings, and lease financing. Each source of funds has a cost, and these costs are the basic inputs in the cost of capital determination.

Capital is a necessary factor of production, and like any other factor, it has a cost. The cost of each type of capital employed by the firm is defined as the *component cost* of that particular capital. For example, if a firm can borrow money at a 14 percent interest rate, the component cost of debt is defined as 14 percent. Although firms obtain capital funds through the use of many financial instruments, we concentrate on debt and equity capital components in this discussion of capital costs. These are the major capital resource categories, and limiting our discussion to them will enable us to examine the basic cost-of-capital concept without getting mired down in too much financial, accounting, and legal detail.

Cost of Debt. The component cost of debt is based on the interest rate investors require on debt issues, adjusted for taxes. If a firm borrows $100,000 for one year at 14 percent interest, its before-tax dollar cost is $14,000, and its before-tax percentage cost is 14 percent. However, interest payments on debt are deductible for income tax purposes. It is necessary to account for this tax deductibility by adjusting the cost of debt to an after-tax basis. The deductibility of interest payments means, in effect, that the government pays part of a firm's interest charges. This reduces the cost of debt capital as follows:

After-Tax Component Cost of Debt = (Interest Rate) × (1.0 − Tax Rate).

Assuming that the firm's marginal tax rate is 50 percent, the after-tax cost of debt will be one half the interest rate.

Note that the cost of debt is applicable only to *new* debt, not to the interest on old, previously outstanding debt. In other words, we are interested in the cost of new debt, or the *marginal cost of debt*. The primary concern with the cost of capital is to use it in a decision making process, the decision being whether to obtain capital to make new investments. The fact that the firm borrowed at high or low rates in the past is irrelevant.

Cost of Equity. The *component cost of equity* is defined as the rate of return stockholders require on the common stock of a firm. Because dividends paid to stockholders are not deductible as a business expense for income tax purposes (dividend payments must be made with after-tax dollars), there is no tax adjustment for the component cost of equity capital.

Although empirical estimation of the cost of equity capital is a complex and often difficult process, most methods employed in this effort are based on one of two relatively simple concepts. The first of these is to recognize that the cost of capital of a risky security such as a common stock consists of a riskless rate of return (R_F) plus a risk premium (P):

$$k = R_F + P.$$

The risk-free return is typically taken to be the interest rate on short-term U.S. government securities. Various procedures are available for estimating P for different securities.

One frequently encountered procedure involves adding a premium of about four to five percentage points to the interest rate on a firm's long-term bonds so that the total risk premium on equity is equal to the difference between the yield on the firm's debt and that on government bonds *plus* four to five percentage points. For example, if government bonds are priced to yield 12 percent and the bonds of a firm yield 14 percent, then Cost of Equity, k_e, would be estimated as:

$$k_e = \text{Bond Rate} + 4\% \text{ to } 5\% \text{ Risk Premium}$$

$$= 14\% + 4\% \text{ to } 5\% = 18\% \text{ to } 19\%.$$

Since

$$k_e = R_F + P,$$

where R_F = yield on government bonds = 12 percent,

$$18\% \text{ to } 19\% = 12\% + P$$

$$P = 6\% \text{ to } 7\%.$$

Analysts who use this procedure generally cite studies of historical returns on stocks and bonds and use the difference between the average yield (dividends plus capital gains) on stocks and the average yield on bonds as the risk premium of stocks over bonds. The primary difficulties with using historical returns to estimate risk premiums are that (1) historical returns differ, depending on the beginning and ending dates used to estimate them, and (2) there is no reason to think that past differences in stock and bond yields precisely indicate future required risk premiums.

A second procedure for estimating P is based on a construct known as the capital asset pricing model (CAPM). This approach assumes that the risk of a stock is based on the sensitivity of its return to changes in the level of return on all securities in the market.

To use this procedure for estimating the required return on a stock we proceed as follows:

Step 1 Estimate the riskless rate, R_F, generally taken to be the short-term U.S. Treasury Securities rate.

Step 2 Estimate the stock's risk by calculating the variability of its return relative to variability of return on the capital market as a whole. This risk index, known as the stock's beta coefficient, b, is a measure of the risk of one security relative to the average risk on the market, or average, stock. Thus, a stock with average risk will have a beta of 1.0; low-risk stocks will have betas less than 1.0; and high-risk stocks will have betas greater than 1.0.[8]

Step 3 Estimate the rate of return on the market, or average, stock. This return, k_M, provides a benchmark for determining how investors are pricing risk as measured by the betas of individual stocks.

Step 4 Estimate the required rate of return on the firm's stock as:

$$k_e = R_F + b(k_M - R_F).$$

The value $(k_M - R_F)$ is the risk premium on the average stock. (Recall that the average stock has a beta of 1.0.) Multiplying this price of risk by the index of risk for a particular stock, b, gives us the risk premium for that stock. To illustrate, assume that $R_F = 9\%$, $k_M = 13\%$, and $b = 0.8$ for a given stock. The stock's required return is calculated as follows:

$$k_e = 9 + 0.8(13 - 9) = 9 + 3.2 = 12.2\%.$$

Had b been 1.7, indicating that the stock was more risky than the average security, k_e would have been estimated as

$$k_e = 9 + 1.7(13 - 9) = 9 + 6.8 = 15.8\%.$$

---

[8] Estimation of betas is a complex task involving regressing of returns for a stock on the average return to all securities. Securities analysts and investment advisory services publish estimates of betas that can be used for estimating equity capital costs.

Yet another procedure for determining the cost of equity is to estimate the basic required rate of return as:[9]

$$\text{Rate of Return} = \frac{\text{Dividend}}{\text{Price}} + \text{Expected Growth Rate}$$

$$k_e = \frac{D}{P} + g.$$

The rationale for this equation is that stockholder returns are derived from dividends and capital gains. If past growth rates in earnings and dividends have been relatively stable, and if investors appear to be projecting a continuation of past trends, then g may be based on the firm's historic growth rate. However, if the company's growth has been abnormally high or low, either because of its own unique situation or because of general economic conditions, then investors will not project the past growth rate into the future. In this case, g must be estimated in some other manner. Security analysts regularly make earnings growth forecasts, looking at such factors as projected sales, profit margins, and competitive factors. Someone making a cost of capital estimate can obtain such analysts' forecasts and use them as a proxy for the growth expectations of investors in general, then combine g with the expected dividend yield, to estimate k_e as

$$k_e = \frac{D}{P} + \text{Growth Rate as Projected by Security Analysts.}$$

In practical work it is best to use all the methods described above and then apply judgment when the methods produce different results. People experienced in estimating equity capital costs recognize that both careful analysis and some very fine judgments are required.

Weighted Cost of Capital. Suppose a particular firm's after-tax cost of debt is estimated to be 6 percent (the interest rate on new debt issues is 12 percent and the firm's marginal income tax rate is 50 percent); its cost of equity is estimated to be 15 percent; and the firm has decided to finance next year's projects by selling debt. The argument is sometimes advanced that the cost of these projects is 6 percent, because debt will be used to finance them.

This position contains a basic fallacy. To finance a particular set of projects with debt implies that the firm is also using up some of its po-

---

[9] The growth rate here is the growth in the price of the firm's stock, but if the dividend payout rate is constant, and if the dividend capitalization rate (k) remains unchanged, earnings, dividends, and the stock price all grow at the same rate.

tential for obtaining new low-cost debt. As expansion takes place in subsequent years, at some point the firm will find it necessary to use additional equity financing or else the debt ratio will become too large. In other words, the interest rate or component cost on debt is not the firm's true opportunity cost of this kind of capital.

To illustrate, suppose the firm has a 6 percent cost of debt and a 15 percent cost of equity. In the first year it borrows heavily, using up its debt capacity in the process, to finance projects yielding 7 percent. In the second year it has projects available that yield 13 percent, almost twice the return on first-year projects, but it cannot accept them because they would have to be financed with 15 percent equity money. To avoid this problem the firm should be viewed as an ongoing concern, and its cost of capital should be calculated as a weighted average of the various types of funds it uses. The proper set of weights to be employed in computing the weighted average cost of capital is determined by the optimal financial structure of the firm.

In general, the risk to investors is lower on debt and higher on common stock; because of risk aversion, therefore, debt is the lowest-cost source of funds, and equity the highest-cost source. Risk increases as the percentage of total capital obtained in the form of debt increases, since the higher the debt level, the greater the probability that adverse conditions will lower earnings to the point where the firm is unable to pay its interest charges and to pay off debt issues as they mature. The fact that interest rates on debt are lower than the expected rate of return (dividends plus capital gains) on common stock causes the overall, or average, cost of capital to the firm to decline as the percentage of capital raised as debt increases. However, the fact that more debt means higher risk offsets this effect to some extent. As a result, it is generally felt that the average cost of capital (1) declines at first as a firm moves from zero debt to some positive amount of debt; (2) hits a minimum (perhaps over a range rather than at some specific amount of debt); and then (3) rises as an increase in the level of debt drives the firm's risk position beyond acceptable levels. Thus, there is an optimal amount of debt for each firm, an amount of debt that minimizes its cost of capital and maximizes its value.

Figure 12.2 shows, for a hypothetical industry, how the cost of capital changes as the debt ratio increases. (The average cost of capital figures in the graph are calculated in Table 12.6.) In the figure each dot represents one of the firms in the industry. For example, the dot labeled 1 represents Firm 1, a company with no debt. Since it is financed entirely with 20 percent equity money, Firm 1's average cost of capital is 20 percent. Firm 2 uses 10 percent debt in its capital structure, and it too has a 6 percent after-tax cost of debt and 20 percent cost of equity. Firm 3 also has a 6 percent cost of debt and a 20 percent cost of equity

Figure 12.2
Hypothetical Cost of Capital Schedules for an Industry

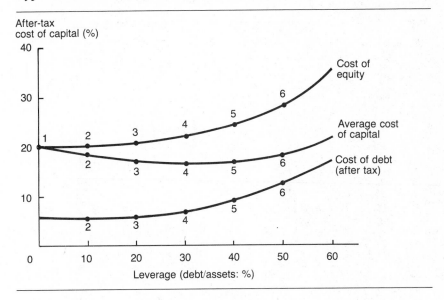

even though it uses 20 percent debt. Firm 4 has a 21 percent cost of equity and a 7 percent cost of debt. It uses 30 percent debt, and a risk premium of 1 percent has been added to the required return on equity to account for the additional risk of financial leverage. Providers of debt capital also feel that because of the added risk of financial leverage at this debt level, they should obtain higher yields on the firm's securities. In this particular industry the threshold debt ratio that begins to worry creditors is about 20 percent. Below 20 percent debt, creditors are totally unconcerned about any risk induced by debt; above 20 percent they are aware of the higher risk and require compensation in the form of higher rates of return.

In Table 12.6 the debt and equity costs of the various firms are averaged on the basis of their respective proportions of the firm's total capital. Firm 1 has a weighted average cost equal to 20 percent; Firm 2 has a weighted average cost of 18.6 percent; Firm 3 has a weighted cost of 17.2 percent; and Firm 4 has a weighted cost of 16.8 percent. These weighted costs, together with those of the other firms in the industry, are also plotted in Figure 12.2. We can see that firms with approximately 30 percent debt in their capital structure have the lowest weighted average cost of capital. Accordingly, proper calculation of the cost of capital requires that the cost of equity for a firm in the industry be given a weight of 0.70 and that debt be given a weight of 0.30.

Table 12.6
Calculation of Average Cost of Capital for Hypothetical
Firms with Different Debt Ratios

		Percentage of Total (1)	Component Cost (2)	Weighted Cost $\frac{(1) \times (2)}{100}$ (3)
Firm 1	Debt	0	6.0	0.00
	Equity	100	20.0	20.00
		100%	Average Cost	20.00
Firm 2	Debt	10	6.0	0.60
	Equity	90	20.0	18.00
		100%	Average Cost	18.60%
Firm 3	Debt	20	6.0	1.20
	Equity	80	20.0	16.00
		100%	Average Cost	17.20%
Firm 4	Debt	30	7.0	2.10
	Equity	70	21.0	14.70
		100%	Average Cost	16.80%
Firm 5	Debt	40	9.0	3.60
	Equity	60	22.5	13.50
		100%	Average Cost	17.10%
Firm 6	Debt	50	12.0	6.00
	Equity	50	24.0	12.00
		100%	Average Cost	18.00%
Firm 7	Debt	60	17.0	10.20
	Equity	40	27.5	11.00
		100%	Average Cost	21.20%

The Post-Audit

A discussion of the *post-completion audit*, or **post-audit**, is necessary in any treatment of capital budgeting. The post-audit involves (1) a comparison of actual results to those predicted in the investment proposal and (2) an explanation of observed differences.

The post-audit has several purposes, including the following:

1. *Improving Forecasts.* When decision makers systematically compare their projections to actual outcomes, estimates tend to improve. Conscious or unconscious biases are observed and eliminated; new forecasting methods will be sought as their need becomes apparent; and people simply tend to work better if they know that their actions are being monitored.

2. *Improving Operations.* Businesses are run by people, and people can perform at higher or lower levels of efficiency. When a divisional team has made a forecast about a new installation, it is, in a sense, putting its reputation on the line. Because of the post-audit these executives have every incentive to make it happen, to fulfill their prophecies. If costs are above predicted levels, sales below expectations, and so on, then managers in production, sales, and related areas will strive to improve operations and bring results into line with forecasts.

The post-audit is a complex process. First, we must recognize that each element of the cash flow forecast is subject to uncertainty, so a percentage of all projects undertaken by any reasonably venturesome firm will prove unsuccessful. This fact must be considered when appraising the performances of the operating executives who submit capital expenditure requests. Second, projects sometimes fail to meet expectations for reasons beyond the control of the operating executives and for reasons that no one could realistically be expected to anticipate. For example, the imposition of price controls in 1971 adversely affected many projects for which price increases had been projected, and the quadrupling of oil prices in 1973 hurt others. Third, it is often difficult to separate the operating results of one investment from those of a larger system. Fourth, if the post-audit process is not used carefully, executives may be reluctant to suggest potentially profitable but risky projects.

Because of these difficulties, some firms tend to play down the importance of the post-audit. However, observations of both businesses and governmental units suggest that the best-run and most successful organizations are those that put the greatest stress on post-audits. Accordingly, the post-audit is one of the most important elements in a good capital budgeting system.

Summary

Capital budgeting is the process of planning expenditures where the returns or benefits are expected to extend beyond one year. Capital budgeting decisions are among the most important faced by a firm's management because of both the size of the expenditures and the long-run nature of the commitments involved. It is a difficult process because one is dealing with estimates of events that are going to occur some distance in the future.

Capital budgeting decision making requires an integration of all the elements of the firm. Demand projections must be developed for the firm's products. Production and cost relationships have to be analyzed.

Personnel requirements must be estimated. The funds necessary to support the investment project have to be procured.

Capital budgeting decisions should be made by comparing the marginal return on investment with the marginal cost of capital. The net present value (NPV) technique was shown to be a theoretically correct method for analyzing investment proposals.

For certain complex capital budgeting situations (those involving capital rationing, mutually exclusive, and closely interrelated projects) the NPV approach may be inappropriate for project selection. Profitability index (PI), or benefit-cost ratio analysis, can sometimes improve decision making in these complex circumstances.

Calculation of the relevant cost of capital is a difficult problem. Proper decision making requires that a weighted average of the costs of the various types of capital employed by the firm should be used for all capital budgeting decisions.

Questions

12.1 Define the term *capital budgeting*.

12.2 How are appropriate discount rates selected for *NPV* analysis?

12.3 How is *NPV* related to the *PI*?

12.4 When is *NPV* analysis appropriate? When should the *PI* method be substituted for *NPV* analysis?

12.5 What major steps are involved in the capital budgeting process?

12.6 The economics of input combination tell us that factors should be used in proportions such that the marginal product/price ratios for all inputs are equal. For capital management policy, this implies that the marginal net cost of debt should be equal to the marginal net cost of equity in the optimal capital structure. Yet we typically see firms issuing debt at interest rates significantly below the yields investors are estimated to require on the firm's equity shares. Does this mean that these firms are not operating with optimal capital structures? Explain.

12.7 New York City licenses taxicabs in two classes: (1) for operation by companies with fleets and (2) for operation by independent driver-owners having only one cab. It also fixes the rates that taxis charge. For many years now, no new licenses have been issued in either class. There is an unofficial market for the medallions that signify the possession of a license. A medallion for an independent cab recently sold for roughly $70,000 in this market.

a) Discuss the factors determining the price of a medallion. For concreteness, develop hypothetical values of the various components that together can be summarized in a price of $70,000.

b) What factors would determine whether a change in the fare fixed by the city would raise or lower the price of a medallion?

c) Cab drivers, whether hired by companies or as owners of their own cabs, seem unanimous in opposing any increase in the number of cabs licensed. They argue that an increase in the number of cabs, by increasing competition for customers, would drive down what they regard as an already unduly low return to drivers. Is their economic analysis correct? Who would benefit and who would lose from an expansion in the number of licenses issued at a nominal fee?

12.8 What important purposes are served by the post-audit?

Solved Problem

12.1 The Metro Communications Company is considering two mutually exclusive capital budgeting projects. These projects have equal lives of two years and identical costs of $8,000. Relevant cash flow data for the two projects is as follows:

		Project A			
	Year 1			Year 2	
Pr.		Cash Flow		Pr.	Cash Flow
0.35		$4,500		0.25	$5,000
0.40		5,000		0.50	6,000
0.25		6,000		0.25	7,000

		Project B			
	Year 1			Year 2	
Pr.		Cash Flow		Pr.	Cash Flow
0.20		$(200)		0.10	$1,000
0.30		4,000		0.30	4,500
0.30		5,000		0.35	6,500
0.20		7,200		0.25	8,000

a) Calculate the expected value of the annual cash flows from each project.

b) Calculate the risk-adjusted *NPV* of each project, using a 14 percent cost of capital for the more risky project, and 12 percent for the less risky one. Use variability of cash flows as an indicator of risk.

c) Calculate the *PI* for each project.

d) Calculate the *IRR* of each project.

e) Rank order the projects, using the *NPV*, *PI*, and *IRR* criteria.

Solution

a) The expected annual cash flow from each project can be calculated as shown on page 516.

Project A

Probability	×	Year 1 Annual Net Cash Flow			Probability	×	Year 2 Annual Net Cash Flow		
0.35	×	$4,500	=	$1,575	0.25	×	$5,000	=	$1,250
0.40	×	5,000	=	2,000	0.50	×	6,000	=	3,000
0.25	×	6,000	=	1,500	0.25	×	7,000	=	1,750

Expected Annual Cash Flow = $5,075.   Expected Annual Cash Flow = $6,000 .

Project B

Probability	×	Year 1 Annual Net Cash Flow			Probability	×	Year 2 Annual Net Cash Flow		
0.20	×	$ −200	=	$ −40	0.10	×	$1,000	=	$ 100
0.30	×	4,000	=	1,200	0.30	×	4,500	=	1,350
0.30	×	5,000	=	1,500	0.35	×	6,500	=	2,275
0.20	×	7,200	=	1,440	0.25	×	8,000	=	2,000

Expected Annual Cash Flow = $4,100 .   Expected Annual Cash Flow = $5,725 .

b) Project B appears to be the more risky since it has a higher variability of cash flows. Project B will thus be discounted at 14 percent. Project A will be evaluated by using a 12 percent cost of capital.

Project A

NPV_A = $5,075 (*PVIF*, 12%, 1 year) + $6,000 (*PVIF*, 12%, 2 years) − $8,000

= 5,075(0.8929) + 6,000(0.7972) − 8,000

= 9,314.67 − 8,000

= $1,314.67.

Project B

NPV_B = $4,100 (*PVIF*, 14%, 1 year) + $5,725 (*PVIF*, 14%, 2 years) − $8,000

= 4,100(0.8772) + 5,725(0.7695) − 8,000

= 8,001.91 − 8,000

= $1.91.

c) The profitability index for each project is:

Project A

$$PI_A = \frac{PV \text{ of Cash Flows}}{Cost}$$

$$= \frac{\$9,314.67}{\$8,000.00}$$

$$= 1.164.$$

Project B

$$PI_B = \frac{PV \text{ of Cash Flows}}{Cost}$$

$$= \frac{\$8,001.91}{\$8,000.00}$$

$$= 1.000.$$

d) The *IRR* is the interest rate that produces an *NPV* equal to zero.

Project A

For Project *A* set

NPV_A = $5,075 (*PVIF*, *X*%, 1 year) + $6,000 (*PVIF*, *X*%, 2 years)
       − $8,000 = 0.

The *IRR* can be easily calculated by many types of hand-held calculators, or by trial and error with various interest rates in the preceding equation.

Interest Rate	NPV
20%	$395.40
24%	−4.61
28%	−372.50

The *IRR* for Project *A* is just under 24 percent.

Project B

For Project *B* set

NPV_B = $4,100 (*PVIF*, *X*%, 1 year) + $5,725 (*PVIF*, *X*%, 2 years)
       − $8,000 = 0.

Using trial and error with various interest rates in the above equation, we find

Interest Rate	NPV
12%	$224.86
14%	1.91
16%	−210.57

The *IRR* for Project *B* is slightly more than 14 percent.

e) The rank order of the two investment alternatives is:

$$NPV: NPV_A > NPV_B \rightarrow A,B$$

$$PI: \quad PI_A > \quad PI_B \rightarrow A,B$$

$$IRR: \ IRR_A > \ IRR_B \rightarrow A,B.$$

Therefore, irrespective of which criterion is adopted, Project A is preferred to Project B.

Solved Problem

12.2 Racine Mill Works Inc. is considering a range of capital budgeting projects. In order to decide on whether or not to accept specific investment proposals, the firm needs to determine its opportunity cost of capital. Racine has learned that new 13 percent bonds can be sold at par, and new common stock can be sold for $30. Earnings per share have been growing at 10 percent, and this growth rate is expected to continue. Dividends per share next year are estimated to be $1.50, and the firm faces a 50 percent corporate income tax rate.

a) What are the values of the component costs that are needed for a cost of capital calculation?

b) Assuming equal weights for the cost of capital components, calculate the weighted average cost of capital.

Solution

a)

$$\text{Cost of Debt} = i(1 - t) = 0.13(1 - 0.5) = 0.065.$$

$$\text{Cost of Equity} = k_e = \frac{D}{P} + g = \frac{1.50}{30} + 0.10 = 0.15.$$

b) The weighted average cost of capital, using equal weights for debt and equity, is:

$$k = (\text{Debt Weight})(\text{Debt Cost}) + (\text{Equity Weight})(\text{Equity Cost})$$

$$= (0.5)(0.065) + (0.5)(0.15)$$

$$= .1075, \text{ or } 10.75 \text{ Percent.}$$

Problem Set

12.1 Max Miller must choose between two mutually exclusive investment projects. Each project costs $10,000 and has an expected life of

four years. Annual net cash flows from each project begin one year
after the initial investment is made and have the following
characteristics:

	Probability	Annual Cash Flow
Project A	0.15	$ 300
	0.35	3,300
	0.30	6,100
	0.20	5,200
	1.00	
Project B	0.05	$2,100
	0.40	3,600
	0.25	3,900
	0.30	3,500
	1.00	

Miller has decided to discount the riskier project using a 14 percent
cost of capital, and the less risky project using 12 percent.

a) Calculate the expected value of the annual cash flows from each
project.

b) Calculate the risk-adjusted *NPV* of each project.

c) Calculate the *IRR* for each project.

d) Rank order the two projects, using *NPV* and *IRR* criteria.

12.2 EZ-Print Inc. is considering three locations in California for a new
printing shop. Each location involves different equipment, set-up costs,
production costs, and expected annual sales volumes. Relevant data on
each location are:

	Anaheim	Santa Ana	Huntington Beach
Annual orders sold	800,000	650,000	450,000
Average order sale price	$ 10.00	$ 12.00	$ 14.00
Average order direct cost	4.00	4.60	5.00
Annual marketing costs	100,000	85,000	65,000
Required investment	4,000,000	3,500,000	3,000,000

Assume: (1) The company's marginal tax rate is 50 percent; (2) the shop
in each location is expected to have a six-year life (involves a six-year
commitment); (3) the firm uses straight-line depreciation; (4) the average
cost of capital is 15 percent; (5) the proposed new printing shops are of
about the same riskiness as the firm's other businesses; and (6) the company has already spent $60,000 on market research, an amount that has
been capitalized and is to be written off over the life of the project.

a) Calculate the expected yearly net cash flows for each potential
location. (*Hint*: Yearly net cash flow equals net profit after taxes
plus depreciation and amortization charges.)

b) Calculate the *NPV* for each location. Rank order the investment alternatives, using the *NPV* criterion.

c) Calculate the *PI* for each location. Rank order the projects, using a *PI* criterion.

d) Discuss any differences in your rank orders for parts b and c above.

e) Suppose that EZ-Print's overall business is quite cyclical, moving up and down with the economy, and the sales from the Anaheim location are expected to be countercyclical? Might this have any bearing on your decision?

12.3 Braun's Drug Store is a medium-sized drug store located in Coral Gables, Florida, which is owned and operated by Paul Braun. Braun's sells pharmaceuticals, cosmetics, toiletries, magazines, and various novelties. Braun's 1984 net income statement is presented next:

Sales revenue:		$1,500,000
Total costs:		
Cost of goods sold	$830,000	
Wages and salaries	200,000	
Rent	100,000	
Depreciation	50,000	
Utilities	40,000	
Miscellaneous	20,000	
Total		1,240,000
Net profit before tax		$ 260,000

The sales and expenses for Braun's have remained relatively constant in the past few years and are expected to remain unchanged in the future.

To increase sales, Braun is considering using some floor space for a small restaurant. Braun would operate the restaurant for an initial three-year period, after which time its profitability would be reevaluated. The incremental investment requirement for the restaurant is $20,000 for furniture, equipment, utensils, and so on. This is the only capital investment required during the initial three year period. At the end of that time, additional capital would be required if the restaurant operation is continued and there would be no capital recovery if it is dropped. The restaurant is expected to have sales of $65,000 and food and materials expenses of $18,000 per year. The restaurant is also expected to increase wage and salary expenses by 8 percent, and utility expenses by 5 percent. Since the restaurant will reduce the floor space available for display of other merchandise, sales for the nonrestaurant items are expected to decline by 1 percent.

a) Develop the relevant cash flows for the restaurant.

b) Assume that Braun has the capital necessary to install the restaurant and places a 15 percent opportunity cost on those funds. Should the restaurant be installed in the store? Why or why not?

12.4 The management of Hauschel Manufacturing Inc. is reviewing investment proposals available for the next fiscal year. Hauschel has historically used the *NPV* method for determining which investment proposals will be accepted. Of course, in order to use *NPV* analyses, the opportunity cost of capital must be determined. Current market conditions indicate that Hauschel can sell new 14 percent bonds at par and new common stock for $40 per share. Additional current financial information about Hauschel is also available:

Price/earnings ratio	8
Earnings per share growth rate	10 percent
(this growth rate is expected to continue)	
Estimated dividend per share next year	$2.50
Earnings/share	$5.00
Company bond rating	AA
Corporate tax rate	50 percent

a) Calculate the component cost values needed to determine the cost of capital.

b) Assuming that Hauschel uses 40 percent debt financing and 60 percent equity financing, calculate the weighted average cost of capital.

c) Assume now that Hauschel's investment banker will purchase from Hauschel all newly issued stock for $4 per share below the current market price. This $4 *flotation cost* is compensation for the cost and risk involved in marketing Hauschel stock to individual and institutional investors. Calculate the effect of flotation costs on Hauschel's component cost of equity.

d) With flotation costs, what is the relevant cost of equity?

12.5 J&J Electronics is a small but rapidly growing electronic equipment manufacturer located in St. Louis, Missouri. As an individual investor, Chris Nicholas is intrigued by the company's rapid growth during the past five years and prospects for more of the same during the next decade. Although Nicholas is impressed with the 6 percent riskless rate of return currently available on U.S. government securities, she finds stocks in general appealing in light of their traditional 5 percent per year risk premium.

While investigating J&J for possible purchase, Nicholas learns that a leading investment advisory service has estimated a beta of 2.0 for the stock. Therefore, J&J is twice as risky as the market as a whole.

a) Calculate the cost of equity capital for J&J.

b) Calculate Nicholas's expected return on J&J should she decide to buy the stock.

12.6 Community Psychiatric Centres Inc. (CPC) provides both inpatient and outpatient psychiatric counseling services in the Dallas Metroplex area. The company has no outstanding debt and has been internally financed by its founder, Dr. Anne Lewis, who owns all 100,000 shares of common stock (equity) outstanding. Following rapid growth in demand for its services, CPC must raise at least $1 million for capital expenditures. In order to meet these capital needs, the company must seek outside funds.

A local bank has offered to lend CPC funds at 16 percent interest but requires that CPC raise at least one half of new capital from equity investors. Given a projected growth rate of 20 percent per year, an investment dealer advises Lewis that additional common stock could be issued and sold at 5 times current earnings of $6.00 per share. Lewis is adamant that there be no current dividend and that she retain at least 80 percent ownership in the company.

    a) Set up and interpret the linear program that CPC would use to minimize the after-tax cost of the additional required capital, using both the inequality and equality forms of the constraint conditions. Assume a 50 percent tax rate.

    b) Using a graph, solve the problem and completely interpret your solution values.

    c) Assuming the cost of equity capital remains at 20 percent, what is the minimum after-tax cost of debt required in order to change the optimal capital structure as calculated?

References

Ben-Horim, Moshe and Levy, Haim. "Management of Accounts Receivable Under Inflation." *Financial Management* 12 (Spring 1983): 42–48.

Bierman, Harold, Jr. *Strategic Financial Planning.* New York: Free Press, 1980.

Brigham, Eugene F. *Financial Management Theory and Practice.* 2d ed. Hinsdale, Ill.: The Dryden Press, 1982.

Brigham, Eugene F. *Fundamentals of Financial Management.* 3d ed. Hinsdale, Ill.: The Dryden Press, 1983.

Copeland, Thomas E. and Weston, J. Fred. *Financial Theory and Corporate Policy.* 2d ed. Reading, Mass.: Addison-Wesley, 1983.

Durand, David. "Comprehensiveness in Capital Budgeting." *Financial Management* 10 (Winter 1981): 7–13.

Ellsworth, Richard R. "Subordinate Financial Policy to Corporate Strategy." *Harvard Business Review* 61 (November–December 1983): 170–182.

Greenfield, Robert L.; Randall, Maury R. and Woods, John C. "Financial Leverage and Use of the Net Present Value Investment Criterion." *Financial Management* 12 (Autumn 1983): 40–44.

Park, Chan S. "Probabilistic Benefit-Cost Analysis." *Engineering Economist* 29 (Winter 1984): 83–100.

Pinches, George E. "Myopia, Capital Budgeting and Decision Making." *Financial Management* 3 (Autumn 1982): 6–19.

Rappaport, Alfred and Taggart, Robert A. Jr. "Evaluation of Capital Expenditure Proposals Under Inflation." *Financial Management* 11 (Spring 1982): 5–13.

Schall, Lawrence D.; Sudem, Gary L. and Geijsbeek, William R. Jr. "Survey and Analysis of Capital Budgeting Methods." *Journal of Finance* (March 1978): 281–287.

Seed, Allen H. III. "Understanding Inflation's Impact." *Journal of Business Strategy* 2 (Fall 1981): 3–13.

Shashua, Leon and Goldschmidt, Yaaqov. *Tools for Financial Management: Emphasis on Inflation.* Lexington, Mass.: Lexington Books, 1983.

Singhvi, Surendra S. *Planning for Capital Investments.* Oxford, Ohio: Planning Executives Institute, 1979.

Chapter 13

Competitive Strategy

Key Terms

Economic censuses	*Learning curve*
Economies of scope	*Growth share matrix*
Gross national product	*Strategic business units*

The theory and practice of competitive strategy are among the most dynamic and fascinating subjects in business. Although a complete treatment of the topic is beyond the scope of an introductory text in managerial economics, a brief introduction can illustrate how the tools and techniques of managerial economics are used in the formulation and implementation of an effective competitive strategy. This process involves an evaluation of current performance and growth opportunities, sometimes referred to as the *strategic audit*, as well as implementation and strategy reevaluation phases. Given the rapidly changing character of markets and competition, a constant reevaluation of the strategic plan and ongoing modification are important for economic success. Feedback throughout the formulation and implementation phases is not only helpful in defining an effective competitive strategy; it is an essential component of successful management.

In this chapter we analyze several important strategic concepts. The first of these is the strategic business unit. Access to reliable data collected on a regular and consistent basis is mandatory if the firm is to identify its various strategic business units, monitor their performance, and identify attractive opportunities. Information made available by the U.S. Department of Commerce on market structure and economic performance in its economic census publications help meet this important data requirement. Thus, we will consider in some detail important characteristics of census information and how these data can be utilized in strategic decision making. We then consider the growth share matrix method of categorizing strategic business units in terms of realized and potential performance. Here information on important economic trends is incorporated into the analysis to learn which among the firm's various businesses are its potential "stars" of the future. Economies of scope is a third important strategic concept that we consider. A major implication of the economies of scope concept is that firms will be successful when they emphasize areas where their special expertise or capability creates a comparative advantage that is not easily imitated by competitors. And finally, we argue that competitive strategy formulation and implementation are likely to be most successful when the process is reflected in the day-to-day operations of the firm. Optimal managerial decisions are only possible when both short- and long-run considerations are consistently incorporated into the decision process.

Strategic Business Units

One of the key competitive strategy concepts is that the various activities of the firm should be analyzed in segments called **strategic business units**, or SBUs. An SBU is defined as an independent business unit offering related products to an identifiable market. SBUs offer a basis for the development and analysis of strategic policy because they enable a company to identify its markets, competitors, and relative position for an entire spectrum of products. For example, rather than basing policy on the general perception that companies A and B are the firm's main competitors in the office equipment business, an integrated manufacturer of office equipment might instead formulate policy on the basis of the firm's dominant position in dry copiers, competitive but nonleading position in typewriters and word processors, and perhaps lagging performance in computers and peripheral equipment. The SBU concept is useful in that it makes it possible for the firm to identify the markets in which it is successful, as well as those in which it is less so. Ideally, by focusing attention on its successes, a firm will become better at understanding the factors that have led to that success. Then, this knowledge can be applied to improving performance in less successful markets, as well as to identify areas for fruitful expansion, maintenance, or perhaps even exit.

As we learned in Chapter 8, a market consists of all firms and individuals willing and able to buy or sell similar competing products. In identifying competing products the key criterion is similarity in *use*. Precise determination of whether or not a specific good is a distinct economic product involves an evaluation of cross-price elasticities for broad classes of goods. When cross-price elasticities are large and positive, goods are substitutes for one another and can be thought of as competing products in a single market. Thus, positive cross-price elasticities identify a firm's competitors. Conversely, large negative cross-price elasticities indicate complementary products. If complementary products are produced by a single firm, these products must be evaluated as a single product line serving the same market. If complementary products are produced by other companies, then evaluating the potential of a given SBU can involve incorporating exogenous influences beyond the firm's control. When cross-price elasticities are near zero, goods are in separate economic markets and can be separately analyzed as serving distinct consumer needs. Therefore, using cross-price elasticity criteria to disaggregate the firm's overall product line into its distinct economic components is an important component in the application of the SBU concept.

In order to identify relevant economic markets and define their characteristics, firms in the United States make extensive use of economic data collected by the Bureau of Census of the U.S. Department of Commerce. Since these data provide valuable information on economic activity across the broad spectrum of U.S. industry, we will briefly consider the method and scope of the economic censuses.

The Economic Censuses

The **economic censuses** provide a comprehensive statistical profile of a large segment of the national economy. Included are censuses of manufacturers (briefly discussed in Chapter 8), retail and wholesale trade, services, minerals, and construction. In 1977, the most recent census year available, these industries accounted for nearly 70 percent of total economic activity originating in the private sector. Principal industry groups not covered were finance, insurance, real estate, agriculture, forestry, communications, public utilities, and transportation. However, limited transportation-related information is collected, including the distance that commodities are shipped and the type of transport employed.

The economic censuses are the primary source of data concerning changes in the number and size distribution of competitors, output, and employment in the economy. They are also used extensively by the government in compiling national income accounts, and as a basis for current surveys of industrial production, productivity, and prices. Census data are also used extensively by government agencies in setting public policy and monitoring economic programs. Manufacturers and distributors rely on census data to analyze current and potential markets. The censuses provide data that can be used for demand and cost forecasting; market penetration analysis; the layout of sales territories; the allocation of advertising budgets; and the location of plants, warehouses, and retail outlets. Trade and professional associations rely on census information to learn about changes in the number, size, and geographic dispersion of firms in their industry. State and local governments and chambers of commerce use census data to assess the business climate, as well as to gauge the success of programs designed to increase business investment and employment opportunities in local areas.

A further important characteristic of the economic censuses is their coverage of geographic trends. For example, the 1977 *Census of Manufacturers* measured industrial activity at the state, county, city, and Standard Metropolitan Statistical Area (SMSA) levels. In recent years, there has been increasing interest in state information in preference to data on broader regions. As a result, the 1977 census gave first precedence to publishing state figures. In addition to the data for legally constituted geographic units such as states, counties, and cities, manufacturing activity levels are also provided on 280 SMSAs. SMSAs are integrated economic and social units with a large volume of daily travel and communication between the central city (having 50,000 or more population) and outlying areas. Each SMSA consists of one whole county or more and may include both industrialized counties and adjoining counties that are largely residential in character. In the 1977 census, detail for various industries is shown at the SMSA level if data for individual companies would not be disclosed, and the industry had at least 250 employees.

In addition to being a comprehensive source of information on economic activity, census data have the compelling virtues of easy access and widespread availability. Census reports can be purchased directly from the Government Printing Office at modest cost or can be consulted free of charge at most major public and college libraries. In addition, census data and reports are often republished and distributed by trade associations, business journals, magazines, and newspapers.

The Census Classification System

Census data are collected on an establishment basis, that is, at a single physical location engaged in a specific line of business. The establishment level is best suited for obtaining direct measures of output, and inputs such as labor, materials, capital, and so on. It is also a useful level of aggregation for providing detailed industry and geographic tabulations. On the other hand, statistics measuring overall income and balance sheet data are best collected at the company or enterprise level. Enterprise statistics on income and balance sheet data are made available to the public by the Internal Revenue Service in its *Statistics of Income* and by the Federal Trade Commission in its *Quarterly Financial Report for Manufacturing, Mining and Trade.*

The census classification of individual establishments by sector, industry group, industry, and products is called the Standard Industrial Classification (SIC) system. Table 13.1 shows the first step in this process and illustrates how the entire scope of economic activity is subdivided into sectors described by two-digit classifications. Below the two-digit major group or sector level the SIC system proceeds to disaggregated levels of increasingly narrowly defined activity. Currently, the SIC system proceeds from very general two-digit industry groups to very specific seven-digit product classifications. To illustrate, Table 13.2 shows the breakdown that occurs as one moves from the two-digit food and kindred products major group, to the seven-digit canned

Table 13.1

Standard Industrial Classifications of Economic Activity

Sector	Two-Digit SIC Codes
Agriculture, Forestry, and Fisheries	01–09
Mining	10–14
Contract Construction	15–17
Manufacturing	20–39
Transportation; Communication; Electric, Gas, and Sanitary Services	40–49
Wholesale and Retail Trade	50–59
Finance, Insurance, and Real Estate	60–67
Services	70–89
Public Administration	91–97
Nonclassifiable Establishments	99

Table 13.2

Census Classification Example

Digit Level	Number of Classifications	Example SIC Code	Description
Two	20	20	Food and Kindred Products
Three	144	202	Dairy Products
Four	452	2023	Condensed and Evaporated Milk Industry
Five	1,500	20232	Canned Milk
Six			(Not currently utilized)
Seven	13,000	2023212	Canned Evaporated Milk

evaporated milk product category. As discussed in Chapter 8, most economists agree that four-digit level classifications correspond quite closely with the economic definition of a market. That is, establishments grouped at the four-digit level produce products that are ready substitutes for one another and thus act as competitors. Therefore, managers who analyze census data to learn about the number and size distribution of actual and potential competitors focus their attention primarily on data provided at the four-digit level. For this reason, we focused our attention on four-digit level concentration data in our earlier discussion of market structure.

Trends in Aggregate Economic Activity

In many instances, fruitful areas for expansion of SBUs are suggested when broad economic trends are analyzed. Therefore, strategic planners must be familiar with recent trends in aggregate measures of economic activity such as gross national product, gross domestic product, and national income.

Gross national product (GNP) is the total value of goods and services produced in the economy. The goods and services included are largely those bought for final use in the market economy. However, a number of inputted values for "income in kind" are also included in GNP, the most important of which is the rental value of owner-occupied housing. Therefore, in a broader context, GNP measures the market value of output attributable to all factors of production (including labor). A related measure, national income is the aggregate of labor and property earnings that can be attributed to current production. It is the sum of employee compensation, proprietor's income, rental income, corporate profits, and net interest. GNP differs from national income mainly in that GNP includes allowances for depreciation and indirect business taxes (sales, excise, and so on).

Figure 13.1 shows the trend in GNP during the post–World War II period. When measured in current dollars, GNP displays a very significant upward trend. These changes in current dollar GNP reflect real changes in the quantity and quality of goods and services produced in the economy, as well as the effects of inflation. In fact, during periods of rampant double-digit inflation, such as that experienced during the late 1970s and early 1980s, current dollar GNP can continue to rise despite constant or even falling rates of real economic activity.

Whereas current dollar GNP figures reflect prices prevailing during that specific period, constant dollar GNP figures reflect prices prevailing in a base period such as 1972. Constant dollar values can be obtained by dividing (or deflating) current dollar figures by an appropriate index of prices prevailing in the 1972 base period and are shown as the broken line in Figure 13.1. From the trend in constant dollar GNP, a short, but

Figure 13.1
Gross National Product, 1945–1982

13.1

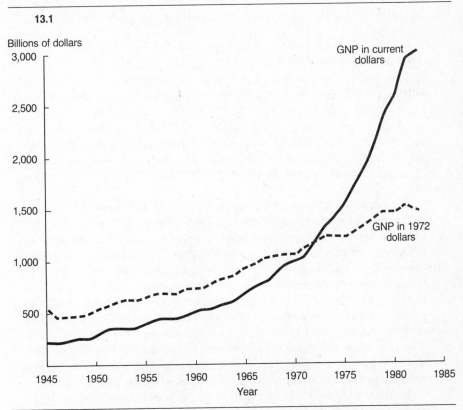

Billions of dollars

Source: *Economic Report of the President* (U.S. Government Printing Office, Washington, D.C.: 1983), pp. 170–171.

sharp, economic recession in 1982, for example, and a longer but less severe decline during the 1973–1975 period are apparent. Thus, by separating out the effects of changes in real economic activity from the effects of inflation, changes in constant dollar GNP provide a more complete picture of trends in the economic environment.

Understanding the direction, magnitude, and duration of changes in the overall economy is of vital importance to the success of firms. Trends in the economy have immediate implications for hiring policy, production, inventory and trade credit decisions, capital investment and capital structure decisions, and so on. Whereas poorly structured or poorly run firms can survive and even prosper for brief periods during vibrant economic expansion, they suffer greatly and often fail during economic contractions. Similarly, firms that ignore basic trends affecting the overall makeup of economic activity risk losing access to large and growing markets. In the United States and many other countries, it is important that firms consider the implications of a rapidly growing services sector for strategic planning. Indeed, perhaps no other economic aspect of the post–World War II period is as striking as the growth in services.

The Services Economy

During 1982 current dollar GNP in the United States totaled $3,073.0 billion. Of this amount, $1,280.9 billion represented the value of goods (durable and nondurable); $1,511.1 billion represented the value of services (private and government); and $281.0 billion represented the value of new construction (structures). This means that roughly one half of total final demand in the economy can be directly accounted for in terms of services such as legal advice, medical care, entertainment, and so on.

However, by only considering final demand one substantially underestimates the relative importance of services in the economy. This is because services account for a large share of intermediate demand in the goods and structures categories. To illustrate, consider a building construction project where, as is typical, the general contractor retains the services of independent plumbers, electricians, painters, and so on. Indeed, these independent contractors may be responsible for a large portion of the cost (value) of the overall project. Nevertheless, the value of their services will not be reflected in the service sector of GNP since the total value of the project will be entered under the heading of structures. Similarly, much of the value of the goods portion of GNP reflects the value of services involved with transportation and distribution.

In order to get an accurate picture of the relative importance of services in the economy, it is necessary to consider the share of GNP and employment that originate in services-producing sectors. Table 13.3 shows the distribution of GNP and employment by industry of origin during 1982. Among private industries, the goods-producing sector includes agriculture, mining, construction, and manufacturing. The services-producing sector includes transportation and public utilities; wholesale and retail trade; finance; services (medical, legal, and so on); government and government enterprise. From the figures in Table 13.3 we see that in 1982 goods-producing industries accounted for $953.7 billion, or 31 percent of GNP, whereas services accounted for $2,072.0 billion, or more than 67 percent of GNP. Thus, when both final and intermediate demand for goods and services are considered, services account for over two thirds of total activity. The importance of services in the economy becomes even more pronounced when we consider that goods-producing industries accounted for only 26.4 percent of total employment in 1982, versus 73.6 percent, or nearly three fourths of total employment, for services. In sum, services currently account for far

Table 13.3

Gross National Product and Employment by Industry of Origin, 1982

	Gross national product		Employment	
	($ billions)	(percentage)	(thousands)	(percentage)
Domestic industries (gross domestic product)	$3,025.7	98.5	96,484	100.0
Private industries	2,661.8	86.6	77,044	79.9
Goods				
Agriculture, forestry, and fisheries	84.3	2.7	1,634	1.7
Farms	74.1	2.4	1,152	1.2
Agricultural services, forestry, and fisheries	10.2	0.3	482	0.5
Mining	116.1	3.8	1,125	1.2
Construction	122.4	4.0	3,871	4.0
Manufacturing	630.9	20.5	18,885	19.6
Durable goods	367.8	12.0	11,115	11.5
Nondurable goods	263.1	8.6	7,770	8.1
Services				
Transportation and public utilities	279.7	9.1	5,077	5.3
Transportation	106.0	3.5	2,779	2.9
Communication	85.6	2.8	1,426	1.5
Electric, gas, and sanitary services	88.2	2.9	872	0.9
Wholesale trade	210.3	6.8	5,324	5.5
Retail trade	279.9	9.1	15,208	15.8
Finance, insurance, and real estate	507.1	16.5	5,500	5.7
Finance and insurance	147.4	4.8	4,429	4.6
Real estate	359.8	11.7	1,071	1.1
Miscellaneous Services (legal, medical, etc.)	431.1	14.0	20,420	21.2
Government and government enterprise	363.4	11.8	19,440	20.2
Government	324.1	10.5	18,705	19.4
Government enterprise	39.3	1.3	735	0.8
Rest of the world	47.3	1.5	−25	0.0
Total	$3,073.0	100.0	96,459	100.0

Source: Survey of Current Business, vol. 63 (July 1983), p. 68.

more than one half of aggregate economic activity in the United States; a ratio of two thirds or three quarters is more nearly accurate.

The dominant role played by services in the U.S. economy today is the result of a process of change spanning several decades. Table 13.4 shows the growing relative importance of service-producing industries, using data compiled by the Bureau of the Census. These data show the breakdown by industry of gross domestic product (GDP) as reported for census years between 1947 and 1982. GDP is the value of

Table 13.4

Gross Domestic Product, by Industry, for Selected Years, 1947 to 1982

Industry Group	(Percentages)							
	1947	1954	1958	1963	1967	1972	1977	1982
Goods								
Agriculture, forestry, and								
fisheries	9.0	5.7	4.9	3.7	3.0	3.0	2.8	2.7
Mining	3.0	3.0	2.8	2.2	1.8	1.6	2.6	3.9
Construction	4.0	4.7	4.7	4.6	4.7	5.1	4.6	4.1
Manufacturing	28.7	29.2	27.7	28.3	28.0	25.0	24.4	20.8
Nondurable goods	*14.2*	*12.5*	*12.1*	*11.8*	*11.2*	*10.2*	*9.8*	*8.7*
Durable goods	*14.5*	*16.7*	*15.6*	*16.5*	*16.8*	*14.8*	*14.6*	*12.2*
Services								
Transportation and public								
utilities	8.9	9.0	9.1	8.9	8.6	8.9	9.0	9.2
Wholesale and retail trade	19.2	16.7	16.8	16.2	16.4	17.0	17.0	16.1
Finance, insurance, and								
real estate	10.1	12.8	14.0	14.4	14.4	14.5	14.6	16.8
Miscellaneous Services								
(legal, medical, etc.)	8.8	8.4	9.5	10.1	10.8	11.6	12.4	14.2
Government and govern-								
ment enterprise	8.4	10.1	10.5	11.1	12.1	13.3	12.5	12.0
Gross domestic product	100.0	100.0	100.0	100.0	100.0	100.0	100.0	100.0

Sources: *Census of Manufacturers*, 1977, and *Survey of Current Business*, July 1983.

goods and services attributable to labor and property located within
the United States and equals GNP minus the net inflow of labor and
property income from abroad. Although this inflow has increased during recent years, GDP still accounts for well over 98 percent of GNP
(see Table 13.3). Thus, trends in GDP, like trends in GNP (see Figure
13.1), provide an interesting perspective on important changes in the
overall economy.

It is apparent from the data in Table 13.4 that the share of economic
output from the goods-producing sector has been in a long-term decline. On an overall basis, the goods share of GDP has fallen from 44.7
to 31.5 percent between 1947 and 1982. The relative decline has been
most severe in agricultural goods but also significant in manufacturing. The rising importance of services has largely been the result of rapid
growth in financial services, final demand for miscellaneous services,
and government. Within the transportation and public utility sector,
rapid growth in communications has largely offset the declining importance of transportation services. Overall, the relative share of services in
GDP has risen from 55.4 percent to 68.3 percent. Although recent trends
suggest that limits on the future growth of government may emerge,

no restrictions on growth in other important service sectors are apparent in the foreseeable future. On the contrary, it is likely to be spurred by such factors as advances in technology and increased education.

Despite obvious measurement and classification problems, it is clear that the services sector of the U.S. economy has grown rapidly in both absolute and relative terms during recent decades. Services now account for well more than one half, and perhaps as much as three fourths of aggregate economic activity in the United States. This has important implications for competitive strategy as it affects both the types of products desired by consumers and the size and organization of successful firms. Strategic business units often consist of a combination of goods and services that together constitute an identifiable product line. Computers, peripheral equipment, and software services, for example, might together constitute an information system's SBU for the integrated office equipment manufacturer described earlier. In light of growing specialization in user needs, software services may ultimately prove to be most important in terms of both revenues and profits. Thus, even when the provision of services involves unique facilities and personnel, the growth in services demand will have important implications for firms producing goods and services alike.

Identifying relevant SBUs is only the first, albeit important, step in the competitive strategy process. Once identified, the realized and future potential of SBUs must be determined in order that appropriate expansion, maintenance, or exit decisions can be made. Just as census data are helpful in identifying SBUs, they are also useful in performance evaluation. Although firm and census data provide necessary information on firm and industry benchmarks for performance evaluation, a useful conceptual framework is provided by a tool called the *market share matrix*. We now turn to this second key strategic concept.

The Growth Share Matrix

The **growth share matrix** is a means of characterizing a firm's current and potential SBUs based on data generated in the information gathering phase of the strategic audit. The growth share matrix shows both the cash generating capabilities of various SBUs and their cash requirements. As shown in Figure 13.2, the box in the upper right-hand quadrant includes units that are "stars" because they have high market share in a rapidly growing market. These units have great potential, given the advantages of dominant firms in growing areas. "Question marks," which have low market share in a rapidly growing market, occupy the lower right-hand quadrant. These units may or may not have an attractive future depending upon the firm's ability to capitalize on the

Figure 13.2
The Growth Share Matrix

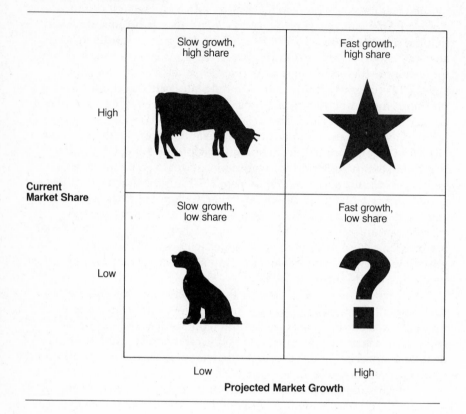

opportunities, while avoiding the pitfalls, of a rapidly changing market. SBUs with a low market share in slowly growing markets are commonly referred to as "dogs." Given their weak market position in stagnant markets, these units offer only a limited future potential and sometimes should be dropped so that available funds and managerial talents might be redeployed in areas with better prospects. And finally, units falling in the low growth and high market share category, the upper left-hand quadrant, are called "cash cows" because high current profits can be "milked" from these businesses and reinvested in other markets with greater growth potential. Although cash cows are clearly not as desirable as stars, few companies seek to divest them, preferring instead to retain them and the degree of stability they lend to profits.

Perhaps the greatest benefit of the growth share matrix approach is that it focuses attention on the various components of a firm's business in terms of both historical results and unrealized potential. This strategic perspective provides a discipline that forces management to characterize proposals from various operating units as either consistent or inconsistent with an overall objective of increasing recognized strengths (stars) or developing new capabilities in areas with significant potential (current question marks). It also forces management to focus on the competitive dynamics of business: How are we doing in relation to our competitors? Are we competing in an area where we can win, or are we likely to lose?

A key proposition of the growth share matrix concept is that rapid industry growth can result in important long-term advantages for leading firms. This is thought to be particularly true when the **learning curve** or experience curve phenomenon discussed in Chapter 6 is important. With learning, rapid industry growth can create a durable relative cost advantage for industry leaders and result in the creation of a profitable market niche. Indeed, it is often argued that the learning curve phenomenon plays an important role in competitive processes and is a key determinant of a firm's future "stars."

Strategic Implications of the Learning Curve Concept

The learning curve can often play a central role in determining a firm's long-run success or failure and therefore plays an important role in competitive strategy. Recall from Chapter 6 that average costs often decline as production experience accumulates because both management and labor become more knowledgeable concerning production techniques. When this knowledge is used to improve production methods so that output can be produced with ever-increasing efficiency, the resulting decline in average costs is said to reflect the effects of the firm's greater learning or experience from cumulated prior production. The point is that if a standardized product is being produced, every successive increment in cumulative output can bring a decrease in the per unit cost of production. For example, a learning rate of 30 percent means that doubling cumulative volume, and thus doubling learning or experience, would produce an average cost decrease of 30 percent.

What makes the learning curve phenomenon crucially important in a competitive strategy context is the importance it can place on achieving and maintaining a dominant leadership position. By virtue of their larger relative volume, dominant firms have a greater opportunity for learning than do smaller, nonleading firms. In some instances, the market share leader may be able to drive down its average cost curve faster than the competition, underprice them, and permanently maintain its leadership position. Nonleading firms would then face an important, and perhaps insurmountable, barrier to a relative improvement in performance. Thus, where the learning curve advantages of leading firms are important, it may be prudent for firms to relinquish nonleading positions in favor of a redeployment of assets to markets where a dominant position can be achieved or maintained.

A classic example illustrating the successful use of the learning curve concept is provided by Texas Instruments (TI). TI is a large and highly profitable growth company headquartered in Dallas, Texas. Despite some well-publicized problems in its consumer products division (personal computers, calculators, video games), TI has long enjoyed a dominant position as a supplier in the producer products segment of the electronics industry. TI's main business is to produce semiconductor chips, a key component used to store information in computers and a wide array of electronic products. With growing applications for computers and "intelligent" electronics during recent years, there is a rapidly growing demand for semiconductors. A number of years ago, TI was one among a number of leading semiconductor manufacturers. At this early stage in the development of the industry, TI made the key strategic decision to price its semiconductors well below then-current production costs on the expectation that learning curve advantages in the 20 percent range would be forthcoming. TI's learning curve strategy proved spectacularly successful. With a low price, volume increased dramatically. Soon TI was making enough chips so that its costs were even lower than anticipated, it could price below the competition, and dozens of competitors were knocked out of the world market. Given a relative cost advantage and strict quality controls, TI rapidly achieved a position of dominant leadership in a market that became a source of large and rapidly growing profits.

Generally speaking, in order for learning or experience to play an important role in an effective competitive strategy, two conditions must be satisfied. First, learning must be significant, resulting in average cost savings of 20 to 30 percent as output is doubled. If only modest effects of learning are present, then relative product quality or customer service are likely to play a greater role in determining firm success than is a modest cost advantage. Learning is likely to be much more important in industries with an abundance of new products and/or new production techniques, rather than in mature industries with stable and well-known production methods. Similarly, learning will be important in industries producing standardized products (such as semiconductors) where price rather than product variety or service competition is prevalent. Second, the learning curve phenomenon must be managed. It is definitely not automatic. The beneficial effects of learning are only realized if management systems that tightly control costs and monitor potential sources of increased productive efficiency are established. A continuous feedback of information between production and management personnel is essential. To ensure the flow of useful information and a cooperative attitude among all employees, incentive pay programs that reward increased productivity are often established, thereby allowing both employees (through their compensation) and employers (through profits) to benefit jointly through learning.

Despite obvious successes and widespread acceptance within the business community, the key strategic concepts discussed above have limitations. First, segmenting a business into SBUs is a process in which mistakes can be, and sometimes are, made. As described above, correct definition of individual SBUs involves a careful consideration of detailed cross-price elasticity information. These data may or may not be readily available. Second, although the learning curve phenomenon is important for new industries producing undifferentiated products, many industries don't fit this new commoditylike product pattern. And third, despite the usefulness of the growth share matrix as a tool for understanding current businesses, it doesn't indicate how various SBUs ended up in various categories, nor does it identify where the next stars will come from. As a result, the key strategic concepts considered so far are supplemented by additional analytical tools including a concept called *economies of scope*.

Economies of Scope

One approach to defining fruitful areas for future expansion is called *field theory* and is based on the economic concept of **economies of scope**. Basically, the approach involves a detailed assessment of a firm's special capabilities and the construction of a strategic plan based upon the firm's recognized strengths.

Economies of scope exist for multiple outputs when the cost of joint production is less than the cost of producing each output separately. In other words, a firm will produce products that are complementary in the sense that producing them jointly is less costly than individual production. For example, suppose a regional airline offers regularly scheduled passenger service between midsize city pairs and that some excess capacity is to be expected. Furthermore, suppose there is a modest local demand for air parcel and small-package delivery service. Given current technology (airplane size, configuration, and so on), it is often less costly for a single firm to provide both passenger and cargo services in small regional markets rather than specialize in one or the other. Thus, regional air carriers often provide both types of services. This can be seen as an example of economies of scope. Other examples of scope economies abound in the provision of both goods and services. Indeed, the economies of scope concept seems to explain best why firms produce multiple rather than single outputs.

An important benefit gained in applying the economies of scope concept is that it forces management to consider both the direct and indirect benefits associated with individual lines of business. For example, on a product line basis, many firms offering financial services regard money market mutual funds as a "loss leader." That is, when one considers just the revenues and costs associated with marketing and running a money market mutual fund, it may yield only a modest profit margin or even be a breakeven operation. However, successful firms such as Merrill Lynch correctly evaluate the profitability of their money market mutual funds within the context of overall operations. These funds are a valuable "delivery vehicle" for the vast array of financial products and services that the firms offer. By offering money market funds on an attractive basis, Merrill Lynch establishes a working relationship with an ideal group of prospective customers for stocks, bonds, tax shelters, and so on. When viewed as a delivery vehicle or marketing device, its money market mutual funds may be one of Merrill Lynch's most profitable financial product lines.

Economies of scope are also important because they permit a firm to transfer superior skill or productive capability in a given product line to unique advantages in the production of complementary products. In terms of business policy, this suggests that an effective competitive strategy would be one emphasizing the development or extension of product lines related to a firm's current stars, or areas of recognized strength. For example, PepsiCo has long been a leader in the soft drink market. Over time, the company has gradually broadened its product line to include various brands of regular and diet soft drinks, Frito's and Dorito's corn chips, Grandma's Cookies, and other snack foods. PepsiCo can no longer be considered just a soft drink manufacturer. Instead, it is a widely diversified snack foods company. In fact, well over one half of total current profits come from non-soft drink lines. PepsiCo's snack foods product line extension strategy was effective because it capitalized on the product development capabilities, distribution network, and marketing skills the firm had developed in its soft drink business. In the case of PepsiCo, snack foods and soft drinks are a natural fit and a good example of how a firm has been able to take the skills gained in developing one star (soft drinks) and use them to develop a second (snack foods).

In sum, the economies of scope concept plays an important role in the formulation of an effective competitive strategy because it offers a useful means for evaluating the potential of current and prospective lines of business. It naturally leads to a definition of those areas in which the firm has a comparative advantage and thus its greatest profit potential. However, formulating an effective competitive strategy using economies of scope and other key strategic concepts is only one aspect, albeit important, of the strategic management process. The implementation phase is equally important. We now turn our attention to the important implementation issue.

Implementing Competitive Strategy

One of the most serious limitations of current approaches to strategic planning is that although much effort is devoted to strategy formulation, relatively little attention has been paid to the implementation issue, at least until recently. Too often, highly detailed and insightful strategic plans developed by outside consultants have foundered because implementation was left to corporate personnel who failed to understand or support key aspects of the analysis. A typical lament has been "The strategy was perfectly good, but the client failed to implement it." However, this excuse begs an important question, namely, How "perfectly good" is any strategy that isn't implemented? Implementation is clearly as important as development.

Today many excellently managed companies such as General Electric (GE) are devoting increased attention to the implementation phase of strategic planning. GE, always a pioneer in strategic planning, is now cutting back on the size of its in-house planning staff and redirecting those who remain to focus on issues of interest to more than one SBU. The GE approach is consistent with the notion that the skills developed by corporate management should be useful in more than one product line, as well as in the strategic planning process itself. After all, who would understand the economies of scope or learning curve potential of a given GE product line better than GE line managers? In short, GE has discovered that for any competitive strategy to be successfully implemented, those in charge of implementation must believe the plan is both appropriate and workable. This requires involvement in developing the strategic plan, as well as a certain amount of persuasion and "selling" within the company. The importance of fostering a cooperative attitude throughout the strategic process cannot be overemphasized. As G. Hugh Tsuruoka, president of Design Promotion Inc., once remarked, "The inside sell is the toughest part. Once company personnel agree that a given plan will work, the rest is easy."

One of the most persuasive arguments for making strategic planning an everyday function of management is that this approach has enjoyed great success in several excellently managed firms. Thomas J. Peters and Robert H. Waterman report in their recent book titled *In Search of Excellence*[1] that highly successful firms tend to incorporate key strategic concepts into day-to-day operating decisions. In their study of 62 U.S. companies in six industry categories, Peters and Waterman found that eight major attributes characterize the excellent, innovative firm. They are the following:

---

[1] Thomas J. Peters and Robert H. Waterman, *In Search of Excellence: Lessons from America's Best Run Companies* (New York: Warner Books, 1984).

1. A bias for action: a preference for doing something—anything—rather than sending a question through endless analyses and committee reports

2. Staying close to the customer: learning customer preferences and catering to them

3. Autonomy and entrepreneurship: encouraging individuals and divisions to act independently and competitively

4. Productivity through people: making sure that *all* employees share in company success

5. Hands-on, value driven: an insistence that management keep in touch with the firm's essential business

6. Stick to the knitting: remaining with the business the company knows best

7. Simple form, lean staff: few administrative layers

8. Simultaneous loose-tight properties: fostering a climate where there is a dedication to the central values of the company combined with a tolerance for all employees who accept those values

On an overall basis, these eight attributes suggest that success lies in store for the firm that is able to exploit its comparative advantages by developing a unique combination of valuable goods and services. We have seen that optimal price/output strategies will depend on the nature of the firm's competitive environment. In addition to affecting all aspects of marketing strategy, the competitive environment will also have important implications for firm policies concerning worker training, capital investment, diversification, mergers, multinational involvement, and so on. Indeed, a clear understanding of current and future trends in the competitive environment and of resulting implications for competitive strategy is essential for a complete understanding of the usefulness of the tools and techniques of managerial economics.

Summary

This chapter has examined a number of important tools and techniques employed in the formulation and implementation of a successful competitive strategy.

The strategic business unit was the first concept introduced. A SBU is defined as an independent business unit offering related products to a single identifiable market. By categorizing its business into SBUs, the firm is able to identify areas of relative strength and weakness in this information gathering phase of the competitive strategy formulation process. Firms rely heavily on economic data regularly published by the U.S. Department of Commerce in its economic censuses. Important aspects of these data on market structure and economic performance in industry are examined in some detail.

After a firm's SBUs have been identified, it becomes necessary to characterize their historical and potential performance. Here the growth share matrix method of classification becomes useful: A firm's high potential "stars" or fast growth and high market share SBUs are identified, as well as its "cash cows" (slow growth, high share); "question marks" (fast growth, low share); and "dogs" (slow growth, low share). To illustrate its potential role in competitive strategy, the strategic implications of the learning curve concept, first introduced in Chapter 6, were analyzed.

Economies of scope are a third concept considered in the competitive strategy formulation process. Economies of scope exist whenever the cost of joint production is less than the cost of producing each product separately. In other words, a firm will enjoy an advantage whenever the skills or resources developed in the production, marketing and distribution of one product allow the firm to produce and market some additional good or service more efficiently than specialized producers. Economies of scope often create market niches that can be profitably exploited, even in the face of intense competition over broader product lines. In fact, many of the stars found in the growth share matrix result from advantages flowing from economies of scope. This makes the economies of scope concept one of the most important considerations in the competitive strategy formulation process.

And finally, we considered the problems involved with the implementation of competitive strategy. The optimal strategic plan is one that accurately perceives areas of future potential, develops a workable plan for exploring that potential by building on the firm's recognized strengths, and is carefully implemented in a timely and efficient manner. Comprehensive involvement of operating personnel in the entire process is essential. Clearly, implementation is as important as the formulation of a successful competitive strategy.

Questions

13.1 What are strategic business units? How are they determined?

13.2 Can you see any problems for evaluating industry performance in light of the fact that census data are collected on an establishment rather than company basis?

13.3 What is the difference between GNP and GDP?

13.4 Is there a simple economic explanation as to why services have accounted for an increasingly important share of GNP over time?

13.5 Describe the elements of the growth share matrix.

13.6 Under what conditions are learning curve advantages likely to be important?

13.7 How do economies of scope differ from economies of scale?

13.8 Cite some examples of economies of scope.

References

Carroll, Peter J. "The Link Between Performance and Strategy." *Journal of Business Strategy* 2 (Spring 1982): 3–20.

Day, George S. and Montgomery, David B. "Diagnosing the Experience Curve." *Journal of Marketing* 47 (Spring 1983): 44–58.

Fruhan, William E. Jr. "How Fast Should Your Company Grow?" *Harvard Business Review* 62 (January–February 1984): 84–93.

Goldhar, J. D. and Jelinek, Mariann. "Plan for Economies of *Scope*." *Harvard Business Review* 61 (November–December 1983): 141–148.

Hax, Arnoldo C. and Majluf, Nicholas S. "The Use of the Industry Attractiveness–Business Strength Matrix in Strategic Planning." *Interfaces* 13 (April 1983): 54–71.

Hax, Arnoldo C. and Majluf, Nicholas S. "The Use of the Growth-Share Matrix in Strategic Planning." *Interfaces* 13 (February 1983): 46–60.

Henderson, Bruce D. "The Application and Misapplication of the Experience Curve." *Journal of Business Strategy* 4 (Winter 1984): 3–9.

Peters, Thomas J. and Waterman, Robert H. *In Search of Excellence: Lessons from America's Best-Run Companies.* New York: Warner Books, 1984.

Porter, Michael E. *Competitive Strategy: Techniques for Analyzing Industries and Competitors.* New York: Free Press, 1980.

Porter, Michael E. "Industrial Organization and the Evolution of Concepts for Strategic Planning." *Managerial and Decision Economics* 4 (September 1983): 172–180.

Robinson, Richard B. Jr. and Pearce, John A. "Research Thrusts in Small Firm Strategic Planning." *Academy of Management Review* 9 (January 1984): 128–137.

Shubik, Martin. "The Strategic Audit: A Game Theoretic Approach to Corporate Competitive Strategy." *Managerial and Decision Economics* 4 (September 1983): 160–171.

Solman, Paul and Friedman, Thomas. *Life and Death on the Corporate Battlefield.* New York: Simon and Schuster, 1982.

Teece, David J. "Economies of Scope and the Scope of the Enterprise." *Journal of Economic Behavior and Organization* 1 (September 1980): 223–247.

Wind, Yoram and Robertson, Thomas S. "Marketing Strategy: New Directions for Theory and Research." *Journal of Marketing* 47 (Spring 1983): 12–25.

Appendix A

Compounding and the Time Value of Money

The concepts of compound growth and the time value of money are widely used in all aspects of business and economics. Compounding is the principle that underlies growth, whether it is growth in value, growth in sales, or growth in assets. The time value of money—the fact that a dollar received in the future is worth less than a dollar in hand today—also plays an important role in managerial economics. Cash flows occurring in different periods must be adjusted to their value at a common point in time if they are to be analyzed and compared. Because of the importance of these concepts in economic analysis, a thorough understanding of the material on future (compound) and present values in this appendix is important for the study of managerial economics.

Future Value (or Compound Value)

Suppose you deposit $100 in a bank savings account that pays 5 percent interest compounded annually. How much will you have at the end of one year? Let us define terms as follows:

PV = present value of your account, or the beginning amount, $100.

i = interest rate the bank pays you = 5 percent per year, or, expressed as a decimal, 0.05.

I = dollars of interest you earn during the year.

FV_n = future value, or ending amount, of your account at the end of n years. Whereas PV is the value now, at the *present* time, FV_n is the value n years into the future, after compound interest has been earned. Note also that FV_0 is the future value *zero* years into the future, which is the *present*, so $FV_0 = PV$.

In our example, $n = 1$, so $FV_n = FV_1$, and it is calculated as follows:

$$FV_1 = PV + I$$

$$= PV + (PV)(i) \tag{A.1}$$

$$= PV(1 + i).$$

We can now use Equation A.1 to find how much the account is worth at the end of one year:

$$FV_1 = \$100(1 + 0.05) = \$100(1.05) = \$105.$$

Your account earned $5 of interest ($I = \$5$), so you have $105 at the end of the year.

Now suppose you leave your funds on deposit for five years; how much will you have at the end of the fifth year? The answer is $127.63; this value is worked out in Table A.1.

Notice that the Table A.1 value for FV_2, the value of the account at the end of Year 2, is equal to

$$FV_2 = FV_1(1 + i) = PV(1 + i)(1 + i) = PV(1 + i)^2.$$

Continuing, we see that FV_3, the balance after three years, is

$$FV_3 = FV_2(1 + i) = PV(1 + i)^3.$$

In general, FV_n, the future value at the end of n years, is found as:

$$FV_n = PV(1 + i)^n. \tag{A.2}$$

Table A.1
Compound Interest Calculations

Year	Beginning Amount, PV	×	(1 + i)	=	Ending Amount, FV_n
1	$100.00		1.05		$105.00
2	105.00		1.05		110.25
3	110.25		1.05		115.76
4	115.76		1.05		121.55
5	121.55		1.05		127.63

Applying Equation A.2 to our five-year, 5 percent case, we obtain

$$FV_5 = \$100(1.05)^5$$

$$= \$100(1.2763)$$

$$= \$127.63,$$

which is the same as the value worked out in Table A.1.

If an electronic calculator is handy, it is easy enough to calculate $(1 + i)^n$ directly.[1] However, tables have been constructed for values of $(1 + i)^n$ for wide ranges of i and n. Table A.2 is illustrative. Table B.1 in Appendix B contains a more complete set of compound value interest factors. Notice that we have used the term *period* rather than *year* in Table A.2. As we shall see later in the appendix, compounding can occur over periods of time different from one year. Thus, while compounding is often on an annual basis, it can be quarterly, semiannually, monthly, or for any other period.

We define the term *future value interest factor* ($FVIF_{i,n}$) to equal $(1 + i)^n$. Therefore Equation A.2 may be written as $FV_n = PV(FVIF_{i,n})$. One need only to go to an appropriate interest table to find the proper interest factor. For example, the correct interest factor for our five-year, 5 percent illustration can be found in Table A.2. We look down the period column to 5, then across this row to the 5 percent column to find the interest factor, 1.2763. Then, using this interest factor, we find the value of $100 after five years as $FV_n = PV(FVIF_{i,n}) = \$100(1.2763) = \$127.63$, which is identical to the value obtained by the long method in Table A.1.

Graphic View of the Compounding Process: Growth

Figure A.1 shows how $1 (or any other initial quantity) grows over time at various rates of interest, or growth. The higher the rate of interest, the faster the rate of growth. The interest rate is, in fact, the growth rate: If a sum is deposited and earns 5 percent, then the funds on deposit grow at the rate of 5 percent per period. Similarly, the sales of a firm or the gross national product (GNP) of a country might be expected to grow at a constant rate. Projections of future sales or GNP could be obtained using the compound value process.

---

[1] For example, to calculate $(1 + i)^n$ for $i = 5\% = 0.05$ and $n = 5$ years, we multiply $(1 + i) = (1.05)$ times (1.05); multiply this product by (1.05); and so on:

$$(1 + i)^n = (1.05)(1.05)(1.05)(1.05)(1.05) = (1.05)^5 = 1.2763.$$

Table A.2
Future Value of $1 at the End of n Periods: $FVIF_{i,n} = (1 + i)^n$

Period (n)	1%	2%	3%	4%	5%	6%	7%	8%	9%	10%
0	1.0000	1.0000	1.0000	1.0000	1.0000	1.0000	1.0000	1.0000	1.0000	1.0000
1	1.0100	1.0200	1.0300	1.0400	1.0500	1.0600	1.0700	1.0800	1.0900	1.1000
2	1.0201	1.0404	1.0609	1.0816	1.1025	1.1236	1.1449	1.1664	1.1881	1.2100
3	1.0303	1.0612	1.0927	1.1249	1.1576	1.1910	1.2250	1.2597	1.2950	1.3310
4	1.0406	1.0824	1.1255	1.1699	1.2155	1.2625	1.3108	1.3605	1.4116	1.4641
5	1.0510	1.1041	1.1593	1.2167	1.2763	1.3382	1.4026	1.4693	1.5386	1.6105
6	1.0615	1.1262	1.1941	1.2653	1.3401	1.4185	1.5007	1.5869	1.6771	1.7716
7	1.0721	1.1487	1.2299	1.3159	1.4071	1.5036	1.6058	1.7138	1.8280	1.9487
8	1.0829	1.1717	1.2668	1.3686	1.4775	1.5938	1.7182	1.8509	1.9926	2.1436
9	1.0937	1.1951	1.3048	1.4233	1.5513	1.6895	1.8385	1.9990	2.1719	2.3579
10	1.1046	1.2190	1.3439	1.4802	1.6289	1.7908	1.9672	2.1589	2.3674	2.5937
11	1.1157	1.2434	1.3842	1.5395	1.7103	1.8983	2.1049	2.3316	2.5804	2.8531
12	1.1268	1.2682	1.4258	1.6010	1.7959	2.0122	2.2522	2.5182	2.8127	3.1384
13	1.1381	1.2936	1.4685	1.6651	1.8856	2.1329	2.4098	2.7196	3.0658	3.4523
14	1.1495	1.3195	1.5126	1.7317	1.9799	2.2609	2.5785	2.9372	3.3417	3.7975
15	1.1610	1.3459	1.5580	1.8009	2.0789	2.3966	2.7590	3.1722	3.6425	4.1772

Figure A.1
Relationships among Future Value Interest Factors, Interest Rates, and Time: Amount to Which Interest Factor Grows after n Periods at Various Interest Rates

Future value interest factor, $FVIF_{i,n}$

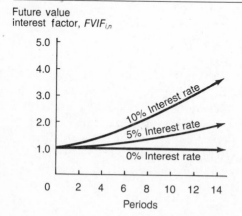

Future value curves could be drawn for any interest rate, including fractional rates. In Figure A.1, we have plotted curves for 0 percent, 5 percent, and 10 percent, using the data from Table A.2.

Present Value

Suppose you are offered the alternative of receiving either $127.63 at the end of five years or X dollars today. There is no question that the $127.63 will be paid in full (perhaps the payer is the U.S. government). Having no current need for the money, you would deposit it in a bank account that pays 5 percent interest. (Five percent is defined to be your *opportunity cost*, or the rate of interest you could earn on alternative investments of equal risk.) What value of X will make you indifferent between X dollars today or the promise of $127.63 five years hence?

Table A.1 shows that the initial amount of $100 growing at 5 percent a year yields $127.63 at the end of five years. Thus, you should be indifferent in your choice between $100 today and $127.63 at the end of five years. The $100 is defined as the present value, or *PV*, of $127.63 due in five years when the applicable interest rate is 5 percent. Therefore, if X is anything less than $100, you would prefer the promise of $127.63 in five years to $X today.

In general, the present value of a sum due n years in the future is the amount which, if it were on hand today, would grow to equal the future sum over a period of n years. Since $100 would grow to $127.63 in five years at a 5 percent interest rate, $100 is defined to be the present value of $127.63 due five years in the future when the appropriate interest rate is 5 percent.

Finding present values (or *discounting*, as it is commonly called) is simply the reverse of compounding, and Equation A.2 can readily be transformed into a present value formula:

$$FV_n = PV(1 + i)^n,$$

which, when solved for PV, gives

$$PV = \frac{FV_n}{(1 + i)^n} = FV_n \left[\frac{1}{(1 + i)} \right]^n. \tag{A.3}$$

Tables have been constructed for the term in brackets for various values of i and n; Table A.3 is an example. For a more complete table, see Table B.2 in Appendix B. For the illustrative case being considered, look down the 5 percent column in Table A.3 to the fifth row. The figure

Appendix A

Table A.3
Present Values of $1 Due at the End of n Periods

$$PVIF_{i,n} = \frac{1}{(1 + i)^n} = \left[\frac{1}{(1 + i)} \right]^n$$

Period (n)	1%	2%	3%	4%	5%	6%	7%	8%	9%	10%	12%	14%	15%
1	.9901	.9804	.9709	.9615	.9524	.9434	.9346	.9259	.9174	.9091	.8929	.8772	.8696
2	.9803	.9612	.9426	.9246	.9070	.8900	.8734	.8573	.8417	.8264	.7972	.7695	.7561
3	.9706	.9423	.9151	.8890	.8638	.8396	.8163	.7938	.7722	.7513	.7118	.6750	.6575
4	.9610	.9238	.8885	.8548	.8227	.7921	.7629	.7350	.7084	.6830	.6355	.5921	.5718
5	.9515	.9057	.8626	.8219	.7835	.7473	.7130	.6806	.6499	.6209	.5674	.5194	.4972
6	.9420	.8880	.8375	.7903	.7462	.7050	.6663	.6302	.5963	.5645	.5066	.4556	.4323
7	.9327	.8706	.8131	.7599	.7107	.6651	.6227	.5835	.5470	.5132	.4523	.3996	.3759
8	.9235	.8535	.7894	.7307	.6768	.6274	.5820	.5403	.5019	.4665	.4039	.3506	.3269
9	.9143	.8368	.7664	.7026	.6446	.5919	.5439	.5002	.4604	.4241	.3606	.3075	.2843
10	.9053	.8203	.7441	.6756	.6139	.5584	.5083	.4632	.4224	.3855	.3220	.2697	.2472

shown there, 0.7835, is the *present value interest factor* ($PVIF_{i,n}$) used to determine the present value of $127.63 payable in five years, discounted at 5 percent:

$$PV = FV_5(PVIF_{i,n})$$

$$= \$127.63(0.7835)$$

$$= \$100.$$

Graphic View of the Discounting Process

Figure A.2 shows how the interest factors for discounting decrease as the discounting period increases. The curves in the figure were plotted with data taken from Table A.3; they show that the present value of a sum to be received at some future date decreases (1) as the payment date is extended further into the future and (2) as the discount rate increases. If relatively high discount rates apply, funds due in the future are worth very little today. Even at relatively low discount rates, the present values of funds due in the distant future are quite small. For example, $1.00 due in ten years is worth about $0.61 today if the discount rate is 5 percent. It is worth only $0.25 today at a 15 percent discount rate. Similarly, $1.00 due in five years at 10 percent is worth $0.62 today, but at the same discount rate $1.00 due in ten years is worth only $0.39 today.

Figure A.2
Relationships among Present Value Interest Factors, Interest Rates, and Time

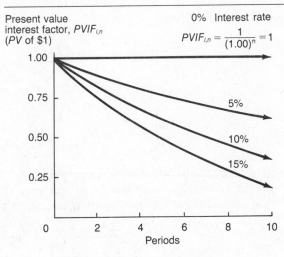

Present value interest factor, $PVIF_{i,n}$ (PV of $1)

0% Interest rate

$$PVIF_{i,n} = \frac{1}{(1.00)^n} = 1$$

Future Value Versus Present Value

Notice that Equation A.2, the basic equation for compounding, was developed from the logical sequence set forth in Table A.1; the equation merely presents in mathematical form the steps outlined in the table. The present value interest factor ($PVIF_{i,n}$) in Equation A.3, the basic equation for discounting or finding present values, was found as the *reciprocal* of the future value interest factor ($FVIF_{i,n}$) for the same i,n combination:

$$PVIF_{i,n} = \frac{1}{FVIF_{i,n}}.$$

For example, the *future value* interest factor for 5 percent over five years is seen in Table A.2 to be 1.2763. The *present value* interest factor for 5 percent over five years must be the reciprocal of 1.2763:

$$PVIF_{5\%,\,5\,years} = \frac{1}{1.2763} = 0.7835.$$

The $PVIF_{i,n}$ found in this manner does, of course, correspond with the $PVIF_{i,n}$ shown in Table A.3.

The reciprocal nature of the relationship between present value and future value permits us to find present values in two ways—by multiplying or by dividing. Thus, the present value of $1,000 due in five years and discounted at 5 percent may be found as

$$PV = FV_n \left[\frac{1}{1+i} \right]^n = FV_n(PVIF_{i,n}) = \$1,000(0.7835) = \$783.50,$$

or as

$$PV = \frac{FV_n}{(1+i)^n} = \frac{FV_n}{FVIF_{i,n}} = \frac{\$1,000}{1.2763} = \$783.50.$$

To conclude this comparison of present and future values, compare Figures A.1 and A.2.[2] Notice that the vertical intercept is at 1.0 in each case, but future value interest factors rise, while present value interest factors decline.

Future Value of an Annuity

An annuity is defined as a series of payments of a fixed amount for a specified number of periods. Each payment occurs at the end of the period.[3] For example, a promise to pay $1,000 a year for three years is a three-year annuity. If you were to receive such an annuity and were to deposit each annual payment in a savings account paying 4 percent interest, how much would you have at the end of three years? The answer is shown graphically as a *time line* in Figure A.3. The first payment is made at the end of Year 1, the second at the end of Year 2, and the third at the end of Year 3. The last payment is not compounded at all; the second payment is compounded for one year; and the first is compounded for two years. When the future values of each of the payments are added, their total is the sum of the annuity. In the example, this total is $3,121.60.

Expressed algebraically, with S_n defined as the future value, R as the periodic receipt, n as the length of the annuity, and $FVIFA_{i,n}$ as the future value interest factor for an annuity, the formula for S_n is:

---

[2]Notice that Figure A.2 is not a mirror image of Figure A.1. The curves in Figure A.1 approach ∞ as n increases; in Figure A.2 the curves approach zero, not $-\infty$.

[3]Had the payment been made at the beginning of the period, each receipt would simply have been shifted back one year. The annuity would have been called an *annuity due*; the one in the present discussion, where payments are made at the end of each period, is called a *regular annuity* or, sometimes, a *deferred annuity*.

Figure A.3
Time Line for an Annuity: Future Value ($i = 4\%$)

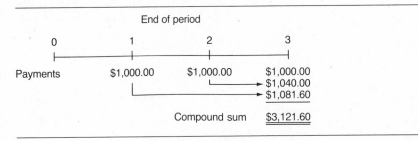

	End of period		
0	1	2	3

Payments $1,000.00 $1,000.00 $1,000.00
                                              → $1,040.00
                                            → $1,081.60

Compound sum $3,121.60

$$S_n = R(1 + i)^{n-1} + R(1 + i)^{n-2} + \ldots + R(1 + i)^1 + R(1 + i)^0$$

$$= R[(1 + i)^{n-1} + (1 + i)^{n-2} + \ldots + (1 + i)^1 + (1 + i)^0]$$

(A.4)

$$= R \sum_{t=1}^{n} (1 + i)^{n-t}, \text{ or } = R \sum_{t=1}^{n} (1 + i)^{t-1}$$

$$= R \, (FVIFA_{i,n}).$$

The expression in parentheses, $FVIFA_{i,n}$, has been calculated for various combinations of i and n.[4] An illustrative set of these annuity interest factors is given in Table A.4.[5] To find the answer to the three-year, $1,000 annuity problem, simply refer to Table A.4, look down the four percent column to the row of the third period, and multiply the factor 3.1216 by $1,000. The answer is the same as the one derived by the long method illustrated in Figure A.3:

$$S_n = R(FVIFA_{i,n})$$

$$S_3 = \$1,000(3.1216) = \$3,121.60.$$

---

[4]The third equation is simply a shorthand expression in which sigma (Σ) signifies *sum up* or add the values of n factors. The symbol $\sum_{t=1}^{n}$ simply says, "Go through the following process: Let $t = 1$ and find the first factor. Then let $t = 2$ and find the second factor. Continue until each individual factor has been found, and then add these individual factors to find the value of the annuity."

[5]The equation given in Table A.4 recognizes that the *FVIFA* factor is the sum of a geometric progression. The proof of this equation is given in most algebra texts. Notice that it is easy to use the equation to develop annuity factors. This is especially useful if you need the *FVIFA* for some interest rate not given in the tables (for example, 6.5 percent).

Table A.4
Sum of an Annuity of $1 per Period for n Periods:

$$FVIFA_{i,n} = \sum_{t=1}^{n} (1 + i)^{t-1}$$

$$= \frac{(1 + i)^n - 1}{i}$$

Number of Periods	1%	2%	3%	4%	5%	6%	7%	8%
1	1.0000	1.0000	1.0000	1.0000	1.0000	1.0000	1.0000	1.0000
2	2.0100	2.0200	2.0300	2.0400	2.0500	2.0600	2.0700	2.0800
3	3.0301	3.0604	3.0909	3.1216	3.1525	3.1836	3.2149	3.2464
4	4.0604	4.1216	4.1836	4.2465	4.3101	4.3746	4.4399	4.5061
5	5.1010	5.2040	5.3091	5.4163	5.5256	5.6371	5.7507	5.8666
6	6.1520	6.3081	6.4684	6.6330	6.8019	6.9753	7.1533	7.3359
7	7.2135	7.4343	7.6625	7.8983	8.1420	8.3938	8.6540	8.9228
8	8.2857	8.5830	8.8923	9.2142	9.5491	9.8975	10.2598	10.6366
9	9.3685	9.7546	10.1591	10.5828	11.0266	11.4913	11.9780	12.4876
10	10.4622	10.9497	11.4639	12.0061	12.5779	13.1808	13.8164	14.4866

Notice that for all positive interest rates, the $FVIFA_{i,n}$ for the sum of an annuity is always equal to or greater than the number of periods the annuity runs.[6]

Present Value of an Annuity

Suppose you were offered the following alternatives: a three-year annuity of $1,000 per year or a lump sum payment today. You have no need for the money during the next three years, so if you accept the annuity you would simply deposit the receipts in a savings account pay-

---

[6]It is worth noting that the entry for each period t in Table A.4 is equal to the sum of the entries in Table A.2 up to period $n - 1$. For example, the entry for Period 3 under the 4 percent column in Table A.4 is equal to $1.000 + 1.0400 + 1.0816 = 3.1216$.

Also, had the annuity been an *annuity due*, with payments received at the beginning rather than the end of each period, then the three payments would have occurred at $t = 0$, $t = 1$, and $t = 2$. To find the future value of an annuity due, (1) Look up the $FVIFA_{i,n}$ for $n + 1$ years, then (2) subtract 1.0 from the amount to get the $FVIFA_{i,n}$ for the annuity due. In the example, the annuity due $FVIFA_{i,n}$ is $4.2465 - 1.0 = 3.2465$ versus 3.1216 for a regular annuity. Because payments on an annuity due come earlier, it is a little more valuable than a regular annuity.

Figure A.4
Time Line for an Annuity: Present Value ($i = 4\%$)

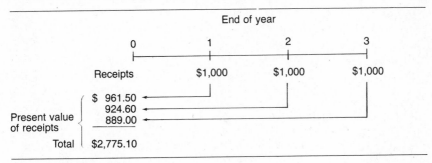

ing 4 percent interest. How large must the lump sum payment be to make it equivalent to the annuity? The time line shown in Figure A.4 will help explain the problem.

The present value of the first receipt is $R[1/(1 + i)]$, the second is $R[1/(1 + i)]^2$, and so on. Defining the present value of an annuity of n years as A_n, and with $PVIFA_{i,n}$ defined as the present value interest factor for an annuity, we may write the following equation:

$$A_n = R\left(\frac{1}{1+i}\right)^1 + R\left(\frac{1}{1+i}\right)^2 + \ldots + R\left(\frac{1}{1+i}\right)^n$$

$$= R\left(\frac{1}{(1+i)^1} + \frac{1}{(1+i)^2} + \ldots + \frac{1}{(1+i)^n}\right)$$ (A.5)

$$= R\sum_{t=1}^{n}\left(\frac{1}{1+i}\right)^t$$

$$= R\,(PVIFA_{i,n}).$$

Again, tables have been worked out for $PVIFA_{i,n}$, the term in parentheses in Equation A.5. Table A.5 is illustrative; a more complete listing is found in Table B.4 in Appendix B. From Table A.5, the $PVIFA_{i,n}$ for a three-year, 4 percent annuity is found to be 2.7751. Multiplying this factor by the $1,000 annual receipt gives $2,775.10, the present value of the annuity. This figure is identical to the long-method answer shown in Figure A.4:

$$A_n = R(PVIFA_{i,n})$$

$$A_3 = \$1,000(2.7751)$$

$$= \$2,775.10.$$

Table A.5
Present Value of an Annuity of $1 per Period for n Periods:

$$PVIFA_{i,n} = \sum_{t=1}^{n} \frac{1}{(1 + i)^t} = \frac{1 - \dfrac{1}{(1 + i)^n}}{i}$$

Period	1%	2%	3%	4%	5%	6%	7%	8%	9%	10%
1	0.9901	0.9804	0.9709	0.9615	0.9524	0.9434	0.9346	0.9259	0.9174	0.9091
2	1.9704	1.9416	1.9135	1.8861	1.8594	1.8334	1.8080	1.7833	1.7591	1.7355
3	2.9410	2.8839	2.8286	2.7751	2.7232	2.6730	2.6243	2.5771	2.5313	2.4869
4	3.9020	3.8077	3.7171	3.6299	3.5460	3.4651	3.3872	3.3121	3.2397	3.1699
5	4.8534	4.7135	4.5797	4.4518	4.3295	4.2124	4.1002	3.9927	3.8897	3.7908
6	5.7955	5.6014	5.4172	5.2421	5.0757	4.9173	4.7665	4.6229	4.4859	4.3553
7	6.7282	6.4720	6.2303	6.0021	5.7864	5.5824	5.3893	5.2064	5.0330	4.8684
8	7.6517	7.3255	7.0197	6.7327	6.4632	6.2098	5.9713	5.7466	5.5348	5.3349
9	8.5660	8.1622	7.7861	7.4353	7.1078	6.8017	6.5152	6.2469	5.9952	5.7590
10	9.4713	8.9826	8.5302	8.1109	7.7217	7.3601	7.0236	6.7101	6.4177	6.1446

Notice that the entry for each period n in Table A.5 is equal to the sum of the entries in Table A.3 up to and including period n. For example, the $PVIFA$ for 4 percent, three periods as shown in Table A.5 could have been calculated by summing values from Table A.3:

$$0.9615 + 0.9246 + 0.8890 = 2.7751.$$

Notice also that for all positive interest rates, $PVIFA_{i,n}$ for the *present value* of an annuity is always less than the number of periods and annuity runs, whereas $FVIFA_{i,n}$ for the *sum* of an annuity is equal to or greater than the number of periods.[7]

Present Value of an Uneven Series of Receipts

The definition of an annuity includes the words *fixed amount*—in other words, annuities involve situations where cash flows are *identical* in

---

[7]To find the $PVIFA_{i,n}$ for an *annuity due*, go through these steps: (1) Look up the $PVIFA_{i,n}$ for $n - 1$ periods, then (2) add 1.0 to this amount to obtain the $PVIFA_{i,n}$ for the annuity due. In the example, the $PVIFA_{i,n}$ for a 4 percent, three-year annuity due is 1.8861 + 1.0 = 2.8861.

every year. Although many managerial decisions involve constant cash flows, some important decisions are concerned with uneven flows of cash. Consequently, it is necessary to expand our analysis to deal with varying payments streams.

The *PV* of an uneven stream of future income is found as the sum of the *PV*s of the individual components of the stream. For example, suppose we are trying to find the *PV* of the stream of receipts shown in Table A.6, discounted at 6 percent. As shown in the table, we multiply each receipt by the appropriate $PVIF_{i,n}$, then sum these products to obtain the *PV* of the stream, $1,413.24. Figure A.5 gives a graphic view of the cash flow stream.

The *PV* of the receipts shown in Table A.6 and Figure A.5 can also be found by using the annuity equation; the steps in this alternative solution process are outlined below:

Step 1 Find *PV* of $100 due in one year:

$$\$100(0.9434) = \$94.34.$$

Step 2 Recognize that a $200 annuity will be received during Years 2 through 5. Thus, we could determine the value of a five-year annuity, subtract from it the value of a one-year annuity, and have remaining the value of a four-year annuity whose first payment is due in two years. This result is achieved by subtracting the *PVIFA* for a one-year, 6 percent annuity from the *PVIFA* for a five-year annuity and then multiplying the difference by $200, as shown on page 559.

Table A.6
Present Value of an Uneven Stream of Receipts

	Stream of Receipts	×	$PVIF_{i,n}$ (6%)	=	PV of Individual Receipts
Year 1	$ 100		0.9434		$ 94.34
Year 2	200		0.8900		178.00
Year 3	200		0.8396		167.92
Year 4	200		0.7921		158.42
Year 5	200		0.7473		149.46
Year 6	0		0.7050		0
Year 7	1,000		0.6651		665.10
			PV = Sum =		$1,413.24

Figure A.5
Time Line for an Uneven Cash Flow Stream ($i = 6\%$)

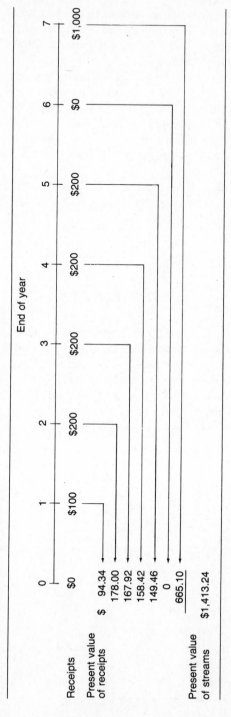

$$PV \text{ of the Annuity} = (PVIFA_{6\%,\,5yrs.} - PVIFA_{6\%,\,1yr.})(\$200)$$

$$= (4.2124 - 0.9434)(\$200)$$

$$= \$653.80.$$

Thus, the present value of the annuity component of the uneven stream is $653.80.

Step 3 Find the *PV* of the $1,000 due in Year 7:

$$\$1,000(0.6651) = \$665.10.$$

Step 4 Sum the components:

$$\$94.34 + \$653.80 + \$665.10 = \$1,413.24.$$

Either of the two methods can be used to solve problems of this type. However, the alternative (annuity) solution is easier if the annuity component runs for many years. For example, the alternative solution would be clearly superior for finding the *PV* of a stream consisting of $100 in Year 1, $200 in Years 2 through 29, and $1,000 in Year 30.

Annual Payments for Accumulation of a Future Sum

Suppose we want to know the amount of money that must be deposited at 5 percent for each of the next five years in order to have $10,000 available to pay off a debt at the end of the fifth year. Dividing both sides of Equation A.4 by *FVIFA*, we obtain:

$$R = \frac{S_n}{FVIFA_{i,n}}. \qquad\qquad \text{(A.6)}$$

Looking up the future value of an annuity interest factor for five years at 5 percent in Table A.4 and dividing this figure into $10,000, we find:

$$R = \frac{\$10,000}{5.5256} = \$1,810.$$

Thus, if $1,810 is deposited each year in an account paying 5 percent interest, at the end of five years the account will have accumulated $10,000.

Annual Receipts from an Annuity

Suppose that on September 1, 1984, you receive an inheritance of $7,000. The money is to be used for your education and is to be spent during the academic years beginning September 1985, 1986, and 1987. If you place the money in a bank account paying 10 percent annual interest and make three equal withdrawals at each of the specified dates, how large can each withdrawal be so as to leave you with exactly a zero balance after the last one has been made?

The solution requires application of the present value of an annuity formula, Equation A.5. Here, however, we know that the present value of the annuity is $7,000, and the problem is to find the three equal annual payments when the interest rate is 10 percent. This calls for dividing both sides of Equation A.5 by $PVIFA_{i,n}$ to derive Equation A.7:

$$R = \frac{A_n}{PVIFA_{i,n}}. \tag{A.7}$$

The interest factor is found in Table A.5 to be 2.4869, and substituting this value into Equation A.7, we find the three annual withdrawals to be $2,815:

$$R = \frac{\$7,000}{2.4869} = \$2,815.$$

This particular calculation is used frequently to set up insurance and pension plan benefit schedules and to find the periodic payments necessary to retire a loan within a specified period. For example, if you want to retire in three equal annual payments a $7,000 bank loan accruing interest at 10 percent on the unpaid balance, each payment would be $2,815. In this case the bank is acquiring an annuity with a present value of $7,000.

Determining Interest Rates

We can use the basic equations developed earlier to determine the interest rates implicit in financial contracts.

Example 1. A bank offers to lend you $1,000 if you sign a note to repay $1,610.50 at the end of five years. What rate of interest are you paying? To solve the problem, recognize that $1,000 is the *PV* of $1,610.50 due in five years, and solve Equation A.3 for the present value interest factor ($PVIF_{i,n}$).

$$PV = FV_n \left[\frac{1}{(1 + i)^n} \right] = FV_n(PVIF_{i,n})$$

$$\$1,000 = \$1,610.50(PVIF_{i,n} \text{ for 5 years})$$ (A.3)

$$\$1,000/\$1,610.50 = 0.6209 = PVIF_{i,5}.$$

Now, go to Table A.3 and look across the row for Year 5 until you find 0.6209. It is in the 10 percent column, so you would be paying a 10 percent rate of interest.

Example 2. A bank offers to lend you $75,000 to buy a house. You must sign a mortgage calling for payments of $9,562.67 at the end of each of the next 25 years. What interest rate is the bank charging you?

1. Recognize that $75,000 is the *PV* of a 25-year, $9,562.67 annuity:

$$\$75,000 = PV = \sum_{t=1}^{25} \$9,562.67 \left[\frac{1}{(1 + i)^t} \right] = \$9,562.67(PVIFA_{i,n}).$$

2. Solve for $PVIFA_{i,n}$:

$$PVIFA_{i,n} = \$75,000/\$9,562.67 = 7.843.$$

3. Turn to Table B.4 in Appendix B, since Table A.4 does not cover a 25-year period. Looking across the row for 25 periods, we find 7.843 under the column for 12 percent. Therefore, the rate of interest on this mortgage loan is 12 percent.

Semiannual and Other Compounding Periods

In all the examples used thus far, it has been assumed that returns were received once a year, or annually. Suppose, however, that you put your $1,000 in a bank that advertises that it pays 6 percent interest *semiannually*. How much will you have at the end of one year? Semiannual compounding means that interest is actually paid every six months, a fact taken into account in the tabular calculations in Table A.7. Here the annual interest rate is divided by two, but twice as many compounding periods are used, because interest is paid twice a year. Comparing the amount on hand at the end of the second six-month period, $1,060.90, with what would have been on hand under annual compounding, $1,060, shows that semiannual compounding is better from the stand-

Table A.7
Compound Interest Calculations with Semiannual Compounding

	Beginning Amount (PV)	× (1 + i/2) =	Ending Amount, FV_n
Period 1	$1,000.00	(1.03)	$1,030.00
Period 2	1,030.00	(1.03)	1,060.90

point of the saver. This result occurs because you earn interest on interest more frequently.

Throughout the economy, different types of investments use different compounding periods. For example, bank and savings and loan accounts generally pay interest quarterly, some bonds pay interest semiannually, and other bonds pay annual interest. Thus, if we are to compare securities with different compounding periods, we need to put them on a common basis. This need has led to the development of the terms *nominal*, or *stated*, *interest rate* and *effective annual*, or *annual percentage*, *rate* (APR). The stated, or nominal, rate is the quoted rate; thus, in our example the nominal rate is 6 percent. The annual percentage rate is the rate that would have produced the final compound value, $1,060.90, under annual rather than semiannual compounding. In this case, the effective annual rate is 6.09 percent:

$$\$1,000(1 + i) = \$1,060.90$$

$$i = \frac{\$1,060.90}{\$1,000} - 1 = 0.0609 = 6.09\%.$$

Thus, if one bank offered 6 percent with semiannual compounding, while another offered 6.09 percent with annual compounding, they would both be paying the same effective rate of interest. In general, we can determine the effective annual rate of interest, given the nominal rate, as follows:

Step 1 Find the *FV* of $1 at the end of one year, using the equation

$$FV = 1\left(1 + \frac{i_n}{m}\right)^m.$$

Here i_n is the nominal rate, and m is the number of compounding periods per year.

Step 2 Subtract 1.0 from the result in Step 1, then multiply by 100. The final result is the effective annual rate.

Example. Find the effective annual rate if the nominal rate is 6 percent, compounded semiannually:

$$\text{Effective Annual Rate} = \left(1 + \frac{0.06}{2} \right)^2 - 1.0$$

$$= (1.03)^2 - 1.0$$

$$= 1.0609 - 1.0$$

$$= 0.0609$$

$$= 6.09\%.$$

The points made about semiannual compounding can be generalized as follows. When compounding periods are more frequent than once a year, we use a modified version of Equation A.2:

$$FV_n = PV(1 + i)^n. \tag{A.2}$$

$$FV_n = PV \left(1 + \frac{i}{m} \right)^{mn}. \tag{A.2a}$$

Here m is the number of times per year compounding occurs. When banks compute daily interest, the value of m is set at 365, and Equation A.2a is applied.

The interest tables can be used when compounding occurs more than once a year. Simply divide the nominal, or stated, interest rate by the number of times compounding occurs, and multiply the years by the number of compounding periods per year. For example, to find the amount to which $1,000 will grow after six years if semiannual compounding is applied to a stated 8 percent interest rate, divide 8 percent by 2 and multiply the six years by 2. Then look in Table A.2 under the 4 percent column and in the row for Period 12. You find an interest factor of 1.6010. Multiplying this by the initial $1,000 gives a value of $1,601, the amount to which $1,000 will grow in six years at 8 percent compounded semiannually. This compares with $1,586.90 for annual compounding.

The same procedure is applied in all the cases covered—compounding, discounting, single payments, and annuities. To illustrate semiannual discounting in finding the present value of an annuity, consider the case described in the section "Present Value of an Annuity": $1,000 a year for three years, discounted at 4 percent. With annual discounting, the interest factor is 2.7751, and the present value of the annuity is $2,775.10. For semiannual discounting, look under the 2 percent column and in the Period 6 row of Table A.5 to find an interest factor of 5.6014.

This is now multiplied by half of $1,000, or the $500 received each six months, to get the present value of the annuity, $2,800.70. The payments come a little more rapidly—the first $500 is paid after only six months (similarly with other payments)—so the annuity is a little more valuable if payments are received semiannually rather than annually.

Summary

Managerial decisions often involve determining the present value of a stream of future cash flows. Also, we often need to know the amount to which an initial quantity will grow during a specified time period, and at other times we must calculate the interest rate built into a financial contract. The basic concepts involved in these processes are called compounding and the time value of money.

The key procedures covered in this appendix are summarized below:

Future Value: $FV_n = PV(1 + i)^n$, where FV_n is the future value of an initial amount, PV, compounded at the rate of i percent for n periods. The term $(1 + i)^n$ is defined as $FVIF_{i,n}$, the *future value interest factor*. Values for $FVIF$ are contained in tables.

Present Value: $PV = FV_n[1/(1 + i)]^n$. This equation is simply a transformation of the future value equation. The term $[1/(1 + i)]^n$ is defined as $PVIF_{i,n}$, the present value interest factor.

Future Value of an Annuity: An annuity is defined as a series of constant or equal payments of R dollars per period. The sum, or future value of an annuity, is given the symbol S_n, and it is found as follows: $S_n = R[\sum_{t=1}^{n}(1 + i)^{t-1}]$. The term $[\sum_{t=1}^{n}(1 + i)^{t-1}]$ is defined as $FVIFA_{i,n}$, the future value interest factor for an annuity.

Present Value of an Annuity: The present value of an annuity is given the symbol A_n, and it is found as follows: $A_n = R[\sum_{t=1}^{n}(1/1 + i)^t]$. The term $[\sum_{t=1}^{n}(1/1 + i)^t] = PVIFA_{i,n}$ is defined as the present value interest factor for an annuity.

Appendix B

Interest Factor Tables[1]

[1] These tables are from E. F. Brigham, *Financial Management: Theory and Practice*, 3rd ed. (Hinsdale, Ill.: The Dryden Press, 1982), pp. 836–844. Copyright © 1982 by The Dryden Press.

Table B.1
Compound Sum of \$1: $FVIF_{i,n} = (1 + i)^n$

Period	1%	2%	3%	4%	5%	6%	7%	8%	9%	10%
1	1.0100	1.0200	1.0300	1.0400	1.0500	1.0600	1.0700	1.0800	1.0900	1.1000
2	1.0201	1.0404	1.0609	1.0816	1.1025	1.1236	1.1449	1.1664	1.1881	1.2100
3	1.0303	1.0612	1.0927	1.1249	1.1576	1.1910	1.2250	1.2597	1.2950	1.3310
4	1.0406	1.0824	1.1255	1.1699	1.2155	1.2625	1.3108	1.3605	1.4116	1.4641
5	1.0510	1.1041	1.1593	1.2167	1.2763	1.3382	1.4026	1.4693	1.5386	1.6105
6	1.0615	1.1262	1.1941	1.2653	1.3401	1.4185	1.5007	1.5869	1.6771	1.7716
7	1.0721	1.1487	1.2299	1.3159	1.4071	1.5036	1.6058	1.7138	1.8280	1.9487
8	1.0829	1.1717	1.2668	1.3686	1.4775	1.5938	1.7182	1.8509	1.9926	2.1436
9	1.0937	1.1951	1.3048	1.4233	1.5513	1.6895	1.8385	1.9990	2.1719	2.3579
10	1.1046	1.2190	1.3439	1.4802	1.6289	1.7908	1.9672	2.1589	2.3674	2.5937
11	1.1157	1.2434	1.3842	1.5395	1.7103	1.8983	2.1049	2.3316	2.5804	2.8531
12	1.1268	1.2682	1.4258	1.6010	1.7959	2.0122	2.2522	2.5182	2.8127	3.1384
13	1.1381	1.2936	1.4685	1.6651	1.8856	2.1329	2.4098	2.7196	3.0658	3.4523
14	1.1495	1.3195	1.5126	1.7317	1.9799	2.2609	2.5785	2.9372	3.3417	3.7975
15	1.1610	1.3459	1.5580	1.8009	2.0789	2.3966	2.7590	3.1722	3.6425	4.1772
16	1.1726	1.3728	1.6047	1.8730	2.1829	2.5404	2.9522	3.4259	3.9703	4.5950
17	1.1843	1.4002	1.6528	1.9479	2.2920	2.6928	3.1588	3.7000	4.3276	5.0545
18	1.1961	1.4282	1.7024	2.0258	2.4066	2.8543	3.3799	3.9960	4.7171	5.5599
19	1.2081	1.4568	1.7535	2.1068	2.5270	3.0256	3.6165	4.3157	5.1417	6.1159
20	1.2202	1.4859	1.8061	2.1911	2.6533	3.2071	3.8697	4.6610	5.6044	6.7275
21	1.2324	1.5157	1.8603	2.2788	2.7860	3.3996	4.1406	5.0338	6.1088	7.4002
22	1.2447	1.5460	1.9161	2.3699	2.9253	3.6035	4.4304	5.4365	6.6586	8.1403
23	1.2572	1.5769	1.9736	2.4647	3.0715	3.8197	4.7405	5.8715	7.2579	8.9543
24	1.2697	1.6084	2.0328	2.5633	3.2251	4.0489	5.0724	6.3412	7.9111	9.8497
25	1.2824	1.6406	2.0938	2.6658	3.3864	4.2919	5.4274	6.8485	8.6231	10.834
26	1.2953	1.6734	2.1566	2.7725	3.5557	4.5494	5.8074	7.3964	9.3992	11.918
27	1.3082	1.7069	2.2213	2.8834	3.7335	4.8223	6.2139	7.9881	10.245	13.110
28	1.3213	1.7410	2.2879	2.9987	3.9201	5.1117	6.6488	8.6271	11.167	14.421
29	1.3345	1.7758	2.3566	3.1187	4.1161	5.4184	7.1143	9.3173	12.172	15.863
30	1.3478	1.8114	2.4273	3.2434	4.3219	5.7435	7.6123	10.062	13.267	17.449
40	1.4889	2.2080	3.2620	4.8010	7.0400	10.285	14.974	21.724	31.409	45.259
50	1.6446	2.6916	4.3839	7.1067	11.467	18.420	29.457	46.901	74.357	117.39
60	1.8167	3.2810	5.8916	10.519	18.679	32.987	57.946	101.25	176.03	304.48

Table B.1
(continued)

Period	12%	14%	15%	16%	18%	20%	24%	28%	32%	36%
1	1.1200	1.1400	1.1500	1.1600	1.1800	1.2000	1.2400	1.2800	1.3200	1.3600
2	1.2544	1.2996	1.3225	1.3456	1.3924	1.4400	1.5376	1.6384	1.7424	1.8496
3	1.4049	1.4815	1.5209	1.5609	1.6430	1.7280	1.9066	2.0972	2.3000	2.5155
4	1.5735	1.6890	1.7490	1.8106	1.9388	2.0736	2.3642	2.6844	3.0360	3.4210
5	1.7623	1.9254	2.0114	2.1003	2.2878	2.4883	2.9316	3.4360	4.0075	4.6526
6	1.9738	2.1950	2.3131	2.4364	2.6996	2.9860	3.6352	4.3980	5.2899	6.3275
7	2.2107	2.5023	2.6600	2.8262	3.1855	3.5832	4.5077	5.6295	6.9826	8.6054
8	2.4760	2.8526	3.0590	3.2784	3.7589	4.2998	5.5895	7.2058	9.2170	11.703
9	2.7731	3.2519	3.5179	3.8030	4.4355	5.1598	6.9310	9.2234	12.166	15.916
10	3.1058	3.7072	4.0456	4.4114	5.2338	6.1917	8.5944	11.805	16.059	21.646
11	3.4785	4.2262	4.6524	5.1173	6.1759	7.4301	10.657	15.111	21.198	29.439
12	3.8960	4.8179	5.3502	5.9360	7.2876	8.9161	13.214	19.342	27.982	40.037
13	4.3635	5.4924	6.1528	6.8858	8.5994	10.699	16.386	24.758	36.937	54.451
14	4.8871	6.2613	7.0757	7.9875	10.147	12.839	20.319	31.691	48.756	74.053
15	5.4736	7.1379	8.1371	9.2655	11.973	15.407	25.195	40.564	64.358	100.71
16	6.1304	8.1372	9.3576	10.748	14.129	18.488	31.242	51.923	84.953	136.96
17	6.8660	9.2765	10.761	12.467	16.672	22.186	38.740	66.461	112.13	186.27
18	7.6900	10.575	12.375	14.462	19.673	26.623	48.038	85.070	148.02	253.33
19	8.6128	12.055	14.231	16.776	23.214	31.948	59.567	108.89	195.39	344.53
20	9.6463	13.743	16.366	19.460	27.393	38.337	73.864	139.37	257.91	468.57
21	10.803	15.667	18.821	22.574	32.323	46.005	91.591	178.40	340.44	637.26
22	12.100	17.861	21.644	26.186	38.142	55.206	113.57	228.35	449.39	866.67
23	13.552	20.361	24.891	30.376	45.007	66.247	140.83	292.30	593.19	1178.6
24	15.178	23.212	28.625	35.236	53.108	79.496	174.63	374.14	783.02	1602.9
25	17.000	26.461	32.918	40.874	62.668	95.396	216.54	478.90	1033.5	2180.0
26	19.040	30.166	37.856	47.414	73.948	114.47	268.51	612.99	1364.3	2964.9
27	21.324	34.389	43.535	55.000	87.259	137.37	332.95	784.63	1800.9	4032.2
28	23.883	39.204	50.065	63.800	102.96	164.84	412.86	1004.3	2377.2	5483.8
29	26.749	44.693	57.575	74.008	121.50	197.81	511.95	1285.5	3137.9	7458.0
30	29.959	50.950	66.211	85.849	143.37	237.37	634.81	1645.5	4142.0	10143.
40	93.050	188.88	267.86	378.72	750.37	1469.7	5455.9	19426.	66520.	*
50	289.00	700.23	1083.6	1670.7	3927.3	9100.4	46890.	*	*	*
60	897.59	2595.9	4383.9	7370.1	20555.	56347.	*	*	*	*

* *FVIF* > 99,999.

Table B.2
Present Value of $1: $PVIF_{i,n} = 1/(1 + i)^n = 1/FVIF_{i,n}$

Period	1%	2%	3%	4%	5%	6%	7%	8%	9%	10%
1	.9901	.9804	.9709	.9615	.9524	.9434	.9346	.9259	.9174	.9091
2	.9803	.9612	.9426	.9246	.9070	.8900	.8734	.8573	.8417	.8264
3	.9706	.9423	.9151	.8890	.8638	.8396	.8163	.7938	.7722	.7513
4	.9610	.9238	.8885	.8548	.8227	.7921	.7629	.7350	.7084	.6830
5	.9515	.9057	.8626	.8219	.7835	.7473	.7130	.6806	.6499	.6209
6	.9420	.8880	.8375	.7903	.7462	.7050	.6663	.6302	.5963	.5645
7	.9327	.8706	.8131	.7599	.7107	.6651	.6227	.5835	.5470	.5132
8	.9235	.8535	.7894	.7307	.6768	.6274	.5820	.5403	.5019	.4665
9	.9143	.8368	.7664	.7026	.6446	.5919	.5439	.5002	.4604	.4241
10	.9053	.8203	.7441	.6756	.6139	.5584	.5083	.4632	.4224	.3855
11	.8963	.8043	.7224	.6496	.5847	.5268	.4751	.4289	.3875	.3505
12	.8874	.7885	.7014	.6246	.5568	.4970	.4440	.3971	.3555	.3186
13	.8787	.7730	.6810	.6006	.5303	.4688	.4150	.3677	.3262	.2897
14	.8700	.7579	.6611	.5775	.5051	.4423	.3878	.3405	.2992	.2633
15	.8613	.7430	.6419	.5553	.4810	.4173	.3624	.3152	.2745	.2394
16	.8528	.7284	.6232	.5339	.4581	.3936	.3387	.2919	.2519	.2176
17	.8444	.7142	.6050	.5134	.4363	.3714	.3166	.2703	.2311	.1978
18	.8360	.7002	.5874	.4936	.4155	.3503	.2959	.2502	.2120	.1799
19	.8277	.6864	.5703	.4746	.3957	.3305	.2765	.2317	.1945	.1635
20	.8195	.6730	.5537	.4564	.3769	.3118	.2584	.2145	.1784	.1486
21	.8114	.6598	.5375	.4388	.3589	.2942	.2415	.1987	.1637	.1351
22	.8034	.6468	.5219	.4220	.3418	.2775	.2257	.1839	.1502	.1228
23	.7954	.6342	.5067	.4057	.3256	.2618	.2109	.1703	.1378	.1117
24	.7876	.6217	.4919	.3901	.3101	.2470	.1971	.1577	.1264	.1015
25	.7798	.6095	.4776	.3751	.2953	.2330	.1842	.1460	.1160	.0923
26	.7720	.5976	.4637	.3607	.2812	.2198	.1722	.1352	.1064	.0839
27	.7644	.5859	.4502	.3468	.2678	.2074	.1609	.1252	.0976	.0763
28	.7568	.5744	.4371	.3335	.2551	.1956	.1504	.1159	.0895	.0693
29	.7493	.5631	.4243	.3207	.2429	.1846	.1406	.1073	.0822	.0630
30	.7419	.5521	.4120	.3083	.2314	.1741	.1314	.0994	.0754	.0573
35	.7059	.5000	.3554	.2534	.1813	.1301	.0937	.0676	.0490	.0356
40	.6717	.4529	.3066	.2083	.1420	.0972	.0668	.0460	.0318	.0221
45	.6391	.4102	.2644	.1712	.1113	.0727	.0476	.0313	.0207	.0137
50	.6080	.3715	.2281	.1407	.0872	.0543	.0339	.0213	.0134	.0085
55	.5785	.3365	.1968	.1157	.0683	.0406	.0242	.0145	.0087	.0053

Table B.2
(continued)

Period	12%	14%	15%	16%	18%	20%	24%	28%	32%	36%
1	.8929	.8772	.8696	.8621	.8475	.8333	.8065	.7813	.7576	.7353
2	.7972	.7695	.7561	.7432	.7182	.6944	.6504	.6104	.5739	.5407
3	.7118	.6750	.6575	.6407	.6086	.5787	.5245	.4768	.4348	.3975
4	.6355	.5921	.5718	.5523	.5158	.4823	.4230	.3725	.3294	.2923
5	.5674	.5194	.4972	.4761	.4371	.4019	.3411	.2910	.2495	.2149
6	.5066	.4556	.4323	.4104	.3704	.3349	.2751	.2274	.1890	.1580
7	.4523	.3996	.3759	.3538	.3139	.2791	.2218	.1776	.1432	.1162
8	.4039	.3506	.3269	.3050	.2660	.2326	.1789	.1388	.1085	.0854
9	.3606	.3075	.2843	.2630	.2255	.1938	.1443	.1084	.0822	.0628
10	.3220	.2697	.2472	.2267	.1911	.1615	.1164	.0847	.0623	.0462
11	.2875	.2366	.2149	.1954	.1619	.1346	.0938	.0662	.0472	.0340
12	.2567	.2076	.1869	.1685	.1372	.1122	.0757	.0517	.0357	.0250
13	.2292	.1821	.1625	.1452	.1163	.0935	.0610	.0404	.0271	.0184
14	.2046	.1597	.1413	.1252	.0985	.0779	.0492	.0316	.0205	.0135
15	.1827	.1401	.1229	.1079	.0835	.0649	.0397	.0247	.0155	.0099
16	.1631	.1229	.1069	.0930	.0708	.0541	.0320	.0193	.0118	.0073
17	.1456	.1078	.0929	.0802	.0600	.0451	.0258	.0150	.0089	.0054
18	.1300	.0946	.0808	.0691	.0508	.0376	.0208	.0118	.0068	.0039
19	.1161	.0829	.0703	.0596	.0431	.0313	.0168	.0092	.0051	.0029
20	.1037	.0728	.0611	.0514	.0365	.0261	.0135	.0072	.0039	.0021
21	.0926	.0638	.0531	.0443	.0309	.0217	.0109	.0056	.0029	.0016
22	.0826	.0560	.0462	.0382	.0262	.0181	.0088	.0044	.0022	.0012
23	.0738	.0491	.0402	.0329	.0222	.0151	.0071	.0034	.0017	.0008
24	.0659	.0431	.0349	.0284	.0188	.0126	.0057	.0027	.0013	.0006
25	.0588	.0378	.0304	.0245	.0160	.0105	.0046	.0021	.0010	.0005
26	.0525	.0331	.0264	.0211	.0135	.0087	.0037	.0016	.0007	.0003
27	.0469	.0291	.0230	.0182	.0115	.0073	.0030	.0013	.0006	.0002
28	.0419	.0255	.0200	.0157	.0097	.0061	.0024	.0010	.0004	.0002
29	.0374	.0224	.0174	.0135	.0082	.0051	.0020	.0008	.0003	.0001
30	.0334	.00196	.0151	.0116	.0070	.0042	.0016	.0006	.0002	.0001
35	.0189	.0102	.0075	.0055	.0030	.0017	.0005	.0002	.0001	*
40	.0107	.0053	.0037	.0026	.0013	.0007	.0002	.0001	*	*
45	.0061	.0027	.0019	.0013	.0006	.0003	.0001	*	*	*
50	.0035	.0014	.0009	.0006	.0003	.0001	*	*	*	*
55	.0020	.0007	.0005	.0003	.0001	*	*	*	*	*

*The factor is zero to four decimal places.

Table B.3

Sum of an Annuity of $1 for N Periods: $FVIFA_{i,n} = \sum\limits_{t=1}^{n} (1+i)^{t-1}$

$$= \frac{(1+i)^n - 1}{i}$$

Number of Periods	1%	2%	3%	4%	5%	6%	7%	8%	9%	10%
1	1.0000	1.0000	1.0000	1.0000	1.0000	1.0000	1.0000	1.0000	1.0000	1.0000
2	2.0100	2.0200	2.0300	2.0400	2.0500	2.0600	2.0700	2.0800	2.0900	2.1000
3	3.0301	3.0604	3.0909	3.1216	3.1525	3.1836	3.2149	3.2464	3.2781	3.3100
4	4.0604	4.1216	4.1836	4.2465	4.3101	4.3746	4.4399	4.5061	4.5731	4.6410
5	5.1010	5.2040	5.3091	5.4163	5.5256	5.6371	5.7507	5.8666	5.9847	6.1051
6	6.1520	6.3081	6.4684	6.6330	6.8019	6.9753	7.1533	7.3359	7.5233	7.7156
7	7.2135	7.4343	7.6625	7.8983	8.1420	8.3938	8.6540	8.9228	9.2004	9.4872
8	8.2857	8.5830	8.8923	9.2142	9.5491	9.8975	10.259	10.636	11.028	11.435
9	9.3685	9.7546	10.159	10.582	11.026	11.491	11.978	12.487	13.021	13.579
10	10.462	10.949	11.463	12.006	12.577	13.180	13.816	14.486	15.192	15.937
11	11.566	12.168	12.807	13.486	14.206	14.971	15.783	16.645	17.560	18.531
12	12.682	13.412	14.192	15.025	15.917	16.869	17.888	18.977	20.140	21.384
13	13.809	14.680	15.617	16.626	17.713	18.882	20.140	21.495	22.953	24.522
14	14.947	15.973	17.086	18.291	19.598	21.015	22.550	24.214	26.019	27.975
15	16.096	17.293	18.598	20.023	21.578	23.276	25.129	27.152	29.360	31.772
16	17.257	18.639	20.156	21.824	23.657	25.672	27.888	30.324	33.003	35.949
17	18.430	20.012	21.761	23.697	25.840	28.212	30.840	33.750	36.973	40.544
18	19.614	21.412	23.414	25.645	28.132	30.905	33.999	37.450	41.301	45.599
19	20.810	22.840	25.116	27.671	30.539	33.760	37.379	41.446	46.018	51.159
20	22.019	24.297	26.870	29.778	33.066	36.785	40.995	45.762	51.160	57.275
21	23.239	25.783	28.676	31.969	35.719	39.992	44.865	50.422	56.764	64.002
22	24.471	27.299	30.536	34.248	38.505	43.392	49.005	55.456	62.873	71.402
23	25.716	28.845	32.452	36.617	41.430	46.995	53.436	60.893	69.531	79.543
24	26.973	30.421	34.426	39.082	44.502	50.815	58.176	66.764	76.789	88.497
25	28.243	32.030	36.459	41.645	47.727	54.864	63.249	73.105	84.700	98.347
26	29.525	33.670	38.553	44.311	51.113	59.156	68.676	79.954	93.323	109.18
27	30.820	35.344	40.709	47.084	54.669	63.705	74.483	87.350	102.72	121.09
28	32.129	37.051	42.930	49.967	58.402	68.528	80.697	95.338	112.96	134.20
29	33.450	38.792	45.218	52.966	62.322	73.639	87.346	103.96	124.13	148.63
30	34.784	40.568	47.575	56.084	66.438	79.058	94.460	113.28	136.30	164.49
40	48.886	60.402	75.401	95.025	120.79	154.76	199.63	259.05	337.88	442.59
50	64.463	84.579	112.79	152.66	209.34	290.33	406.52	573.76	815.08	1163.9
60	81.669	114.05	163.05	237.99	353.58	533.12	813.52	1253.2	1944.7	3034.8

Table B.3
(continued)

Number of Periods	12%	14%	15%	16%	18%	20%	24%	28%	32%	36%
1	1.0000	1.0000	1.0000	1.0000	1.0000	1.0000	1.0000	1.0000	1.0000	1.0000
2	2.1200	2.1400	2.1500	2.1600	2.1800	2.2000	2.2400	2.2800	2.3200	2.3600
3	3.3744	3.4396	3.4725	3.5056	3.5724	3.6400	3.7776	3.9184	4.0624	4.2096
4	4.7793	4.9211	4.9934	5.0665	5.2154	5.3680	5.6842	6.0156	6.3624	6.7251
5	6.3528	6.6101	6.7424	6.8771	7.1542	7.4416	8.0484	8.6999	9.3983	10.146
6	8.1152	8.5355	8.7537	8.9775	9.4420	9.9299	10.980	12.135	13.405	14.798
7	10.089	10.730	11.066	11.413	12.141	12.915	14.615	16.533	18.695	21.126
8	12.299	13.232	13.726	14.240	15.327	16.499	19.122	22.163	25.678	29.731
9	14.775	16.085	16.785	17.518	19.085	20.798	24.712	29.369	34.895	41.435
10	17.548	19.337	20.303	21.321	23.521	25.958	31.643	38.592	47.061	57.351
11	20.654	23.044	24.349	25.732	28.755	32.150	40.237	50.398	63.121	78.998
12	24.133	27.270	29.001	30.850	34.931	39.580	50.894	65.510	84.320	108.43
13	28.029	32.088	34.351	36.786	42.218	48.496	64.109	84.852	112.30	148.47
14	32.392	37.581	40.504	43.672	50.818	59.195	80.496	109.61	149.23	202.92
15	37.279	43.842	47.580	51.659	60.965	72.035	100.81	141.30	197.99	276.97
16	42.753	50.980	55.717	60.925	72.939	87.442	126.01	181.86	262.35	377.69
17	48.883	59.117	65.075	71.673	87.068	105.93	157.25	233.79	347.30	514.66
18	55.749	68.394	75.836	84.140	103.74	128.11	195.99	300.25	459.44	700.93
19	63.439	78.969	88.211	98.603	123.41	154.74	244.03	385.32	607.47	954.27
20	72.052	91.024	102.44	115.37	146.62	186.68	303.60	494.21	802.86	1298.8
21	81.698	104.76	118.81	134.84	174.02	225.02	377.46	633.59	1060.7	1767.3
22	92.502	120.43	137.63	157.41	206.34	271.03	469.05	811.99	1401.2	2404.6
23	104.60	138.29	159.27	183.60	244.48	326.23	582.62	1040.3	1850.6	3271.3
24	118.15	158.65	184.16	213.97	289.49	392.48	723.46	1332.6	2443.8	4449.9
25	133.33	181.87	212.79	249.21	342.60	471.98	898.09	1706.8	3226.8	6052.9
26	150.33	208.33	245.71	290.08	405.27	567.37	1114.6	2185.7	4260.4	8233.0
27	169.37	238.49	283.56	337.50	479.22	681.85	1383.1	2798.7	5624.7	11197.9
28	190.69	272.88	327.10	392.50	566.48	819.22	1716.0	3583.3	7425.6	15230.2
29	214.58	312.09	377.16	456.30	669.44	984.06	2128.9	4587.6	9802.9	20714.1
30	241.33	356.78	434.74	530.31	790.94	1181.8	2640.9	5873.2	12940.	28172.2
40	767.09	1342.0	1779.0	2360.7	4163.2	7343.8	22728.	69377.	*	*
50	2400.0	4994.5	7217.7	10435.	21813.	45497.	*	*	*	*
60	7471.6	18535.	29219.	46057.	*	*	*	*	*	*

*FVIFA > 99,999.

Table B.4

Present Value of an Annuity of \$1 for n Periods: $PVIFA_{i,n} = \sum_{t=1}^{n} \dfrac{1}{(1+i)^t}$

$$= \dfrac{1 - \dfrac{1}{(1+i)^n}}{i}$$

Number of Pay-ments	1%	2%	3%	4%	5%	6%	7%	8%	9%
1	0.9901	0.9804	0.9709	0.9615	0.9524	0.9434	0.9346	0.9259	0.9174
2	1.9704	1.9416	1.9135	1.8861	1.8594	1.8334	1.8080	1.7833	1.7591
3	2.9410	2.8839	2.8286	2.7751	2.7232	2.6730	2.6243	2.5771	2.5313
4	3.9020	3.8077	3.7171	3.6299	3.5460	3.4651	3.3872	3.3121	3.2397
5	4.8534	4.7135	4.5797	4.4518	4.3295	4.2124	4.1002	3.9927	3.8897
6	5.7955	5.6014	5.4172	5.2421	5.0757	4.9173	4.7665	4.6229	4.4859
7	6.7282	6.4720	6.2303	6.0021	5.7864	5.5824	5.3893	5.2064	5.0330
8	7.6517	7.3255	7.0197	6.7327	6.4632	6.2098	5.9713	5.7466	5.5348
9	8.5660	8.1622	7.7861	7.4353	7.1078	6.8017	6.5152	6.2469	5.9952
10	9.4713	8.9826	8.5302	8.1109	7.7217	7.3601	7.0236	6.7101	6.4177
11	10.3676	9.7868	9.2526	8.7605	8.3064	7.8869	7.4987	7.1390	6.8052
12	11.2551	10.5753	9.9540	9.3851	8.8633	8.3838	7.9427	7.5361	7.1607
13	12.1337	11.3484	10.6350	9.9856	9.3936	8.8527	8.3577	7.9038	7.4869
14	13.0037	12.1062	11.2961	10.5631	9.8986	9.2950	8.7455	8.2442	7.7862
15	13.8651	12.8493	11.9379	11.1184	10.3797	9.7122	9.1079	8.5595	8.0607
16	14.7179	13.5777	12.5611	11.6523	10.8378	10.1059	9.4466	8.8514	8.3126
17	15.5623	14.2919	13.1661	12.1657	11.2741	10.4773	9.7632	9.1216	8.5436
18	16.3983	14.9920	13.7535	12.6593	11.6896	10.8276	10.0591	9.3719	8.7556
19	17.2260	15.6785	14.3238	13.1339	12.0853	11.1581	10.3356	9.6036	8.9501
20	18.0456	16.3514	14.8775	13.5903	12.4622	11.4699	10.5940	9.8181	9.1285
21	18.8570	17.0112	15.4150	14.0292	12.8212	11.7641	10.8355	10.0168	9.2922
22	19.6604	17.6580	15.9369	14.4511	13.1630	12.0416	11.0612	10.2007	9.4424
23	20.4558	18.2922	16.4436	14.8568	13.4886	12.3034	11.2722	10.3711	9.5802
24	21.2434	18.9139	16.9355	15.2470	13.7986	12.5504	11.4693	10.5288	9.7066
25	22.0232	19.5235	17.4131	15.6221	14.0939	12.7834	11.6536	10.6748	9.8226
26	22.7952	20.1210	17.8768	15.9828	14.3752	13.0032	11.8258	10.8100	9.9290
27	23.5596	20.7069	18.3270	16.3296	14.6430	13.2105	11.9867	10.9352	10.0266
28	24.3164	21.2813	18.7641	16.6631	14.8981	13.4062	12.1371	11.0511	10.1161
29	25.0658	21.8444	19.1885	16.9837	15.1411	13.5907	12.2777	11.1584	10.1983
30	25.8077	22.3965	19.6004	17.2920	15.3725	13.7648	12.4090	11.2578	10.2737
35	29.4086	24.9986	21.4872	18.6646	16.3742	14.4982	12.9477	11.6546	10.5668
40	32.8347	27.3555	23.1148	19.7928	17.1591	15.0463	13.3317	11.9246	10.7574
45	36.0945	29.4902	24.5187	20.7200	17.7741	15.4558	13.6055	12.1084	10.8812
50	39.1961	31.4236	25.7298	21.4822	18.2559	15.7619	13.8007	12.2335	10.9617
55	42.1472	33.1748	26.7744	22.1086	18.6335	15.9905	13.9399	12.3186	11.0140

Table B.4
(continued)

Number of Pay-ments	10%	12%	14%	15%	16%	18%	20%	24%	28%	32%
1	0.9091	0.8929	0.8772	0.8696	0.8621	0.8475	0.8333	0.8065	0.7813	0.7576
2	1.7355	1.6901	1.6467	1.6257	1.6052	1.5656	1.5278	1.4568	1.3916	1.3315
3	2.4869	2.4018	2.3216	2.2832	2.2459	2.1743	2.1065	1.9813	1.8684	1.7663
4	3.1699	3.0373	2.9137	2.8550	2.7982	2.6901	2.5887	2.4043	2.2410	2.0957
5	3.7908	3.6048	3.4331	3.3522	3.2743	3.1272	2.9906	2.7454	2.5320	2.3452
6	4.3553	4.1114	3.8887	3.7845	3.6847	3.4976	3.3255	3.0205	2.7594	2.5342
7	4.8684	4.5638	4.2883	4.1604	4.0386	3.8115	3.6046	3.2423	2.9370	2.6775
8	5.3349	4.9676	4.6389	4.4873	4.3436	4.0776	3.8372	3.4212	3.0758	2.7860
9	5.7590	5.3282	4.9464	4.7716	4.6065	4.3030	4.0310	3.5655	3.1842	2.8681
10	6.1446	5.6502	5.2161	5.0188	4.8332	4.4941	4.1925	3.6819	3.2689	2.9304
11	6.4951	5.9377	5.4527	5.2337	5.0286	4.6560	4.3271	3.7757	3.3351	2.9776
12	6.8137	6.1944	5.6603	5.4206	5.1971	4.7932	4.4392	3.8514	3.3868	3.0133
13	7.1034	6.4235	5.8424	5.5831	5.3423	4.9095	4.5327	3.9124	3.4272	3.0404
14	7.3667	6.6282	6.0021	5.7245	5.4675	5.0081	4.6106	3.9616	3.4587	3.0609
15	7.6061	6.8109	6.1422	5.8474	5.5755	5.0916	4.6755	4.0013	3.4834	3.0764
16	7.8237	6.9740	6.2651	5.9542	5.6685	5.1624	4.7296	4.0333	3.5026	3.0882
17	8.0216	7.1196	6.3729	6.0472	5.7487	5.2223	4.7746	4.0591	3.5177	3.0971
18	8.2014	7.2497	6.4674	6.1280	5.8178	5.2732	4.8122	4.0799	3.5294	3.1039
19	8.3649	7.3658	6.5504	6.1982	5.8775	5.3162	4.8435	4.0967	3.5386	3.1090
20	8.5136	7.4694	6.6231	6.2593	5.9288	5.3527	4.8696	4.1103	3.5458	3.1129
21	8.6487	7.5620	6.6870	6.3125	5.9731	5.3837	4.8913	4.1212	3.5514	3.1158
22	8.7715	7.6446	6.7429	6.3587	6.0113	5.4099	4.9094	4.1300	3.5558	3.1180
23	8.8832	7.7184	6.7921	6.3988	6.0442	5.4321	4.9245	4.1371	3.5592	3.1197
24	8.9847	7.7843	6.8351	6.4338	6.0726	5.4510	4.9371	4.1428	3.5619	3.1210
25	9.0770	7.8431	6.8729	6.4642	6.0971	5.4669	4.9476	4.1474	3.5640	3.1220
26	9.1609	7.8957	6.9061	6.4906	6.1182	5.4804	4.9563	4.1511	3.5656	3.1227
27	9.2372	7.9426	6.9352	6.5135	6.1364	5.4919	4.9636	4.1542	3.5669	3.1233
28	9.3066	7.9844	6.9607	6.5335	6.1520	5.5016	4.9697	4.1566	3.5679	3.1237
29	9.3696	8.0218	6.9830	6.5509	6.1656	5.5098	4.9747	4.1585	3.5687	3.1240
30	9.4269	8.0552	7.0027	6.5660	6.1772	5.5168	4.9789	4.1601	3.5693	3.1242
35	9.6442	8.1755	7.0700	6.6166	6.2153	5.5386	4.9915	4.1644	3.5708	3.1248
40	9.7791	8.2438	7.1050	6.6418	6.2335	5.5482	4.9966	4.1659	3.5712	3.1250
45	9.8628	8.2825	7.1232	6.6543	6.2421	5.5523	4.9986	4.1664	3.5714	3.1250
50	9.9148	8.3045	7.1327	6.6605	6.2463	5.5541	4.9995	4.1666	3.5714	3.1250
55	9.9471	8.3170	7.1376	6.6636	6.2482	5.5549	4.9998	4.1666	3.5714	3.1250

Index